DO NOT
CIRCULATE

D0161840

CENTRAL LIBRARY
IRVING PUBLIC LIBRARY SYSTEM
IRVING, TEXAS 75060

jR 305.235 SHE   CC
              33163008603190
Sherrow, Victoria.
Encyclopedia of youth and
war : young people as

WITHDRAWN

CHILDREN'S COLLECTION

CENTRAL LIBRARY

Encyclopedia of Youth and War

Young People as Participants and Victims

by Victoria Sherrow

Oryx Press

2000

3 3163 00860 3190

The rare Arabian Oryx is believed to have inspired the myth of the unicorn. This desert antelope became virtually extinct in the early 1960s. At that time, several groups of international conservationists arranged to have nine animals sent to the Phoenix Zoo to be the nucleus of a captive breeding herd. Today, the Oryx population is over 1,000, and over 500 have been returned to the Middle East.

© 2000 by Victoria Sherrow
Published by The Oryx Press
4041 North Central at Indian School Road
Phoenix, Arizona 85012-3397

All rights reserved. No part of this publication may be reproduced or transmitted in any form or by any means, electronic or mechanical, including photocopying, recording, or by any information storage and retrieval system, without permission in writing from The Oryx Press.

Published simultaneously in Canada
Printed and bound in the United States of America

∞ The paper used in this publication meets the minimum requirements of American National Standard for Information Science—Permanence of Paper for Printed Library Materials, ANSI Z39.48, 1984.

Cover photo by Kimberly Butler, United Jewish Communities.

Library of Congress Cataloging-in-Publication Data

Sherrow, Victoria.
    Encyclopedia of youth and war : young people as participants and victims / Victoria Sherrow.
        p. cm.
    Includes bibliographical references and index.
    ISBN 1-57356-287-4 (alk. paper)
    1. Children and war. 2. Youth. I. Title.
HQ784.W3 S54 2000
305.235—dc21
                                                                99-043452

CONTENTS

PREFACE

The *Encyclopedia of Youth and War: Young People as Participants and Victims* examines the impact of war on young people throughout the world and at different times in history, beginning with the Thirty Years' War (1618–1648). That conflict was taken as the book's starting point because it was the first time the number of civilian casualties exceeded the number of military casualties, and thus was the first modern war of long duration to have a significant effect on children and families.

The *Encyclopedia* defines "youth" as boys and girls age 18 or younger, although some entries do follow the activities of specific individuals from their teens into their early 20s. With over 300 entries, the *Encyclopedia* covers the activities of young people in most of the important wars, revolutions, and conflicts of the last 400 years, and especially those of the last century. Entries also discuss the various ways youth took part in war—as combatants, support personnel, defense plant workers, spies, couriers, resistance fighters, protestors, volunteers, or simply as children growing up on the home front. Entries on such topics as food, disease, education, rationing, clothing shortages, blackouts, holidays, and sports describe the daily life of young people in war-torn countries. Other entries profile individual children who illustrate particular wartime activities or hardships, such as dealing with combat, internment, concealment, or shortage, or who won fame as diarists, rescuers, spies, or resistance group leaders.

The book also includes entries on adults and organizations that have worked to rescue children, to relieve their suffering, or to promote their welfare during and after wars. People who planned and perpetrated violence against children during the course of a war or revolution are also discussed. Entries on such subjects as radiation sickness, post-traumatic stress disorder, land mines, displaced persons, unaccompanied children, refugees, and adoption show how wars continue to affect children even after the fighting stops.

Many entries cover twentieth-century wars and topics, particularly World War II and the Holocaust, which together claimed the lives of millions of children around the world and seriously affected the lives of millions more. The Holocaust and other entries involving genocide (e.g., the Armenian-Turkish Conflict, Bosnia, Kosovo, Cambodia, Rwanda, Romani) receive extensive coverage because many of these conflicts are recent or ongoing, and because they illustrate how children have been deliberately targeted for mass murder.

The material for this book was collected over a period of three years and includes numerous primary and secondary sources. Many primary accounts of a young person's experiences during World War II or the Holocaust, or during one of the smaller conflicts of the late twentieth century, are available in English or in translation. Excerpts from such accounts have been used frequently in the entries to put a human face on discussions of events and experiences. Both primary and secondary sources are found in the Further Reading listings at the ends of entries. Sources of quotations are also supplied in the entries.

A comprehensive listing of significant people, places, conflicts, and events related to this vast and vital topic would be far more than a single volume could accommodate. However, the selection of entries included in the *Encyclopedia* will show readers the many and diverse ways in which young people are involved in and affected by war and revolution. Numerous cross-references and an extensive bibliography make the *Encyclopedia*'s information more accessible and offer further information for interested users, whether they are students (from grade school to college), teachers, researchers, or the general public. The *Encyclopedia of Youth and War* is the first reference book of its kind to bring together so much information about how war has affected young people around the world.

INTRODUCTION

Childhood is often called a time of innocence, a time to grow and learn, free from the heavy responsibilities that typify adulthood. At its best, childhood is spent in a safe environment with a loving family and adequate food, shelter, clothing, and health care. A child spends his or her days going to school and helping with chores, with time for friends, play, sports, spiritual observances, and community activities.

For children in the midst of war, life is quite different. Youth in war-torn countries live with hunger, fear, anger, family separations, upheaval, and destruction. They may be deprived of their most basic needs, forced out of their homes or homelands, sent into combat, abused, imprisoned, even tortured and killed. As a result of war, many children lose a family member or are separated from their families, sometimes permanently. Many face the future with weakened health, a disrupted education, lost limbs, broken communities, and broken hearts.

In more fortunate cases, wartime experiences strengthen character and enable young people to prove their strength, courage and leadership abilities. They develop a deeper appreciation for life and human relationships. Families have grown closer after coping with the threats that wars bring. As a result of their wartime experiences, some young people go on to devote their lives to helping others or to working for social causes, including world peace. In any case, war has profound and life-changing effects on youth.

Throughout history, children have endured countless wars. Each century has brought more destructive wars and more civilian casualties. The twentieth century saw a dramatic increase in young casualties of war, both military and civilian. In its 1996 study of children around the world, UNICEF—the United Nations Children's Fund—reported that, from 1986 to 1996, 2 million children were killed by wars, 4 to 5 million were disabled, and more than 12 million were left homeless (Vittachi, 1993, p. 9).

Of young victims of war, author Philip Hallie writes,

For us, children are the springtime, the creative burgeoning of human life. They are not only *in* that springtime, they *are* that springtime. . . . And when they are tortured, when they are deliberately broken and killed, it is spring that is being attacked. It is as if the living center of human life were being dirtied and then smashed. (Hallie, 1979, pp. 274–75)

Historic Roots

War has been a regular occurrence throughout human history and has continued to escalate both in scope and destructive potential. Historians point to greed, fear, revenge, aggression, racism, religious zeal, nationalism, self-defense, and a desire for economic or political dominance as reasons why people go to war.

In ancient times, people fought with their hands or with relatively simple weapons, including clubs, bows and arrows, and stones. The lack of fast, efficient means of transportation, along with the limitations of hand-to-hand combat and short-range weapons, confined fighting to relatively small areas and meant that wars did not affect large numbers of people. Rural peoples or nomads might fight others in the region for a piece of desirable land, for instance. Nearly all the casualties were the combatants themselves.

The use of horses and wheeled vehicles, along with the development of more sophisticated and destructive weapons, made it possible to engage in distant wars and to affect growing numbers of people. Armies intimidated their enemies by threatening their communities and families. Towns or fortresses that were the targets of invasion might be "sacked"—looted, burned, destroyed. Invading soldiers did not spare women or children. Victims of all ages were sometimes abused, injured, killed, or sold into slavery. Savage and brutal acts against civilians were documented in ancient Assyria, Egypt, Greece, Rome, Asia, and the Americas. Certain conquerers, such as the Mongol leader Genghis Khan, were renowned for their aggressive attacks on civilians. Massacres—mass killings of people by enemy forces—took place during the Crusades of the Middle Ages. As European conquerers invaded the West Indies and the Americas, some of them killed and enslaved the inhabitants of these lands.

The Thirty Years' War, which was fought in Western Europe from 1618 to 1648, is regarded as a historical turning point. During this prolonged series of battles, more civilians died than soldiers. Numerous cities, towns, and villages were under siege as invading troops surrounded and attacked them, causing deaths and destruction. Young people went hungry as farms and crops were burned, along with factories and shops. Massacres occurred in numerous places. Some historians estimate that up to half the population of Germany may have perished during the war.

Early in history, military troops were composed of trained soldiers. That, too, changed through the centuries as larger armies were formed. Civilians were recruited and given varying amounts of training. More civilians than ever before fought during the nineteenth century in the U.S. Civil War and Napoleonic Wars in Europe. New weapons, including more destructive guns and cannons, were also developed during the 1800s.

Children were also placed in harm's way when they went to conflict-ridden zones with their parents. In North America, children and wives accompanied men to forts where they were stationed as soldiers. British children went to India where their fathers were stationed with the army that maintained British control of that country. Between January 1819 and November 1836, 183 children living with British troops of the 1st Nottinghamshire Regiment died.

Devastating World Wars

The two world wars and numerous regional wars of the twentieth century had profound effects on young people. Chemical weapons plagued infantry soldiers during World War I, many of them under age 21. Weapons of mass destruction appeared during that same war and were later used on a large scale during World War II, which also marked the first time nuclear weapons were used. Bombings killed and injured tens of thousands of children and young adults and orphaned many others.

The First World War left many children in Europe homeless and hungry, surrounded by ruined towns and cities. During those same years, conflicts in Russia (later the Soviet Union) and Turkey led to the deaths of thousands of children and caused massive displacement. Massacres and genocide were perpetrated on civilians of all ages.

Moved by the terrible suffering, individuals and groups took action. New organizations were formed to help war victims, particularly children. Englishwoman Eglantyne Jebb organized food shipments for civilians both in allied countries, including France and Belgium, and on the German side. As a result, Jebb was charged in the United Kingdom with aiding the enemy. At her court hearing, she told the judge, "My Lord, I have no enemies below the age of 11" (Vittachi, 1993, p. 9). In the end, Jebb was acquitted and went on to found the international relief organization Save the Children.

Young conscientious objectors also found ways to help victims of World War I. The American Friends Service Committee (AFSC) was among the organizations that developed both to help those who were suffering and to enable noncombatants to serve in peaceful ways.

Although World War I was called "the war to end all wars," within less than 30 years, an even more devastating war had begun. Beginning in 1939, World War II spread to dozens of countries. When the war ended in 1945, there were about 50 million casualties, including millions of youth. About 17 million were military casualties, but most were civilians. Eleven million people had died in concentration camps alone. Millions of young people died in combat or in bombings, from disease, hunger, or exposure. About 20 million people were homeless after World War II. Hundreds of thousands of young people were also refugees.

Children and World War II

During World War II, some children were deliberately targeted for death. Nazi Germany, under its leader Adolf Hitler, set out to annihilate Jews and Romani (also called Gypsies) of all ages, along with children who had physical or mental disabilities. The Nazis killed children in ghettos and death camps and rounded them up with their elders to be shot by mobile killing squads in Poland and the Ukraine. An estimated 1.5 million Jewish victims of the Nazis were children, ranging in age from birth to 14.

Babies were helpless victims of genocide. Most babies were killed upon arriving at Nazi concentration camps but a few managed to survive in hiding. In March 1945, at the German camp Ravensbruck, which was set up for women, Nazi guards found some 32 infants whom the inmates had concealed. These infants were gassed to death just one month before the camp was liberated by Russian troops. In Poland, the International Red Cross guessed that 40,000 babies born in prisons, labor camps, and concentration camps had been taken from their mothers during the war. Most were killed, while a few were given to other families to be adopted (Laska, 1984, pp. 19–20, 206).

Young children were particularly baffled by the violence that surrounded them, and could not understand why they were being persecuted. Rudolf Reder witnessed a mother and daughter as they were sent into the gas chambers at the Nazi death camp at Belzec. The child was saying, "Mother it's dark, it's so dark, and I was being so good" (Levy and Tillard, 1969, p. 50).

New and more destructive weapons emerged during the Second World War. Incendiary bombs were dropped on both Allied and Axis countries, and children learned how to take shelter and other precautions during air raids. Lionel King, an English boy who was eight years old during the 1944 German bombing raids, later recalled a week when so many bombers appeared in the skies that the authorities no longer bothered to sound the sirens. King wrote, "When a bomb announced its approach, [my friend] Doug and I dived for the shelter, not forgetting to grab our cat Jimmy if he was in sight" (Westall, 1985).

Families have been torn apart by war for centuries when members entered the military, fled from war zones, or died in combat or as a result of wartime conditions. As a result of World War II, and numerous civil wars in the late 1900s, family separations reached historic levels. Some separations were a consequence of war, while others were deliberately planned and carried out by invading forces.

During the Holocaust, the Nazis purposely separated families. Hirsh Altusky, who was deported from his native Poland on board a Nazi train, recalled, "Our transport was sent to Maidanek [a death camp in Poland], and I was separated from my father. When I tried to join him, the Nazis said, 'You don't need your father. We are your father now'" (Adler, 1989, p. 67).

Other children lost parents or other relatives from bombings. Kayano Nagai, a survivor of the atomic bombing of Nagasaki, Japan, later recalled,

> I can remember when I was little, but mostly bad things; I mean mostly times when I was scared and things like that. The year I was born, the war began. The whole time I was little there were air raids all the time. It was awful but anyhow I had my Mummy then, so it was so nice; I was so happy. . . . [But then came] the atom bomb. I was four then. I remember the cicadas chirping. The atom bomb was the last thing that happened in the war and no more bad things have happened since then, but I don't have my Mummy any more. So even if it isn't bad any more, I'm not happy. (Nagai, 1951, p. 6)

Post-War Adjustments

Young people rejoiced with their elders to see the end of World War II, which had brought so much fear and so many losses and hardships. A teenage girl from Eindhoven recalled September 9, 1944, when her region of Holland was liberated:

> Looking out of the window towards a nearby airfield, I saw the most wonderful sight—the sky was full of parachutes. Everyone was crying and laughing at the same time and shouting, "It's the Tommies!" . . . I remember going into town on my way to work and seeing tanks and lorries full of British soldiers— people at the roadside waving Dutch flags and sometimes grabbing hold of a soldier and hugging and thanking him. (Westall, 1985, pp. 214–15)

After the war, the contributions of youth were publicly acknowledged in many countries. Young people were praised for their courage and endurance, and monuments were erected to honor their heroic deeds or to memorialize their untimely deaths. On June 8, 1945, a message from British monarch George VI held words of praise and inspiration for that nation's youth.

Today, as we celebrate victory, I send this personal message to you and all other boys and girls at school. For you have shared in the hardships and dangers of a total war and you have shared no less in the triumph of the Allied Nations. . . . courage, endurance and enterprise brought victory. May these qualities be yours as you grow up and join in the common effort to establish among the nations of the world unity and peace. (Westall, 1985, p. 235)

Young people still faced many difficulties and adjustments after the war. They lacked food, shelter, clothing, health care, and other basic needs. They had suffered many losses, large and small. Some were hospitalized, sick, or wounded. Many bomb victims in Hiroshima and Nagasaki were horribly disfigured or would later suffer and die from exposure to radiation. An English teenager described the sad changes that surrounded him: "People you knew were no longer around. Schoolfriends had been killed. Familiar buildings had been destroyed" (Westall, 1985, p. 220).

Some children were too young to recall a time when there had been no war. Rachelle Silberman Goldstein said,

People would always be talking to me about "before the war". . . . and I remember going to people saying, "What is it? What was it like before the war?". . . And they would go into rhapsodies of all the things they had. I didn't know what they were talking about. I had absolutely no idea of what they were talking about. They would talk about after the war and say, "We will have all these things again." (Greenfield, 1993, p. 47)

Jewish children who survived faced more than the usual post-war adjustments. Many had lost one or both parents, siblings, grandparents, and other relatives and friends. They were often homeless, without a community to return to. Their families had lost all their material possessions, their jobs, and their way of life. When some Jews tried to return to their former towns or neighborhoods, they experienced hatred and violence. Some had to move from place to place for several years, living in displaced persons' camps, waiting for a chance to emigrate.

Historian Dorothy Macardle, who conducted an extensive study of children who had been affected by World War II, wrote, "Never has childhood been so assailed and tormented since the beginning of man" (Macardle, 1951, p. 13).

New Conflicts

The development of nuclear weapons and an escalating arms race between the Western allies and the Soviet bloc added tension to life after the war. Nations developed thermonuclear weapons capable of destroying whole countries, along with new and faster missiles that could carry these warheads across continents.

During the last half of the twentieth century, the world was no longer engulfed in a far-reaching war, but regional wars took place on different continents. During the Six-Day War between Israel and Arab countries, a 12-year-old boy expressed the fears of many other youth when he wrote,

If there is a war, it will be a world war. And there will be nothing more dangerous for the people of the world. Because there are atom bombs now and other powerful weapons. That is why it does not pay to have a war. In the First World War several million human beings perished; in the Second World War—tens of millions and among them many Jews. And now, there will be a Third World War—hundreds of millions will die. And that will be terrible (Kovner, 1971, p. 21).

Wars in Southeast Asia caused immense suffering for civilian youth in Vietnam, Cambodia, and Laos, as well as for young soldiers fighting on both sides of these conflicts. Civilian children were killed by troops fighting on both sides of this civil war, in which the United States aided South Vietnam and the Soviets aided North Vietnam. Author Dean Brelis wrote of a night in Vietnam when he saw bombs dropping.

> I looked and it was a bizarre sight—a small silhouette of a boy, running around the paddy field, chasing after the sound of the C-123 above him, running as if he were flying a kite because his arms were raised and he seemed to be having fun. And then the tracers from the machine gun reached out for him like a distorted broken finger, and the kid danced away and fell to the ground. . . . The machine gun bullets had killed him. I knew it. The machine gunner knew it, and the two Marines knew it. We went out to where the body was and it was a little boy; he looked like eight, but he was probably twelve. The diet is poor in Vietnam and the bodies are smaller. He was lying down in the wet paddy field, and the machine-gun bullets had practically chopped him in half. In his hand were the parachute flares he had been collecting. (Brelis, 1967)

Betty Jean Lifton, who has written about young victims of Hiroshima and Vietnam, spent years as a journalist in Vietnam, wrote, "I went through orphanages, hospitals, and shelters in Saigon, and then flew to a few of the provincial hospitals and orphanages in My Tho, Qui Nhon and Danang. There seemed no words to convey the misery of it all, the scope of this tragedy" (Lifton and Fox, 1972, afterword).

Refugees were another tragic consequence of these wars. Civil wars plagued Angola during the 1970s. One of the young refugees, Julio Leitao, was nine years old when his family fled to Zambia, and then to Portugal. "We created our own Africa in Portugal. Whenever we went to sleep, my mother sang. In my dreams, I walked through my father's garden and smelled the lemon grass. That's the way you survive when you don't have a home—your dreams, and the music and dance, keep you going." Leitao later moved to New York City, where he decided to help children by starting the Batoto Yetu children's dance troupe in Harlem. Children in the troupe learn traditional African dances. His work with the dance troupe, says Leitao, has given him a chance "to live the childhood that was taken from [him]" (Dougherty and Kahn, 1996, p. 105).

Millions of people became refugees as a result of wars in Asia, Africa, Europe, and the Americas. During the mid-1990s, people of Mayan descent suffered from civil war violence in Chiapas, the southern-most state in Mexico. Wealthy landowners in the region organized civilian para-military forces to suppress impoverished inhabitants of Chiapas. After state and local law enforcement agencies did not protect citizens, they organized their own armed forces, called the Zapatista National Liberation Army (EZLN). Hundreds of civilians died in 1994 when fighting broke out between these groups. Thousands of refugees fled to neighboring villages, which lacked the resources to accommodate them (Friends Committee, 1998, p. 3).

Young Soldiers

The late twentieth century brought renewed concerns about the use of child soldiers, usually defined as combatants under the age of 18. Youthful soldiers have existed since ancient times. For example, in Sparta, in ancient Greece, male citizens were required to begin military training between ages 7 and 10. The fostering of military attitudes began at birth. Boys were trained to endure pain and to withstand the elements by wearing light summer clothes during the winter. To check their endurance, they were flogged at the altar of Artemis. At 20, they became soldiers. After 10 years, a soldier gained the privilege of being allowed to vote. Those with 10 or more years of service were esteemed as an elite corps of officers.

During modern times, young women as well as men were increasingly involved in military activities, including combat. For example, during the Algerian rebellion against the colonial French government in the 1950s, young girls often served as couriers for the rebels. Like other rebels and spies who were caught, the girls were tortured until they confessed the whereabouts of their leaders.

Child welfare groups became increasingly alarmed by the large number of youths fighting in civil wars. One 11-year-old soldier, who was interviewed by Swiss journalist Robert Bourgoing, said he had seen his father killed and his mother fleeing their village in terror when he was seven years old. He then joined the Movement for Freedom and Democracy in Liberia (ULIMO) as a commander's servant. He was equiped with a pistol and taught how to shoot, and later was shown how to operate larger weapons. The boy left the army after four years but claimed he continued to have nightmares in which he saw the faces of people he had killed. "Sometimes I sit down and cry. I don't want to kill them anymore. I want to forget them" (Toney, 1997, pp. 36, 39).

As of 1998, an estimated 200,000 children from 34 countries were taking part in armed conflicts in some region of the world on any given day (Radda Barnem, 1996, p. 7). Organizations that studied this situation found that many youths were recruited into the armed services by coercion, physical force, severe economic need, or deception. Some military leaders regarded young soldiers as easier to control and more willing to take risks than older soldiers. The United Nations and other concerned individuals and groups worked to ban the use of child combatants.

A Declaration of Rights

The United Nations (UN) has become a vocal advocate for children around the world and has set up the United Nations International Children's Emergency Fund (UNICEF) to respond to their needs. The UN declared 1979 the International Year of the Child and set forth a list of rights that should apply to all children. The declaration of rights reads, in part:

> To this end we declare that every child, whatever their race or nationality, has the inalienable right to a life free from the threat of a nuclear war, protection and shelter, pure air and water, nourishing food, free relationship with other children, access to the most current and relevant knowledge, and the best of medical care.
>
> For each young child we claim the right to explore, to experiment; to climb a mountain, fish a stream; to sail, to fly, to dream; to laugh, to dance, to sing, to read, to write, to create, to learn; to respect and be respected; to know the joy of belonging to the human race and of finding their unique place in life.
>
> For older children we claim the right to participate freely in forming the future, and to pursue the paths they feel will lead to greater awareness of the world's oneness; the right to heed their conscience in refusing to participate in war. . . . (Kome and Crean, 1986, p. 174).

Civil Wars

Despite these lofty goals, during the 1990s, civil wars devastated youth and other civilians in Africa and the former Yugoslavia. Analysts pointed to the disturbing fact that war was being routinely waged against unarmed civilians. This occurred during the war that began in Liberia in 1990, and later in Somalia, Sierra Leone, the Central African Republic, the Congo Republic, Rwanda, and Uganda, among other places.

The war in Liberia saw heavy civilian casualties, genocide, and the use of child soldiers. Heavy shelling of cities did not distinguish between military and civilian targets. Ethnic conflicts in Liberia and in Rwanda and Burundi led to hideous massacres of people and entire villages. Children were recruited into the military for combat.

The Liberian war began when the National Patriotic Liberation Front (NPLF) invaded the Ivory Coast late in 1989. A peace-keeping force, including soldiers from Ghana, was stationed in West Africa and fought to prevent NPFL troops from taking over the Liberian capital, Monrovia. In response, the NPLF attacked that densely populated city, killing many civilians. Government troops also killed civilians. In 1990, soldiers slew more than 600 people in a Lutheran church in Monrovia. This genocidal attack was based on the ethnicity of the victims, who were members of tribal groups in conflict with the Gio and Mano tribesmen who comprised the NPLF forces.

After the war ended, Janet Fleischman, director for Africa for Human Rights Watch, said, "All of the factions killed civilians, looted civilians, and raped civilians. And because they all took part in these acts, none of them have any interest in seeing any accounting for what happened" (French, 1998, p. A3).

As often happened during wartime, many African children died from diseases, which proliferated when people lacked adequate nutrition, shelter, clean water, and health care. In 1997, journalist Jeffrey Goldberg wrote

> It's not hard to find the winner in the Sudanese war, or in any war in Africa: it is the microbes that always emerge victorious. Infectious disease flowers in conditions of anarchy. Measles, cholera, malaria, AIDS, sleeping sickness, leprosy. . . . It is an endless cycle of misery: war and corruption mean no health care and no family planning; no health care and no family planning mean too many sick people; too many sick people create desperation and poverty, which lead back to corruption and war. (Goldberg, 1997, p. 35)

The fear and despair of growing up in a war zone were expressed by Zlata Filopovic of Sarajevo, in the former Yugoslavia. In the following diary entry dated June 29, 1992, Filopovic described the misery she experienced during the Bosnian civil war:

> BOREDOM!!! SHOOTING!!! SHELLING!!! PEOPLE BEING KILLED!!! DESPAIR!!! HUNGER!!! MISERY!!! FEAR!!! That's my life! The life of an innocent eleven-year-old schoolgirl!! A schoolgirl without a school, without the fun and excitement of school. A child without games, without friends, without the sun, without birds, without nature, without fruit, without chocolate or sweets, with just a little powdered milk. In short, a child without a childhood. A wartime child. I now realize that I am really living through a war, I am witnessing an ugly, disgusting war. I and thousands of other children in this town that is being destroyed, that is crying, weeping, seeking help, but getting none. (Filopovic, 1994, p. 65)

Yearning for Peace

In her famous diary, written while her family was hiding from the Nazis during World War II, Anne Frank wrote, "What, oh, what is the use of war? Why can't people live peacefully together? Why all this destruction?" (Frank, 1967). These thoughts and the dream of a peaceful world have been expressed by young people around the world.

In 1983, an American girl from Maine became a symbol of the hope for world peace when she made a trip to the Soviet Union as an unofficial peace envoy. When she was 10 years old, Samantha Smith wrote to Soviet leader Yuri Andropov about her hopes that people would find peaceful ways to resolve their conflicts so that wars would be avoided in the future. Smith and her parents were invited to visit with Soviet leaders. Tragically, Smith and her father were killed in an airplane crash two years later. The Samantha Smith Foundation, established in her honor, promoted the cause of world peace in Smith's name. For example, in 1986, the foundation sponsored a worldwide art contest for young people in which they created works promoting international goodwill. Artworks by the winners were displayed at the first Goodwill Games, an athletic event that took place in Moscow that year.

Like Samantha Smith, many other young people throughout the world, whether they've had firsthand experience of modern war or have only seen it depicted on television news programs, are working in whatever ways they can to bring peace to the world. Their hope is that the wartime experiences of earlier children described in this volume will not be repeated.

References

Adler, David A. *We Remember the Holocaust*. New York: Henry Holt, 1989.

Brelis, Dean. *The Face of South Vietnam*. Boston: Houghton Mifflin, 1967.

Dougherty, Steve, and Kahn, Toby. "Moving Lessons." *People* (March 4, 1996), pp. 102-05.

Filipovic, Zlata. *Zlata's Diary*. New York: Viking, 1994.

Frank, Anne. *The Diary of a Young Girl*. Translated by B.M. Mooyart. Garden City, NY: Doubleday, 1967.

Friends Committee on National Legislation. "A Climate of Violence in Southern Mexico." *Indian Report* (Winter 1998).

Goldberg, Jeffrey. "Our Africa." *The New York Times Magazine* (March 2, 1997), pp. 34-35.

Greenfeld, Howard. *The Hidden Children*. New York: Houghton Mifflin, 1993.

Hallie, Philip. *Lest Innocent Blood Be Shed: The Story of the Village of Le Chambon and How Goodness Happened There*. New York: Harper and Row, 1979.

Kome, Penney, and Crean, Patrick, eds. *Peace: A Dream Unfolding*. San Francisco: Sierra Club Books, 1986.

Kovner, Abba, ed. *Childhood Under Fire: Stories, Poems, and Drawings by Children During the Six Days of War*. Tel Aviv, Israel: Sifriat Poalim, 1971.

Laska, Vera, ed. *Women of the Resistance and in the Holocaust*. Westport, CT: Greenwood Press, 1984.

Levy, Claude, and Tillard, Paul. *Betrayal at the Velodrome d'Hiver*. Translated by Inea Bushnaq. New York: Hill and Wang, 1969.

Lifton, Betty Jean, and Fox, Thomas C. *Children of Vietnam*. New York: Atheneum, 1972.

Macardle, Dorothy. *Children of Europe: A Study of Children of Liberated Countries, Their War-Time Experiences, Their Reactions, and Their Needs, with a Note on Germany*. Boston: Beacon Press, 1951.

Nagai, Takashi. *We of Nagasaki: The Story of Survivors in an Atomic Wasteland*. New York: Meredith Press, 1951.

Radda Barnen (Swedish Save the Children). *Children of War*. Stockholm: Radda Barnen, June 1996.

Toney, Raymond. "The Children of War." *Christian Social Action* (March 1997), pp. 36-39.

Vittachi, Varindra T. *Between the Guns: Children as a Zone of Peace*. London: Hodder and Stoughton, 1993.

Westall, Robert. *Children of the Blitz: Memories of Wartime Childhood*. New York: Viking, 1985.

A

Adana Massacres. *See* ARMENIAN-TURKISH CONFLICT

Addams, Jane (1860–1935)

The first American woman to receive the Nobel Peace Prize, Jane Addams was a social worker and reformer who spent more than 20 years working for the cause of world peace. During World War I, Addams led relief efforts for children in Europe and helped to found an international organization that promotes peace and operates programs that aid youth in war-torn countries.

Addams grew up in an affluent Quaker family in Cedarville, Illinois, where her widower father, John Addams, was known for his abolitionist work and philanthropy. Unlike most women of her era, Addams attended college. In 1881, she graduated first in her class from Rockford Seminary. Health problems forced her to give up plans to study medicine, but a trip to Europe (1883–85) renewed her concern for the poor. She visited orphanages and institutions set up to help the poor, both in Europe and in the United States.

Addams used her inheritance from her father to buy a house in a low-income Chicago neighborhood. There, she and her friend Ellen Starr opened a settlement house, modeled on Toynbee Hall in London, where the two women could live and work among the people they served. Hull-House, as it was

called, offered members of the community a day-nursery, youth groups, kindergarten classes, a library, and English classes for immigrants.

During the 1890s and early 1900s, Addams worked to end child labor and supported rights for women and African Americans. By 1910, she had received many honors and became the first woman president of the National Conference of Charities and Corrections.

After World War I began in Europe in 1914, Addams organized the Women's Peace Party of the USA. In 1915, she chaired an international congress of more than 1,000 women delegates from 12 nations who gathered at The Hague in the Netherlands to discuss ways to end the killing. Addams opposed American entry into the war but supported young servicemen and held farewell meals for them at Hull-House.

With the end of war in 1918, Addams joined the Department of Food Administration, headed by Herbert Hoover, to help the victims of the war. In 1919, she attended the second International Congress of Women in Zurich, Switzerland, where she became the first president of the Women's International League for Peace and Freedom (WILPF), a permanent organization formed by the delegates to the Congress. Addams held the WILPF presidency until 1929.

Before leaving Europe, Addams took food supplies to hungry German children, and,

In 1919, Jane Addams (with cane) attended the second International Congress of Women in Zurich, becoming the first president of the Women's International League for Peace and Freedom. *Corbis.*

once back in the U.S., began raising money to ship food abroad. When she told Americans about the plight of German children, some people responded, but others criticized Addams for helping a former enemy.

During the 1920s, Addams continued to work for Hull-House and the WILPF. She made goodwill tours in Europe and Asia promoting the cause of world peace. After 1929, Hull-House provided food and other help to Americans suffering the effects of the Great Depression. In 1931, Addams, then 71, became the first American woman to win the Nobel Peace Prize. She donated her $16,000 prize-money to aid WILPF and her Hull-House neighbors. Addams died of cancer in 1935. *See also* HUNGER/MALNUTRITION; WOMEN'S INTERNATIONAL LEAGUE FOR PEACE AND FREEDOM (WILF); WORLD WAR I.

Further Reading: Jane Addams, *Twenty Years at Hull-House.* (1910) and *The Second Twenty Years at Hull-House* (1930); John C. Farrell, *Beloved Lady* (1967); Emily Cooper Johnson, ed., *Jane Addams* (1960).

Adolf Hitler Schools

In 1937, Germany's Nazi government founded the Adolf Hitler Schools to train future Nazi leaders. These schools operated outside the regular German education system under the direction of the Hitler Youth organization.

Local Nazi Party leaders selected candidates for the schools from among boys aged 12 to 18 who showed leadership ability and dedication to Nazism. The courses in the schools stressed athletics and paramilitary activities rather than academics. Most graduates were expected to go on to a three-year training program at the Nazi Order Castles, which were organized in 1937 as military academies. However, these academies were closed in 1939 when the German invasion of Poland began World War II and required more young German men to enter active military service. *See also* HITLER, ADOLF; HITLER YOUTH; WORLD WAR II.

Further Reading: Richard Grunberger, *The 12-Year Reich* (1971); Alfons Heck, *A Child of Hitler* (1985);

Eileen Heyes, *Children of the Swastika* (1993); H.W. Koch, *The Hitler Youth* (1975).

Adoption

As a result of war, children and young people have sometimes been adopted by relatives, friends, or strangers. Throughout history, wartime events have left children around the world without one or both parents. Before the mid-twentieth century, wars most often cost children their fathers, who were killed while serving in the military or fighting in resistance or partisan groups. Children lost mothers as a result of sieges, massacres, or executions, or through the malnutrition, starvation, and illnesses that often accompany war. In more recent wars, women have been killed serving in the military or while working with resistance efforts in occupied countries. In some cases, children have been left without parents when enemy troops imprisoned civilians or took them away for forced labor. Recent wars have brought higher numbers of civilian casualties, and bombings, forced labor, and radiation sickness have killed many parents.

During World War II, Nazi Germany organized a plan of forced adoptions in some occupied countries. They removed children from orphanages and also from intact families and sent them to Germany for adoption by German families. Some Jewish and Slavic children, primarily from Poland, were removed from the concentration camps and sent to Germany for adoption. These adoptees were mostly babies and toddlers who were regarded as inexperienced enough to adjust to a new life and too young to remember their origins.

For adoption, the Nazis chose children they regarded as "Aryan" in appearance, with the features they considered most desirable— blonde hair, fair skin, and blue or gray eyes. In 1944, Heinrich Himmler, the head of the Nazi secret police (Gestapo), declared that children who fit this description were to be taken from occupied countries even "by robbing or stealing," if necessary. Historians have estimated that at least 200,000 children in Poland were taken from the streets or kid-napped from schools and homes. These children were brought to special centers where they were evaluated. Children who were deemed unfit for the Germanization process were either killed or put out on the street.

Forced removal of children from their families has also been carried out in other countries. During a military takeover in Argentina in the mid-1970s, the revolutionary government sometimes punished political enemies by taking children from their families and arranging for their adoption. These children became known as *"los desaparecidos"* ("the disappeared ones"). The adopting families did not usually know where the babies had come from, and most did not ask questions. A film called *The Official Story* portrays the heartwrenching experiences of a family whose child was taken and of the adoptive family, who comes to realize that their child was stolen from its parents.

About 30,000 people "disappeared" in Argentina, and hundreds of them were children. Some infants were seized from women who gave birth in concentration camps run by the government, and the mothers themselves were killed. These babies were given to military families and their friends.

In 1976, thousands of mothers in Argentina began holding silent protests in front of government offices. The women wore black dresses and rosebuds—white ones if they believed their loved ones were alive and red rosebuds if they were dead.

Several organizations, including the Abuelas de Plaza de Mayo (Grandmothers of May Square) have worked to find missing children. As of 1999, 58 children had been located. Eight had been murdered; 33 were reunited with their legitimate families. Others learned about their roots and were able to contact their relatives. The Blood Center of New York and the Association for the Advancement of Science (U.S.) helped to conduct specialized genetic blood tests to prove the children's identity.

Stealing children for purposes of adoption has taken place in other modern wars, including the civil war in El Salvador, the 36-year civil war in Guatemala, and in Turkey, where Kurdish parents have described the disappearance of their children. Thousands of Guatemalan children have been reported missing.

When wars end, orphaned children are sometimes adopted by people in their homelands or by people in other countries. The number of war orphans adopted by foreign parents increased during the twentieth century. International adoption by families in the United States increased greatly between the 1970s and the 1990s. These adopted children came from many countries, including Vietnam, Cambodia, Bosnia, and Latin America. By adopting children from Southeast Asia, well-known people, such as the American actress Mia Farrow, have increased public awareness of the children's plight and encouraged more people to consider adopting foreign children who need homes. *See also* ARMENIAN-TURKISH CONFLICT; AYLWARD, GLADYS; BOSNIA; COORDINATION COMMITTEE; HIROSHIMA; HOLOCAUST; LEBENSBORN; MOZAMBIQUE; NINOSHIMA; ORPHANS; POLAND (WORLD WAR II); RED CROSS; RIGHTEOUS GENTILES; VIETNAM WAR; WORLD WAR II.

Further Reading: Claudia Kalb et al., "Bringing Kids All the Way Home," *Newsweek,* June 16, 1997, pp. 60–65; Richard C. Lukas, *Did the Children Cry?* (1994); Richard C. Lukas, ed., *Out of the Inferno* (1989); Tina Rosenberg, "What Did You Do in the War, Mama?" *The New York Times Sunday Magazine,* February 7, 1998, pp. 52ff; Kiryl Sosnowski, *The Tragedy of Children Under Nazi Rule* (1983).

Afghanistan

Young people in Afghanistan and the surrounding region have endured the effects of wars and internal tribal disputes for hundreds of years. Located in central Asia and bordering Russia, China, and Pakistan, Afghanistan has been invaded and occupied by Greeks, Kushans, Huns, and Arabs. During the twelfth century, Genghis Khan's Mongol horsemen attacked Muslim communities throughout Afghanistan. They massacred whole cities and destroyed homes, farms, and Balkh, the country's capital. Other conquerers followed in the fourteenth and the sixteenth centuries; in the eighteenth and nineteenth centuries, the people now called Afghans fought off the British and Russians, both of whom wanted to control the region. Modern Afghanistan was born in 1921.

In 1979, civil war erupted when many Afghans rebelled against the Soviet-backed regime of Hafizullah Amin, an Afghan communist who had taken control of Afghanistan by force in 1978. When the government had trouble maintaining control, the Soviet Union sent 110,000 troops into the country and replaced Amin (who was killed) with another communist politician. The war persisted for more than eight years as government troops fought against guerillas.

Government bombing attacks killed civilians of all ages. More than 1.5 million people died, including several hundred thousand civilians. Four to five million men, women, and children (about one-third of the population) fled the country as refugees. Thousands of Afghans were arrested for such crimes as listening to foreign radio stations.

Between 1979 and 1993, the Afghan government lowered the age at which young men could be conscripted into the military from 19 to 15. Exceptions were made for the sons of Communist Party members. Many Afghan youths joined the military to escape poverty. Most volunteers under age 25 came from the Democratic Youth Organization, which all youth were required to join at age 15. Many young men were forced into the army, and boys between 16 and 18 had to serve in the Organization for Civil Defense.

In 1982, military training in the public schools became mandatory for youths ages 10 to 15. Youth militias called Young Pioneers were also formed, and children as young as 12 were armed and assigned to guard duty. Members of the Democratic Youth Organization were used for military purposes, such as guard duty, surveillance, and propaganda in the schools. Armed groups of youths were assigned to defend various towns. An elite guard, which included many members under 18 years old, was assigned to defend Kabul, the capital.

Journalists covering the war reported that guerrilla units recruited 15- and 16-year-old boys. Boys from refugee camps also sometimes joined these troops, often because they wanted the security and status of belonging to a group. Casualties in these guerilla fighting units were high. Early in the war, military leaders ended the practice of using untrained children for short-term fighting.

French author Alain Louyot investigated the treatment of young prisoners of war who were captured during the battle over Jalalabad. He found that some boys who had been kept in underground cells at the Soviet-Afghan base were beaten and tortured, sometimes with attack dogs. Of the 1,400 prisoners confined in the central prison at Jalalabad, 66 were between the ages of 12 and 16. The commander of this facility permitted 10 prisoners between the ages of 12 and 15 to return home.

The war affected young Afghans in many ways. Schooling was interrupted and the education system changed significantly. Between 1979 and 1991, hundreds of schools were also destroyed and others were damaged by Soviet- and Kabul-ordered bombings. Classes at the university at Kabul were also frequently interrupted during the war years. The Russian language was promoted over other foreign languages. New textbooks coming from the Soviet Union included the study of communism and politics. From 1980 to 1989, some 130,000 Afghan children were sent to schools in the Soviet Union and were trained to support Soviet beliefs and practices.

Young people were among the millions of Afghans who became refugees during these years. By 1989, 2.3 million Afghan refugees were in Pakistan and another 2.3 million had fled to Iran. Soviet troops withdrew from the country in 1989 after failing to make real gains. When Afghanistan signed an agreement with Pakistan in 1989, some refugees returned home, but another 80,000 Afghans fled the continued fighting. The United Nations (UN) set up schools for Afghan youths living in refugee camps in Pakistan. These schools included girls as well as boys, a practice that went against the Afghan tradition of not sending girls to school. UNICEF estimates that 4 million Afghan children have died since 1979 of shelling, land mine explosions, malnutrition, or disease.

Political unrest in Afghanistan continued into the 1990s as Islamic rebels belonging to the group called Taleban fought against the government and other warring factions. Numerous land mines also remained in the Afghan countryside where they posed an ongoing threat to children. *See also* LAND MINES; SOLDIERS, CHILD

Further Reading: "Afghanistan: Marshalling Aid for Orphans," *ICRC (International Committee of the Red Cross) News*, January 30, 1997; Jon Anderson, "Children Cast into Afghan Front Line," *The Sunday Times (London)*, June 4, 1989; George Arney, *Afghanistan* (1989); Barnett R. Rubin, *The Search for Peace in Afghanistan* (1999); United Nations Children's Fund, *Children on the Front Lines* (1989); Dorothea E. Woods, ed., *Child Soldiers* (1993).

Africa

During the twentieth century, African nations experienced numerous wars for independence from European colonial rulers and many civil wars. Young people suffered both as civilians and as combatants. Most African children who died during civil wars lost their lives because of the conditions that ensued. As of 1997, a lack of food and medical services and the stress of fleeing from combat areas had combined to kill 20 times more people than armaments.

Deaths in combat included young people in their teens. For example, during the civil wars in Chad during the mid to late 1980s, teenagers under 18 fought on both sides, and some young Chadian soldiers were later captured during Chad's desert war against Libya.

In 1995, the United Nations Children's Fund (UNICEF) commissioned a study of African youth from war-torn regions. The study found that 75 percent of those interviewed had seen somebody being killed; more than half had witnessed the killing of a family member; most had seen at least one mass killing in a village, school, church, or other location; and 80 percent had feared for their own lives at least once. To draw attention to the plight of African children, UNICEF sponsored the Day of the African Child on June 16, 1995, the anniversary of the killing of 600 people, mostly youths, on June 16, 1976, in Soweto, South Africa, during the struggle against apartheid. UNICEF urged that schools around the world spend part of that day each year teaching their students about

These children are part of a group of Kikuyu prisoners taken during the Mau Mau Rebellion against British rule in Kenya in the 1950s. *Corbis/Hulton-Deutsch Collection*.

the African continent and its cultures and increasing their awareness of how children live in Africa.

To mark the 1995 Day of the African Child, UNICEF increased its efforts to help child victims of war, including projects to improve child nutrition and family life. The Trauma Recovery Program was set up in 1994 to address the short- and long-term traumatic psychological effects of war on African youth. UNICEF also opened a national recovery center that supported a clinic for children suffering from severe trauma. Young people who were treated at the center suffered from intense fears, nightmares, depression, and other effects of their ordeals. *See also* ALGERIA; ANGOLA; DISEASE; GENOCIDE; LIBERIAN CIVIL WAR; MASSACRES; MOZAMBIQUE; POST-TRAUMATIC STRESS DISORDER (PTSD); RELIEF ORGANIZATIONS; RWANDA; SAVE THE CHILDREN; SOLDIERS, CHILD; SOMALIA; SUDAN; UGANDA; UNITED NATIONS CHILDREN'S FUND (UNICEF); ZAIRE.

Further Reading: James Cameron, *The African Revolution* (1961); Mark Dennis, "Hurt, But Not Yet Beaten," *Newsweek*, June 30, 1997, p. 45; Wanda S. Franklin, "A Light of Hope: Reuniting Displaced Children with Their Families," *Time,* May 31, 1995; "The Toyota War," *Time,* April 23, 1984; United Nations Children's Fund, *Children on the Front Lines* (1989); Dorothea E. Woods, ed., *Child Soldiers* (1993).

Agent Orange

Agent Orange is a defoliant chemical substance that was used in Vietnam by the American military between 1962 and 1971. U.S. aircraft dumped some 19 million tons of chemicals over jungle areas of South Vietnam to kill foliage that could conceal enemy guerrillas and infiltrants.

The impact of Agent Orange (and Agents Blue and White, which were named for colored stripes on their containers) was far-reaching. Veterans, many of them young soldiers ages 18 to 21, developed health problems they attributed to their exposure to these defoliants. Children born to Vietnam veterans had higher than normal rates of birth defects. Defoliants also created ongoing problems for Vietnamese youth and their families.

After leaving Vietnam, American veterans began complaining of symptoms that could be linked to their exposure to Agent Orange. The men who were most affected were usually ground combat soldiers who walked through contaminated areas, drank water that was tainted with chemicals, and wore contaminated uniforms for extended periods of time. Studies showed that these veterans had higher than normal rates of rare cancers, diseases of the blood, liver problems, and nervous system disorders.

Some veterans who showed high levels of dioxin in their systems aged prematurely and experienced severe hair loss, weight loss, palsies, and strange nervous disorders. Scientists concluded that the chemical dioxin, which is part of Agent Orange, harms the immune system.

Researchers also investigated how exposure to defoliant chemicals had damaged the veterans' genes and thus harmed children born to them after they were exposed to the chemicals. During the 1990s, government reports showed children of Vietnam veterans had higher than normal rates of birth defects. One study found that infants of veterans exposed to Agent Orange were four times more likely to die of Sudden Infant Death Syndrome (SIDS) than babies in the general population. Children born to these same men before they were exposed to Agent Orange did not have these same problems.

Vietnamese people, especially those who were children during the war, also appear to have suffered ill effects from Agent Orange. In a 1996 report, scientist Hoang Dinh Cau estimated that from 200,000 to 300,000 Vietnamese children were adversely affected by Agent Orange in some way. Thousands suffered from skin diseases and exhibited below average physical and mental development. Children living in defoliated areas had been diagnosed with mental retardation more often than children who had not been exposed to Agent Orange.

The Vietnamese government lacked enough funds and technology to help all these victims. Operating with funds contributed by the United States and other nations, the Hanoi Peace Village and medical center, near the Vietnamese capital, provided medical care to some of the children who had been harmed by defoliants. These services were organized after U.S. troops left Vietnam in 1975.

In addition to harming the health of individuals, defoliants damaged the ecology and economic resources of communities throughout the country. Because the Vietnamese were primarily farmers, the use of these chemicals destroyed their livelihoods in numerous areas. Defoliants had poisonous effects both on the soil and the water, including drinking water. As a result, children who lived in the affected regions experienced more hunger, malnutrition, and other problems than children in unaffected areas, and these problems persisted for decades after the end of the Vietnam War. *See also* INTERNATIONAL RESCUE COMMITTEE (IRC); VIETNAM WAR.

Further Reading: "Agent Orange," David Compton, reporting for Cable News Network (CNN), April 13, 1996; Janet Gardner, "New Agent Orange Research: Answers at Last?" *The Nation* 244, April 11, 1987, p. 462; Ellen K. Silbergold, "Agent Orange Claims

Should Be Paid Now," *The American Legion Magazine* 128, July 1989, p. 46; "Vietnam Veterans Sustain Throat Cancer," *Science News* 137, April 14, 1990, p. 17.

Air Raid Drills. *See* AIR RAIDS; GAS MASKS; WORLD WAR II

Air Raid Shelters. *See* AIR RAIDS

Air Raids

After World War II began in 1939, government officials in various countries prepared their citizens for the possibility of air raids. Bomb shelters were built and special equipment was manufactured and distributed. British leaders believed that Adolf Hitler might use poison gas against civilians in Allied countries, so they passed out gas masks along with other equipment.

British schoolchildren practiced for real air raids by taking part in drills. When the air raid siren sounded, they were expected to immediately put on their gas masks and coats and head for the nearest shelter, carrying their emergency rations. These rations were kept

During World War II, Soviet children in Leningrad take cover in a bomb shelter. *Sovfoto.*

in a tin and carried to school and other places in case they were needed. Some tins included candy bars.

During the war, air raids became an on-going threat for youth and other civilians as warplanes from the opposing sides attacked enemy cities with conventional bombs. During the so-called Blitz in 1940, Germany bombed England, especially London, hundreds of times. Hundreds of public air-raid shelters were built in basements, churches, subway stations, or other underground structures throughout London. Some citizens received portable shelters, and people who lived far away from group shelters built their own. Shelters had to be made to careful specifications—three feet deep with no wood floors or wooden doors. A British man later recalled his experiences in Tyneside when he was nine years old.

> Council workmen just came with a lorry [truck] and dumped the bits on your front lawn and left you to get on with it. We didn't think much of the bits, lying out in the rain, gathering rainwater. Just thin bits of corrugated iron, like some old shed. (Westall, 1985)

Dugouts, or underground shelters, were also built by homeowners in case they could not reach other shelters. Some were dug out of the earth and covered with iron or other strong materials and topped with more earth. When a siren went off, people hustled to the shelter. One child told of having to lie inside the shelter quietly and recalled that "everyone was scared stiff."

A Japanese child who was four years old during a bombing described the experience as follows:

> We had many air raids. There got to be more and more of them—they began coming every day, but that was near the end of the war. The sirens got to be very loud, and we used to run around and get all excited at my house, and so did they next door and across the road, too. Mummy used to put heavy clothes on me and make me wear an air-raid cap. It was stuffed with cotton so that I could wear the heavy helmet without being hurt. She made all of us

carry knapsacks on our backs and put on our leather shoes to run faster; and then she took us to the air-raid shelter. (Nagai, 1951)

The same Japanese woman described the shelter as a dark, cramped place where mosquitoes thrived in the damp air. At school, air raids were signaled by bells that caused children to run to shelters.

When Allied bombers hit Germany, people hurried to public shelters or to shelters they had built on their own property. Ilse Koehn, a German girl who was 13 in 1942, recalled that time as follows:

> There's seldom a night without an air raid anymore. Everyone is tired. For the first hour or two in school we talk of nothing but where the bombs fell last night, what they hit. The teachers join in. A hundred people killed in that one shelter? No, two hundred, five hundred. How do you know? (Koehn, 1987)

See also BLACKOUTS; BLITZ, LONDON; BOMBINGS (WORLD WAR II); BOSNIA; GAS MASKS; HUNGARY (WORLD WAR II); JAPAN (WORLD WAR II); PERSIAN GULF WAR; POLAND (WORLD WAR II); SOVIET UNION (WORLD WAR II); WORLD WAR I; WORLD WAR II.

Further Reading: Ilse Koehn, *Mischling, Second Degree* (1977); Takashi Nagai, *We of Nagasaki* (1951); Dirk van der Heide (pseud.), *My Sister and I* (1941); Robert Westall, *Children of the Blitz* (1985).

Albania. *See* KOSOVO

Algeria

In North Africa in the 1950s, the Algerians fought a war for independence from French colonial rule. Air raids and artillery killed civilians, including children, and many people became refugees. Beginning in 1992, Algerian children endured a civil war that led to more than 60,000 deaths by 1997. Fighting with the rebel troops, called the Islamic Salvation Front, were teenage boys as young as 15. One of these young soldiers told an undercover journalist, Mark Dennis, that he had killed seven men in one week.

In the summer of 1997, many Algerian children died during massacres. In the village of Rais, between 100 and 300 children and adults were killed in August and witnesses said the soldiers then abducted about 20 young girls. The Armed Islamic Group was blamed for the killings.

During the spring of 1999, Algerians had reason to believe the war was finally coming to an end. A presidential election was scheduled for April 15, and 11 diverse candidates were expected to appear on the ballot. The military promised it would not interfere with the election, as it had done in past elections. However, most parties ended up boycotting the April elections and Abdelaziz Bouteflika was elected unopposed. The general assembly (parliament) was formed with a majority of members from the RND (Rassemblement national pour la democratie); MSP (Ovuvement de la societe pour la paix), and FLN (Fron pour la Liberation Nationale) parties. For the people of Algeria, the cost of the war was high. The *New York Times* reported that at least 80,000 people had died since the war began in 1992 and that "in many cases, the dead were civilian women and children, sometimes babies only a few months old" (Burns, 1999). Some died in the Casbah (old Turkish section) of Algiers, which Islamic guerillas had used as a base for bombings, ambushes, and assassinations. *See also* Africa; Massacres.

Further Reading: John F. Burns, "Unforeseen, Strife Eases for Algeria," *New York Times,* March 7, 1999, pp. 1, 6; Craig R. Whitney, "98 Die in One of Algerian Civil War's Worst Massacres," *The New York Times,* August 30, 1997, p. 3.

American Civil War (1861–1865)

The bloodiest war fought on American soil began on April 12, 1861, when Confederate troops fired on Fort Sumter in Charleston, South Carolina. Less than two days later, Union soldiers at the fort surrendered. The Confederacy consisted of southern states that had seceded from the Union. President Abraham Lincoln rejected secession and called for volunteers from northern states to preserve the Union by fighting the Confederacy and putting down the insurrection.

Eighteen was the legal minimum age for enlistees in both the Union and Confederate armies, and about 80 percent of the soldiers in the Civil War were between ages 18 and 25. Tens of thousands of underage boys joined both armies. Recruiters could not usually determine a boy's age, and many looked tall enough to pass for 18 or they dressed themselves to appear older. Since only a minority of parents approved of underage sons joining the army, most of the boys had to deceive recruiters.

Army statisticians have been unable to ascertain the exact number of these underage soldiers, but estimate that between 10 and 20 percent of all soldiers were younger than 18 at the time of their enlistment—a total of between 250,000 and 420,000 soldiers. Because musicians did not have to meet age

Many teenaged soldiers fought on both sides in the Civil War. Shown here is a young Confederate private named Edwin Francis Jemison. *Library of Congress LC-B8184-10037.*

requirements, thousands of underage boys enlisted as drummers and buglers. A total of about 60,000 boys, often as young as 9 or 10, held these noncombatant roles in the Union and Confederate armies.

Boys who were far too young to take an active part in the war could "play soldier" at home. Replicas of different uniforms were sold in stores. Northern boys favored a bright red and blue outfit called a Zouave uniform and the cavalry uniforms. President Lincoln's young son Tad prized a blue cavalry uniform worn by northern officers. Children also played with war toys, including toy soldiers, marching drums, sabers, and guns. Books used in schools sometimes featured themes or storylines related to the war.

A number of young soldiers joined for patriotic reasons, for example, northerners who joined to make the rebellious South stay in the Union. Southerners often felt they were being oppressed by the North. Young men from both sides wanted adventure and new experiences.

Most young recruits had grown up in small towns or on farms in rural areas. Few had ever been away from home before. They faced many difficulties, especially early in the war when the armies were ill-equipped and could not even provide uniforms for soldiers. Some new recruits found uniforms on the battlefields, where they gathered up the clothing and equipment of the dead. Soldiers spent hours marching in hot and cold weather along dusty or muddy roads. Food was also a problem, and meals were simple at best and often inadequate. Camp conditions were unsanitary and water was often contaminated. Soldiers frequently slept on the cold wet ground. Many contracted malaria, pneumonia, scurvy, dysentery, and other illnesses. While many soldiers died in battle, historians think more than half of the casualties in the Civil War resulted from illness.

Young soldiers were teased and criticized by their elders, who told them they were too young or small to do the job. Many also suffered from homesickness. After the fighting began, many young soldiers became terrified and wished to return home. Some deserted their units. As they became more experienced, young soldiers became familiar with death

and the horrible sights of battle. One expressed these new feelings in a letter he wrote home: "Such sights do not affect me as they once did. I can not describe the change nor do I know when it took effect, yet I know that there is a change for I look on the carcass of a man with pretty much feeling as I would do were it a horse or hog" (Wheeler, 1976).

Many boys wrote home about their fear of dying, especially alone. Soldiers feared that if they died on the battlefield their body might be left unclaimed, their identity unknown. To show respect for fallen comrades, groups of soldiers searched the fields after the fighting ended. They gathered the bodies and tried to recognize their fallen comrades, whom they buried with headboards to mark the site. Those who could not be identified were buried in mass, unmarked graves. Thousands of soldiers met this fate.

Some young soldiers were captured and imprisoned by the enemy. As the war dragged on, prison camps became overcrowded and filthy. Prisoners were exposed to extremes of hot and cold. Diseases spread rapidly and food became even scarcer and poorer in quality. Letters described how soldiers hunted rats for food and sold extra rats to other hungry prisoners. Thousands of prisoners of war died, especially in the Confederate prisons.

Many young soldiers distinguished themselves in battle, and thousands were wounded or killed in action. A number of young soldiers received the Medal of Honor and other medals and citations.

After the war, numerous young survivors were left sickly or disabled. The shells and bullets used in the war were powerful enough to rip off limbs and blind people, among other injuries. William Black, age 12, had his hand and arm shattered by shellfire. He is thought to be the youngest soldier wounded during the Civil War.

Medical treatments could do little for the victims, and there were few medics near enough to the battlefields to aid the wounded promptly. Wounds often became infected. The usual treatment was to amputate an infected limb to save the soldier's life. There were no truly effective anesthetics to put the patient to sleep during this frightening procedure. Doctors administered chloroform or, if none was available, patients drank liquor to dull their senses.

Young people's lives were dramatically affected on the homefront, too. In some cases, young people living in the North had relatives in the South. Different political loyalties sometimes tore families apart, and war prevented them from seeing each other. Many children left school to work on farms or in factories after their fathers and older brothers left for the army. Families were hard-pressed to keep farms running with older men gone. Children had to do hard physical labor and learn new tasks. Because many mothers had to work in the fields or in factories, children assumed new duties at home, such as doing laundry, ironing, cleaning, cooking, and baking.

After the war ended in 1865, people all over the United States faced many adjustments. More than 620,000 people had been killed during the war, and over 1,200,000 were wounded. Most of the civilian casualties and destruction took place in the South. These deaths and injuries affected millions of families and communities in every part of the country as people worked to rebuild homes, farms, and lives. Some families in the North found themselves more prosperous after the war. Companies had produced more efficient machines for running farms with less manpower, and many farmers purchased these items for the first time. Young people learned to operate horse-drawn mowers and rakes and other new tools. In some cases, they improved the productivity of their family farms during the war. *See also* BOYD, ISABELLE "BELLE"; CLEM, JOHNNY; DRUMMER BOYS; NEW MARKET, BATTLE OF.

Further Reading: Bruce Catton, *This Hallowed Ground* (1956); Burke Davis, *The Civil War* (1982); Paul Fatou, *Letters of a Civil War Surgeon* (1961); James Marten, *The Children's Civil War* (1998); Jim Murphy, *The Boys' War* (1990); Emmy E. Werner, *Reluctant Witnesses* (1998); Richard Wheeler, *Voices of the Civil War* (1976).

American Friends Service Committee (AFSC)

The American Friends Service Committee (AFSC), an independent Quaker organization, was founded in 1917 to establish relief programs for people in war-torn countries. The AFSC offered conscientious objectors, who did not engage in combat, a chance to aid civilian victims of World War I. Besides direct relief, the AFSC expanded its programs to provide peace education, foster community development, and promote human rights in the U.S. and more than 20 other countries. Programs are designed to combat poverty and social injustice, which the AFSC regards as the root causes of war. The organization receives support from people of various religions, races, and cultures.

The AFSC was founded on the principles of the Society of Friends (Quakers), who oppose war and advocate nonviolent means to resolve problems. During World War I, the AFSC trained hundreds of conscientious objectors, many of them young men, to do relief and reconstruction work in France. The AFSC provided food, clothing, housing, and health care. After the war, the AFSC helped feed one million hungry children in Germany and Austria, and helped other war victims rebuild their lives and communities. In the years that followed, the organization provided relief in other conflicts and smaller wars throughout the world. AFSC workers distributed milk, food, and medicine to people in Russia during the revolution (1917) and helped both sides during the Spanish Civil War (1936–1939) and the Chinese Civil War (1940s). They aided both Hindus and Muslims in India when civil war broke out there in the early 1940s and provided war relief in Korea (1950–1953).

The AFSC was active in numerous countries throughout World War II. During the 1930s and 1940s, AFSC staff and volunteers helped Jews of all ages to leave Germany and other occupied countries and worked to hide Jewish refugees in France and other countries. The group sponsored orphanages and safe houses for Jewish children and provided food to refugee camps. In the United States,

AFSC staff and volunteers helped Japanese Americans who were forced to live in internment camps. In 1942, the AFSC helped 2,866 young people scheduled for internment to be placed instead in hundreds of American colleges and universities, many of them Quaker-affiliated. The AFSC also assisted individual internees and helped to protect Japanese Americans' pre-war property while they were gone. In 1943, the AFSC aided Japanese Americans with resettlement after they left the camps.

After World War II, the AFSC helped to resettle refugees and carry out reconstruction work in Europe, Japan, China, and North Africa. It operated milk stations and shipped food to orphanages. In 1947, the AFSC, along with the British Friends Service Council (BFSC), was awarded the Nobel Peace Prize for post-war relief work.

Since 1948, the AFSC has worked in the Middle East, beginning with relief work for hundreds of thousands of Palestinian refugees after the 1948 Arab-Israeli War. Along with material aid, the group ran schools for children living in the war-torn Gaza Strip. The organization has sponsored numerous programs to help refugees in Algeria (1962), Nigeria (1970), Nicaragua (1985), and other countries. Besides food, clothing, medicine, and health care, the AFSC offers children school supplies and educational programs.

From 1954, when military conflict began to escalate in Southeast Asia, until the Vietnam War ended in 1975, the AFSC protested U.S. involvement in the region while operating programs to help people who were afflicted by the war. In 1966, the AFSC set up a rehabilitation center for youth who had lost limbs. Other health care facilities were set up in Vietnam, Cambodia, and Laos. In the United States, the AFSC operated programs to counsel young men who objected, as a matter of conscience, to serving in combat-related positions during the Vietnam War. These men were encouraged to do community service or relief work.

Today, AFSC activities have expanded to include many service projects. In the United States, the AFSC works with inner-city youth and in poverty-stricken regions such as Appalachia. Programs include mentoring, tutoring, job training, anti-violence education, and help with farming, community organization, famine relief, and medical care. Such programs help communities raise and harvest food, finance farm machinery, and develop clean drinking water supplies. These activities are viewed as important ways to prevent conditions that give rise to war, such as poverty, hopelessness, and misunderstandings and hatreds among people of different races, religions, and nationalities.

To promote peace, the AFSC has also sent delegations to war-torn countries, such as Somalia, to encourage both sides to work out their problems peacefully. The AFSC works with NGOs (Non-Governmental Organizations) that cooperate with people in nations with whom the United States has suspended diplomatic relations, such as Cuba.

Young people are active in various AFSC undertakings, including exchange programs to promote goodwill between nations and youth groups that travel the U.S. as part of Peace Caravans, speaking about ways to attain world peace. They present their views using videos, dance and rap music, and slideshows. Young people in various communities also attend and organize peace education groups and meetings.

Other programs involve youth abroad. In 1996, the AFSC began developing a coalition of youth-serving groups in Palestine, beginning with a meeting of young people from the Gaza Strip, West Bank, Egypt, Israel, and Jordan. Other meetings have been convened for youth on opposing sides of various international conflicts. *See also* CONSCIENTIOUS OBJECTORS; INTERNMENT CAMPS (U.S.); LE CHAMBON-SUR-LIGNON; QUAKERS (SOCIETY OF FRIENDS).

Further Reading: American Friends Service Committee, Fact Sheets: "Introduction to the American Friends Service Committee," Philadelphia: AFSC, October 1994; Philip Hallie, *Lest Innocent Blood Be Shed* (1979).

Santiago (Jimmy) McKinn (center), shown here with a group of Apache children, was a white boy captured by Apaches in 1885 in New Mexico. He was freed in 1886. *Photo by Camillus S. Fly, Courtesy of Museum of New Mexico, Neg. No. 11649.*

American Indian Wars

The Indian Wars were a series of conflicts in the western United States in the late nineteenth century between Native Americans and the white settlers who were moving into the Indians' ancestral lands. These battles came after decades of conflicts and suffering on both sides. Often, one attack followed another as people on both sides sought revenge. For instance, after whites killed some young Creek warriors in 1811, Chief Red Eagle led raids against white settlers. At Fort Mims, near present-day Mobile, Alabama, about 573 people, mostly women and children, were murdered during one of these raids. Only 36 people escaped, few of them children. An African-American girl from the fort, who managed to float down a river to safety after being wounded, told people what had happened. When white troops led by Andrew Jackson attacked Creek settlements, hundreds of Indian women and children were killed or fled into the woods with no food.

Anger over these kinds of events increased hostility among white soldiers and Native American warriors. Many soldiers who fought in U.S. cavalry units assigned to the West took their families to live with them in forts or frontier outposts. The children, who were called "army brats," had to learn to protect themselves in case a post was attacked while the men were gone. They learned to ride horses and to shoot. Occasionally, when relations with nearby tribes were peaceful, they became friends with Indian children. Sometimes, white children were taken as hostages after Indian attacks on their settlements and were raised in Indian families. Some tribes, such as the Apaches, treated captive women and children as equals.

Indian boys in their teens often fought with older warriors, especially when white soldiers attacked their settlements. During the November 1868 Battle of Washita, led by General George Custer against a group of Cheyenne, Captain Frederick Benteen noted the bravery of a boy who looked no older than 14. During that attack, U.S. troops burned down hundreds of tipis, and destroyed the Indians' pots, pans, stores of food, and other possessions. More than 100 Indians were killed. When the battle ended, the Cheyenne had killed two white children and a white woman in their camp to keep them from being rescued.

Similar battles took place throughout the West. In November 1876, U.S. cavalry attacked the Cheyenne camp of Chief Dull Knife on the Powder River of Wyoming and drove out the people, destroying their tipis, clothes, weapons, horses, and food. The surviving Cheyenne became so cold that some children froze to death as they wandered on foot after their camp was destroyed.

Certain tribes, such as the Apache of the Southwest, were known for their fierce warriors. Apache men began training in physical strength and bravery early in life. As children, they learned to run miles a day, in bare feet, across the desert and up steep hills. They were also good horsemen but did not depend only on their horses to carry them around. Children learned the location of water sources, hiding places, and trails to help them escape from their enemies.

Geronimo, the fierce Mibres Apache leader, became a warrior after Mexicans under General Carasco killed a group of his people, including his wife and three children. After years of fighting, the remaining Apaches were sent to a reservation in Florida in 1886. The climate and conditions there were so different from the Southwest that hundreds of children sickened and died, along with many adults.

A number of famous leaders, such as the Sioux chief Sitting Bull, became known as warriors while still in their teens. In 1874, one of the best-known war chiefs was 18-year-old Quanah Parker, whose mother was white and whose father was Comanche. Parker was with a group of Indians gathered at Palo Duro Canyon in northwestern Texas. Thousands of men, women, and children were taking part in a traditional buffalo hunt. General William T. Sherman had sent telegrams ordering U.S troops to find the Indi-

ans, destroy their possessions, and send them to Fort Sill. When the Comanches saw Colonel Mackenzie's cavalry, they fled, but the troops then burned all the Indians' belongings. The Comanches were left to wander cold and hungry during the next winter. The survivors gradually arrived at Fort Sill from where they were forced to move to reservations.

In an attack in December 1890 on Sitting Bull's camp in South Dakota, the chief was killed and his 17-year-old son was shot by cavalry officers. Thirty-eight people managed to escape and took refuge in the camp of Big Foot at Wounded Knee on the Pine Ridge Reservation in South Dakota. The final confrontation of the Indian Wars ended in this camp in December 1890.

As a result of the Indian Wars and other efforts by the U.S. government to remove Native Americans, thousands of children became displaced from their ancestral homelands and lost parents and loved ones. They also experienced hunger and deprivation, and many died from diseases brought to their lands by white settlers. These diseases were new to the Native peoples and they had not developed any immunity. Some historians believe that diseases were deliberately brought into Indian communities by means of blankets and other items that were infected with the smallpox virus.

Children were also forcibly separated from their culture and communities when the federal government implemented a policy of assimilation—the idea that Native Americans should blend in with white society and give up their own customs and religions in exchange for white ways, which were viewed as "superior." In 1865, while the Indian Wars were underway, the U.S. government passed a law requiring Indian children to attend government-run boarding schools. For decades, the children were taken to these schools, given haircuts and the clothing of white people and ordered not to speak their native languages or follow their cultural traditions or religions.

During the 1880s, U.S. soldiers were sent into Native American villages, such as those of the Hopi in the Southwest, to take children by force. In 1891, 104 Hopi children were kidnapped from the village of Oraibi in present-day Arizona. Indian leaders living with their tribes on reservations were also threatened with the loss of food rations and other needed supplies if they refused to let children attend the schools. *See also* DEERFIELD RAID; NEZ PERCE WAR; SAND CREEK MASSACRE; SEMINOLE WARS; WOUNDED KNEE MASSACRE.

Further Reading: Ralph K. Andrist, *The Long Death* (1964); Fairfax Downey, *Indian-Fighting Army* (1941); Odie B. Falik, *Crimson Desert* (1974); Stanley Vestal, *Sitting Bull* (1957).

American Near East Refugee Aid (ANERA)

American Near East Refugee Aid (ANERA) is a nonprofit American group that operates programs to provide education, health care, and jobs for Palestinian and Lebanese young people living in the West Bank, Gaza, and Lebanon, all areas of the Middle East that have been afflicted by ongoing conflicts and violence.

The organization, which was founded in 1968, raises money to supply housing, food, books, and equipment, and to fund teachers' salaries. As of 1997, ANERA sponsored six schools and dormitories for impoverished children in the Middle East, East Jerusalem, Gaza, and other places. A number of the children served by ANERA are orphans and some have physical or mental handicaps. For example, the Atfaluna Center in Gaza serves deaf children. The Sun Day Care Center in Gaza works with children who have various disabilities, including hearing problems. The Al-Kafaat Rehabilitation Institute in Beirut, Lebanon, educates children with mental and physical disabilities. *See also* ARAB-ISRAELI WARS; ARMENIAN-TURKISH CONFLICT; LEBANESE CIVIL WAR.

Further Reading: American Near East Refugee Aid (ANERA), Information pamphlet, 1997.

American Revolution (1775–1783)

Young people were affected in numerous ways by the American Revolution and the war fought by American colonists between 1776

and 1781 to win their independence from Great Britain. Young people witnessed and participated in heated discussions as differ-

The American Revolution is symbolized in this painting by A.M. Willard entitled "Spirit of '76." *Corbis-Bettmann*

ent generations disagreed about the war and neighbors took different political positions. Some children were forbidden to associate with former friends who were loyal to a different side.

A number of children lived in homes that were turned into military headquarters or where military leaders met from time to time. Their lives changed as soldiers took over different rooms and used the family's food and other possessions. At times, friendly troops were invited to use a particular home.

Within families, young people saw fathers and older brothers go off to fight. Mothers often had to assume new roles and duties, as did the children themselves, as families struggled to run households, stores, businesses, and farms without men and older brothers. Teachers were harder to find, so many young people could not continue their educations. Families had to do without many things children used and needed. Food and clothing were in short supply. Farm families were sometimes raided by British troops seeking food and livestock. Children were sent door-to-door to collect rags that could be made into paper, which was scarce during the war.

Young people worked for the war effort in numerous ways. They helped sew military uniforms, knit clothing, roll bandages, and collect money and other goods for the troops. They performed duties in hospitals where soldiers were treated for wounds and illnesses. In some towns, young people helped erect fortifications to protect the community.

At times, young people fought to protect their homes from the enemy. When British Loyalists (those colonists who supported the British Crown) came to the North Carolina home of Jane Thomas to confiscate the ammunition that had been stored there, Thomas's daughters and a young man who lived with the family helped Thomas fend them off. She and the young man fired at the troops while the girls hurriedly loaded and reloaded the guns.

Many young people made substantial contributions to the war effort as spies and messengers. Because they looked innocent, children were often able to carry secret messages without being stopped and searched. Some of them were sent on horseback or by boat to carry important information to members of the military. Other daring young people spied and served as scouts.

Some young people worked to help the British defeat the Patriots. Eighteen-year-old Thomas Hickey was executed by the Americans after being found guilty of taking part in a plot to kidnap George Washington and turn him over to the enemy. In the early days of the war, Hickey had been one of Washington's personal guards.

Family members might also become camp-followers. Young wives sometimes accompanied their husbands to military camps. Some women who accompanied male relatives to camps brought their children along. Young children made themselves useful by carrying water or firewood for meal preparation. Older children cooked, washed and mended clothing, ran errands, and performed other chores. Most of these tasks fell to young

women or wives because domestic chores were still viewed as "women's work."

Thousands of young men joined the army. Some boys under 18, the age limit for becoming a soldier, pretended to be older so they could join the army. Some boys as young as 12 served as soldiers. These youths, such as 14-year-old Theophilus Sargent, who fought with the revolutionary troops, managed to hide their true ages long enough to take part in one or more battles. Those recruits who were found to be underage were not allowed to fight but were assigned to be drummers or cooks' helpers, or to hold other nonfighting jobs. *See also* DALE, BETTY; DARRAGH, JOHN; DOWDY, BETSY; GEIGER, EMILY; MCBRIDE, MAGGIE; MOORE, BETH.

Further Reading: Elizabeth Anticaglia, *Heroines of '76* (1975); Katherine Bakeless and John Bakeless, *Spies of the Revolution* (1962); Wallace Brown, *The Good Americans* (1969); Charles E. Claghorn, *Women Patriots of the American Revolution* (1991); Henry Steele Commager and Richard B. Morris, *The Spirit of "Seventy-Six"* (1967); Linda Grant DePauw, *Founding Mothers* (1975); Phebe A. Hanaford, *Daughters of America,* (1882); Mary Beth Norton, *Liberty's Daughters* (1980); Howard Zinn, *A People's History of the United States* (1980).

AmeriCares Foundation

AmeriCares, an international relief and humanitarian organization based in New Canaan, Connecticut, aids children who are victims of war and other disasters. The organization was founded in 1982 to help people around the world, of any race, creed, or political persuasion. In 1998, AmeriCares airlifted tons of medical supplies and other materials to Albanian refugees fleeing from the Kosovo region of Serbia, part of the former Yugoslavia. Tens of thousands of refugees, including many children and young people, were displaced by fighting in the region. In April, the organization delivered 32,000 pounds of medical supplies to Tirana, the Albanian capital, and in July, AmeriCares sent more than 35,000 pounds of medications, antibiotics, hospital supplies, and various materials needed to provide care for children and newborn infants. *See also* BOSNIA; KOSOVO.

Angola

Further Reading: "About AmeriCares"; "International Programs" at <http://www.americares.org>; AmeriCares, 161 Cherry St., New Canaan, CT 06840.

"Angel of Death." *See* MENGELE, JOSEF

Angola

Between 1956 and 1975, Angolans fought for their independence from Portugal, which had controlled the southwest African colony since the seventeenth century. Children served as soldiers with the National Front for the Liberation of Angola and the National Union for the Total Independence of Angola (UNITA). Both boys and girls of all classes were recruited by the Popular Movement for the Liberation of Angola (MPLA).

In 1975, when independence from Portugal was finally achieved, a civil war destined to last 15 years broke out between the MPLA-controlled government and UNITA guerillas. Young people under age 18 were brought into the military, where they served in village militias and in combat units. Both sides recruited young boys for their armies. Young soldiers in the MPLA received only two or three months of training before they were sent into combat. Some had been kidnapped from school and forced into service.

UNITA also used captured child soldiers, some only 14 years old. The guerillas gave military training to young children, using those under 16 to transport supplies and for other noncombat functions. Young soldiers received no pay. Those who volunteered were drawn to the army for patriotic reasons, and often because they would receive food and clothing.

During the civil war, civilians suffered severely; villages were attacked and UNITA troops destroyed water and food supplies and electrical lines. An estimated 330,000 Angolan children died from war-related causes between 1980 and 1988. Children and young people died of hunger and disease brought on by lack of food. UNITA forces placed land mines on food-producing land so that the opposing side could not produce what it needed. More than 10,000 people died

from famine in the province of Benguela, and another million went hungry throughout Angola. Many families fled to refugee camps in Zambia, then moved to Portugal where they were sheltered in an abandoned jail.

Surveys by relief organizations show the impact of war on Angolan youth. A 1995 study conducted by the United Nations Children's Fund (UNICEF) showed that 20 percent of the children in Angola had been separated at some time from their families. Most of these separations were accidental. In 1995, the Christian Children's Fund conducted interviews with 200 boys and girls ages 8 to 16 from 10 Angolan provinces. Ten percent of the children had lost one or more brothers in the war, while 24 percent had lost at least one parent. Nearly 60 percent had lost relatives. Almost all had seen shooting exchanges, while 90 percent had witnessed shellings and 80 percent had seen aerial bombings. Nearly 70 percent had observed land mine explosions. Ninety percent of these 200 young people had seen dead and wounded persons, and a full 70 percent had witnessed murders and torture. Relief organizations worked to help young people deal with the emotional trauma as well as the devastating physical impact of the war.

More thousands of children became refugees and suffered from hunger and starvation in 1998 and 1999 as the UNITA forces attacked the cities of Cuito, Huambo, and Malanje. The United Nations estimated that 780,000 people fled from their homes between April 1998 and April 1999. Ten people were killed each day in April 1999 as UNITA shelled the city of Cuito. Overpopulation was a serious problem as refugees poured into the three cities. Many families left behind their maize, wheat, and rice crops when they were forced to flee their homes. More children became ill from malnutrition and infectious diseases and diarrhea resulting from inadequate sanitary facilities and unclean water.

Polio, which attacks the motor nerves in the body, posed another threat. More than 600 cases of polio and 33 deaths from the disease were reported in Angola. To prevent the spread of polio, health workers from international agencies vaccinated 600,000 children under age five.

To help Angolans, the United Nation's World Food Programme worked to bring food into Angola by air. China, Italy, and France were among the nations that sent millions of dollars in food and humanitarian aid. *See also* AFRICA; REFUGEES; SOLDIERS, CHILD; UNITED NATIONS CHILDREN'S FUND (UNICEF).

Further Reading: Action for South Africa (ACTSA), "Humanitarian Disaster Looms," *"Angola Peace Monitor,"* 29, no. 7, March 26, 1999; Action for South Africa (ACTSA), "Hunger Stalks Besieged Cities," *Angola Peace Monitor,* 29, no. 8, April 29, 1999; United Nations Children's Fund, *"Angola: Alliance for Life"* and "Famine and Disease" in *The State of the World's Children, 1996* (1996); United Nations Children's Fund, *Children on the Front Lines* (1989); Dorothea E. Woods, ed., *Child Soldiers* (1993).

Anielewicz, Mordechai (1919–1943)

During World War II, Mordechai Anielewicz, a young man trapped in the Warsaw Ghetto, led members of a resistance group called the Jewish Fighters Organization (JFO). Born in a poor section of Warsaw, he moved to Russia during his teens and joined a Zionist youth group called *Hashomer Hatzair.* Anielewicz returned to Poland in 1939 to help his countrymen fight the Nazi invaders.

After he and other Jews were confined in the ghetto, he concluded it would be better to die fighting, because the Nazis would kill them anyway. Ghetto historian Emmanuel Ringelblum wrote, "[Anielewicz] was sure that neither he nor his combatants would survive the liquidation of the Ghetto. He was sure that they would die like stray dogs and no one would even know their last resting-place." (Ringelblum, 1958)

Anielewicz ran a secret radio station to inform ghetto residents about what was happening outside and he wrote articles for an underground paper that also circulated outside the ghetto and was read throughout Poland. Children helped to distribute the papers.

As the Germans began rounding up people in 1943, Anielewicz was among those who resisted deportation. In April 1943, the Nazis set out to arrest all the Jews who remained in the ghetto. Two thousand heavily armed German soldiers arrived in tanks and trucks. They were shocked to be met by the armed JFO, which fought them for 11 hours before the soldiers retreated. In a letter, Anielewicz described the JFO's gallant effort: "The dream of my life has become true. Jewish self-defense in the ghetto has become a fact. Jewish armed resistance and retaliation have become a reality" (Kermish, 1986).

Before the resistance was crushed, Anielewicz wrote to one of his group members about the urgent need for more guns, ammunition, and grenades. It was his last letter. As the Germans overpowered the ghetto, Anielewicz and most other JFO fighters were killed. A few young resisters managed to escape and join partisan units. After the war, a memorial statue to Anielewicz was built in Tel Aviv, Israel, near a kibbutz named Yad Mordechai. *See also* BIELSKI BROTHERS; HOLOCAUST; JEWISH FIGHTERS ORGANIZATION (JFO); POLAND (WORLD WAR II); RESISTANCE MOVEMENTS (WORLD WAR II); WARSAW GHETTO; WORLD WAR II.

Further Reading: Joseph Kermish, ed., *To Live with Honor and Die with Honor* (1986); Dan Kurzman, *The Bravest Battle* (1976); Emmanuel Ringelblum, *Notes from the Warsaw Ghetto* (1958).

Anti-War Movement (Vietnam War)

One of the largest and best-known anti-war movements propelled by youth began in the 1960s when students across the United States and in such countries as France and Great Britain protested Western involvement in the Vietnam War.

In the U.S., young people passed out flowers as a symbol of love and peace. They displayed posters and buttons that read, "Make Love Not War" and "War Is Not Healthy for Children and Other Living Things." Some young people chanted angry slogans criticizing President Lyndon B. Johnson, such as, "Hey, hey, LBJ, how many kids did you kill today?" Students and young people who became known as "Flower Children" or "Peaceniks" produced and distributed underground newspapers and anti-war pamphlets.

Vietnam War protestors burn their draft cards at an anti-war rally in New York's Central Park in April 1967. *Corbis-Bettmann.*

Students at Columbia University and other campuses staged anti-war strikes and sit-ins, seizing control of administration buildings or refusing to move from certain places on campus. About 750,000 people, many of them youths and students, gathered at the Lincoln Memorial in Washington, D.C., for a peace rally in 1969.

Prior to 1966, college students were automatically exempt from military service. However, that year, because of the escalating war in Vietnam, the Selective Service System changed its policy and decided to end automatic student deferments. Under the new system, only students with good grades would receive deferments. Students with a low academic ranking could receive a one-year deferment if they passed a test given each year by the Selective Service in May and June. Those who failed were immediately eligible for the draft.

During the mid- to late 1960s, students demonstrated against the war on streets, blocked military recruiters on campus, picketed when public officials appeared to give speeches, and sat-in at places like Dow Chemical Corporation, a company that manufactured napalm. Protesters handed out anti-draft leaflets at military induction centers and gave young men information about how to avoid the draft. Some young men left the country and moved to Canada to avoid the draft. Young males publicly burned their draft cards, often in front of induction centers. Men who did so faced prison terms.

Protests escalated in 1970 as the war expanded and U.S. troops moved into Cambodia. Tragedy struck on May 4, 1970, during an anti-war demonstration at Kent State University in Kent, Ohio. For two years, anti-war groups had been active on that campus. In 1968, they objected to the presence of military and police recruitment drives at the university. The next year, members of a group called Students for a Democratic Society (SDS) objected to the campus ROTC program. The college then banned the SDS from campus. Students organized a large protest at Kent State on April 30, 1970, when President Richard Nixon declared that the U.S.

would send military troops to Cambodia, which borders Vietnam. During two days of demonstrations, the ROTC building was set on fire.

Governor James Rhodes ordered the Ohio National Guard to the campus to restore order. However, more students seemed to join the demonstration after the Guardsmen arrived. On May 4, large numbers of students joined a gathering on the campus commons. Guardsmen threw tear-gas canisters at the crowds of students, and some of them fired their weapons. Four students were killed by gunfire. Students across the country expressed horror and anger at these deaths, and the anti-war movement grew larger. Demonstrations involving millions of students were held on at least half of the nation's campuses. As more demonstrations took place, some 500 colleges and universities cancelled classes, and violence against ROTC buildings and other threats prompted more colleges to seek help from the National Guard. Fifty campuses never restored order and closed their campuses for the rest of the term.

By 1971, the anti-war movement had grown to include more politicians and adult Americans. Most of the people and all the speakers at a mass rally in Washington that year were over age 30. President Nixon pledged to end the war, and negotiators at the Paris Peace Talks reached an agreement in 1973. The last U.S. troops left Vietnam in 1975. *See also* COLD WAR; CONSCIENTIOUS OBJECTORS; CONSCRIPTION; THE RIBBON; SELECTIVE SERVICE ACTS; *TINKER V. DES MOINES*; VIETNAM WAR.

Further Reading: Scott L. Bills, ed., *Kent State/May 4* (1988); Thomas R. Hensley et al., *The Kent State Incident* (1981); Milton Meltzer, *Ain't Gonna Study War No More* (1985); Caleb S. Rossiter, *The Chimes of Freedom Flashing* (1998); Milton Viorst, *Fire in the Streets* (1979).

Arab-Israeli Wars

Arab-Jewish conflicts in the Middle East date back thousands of years. Contemporary disagreements center around who should rightfully occupy various parts of the land once called Palestine, and involve cultural and religious conflicts as well as legal and territorial disputes. Young people have served in the military on various sides of these recent conflicts and have been assigned to peacekeeping forces in the region. Children growing up in the region have experienced fear and have learned to mistrust and often hate the opposing side. They have also experienced many kinds of deprivation, including lack of food and shelter, and loss of opportunities for education and community life.

During the late 1800s, Zionists (Jews committed to founding a modern Jewish state in their biblical homeland) began settling in Palestine, which was part of the Turkish Empire and came under British control in 1917. Zionists contended that as long as Jews had no national state or country of origin they would be vulnerable to continuing persecution and deprived of protection under international laws no matter where they lived, even if their families had been there for centuries. Jewish organizations bought land in Palestine and Jews moved there to build a homeland.

The British government supported the Zionist cause in 1917, but Arab opposition led them to limit this support. During the 1930s, Jews tried to flee from Nazi-occupied Germany and Austria, but the British imposed strict limits on Jewish immigration to Palestine. Antagonism between Arabs and Jewish settlers led to violence and many acts of terrorism that affected young people. Terrorist attacks and conflicts increased during World War II when Jews defied British immigration laws to smuggle men, women, and children into Palestine. Many new settlers were Holocaust survivors who had lost everything during the war. Among them were young Jews and Jewish orphans, who came to live in communal settlements or with adoptive families.

Young Palestinians have experienced years of war and political unrest in the conflict-ridden Middle East. In 1947, a decree by the United Nations divided the land in what was then called Palestine into two areas. The portion along the west bank of the Jordan River was allocated to Palestinians while the portion along the Mediterranean Sea became the new nation of Israel. Arab nations did not accept this plan, and terrorist acts perpetrated by both Arabs and Israelis caused deaths and injuries in the years that followed. Palestinian children were among the more than 250 victims of the Bir Yassin massacre carried out by the Israeli group Irgun early in 1948. Likewise, Palestinian terrorists killed and injured Israelis of all ages.

In 1947, when Arabs made up more than two-thirds of Palestine's population, compared to about 600,000 Jews, the British withdrew from Palestine and gave control to the United Nations (UN), which divided the land into a Jewish area and three Palestinian areas that were to be united as one. In April 1948, fighting broke out between Jews and Palestinians for control of Jerusalem. On April 8, Jewish terrorists killed 254 men, women, and children in the village of Bir Yassin. Four days later, Arabs retaliated by killing 77 Jewish doctors, nurses, teachers, and students who were en route to a hospital. Attacks by both sides on villages and kibbutzim (Jewish agricultural settlements) resulted in the deaths of women and children, as well as other civilians.

On May 14, 1948, one day before the departure of the British, Jewish leader David Ben-Gurion declared Palestine the independent Jewish state of Israel. United Arab forces consisting of Egyptians, Jordanians, Iraqis, Syrians, and Saudia Arabians fought Israeli troops in a war that lasted eight months. Soldiers on both sides included men and boys under the age of 21. During that time, bombs exploded on streets and in Jewish buildings in Jerusalem, killing young people and others. Teenage nurses were among those who accompanied groups of Israeli soldiers who were sent out in convoys to guard the streets leading into Jewish areas of the city.

Arab forces requested a cease-fire, which took effect in January 1949, but still refused to recognize the state of Israel. By 1949, Israel controlled an area slightly larger than that which the United Nations had allocated to it. The cease-fire gave Egypt, Jordan, and Syria control over other parts of western Palestine. About 750,000 Palestinian Arabs had become refugees after leaving their former homes in Israeli territory. The Palestinians, including

tens of thousands of young people, were left without the country the UN had marked out for them. Most of the refugees lacked the means to travel and had to live in camps the UN set up for them outside Israeli borders. These homeless men, women, and children endured grim conditions, and their plight continued to trouble many people in the decades that followed.

Hostilities between Palestinians and Israelis persisted after 1949 and sometimes exploded into acts of terrorism as well as wars. Five wars and numerous attacks, initiated by both sides, afflicted civilians and claimed thousands of young lives. Resources and jobs became scarcer as more Jewish refugees arrived from the Soviet Union and other countries and the Palestinian population also increased.

In 1964, Arab allies formed the Palestinian Liberation Organization (PLO). Young men were an active part of this organization, which declared it would destroy Israel. Raids on both sides of the Israeli border increased in 1966 and 1967, and Arab leaders announced they would invade Israel. Egyptian leader Gamal Abdel Nasser blockaded Israeli ports in 1967 and ordered UN peacekeeping patrols to leave the Sinai Peninsula. Israel then launched an attack on Egypt known as the Six-Day War. On June 5, 1967, Israeli bombers struck military targets in Egypt, Iraq, Jordan, and Syria. To increase safety around its borders, Israel claimed new territory—the Sinai Peninsula, the West Bank of the Jordan River, Gaza, and the Golan Heights on the border with Syria. Tensions increased as more Palestinians found themselves living inside Israeli territory. Children in Gaza had many needs and relief organizations came to the region. Responding to a request from the United Nations, the American Friends Service Committee (AFSC) set up preschool and kindergarten programs for Arab children in Gaza.

The Six-Day War ended when Egypt and Syria agreed to a cease-fire. The war caused fear for young people on both the Arab and Israeli sides of the conflict. One 10-year-old Israeli child wrote,

I got into bed frozen with fear. The room was dark and the darkness frightened me even more. You could hear the shelling far away and the house was shaking. Airplanes roared overhead. I was afraid the ceiling would fall any minute and perhaps the house would collapse too. (Kovner, 1971)

During the war, older boys from Israeli schools took over farm jobs as older men went to military duty. After the nation was founded in 1948, both men and women were required to serve for three years in the Israeli military beginning at age 19. Younger children worked for the war effort by digging ditches and filling sandbags. Israeli children spent much time inside bomb shelters supplied with blankets and pillows. They ate rice soup, potatoes, eggs, vegetable salad, and bread. While they were in a shelter, two fourth-grade girls in Kibbutz Barkai made drawings of the shelter and wrote on them: "If we had died, they would have found our drawings and known we had been here" (Kovner, 1971).

After the 1967 war, the UN passed a resolution asking the Arab nations to formally recognize Israel and asking the Israelis to withdraw from the territories seized during the war, but both sides refused. Another war, lasting for three weeks in 1973, ended in a stalemate. Through the Organization of Petroleum Exporting Countries (OPEC), Arab nations exerted pressure on other countries to support their cause. They raised oil prices and threatened to drastically reduce exports. The results of this "oil crisis," affected people of all ages around the world because oil plays a major role in the world economy.

Some Palestinians resorted to terrorism as a drastic method to bring more public attention to their cause. During the 1970s, they hijacked airplanes and set bombs in public places in various countries. Hostages were taken by members of the PLO. Many PLO groups lived in Lebanon, and Israeli forces invaded that country in 1977 and in 1982, actions that marked the onset of a new war in Lebanon. During this bloody war, Lebanese soldiers attacked some of the Palestinian camps and killed children and adults.

Meanwhile, the Palestinians endured poor housing and overcrowding in tents and then in cement block shelters. They lacked adequate water and sanitary facilities and did not have enough jobs to support themselves. Starting in December 1987, Palestinians of all ages protested the Israeli occupation of these areas through an uprising that featured mainly acts of civil disobedience, such as refusing to pay taxes and throwing stones at Israeli soldiers.

Palestinian children were active in this resistance, called the Intifada. It pitted young people against each other; young Israeli soldiers were attacked by gangs of young Palestinians with stones and grenades. Israeli soldiers retaliated by shooting at people suspected of launching attacks, by searching homes, by imposing curfews on towns, and by arresting people. Children were arrested, wounded, and killed during the Intifada. Schools closed down or were interrupted numerous times by violence and labor strikes. Young Palestinians told journalists that they felt hopeless about the future because they had few chances to get an education or a good job. They declared their intention to continue fighting for Palestinian independence.

Young Palestinians have also joined the fundamentalist Islamic Resistance Movement, called Hamas. The group operates clinics and schools for Palestinians, using donations from Iran and other Arab countries. Hamas also participates in demonstrations and acts of violence against Israel and has pledged to establish an Islamic state of Palestine.

In September 1993, Arab and Israeli leaders signed a peace accord that allowed limited self-rule to Palestinians in the occupied territories. However, Israelis opposing the terms of this agreement clashed with their Palestinian neighbors in the West Bank and Gaza Strip. Violence took lives on both sides. Palestinians were outraged when a Jewish settler opened fire on Muslims worshiping at a mosque in Hebron, killing at least 40 people.

More terrorist attacks killed a number of children in 1996, as members of militant Palestinian groups targeted buses and public places in Tel Aviv and Jerusalem for suicide bombing missions. Author David Grossman of Jerusalem described how fear plagued young people, including his 11-year-old son. Upon awaking one morning, the boy asked his father, "Has today's bombing happened already?" (Adler, 1996).

See also AMERICAN FRIENDS SERVICE COMMITTEE (AFSC); AMERICAN NEAR EAST REFUGEE AID (ANERA); EDUCATION; INTIFADA; LEBANESE CIVIL WAR; REFUGEES.

Further Reading: David J. Abodaher, *Youth in the Middle East* (1990); Jerry Adler, "Israel at War," *Newsweek,* March 18, 1996, pp. 34–40; Randolph S. Churchill and Winston S. Churchill, *The Six Day War* (1967); William Dudley, ed., *The Middle East* (1992); Abba Kovner, ed., *Childhood Under Fire* (1971); Roderick Macleish, *The Sun Stood Still* (1967); Everett Mendelsohn, *A Compassionate Peace* (1989).

Armenian-Turkish Conflict

Throughout the history of Turkey, wars have broken out between the Armenians and Turks. In ancient times, Armenia was an independent country in western Asia, but the country was later conquered and different sections of Armenia came under the control of Turkey, Iran, and Russia. Between 1894 and 1896, massacres by Turks killed more than 200,000 Armenians living in Turkish Armenia. Turkish troops carried out the killings under orders from the government. On one day in 1896, 3,000 men, women, and children died when troops set fire to an Armenian cathedral where they were hiding from their enemies.

Beginning in 1909, another series of killings called the Adana Massacres took place in the Cilicia region of Turkey. About 20,000 Armenians died. Again, many victims were burned inside churches where they had fled for refuge. In 1915, the Turkish government ordered that about 2.5 million Christian Armenians living in Turkey be sent away to Palestine and Syria. Christians in the country had been working for Armenian independence, and the Turkish government feared that they might help the enemy during World War I. About 1.5 million Armenians died between 1915 and 1923. These events have been called the first genocide of the twentieth century.

Police and military units rounded up men, women, and children all over the country. These people were then forced to march across hundreds of miles of rough terrain, including mountains and deserts. Numerous eyewitnesses described the atrocities that were committed against these unarmed people. They were beaten, shot, drowned, and tortured. Some were locked inside buildings then set on fire.

Kerop Bedoukian and his family, which included three sisters and two brothers, were among the victims of these events. He was nine years old in 1915 when the violence broke out. His family lived in the town of Sivas. After his father was taken away by soldiers, the family had little time to get ready for forced deportation as part of the thousands who would have to march to Aleppo. Bedoukian later recalled the "yelling and weeping by some women who were being forced out under the whips of the guards."

> I looked around me. About fifty wagons and hundreds of animals were parking helter-skelter. The voices of women and the cries of babies and children reached such a pitch that to carry on a conversation was impossible. . . . The caravan stretched out for miles, wagon wheels squeaking, guards on horseback galloping back and forth, whipping anyone who straggled behind. (Bedoukian, 1979)

Tens of thousands of children died during the death marches. Some were killed outright; others died from thirst, starvation, and illness during the marches. Many women and young girls were abducted and raped by Kurd soldiers and others, who allowed these girls to be raped again in the villages they were passing through. Girls were also taken away or sold as slaves.

During times when food was especially scarce, some parents saved their children by giving them their own rations of bread and water. They also made the sacrifice of giving their children to families who were willing to adopt them so the children could live. Parents left children behind as they themselves were rounded up for deportation, and, in most cases, killed. Some Turks reached out to help children and hide them from the troops. They also fed and sheltered needy children who had been orphaned.

One group from Sivas was forced to march in 110-degree weather in July 1915 from Harput to Aleppo. Of the 5,000 who survived the journey, about half were children. Within three months, only about 150 women and children were left alive of a population that had numbered about 300,000.

After the war ended in 1918, Armenian orphans were placed in institutions built with donations from people in the United States and Europe and staffed by Americans and Europeans. Millions of dollars worth of supplies were also sent from the U.S. Efforts were made to find orphaned children, some of whom were surviving as best they could on the streets, and bring them into the orphanages. Other orphans were being kept in homes or farms where they were forced to work long hours and were sometimes abused.

Many children had serious health problems, often related to malnutrition, and they were infested with lice. Some had lost not only parents but siblings and other relatives. Emotional wounds came from witnessing violence and being subjected to abuse themselves. One survivor, a young boy, reported having seen a Turkish youth beat an Armenian baby to death for no reason. Children had also been torn away from their culture and their institutions; some could not recall their native language.

To help these children, surrogate Armenian mothers were assigned to individual youths. The young people attended school, while orphanage officials tried to locate parents and other family members who might have survived. Occasionally, joyful reunions between siblings occurred at the orphanages. One girl from Sivas, who went to an orphanage, recalled,

> I was very happy in the orphanage. We all had the same story in that we all were Armenians who had gone through the deportation and had lost family. It was very clean . . . . The food was good and regular. Every morning we had a brief prayer meeting and then we went to classes. . . . We

had medical help as well, and in the summers they took us on retreat to another village. (Miller and Miller, 1993)

Another survivor said, "We used to dance and sing. We would sing a lot of sad songs and cry together. We used to teach each other the dances we knew according to the places we came from. We were sad, but happy with each other" (Miller and Miller, 1993).

In 1922, the Turkish government pressed these institutions to move the children out of the country, and some were sent to Greece, Egypt, or Lebanon. By then, many of the youths had learned trades or were prepared to study nursing or teaching. Some young men became apprenticed to tailors, shoemakers, carpenters, or other tradespeople in their new homelands. *See also* GENOCIDE; POST-TRAUMATIC STRESS DISORDER (PTSD).

Further Reading: Kerop Bedoukian, *Some of Us Survived* (1979); Donald E. Miller and Lorna Touryan Miller, *Survivors* (1993); Barbara Rogasky, *Smoke and Ashes* (1988).

Arrow Cross. *See* HUNGARY (WORLD WAR II)

Aryan Youth. *See* ADOLPH HITLER SCHOOLS; HITLER YOUTH; HOLOCAUST

Auerbacher, Inge (1934–)

Inge Auerbacher, a German Jew, survived the Holocaust and World War II as a young child. Her acclaimed autobiography, *I Am a Star*, details her harrowing experiences during those years. The title of the book refers to a Nazi edict issued in 1942. The edict required all Jewish persons over age six living in Germany, Austria, or occupied countries to wear some mark that identified them as Jewish, most commonly a yellow cloth Star of David, prominently sewn on their outer clothing, or an armband with a Star of David.

Auerbacher grew up in Kippenheim, in southern Germany, where her family had lived for generations. About 2,000 people lived in Kippenheim, including 60 Jewish families. One of Auerbacher's uncles was

Berthold Auerbach, a popular German folk writer. Auerbacher later wrote, "We were a happy community in Kippenheim until the sound of marching boots shattered the peace of our tranquil village. . . . [Kristallnacht (Crystal Night)] marked the beginning of terror that would continue for seven years" (Auerbacher, 1987). Inge was only three years old when her father and grandfather were taken off to Dachau on Crystal Night, November 9, 1938.

During the war, Auerbacher saw classmates disappear, and her grandmother was deported and killed by the Nazis. In 1942, she and her parents were sent to a concentration camp called Theresienstadt (Terezin) in German-occupied Czechoslovakia. Thousands of children were confined to this camp during the war. Auerbacher was one of only about 100 children who survived. See also CONCENTRATION CAMPS (WORLD WAR II); HOLOCAUST; KRISTALLNACHT; TEREZIN (THERESIENSTADT).

Further Reading: Inge Auerbacher, *I Am A Star* (1985).

Auschwitz. *See* AUSCHWITZ-BIRKENAU

Auschwitz-Birkenau

Auschwitz-Birkenau was the largest of six death camps built in Poland by the Nazis for the purpose of genocide. It was constructed in the Polish village of Oswiecim (Auschwitz in German) in 1940. A second camp, Auschwitz II-Birkenau, was built in 1941, and a third camp called Auschwitz III-Buna-Monowitz was completed early in 1942. This section contained a rubber factory and other industry where many prisoners, including young people, were forced to work as slaves.

At least 1.25 million people were murdered at this camp between May 1942 and the end of World War II in 1945. The Birkenau section of the camp contained gas chambers where people were killed with poison gas, after which their bodies were burned in the crematoria. High walls laced with electrified barb wire surrounded the camp, and guards could be seen throughout the camp.

When teenager Ernest Honig arrived there from Hungary with his brother, they saw "huge chimneys belching forth black smoke. There was a strange smell, like burning the feathers off a chicken before it was cooked. I didn't know that the smoke and the smell were not from chickens. I didn't know, until I found out later, that I was smelling our own flesh, our own families burning" (Adler, 1989).

A selection process took place when new trainloads of prisoners arrived. They were divided into groups, sent to a line on the right or on the left, depending on whether they would be put to work or killed. Those selected for slave labor had their heads and bodies shaved, and a number tattooed on their forearm with blue ink. Boys and girls younger than 14 were routinely killed shortly after arrival.

Older children (or those who could pass for at least 14) who were not killed outright faced a horrifying existence marked by exhausting labor, chronic hunger, exposure to the elements, lice, diseases, and cruel treatment by their captors, including physical abuse, acts of degradation, and sexual abuse. Some young people were also the victims of inhumane quasi-medical experiments.

At times, adults in the camp tried to save the lives of young people by hiding them before they were sent to the gas chambers. However, newborn infants were doomed to die if they were discovered, as were their mothers, in most cases. Children and young people had to be amazingly resourceful, as well as lucky, to stay alive in the cruel, unpredictable place that inmates called "hell on earth." Their main task was to obtain enough food to stay alive, since camp rations—pieces of bread, watery soup, coffee—were too meager to sustain life. Survivor Kitty Hart of Poland, sent to Auschwitz as a teenager, later wrote that she quickly learned the importance at the camp of the word "'organize' . . . It meant: to steal, buy, exchange, get hold of. My very first lesson was that anything here could be used for currency. Even water" (Hart, 1981).

In August 1944, about 3,000 people, mostly women and children, living in the Gypsy Family Camp were gassed to death as the camp was destroyed. About 23,000 Austrian and German Romani (usually but incorrectly called Gypsies) were sent to Auschwitz during the war. Only 3,000 survived. These survivors were people who were transferred out of the camp to work as slave laborers.

In January 1945, the Germans were close to defeat and Soviet troops were approaching the camp. German SS units ordered some 66,000 prisoners on forced marches to other camps in Poland and Germany. The prisoners, who lacked warm clothing and sometimes had no shoes, covered hundreds of miles in sub-zero temperatures. Eleven-year-old Thomas Buergenthal, a Czech, was one of only three children known to have survived the three-day march from Auschwitz. Hundreds of other people, including some under age 18, had been too sick to go on these death marches. The Germans shot many of them. When Soviet troops reached the camp on January 27, there were about 7,000 seriously ill and weak prisoners still there, of whom 150 were children. Some died of their illnesses within weeks after the camp was liberated.

Among the young survivors of Auschwitz was Elie Wiesel, who is today a well-known author and educator. Arriving at the camp in 1943 from Romania, Wiesel lost his father, mother, and young sister during the Holocaust. He later described the horrors of these years in his book *Night* and in his other books and writings on the Holocaust. *See also* CANDLES; DEATH CAMPS (WORLD WAR II); DEATH MARCHES; DEKEL, ALEX SCHLOMO; EXPERIMENTS, NAZI; FINAL SOLUTION; GENOCIDE; HART, KITTY FELIX; HOLOCAUST; MENGELE, JOSEF; ROMANI (GYPSIES); WIESEL, ELIE.

Further Reading: David A. Adler, *We Remember the Holocaust* (1989); Danuta Czech, *The Auschwitz Chronicle* (1997); Lucy Davidowicz, *The War Against the Jews, 1933–1945* (1975); Konnilyn Feig, *Hitler's Death Camps* (1979); Kitty Hart, *Return to Auschwitz* (1971); Primo Levi, *Survival in Auschwitz* (1971); Judith Miller, *One by One by One: Facing the Holocaust* (1990); Elie Wiesel, *Night* (1972).

Austria (World War II)

Austria was allied with Nazi Germany and fought with the Axis forces during World War II. Children and young people on the home front in Austria suffered ever worsening shortages of food, clothing, shoes, fuel, and other goods. However, no major battles were fought on Austrian soil and no bombings destroyed Austrian cities.

Nazism had much support in Austria and thousands of young Austrians joined the Hitler Youth and the military. They held various posts as police and as guards in concentration and death camps, and they helped round up and transport people targeted by the Nazis.

Young Jews suffered intense persecution after Germany annexed Austria in March 1938. Some youths fled with or without their families to other countries in Europe or to parts of North America. After Nazi officials arrived in Austria, they imposed the same anti-Jewish measures as in Germany. Jews were no longer citizens and lost all their rights. People were abused, beaten, and humiliated, often in public. Nazi police degraded Jews in various ways, such as forcing them to clean public toilets and to crawl on the ground and eat grass. Children saw their families and friends suffer. Thea Sonnenmark, a child in pre-war Vienna, recalled what happened in March 1938.

> [A]s my father went to open his grocery store, the SA gave him a toothbrush and ordered him to scrub the street. Some of his non-Jewish customers came by, and when they saw my father there, they laughed and jeered. These were customers of long standing. He considered them to be his friends. (Adler, 1989)

Erika Weihs, also a child in Vienna in 1938, recalled, "I heard marching boots everywhere. It seemed everyone had his radio on. I heard Hitler's voice from every window. I saw a girl I knew on her knees, cleaning the street with a brush. A few SS men were standing over her" (Adler, 1989).

On April 26, 1938, Jews were told that they must register all their property with the authorities. Eventually, the government confiscated all their property. Young people suffered from many kinds of deprivation and were banned from Austrian schools, parks, libraries, and recreation facilities, among other things. Some young Austrian Jews were taken to farms in the Austrian countryside where they could be safe from the violence taking place in Vienna and other cities and also learn trades and agricultural skills. Later, some fled to Palestine where Jews hoped to build a Jewish state. Among the young Viennese who helped their fellow Jews escape the country was Ehud Avriel, who was 21 in 1938. He worked with the group Haganah and parachuted into Nazi-occupied lands during World War II to aid resistance and help people to leave. Avriel later described his wartime experiences in a book called *Open the Gates.*

Austria was also the location of a harsh labor camp called Mauthausen where Jews and political prisoners were forced to work in a huge stone quarry. As they arrived at the railroad station near Mauthausen, many inmates were taunted by villagers, including local children who threw stones. Some Austrians were deeply upset when they found out what was happening in Mauthausen. Anna Strasser, a 20-year-old Austrian woman, worked at an accounting office in a company near the camp. She recalled her horror at the sight of prisoners laboring in the stone quarry: "One absolutely lost one's wits. . . . I simply could no longer endure this great burden. So one day I broke down. I cried and cried. For many weeks I was registered sick" (Horwitz, 1990). *See also* CONCENTRATION CAMPS (WORLD WAR II); DEATH CAMPS (WORLD WAR II); GERMANY (WORLD WAR II); HITLER, ADOLF; HITLER YOUTH.

Further Reading: David A. Adler, *We Remember the Holocaust* (1989); Ehud Avriel, *Open the Gates!* (1975); Robert Goldston, *The Life and Death of Nazi Germany* (1967); Gordon J. Horwitz, *In the Shadow of Death* (1990).

Aylward, Gladys (1902–1970)

Gladys Aylward, a Christian missionary who courageously helped children during World War II, was born in London in 1902. As a young woman, she applied to the China In-

land Mission Training School but was not accepted. For a few years, she worked as a parlormaid, saving her earnings to buy a one-way ticket to China, where she planned to assist Jennie Lawson, a Scottish widow who had been a missionary in Yangcheng for 50 years.

Gladys Aylward, whose work with Chinese children during World War II spawned both a book and a movie, is shown here in Hong Kong in 1958. *AP/Wide World Photos.*

In 1929, Aylward traveled by train through Europe and across Russia to Japan, before reaching the Missionary Society Home in Tientsin, China. After Aylward mastered the local dialect and learned the local customs and culture, she helped Lawson operate a mule train stop and inn at the mission and provided food to travelers, with whom she shared Bible stories. Her Chinese neighbors called her "Ai Weh Teh"—the small woman.

Chinese politics in the 1930s was complex. China was then a Nationalist Republic under President Chiang Kai-shek, who was headquartered in Nanking. His wife had been born a Methodist, and Chiang Kai-shek himself had been baptized in that faith by a Chinese-born Methodist. However, missionaries still faced many obstacles in China, where regional warlords and local leaders called mandarins exercised great power. In the south,

Mao Tse-tung had established a Chinese Soviet Republic.

Just a year after Aylward arrived, Lawson died, leaving Aylward in charge of the mission. She started a children's school at the mission and gained the respect of the local mandarin, who asked her to serve as inspector of feet in the region. The binding of baby girls' feet was a longstanding Chinese custom, based on the idea that small feet were desirable in women. Chinese officials sought to end foot-binding, and Aylward assisted them by urging people to abandon the custom.

In 1935, Aylward was granted Chinese citizenship, which meant that she gave up her right to British protection. By 1936, fighting had broken out between Chinese soldiers and Japanese troops who invaded China. By late 1937, northeastern China was under Japanese control. Yangcheng was bombed by the Japanese, and ground troops swarmed into the area.

Aylward adopted four orphans and brought more orphaned children to live at the inn. Throughout the countryside, she saw immense suffering and wounded children. She offered food and other aid to victims and helped refugees find shelter. The Japanese tracked her movements and noted her friendship with Nationalist Chinese intelligence officer Colonel Lin. In 1940, they branded Aylward a spy and offered a $100 reward for her capture. If she were arrested, Aylward was to be brutally tortured before being killed.

Aylward decided she could protect the children from her orphanage by relocating to Sian across the Yellow River. Her group included 20 girls between the ages of 13 and 15, seven boys between the ages of 11 and 15, and more than 70 boys and girls aged 4 to 8. Two men accompanied the group to carry food and other supplies, and some other Christian converts joined them.

The trip lasted about three weeks. Along the way, they boiled water from streams to cook millet and drank tea brewed from twigs, sleeping in mountain villages after long, tiring days of walking. After a few days, there were no more villages along the trail, so they camped in the open. For a while, they stayed in a cave. Aylward and the older boys carried the small ones. Some boys went ahead to act as scouts in case Japanese soldiers or planes appeared. At the Yellow River, Aylward's group found themselves trapped with no way to cross. After three days, a Chinese officer found a small ferry that transported them a few people at a time. There were so many refugees at Sian that Aylward's group went inland to Fufeng. After she had brought the children to safety, Aylward's health broke, and she contracted both typhoid fever and pneumonia. Missionaries and members of the Red Cross helped her to recover.

Aylward spent the rest of World War II in China where she continued to work as a missionary and to help children. In 1949, her friends raised funds so she could return to England and visit her family. For 10 years, Aylward lectured and preached throughout Europe. The "small woman of China" became famous and a biography was written about her. Her life was also the subject of a radio program and a 1958 movie, *The Inn of the Sixth Happiness,* starring Ingrid Bergmann.

In 1957, Aylward returned to China. By then, communist forces had overwhelmed the Nationalist government of Chiang Kai-shek. Opposed to communism, Aylward founded the Hope Mission in Hong Kong. The Nationalists had settled on the island of Formosa (present-day Taiwan), and Aylward moved there to teach Mandarin Chinese and start the Gladys Aylward Orphanage. To fund these projects, Aylward lectured and sponsored religious crusades in England, the U.S., Canada, Australia, and other countries. She died of pleurisy in 1970 at age 68. Her gravesite is on a hillside near Taipei, where a memorial looks toward the coast of Fukien where Aylward served as a missionary. *See also* CHINESE CIVIL WAR; JAPAN-CHINA WAR; LONG MARCH.

Further Reading: Alan Burgess, *The Small Woman* (1957).

B

Babi Yar. *See* MASSACRES, WORLD WAR II

Bangladesh

In March 1971, the Bengali people of East Pakistan declared themselves independent from West Pakistan. West Pakistani troops responded by massacring citizens of East Pakistan (East Bengal), including children and young people. Between March and December 1971, about 10 million refugees fled from East Pakistan into neighboring India. Young people were among the freedom fighters, called Mukti Bahini, who fought with Indian soldiers against the West Pakistanis. On December 16, 1971, the West Pakistani forces surrendered and the nation of Bangladesh was born.

Before the war for independence, few foreigners knew much about Bangladesh or its people. Their plight sparked prominent rock musicians to come to their aid. Former Beatle George Harrison organized a benefit concert for the people of Bangladesh. Joined by Eric Clapton and other musicians, Harrison performed at Madison Square Garden in New York City on August 1, 1971. Many young people attended the concert and even more bought the recording, *The Concert for Bangla Desh*. A film of the concert was also produced. In 1991, the album was reissued in compact disc form. Proceeds from the record album and compact disc were channeled to UNICEF—the United Nations Children's Fund—which distributed the funds to help children in Bangladesh. The profits of the concert, album, and compact disc totaled $13 million as of 1991.

Various organizations and governments have worked to improve conditions for children in Bangladesh. Save the Children operated programs to ease suffering and improve the quality of life in the country. During the 1970s and 1980s, the largest amount of financial aid to Bangladesh came from the United States. As of 1981, donations from Japan reached a similar level. Economic aid enabled Bangladeshi children to receive health care and education, as well as food and other material aid. *See also* PERSIAN GULF WAR; SAVE THE CHILDREN; UNITED NATIONS CHILDREN'S FUND (UNICEF).

Further Reading: Craig Baxter, *Bangladesh: From a Nation to a State* (1997); Ranabira Samaddara, *The Marginal Nation* (1999); Richard Sisson and Leo E. Rose, *War and Secession* (1991).

Barbie, Klaus (1913–1991)

During World War II, Nikolaus Klaus Barbie, a native of Bonn, Germany, was a prominent Nazi leader in occupied France. As the chief Gestapo officer in Lyon, his brutality toward Jews and opponents of the Nazis earned him the nickname "Butcher of Lyon." He was notorious for his cruelty toward Jewish children.

As a boy, Barbie joined the Hitler Youth Movement, and by age 20, he was the leader of his local chapter. He graduated from high school with grades below those needed for college, so Barbie found a job with a public works organization. He was accepted in Hitler's elite secret service organization, the SS, in 1935 and moved up the ranks. At age 29, Barbie was assigned to head the SS Section IV in Lyon, France. This position allowed him to use any methods he chose to stamp out anti-Nazi resistance in the region. He had a torture chamber built in the basement of a prison to victimize people suspected of anti-Nazi activities.

In one case, he discovered that 41 Jewish children were being sheltered by villagers in Izieu. The children, who ranged in age from 3 to 13, were being hidden in a farmhouse by local people who fed and cared for them. Barbie raided the house in April 1944 and loaded the children and their teachers onto trucks. He had the teachers executed and sent the children to their deaths at Auschwitz. In July 1944, Barbie authorized a massacre of hundreds of civilians at the village of Villars les Dombes.

After the war, Barbie's victims described how he had tortured, murdered, and deported Jewish children and adults. Klaus Barbie was sought as a war criminal but evaded prosecution by using fake identity papers and hiding out in French villages, where he found work as a farmhand. He moved to Germany early in 1946, again using false names, and narrowly escaped being captured more than once. Through a fellow German, he found a way to work as an agent for the U.S. Counter-Intelligence Corps (CIC) in Germany until France informed the CIC that he was a wanted war criminal and must be prosecuted. However, the CIC did not deliver Barbie to French authorities.

In 1951, he fled to South America where he lived under an assumed name. He was finally tracked down in Bolivia in 1983 by two famous Nazi-hunters: Serge Klarsfeld, a Romanian-born Jewish lawyer whose father had been arrested by Barbie, and Klarsfeld's German-born, Protestant wife Beate. Serge Klarsfeld was a child hiding with his parents and sister in southern France when their hiding place was discovered in 1943. His father was dragged away as Klarsfeld waited, terrified, inside a cabinet in that room. His father later died in the Nazi death camp at Auschwitz-Birkenau. The Klarsfelds have devoted their lives to bringing Nazi criminals to justice and to bringing public attention to the Holocaust.

In 1987, Barbie was finally brought to trial. A French court found him guilty of deporting more than 7,000 people to their deaths, including the children from Izieu. The court ruled that Barbie had personally played a role in the murders of 4,342 people and tortured more than 15,000 members of the French Resistance. At trial, Beate Klarsfeld produced as evidence a letter Barbie had written detailing the raid on the Home for Jewish Children at Izieu. In the letter, he apologized to his superiors for not finding any valuables during the raid.

Barbie was convicted of crimes against humanity and sentenced to life in prison, where he died in 1991. When he was interviewed after the Barbie trial, Serge Klarsfeld said that, to him, the verdict meant "the children of Izieu will not die. For me, that's a satisfaction" (Klarsfeld, 1996). *See also* FRANCE (WORLD WAR II); HOLOCAUST; MASSACRES.

Further Reading: Charles Ashman and Robert J. Wagman, *The Nazi Hunters* (1988); Tom Bower, *Klaus Barbie* (1984); Serge Klarsfeld, *The Children of Izieu* (1984); Serge Klarsfeld, *French Children of the Holocaust* (1996).

Bates, Rebecca (1793–1875) and Bates, Abigail (1797–1882)

During the War of 1812 between the United States and Great Britain, Rebecca Bates, age 19, and her sister Abigail Bates, age 15, devised a clever plan to prevent a British warship from entering and raiding their town. The Bates family lived in Scituate, Massachusetts, where their father Simeon was the lighthouse keeper. The British had already raided Scituate in June 1814. On September 1, 1814, Simeon Bates went into town for supplies, along with the American soldiers who were stationed at Scituate Light. When Rebecca and Abigail saw a British ship heading toward the harbor, they became alarmed. The *La Hogue* dropped anchor and two barges of soldiers were dropped into the water.

After consulting with each other, the girls decided to trick the British. They grabbed a fife and drum the American soldiers had left at the lighthouse and began to play them loudly, marching back and forth behind some sand dunes. The sounds of "Yankee Doodle" drifted across the water to the *La Hogue.* The British commander, believing a group of soldiers was drilling near the lighthouse, ordered the barges full of soldiers to return to the ship, and the town of Scituate was spared another British raid. The teenage Bates sisters were widely praised for their quick thinking.

Further Reading: Robert Carse, *Keepers of the Light* (1969); Scituate Historical Society pamphlet; Scituate Town Report: Paper Read at a Meeting of the Chief Justice Cushing Chapter of the Daughters of the American Revolution (D.A.R.) (September 5, 1908); Edward Rowe Snow, *Lighthouses of New England* (1984).

Battle of Britain. *See* BLITZ, LONDON; BOMBINGS (WORLD WAR II)

Baublis, Petras

During World War II, Dr. Petras Baublis was the director of a home for infants in Kovno, Lithuania. He arranged to smuggle Jewish children out of the ghetto the Nazis had set up in Kovno. Children in this ghetto faced starvation, disease, and death, as did anyone who was forced to live there. Working with Catholic clergy, Baublis created false birth certificates for Jewish children. These forged papers labelled them as Christians, which meant they were not subject to anti-Jewish persecution by the Nazis. After sneaking children to the Aryan side of the town, Baublis hid them inside the children's home he administered. He saved at least nine children this way. *See also* HOLOCAUST; RIGHTEOUS GENTILES.

Further Reading: Richard C. Lukas, *Did the Children Cry?* (1994).

Baum, Froim (1926–)

Froim Baum, a young Polish Jew who survived the Nazi Holocaust, described his wartime experiences in a memoir entitled *Child of the Warsaw Ghetto,* written by David Adler. Baum was the youngest of seven children born to a poor Jewish tailor and his wife in Warsaw. His father died in 1932, a year before Adolf Hitler rose to power, and his mother struggled to support the family during the following years of economic depression and war. Froim helped his family, which was sometimes homeless, by getting odd jobs sweeping stores or shops and by working in a factory. Nonetheless, Froim and his brother Icek were eventually sent to the Orphans' House on Krochmalna Street that was run by the Jewish physician and author, Henryk Goldszmidt. Known by his pen name Janusz Korczak, Goldszmidt was renowned for his loving care of the orphans at the home.

On September 1, 1939, Nazi Germany invaded Poland; Warsaw, like the rest of Poland, surrendered to the Germans on September 27. As they had done in their own country, Nazi officials passed laws that deprived Jews of jobs, property, access to education, and all civil rights. Within a month, the Germans were kidnapping young Jewish men for forced slave labor. David, Froim's brother, was among them. He later returned badly beaten.

Like other Jews, the Baum family was forced to move into the Warsaw Ghetto in 1940. They shared a small attic room with no running water and piles of straw on the floor for beds. Korczak's orphanage was also moved inside the ghetto, and Froim alternated between living with his family and at the orphanage. The ghetto gates were sealed on November 16, 1940, and people were forbidden under penalty of death to leave. With winter coming on, the Germans denied the ghetto occupants coal or other fuel and kept them on starvation rations. These conditions forced Froim to become one of the child smugglers of the ghetto. His usual method was to jump over the wall as a car went by and keep moving alongside. After buying bread, he would return to the ghetto. One day, a policeman caught him, beat him, and took away the bread.

In July 1942, deportations from the ghetto to the death camp at Treblinka began. Dr. Korczak had given up chances to go free to stay with the children in his orphanage. When the soldiers came, he led his children out quietly. The child at the front of the line carried a flag bearing the Star of David. Froim had slept in his family's room the night before. Now, he ran to the train station to see his friends taken away. Because he was not wearing his armband identifying him as Jewish, a policeman ordered Froim away rather than forcing him to board the train.

To escape deportation, the Baums hired a professional smuggler to take them to Mrs. Baum's sister's house in Plonsk. However, they were caught in November 1942 and taken to Auschwitz-Birkenau, where Mrs. Baum and the girls were killed at once. Froim's three brothers were chosen as workers and sent to the men's line. Froim was led to a line of old men and children, but he joined his brothers when the guards looked away. One brother died at Auschwitz a week later.

Froim endured three other camps before the war ended in 1945. He was among those liberated at Dachau by American soldiers. He was later reunited with his two surviving brothers and emigrated to the United States during the 1950s. *See also* HOLOCAUST; KORCZAK, JANUSZ; POLAND (WORLD WAR II); WARSAW GHETTO; WORLD WAR II.

Further Reading: David Adler, *Child of the Warsaw Ghetto* (1995).

Baum, Herbert and Baum, Marianne.
See BAUM GROUP

Baum Group

In 1937, a group of young Jews, most between the ages of 11 and 14, began meeting in Berlin, Germany, to organize anti-Nazi activities. The group, which included Zionists and Communists, was led by two young married couples—Herbert and Marianne Baum and Sala and Martin Kochmann. In 1938, Herbert Baum and Martin Kochmann were among 1,000 young Jewish men forced by the Nazis to work in the Siemens electric motor plant in Berlin. Appointed as the factory overseer in charge of the Jewish unit, Baum used his position to recruit more people to work for the underground. For the next two years, members of the group did social work activities for the Jews in their community. Baum also tried unsuccessfully to improve working conditions for his men.

In 1941, the Baum group began riskier activities. They were aided by two non-Jewish clerical workers, young women who did typing at home to help produce printed materials for the group. Members passed out anti-Nazi pamphlets and leaflets, warning people that Hitler would destroy Germany with his aggressive war. These materials reached homes, offices, factories, and houses of worship. Riskier still, members of the group painted anti-Nazi slogans and messages on walls during the night. The group's leaders struggled to obtain food and other things members needed to survive in Nazi Germany. Baum managed to get false identity papers that labelled him and several friends as gentiles (i.e., non-Jews).

In May 1942, the group attacked a Nazi propaganda exhibit in Berlin. Called "The Soviet Paradise," the exhibit was designed to convince Germans to support the war against Soviet Russia, which German troops were losing. Herbert and Marianne Baum led a group of seven people into the exhibit hall to plant explosives, which caused a fire destroying the exhibit. All seven members of the Baum group were arrested by the Gestapo before they could leave the hall. Herbert Baum was tortured and brutally beaten to death after he refused to name other group members. Within months, other members of the Baum group were tracked down. The men were beheaded, and the three women were sent to concentration camps where they died before the war ended in 1945. *See also* FORCED LABOR (WORLD WAR II); HOLOCAUST; RESISTANCE MOVEMENTS (WORLD WAR II); WORLD WAR II.

Further Reading: Milton Meltzer, *Never to Forget* (1976); Yuri Suhl, *They Fought Back* (1975); Leni Yahil, *The Holocaust* (1990).

Becker, Sally. *See* BOSNIA

Beirut, Siege of. *See* LEBANESE CIVIL WAR

Belgium (World War II)

In May 1940, Belgium was invaded by Nazi Germany. After 18 days of fighting, the Belgian troops surrendered and German troops occupied the country, which contained nearly two million refugees from other countries, including thousands of Jews who had fled from Germany, Austria, and Eastern Europe. The Nazi occupation imposed severe restrictions on people and limited their freedom and civil rights. Newspapers and radio were censored, and children whose families listened to the British Broadcasting Company (BBC), the Allied radio station in Europe, had to do so secretly. Food, clothing, and other necessary commodities were strictly rationed. The Nazis also seized crops, dairy products, and livestock for their own use and for shipment to Germany. Young men were kidnapped, even from schools, and used as forced labor in German factories or on other work projects.

An active Belgian resistance movement made up of organized groups and individuals included many students and teenagers. As in other countries, young people served as couriers and delivered underground newspapers. They painted a "V" for Victory on sidewalks and walls after a Belgian refugee in England first used this symbol in shortwave radio transmissions sent to occupied Belgium. In some cases, young resistance workers paid a heavy price. Hortense Daman, who began working with the Resistance at age 13, completed several dangerous missions but was caught and imprisoned at the Ravensbruck concentration camp where she was tortured and forced into hard labor.

Concerned non-Jews, including Belgian clergy, worked to save Jewish children from the Nazis. Belgian clergy helped to hide about 3,000 children. Pere Bruno, a Belgian monk who was in his early 30s during the war, worked with the resistance to rescue Jewish children. One of his main roles was to accompany children by train to safe hiding places. He also provided young people and adults with false identity papers so they could hide from the Nazis, who stepped up their relentless hunt for all Jews in occupied lands in 1942. Bruno saved about 400 children and 100 adults. He was aided by an escape network that included university students and other young Belgians. *See also* ESPIONAGE; HIDDEN CHILDREN; HOLOCAUST; RIGHTEOUS GENTILES; UNDERGROUND PRESSES; WORLD WAR II.

Further Reading: Mark Bles, *Child at War* (1991); Ina Friedman, *Escape or Die* (1982); Howard Greenfeld, *The Hidden Children* (1993).

Belzec. *See* DEATH CAMPS (WORLD WAR II)

Berg, Mary (1924–)

Mary Berg, a young Polish Jew whose mother was an American citizen, kept a diary about her experiences in wartime Poland, including daily life in the Warsaw Ghetto. The family was living in Warsaw when the war began in 1939. Forced into the ghetto in 1940 at age 16, Berg wrote movingly in her diary of the plight of fellow ghetto children.

> There are a great number of almost naked children whose parents have died, and who sit in rags on the streets. Their bodies are horribly emaciated. . . . They no longer have a human appearance and are more like monkeys than children. They no longer beg for bread, but for death. (Berg, 1945)

As ghetto residents were being deported to various death camps in Poland, Berg was sent to a regular prison instead. In March 1944, the Nazis permitted Berg to leave the country because she was a U.S. citizen. She and her parents made their way to Spain and then boarded a ship for the United States. Berg's diary, which was published in the

United States in 1945, shows how young people suffered in wartime Poland and gives a vivid picture of life in the ghetto. It also portrays the special challenges of growing up in this environment. In the following passage, Berg described the dismal housing of the ghetto residents:

> It is a desolate building. The former walls of the separate rooms have been broken down to form large halls; there are no conveniences; the plumbing has been destroyed. Near the walls are cots made of boards and covered with rags. . . . On the floor I saw half-naked, unwashed children lying listlessly. (Berg, 1945)

See also DIARIES; POLAND (WORLD WAR II); WARSAW GHETTO; WORLD WAR II.

Further Reading: Mary Berg, *Warsaw Ghetto* (1945); Gail B. Stewart, *Life in the Warsaw Ghetto* (1992); Leni Yahil, *The Holocaust* (1990).

Bergen-Belsen

Bergen-Belsen, a World War II concentration camp located in Germany near Hannover on the western border, was originally planned as a "model camp" to be shown to Red Cross inspectors. It was also used as an exchange camp to house prisoners scheduled to be traded for German prisoners. A number of young people were imprisoned there, among them the famous diarist Anne Frank and her sister Margot, both of whom perished at Bergen-Belsen.

Although Bergen-Belsen was not designed as a death camp, with gas chambers and crematoria, thousands of inmates died from illnesses, especially typhus, tuberculosis, and scarlet fever. The camp was filthy and diseases spread rapidly. Nearly everyone carried typhus, which was spread by body lice. Thousands more people in the camp died of malnutrition, starvation, and exposure to foul weather. They also suffered from scabies, fleas, bedbugs, frostbite, and exhaustion. One inmate, Hadassah Rosensaft, organized a group of other Jewish women who helped children afflicted with typhoid fever and other diseases. Her group cared for 150 Jewish orphans at the camp.

Children in the camp witnessed death and suffering daily. One eight-year-old girl had to nurse her sick younger brother then watch her mother die of typhus. A former prisoner, Irma Sonnenberg Menkel, later recalled the stark hunger as follows:

> In my early days there, we were each given one roll of bread for eight days, and we tore it up, piece by piece. One cup of black coffee a day and one cup of soup. And water. That was all. Later there was even less. When I asked the commandant for a little gruel for the children's diet, he would sometimes give me some extra cereal. . . . It was only for the little children, only a little bit. The children died anyway. (Menkel, 1997)

A large group of Dutch children were among those sent to the camp. Some of the older girls tried to help them, nursing them when they were sick, comforting them, and helping them with their schooling. Anne and Margot Frank arrived after their hiding place in Amsterdam was discovered during the last months of World War II. Both girls became fatally ill with typhus. In January 1945, Margot died. Anne died a few days later, just months before Bergen-Belsen was liberated in April by British troops who were shocked to see nearly 10,000 unburied bodies, most of them victims of typhus and starvation. Another 28,000 inmates from Bergen-Belson survived the war only to die within months after liberation from illnesses they contracted in the camp. *See also* CONCENTRATION CAMPS (WORLD WAR II); FRANK, ANNE; HOLOCAUST; WORLD WAR II.

Further Reading: Vera Laska, ed. *Women of the Resistance and in the Holocaust* (1984); Willy Lindwer, *The Last Seven Months of Anne Frank* (1991); Irma Sonnenberg Menkel, "I Saw Anne Frank Die," *Newsweek,* July 21, 1997, p. 16; Klara Samuels, *God Does Play Dice* (1999).

Berlin Airlift. *See* COLD WAR

Bicycles

For young people not old enough to drive or lacking access to cars, bicycles have often provided a form of independent transportation. Wars have often deprived youths of their bicycles because rubber and metal were needed for war-related materials. Some young people have tried to circumvent wartime shortages by riding bicycles without tires or by improvising tires out of wooden slats and other materials.

During the two world wars, many young people in occupied countries used their bicycles while working with the resistance. They carried secret messages, transported black-market food or other goods, or delivered underground newspapers and other printed material on bicycle. Some young resisters during World War II carried fake identity cards to people in hiding by stuffing these papers into their bicycle handles.

Youth in occupied Belgium, China, France, and other lands also used their bicycles to carry out sabotage operations. They were able to move swiftly in and out of tight spaces and through different kinds of terrain without the noise of an engine to expose them. Bicycles also could often be concealed more easily than motor vehicles. Near the end of World War II, German occupation forces began stopping cyclists on the street to confiscate bicycles for their own use. People purposely hid their bicycles or tried to make them look shabby and non-functional. After the war ended, one of the most cherished gifts a young person could receive was a working bicycle.

During the Vietnam War in the 1960s and 1970s, young Vietnamese often used bicycles to run errands, carry supplies, and perform other chores for North Vietnamese troops. Some youths transported explosives on their bicycles to carry out attacks in enemy territory. In one incident in Saigon, South Vietnam, a bicycle loaded with explosives was left near a restaurant in a busy part of town. An 11-year-old Vietnamese boy, his younger sister, and his mother were among those killed when the bicycle exploded. Dozens of other pedestrians and restaurant patrons suffered serious burns, cuts, and wounds. Hundreds of other bicycles packed with explosives were left in places throughout South Vietnam.

Such bicycle bombs caused death, suffering, and fear among Vietnamese civilians. *See also* FRANCE (WORLD WAR II); RESISTANCE MOVEMENTS (WORLD WAR II); UNDERGROUND PRESSES; VIETNAM WAR.

Further Reading: Martin Caidin and Jay Barbree, *Bicycles in War* (1974); Miep Gies, *Anne Frank Remembered* (1987); Victoria Sherrow, *Cities at War: Amsterdam* (1992).

Bielski Brothers

During World War II, Tuvia Bielski and his two brothers organized a Jewish partisan group in the Soviet republic of Byelorussia, that offered young people and their families some protection from the enemy. The Bielski's parents had been killed by the Nazis in December 1941. Operating east of the Polish border and southeast of the town of Vilna (Vilnius), the Bielski group was the largest partisan unit in Europe. Beginning with about 20 men and a few rifles bought from a local peasant, the group set out to fight Germans and to offer protection to Jews trying to survive the war. They dynamited supply trains, interfered with communication systems, and destroyed granaries and farms the Germans were using to feed their troops. As other Jews heard about the group, it grew to about 500 members by the end of 1942 and about 1,200 men, women, and children by 1944. The people who joined the Bielski group for protection regarded themselves as a family. They helped each other in many ways—cooking, carrying supplies, nursing the wounded, and setting up barracks. The group performed important tasks for other partisans, such as repairing guns, resoling shoes, and gathering needed supplies. Children in the group carried out many tasks to help the group survive. Teenagers and youths in their early 20s took part in the more dangerous activities.

The Bielskis left the region during the summer of 1944, and members joined other Byelorussian resistance units to fight during the final battles of the war. About 1,000 of these people survived the war. Of the three Bielski brothers, Tuvia alone survived. *See also* HOLOCAUST; RESISTANCE MOVEMENTS (WORLD WAR II); WORLD WAR II.

Further Reading: Nechama Tec, *Defiance: The Bielski Partisans* (1993); Leni Yahil, *The Holocaust* (1990).

Biological Warfare

Biological (germ) warfare refers to the military use of disease-causing microorganisms or toxins on a targeted population to kill or incapacitate them or to destroy animals or vegetation. These biological agents can be released into the air or spread through water or soil. Among the best-known are anthrax, a bacteria that spreads through contaminated air and is nearly always fatal; botulism, which releases toxins that cause severe illness and death; bubonic plague; and various fever-producing organisms such as dengue, brucellosis, yellow fever, and Q fever. In addition, vaccines that might protect against some dangerous biological agents have not been thoroughly tested on children or pregnant women. To protect children against potential biological attacks by neighboring countries, Israel has been acquiring gas masks for its citizens.

Biological weapons have been used by warring nations for more than a century. During the American Indian Wars, for example, some U.S. troops were accused of deliberately spreading smallpox among Indians by means of infected blankets. During the twentieth century, dangerous new biological weapons were developed and stockpiled, especially in the 1980s and 1990s. Such weapons pose grave threats to both military troops and civilians. Children are at special risk because their bodies are still growing and their immune systems are less developed than adults' systems. Young people also must depend on others for access to medical treatment and various means of protecting themselves from attacks by these weapons.

Concerns about the development and potential use of such weapons prompted 99 nations, including the United States, to sign a treaty at the Biological Weapons Convention of 1972. These nations pledged that they would not develop, produce, or stockpile biological agents or toxins and that they would also destroy existing stocks of such weapons.

In 1969, the United States had unilaterally halted the production of such weapons and urged that a convention be held.

Despite the treaty, biological weapons continued to be produced and even used. After Iraq came under suspicion of using biological weapons during the Persian Gulf War of 1991, Iraqi leader Saddam Hussein was obliged to permit United Nations teams to investigate sites where such weapons might be hidden. Throughout the late 1990s, Hussein resisted inspections, prompting the United States and Great Britain to threaten military force unless inspectors were allowed access to various sites.

Investigations also showed that other countries had developed and stored biological weapons. For instance, informers from the former Soviet Union described stockpiles of deadly strains of botulism, anthrax, and other germs that could wipe out the populations of whole cities within days after being released. *See also* CHEMICAL WARFARE; PERSIAN GULF WAR.

Further Reading: Elaine Landau, *Chemical and Biological Warfare* (1991); Jeanne McDermott, *The Killing Winds* (1987); Robert Harris and Jeremy Paxton, *A Higher Form of Killing* (1982); U.S. Department of State, "Fact Sheet: Chemical-Biological Warfare, Washington, DC, February 14, 1998.

Black Sabbath Round-Up. *See* ITALY (WORLD WAR II)

Blackouts

During wartime, children often have to adjust to many new rules, including curfews and blackouts. For example, during World War II in Great Britain, all lights in cities under threat of bombing were turned off at a certain time, and no lights were permitted to show out of any homes. People bought special blackout curtains and plugged the cracks in their shutters with rags or newspapers. Evening activities were curtailed or limited by this lack of lighting. Children were often responsible for turning off lights and making sure that the curtains and shutters were in place. They often did their homework or other evening activities by candlelight. Blackouts meant that the streets were dark much earlier in the evening. During the wintertime in World War II Scotland, with the lights extinguished, the sky grew dark at about 3 o'clock when children were walking home from school.

The United States was not bombed during this war, but blackouts were carried out around the country. Communities developed civil defense plans and required citizens to follow blackout procedures, then checked the area to make sure no lights could be observed.

Although blackouts restricted activities, people who grew up during these years have some fond memories of "blackout" nights. Henk Aben, who was a teenager in Holland during World War II, recalled a time of family togetherness.

> No gas, no electricity, no water. Problems everywhere. But many will remember the long nights with just one candle, doing games or listening to the jammed BBC [British Broadcasting Company] by radio, or Radio Orange [run by the Dutch government-in-exile] in London. Strange enough, those evenings were considered *gesellig* [cozy]. (Abenletter, 1991)

See also AIR RAIDS; BLITZ, LONDON; BOMBINGS (WORLD WAR II); HOLLAND (WORLD WAR II); WORLD WAR II.

Further Reading: Letter from Henk Aben to the author, February 11, 1991; Michael Kronenwetter, *Cities at War: London*, New York (1992); Robert Westall, *Children of the Blitz* (1985).

Blitz, Dresden. *See* GERMANY (WORLD WAR II)

Blitz, London

In September 1940, German bombers began a fierce air attack on London that lasted over eight months through the spring of 1941. These bombings became known as the Blitz, from the German word *blitzkrieg*, or "lightning war." Through the bombings, Adolf Hitler planned to gain control of the air over England and to demoralize the English people, thereby paving the way for a German invasion.

As they looked into the sky on September 7, 1940, the day the attacks began, children living in and around London saw hundreds of bombers. Some even saw the bomb racks opening as the weapons were released. Bombs struck factories, warehouses, docks, and neighborhoods around the city. The bombs made frightening noises and started numerous fires. Thousands of people, mostly poor residents of London, became homeless. Families loaded their remaining belongings onto wagons or baby carriages and fled from burning buildings. Children searched for their parents among the rubble; many became orphans that day and during the weeks that followed. Young people saw their homes destroyed and their friends and neighbors killed. Some teenagers assisted the rescue teams that tended the injured and removed the dead.

Schools were closed after the first bombings. When they reopened, air raids were common during the school day. At the sound of the siren, children shoved their books inside their desks and lined up to go to the shelters. During bombings, they waited on the floor or on wooden benches until the attack ended. Despite these difficulties, schools stayed open during most of the war. As one survivor recalled,

> Much of our time was spent in the air-raid shelter, which paradoxically was a cloakroom with bricked-up windows, three storeys up in the building! The nightly raids meant that even though we had beds in the shelter we didn't get much sleep. . . . It became necessary to organize firewatchers to quickly extinguish any [explosives] that fell. My brother organized street-watches." (Westall, 1985)

On the night of May 10, 1941, more than 500 German bombers flew over London, launching incendiary bombs that caused fires all over the city. People died inside shelters that were directly hit by bombs. Rescue workers also found bodies lying outside shelters. Families sometimes perished together in backyard shelters that did not provide enough protection.

Some families sent members to sit in public shelters during the day so the others would have a spot during the next raid. On some days, so many bombings occurred that people only left the shelters to go to work. Children passed the time by reading, sewing, mending, and doing their homework. As survivor Bernard Kops later recalled,

> I heard sirens. And sirens and sirens. Early in the morning, in the afternoon and in the evening. And we went underground to get away from the sirens and the bombs. Yet they followed me and I heard sirens until the world became a siren. One endless cry of torture. It penetrated right into the core of my being, night and day was one long night, one long nightmare, one long siren, one long wail of despair. (Kops, 1963)

Displacement after the bombings also caused problems. In camps set up away from the stricken areas, children had to adjust to new surroundings. In one reported case, a mother at a camp lost track of her toddler who disappeared near near the water and was drowned.

When the Blitz ended, countless people had been killed and about 90,000 had been injured. Many children knew at least one person who had died, lost a loved one, or been injured. As one survivor, who was 12 in 1940, later wrote, "Every day brought its own tale of war" (Westall, 1985). In the summer of 1944, the Germans began bombing London with new weapons. Their V-1 missiles could travel in any kind of weather and were sent from launching pads in occupied France. British anti-aircraft had a harder time defending against the V-1s. That September, the Germans introduced an even more powerful version called the V-2. Between September 1944 and March 1945, more than 500 V-2s fell on England. These bombings killed at least 2,700 people. *See also* AIR RAIDS; BOMBINGS (WORLD WAR II); EVACUATIONS (WORLD WAR II); GREAT BRITAIN (WORLD WAR II); WORLD WAR II.

Further Reading: Tom Harrison, *Living Through the Blitz* (1976); Bernard Kops, *The World Is a Wedding* (1963); Robert Westall, *Children of the Blitz* (1985).

Block Ten. *See* EXPERIMENTS, NAZI

Bloody Sunday. *See* RUSSIAN REVOLUTION

Bloody Thursday. *See* MASSACRES

Boat People. *See* CAMBODIA; REFUGEES; VIETNAM WAR

Boer War (1899–1902)

Youth suffered from the effects of imprisonment and sieges and died in combat during the Boer War, as British troops fought in South Africa against the Boers, the descendants of Dutch, German, and French settlers. The Boers, whose ancestors had settled the Cape region in the seventeenth century, resented the intrusion of British miners and prospectors into the independent states the Boers had established in southern Africa. When the British ignored a Boer order to leave, war broke out.

Early in the war, the Boers conducted three sieges—in Kimberley, Mafeking, and Ladysmith. Thousands of troops and civilians of all ages were under siege at Ladysmith for 120 days. The people resorted to eating mules and horses. The bread became stale and moldy. Water was also scarce, and the temperatures were high. People became sick with dysentery. The garrison at Mafeking was under siege for 217 days (October 1899 through May 1900). Reporter J.E. Neilly described the starving people he saw there as follows:

> Hunger had them in its grip, and many of them were black spectres and living skeletons. I saw them crawling along on legs like the stems of well-blackened "cutties," with their ribs literally breaking through their shrivelled skin—men, women, and children. . . . The sufferers were mostly little boys—mere infants ranging in age from four or five upwards. (Carey, 1988)

Some children survived with the help of soup kitchens that were set up for hundreds of people ranging in age from infancy to adulthood. Desperately hungry, people made soup from dead horses. Later, they gathered locusts to eat. In all, about 20,000 civilians died in the camps. Young men were also among the 28,000 British soldiers and 4,000 Boer soldiers who perished.

Other children suffered and died after British General Horatio Kitchener implemented a "scorched earth" policy toward the Boers. The British burned Boer farms and settlements where guerrillas had been hiding and destroyed all provisions they found. The loss of their crops and livestock caused widespread hunger among the Boers.

The British began ordering Boer women and children of all races into concentration camps early in 1901. Eventually, there were 31 such camps. About one fourth of the Boer population (116,572 persons, nearly all women and children) were kept in the camps. Eyewitnesses reported that several families often had to share one tent in the camps, and the camps offered little or no protection in bad weather. Children in the camps suffered from high rates of typhus, measles, dysentery, and other infectious diseases. The inmates tried to help the children by operating schools, because their education was also interrupted by their imprisonment.

English reformer Emily Hobhouse reported, "The children have been the hardest hit. They wither in the terrible heat and as a result of insufficient and improper nourishment. . . . To maintain this kind of camp means nothing less than murdering children" (Weber, "The Boer War Remembered" Web site). The Boers claimed that many children died of starvation after the British cut their rations in half to put more pressure on the Boer soldiers to surrender. Babies did not receive milk, and fruits and vegetables were not available to the inmates. Waste disposal facilities were inadequate and people lacked enough water to keep themselves clean, all of which hastened the spread of diseases. There were few doctors or nurses in the camps.

Official reports at the end of the war showed that 27,927 Boers had died in the camps; 26,251 of them were women and children and 22,074 of that total were children under age 16.

Further Reading: John Carey, *Eyewitness to History* (1988); John Keegan, *A History of Warfare* (1993); Hans A Schmitt, *Quakers and Nazis* (1997); Mark Weber, "The Boer War Remembered," <*http://www.boer.co.za/boerwar/weber.html*>.

Bomb Shelters. *See* AIR RAIDS; COLD WAR

Bombardment. *See* AIR RAIDS; ARAB-ISRAELI WARS; BLITZ, LONDON; BOMBINGS (WORLD WAR II); GERMANY (WORLD WAR II); HIROSHIMA; JAPAN (WORLD WAR II); NAGASAKI; VIETNAM WAR; WORLD WAR II

Bombings (World War II)

By the end of World War I in 1918, bombs had become a standard weapon of modern warfare. They were used by all major combatants during World War II. German planes bombed Great Britain in an attempt to demoralize the people and drive them out of the war. To children, the German Stuka bombers were the ultimate in horrifying weapons. One night in April 1941, the Foreman household, located in the village of Pakefield on the Suffolk coast, was hit by an incendiary, or fire, bomb. Michael Foreman, a child at the time, later wrote,

> I woke up when the bomb came through the roof. It came at an angle, overflew my bed by inches, bounced up over my mother's bed, hit the mirror, dropped into the grate, and exploded up the chimney. . . . My brother Ivan appeared in pyjamas and his Home Guard tin hat. Being in the Home Guard, he had ensured that all the rooms in our house were stuffed with sandbags. Ivan threw sand over the bomb but the dry sand kept sliding off. He threw the hearthrug over the bomb and jumped up and down on it. (Foreman, 1989)

The family had to pile wet sand on the bomb to quench the flames. Michael Foreman's

A baby cries on the bomb-devastated streets of Shanghai, China, in 1938. *Corbis.*

mother hustled her three children out of the house and across the street into a bomb shelter just as the village church exploded.

Some boys were playing ball near Kenley Airfield in August 1940 when it was bombed. Eight-year-old Brian Crane was among them. Crane later said that they ran as fast as they could toward home as the bombs began falling. People shouted, "Get off the streets," and one woman made them take cover in her house (Price 1980). They stayed there under the stairs eating milk and cookies until the bombing ended. Another child was inside a movie theater when the street was bombed. Crane recalled the dust caused by the bombs and the exit-doors being blown off their hinges.

Homes were also destroyed. One girl, age 18 in 1941, recalled leaving an air-raid shelter one day to go home: "There was no home. All that was left was a pile of bricks. We had nowhere to live except the shelter, and that was to be our home for six months. We had our meals at different relations" (Westall, 1985). People whose homes had been destroyed by bombs were sheltered in group housing called "rest centres." These centers were located throughout Great Britain.

Numerous other countries suffered from bombings during the Second World War. Poland was hard-hit in September 1939, and several cities were virtually demolished. In May 1940, the German *Luftwaffe* (air force) struck The Netherlands. Fifty-four bombers devastated Rotterdam to force a Dutch surrender. Water mains burst and fires destroyed 750 city blocks, leaving 78,000 homeless and thousands of people injured. A 12-year-old boy, Dirk van der Heide, described the scene in the city:

> One bomb landed on the lawn by our air shelter and one side of the shelter caved in. . . . The whole house rocked when the bombs came close. . . . I went out for a

while and they were taking dead people out of the bombed houses. . . . Three men were killed trying to get a bomb away that hadn't gone off yet. One of the men was our postmaster and I loved him very much. He gave me my first bicycle. It is awful to watch the people standing by their bombed houses. They just walk around and look at them and look sad and tired. (Van Der Heide, 1941)

Later in the war, Allied planes attacked strategic targets in France and cities throughout Japan. German cities were also targets of Allied bombs. "We were sitting in the cellars day and night . . . and the walls were trembling," recalled a Dusseldorf schoolboy who lived through World War II. About 93 percent of the houses in Dusseldorf were destroyed. Allied aircraft bombed the city of Dresden, Germany, on February 13, 1945, in the last months of World War II. About 350,000 people died from the bombing and the firestorms that it caused. The city was devastated. Eva Beyer, 17 years old at that time, later described the aftermath:

People were running around searching for a father, a mother, for children, for relatives. They got down on their hands and knees and tried to scrape away earth and stones of the rubble of homes in the vague hope of finding a beloved human being. Again and again, I heard children screaming for mummy and daddy, and nobody could help them. As I made my way to the center of the town . . . what my eyes saw can hardly be described. Nothing but parts of bodies, arms, legs, heads, hands, and torsos, being shoveled in a big heap with forks by men of the ARP, the army and the Red Cross. . . . Lorries came all the time and brought more of these dismembered people. (McKee, 1982)

See also AIR RAIDS; BICYCLES; BLITZ, LONDON; CAMBODIA; EVACUATIONS; GAS MASKS; GERMANY (WORLD WAR II); HIROSHIMA; HOLLAND (WORLD WAR II); JAPAN (WORLD WAR II); NAGASAKI; WORLD WAR II.

Further Reading: Eleanor Ayer, *Cities at War: Berlin* (1992); Michael Foreman, *War Boy* (1989); Tom Harrison, *Living Through the Blitz* (1976); Michael Kronenwetter, *Cities at War: London* (1992); Alexander McKee, *Dresden 1945, The Devil's Tinderbox* (1982); Alfred Price, *The Hardest Day* (1980); Dirk Van der Heide (pseud.), *My Sister and I* (1941); Robert Westall, *Children of the Blitz* (1985).

Bosnia

After World War II ended in 1945, Bosnia (also called Bosnia-Herzegovina) was one of six republics in the nation of Yugoslavia, located in the Balkans region of southeastern Europe. The population of Bosnia was about 4 million, including Muslims (44 percent), Serbs (32 percent), and Croatians (17 percent). Although these three groups had different cultural and religious traditions, they had lived together for years, sometimes intermarrying.

In March 1992, Bosnia declared its independence from Yugoslavia, following the example of Croatia, Slovenia, and Macedonia, actions which split Yugoslavia into separate and independent republics. Serbia and Montenegro remained united to form the Federal Republic of Yugoslavia.

Conflicts occurred shortly after the Bosnian declaration. On April 5, 1992, people in Sarajevo, the Bosnian capital, began gathering for a peace march. About 7,000 people, including many young people waving Yugoslav flags, gradually joined the march, which assembled in the center of the city. The diverse gathering represented the various ethnic groups in the region, and the marchers hoped that this showing of solidarity would help ease tensions. However, fighting had already begun in the southern part of the city. As the marchers reached that area, some of them were shot. A female medical student, Suada Dilberovic, was shot to death and became the first civilian casualty of what became a bloody war.

The war that broke out among the Serbs, Croats, and Muslims continued for more than four years, resulting in the deaths of more than 200,000 people, including at least 17,000 children. Many children were also among the 2 million people who lost their homes. Numerous other young people suffered injuries, emotional trauma, poverty, and homelessness.

The war involved atrocities against young people and other civilians and attempts at genocide. With the goal of "ethnic cleansing," new groups tried to eliminate residents of a region they intended to occupy themselves. Young Muslim women were raped and brutalized by Serbs. Romani (commonly but incorrectly called Gypsies) were abused by both Croatians and Serbs. They were cast out no matter which group of soldiers controlled the regions in which they lived. As part of ethnic cleansing, people tried to eliminate all traces of the opposing group and its cultural institutions. For instance, Serbs demolished the homes and churches of their enemies, while Croats wiped out the villages and mosques of Muslims. Children were victims and witnesses to these acts.

Boys as young as 15 and 16 served with Serbian forces or were part of armed militias that defended towns and guarded crops. A documentary film about the war, shown on French television in September 1992, showed teams of Serbian snipers, of whom half were under age 20.

Orphanages were set up to house children who had lost both parents. Conditions of war made life difficult there, too. For example, the orphanage at Sarajevo lacked heat and enough food and medicines. Some young people lived on the streets or found housing in abandoned railroad cars or shelled out buildings. One 13-year-old recalled the terror of shootings.

> A grenade had landed on our shelter. We had to climb over the dead bodies to get out. Meanwhile the snipers kept shooting at us. My father was one of those wounded and was taken away to the hospital. We've not seen him since, but I hope that he is still alive, perhaps in one of the detention camps. I try not to talk about these things, but I get so upset and keep having nightmares about what happened. (Greenberg and Isaac, 1997)

People around the world became aware of the horrors taking place in Bosnia. In the fall of 1992, the United Nations Children's Fund (UNICEF) provided aid during what they called a "week of tranquility." Opposing forces agreed to stop fighting during this seven-day period so that UNICEF could bring in food, medicine, and clothing before the winter started.

The war had many devastating effects on children. John Isaac, a photographer from UNICEF who worked in Bosnia, described the artwork he saw in a children's school.

> Instead of sunny pictures of kids playing and flowers blooming, the drawings that hung there were brutal pictures of war: scared people, bombs falling on buildings, destruction and sadness, The kids sang songs about peace and proudly displayed banners of peace signs and doves. (Greenberg and Isaac, 1997)

As Isaac was visiting with the children, a bomb fell and the school walls shook, but the children seemed to take it in stride because such violence had become so frequent.

Organizations and individuals tried to help victims of the war. A British woman named Sally Becker rescued several groups of children in battle-torn western Bosnia. She led them to a safe area where they could receive medical attention.

As of 1995, 278,000 people in Bosnia (about 6.3 percent of the population) were dead or missing, and more than half (about 58 percent) had been driven from their homes. About 60 percent of the homes in Bosnia had been damaged or destroyed. A total of 475 villages had been destroyed and 57 cities were occupied or under siege. A ghastly massacre had taken place in July 1995 when Bosnian Serbs killed as many as 8,000 Muslims in the area around Srebrenica.

The loss of parents, relatives, and their homes caused profound suffering for children and young adults. One family that fled from Srebrenica included two teenagers, a two-year-old, and their widowed mother. They fled to a refugee camp where they had to live in one small room that measured about six feet across with one bed and a wood stove. They had only cabbage and some potatoes to eat.

The United States and other nations urged opposing leaders to negotiate terms for peace. A meeting took place between the heads of

Serbia, Croatia, and Bosnia in November 1995 in Dayton, Ohio. Under the agreement that followed, United Nations peace-keeping forces were stationed in the region to maintain the truce.

Youth still suffered greatly after the treaty was signed and sporadic fighting still occurred. About 1.5 million children had been displaced during the war. After the fighting started, buses and convoys took children away from the war-torn area to various places inside and outside the former Yugoslavia. Siblings who left on different days had been taken to different destinations, and most youth traveled without their parents. By 1996, more than 2,000 children had suffered missing limbs and other disabilities, and had been scattered throughout Eastern and Western Europe, the Middle East, and Asia. Some children were put to work in factories or homes where they were poorly treated or abused. They could no longer attend school.

According to Dr. Vesna Bosnjak, director of a project called Unaccompanied Children in Exile, "Many of the children are completely out of contact with their families. They are more plagued by depression, sadness, insomnia, and nightmares than children who are able to communicate directly with a parent by phone or letter." Bosnjak's organization worked to protect the children from illegal adoptions, illicit trafficking, and other abuse, and to see that each child had a name, nationality, and family. After locating displaced children, the project workers interviewed and registered the child and maintained contact as they helped reunite families and repatriate the children.

Relief workers also saw high levels of post-traumatic stress in young people, including depression, weeping spells, and suicide attempts. Rates of aggressive behavior and delinquency rose during and after the war. Individuals also worked to help Bosnian children. Among them was Ellen Blackman, a Chicago businesswoman who organized rescue operations to evacuate sick babies and children. *See also* CROATIA; FILIPOVIC, ZLATA; GENOCIDE; KOSOVO; POST-TRAUMATIC STRESS DISORDER (PTSD); SAVE THE CHILDREN; SEXUAL ABUSE; UNACCOMPANIED CHILDREN; UNITED NATIONS CHILDREN'S FUND (UNICEF).

Further Reading: Mark Almond, *Europe's Backyard War* (1994); Ellen Blackman, *Harvest in the Snow* (1997); Zlata Filipovic, *Zlata's Diary* (1994); Keith Greenberg and John Isaac, *Children in Crisis: Bosnia,* (1997); Lara Marlowe, "Muslim Victims Locked Up in Cattle Shed," *Financial Times (London),* September 2, 1992; Edgar O'Ballance, *Civil War in Bosnia* (1995); William Pfaff, "No Salvation in Sight for the Damned of Sarajevo," *International Herald Tribune,* September 24, 1992; Everett M. Ressler et al., *Children in War* (1993).

Boyd, Isabelle "Belle" (1844–1900)

Belle Boyd was a Confederate spy during the Civil War. A native of Martinsburg, Virginia, and the daughter of a federal official, Boyd was 17 years old when the war broke out. Union soldiers invaded her hometown in 1861 and hung a Union flag on the Boyd home, enraging her staunchly Confederate mother. When a Yankee soldier physically pushed Mrs. Boyd, Belle shot him dead with a pistol. She was arrested but the prosecutor released her, ruling that she had acted in self-defense. Boyd later described the shooting as a turning point in her life—"My indignation roused beyond control; my blood boiling in my veins" (Davis, 1968).

Because federal officers and Union soldiers occupied Martinsburg, Boyd could discover their plans and pass this information on to the Confederate army. Using her charm and flirtatious manners, Boyd mingled with officials and soldiers to gain information that would help the South. Sometimes she asked male friends to carry messages behind battle lines. At other times, she boldly delivered messages in person.

On May 23, 1862, Boyd braved gunfire to enter a battle zone, where she told General Thomas "Stonewall" Jackson that Union troops were preparing to attack him. Jackson increased his forces and won the battle. He later wrote a personal letter thanking Belle Boyd for her help.

Boyd had eluded capture on several occasions but was finally arrested and put on trial for spying. She was caught more than once and spent 17 months in prison during the years 1862 and 1863. Inside her cell, Boyd hung a picture of Confederate president Jefferson Davis. To pass messages from prison, she hid them inside rubber balls she had smuggled into her cell and then tossed them outside her window. A man she knew by the initials "C.H." received these coded messages. Through her charm and connections, Boyd was able to gain her release after each confinement. In addition, Union military officials were reluctant to keep women in prison for long periods of time.

After Boyd was exchanged for a Northern prisoner and released, she resumed spying. Near the war's end, she was again imprisoned, for the sixth time, and placed in a Union ship. There, she fell in love with Lieutenant Sam Wylde Hardinge. They were married, but Hardinge died in 1864.

The next year, Boyd published a book about her wartime exploits called *Belle Boyd in Camp and Prison, Written by Herself.* People across the United States heard about the famous rebel spy, and Boyd was invited to lecture in the United States and England. Wearing a grey Confederate soldier's uniform, she recounted her war experiences. Throughout her life, she continued to make public appearances and give readings from her biography.

Boyd married John Hammond, but they divorced in 1884. She remarried in 1885. In all, she had three children. While appearing onstage in Wisconsin, Boyd died of a heart attack at age 56. The women's auxiliary of the Grand Army of the Confederacy paid the bills for her burial, and an admiring Confederate veteran later provided a new granite tombstone for her gravesite. Although just a teenager at the time, the "Belle Rebelle," as she was called, became perhaps the best-known female spy of the war. *See also* AMERICAN CIVIL WAR; ESPIONAGE.

Further Reading: Curtis Carroll Davis, *Belle Boyd in Camp and Prison* (1968); Donald E. Markle, *Spies and Spymasters of the Civil War* (1994); Ronald Seth, *Some of My Favorite Spies* (1968).

Boy's Island. *See* NINOSHIMA

The Bridge. *See* WAR FILMS

British Academic Exchange Service. *See* REFUGEES

Broken Families. *See* ADOPTION; BOMBINGS (WORLD WAR II); DEPORTATIONS; EVACUATIONS (WORLD WAR II); GHETTOS (WORLD WAR II); HOLOCAUST; ORPHANS; SEPARATIONS, FAMILY

Bruno, Pere (Reverend Bruno Reynders). *See* BELGIUM (WORLD WAR II)

Buchenwald

Buchenwald, a concentration camp, was set up by Nazi leaders in Germany in 1937. Like other camps, Buchenwald was built to confine, punish, and terrorize people, as well as to deter those on the outside who might defy Adolf Hitler and his government. Prisoners were humiliated, beaten, and tortured. They were forced to work in stone quarries and at other hard labor, sometimes to the death, and they received inadequate food, clothing, and shelter.

As Hitler's troops invaded more European countries and took more captives, Buchenwald was enlarged. Most inmates were adult males, but some were in their teens. Nearly all were Jewish. Non-Jewish inmates at the camp included male clergy who opposed Hitler and members of the Jehovah's Witnesses religion, who were arrested for refusing to give the Nazi salute, recite the Nazi pledge of allegiance to Hitler, join the Hitler Youth, or serve in the military, which was compulsory for males over age 18.

Some Nazi guards at the camp were young men. Rabbi Georg Wilde, who spent 11 days in Buchenwald in 1938, described with dismay the lack of compassion or remorse shown by the young guards: "I realized that these eighteen-year-old or twenty-three-year-old boys were being systematically trained to display brutality towards everyone in the execution of their orders, whether young or old, innocent or guilty" (Thalmann and Feinerman, 1974).

The famous author and Holocaust historian Elie Wiesel arrived as a teenager in Buchenwald in January 1945 after being forced on a "death march" from the Auschwitz death camp in Poland. He spent several months in the children's block, which housed about 600 young people near the end of the war. Wiesel later described these experiences in his book, *Night. See also* CONCENTRATION CAMPS (WORLD WAR II); HOLOCAUST; JEHOVAH'S WITNESSES; KALINA, ANTONIN; WIESEL, ELIE.

Further Reading: Gay Block and Malka Drucker, *Rescuers* (1992); Martin Gilbert, *The Boys* (1997); Raul Hilberg, *The Destruction of the European Jews* (1985); Rita Thalmann and Emmanuel Feinermann, *Crystal Night* (1974); Jack Werber and William B. Helmreich, *Saving Children* (1996); Elie Wiesel, *Night* (1972).

Bund Deutscher Madel. *See* LEAGUE OF GERMAN GIRLS

Burma

The military government in the Asian country of Burma, now called the Myanmar Union, fought against ethnic minorities during the late 1980s and early 1990s. The Shans, Karens, and Rakhines are some of the ethnic or tribal groups that live in the Myanmar Republic and that have rebelled against the government. A regional civil war in Kachin took place from 1948 to 1994; a regional civil war in Shan took place from 1948 to the 1990s; a general civil war has been going on since 1991. Teenagers were forced into military service, beginning with students who had demonstrated against the government. Others were sent into combat with little training. Journalists found that a number of boys 15 years old were among the prisoners of war captured during the battle over Mannerplaw, which was a center of anti-government resistance.

Anti-government guerilla forces among the Karens included thousands of students. At one camp, more than a hundred teenagers between the ages of 14 and 18 were training. Among them were the children of poor peasant farmers who were sent by their parents so they could receive clothing and two meals a day. Other boys went voluntarily because they wanted a sense of belonging to the cause of freedom. A number of the young recruits suffered from illnesses like malaria. They did not have enough equipment to protect themselves from the better-equipped government troops.

Two other major anti-government groups, the Paos and Shans, also used child soldiers. The Shans, who managed a large drug trade, included over 10,000 boys and young men between the ages of 8 and 18. Recruiters coerced them to join, or they enlisted to escape poverty. In some locales, the military was the only type of education or training available for poor families. A youth brigade that included boys as young as eight was taught to march and drill with weapons. They learned jungle warfare and were warned that deserters could be executed. Teenagers in the Shan units were used to carry opium across the border into Thailand.

Further Reading: Barbara Crossette, "Burma's Insurgents Go Inland to Step Up the Raids," *International Herald Tribune*, June 2, 1988; Melinda Liu, "Burma's New Guerillas," *Newsweek*, October 14, 1988; Dan Smith, *The State of War and Peace Atlas* (1997).

Burzminski, Stefania Podgorska (1925–)

During World War II, Stefania Podgorska Burzminski, a Polish Catholic, risked her life to save 13 Jews from the Nazi Holocaust. As a 16-year-old in 1941, Burzminski was virtually supporting herself and her 6-year-old sister Helena. Her father had died, her older siblings had moved away, and her mother and brother had been shipped against their will to Germany for forced labor.

Burzminski had Jewish friends who were trapped in the local ghetto, and she began sneaking them food. Moved by the anguish of people in the ghetto, she took in a Jewish man who was fleeing from the Nazis. The man's brother and his wife also needed a refuge outside the ghetto before the Nazis deported the people inside to death camps. Burzminski's apartment was too small to conceal more people, but finding another home in this war-ravaged town was unlikely. After searching in vain one day, she prayed for help and heard a woman's voice direct her to a certain street. There she found a two-room cottage with a kitchen and attic, well-suited for her needs.

Within weeks, she was hiding 13 people there. They remained for two years, during which time Burzminski sacrificed her personal life and safety to meet their needs. Shortly before the war ended, the group faced a new crisis when Germans set up a hospital across the street and ordered Burzminski to vacate her house so they could use it. Again, she prayed and received guidance. She remained in the house and the Germans took only one room. The group in the attic was undetected, even though Germans lived under the same roof for eight months. Author Eva Fogelman, who interviewed this brave woman for her book *Conscience and Courage* (1994), wrote, "Thirteen men, women, and children are alive today because a teenager believed in miracles."

Burzminski later married one of the men she had saved and they moved to the United States. She was honored as a Righteous Gentile by Yad Vashem and is featured in an exhibit on courageous rescuers at the United States Holocaust Memorial and Museum in Washington, D.C. *See also* GHETTOS (WORLD WAR II); HOLOCAUST; POLAND (WORLD WAR II); RIGHTEOUS GENTILES; UNITED STATES HOLOCAUST MEMORIAL AND MUSEUM; WORLD WAR II; YAD VASHEM.

Further Reading: Gay Block and Malka Drucker, *Rescuers* (1992); Eva Fogelman, *Conscience and Courage* (1994).

C

Cadet Nurse Corps

The Cadet Nurse Corps was formed in the United States during World War II to ease the desperate shortage of nurses to fill both military and civilian needs. In 1942, shortly after the United States entered the war, the U.S. Public Health Service determined that 55,000 new nursing students would be needed, a number experts expected would rise to 65,000 by 1943. The nursing profession had long been dominated by women, but many women were now working in defense plant jobs, which offered higher salaries than most jobs then available to women and did not require additional years of schooling.

At that time, nurses usually began training at age 17 or 18 after graduating from high school, and most training programs lasted three years. To attract more people into nursing, Representative Frances Bolton of Ohio introduced a new bill early in 1943. Enacted by Congress in May 1943, the bill created the Student Nurse Corps (SNC), later called the Cadet Nurse Corps (CNC). Under the new law, the federal government paid the tuition of all students who agreed to serve in any vital nursing job for the duration of the war plus six months. Students were also to receive free uniforms and monthly stipends while in school. To qualify, students had to be at least 17 years old. Many young women responded, and high school counselors encouraged capable graduates to study nursing.

Nursing schools also accelerated their programs, operating 12 months a year and helping students to complete their courses in less than three years. As a result of the CNC, thousands more young nurses were graduated and served in the army and navy nurse corps during World War II.

Military nurses, many of them new graduates in their early 20s, served in Europe, the Pacific, and other theaters of operation, as well as on board ships, as flight nurses, and in field hospitals. Young nurses also worked in veterans' hospitals where they nursed men who were recovering from war-related injuries and health problems. *See also* WORLD WAR II.

Further Reading: Edith Aynes, *From Nightingale to Eagle* (1973); Mary M. Roberts, *American Nursing* (1954); U.S. Department of the Army, *Highlights of the History of the Army Nurse Corps* (1987).

Cambodia

The people of Cambodia, a small Southeast Asian country west of Vietnam, suffered through five wars between 1953 and 1993. Child soldiers fought in each conflict. Often, these youths were kidnapped and forced into service, where they received inadequate training and equipment. Others joined the army for patriotic or economic reasons.

During five years of civil war between 1970 and 1975, the United States bombed the country numerous times in an effort to defeat the communist Khmer Rouge. In 1975, the communists seized control of the government and their radical leader, Pol Pot (born Saloth Sar in a village north of the capital, Phnom Penh), set up a brutal authoritarian regime to crush all opposition. Pol Pot, who had joined the anti-French Cambodian resistance when he was still a teenager, became head of the Khmer Rouge in 1963.

Between 1975 and 1979, Pol Pot's four years in power, almost a quarter of the Cambodian people, including entire families, died. Some 100,000 Cambodians, including young people, were killed outright; more than a million died from causes related to the war, including terrorism. During one rocket attack on downtown Phnom Penh, 12 schoolchildren were killed and many others were injured.

Pol Pot forbade the practice of Buddhism, the major religious faith in Cambodia, and destroyed houses of worship, killing religious leaders. He outlawed commerce, education, and cultural life and executed intellectuals as well as other people who might pose a threat to the Khmer Rouge. People who were educated, wealthy, or showed signs of resistance were executed. Some wealthy families committed group suicide to avoid being killed by the Khmer Rouge.

Children were told to report parents or other adults who criticized the government. Those Cambodians who rebelled against the new government were killed, some by being buried alive. The Khmer Rouge forces included many teenage soldiers who were trained to carry out government-ordered killings. Children were recruited at age 12 into a group called the Revolutionary Youth. As the war went on, a number of teenage soldiers wanted to return home, but any caught deserting the army were killed.

A major goal of Pol Pot's military forces was to wipe out all urban life and force every citizen into the countryside, where most of them were forced to work in rice fields. City-dwellers were removed to rural areas and forced into slave labor. In just four years, between one and two million people may have been killed. Young soldiers helped to carry out the forced movement of people into the country, serving as guards and patrols. Children suffered from displacement and cruel treatment; many became orphans and refugees. They died from executions, starvation, overwork, and disease.

More child soldiers, including some as young as seven, were pressed into service as the war continued. Orphaned refugees found in camps near the border with Thailand were ordered to serve by taking supplies and ammunition into central Cambodia. Some young refugees joined the army to gain food and protection. Boys as young as 14 were also taken from schools, orphanages, and the streets. (A film describing the lives of these child soldiers, *I Am Twelve Years Old and I Wage War,* was produced by Gilles de Maistre. It first aired in Switzerland on April 5, 1980, and aroused public opposition to child soldiers.)

In 1979, Vietnamese troops invaded Cambodia. Tens of thousands of refugees fled the country and about 150,000 were resettled in the United States. These "boat people," as they were called, were usually totally impoverished, having left all or most of their belongings behind. International aid helped refugees to begin new lives in other countries. People who worked with the refugees reported that the children and young people often suffered from post-traumatic stress disorder as a result of the horrors they had experienced in their homeland. They had many adjustments to make in new and unfamiliar lands. As of 1993, when the wars ended, nearly 350,000 Cambodian refugees remained in Southeast Asia, most of them living on the Thai border. Although finally able to begin returning home, they faced many new adjustments in rebuilding their lives.

In the years since the fighting ended, Cambodian children have continued to suffer. Thousands of them were the victims of land mines. Children usually did not survive when they stepped on these lethal mines that were buried in the ground during the war years. Those who did survive often lost feet, hands, limbs, eyes, or sustained other injuries. Many children also suffered grief and economic losses after their parents were hurt by the mines. As of 1997, one in every 250 Cambodians, a total of about 40,000, had lost limbs to land mines. Most of them were farmers, wood-cutters, or village-dwellers.

In 1998, experts estimated that from 4 to 8 million more land mines were still buried in Cambodia's forests and fields. The total amount of land that contained mines covered about 1,400 square miles. Progress had been made in clearing land mines from fields but those in forests are extremely hard to find and may never be removed. The American Friends Service Committee (AFSC) was among the relief organizations that sent prosthetic limbs and medical personnel to aid land mine victims. Some of the Cambodians who lost limbs found jobs in the centers that manufacture artificial limbs while others have gone to work on crews that clear land mines from the country.

In 1998, the dead body of 73-year-old Pol Pot was discovered. The Cambodian leader had been in hiding from international authorities that planned to put him on trial and from the Cambodian army. The cause of his death was not clear. People speculated that Pol Pot may have committed suicide, been killed by people who feared what he might say if he testified in a trial, or from natural causes such as heart disease. Other Khmer Rouge officials were also being sought for trial on charges of war crimes and gross human rights abuses.

In 1998, a journalist said, "Virtually every Cambodian alive today has lost a relative" (Mydans, 1998). Haing Ngor, a Cambodian physician who survived the war and returned to Cambodia to aid refugees said, "It's important to save the children. My generation is already gone. If these children disappear, the entire Cambodian civilization will vanish with them" ("Death in LA's Killing Fields," 1996). Dr. Ngor, who became an Oscar-winning actor, used his earnings as an actor, author, and public speaker to help support two clinics and a school in Cambodia and to assist individual Cambodian refugees, particularly orphans. See also AMERICAN FRIENDS SERVICE COMMITTEE (AFSC); ANTI-WAR MOVEMENT (VIETNAM WAR); LAND MINES; POST-TRAUMATIC STRESS DISORDER (PTSD); REFUGEES; SOLDIERS, CHILD; UNITED NATIONS CHILDREN'S FUND (UNICEF); VIETNAM WAR.

Further Reading: Jerry Adler and Ron Moreau, "The Devil's Due," *Newsweek,* June 30, 1997, pp. 40ff; Elizabeth Becker, *The Armies of Cambodia,* (1986); "Death in L.A's Killing Fields," *Los Angeles Times,* February 28, 1996, p. B-8; Nancy Moyer, *Escape from the Killing Fields* (1991); Seth Mydans, "In Cambodia, Wars End, But the Dying Continues," *The New York Times,* December 4, 1997, p. A14; Seth Mydans, "Pol Pot, Brutal Dictator Who Forced Cambodians to Killing Fields, Dies at 74," *The New York Times,* April 17, 1998, A14; Haing Ngor, *A Cambodian Odyssey* (1987); Dith Pran, comp. *Children of Cambodia's Killing Fields* (1997); Philip Shenon, "Khmer Rouge Rush to Cremate Pol Pot's Body without Autopsy," *The New York Times,* April 18, 1998, p. A1, A5; Francois Sully, *Age of the Guerilla* (1968); Sara Terry and Kristin Helmore, "Children in Darkness: The Exploitation of Innocence," *Christian Science Monitor,* July 7, 1987, p. 6.

Camp Followers. *See* AMERICAN REVOLUTION

CANDLES. SEE CHILDREN OF AUSCHWITZ NAZI DEADLY EXPERIMENTS SURVIVORS

Canteens. *See* VOLUNTEERS

CARE

The American relief organization CARE was founded in 1945 to help survivors in war-torn Europe. Twenty-two groups in the United States joined together to form this nonprofit, nonpolitical, nonsectarian organization. CARE Canada joined the effort in 1946. The new organization received strong support from President Harry Truman, former President Herbert Hoover, and General Dwight D. Eisenhower.

Supporters donated materials for millions of CARE packages containing food, clothing, and items needed for personal hygiene. Packages began arriving in France, then 11 other countries, in 1946. During the postwar years, American and Canadian school-

A Somali CARE worker, protected by American Marines, carries a bag of beans into a warehouse in Mogadishu, Somalia, in December 1992. *Jerome Delay, AP/Wide World Photos.*

children took part in this charitable effort, donating soap, hairbrushes, shampoo, small toys, and other items for CARE packages to be sent abroad. In later years, Europeans who received CARE packages as children remembered these gifts with gratitude. As adults, some of them helped to develop new branches of CARE in Europe as the organization was internationalized and expanded its activities.

In the years after World War II, CARE airlifted food into Berlin (1948) and provided meals to millions of undernourished children. The Food for Peace program, instituted in 1954, made surplus American farm produce available for shipment overseas. CARE also used its resources to build schools and it encouraged community development by sending farming tools and other equipment abroad. During the 1960s, CARE helped to train Peace Corps volunteers in Latin America.

While earlier CARE packages had contained tinned meats, margarine, honey, fruit preserves, raisins, chocolate, sugar, milk powder, and coffee, later packages included the dietary favorites of the country receiving the packages, along with tools, blankets, school supplies, and medicine. Between June 1946 and 1965, CARE delivered about 100 million packages to people in need in Europe and later in Asia and other regions.

The acronym CARE, which originally stood for Cooperative for American Remittances to Europe was changed to Cooperative for Assistance and Relief Everywhere. CARE USA became one of 10 member nations of CARE International. By the late twentieth century, CARE was one of the world's largest relief organizations. It delivered $339 million in aid in 1998. During the 1980s and 1990s, CARE assisted children around the world, including refugees in war-torn Somalia and Ethiopia.

Further Reading: "About CARE," "CARE International," Fact Sheets from CARE, 1998 available at <http://www.care.org/html>.

Casualties, Civilian

Prior to the twentieth century, most forms of military combat confined most casualties to the battlefield. Nonetheless, civilians, including children and young adults, have often been casualties of war. They died when armies invaded their communities, executed civilians, conducted massacres or sieges, forced people into hard labor, or caused food shortages and other adverse conditions that bred illness, injury, and death.

Modern warfare brought new weapons, such as bombs, that enabled opposing sides to kill large numbers of civilians indiscriminately. Bombings have dramatically increased the numbers of young casualties during the twentieth century. Land mines placed in the ground caused other casualties long after conflicts ended.

Plans to murder whole groups of people through a policy of genocide have made children and young people direct targets of killing in recent wars. During World War II, Adolf Hitler and other Nazi leaders planned to murder all European Jews, Romani (Gypsies), and other groups of people, such as those with certain kinds of physical and mental disabilities. Many victims were newly born. It is especially difficult to estimate the number of Jewish infants who died at the hands of the Nazis. Many births were not recorded individually or in any form. Some women in ghettos or concentration camps aborted pregnancies, often with the help of sympathetic doctors, so that they and their babies would not meet certain death. Civilian children have also been targeted for death in other conflicts, such as those in Armenia, Cambodia, Bosnia, and Rwanda.

World War II brought the highest number of casualties both for the military and civilians. In addition to those who died during bombings with conventional and atomic weapons, millions died as a result of foreign occupation or after being deported to work camps or death camps. Starvation, disease, and exposure killed millions more people. Historians find it difficult to determine the exact number of young people who died in World War II or in other wars. In Vietnam, for instance, many children died instantly during bombings and their deaths might never have been reported to authorities. Children died while being taken to hospitals or while in areas controlled by the Viet Cong, which American medics could not reach.

By the late twentieth century, military personnel no longer made up most wartime casualties. In recent wars, combatants have deliberately targeted children for aggression in war zones as a way to terrorize and cause profound distress to the adults they perceive as their enemies. According to Laura Herbst, writing in *Children in War: Community Strategies for Healing* (1995),

> In today's wars that involve ethnic and religious conflict, national liberation, counterinsurgency, and guerilla warfare, most of the victims are women and children. Modern weaponry—automatic guns, mines, bombs—makes carnage difficult to contain. War destroys infrastructures and landscapes; for the child, this means homelessness and no way for his family to grow or earn a meal.

See also AFGHANISTAN; AFRICA; AMERICAN CIVIL WAR; ANGOLA; ARMENIAN-TURKISH CONFLICT; BOER WAR; BOSNIA; CAMBODIA; CONCENTRATION CAMPS (WORLD WAR II); CROATIA; DEATH CAMPS (WORLD WAR II); GENOCIDE; HIROSHIMA; HOLOCAUST; KOSOVO; LAND MINES; LIBERIAN CIVIL WAR; MASSACRES; NAGASAKI; PEARL HARBOR; ROMANI (GYPSIES); RWANDA; SIERRA LEONE; SOMALIA; VIETNAM WAR; WORLD WAR I; WORLD WAR II; ZAIRE.

Further Reading: Helen Epstein, *Children of the Holocaust* (1979); Martin Gilbert, *The Fate of the Jews in Nazi Europe* (1979); John Keegan, *The Second World War* (1989); Serge Klarsfeld, *French Children of the Holocaust* (1996); Vera Laska, ed., *Women of the Resistance and in the Holocaust* (1984); Jacob Presser, *The Destruction of the Dutch Jews* (1969); Roger Rosenblatt, *Children of War* (1984); Leni Yahil, *The Holocaust* (1990).

Casualties, Military

Young male combatants have been killed during wars since ancient times. Some of these casualties were under the age of enlistment set by the military in their countries because the young men concealed their true age when they enlisted. Others were permitted or required to join the military at young ages.

Young people on the home front have also suffered when soldiers died. Family members grieved after receiving news that relatives had been killed in battle. An English teenager wrote the following description of the death of his 18-year-old cousin, who died during the D-Day invasion in 1944:

> He was very little so they made him into a tank gunner, because there's not much room in a tank turret. His tank commander wrote to my Aunt Edith, saying that their tank was hit by a shell in a tank-duel with Panzers. He and my cousin got out quick, as the tank was starting to "brew up" and about to explode. The last time he saw my cousin, he was running for cover. . . . I thought about him a lot after he was killed. He was only eighteen, and his life seemed to have hardly started. (Westall, 1985)

An American who was in her late teens during World War II recalled that

> Death got to be a common thing with us. Every day they'd have a big list in the paper and a friend might be on the list. At the time you'd think it was too bad, but you got so saturated with deaths and people missing that you just accepted it as natural. It went on and on and on for four years. (Westall, 1985)

See also AFGHANISTAN; AFRICA; ALGERIA; AMERICAN CIVIL WAR; BOSNIA; CAMBODIA; CHECHNYA; CROATIA; D-DAY; FRENCH REVOLUTION; LIBERIAN CIVIL WAR; PEARL HARBOR; REFUGEES; RWANDA; SIERRE LEONE; SOLDIERS, CHILD; UGANDA; VIETNAM WAR; WORLD WAR I; WORLD WAR II; ZAIRE.

Further Reading: John Keegan, *The Second World War* (1989); Archie Satterfield, *Home Front* (1981); Robert Westall, *Children of the Blitz* (1985).

CENTOS

CENTOS (*Centrala Opieki nad Sierotami*) was a Jewish organization formed in Poland after World War I to help children who had been orphaned or injured. CENTOS' funding came from its members throughout Po-

land, who numbered about 60,000, and from the government, municipalities, and the JDC (American Jewish Joint Distribution Committee). CENTOS took care of about 10,000 orphans, who were housed in institutions and foster homes. During World War II, under director Adolf Berman, the group ran public kitchens, child centers, clinics, dormitories, orphanages, and boarding schools. Besides meeting the physical needs of young people, CENTOS also tried to boost their morale and care for their educational and emotional needs. The group strived to keep children safe from the dangers that surrounded them daily in the ghettos, where Jews were forced to live. Fund-raising efforts in 1941 yielded one million zlotys, which CENTOS used to plan educational and cultural activities to enrich young people's lives. A second series of cultural events was planned for August 1942, but before they could take place, the Nazis began liquidating the Warsaw Ghetto and deporting Jewish residents to death camps. *See also* DEATH CAMPS (WORLD WAR II); DEPORTATIONS; HOLOCAUST; POLAND (WORLD WAR II); WARSAW GHETTO; WORLD WAR II.

Further Reading: Yehuda Bauer, *American Jewry and the Holocaus* (1981); Celia S. Heller, *On the Edge of Destruction* (1977); Leni Yahil, *The Holocaust* (1990).

Centrala Opieki nad Sierotami (National Society for the Care of Orphans). *See* CENTOS

Chaillet, Pierre. *See* FRANCE (WORLD WAR II)

Chalmers, Burns. *See* Le Chambon-sur-Lignon; Quakers (Society of Friends)

Chechnya

In 1994 in Chechnya, a Muslim province located in southern Russia, fighting broke out between Chechen rebels and Russian troops. Bombings injured and killed children, as well as other civilians, as the war continued into 1996. Shahpari Kashoggi, who undertook a relief mission in Chechnya, found children who had been separated from their families scavenging for food in the streets. They were suffering from malnutrition and a lack of health care. According to Kashoggi, "So many buildings have been destroyed that people mostly are living underground. There's no food, no water, no electricity, no order and no relief in any way. . . . We have to convince people this is not a children's war, so why are we letting the children suffer?" ("Liz to Add Glitz," 1997). After her visit to the city of Grosny and the surrounding area, Kashoggi began organizing fund-raising efforts to help these children.

Children also made up a large percentage of the 350,000 refugees who fled from Chechnya to neighboring Ingushetia and other nearby regions. Some refugees found housing with local residents. The cultural traditions of these people oblige them to shelter those in need. There was not enough housing for the refugees, and some people had to stay in passenger trains or schoolrooms while government authorities sought places where they could live. Several families shared small rooms, and many refugees lacked hot water, cooking facilities, and places to wash clothing. Cholera, diphtheria, typhus, and other infectious diseases broke out during the war, and more than 20 children in one camp died from these diseases.

A large number of teenagers and boys and girls as young as 11 became soldiers during this war, and many were combatants. Relief workers who talked with these children after the war reported that they experienced intense fear of being killed and were horrified by the violence they witnessed. Workers described many boys as angry and hostile.

Organizations from around the world sent medical supplies and people to help the refugees but were often hindered in their efforts when combatants shot at them. These relief groups included the International Committee of the Red Cross (IRC) and a French-founded group called Médecins Sans Frontières (Doctors without Borders). During 1995, health workers inoculated thousands of children against diphtheria and polio. Health workers who aided the refugees said

the children had been emotionally traumatized by the bombings they had seen. Some of the children would begin to cry whenever airplanes flew overhead. An organization called War Child helped children in Chechnya. In 1996, War Child helped to pay for medical supplies and Family Packs that contained enough food for a family of four for one month.

The Red Cross estimated that more than 6,000 children had lost at least one parent. Orphanages were overcrowded and did not have enough staff or health care personnel for all the children. After visiting an orphanage, journalist Geoffrey York reported that children shaped clay into replicas of weapons and tanks. "The children of this orphanage have seen many things—war, death, bombs, destruction on an unimaginable scale. They have survived explosions, served as spies behind Russian lines and flung corpses into bomb craters to bury them" (York, 1997). One 14-year-old boy described his reconnaissance missions into dangerous territory; others told of seeing people blown apart by bombs before their eyes. *See also* POST-TRAUMATIC STRESS DISORDER (PTSD); RED CROSS; REFUGEES; WAR CHILD.

Further Reading: Alan Cooperman, "A Trail of Tears from Grozny to Nowhere," *U.S. News and World Report,* February 27, 1995; Doctors without Borders at <http://www.dwb.org>; "Liz to Add Glitz to Chechnya Benefit," *USA Today,* January 20, 1997; Geoffrey York, "Grozny's War-Hardened Orphans Trying to Be Kids Again," *Toronto Globe and Mail,* January 29, 1997.

Chemical Warfare

As the twentieth century drew to a close, the use of chemical substances in warfare posed a growing threat to civilians and military personnel. Simpler chemical weapons, including poisonous gases, had existed for decades. At the First International Peace Conference in The Hague, The Netherlands, in 1899, several nations signed a pact agreeing not to use "projectiles, the object of which is the diffusion of asphyxiating or deleterious gases." Nonetheless, poison gas was used during World War I. Germany had signed the pact at The Hague, but in 1915, German

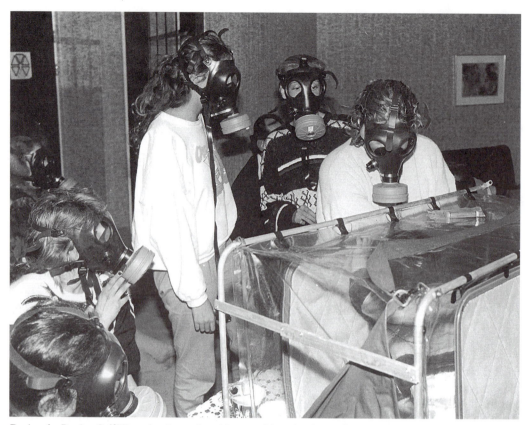

During the Persian Gulf War, when it was feared Iraq would use its chemical weapons, an Israeli mother wears a gas mask and places her child in a "safe tent" during a missile attack on Tel Aviv in January 1991. *Martin Cleaver, AP/Wide World Photos.*

soldiers distributed thousands of cylinders containing liquid chlorine in trenches along a stretch of Flanders Field near the Belgian town of Ypres. When artillery was fired on these trenches, the cylinders burst open, releasing deadly fumes. The German government claimed it had adhered to the agreement because no projectiles were used to deliver the gas. Later, German soldiers also used mustard gas on Allied soldiers. By the war's end, both sides had used chemical weapons. Soldiers young and old suffered serious effects from these chemicals. Nearly 100,000 died and some were left disabled and suffered from permanent nerve injuries.

New and more deadly chemicals were devised during World War II. A top-secret Japanese chemical plant operated on the island of Okunoshima from 1937 to 1944. Children were among the workers at this plant, which stayed open 24 hours a day. Although workers had safety gear, it did not

fully protect them from the effects of gas leaks. The masks had been made for adult males and did not fit women or children properly. Their skin became discolored and they suffered from sore eyes and throats. Some fainted and coughed up blood. Students from the Adamoumi Pacific Girls High School who worked at the plant complained of the awful smells. Later in life, these former workers had an unusually high incidence of cancers and chronic bronchitis.

Concern over chemical warfare increased in the 1950s as more nations developed and stockpiled these kinds of weapons and found more efficient ways to unleash them. Because chemical weapons are relatively cheap and can be produced in pesticide factories without much technology, Third World countries began amassing them. They were able to purchase equipment and materials from companies in the West and in Asia.

Terrorists have used deadly chemicals on groups of people. For example, in Japan, terrorists released cans of sarin, a poisonous nerve gas, in five Tokyo subway cars on March 20, 1995. Twelve people were killed and 5,500 were injured. On April 19, 1995, terrorists struck again, releasing the toxic gas phosgene in a crowded train in Yokohama, Japan.

Iraq, under its leader Saddam Hussein, was accused of using chemical weapons on both its enemies and on its own people during the Iran-Iraq War in the 1980s and during the Persian Gulf War of 1991. Field investigators from the United Nations determined that Iraq had used these weapons, including nerve agents and mustard gas (yperite), on Iran in 1984, 1985, and 1986. In 1988, investigators concluded that Iraq had delivered poison gas on Kurds in the Iraqi town of Halabja. These agents killed thousands of unarmed civilians, including children. Survivors experienced pain, disability, and ongoing illness. People around the world saw photographs of Kurdish mothers trying to protect their children from the poisonous air.

During the Persian Gulf War, Israel and other nations worried about chemical weapons. Thousands of people bought gas masks for themselves and their families. The Israeli government purchased and stored more than 4.2 million gas masks for civilians. Some people spent $2,000 apiece on special motor-driven masks that could be worn by children who were too small to use the standard sizes. Young people in both Israel and Kuwait attended special meetings in which they were taught what to do in case of a chemical weapons attack. In 1997 and 1998, the United Nations continued to insist that Iraq be open to U.N. inspections to determine if chemical weapons were being manufactured and stored. Conflicts over weapons inspections in Iraq continued in 1999 as U.N. inspectors contended that they could not gain access to some of the sites they believed might contain weapons. *See also* AGENT ORANGE; BIOLOGICAL WARFARE; GULF WAR SYNDROME; IRAN-IRAQ WAR; PERSIAN GULF WAR; WORLD WAR I; WORLD WAR II.

Further Reading: Louise Lief and Steven Emerson, "The Uphill Battle to Contain Chemical Weapons," *U.S. News & World Report,* January 9, 1989, p. 42; Robert Harris and Jeremy Paxton, *A Higher Form of Killing* (1982); Yuka Tanaka, "Poison Gas: The Story Japan Would Like to Forget," *Bulletin of the Atomic Scientist,* October 1988, p. 14; "The Poison This Time," *Time,* January 30, 1989, p. 45; Patrick E. Tyler, "U.S. Prepares for High Poison Gas Toll," *The New York Times,* August 20, 1990, p. 24.

Child Refugee Bill (Wagner-Rogers Bill)

The Child Refugee Bill of 1939 was proposed in the U.S. Congress in response to the rising violence against Jews in Nazi Germany. Introduced by Senator Robert F. Wagner and Congresswoman Edith Nourse Rogers, the bill would have admitted into the United States 20,000 German Jewish and non-Jewish refugee children above the usual immigration quota. The sponsors hoped the bill would offer more young people a safe haven from persecution and terror. Although both First Lady Eleanor Roosevelt and former President Herbert Hoover and various religious and labor leaders supported it, the Wagner-Rogers Bill was withdrawn after various groups throughout the country strongly opposed it. These groups included the DAR and American Legion. Personal correspondence between the president and the first lady show that Franklin D. Roosevelt also wanted the bill to succeed but political advisors told him that if he openly supported it and it failed, he might jeopardize chances to bring increased numbers of refugee children into the United States. During the late 1930s, the United States was still trying to recover from the Great Depression that had caused massive poverty since 1929. Many Americans feared that more immigrants would aggravate unemployment and further burden institutions and social services that were struggling to meet people's needs. Some Americans, including people in government positions, also had anti-Semitic (anti-Jewish) attitudes. Because most countries around the world closed their doors to them, Jewish refugees were forced to remain in European countries controlled by the Nazis during World

War II. *See also* CHILDREN'S TRANSPORTS; HOLOCAUST; REFUGEES; *ST. LOUIS*; WORLD WAR II.

Further Reading: David A. Adler, *We Remember the Holocaust* (1989); Richard Breitman and Alan M. Kraut, *American Refugee Policy and European Jewry* (1987); Henry L. Feingold, *The Politics of Rescue* (1970); Joseph P. Lash, *Eleanor and Franklin* (1971).

Child Soldiers. *See* SOLDIERS, CHILD

Children of Auschwitz Nazi Deadly Experiments Survivors (CANDLES)

Children of Auschwitz Nazi Deadly Experiments Survivors (CANDLES) is an international group for the victims, mainly twins, who were subjected to cruel Nazi quasi-medical experiments at the Auschwitz-Birkenau death camp in Poland during World War II. The group was founded by twin sisters, Eva and Miriam Mozes, who both endured experiments conducted at Auschwitz by Dr. Josef Mengele. In 1984, after attending a 1983 conference for Holocaust survivors in Washington, D.C., the sisters wrote letters to American journalists and newspapers, urging them to tell the public about Mengele's deadly experiments and his child victims.

Syndicated columnist Jack Anderson was among those who responded. His associate, Lucette Lagnado, interviewed Eva Mozes and wrote her account of the brutal surgeries, the murder of her sisters and parents, and Mengele's activities. Twins had been subjected to blood tests, radiation, unnecessary surgery and injections, starvation diets, and exposure to cholera and tuberculosis organisms, among other things.

Through the Israeli press, Eva Mozes and her sister asked other survivors to contact them. Mozes later said,

> I thought that maybe if I could locate the twins, we could sit down and piece together what had happened to us in the concentration camp. And then one day, it occurred to me that there was one person who knew exactly what was done to us—Dr. Mengele. I found out that Mengele had been free

since the end of the war. I thought, "That is impossible." (Lagnado and Dekel, 1991)

Nearly 100 survivors were identified. After they held a reunion in Israel, the Mozes sisters decided to form CANDLES. Their goal was to raise public awareness, to prompt more investigations into the Nazi experiments, and to spur law enforcement officials to bring Mengele to justice.

In September 1984, Jack Anderson wrote a feature story on the Auschwitz twins. In January 1985, members of CANDLES traveled to Auschwitz on the fortieth anniversary of the camp's liberation. They also retraced the steps of their Death March across the snow. The trip was widely covered by the world press, leading Eva Mozes to say, "Since the Holocaust, I had always felt that if only the world knew our story, it would care. At Auschwitz, surrounded by all those reporters, I felt, people do care" (Lagnado and Dekel, 1991).

In Tel Aviv, some of the twins met with foreign dignitaries and officials to hold a mock trial in which they charged Josef Mengele with war crimes and crimes against humanity. Their stories prompted a new search for Mengele that turned up evidence that he had died in 1979 in Brazil. CANDLES continues as a support group for surviving victims. *See also* AUSCHWITZ-BIRKENAU; DEATH MARCHES; DEKEL, ALEX SCHLOMO; EXPERIMENTS, NAZI; HOLOCAUST; MENGELE, JOSEF; POLAND (WORLD WAR II); ROMANI (GYPSIES) WORLD WAR II.

Further Reading: David A. Adler, *We Remember the Holocaust* (1989); Lucette Matalon Lagnado and Sheila Cohn Dekel, *Children of the Flames* (1991); Nancy L. Segal, "Holocaust Twins: Their Special Bond," *Psychology Today,* August 1985, pp. 52-58; Simon Wiesenthal, *The Murderers Among Us* (1967).

Children of War Tour

In 1986, the Religious Task Force (RTF) of the Mobilization for Survival organized the Children of War Tour to mark the start of their international peace and justice program. The tour brought together 38 teenagers from 14 war-torn countries around the world. The teenagers embarked on a 54-city tour of the

United States during which they spoke to groups in schools, churches, synagogues, and community centers. These youths told audiences about the horrors of war and its special impact on the lives of children and young people. Many spoke to other teens in the United States and urged American youths to join efforts to promote worldwide peace.

Children's Evacuation. *See* EVACUATIONS (WORLD WAR II)

Children's Garden. *See* YAD VASHEM

Children's Monument. *See* PEACE MONUMENT

Children's Transports (*Kindertransport*)

In 1938, as the Nazis accelerated their attacks against Jews in Germany and its territories, people in Great Britain organized a project called the World Movement for the Care of Children from Germany and Austria. Through a program known as the Children's Transports, endangered children were moved to safe havens elsewhere in Europe. Most would never see their families again.

Priority was given to children who had been orphaned, were homeless, or whose fathers had been imprisoned by the Nazis, leaving the family with no means of support. Older children whose lives were threatened by the Nazis were also placed on transports. Most evacuees were female because they were easier to place in households. Boys over 12 years of age were in the minority. The first transport arrived in Harwich, England, on December 2, 1938, and included 320 children. One of the young people who went on this transport later recalled that

> During the time my father was in the concentration camp, my mother, trying everything to have him released, was advised by the Jewish committee to send my sister and me to England with the first children's transport leaving Berlin. This terrible de-

cision fell on her shoulders alone—but what else could she do, at least it would mean safety for her children. . . . She sent us not knowing what would become of us or if she would ever see us again. My sister was eleven and I was twelve years old. (Gershon, 1966)

Another member of the transport said, "I was ten years old and my total possessions were one small rucksack containing one change of clothes, some socks, handkerchiefs, a mouth organ and some medical supplies for my ear" (Gershon, 1966).

The children faced many adjustments. Most of them spoke German, Czech, or Polish, but little or no English. Some were also aware that they were refugees and had escaped from danger. They had been separated from their families, friends, schools, and other normal activities. One 12-year-old girl from Vienna wrote in her diary, "When I am dead they will have to put on my grave that here lies a child who died of homesickness" (Gershon, 1966).

When they first arrived, many of the children had to stay in uncomfortable camps until arrangements were made for them to travel to their destinations. It was a cold winter, and hundreds of children were housed together in barracks, but the food was adequate. One former refugee recalled, "Every evening lists of names were read over the loudspeaker, of children who would be leaving the camp the following day. One night I heard my name. . . . I was to go to a boarding school in Manchester. I did not even know what the term boarding school meant" (Gershon, 1966).

Some communities formed special committees to help receive and place refugee children. Prospective foster parents visited the camps and offered to take specific children home with them. Individuals and organizations set up homes to welcome groups of children. One such place was Welcome House, run by a woman named Freeman. Farm School at Whittingehame House in Scotland was part of the English Youth Aliyah Movement that prepared young Jews to move to Palestine later on. It opened in February 1939. Jewish citizens in various areas organized hostels and boarding schools where children lived comfortably and received good educations. A number of Jewish children were taken in by non-Jewish families, although the Jewish Refugee Committee tried to match people of the same religious faiths.

Some of the young people had to give up their dreams of more education and chosen careers. One former refugee recalled being interviewed by a woman filling out a form: "When I was asked what I wanted to be, I said a doctor. The woman who was filling in the form said: 'I can't put that down—you must remember that you are a refugee'" (Gershon, 1966). A number of the young people quit school at age 14 to take jobs and support themselves. They worked in hospitals, mines, tailor shops, and as clerks, in printing businesses, and at various other jobs.

By September 1939 when World War II broke out, 9,354 children had left Germany through this program. Of this total, 7,482 were Jewish. Some of these children had relatives or friends in England who agreed to sponsor them after they arrived. Others were placed in private homes, schools that agreed to sponsor them, or households that wanted to hire older children as servants.

According to Professor Norman Bentwich, more than 1,000 of these refugees, including several hundred girls, served with the British forces during World War II. They were drivers, clerks, mechanics, gunners, wireless operators, nurses, tank crew members, translators, and pilots, among other things. Thirty of them lost their lives.

Others came of age (18) when the Essential Works Order was in force. Like others, they signed up for war work deemed necessary and compulsory for every able person between ages 18 and 50.

Former refugees formed a group called Hyphen in 1948 to share their experiences and keep in touch with people from their homelands while still promoting adjustment to British life. They organized lectures, study groups, social events, and volunteer work to help sick and elderly refugees. *See also* HOLOCAUST; *KRISTALLNACHT;* REFUGEES; YOUTH ALIYAH.

Further Reading: Norman Bentwich, *They Found Refuge* (1956); Olga Levy Drucker, *Kindertransport* (1992); Karen Gershon, ed. *We Came as Children* (1966); Elaine Landau, *We Survived the Holocaust* (1991); Dorothy Macardle, *Children of Europe* (1951).

Chinese Civil War

Conflicts between nationalist and communist groups had occurred off and on for more than 10 years when the Chinese civil war ended in 1949, a time when the population of this vast country was more than 450 million. In addition, both nationalist and communist forces had engaged in nearly constant warfare with Japanese troops between 1933 and 1945. In 1949, the Nationalist government, under leader Chiang Kai-shek, was overturned by Communists under Mao Tse-tung. Children on both sides of this long internal conflict suffered displacement, the loss of family members, and numerous deprivations.

The Chinese Communist Party had been founded in 1921 and included students and other young people, many of them discontented peasants and workers. Communist leaders believed that they must mobilize young people to gain and maintain power. In 1926, Mao Tse-tung told a group of Central Committee leaders that "The young people are the main force of the Cultural Revolution. They must be fully mobilized" (Robottom, 1969).

Thousands of young girls and boys joined the revolutionary groups that took part in the Nationalist Revolution of 1927. They attended schools, such as the Central Military and Political Academy, where they trained to become soldiers. Afterwards, many young revolutionaries found themselves arrested as the political parties were reorganized and the government imprisoned some communists.

During the early 1930s, communist troops headed for remote areas of China to regroup and plan their next moves against the nationalists. When the Red Army, as Mao Tse-tung's troops were called, marched north in October 1934 to escape pursuing nationalists, about 1,000 young boys, most of them orphans, accompanied the troops to serve as nurses and aides. These Young Vanguards, as they were called, ranged in age from 11 to 17. During this arduous journey, the boys cared for wounded men and rubbed the feet of men whose circulation was impaired by exposure to cold. Only 300 of the boys survived this march. Some died when they fell into swift-moving rivers, which had to be crossed on rope bridges. Others died from hunger, since raw wheat was sometimes the only food available.

During the years of civil war, many peasants' and workers' children were orphaned or went hungry. Families who possessed wealth or land were stripped of their holdings, and many landowners were killed, leaving children without parents or a means of support. At times, relief organizations, such as the United Nations Relief and Rehabilitation Association (UNRRA), sent stores of food but the government did not distribute them efficiently. One former Nationalist government general told an American reporter,

> I shall never forget an American girl who had volunteered to take care of some of the orphans. UNRRA had sent her supplies of food for them, but Chiang's [Chiang Kai-shek's] officers prevented her from getting the food. Many of the children had died while the food that would have saved them was being sold out of a warehouse around the corner. (Hoff, 1965)

Soldiers on both sides included young men. Communist guerillas often included disgruntled peasant teenagers. When the civil war ended, young children guarded the entrances to villages now committed to the new Communist government. *See also* JAPAN-CHINA WAR (1930S); UNITED NATIONS RELIEF AND REHABILITATION ADMINISTRATION (UNRRA): WORLD WAR II.

Further Reading: Rhonda Hoff, *China: Adventures in Eyewitness History* (1965); Hsieh Ping-ying, *Girl Rebel* (1940); John Robottom, *China in Revolution* (1969); Nym Wales, *Inside Red China* (1939).

Christian Children's Fund. *See* RELIEF ORGANIZATIONS

CIMADE

CIMADE (*Comite d'Inter Mouvements Aupres des Evacues*) was a rescue group founded by Protestants in occupied Europe during World War II. The group, whose members were mostly French and Swiss women, helped Jewish children and young adults. CIMADE did relief work, found safe houses for Jews, and provided people in hiding with food, fake identity papers, medicines, and other needs. They also conducted people to safe houses and smuggled refugees across the French-Swiss border into neutral Switzerland. This ecumenical organization, based in Paris, France, continues to actively work for human rights and to assist refugees from countries around the world. *See also* FRANCE (WORLD WAR II); HOLOCAUST; REFUGEES; RIGHTEOUS GENTILES; WORLD WAR II.

Further Reading: Philip Friedman, *Their Brother's Keepers* (1978); Philip Hallie, *Lest Innocent Blood Be Shed* (1979); Carol Rittner and Sondra Meyers, eds., *The Courage to Care* (1986).

Civil Defense

During wartime, teenagers have been assigned to various duties in civil defense. In some countries, young people were required to register for this type of work or other war-related jobs at a certain age, often 16 or 18. The tasks performed by young people in Great Britain during World War II are typical of the work done by youths in various countries during that war. British teens too young to be drafted worked in the British Home Guard and received training at night on ways to protect the nation if it were invaded by parachute troops or by sea. These youths also served as messengers. At age 18, they were allowed to serve on patrols. They reported bombings and directed rescue workers to people in need of help. Some young people helped to put out fires that were caused by incendiary bombs. They also played the roles of victims in training exercises set up to help people practice evacuating the injured and giving first aid. Some worked with rescue crews that helped people after bombings. Other young people drove and helped to repair and maintain trucks and other vehicles used by the city of London. *See also* AIR RAIDS; BLITZ, LONDON; BOMBINGS (WORLD WAR II); COLD WAR; ELIZABETH II; GERMANY (WORLD WAR II); JAPAN (WORLD WAR II).

Further Reading: Mark Jonathan Harris et al. *The Homefront* (1984); Robert Westall, *Children of the Blitz* (1985).

Civil War. *See* AMERICAN CIVIL WAR

Clem, John Lincoln (Johnny) (1850–1937)

Johnny Clem, a drummer in the Union army during the American Civil War, was known as the "Drummer Boy of Shiloh." Born in Newark, Ohio, Clem left home in 1861 at age 10 to join the Twenty-second Michigan Regiment as drummer boy, a position that paid him $13 a month. One observer, Mrs. Annie Wittenmyer, described the 11-year-old as "a fair and beautiful child . . . small for his age . . . about thirty inches high and weighed about sixty pounds" (Robertson, 1984).

Clem earned his nickname—"Johnny Shiloh"—in April 1862 at the Battle of Shiloh in Tennessee. During this battle, a cannon shell burst on a tree stump and fragments hit Clem's drum. He obtained another drum, but that, too, was hit during the battle.

Clem then grabbed a musket and began shooting with the troops. From then on, Clem fought as a soldier. He saw action in the Battle of Chattanooga and several other battles, where he used a sawed-off musket. Clem was said to have killed a Confederate colonel who tried to capture him at Chattanooga, and he was praised for his bravery. He was wounded at least once. In 1863, Johnny Clem was promoted to the rank of sergeant.

Clem remained in the army and was the last man active in the armed forces who had fought in the Civil War when he retired as a major general in 1916 at age 65. Clem was living in Texas when he died in 1937; he was buried with full military honors at Arlington National Cemetery. *See also* AMERICAN CIVIL WAR; DRUMMER BOYS.

Further Reading: Bruce Catton, *This Hallowed Ground* (1956); Jim Murphy, *The Boys' War* (1990);

James I. Robertson, *The Civil War* (1984); Richard Wheeler, *Voices of the Civil War* (1976).

Clothing Shortages (World War II)

During wartime, young people have faced shortages of food, shelter, and other basic needs, including clothing. Clothing shortages have affected young people serving in the military as well as in civilian life. Many young civilians were deprived of the clothing they would have normally worn for school, dances, dating, or other special occasions. They often felt self-conscious about wearing ill-fitting or shabby clothes and shoes.

In some cases, a lack of adequate clothing caused much more serious health problems, even death. During World War II, when

Like many children during World War II, this Korean boy overcomes clothing shortages by wearing an oversize pair of GI combat boots. The picture was taken in Seoul, South Korea, in December 1952, shortly after the visit there of President-elect Dwight Eisenhower. *UPI/Corbis-Bettmann.*

the Nazis forced Jews to live in ghettos and concentration camps, these victims lacked overcoats and other warm garments and suffered greatly in bitter winter weather. Without adequate fuel, blankets, and warm clothing, some children froze to death in ghettos and Nazi-run camps. Their bodies were exposed to damp, cold conditions and could not resist infections, which led to illnesses.

Clothing was in short supply in many countries during World War II. Shortages led to a rationing system in countries occupied by Nazi Germany and in Allied nations that were using their resources to fight the Axis countries (Germany, Japan, and Italy). People made do with fewer clothes and waited until they had saved enough ration coupons to buy a new raincoat or pair of pajamas, for instance. To compound shortages, occupying forces sometimes collected warm clothing and ordered people to give up furs, warm coats, and other items.

Young people in Holland (The Netherlands) endured a harsh five-year Nazi occupation beginning in May 1940. By the last years of the war, most people wore shabby, worn clothing and shoes without heels. They lacked stockings, coats, and hats. People turned clothes inside out and mended and patched any items that could be worn longer. They wore wooden shoes when no other footwear was available.

Shoes were a special problem for many young people during the war. Footwear that did not wear out became too small as a child's feet grew larger. Worn-out soles allowed water inside the shoes when children were outdoors. Because leather was scarce, people made new soles out of wood or pieces of cardboard cut to fit. They lined thin shoes with newspapers for warmth. Some parents cut the toes off shoes to allow more room for their children's growing feet.

Resourceful parents devised ways to dress their children for school and other occasions. They unraveled sweaters and used the old yarn to knit dresses. One young girl in England recalled that

> You could hardly get wool and so my Mum used to undo all my Dad's old jumpers to make us hats, gloves, wool socks and scarves; if she had enough wool, all to match, I was the envy of the neighborhood. (Westall, 1985)

Scraps or bits of linen were also made into clothing in Great Britain during World War II. Bolts of new cloth were highly prized throughout war-torn Europe, when they could be purchased or if relatives or friends abroad sent them as gifts. In Germany, Allied blockades prevented imported cotton and wool from arriving, so childen wore old clothing throughout the war years. Shoes also wore out more quickly because only about half the population was allowed to buy overshoes or rubber boots during a calendar year. The leather shortage also meant that worn-out soles could not be replaced. *See also* AMERICAN CIVIL WAR; CONCENTRATION CAMPS (WORLD WAR II); FRANCE (WORLD WAR II); GENEVA CONVENTIONS; GERMANY (WORLD WAR II); GHETTOS (WORLD WAR II); HOLLAND (WORLD WAR II); JAPAN (WORLD WAR II); REFUGEES; RELIEF ORGANIZATIONS; WORLD WAR I; WORLD WAR II.

Further Reading: Penny Colman, *Rosie the Riveter* (1995); Miep Gies, *Anne Frank Remembered* (1987); Walter B. Maas, *The Netherlands at War* (1970); Archie Satterfield, *Home Front* (1981); Robert Westall, *Children of the Blitz* (1985).

Cold War

After World War II ended in 1945, political conditions led to a tense period in international relations called the Cold War. From time to time, the Cold War heated up, causing fears that major world powers might go to war, this time using deadly nuclear weapons that had proliferated in the post-war era. The threat of nuclear war hung over generations of people born after the war. Young people growing up in the nuclear age have lived with the ominous knowledge that humankind could virtually destroy life on earth within minutes.

The Cold War began in 1945, when the Soviet Union, which had driven the Germans out of Eastern and Central Europe, set up Soviet-controlled regimes in Poland, Hungary, Romania, Yugoslavia, Czechoslovakia, and East Germany. These nations became known as the Eastern Bloc, as opposed to the Western Bloc of nations led by the United States and its allies in Western Europe. In 1946, a number of these Western nations formed NATO—the North Atlantic Treaty Organization.

The Berlin Airlift is often called the first crisis of the Cold War. In April 1948, Soviet troops cut off access to the British, French, and American sectors of Berlin. People living in these parts of Berlin could not receive fuel, food, medicine, and other supplies. The United States joined with Great Britain and France to conduct the largest airlift in history, flying coal and other supplies over the blockaded areas. During an 11-month period, they flew 2.3 million tons of food and fuel into the city.

During the Berlin Airlift, a U.S. pilot named Gail Halvorsen from Utah was one of hundreds of pilots who ran the blockade. During an afternoon visit to Berlin, he was mobbed by a group of children who were eager to see a pilot. He handed out the two sticks of chewing gum he had in his pocket, promising to return in his plane the next day with more goodies. Halvorsen decided to start dropping tiny parachutes (made from handkerchiefs), rigged to pieces of candy and chewing gum, from his cargo compartment while he was en route to deliver the regular cargo. The grateful children of Berlin called him the Candy Bomber and the Chocolate Pilot. They could tell he was coming by the way he dipped the wings of his C-54 in the air before dropping the sweets.

Other pilots followed his lead. Like Halverson, they signaled the children by wiggling the wings of their bombers so the children would know which planes were going to drop the candy. Candy companies and individuals in the United States donated more than three tons of chocolate bars, chewing gum, and other treats. American schoolchil-

Split by the Cold War, members of a German family meet across a barbed wire fence dividing East Berlin from West Berlin. *Corbis/Hulton-Deutsch Collection.*

dren made the parachutes used to hold the candy.

More than 100,000 German children received parcels from the Candy Bombers. During an interview in 1998, Halvorsen said, "I can still see the kids' smiling faces, waiting for a pack of gum or a piece of chocolate to come floating from the blue." One of those children who received the packages, Ingrid Preston, recalled, "There was never enough to eat. It was like Christmas every time they dropped the candy" (Guthrie and Free, 1998).

The Cold War continued after the airlift ended in a Soviet withdrawal. Both East and West possessed nuclear weapons and became involved in an escalating arms race, with each side building new and more powerful nuclear devices and missiles. In 1949, after years of conflict, Mao Tse-tung's communist forces in China overturned the Nationalist government of Chiang Kai-shek. Mainland China, the most heavily populated country in the world, became known as the People's Republic of China and was allied with other communist nations. China also developed its own nuclear arsenal.

During the 1950s and 1960s, American children commonly discussed the possibility of a nuclear war. Children speculated about which cities or regions of the country might be likely targets for bombs from Soviet Russia or Red China. A minority of people even built backyard bomb shelters to house their families in the event of a nuclear war. Families could order a bomb shelter from magazine ads. Shelters sold for between $2,000 and $3,000 in 1955. Nationwide, about one million households owned shelters in 1960.

In 1951, young people around the country watched a filmstrip called "Survival Under Nuclear Attack" and practiced dropping to the ground or floor or moving inside a fallout shelter. "Duck and Cover" was a well-known civil defense slogan. A film by that same name, featuring Bert the Turtle, was presented in elementary school classrooms. The movie showed children how to take cover from flying glass and other debris that would occur during an attack. A pamphlet featuring cartoon strips with Bert the Turtle and a

sheet music version of "Duck and Cover" reinforced these messages.

For millions of children, the Cuban Missile Crisis of 1962 was perhaps the most frightening event of the Cold War. Relations between the United States and Cuba, its neighbor in the Caribbean, had deteriorated after Fidel Castro became prime minister in 1959. Following a successful revolution to overturn the old government, Castro installed a communist regime.

In October 1962, President John F. Kennedy announced that U.S. surveillance planes had spotted offensive missile sites being built in Cuba. Jet bombers capable of carrying nuclear weapons were found in these areas. Kennedy ordered a naval and air quarantine of Cuba, which was to continue until all offensive weapons were removed from Cuba under the supervision of the United Nations. The missiles had come from the Soviet Union. Kennedy further declared that if nuclear weapons were launched against any nation in the Western Hemisphere, the United States would view this as an attack on the United States and retaliate against the Soviet Union. Tense negotiations began with Soviet Premier Nikita Khrushchev.

For eight days, people feared a war might ensue. Children heard their parents and teachers discussing the possibility of nuclear war and what people would do in case of an attack. Some families discussed the possibility of barricading themselves in bomb shelters if bombs fell nearby.

Young people discussed their fears about nuclear war and speculated if anyone would survive. If so, what would happen to them if radioactive fallout killed the plants and animals people needed to live and contaminated the air, water, and land? They wondered if their towns were safe from attack or if they were located too near important military, political, or industrial establishments. The Cuban Missile Crisis affected children around the world. Children of U.S. military personnel recalled seeing troops being called back to the base and preparing for possible emergencies. During the tense Cold War years, they sometimes had fallout drills and nuclear alerts.

The Cuban Missile Crisis ended when Soviet leaders agreed to remove the missiles. A deadly confrontation was avoided, but for many young people, fears of nuclear war lingered long after the crisis was over. Some of these youths would later join groups that opposed new nuclear weapons and the arms race. They would work with organizations that promoted world peace and non-military solutions to political conflicts. *See also* ANTI-WAR MOVEMENT (VIETNAM WAR); CUBAN REVOLUTION; NUCLEAR TESTING.

Further Reading: Michael Barson, *Better Red Than Dead* (1992); Bruce Guthrie and Cathy Free, "Sweet Memories," *People*, June 29, 1998, pp. 54–56; David Halberstam, *The Fifties* (1993); David Parrish, *The Cold War Encyclopedia* (1996); Louis A. Perez, Jr., *Cuba Between Reform and Revolution* (1988); Robert Smith Thompson, *The Missiles of October* (1992); Peter Wyden, *Bay of Pigs* (1979).

Collection Center Drives (World War II)

During World War II, people in the United States and other countries collected materials needed for the war effort. Key materials for collection included scrap metal, rubber, and paper that were then used to make military supplies. Young people gathered newspapers, used metal such as tin cans and lead foil, and discarded tires. American youths also collected used clothing and shoes for Victory Clothing Drives, as well as phonograph records (for wax), and cooking fats saved by homemakers. Individual youths, school or church groups, and organizations took part in collection drives. Among the organized youth groups that participated were the Boy Scouts and Girl Scouts. After President Franklin Roosevelt issued a national appeal in 1942, the Scouts organizations in the U.S. collected about 54,000 tons of rubber. Another youth group called the Junior Commandos also contributed a great deal to wartime scrap drives.

Further Reading: Penny Colman, *Rosie the Riveter* (1995); Archie Satterfield, *Home Front* (1981).

Combat. *See* AMERICAN CIVIL WAR; AMERICAN REVOLUTION; CASUALTIES

MILITARY; CLEM, JOHN LINCOLN; FRENCH REVOLUTION; SOLDIERS, CHILD; SUDAN; VIETNAM WAR; WORLD WAR I; WORLD WAR II

Comite d'Inter Mouvements Aupres des Evacues. See CIMADE

Committee of Responsibility (COR)

The Committee of Responsibility (COR) was a group of American doctors and laypeople organized to help injured children in Southeast Asia during the Vietnam War. Funding for COR's work came from concerned individual Americans and from religious, civic, and other groups.

COR sought permission from the U.S. and Vietnamese governments to bring badly wounded children to the United States for medical treatment. Both of these governments expressed concern that problems might result from removing these children from their homelands and families. However, critics of the U.S. government charged that U.S. officials were more concerned about how Americans would react when they saw these terribly injured young victims of an unpopular war.

By 1970, COR had convinced the U.S. government to let them fly 76 children to hospitals in the United States. These children received extensive care, sometimes in more than one health care setting. Many of these victims had infections and other injuries that worsened during the months they had been in Asia without proper treatment. Some needed several different operations to remove metal fragments. Youths with missing limbs needed braces, artificial limbs, and ongoing physical therapy. The children also had intense emotional needs as they adjusted to new situations and struggled to communicate in a foreign environment. Some had mental problems resulting from brain injuries or from the emotional trauma they had endured.

As COR had promised, the children were returned to their homeland after they completed their treatments. Some members of COR accompanied the children and stayed with them until they had readjusted. They helped to arrange for ongoing care in Vietnam. *See also* ANTI-WAR MOVEMENT (VIETNAM WAR); LAND MINES; POST-TRAUMATIC STRESS DISORDER (PTSD); VIETNAM WAR.

Further Reading: Betty Jean Lifton and Thomas C. Fox, *The Children of Vietnam* (1972).

Con Lai. *See* MULTIRACIAL CHILDREN

Concentration Camps (World War II)

During World War II, the German Nazi regime under Adolf Hitler built and operated dozens of concentration camps in Germany, Austria, and certain occupied countries. The camps, labeled as work camps, were set up to confine and punish people the Nazis regarded as their enemies. The camps were also used to deter people from opposing Nazism or engaging in anti-Nazi activities. The phrase "concentration camps," as used here, refers to camps where confinement, not murder, was the main goal. The Nazis also ran six death camps. However, many concentration camp inmates died of overwork, starvation, illness, beatings, shootings, and other abuse.

Hundreds of thousands of children, most of them Jewish, were sent to concentration camps. These children came from Germany and other countries the Nazis occupied, such as Austria, Poland, Denmark, France, Norway, The Netherlands, Belgium, Greece, Romania, Czechoslovakia, Yugoslavia, Russia, Italy, Lithuania, and Hungary. In addition, Romani (Gypsy) children and children of political prisoners were sent to camps, as were young partisans, resisters, and Jehovah's Witnesses and other religious groups persecuted by the Nazis.

The first concentration camp was opened in 1933 at Dachau, outside Munich, Germany. Political prisoners, including Jews, communists, and Nazi protesters made up most of the population. Other camps included

Youthful inmates of the Nazi concentration camp at Dachau greet their liberators on May 3, 1945. *Corbis/Hulton-Deutsch Collection.*

Buchenwald, Bergen-Belsen, Terezin (Theresienstadt), Mauthausen, Ohrdruf, Moringen, and Osthofen. Ravensbruck in Germany was a women's camp where young girls were also detained.

Some young people went to more than one camp. Sophia Hausman, a Dutch teenager from Rotterdam, spent about 27 months in different ghettos and camps between her seventeenth and nineteenth birthdays, including Sobibor, Maidanek, Auschwitz, Bergen-Belsen, and Terezin. Life in the camps was frightening and unpredictable. Harrowing incidents of brutality occurred daily. For example, 14-year-old Sandor Braun, a Romanian Jew, was transferred from Auschwitz to Dachau in 1944. He later recalled this horror.

> One day, a camp guard, promising extra food, entered his [Braun's] barracks holding a violin, and asked if anyone could play. Sandor and two others volunteered. The first two prisoners did not please the guard, and they were both killed before Sandor's eyes. Sandor, however, played the "Blue Danube" waltz, and received an extra ration of food for his performance. (Bachrach, 1993)

The camps were designed so that nobody lived very long. Yet some people survived months, even years, and lived to tell their stories. One inmate, sent to a camp at age 15, later told author Barbara Rogasky (1988), "Some of us had to live, to defy them all, and one day to tell the truth."

When the children survivors of the camps finally could leave, they set out to find any remaining family members. Many found they were orphans, with no surviving relatives. Some were even the only surviving members of their entire pre-war villages. A few turned to displaced persons camps for help.

During the war, young people from Germany, Austria, and their allied countries also worked in concentration camps. Youthful guards were assigned to various duties and sometimes cruelly abused the prisoners. Chief SS supervisor Dorothea Binz arrived at the Ravensbruck camp, where all prisoners were women, when she was 19 years old. Inmates who survived the camp later described her as a malicious person who carried a whip and brought a vicious dog along with her as she made her inspections. She was known to harass and beat prisoners and had some young women subjected to unnecessary medical operations carried out under cruel conditions.

Few children survived in these camps. When the camps were liberated at the war's end, there were about 1,000 children survivors in Buchenwald, 500 at Bergen-Belsen, 500 at Ravensbruck, 1,400 at Dachau, and 100 in Terezin (Theresienstadt). *See also* AUERBACHER, INGE; AUSCHWITZ-BIRKENAU; BERGEN-BELSEN; BUCHENWALD; CROATIA; DEATH CAMPS; DEATH MARCHES; DRANCY; HITLER YOUTH; HOLOCAUST; TEREZIN (THERESIENSTADT).

Further Reading: Susan Bachrach, *Tell Them We Remember* (1993); Sir Martin Gilbert, *The Boys* (1997); Vera Laska, ed., *Women of the Holocaust and in the Resistance* (1984); Barbara Rogasky, *Smoke and Ashes* (1988).

Congo. *See* ZAIRE

Conscientious Objectors

Conscientious objectors are individuals who refuse to serve in their country's military for reasons of conscience. Many men who refused to fight or kill did so because of their religious principles. They belonged to a traditional peace church, such as the Society of Friends (Quakers), Mennonites, Moravians, Amish, Dunkards, or other pacifist sects. For refusing to fight, conscientious objectors have often been ostracized and accused of cowardice or a lack of patriotism.

In the United States, laws were developed early in the nation's history to accommodate such beliefs. During the American Civil War, men could be drafted at age 18. They were required to register with the Selective Service for this purpose on their eighteenth birthday. Formal procedures were set up for those who wished to request a legal exemption from military service for reasons of conscience.

The Society of Friends (Quakers) led an effort that prompted the U.S. Congress to pass an alternative service law in 1864. Members of certain religious groups, including Quakers, Nazarenes, Shakers, and Rogerenes, were exempt from service but had to pay a fee of $300 or work in a hospital as a substitute for military duty. Young Quaker men of draft age could turn to special committees run by the Society of Friends, which advised them on how to deal with the draft board and helped them to perform their alternate service. Most did not believe it was morally right to pay for another person to fight in their place.

Some young objectors went to jail rather than fight. These men were often treated badly in prison and died there from abuse or illness. People who refused to fight were called "nonresistants" until World War I when the term conscientious objector—shortened to "CO"—came into use. Young men also became conscientious objectors in World War II. However, some individuals of draft age who belonged to pacifist churches opted to fight in this war because they believed that the evil they were battling overrode their usual opposition to war. The number of conscientious objectors and resistors of draft registration peaked in the United States during the Vietnam War, which became increasingly unpopular. The issue became moot in 1972 when the U.S. abolished the draft.

Other nations have also confronted the issues surrounding conscientious objectors. In Nazi Germany during World War II, members of the Jehovah's Witnesses, a small, pacifist Christian group, were punished for refusing to serve in the military. Witnesses were persecuted, physically punished, imprisoned, and killed for following their beliefs. In many cases, their families were also punished, and their children were removed from the home when men refused to serve in the German military.

Different countries have developed different procedures for dealing with young people who object to military service. Some have legal procedures through which people can be declared exempt. The Fellowship of Reconciliation (FOR), founded in England in 1914, helped to promote legal recognition of CO rights in that country as of 1917.

Laws have been changing in countries that previously did not recognize conscientious objection. For example, in 1997, Greece drafted new legislation that permitted young men to perform alternative civilian service or noncombatant service for reasons of conscience. Some countries still do not have such laws. During 1997 and 1998, conscientious objectors were imprisoned in Turkey, Colombia, and other places. *See also* ANTI-WAR MOVEMENT (VIETNAM WAR); CONCENTRATION CAMPS (WORLD WAR II); CONSCRIPTION; JEHOVAH'S WITNESSES; NATIONAL INTERRELIGIOUS SERVICE BOARD FOR CONSCIENTIOUS OBJECTORS (NIBSCO); QUAKERS (SOCIETY OF FRIENDS); SELECTIVE SERVICE ACTS; VIETNAM WAR.

Further Reading: Ina Friedman, *Escape or Die* (1982); Milton Meltzer, *Ain't Gonna Study War No More* (1985); National Interreligious Service Board for Conscientious Objectors, "News Briefs," *The Reporter,* NIBSCO, Spring 1997.

Conscription

Conscription (draft) laws have required young men and women under the age of 21 to register for military service or to serve in the military. Youth in many countries have also protested mandatory conscription, which tends to affect them more than it does older citizens.

Conscription laws specify the age of conscriptees and whether only men or both men and women will be drafted. They also state the length of time people will be required to serve. While some countries have a policy of universal conscription, others draft only men, and some countries have no compulsory draft. For example, the United States has had an all-volunteer army since 1973. However, American males are still required to register with the Selective Service Administration at age 18.

Congress enacted the first mandatory draft in the United States in 1863, during the last two years of the Civil War. President Abraham Lincoln signed the Conscription Act, because the number of volunteers had declined as the war dragged on and soldiers were badly needed. Under the act, young men could be drafted at age 18.

One clause of the act allowed men whose names came up for conscription to pay a $300 fee for a volunteer to take their place. The government then offered the money to a volunteer as a bonus payment. Youths who were poor and unskilled were tempted to enlist to receive this money, along with the financial incentives that states and local communities also offered.

Congress passed a new Conscription Act in 1917 after the United States entered World War I. Men between the ages of 18 and 35 were ordered to register for the draft. Some critics called the draft inequitable because rich young men could often elude service while poorer ones and minorities, such as African Americans, were more likely to serve. Students also received different treatment. During World War I, 145,000 young men who were enrolled in the Student Army Training Corps did not have to serve in the regular army but could continue their education so long as they attended drills. The law exempted members of a well-organized religious group "whose existing creed or principles forbid its members to participate in war in any form." These objectors (including Quakers, Mennonites, Hutterites, Brethren, and Jehovah's Witnesses) did, however, have to perform non-combatant services.

Around the world, complaints about inequity in draft laws are not new. Some nations have also used conscription laws to persecute certain groups in the population. For example, during the 1820s, the Russian tsarist government forcibly drafted Jewish boys at age 12 and required them to serve for as long as 25 years. Most of these boys never returned home after they left for the army. To avoid this fate, some parents concealed their sons or even injured them so they would not pass the physical exams given to new draftees.

During certain wars, draft laws were changed to require both sexes to serve. For example, in the Soviet Union during World War II, both women and men were drafted. Young people around the world have expressed opinions about conscription and some have opposed laws that force them to register for the draft and serve in the military. Nearly 2,000 young people in Chile marched to protest mandatory military service in March 1997. *See also* AMERICAN CIVIL WAR; ANTI-WAR MOVEMENT (VIETNAM WAR); CONSCIENTIOUS OBJECTORS; JEHOVAH'S WITNESSES; NATIONAL INTERRELIGIOUS SERVICE BOARD FOR CONSCIENTIOUS OBJECTORS (NIBSCO); QUAKERS (SOCIETY OF FRIENDS); SOVIET UNION (WORLD WAR II); WORLD WAR I; WORLD WAR II

Further Reading: Peter Brock, *Pacifism in the United States from Colonial Era to the First World War* (1968); Frederic C. Giffin, *Six Who Protested* (1977); Milton Meltzer, *Ain't Gonna Study War No More* (1985).

Convention on the Rights of the Child

In 1989, the United Nations General Assembly adopted the Convention on the Rights of the Child, which states that "all people under age eighteen have the right to develop to their full potential, free from hunger and want, neglect, exploitation, and the abuses of war." By 1995, 179 countries had ratified the convention, and the United Nations Children's Fund (UNICEF) began pursuing a goal of universal ratification. UNICEF mobilized the Committee on the Rights of the Child to monitor ratifying countries as they moved to implement the provisions of the convention.

The convention is based on the premise that each child is a complete individual with an identity that is distinct from the parents or nurturers and that must be protected by the community. It further states that the overriding principle in determining custody and guardianship should be the child's best interests. The declaration covers children's social, economic, and civil and political rights, asserting that children have rights to survival and early development, education, health care, and social welfare support. They also have the right to a name and nationality; to freedom of expression; to participate in decisions affecting their well-being; to protection from discrimination on the basis of gender, race, or minority status; and to protection from exploitation, sexual and otherwise.

The convention specifically addresses the rights of children during wartime, such as rights to survival, family support, education, health care, and adequate nutrition. Other rights named in the convention are protection against exploitation, violence, torture, and other forms of cruel or degrading treatment or punishment.

Article 38 calls on States Parties (governments) to apply rules of international humanitarian law that apply to children and to make every feasible effort to "ensure protection and care of children who are affected by armed conflict." Article 39 of the Convention stresses the need for the physical and psychological recovery of children after wars have ended. Child victims of war often need special help to re-adjust to society when conflicts end.

The convention also says that governments should refrain from recruiting for the military anyone under the age of 15 and to make every effort to prevent young people under 18 from joining the military. However, the United Nations and many other nations have been trying to raise this age limit to 18 throughout the world. UNICEF hopes that nations will eventually adopt the Optional Protocol to the convention which would make 18 the age limit for military recruitment. *See also* SOLDIERS, CHILD; UNITED NATIONS CHILDREN'S FUND (UNICEF).

Further Reading: Laura Herbst, *Children in War* (1995); United Nations Children's Fund, *Convention on the Rights of the Child,* 1989.

Coordination Committee

At the end of World War II, four Zionist groups organized the Coordination Committee for the purpose of locating and assisting Jewish youth who had survived the Holocaust. Some funding for their work came from the American Joint Distribution Committee, a Jewish organization based in the United States. The four groups sent representatives to Warsaw, Poland, early in 1945 to coordinate their work. The committee then searched for young survivors in towns, cities, and displaced persons' camps. When they found children whose families had died during the war, they usually arranged for these youths to emigrate to Palestine. At that time,

Palestine was still under the control of Great Britain and the Jewish homeland, Israel, was not yet established. Some ships secretly brought groups of displaced children, as well as adults, from Germany and Austria to the Mediterranean.

By 1947, a total of 122,313 Jews from Poland were living in Israel, and thousands of them were children and young people. Most of the orphans, as well as many youth with families, lived in groups of 70 to 80 people called kibbutzen. Kibbutzen residents aimed to live cooperatively and help build a Jewish homeland in Israel. *See also* ADOPTION; DISPLACED PERSONS (DPS); HOLOCAUST; ORPHANS; REFUGEES; POLAND (WORLD WAR II); WORLD WAR II.

Further Reading: Richard C. Lukas, *Did the Children Cry?* (1994).

Croatia

During the twentieth century, the Balkan country of Croatia has endured both occupation and civil war. During World War II, a Nazi puppet government was installed in Croatia and hundreds of thousands of Serbian people were killed. Among them were 11,000 Serbian children who had lived in the Kozara Mountains. It is estimated that anywhere from tens of thousands to hundreds of thousands of Serbs, young people among them, also met their deaths in the Ustache concentration camp in Jasenovac.

After World War II, Croatia became part of Yugoslavia. In 1991, Croatian nationalists and Serbs began fighting after Croatia seceded from the former Yugoslavia. Ethnic Serb civilians were attacked and killed in Gospic and other towns and villages throughout the country. Homes were blown up, and their occupants were dragged away to be executed. Children became orphans after parents were killed. Families were also forced to separate as various members struggled to survive. *See also* BOSNIA; WORLD WAR II.

Crystal Night. *See Kristallnacht*

Cuban Missile Crisis. *See* COLD WAR

Cuban Revolution (1956-1958)

Between 1956 and 1958, Cuban rebels led by communist Fidel Castro fought to overthrow the government of President Fulgencio Batista. During a bloody civil war that killed over 20,000 people, young Cubans assisted Castro's rebels, suffering hardships during the revolution and helping to rebuild the country afterwards with a new communist form of government.

Among the men who fought with Castro for the revolutionary cause were peasant youths and university students from the capital, Havana. In 1957, university students tried to enter the presidential palace by force, planning to assassinate President Batista. They believed that Cuban capitalism was responsible for many social ills, including poverty, illiteracy, class distinctions, diseases, and prostitution. Students also organized an unsuccessful strike against the Batista government in April 1958. Enrique Meneses (1967), a journalist on the scene, later described what he saw in Havana.

> [I]n Avenida del Prado a crowd had gathered to watch a column of smoke and fire shooting up from the sidewalk—the bomb had exploded and set fire to the gas pipes.

In the old part of the city everything was over in fifteen minutes. Several youths had been killed by the police and others fled for their lives, disposing of their arms in garbage bins so as not to be caught red-handed.

Battista fled from Cuba on New Year's Eve 1958 and the rebels took over the government on January 1, 1959. As a result of the revolution, many families experienced separations because some relatives fled to other countries while others were not allowed to leave communist Cuba. Because Castro's regime diminished the role of the Catholic Church, children no longer took part in certain religious activities. Christmas was no longer a public holiday. School curricula changed to reflect communist beliefs, and the education system was expanded throughout the country. Schools distributed uniforms and served meals, which were often the heartiest meals a child received during the day. State-operated health care for all was also established.

Further Reading: Terence Cannon, *Revolutionary Cuba* (1981); Enrique Meneses, "First Days of the Cuban Revolution," in Overseas Press Club, *How I Got That Story* (1967); Hugh Thomas, *The Cuban Revolution* (1977).

D

Dachau. *See* CONCENTRATION CAMPS (WORLD WAR II); EXPERIMENTS, NAZI

Dale, Betty (1765–?)

During the American Revolution, 12-year-old Betty Dale made a famous horseback ride to warn General George Washington of approaching British forces. Ann and Ezra Dale, Betty's parents, were Quakers who lived in southeastern Pennsylvania. Although their religious principles prevented them from taking a combat role in the war, the Dales supported the Patriot cause.

One day in 1777, when her parents were away buying food and Betty was alone, a group of American soldiers appeared with the frightening news that 300 British soldiers were attacking Chichester, where the Quaker meetinghouse had been turned into a fort. They begged Betty to notify her father that the British cavalry were about to attack. Mounted on her horse Daisy, Dale sped forward, although British soldiers began to fire at her when she refused their order to halt. Pursued by the British, Dale hid behind dense trees at a crossroads where the British took the upper road. Dale then emerged from hiding and followed a shortcut on the lower road to General Washington's camp.

After she delivered her message, Dale collapsed from the strain of her ride. Continental soldiers hurried to Chichester, and Betty Dale was taken home where she spent sev-eral days recuperating. Washington praised the girl's courage and called her "an honor to her country." *See also* AMERICAN REVOLUTION.

Further Reading: Elizabeth Anticaglia, *Heroines of '76* (1975); Charles E. Claghorn, *Women Patriots of the American Revolution* (1991); Mary Beth Norton, *Liberty's Daughters* (1975).

Darragh, John (1763–?)

During the American Revolution, teenager John Darragh helped carry secret messages to colonial troops under the command of General George Washington at Whitemarsh, Pennsylvania. The Darragh family, which included nine children, lived in Philadelphia and belonged to the Religious Society of Friends (Quakers). When British troops occupied Philadelphia in the fall of 1777, British officers took over rooms in the Darragh house and sometimes held meetings there to discuss military plans. Although Quakers were pacifists, Lydia Barrington Darragh, John's mother, secretly listened to the conversations and wrote down coded messages. She then folded these messages, stuck them inside four large buttons she sewed on John's coats, and covered the buttons with cloth to match John's suit.

With the messages thus hidden, John Darragh visited his older brother Charles, who was a lieutenant in Washington's army at Whitemarsh. To get to his brother, Darragh had to pass through British guard stations along the way. He met Charles at the home of their Aunt Sally, where Charles removed the bits of paper and decoded the messages. Thus forewarned, the American troops were able to predict some of their enemies' actions and were prepared for a "surprise" attack in December 1777. *See also* AMERICAN REVOLUTION; ESPIONAGE.

Further Reading: Katherine Bakeless and John Bakeless, *Spies of the Revolution* (1962); State Historical Society of Pennsylvania.

Day of the African Child. *See* AFRICA

D-Day (June 6, 1944)

Thousands of soldiers under age 21 fought with troops on both sides on D-Day, the beginning of a major battle and turning point of World War II. On June 6, 1944, thousands of Allied soldiers landed on the Normandy coast, planning to move inland and liberate France and Europe, from German occupation. The Allies sent 155,000 troops, more than 5,000 boats and ships, and 12,000 aircraft.

Fighting with the German troops were young boys who had been forced into service from countries occupied by the Nazis. In addition, Hitler Youth units were sent from Germany to fight against the Allies as they moved into France after D-Day. In June 1944, nearly 200 teenage boys in a Hitler Youth unit worked to dig defensive trenches on the German border with Luxembourg. Their leader was 16-year-old Alfons Heck.

On the beaches, the German commander, Field Marshal Erwin Rommel, had assembled trenches, pillboxes, land mines, and other obstacles. Young casualties were high as Allied soldiers landed on the beach and attempted to move forward. By the end of July, about one-fifth of the Allied tank division members were dead; another 40 percent of these men were missing or wounded. Eventually the Allies won the battle and were able to push inland.

Hitler had ordered his troops to fight to the last man, and General Karl Wilhelm von Schlieben, commander of the garrison in Cherbourg, France, told his troops that "withdrawal from present positions is punishable by death." However, many of these young men were not loyal to the Nazis and deserted or surrendered to U.S., Canadian, and British troops. Some young deserters became Allied prisoners of war.

U.S. Army Private First Class Robert D. Slaughter was one of the young soldiers who landed on Normandy on D-Day. Slaughter was part of Company D, 1st Battalion, 116th Infantry Regiment of the 29th Division, which landed on Omaha Beach. He had lied about his age (15) in 1940 to join the National Guard in Virginia, and his unit shipped out to England in 1941. Slaughter was 19 years old on D-Day. During the 1990s, Slaughter spearheaded an effort to construct a National D-Day Memorial and education center at a site in Bedford, Virginia, a small town that suffered 21 casualties among the 35 residents who fought on D-Day as part of Company A. The memorial is scheduled to open on June 6, 2000. *See also* HITLER YOUTH; WORLD WAR II.

Further Reading: John Barry, "Why the Allies Won," *Newsweek,* May 23, 1994, pp. 30-31; Alfons Heck, *A Child of Hitler* (1985); John Keegan, *The Second World War* (1989); Patrick Rogers and Gerald Burstyn, "In Memory's Cause," *People,* November 19, 1998, pp. 60-62.

Death Camps (World War II)

During the Holocaust, the German Nazi regime under Adolf Hitler built and operated six camps in isolated areas of Poland for the purpose of mass murder: Chelmno, Belzec, Auschwitz-Birkenau, Sobibor, Maidanek, and Treblinka. Some camps had no barracks to house people because inmates were killed upon arriving. After they were stripped of their belongings and ordered to undress, victims were forced into sealed rooms where poison gas was piped in. Their bodies were then burned in ovens called crematoria.

In December 1941, Chelmno became the first death camp to begin operation. Belzec followed in March 1942, at which time 15,000 people were deported to Belzec from the Lublin Ghetto. More than 6,700 were killed by poison gas within days. In the same month, another 15,000 Jewish men, women, and children were brought to Belzec from Lvov in eastern Poland; all were killed. By the end of the war in 1945, 600,000 Jews and 1,200 non-Jews had been murdered at Belzec.

Historians have found that every transport to death camps included children or young adults. According to author Richard C. Lukas (1994), about 1,000 empty prams (baby strollers) were stored at Auschwitz-Birkenau every day. During a 47-day period in late 1944, about 100,000 sets of children's clothing were sent from Auschwitz to Germany.

The Nazis killed people they regarded as "useless eaters," so they scrutinized all new arrivals and allowed only people capable of working to live. Few children survived this initial selection process. Children whom the guards concluded were younger than age 14 were usually killed upon arrival. Women who were obviously pregnant were killed. Some managed to survive, and babies were actually born in the camps. In some instances, fellow prisoners helped to hide the woman and her newborn. Guards killed babies they found in the barracks, sometimes in front of their mothers.

Young people imprisoned in death camps found themselves in a situation from which there was no escape. Camps were surrounded by high fences and electrified barbed wire. Armed guards stood on watchtowers equiped with searchlights, and other guards patroled the grounds and barracks day and night. Inmates were required to show up for roll calls two or more times a day, at which time they lined up, sometimes for hours, and called out the numbers that had been tattooed on their arms for identification. They lacked warm clothing, and food rations were inadequate for daily needs. The demands of forced labor and a lack of food had a particularly harsh effect on children and young people whose bodies were still growing. Many young women who had reached the age of puberty stopped having menstrual periods as a result of malnutrition and other stress.

When the Allies liberated various camps in 1945, they found only a few hundred children had survived in the death camps. Only 500 remained at Auschwitz-Birkenau, where survivors included some of the twins who had been used as guinea pigs by Nazi Dr. Josef Mengele in his so-called "medical experiments." Most of these children and young people were ousted from this camp in January 1945 and forced to embark on what people called "death marches." Those who survived reached the Mauthausen concentration camp in Germany. Others who eluded this roundup stayed at Auschwitz with no food or other supplies. When Russian troops arrived there to liberate the camp on January 27, they found starving children huddling for warmth inside the barracks. Many suffered from dysentery and typhoid fever (typhus), which had raged throughout the camp. The soldiers gave them blankets and clothing.

The next day, Russian photographers filmed the childrens' departure from the camp and the horrendous conditions in which they had lived. The departing children left behind dead family members and friends who had been murdered in the gas chambers. Of the 400,000 Polish prisoners who survived the death camps, 17,750 were children. Many of these children suffered from long-term health problems, as well as from the emotional distress resulting from their ordeal. Only 9,500 were still alive 25 years later.

Troops that arrived to liberate the Nazi camps saw stark evidence of dead children. At Maidanek, a warehouse held children's clothes and thousands of their possessions ready to ship to Germany. One eyewitness, Alexander Werth (1988), recalled that "In the next room were piled up children's toys: teddy-bears, and celluloid dolls and tin automobiles by the hundreds, and simple jigsaw puzzles, and an American-made Mickey Mouse. . . . And so on, and so on. . . . What hideous story is behind this?"

One survivor of Auschwitz, 11-year-old Menache Lorinczi, was interviewed by members of the world press. He guided reporters and Russian troops through the camp, explaining what the Nazis had done there.

Lorinczi was the first child survivor of the death camps to be quoted in the press. He and many other children had to be hospitalized after their ordeal. Lorinczi experienced numerous health problems, including tuberculosis and a lung infection. Many children had also lost their teeth as a result of starvation, and most suffered from skin diseases. Some children's digestive systems no longer worked properly, while others had visual and hearing disturbances.

Children who did not have serious health problems were taken to a monastery in Katowice, not far from the camp. The nuns gave them warm clothing, three meals a day, and playthings. In town, they were allowed to ride for free on streetcars and spent time enjoying their newfound freedom to play and explore their surroundings. Eva Mozes, one of the children who stayed in Katowice, recalls that she and her twin sister Miriam stayed in "a beautiful room with a large bed, covered by the whitest sheets I had ever seen. The room was filled with toys" (Lagnado and Dekel, 1991).

The exact number of children confined to death camps and killed there is uncertain. Young children were often murdered soon after they arrived, before the Nazis registered their arrival or listed them on camp rosters. The numbers on Nazi lists do not always show how many victims were adults and how many were children. However, by comparing pre-war and post-war population figures, it is estimated that 89 percent of all the Jewish children alive in Europe before the war had been killed. A total of 600,000 of these young victims were Polish Jews. *See also* Auschwitz-Birkenau; Concentration Camps (World War II); Death Marches; Dekel, Alex Schlomo; Deportations; Euthanasia; Experiments, Nazi; Final Solution; Genocide; Hart, Kitty Felix; Hitler, Adolf; Holocaust; Mengele, Josef; Poland (World War II); Round-Ups; Selection Process at Concentration Camps (World War II); World War II; Zyklon B.

Further Reading: Raul Hilberg, *Perpetrators, Victims, Bystanders* (1992); Lucette Matalon Lagnado and Sheila Cohn Dekel, *Children of the Flames* (1991); Primo Levi, *Survival in Auschwitz* (1971); Richard C. Lukas, *Did the Children Cry?* (1994); Barbara Rogasky, *Smoke and Ashes* (1988); Alexander Werth, "The Nazi Extermination Camp, Maidanek," in John Carey, *Eyewitness to History* (1988); Elie Wiesel, *Night* (1972); Leni Yahil, *The Holocaust* (1990).

Death Marches

At the end of World War II, prisoners who were still alive in the Nazi concentration and death camps were forced to leave on foot. Nazi officials ordered camp guards to hide evidence of mass murder at the camps and to bring the remaining captives to Germany before the Allies arrived. At Auschwitz-Birkenau, the few child survivors were those who had been kept alive for diabolical "medical" experiments in the Twins' Block run by Dr. Josef Mengele. These survivors, some under age 10 at the time, later recalled how in January 1945 the Nazis set the camp on fire and tried to destroy evidence of war crimes. Many Nazis fled to avoid capture.

Armed troops led the children and adults out of Poland. In freezing weather, without adequate food, water, or clothing, they had to walk across the snow through Czechoslovakia and into the Mauthausen camp in Austria. Less than 3,000 people survived out of the 20,000 or so who began the journey. Thomas Buergenthal, a Czechoslovakian Jew, later described how he and two young friends survived a death march out of Auschwitz that began in January 1945. Buergenthal was 11 years old at that time.

> The children's camp group was put in front when we first marched out. . . . After about a 10 to 12 hour walk we began to be very tired. The children began to fall back. . . . Three of us developed a system of resting, which was to run up to the front, and then sort of stop almost, until we reached the back. And by that time, we had rested, and then we could run up again and we would stay warm. (Berenbaum, 1993)

In the evening, the guards ordered all the children to come to the front of the line because they were going to be put "on a farm." Most of the children complied, but Buergenthal and his friends were suspicious. The children who moved forward were not seen again, and people realized they had been shot.

Vera Blau also survived a death march from Auschwitz. Blau told author Lucette Lagnado that when her younger sister Rachel said she was too weak to go on, Vera "grabbed her by her coat and dragged her through the snow." At one point, Blau's captors gave them hot water to drink. Says Blau, "I spilled the hot water, and it fell into my shoe. It was so cold, my foot got frozen" (Lagnado and Dekel, 1991).

Survivor Leah Stern recalled that they were not even allowed to drink snow to quench their thirst during the long days and nights. "I was so weak I kept wanting to stop, but my twin wouldn't let me." To lighten their load, these girls threw away their blanket and even some bread they had saved for weeks and brought along. "When it looked like I was going to collapse, Hedvah [her twin sister] hoisted me on her shoulder and carried me. She saved my life" (Lagnado and Dekel, 1991). *See also* AUSCHWITZ-BIRKENAU; DEATH CAMPS (WORLD WAR II); DEKEL, ALEX SCHLOMO; EXPERIMENTS, NAZI; HOLOCAUST; MENGELE, JOSEF; POLAND (WORLD WAR II); WIESEL, ELIE.

Further Reading: David A. Adler, *We Remember the Holocaust* (1989); Michael Berenbaum, *The World Must Know* (1993); Lucy Davidowicz, *The War Against the Jews* (1975); Lucette Matalon Lagnado and Susan Cohn Dekel, *Children of the Flames* (1991).

Deerfield Raid

Young settlers in the American colonies were affected by Queen Anne's War, which began in 1703 and lasted 10 years. Queen Anne's War was the American phase of a simultaneous European war between Great Britain and France. During Queen Anne's War, French troops and their Native American allies attacked frontier English villages. A major raid took place in Deerfield, Massachusetts, on February 29, 1704. French and Abenaki forces attacked this stockaded village and burned it. They kidnapped 111 people and forced them to march to Canada in freezing weather. Families or friends were forced to pay money if they wanted the cap-

tives returned. Some of the children from Deerfield were kept in Canada permanently. Eunice Williams, who was 10 in 1704, stayed with the Indians and married a Mohawk. A former captive later said that the captives suffered a great deal. Some of the children went hungry during the march to Canada when they had only roots to eat.

The Deerfield raid increased hostilities among French, English, and Native Americans. Children living in fortified frontier settlements worried about being attacked, and hundreds experienced raids. Young people helped their elders prepare against attacks, and older youths helped defend forts.

Further Reading: Edward P. Hamilton, *The French and Indian Wars* (1962); John Williams, *The Redeemed Captive, Returning to Zion* (1976).

Defense Plants

Young adults and children in various countries worked in defense or munitions plants during World War I and World War II. These youthful workers were primarily young women because most able young men were expected to join the military. Women could earn higher salaries than they had in jobs that were traditionally open to them—e.g., clerical, secretarial, bookkeeping, teaching, and nursing or domestic work or service jobs in hotels and restaurants. They performed many functions and worked different shifts. In England, for example, 18-year-olds might work the night shift from 10 p.m. until 6 a.m. cleaning bomb casings or putting airplane parts together.

Young women in defense jobs were most numerous during World War II. More than a million teenage women in Great Britain worked in defense plants. In the United States, millions of women also entered the labor force to replace men who had gone to war. They built airplanes, tanks, ships, guns, ammunition, and parachutes and were skilled metal workers, welders, machinists, and draftspeople.

By 1943, more than 3 million young people between the ages of 12 and 16 were working in U.S. factories. Pre-teens were able to work after school and on weekends when child labor laws were not enforced. For many young women, this was their first job. They gained more economic independence at an earlier age than previous generations of American women. They also expressed satisfaction at holding down these kinds of jobs and aiding the war effort. As a result, after the war, women had new attitudes about themselves and their capabilities. Many women remained in the workforce after the war, and the percentage of women entering previously male-dominated professions increased. Some historians have said that this newfound confidence contributed to the women's rights movement that grew during the 1960s and 1970s.

Youth who did not work in defense plants were affected by these events in other ways. Some young people had to move to new homes, adjust to new schools, and make new friends when their parents relocated to Detroit, San Diego, or other cities where large plants were located. Many families moved to a different region—for example, from the rural South to the industrial North. In some cases, defense jobs enabled families to escape poverty. Minority families benefited from the higher wages they could earn at defense plants. African Americans had more access to these jobs after President Franklin Roosevelt signed Executive Order 8008, which banned racial discrimination in defense industry jobs.

For many children, the war was the first time their mothers had worked outside the home. Some stayed at the homes of relatives while their mothers were gone, while others were taken to day-care centers. Douglas Aircraft in Santa Monica, California, and the Kaiser Shipyard in Portland, Oregon, were among the plants that operated on-site day-care centers for working mothers. The Kaiser center accommodated children 18 months and older and operated around the clock. The cost was 75 cents a day for the first child and 50 cents for each additional child. Older children were given more child-rearing and housekeeping responsibilities after their mothers went to work. *See also* CHEMICAL WARFARE; ROSIE THE RIVETER; WORLD WAR II.

Further Reading: Sherna Berger Gluck, *Rosie the Riveter Revisited* (1987); Nancy Baker Wise and Christy Wise, *A Mouthful of Rivets* (1994).

Dekel, Alex Schlomo (1930–1983)

Born in Cluj, Romania, Alex Schlomo Dekel was 13 years old when he was deported to Auschwitz. The tall, German-speaking youth was sent to live in the Twins' Block although he was not a twin. As an inmate in this section, Dekel was subjected to Nazi Dr. Josef Mengele's cruel quasi-medical experiments. Dekel managed to survive the experiments and the deprivations and epidemics at the camp. His mother had also been sent there, and, since young people in the Twins' Block received a little more food each day than the other inmates, Dekel tried to pass some through the barbed-wire fence to his mother. Concerned for her son, Mrs. Dekel refused the food, and Dekel would throw it over the fence so she would take it. Nonetheless, his mother was later killed in the gas chambers. Dekel's brother also died there.

In November 1944, with Russian troops approaching the camp, the Nazis sealed off the Twins' Block so that the only possible escape was through small windows that were about five feet from the ground. As Dekel later recalled,

> I jumped up to one of those small windows. It was impossible to reach, but I jumped. Somehow I reached it, and I just hung there, barely grasping the windowsill with my fingers. Then, I do not know how, I managed to jump outside. I landed in the snow and saw a building in front of me. I climbed through the window and found myself in a toilet. Outside, I heard truck engines. And so I jumped down into the toilet. (Lagnado and Dekel, 1991)

Although a German guard searched the room with a flashlight, Dekel remained undetected. He stayed in the toilet all night and was alive when Russian soldiers liberated the camp.

After the war, Dekel settled in Israel and worked in various government jobs. He married American Sheila Cohn, an author, in 1963. Dekel devoted his life to finding war criminals, especially Josef Mengele, who had escaped after the war and managed to evade prosecution. Israeli intelligence officers tracked down Mengele to South America, where he had been allowed to live in Paraguay.

Dekel wrote and spoke about his experiences and worked with authors who publicized the use of child subjects for Nazi experiments. He died in 1983. *See also* AUSCHWITZ-BIRKENAU; CHILDREN OF AUSCHWITZ NAZI DEADLY EXPERIMENTS SURVIVORS (CANDLES); DEATH CAMPS (WORLD WAR II); MENGELE, JOSEF; EXPERIMENTS, NAZI.

Further Reading: Lucette Matalon Lagnado and Sheila Cohn Dekel, *Children of the Flames* (1991).

Delagazione Assist enza Emigrant Ebitei. See ITALY, WORLD WAR II

Delasem. *See* ITALY, WORLD WAR II

Delinquency. *See* Wild Children

Denmark (World War II)

In April 1940, the small Scandinavian nation of Denmark was invaded by German troops.

For five years, the Danes found themselves under Nazi rule. Denmark developed a strong resistance organization that included many young people. These youthful resisters produced and distributed underground newspapers, carried secret messages, and engaged in sabotage operations to destroy German targets. An estimated 500,000 of the four million Danes took an active part in the resistance. Children whose parents were involved in resistance work also had to make adjustments and be careful they did not reveal these secret activities. They had to cope with the fear of discovery and endured other hardships when a parent was caught and arrested.

Young people played an important role in the rescue of Danish Jews. The Danes objected to anti-Jewish measures and protested in 1942 when Nazi officials decreed that all Jews over age six in occupied countries must wear a yellow cloth Star of David on their clothing. The Danish King Christian X and his family announced that they would also wear the star "as a badge of honor." The king opposed Nazi anti-Semitism and Nazi persecution, saying that Jews were part of the Danish nation like other citizens.

This photo from October 1943 shows a group of Danish Jews who have just arrived in Malmo, Sweden, after having fled in small boats from their Nazi-occupied homeland. *UPI/Corbis-Bettmann.*

In the fall of 1943, Danes organized a massive rescue operation after they heard the Nazis planned to deport Danish Jews in October. Throughout the country, people warned those who might be in danger. Individuals and groups began hiding men, women, and children in their homes and other places, such as hospitals or funeral parlors.

By boat, the Danes transported thousands of people across the sea to neutral Sweden. Nearly 8,000 people—Jews, people with some Jewish ancestry, and spouses of Jews—were carried across the Kattegat Sound, a total of 98.5 percent of the Danish Jews and refugees from other lands who were living in Denmark. To prepare young children for the journey, doctors gave them sedatives to keep them quiet. Children were often wrapped in rugs or other disguises. Some children were hidden in farm wagons beneath sacks of vegetables or grain. Young people involved in the rescue missions carried messages, fed and cared for refugees, and guided people to safe homes and to boats for the trip to Sweden. Young men were among the sailors who operated the boats that carried people to safety. As a result of this concerted effort, nearly all the Jews who lived in Denmark as of 1940 survived the war. As a nation, the Danes were later honored by Yad Vashem for their heroism and humanitarian response to Nazism. *See also* RESISTANCE MOVEMENTS (WORLD WAR II); UNDERGROUND PRESSES, YAD VASHEM.

Further Reading: Lore Cowan, ed., *Children of the Resistance* (1969); Harold Flender, *Rescue in Denmark* (1963); Vera Laska, ed., *Women of the Resistance and in the Holocause* (1984); Milton Meltzer, *Rescue* (1988); Margaret Rossiter, *Women in the Resistance* (1986); Leni Yahil, *The Rescue of Danish Jewry* (1969).

Deportations

Deportation is the forced removal and relocation of whole populations. Especially in the twentieth century, children have been the victims of deportations caused by wars and civil conflicts. Deportation has caused family separations, displacement, loss of community life and education, health problems, and death. Deportations of young people occurred on a massive scale during World War II, when more than one million children were deported by the Nazis. Most were Jews, but large numbers of young Poles and members of other groups targeted by the Nazis (for example, the Romani, commonly called Gypsies) were also deported. The deportees were forced to live in ghettos or camps the Nazis set up to imprison millions of people. These included transit camps, concentration camps, and death camps located in various countries.

Early in the occupation of Poland, in 1939 and 1940, Nazi leaders announced that all Poles living in western Poland must leave. Nazi leaders had annexed this land to Germany. About half of the 600,000 Poles deported from the Wartheland region of Poland were children. Deportees were given little or no time to gather whatever belongings the Nazis allowed them to take along before armed soldiers forced their departure. Many men were separated from their wives and children and taken to labor camps from which thousands never returned. Women and children stayed for a while in a camp at Lodz where many died from hunger, disease, or unsanitary conditions. Some died from drowning in unsafe lavatories. Historians are uncertain how many children died in the camp at Lodz but estimate that there were thousands of casualties.

From Lodz, Poles were taken in unheated, sealed freight cars to another region known as the General Government. Some children died during these train trips, which took place in freezing weather. Starting in 1942, mass deportations were carried out to remove Jews from Nazi-occupied lands, including Germany, Austria, Poland, Czechoslovakia, The Netherlands, Belgium, and France. Roundups were conducted in ghettos as well as in cities where victims could be identified from official lists of Jewish residents. To keep people calm and cooperative, the Nazis told Jews they were being taken to labor camps or to "resettlement" areas in the east. However, some people heard or guessed that Jews were being deported to their deaths. Believing these stories, some young people sought to escape from the ghetto before they were deported. A small number of others managed to escape during the trip itself, although this was extraordinarily difficult.

The threat of deportation caused family separations because various people went into hiding or were taken away. In some cases, whole families went into hiding to avoid deportation. One well-known example is the family of Anne Frank, a German Jewish teenager whose family had fled to Holland in the early 1930s. When 16-year-old Margot Frank received an order from the Nazis to report for a "work assignment" in Germany, the Franks went into hiding earlier than they had anticipated.

At 17, Mendy Berger was deported from the ghetto in Munkacs, Hungary. He later gave the following description of his deportation:

> We were chased from the ghetto to the train station. As we ran, and some of us were killed, the Christian people of the community were watching as if it was a parade, applauding, laughing. One man whom my father and uncle had helped many times smiled and yelled at us in Hungarian, "Shoho vissa—You will never return." (Kahn and Hager, 1996)

Although these bystanders showed hostility toward Jewish victims, others in Europe were appalled by the sight of children being deported and detested the brutality that often accompanied deportations. Some Nazi police beat children or abused them as they loaded them onto trucks or railroad cars. They grabbed them by the limbs or hair and pushed them onto trucks. Marion von Binsbergen, a Dutch university student who went on to rescue Jewish children, saw Nazis arrest some women who tried to stop police from hitting children as they loaded them onto a truck. Others also were spurred to join resistance movements or rescue groups after witnessing the abuse of children being deported.

Packed into freight trains with no food, water, toilets, or blankets, children cried out in thirst and hunger, and their parents were unable to help them. Unbearably cold in winter and stifling hot in the summer, the cars were also dark, with only tiny slats along the side to admit cracks of light. Mendy Berger described conditions in the cars as "no food, no water, people dying, the smell of the dead, and we had no toilets" (Kahn and Hager, 1996).

Leo Fischelberg, who was imprisoned at the concentration camp at Bergen Belsen at age 15, was ordered to remove from the trains the bodies of those who had died en route. He later described his horror: "We carried them by their legs and arms and had to throw them onto a wagon, then bring them to an open pit and drop them in. I did this for five months" (Adler, 1996).

As Jewish children were rounded up to be deported, their non-Jewish friends and classmates saw them being taken away or realized they were gone when school reconvened. Jean-Louis Besson recalled that in October 1942 his history professor began class by saying,

> You have probably noticed that some of your fellow students haven't returned. I'm talking about those who wore yellow stars. You went on vacation, and they also went away. No one can say exactly where they are, of course. Probably far away, in a camp, performing hard labor like breaking rocks to repair roads. They may come back one day, or you may never see them again. No one knows. I ask you to think of them for a moment, you who are lucky enough to be in this class, and close to your families, too. (Besson, 1995)

See also ARMENIAN-TURKISH CONFLICT; AUSCHWITZ-BIRKENAU; CONCENTRATION CAMPS (WORLD WAR II); DEATH CAMPS (WORLD WAR II); DRANCY; FINAL SOLUTION: FRANCE (WORLD WAR II); FRANK, ANNE; GHETTOS (WORLD WAR II); GIES, MIEP AND GIES, JAN; HOLLAND (WORLD WAR II); HUNGARY (WORLD WAR II); ITALY (WORLD WAR II); KORCZAK, JANUSZ; POLAND (WORLD WAR II); PRITCHARD, MARION VON BINSBERGEN; RIGHTEOUS GENTILES; RIVESALTES; ROUND-UPS; SCHINDLER, OSKAR; WALLENBURG, RAOUL; WARSAW GHETTO; WESTERWILL, JOOP.

Further Reading: David A. Adler, *We Remember the Holocaust* (1989); Jean-Louis Besson, *October 45*

(1995); Deborah Dwork, *Children with a Star* (1991); Leora Kahn and Rachel Hager, eds., *When They Came to Take My Father* (1996); Carol Rittner and Sondra Meyers, eds., *The Courage to Care* (1986); Leni Yahil, *The Holocaust* (1990).

Diaries

Diaries and journals written by young people have provided some of the most informative and moving first-hand accounts of wartime. Young writers have documented the historical events, day-to-day life, family relationships, hardships, and tragedies that occur during wartime. Their words have helped to personalize statistics. In some cases, young people were already keeping diaries before war broke out and they continued to record their thoughts and feelings. Others started keeping diaries after a revolution or war began. Many adults encouraged journal-writing and believed this form of expression might help young people cope with their experiences and feelings, as well as provide a constructive way to pass the time. These writings have also been regarded as valuable historical records for others to read. For some people, a diary or journal was the only way their words and ideas could live on if they did not survive the war.

A number of diaries by young people were kept during World War II. Youth in various countries described their experiences during bombings, occupation, and combat, or while they were in hiding, confined to concentration camps, or forced into labor. They also shared their experiences working with resistance movements. Jews trapped in the Warsaw Ghetto were urged to keep daily journals. Emmanual Ringelblum, a historian in the ghetto, told people to document daily life. Ringelblum himself wrote a detailed diary that was later published. He and other courageous people in the ghetto hid these eyewitness accounts and other documents in places where they would later be found, or they smuggled them outside the ghetto walls so that people would know what was happening inside. One diarist, teenager Mary Berg, was able to share her writings after she was freed from the ghetto because of her U.S. citizenship.

Some writings, such as the diary kept by teenager Anne Frank, a German Jew who hid from the Nazis in Amsterdam during World War II, have become famous. *Zlata's Diary*,

This display in the Piskaryovskoye Memorial Cemetery Museum memorializes the diary of a girl named Tanya, who recorded her experiences during the German siege of Leningrad. *Oleg Porokhovnikov, Itar-Tass/Sovfoto.*

written by a young girl who lived in wartime Bosnia during the 1990s, was widely read and publicized. It helped increase public awareness of the plight of youth in this war-torn region. *See also* BERG, MARY; FILIPOVIC, ZLATA; FRANK, ANNE; HIDDEN CHILDREN; GHETTOS (WORLD WAR II); RINGELBLUM ARCHIVES; TOLL, NELLY LANDAU; WARSAW GHETTO.

Further Reading: Anne Frank, *The Diary of a Young Girl* (1967); Israel Gutman, *Resistance* (1994); Gertrude Schneider, *Journey into Terror* (1979); Gail B. Stewart, *Life in the Warsaw Ghetto* (1992); Nelly S. Toll, *Behind the Secret Window: A Memoir of a Hidden Childhood During World War II* (1993); Tatjana Wassiljewa, *Hostage to War* (1997).

"Disappeareds." *See* ADOPTION; EL SALVADOR

Disease

Wars create conditions that foster serious and often fatal diseases. Children have died of illnesses and infectious diseases brought on by food and clothing shortages, unsanitary conditions, lack of fuel, a breakdown of medical and social services, and other consequences of armed conflicts, barricades, sieges, and other wartime events.

Typhus was especially widespread during World War II. People died of typhus in ghettos and concentration camps and on ships and in jails. The organism that causes typhus was spread by rats, fleas, sewage, and unsanitary water. Young people's immune systems were severely weakened by hunger, fatigue, exposure to the elements, and other stressors.

Conditions after both world wars ended also increased the rate of various diseases among children in countries where war caused a widespread lack of adequate shelter, nourishing food, sanitation, and clean water. The lack of organized health care, inadequate numbers of nurses and doctors, and shortages of medicines and other supplies worsened these problems.

In the late twentieth century, diseases have run rampant in areas of Africa ravaged by civil war. For example, in the Sudan during the 1990s, diarrhea caused thousands of

deaths, as did epidemics of measles and other diseases. Journalist Jeffrey Goldberg wrote in 1997, "It's not hard to find the winner in the Sudanese war, or in any war in Africa: it is the microbes that always emerge victorious. Infectious disease flowers in conditions of anarchy. Measles, cholera, malaria, AIDS, sleeping sickness, leprosy. . . ." *See also* ADDAMS, JANE; AFGHANISTAN; AGENT ORANGE; ANGOLA; AUSCHWITZ-BIRKENAU; BERGEN-BELSEN; BIOLOGICAL WARFARE; BOER WAR; CONCENTRATION CAMPS (WORLD WAR II); DEATH CAMPS (WORLD WAR II); DISPLACED PERSONS (DPs) (WORLD WAR II); DRANCY; EXPERIMENTS, NAZI; FRANK, ANNE; GERMANY (WORLD WAR II); GHETTOS (WORLD WAR II); GREECE (WORLD WAR II); GULF WAR SYNDROME; HIDDEN CHILDREN; HOLOCAUST; HUNGER/MALNUTRITION; HUNGER WINTER; JAPAN (WORLD WAR II); MOZAMBIQUE; RADIATION SICKNESS; REFUGEES; RWANDA; SOVIET UNION (WORLD WAR II); SUDAN; UGANDA; VIETNAM WAR; WARSAW GHETTO; WORLD WAR I; WORLD WAR II; ZAIRE.

Further Reading: Helen Epstein, *Children of the Holocaust* (1979); Miep Gies, *Anne Frank Remembered* (1987); Martin Gilbert, *Final Journey* (1979); Jeffrey Goldberg, "Our Africa," *The New York Times Magazine,* March 2, 1997, pp. 34ff; Kiryl Sosnowski, *The Tragedy of Children Under Nazi Rule* (1983); United Nations Children's Fund, *The State of the World's Children, 1996* (1996).

Displaced Persons (DPs) (World War II)

After World War II, Europe had nearly 10 million displaced persons, including millions of Jewish children. Their homes and often their whole communities had been destroyed, and many children in the refugee camps were orphans. Young non-Jewish Europeans who had been taken to Germany or other places for forced labor also sometimes found themselves in displaced person (DP) camps. People spent weeks and sometimes months trying to find transportation home.

Relief organizations and concerned individuals began efforts to resettle displaced children, but the problems of the postwar world left many displaced persons homeless for years. About 750,000 people were still in displaced person camps in 1947. Such camps were organized in Germany, Austria, and Italy. The early camps were often dirty and poorly organized. In Poland, the Russians who were in charge did not set up any camps, and the one million people who were liberated from Nazi camps in this country usually had nowhere to turn. They suffered more deprivations after the war and many died.

Allied military units were in charge of many DP camps. In 1945, President Harry Truman authorized a plan to provide for people who had been devastated by the war. In the fall of that year, the U.S. government also authorized special plans to help meet the needs of Jewish survivors. General of the Army Dwight D. Eisenhower was told to implement these humanitarian measures in DP camps.

In some camps, children were able to take part in educational activities and sports. Children were also born in displaced persons' camps. Florence Bauman Weiner and her brother were born in Bergen-Belsen, Germany, a former concentration camp that was turned into a DP camp in 1945. Her parents met at the camp that year and the family had to remain there for several years.

Groups run by the Quakers, the United Nations, the International Red Cross, and Jewish relief agencies worked together to meet the refugees' physical needs for food, clothing, and shelter, and to provide medical care. They hoped to reunite displaced children with any surviving family members and help them start new lives wherever it was possible. Some displaced children left the camps after relatives or friends came to find them. Relief organizations also helped place orphaned children with relatives or new families. Displaced people waited to gain admittance to other countries, primarily the United States, Palestine, and South Africa. Some children spent time in group homes, orphanages, and Red Cross hospitals, and were moved to more than one DP camp before they were finally resettled.

Young people made their way to these camps either on their own or with an adult. Some eventually made their way home.

Hedvah Stern, a 14-year-old at the time, managed to reach her town in Hungary with her twin sister Leah in the spring of 1945. They were accompanied by an adult woman they had met in a DP camp. The only surviving family members were two widowed uncles. The family home had been ransacked and all their possessions were gone (Lagnado and Dekel, 1991).

Menache Lorinczi, aged 12 in 1945, reached his former home in Cluj, Romania, with his twin sister Lea. He recalls that thousands of survivors were roaming Eastern Europe, hoping to go home. Their father had survived and he managed to find his children after reading an interview Menache gave to the press after the liberation.

In some German camps, youths from Poland who formed close friendships with Allied soldiers became known as "G.I. mascots." Soldiers often felt sympathy for these young people and gave them candy, food, and other gifts. Some children hoped they would be taken to the United States, a country they regarded as prosperous and safe. They were disappointed when the soldiers were transferred or went home. Some of the so-called mascots had a great deal of trouble adjusting and were sent to a special camp run by the Young Men's Christian Association (YMCA) to give them special help in resuming their lives after the war.

Polish and Russian children who had been sent illegally to Germany were also considered displaced persons. Some had been adopted and others had been used for forced labor. The Polish government sent printed materials to Germany urging Poles to return to their homeland. One popular slogan read, "Your country is calling." Young Poles added their own messages to these fliers, urging their peers to come home after the war to help rebuild the country.

In *Did the Children Cry?* (1994), author Richard C. Lukas described the homecoming of the first group of Polish children to return home after the war. They arrived on a repatriation train early in June 1946. Polish Red Cross personnel, including nurses and physicians, accompanied the group to

Katowice. As the train arrived, the children sang Polish songs and waved flags. They were greeted by a band, flowers, and Polish boy scouts, and by family members who waited eagerly at the station.

A 1996 documentary film, *The Long Way Home*, portrayed the anguish of displaced persons after World War II. The film includes first-person accounts from people who were children or teenagers during the time they spent in the displaced persons' camps. The film won the Academy Award for best documentary. *See also* ADOPTION; COORDINATION COMMITTEE; FORCED LABOR (WORLD WAR II); LEBENSBORN; POLAND (WORLD WAR II); RED CROSS; REFUGEES; RELIEF ORGANIZATIONS; TOLL, NELLY LANDAU; UNITED NATIONS CHILDREN'S FUND (UNICEF); WORLD WAR II.

Further Reading: David A. Adler, *We Remember the Holocaust* (1989); Yehuda Bauer, *A History of the Holocaust* (1982); Lucette Matalon Lagnado and Sheila Cohn Dekel, *Children of the Flames* (1991); Richard C. Lukas, *Did the Children Cry?* (1994); Dorothy Macardle, *Children of Europe* (1951).

Dowdy, Betsy (c.1759–?)

During the American Revolution, teenager Betsy Dowdy made a courageous horseback ride on a cold winter night to warn Continental troops that British loyalists planned to attack them. Dowdy lived on a farm in North Carolina in an area called the Outer Banks, which is located on the northern tip of North Carolina's eastern shore. During the early months of the Revolution, she saw British raids destroy local property and British loyalists burn down her family's barn.

Because she was an expert horsewoman and might fool British guards, Dowdy was chosen to deliver a vital message to General Skinner's encampment at Great Dismal Swamp. On a cold, foggy night in December, Dowdy mounted her banker pony and set off on a journey of about 50 miles of steep cliffs, banks, dunes, and swamplands. After reaching the camp, Dowdy warned General Skinner about the impending raid on the Eastern Shore of Virginia. Skinner organized his troops and joined the Virginia Continental army to defeat the 1,200 loyalists under

Governor John Dunsmore. For her brave ride, Dowdy became a local heroine of the Revolution. *See also* AMERICAN REVOLUTION.

Further Reading: R.D.W. Connor, *Makers of North Carolina History* (1930); Nell Wise Wechter, *Betsy Dowdy's Ride* (1960).

Draft. *See* CONSCRIPTION; SELECTIVE SERVICE ACTS

Drancy

During World War II, Drancy, located about three miles northeast of Paris, was the site of the largest Nazi detention, or transit, camp in France. A four-story concrete compound there was used as a "holding place" for thousands of people who were to be sent to Nazi death camps in Poland in successive transports. On July 17, 1942, 13,000 non-French Jews living in Paris were rounded up and taken to a stadium that had been used for bicycle races. These frightened people were crammed into buses for the overnight trip to the stadium. Among them were more than 3,000 children ranging in age from infancy to 12. Most of the children were transferred to Drancy, usually without their parents. Eyewitnesses said that younger children were terrified at being separated from their families.

At Drancy, children had little to eat, mainly watery cabbage soup, and were exposed to diseases and germ-carrying lice. Many suffered from diarrhea and skin diseases. A young woman described the conditions at Drancy as follows: "The misery and distress around us are beyond description. Just along the way are nine orphans from a boarding school. The regime is the regime of a military prison. Filth of a coal mine. Straw mattresses full of lice and fleas. Horrid overcrowding" (Josephs, 1989).

During the summer, Nazi leaders set quotas that required a certain number of people to be sent by train to the death camps. Each day, another group of children from Drancy were awakened at about 5:00 a.m. and forced to go down to the yard where their names were called. Some screamed in fear as they were physically carried out to the yard. They were then loaded onto freight trains. An eyewitness, Georges Wellers, later recalled that

> In the yard they waited to be called; they often answered wrongly when their names were called out. The older ones held on to the little ones' hands and would not let go of them. There was a certain number of children in each transport added at the end: those whose names were unknown. They were entered on the list by a question mark. (Josephs, 1989)

Seventeen train cars left Drancy on August 21, 1942 carrying 1,000 people, 614 of them children. Ten of these children were younger than 2 1/2 years of age, and another 252 were younger than 10. Those who survived the arduous journey in the airless, cramped cars arrived at the notorious death camp, Auschwitz-Birkenau. At Auschwitz, 892 of the passengers were gassed at once. A few were abused in pseudo-medical experiments conducted at the camp by Nazi doctors or were used as slave laborers. Most of these young victims were killed within hours after their arrival. Of the 13,000 people who were arrested on July 12, only about 30, all over age 12, survived the war.

Beginning in June 1943, Drancy was under the direction of high-ranking SS commandant Alois Brunner, who referred to Jewish children, even infants, as "future terrorists" who must be deported to their deaths. He ruthlessly sought out all Jewish children in the region. Tens of thousands of new victims were brought to the camp during 1943 and 1944, then deported in groups by train to Auschwitz-Birkenau and other camps. These victims included hundreds of children from orphanages outside Paris and Lyons. The last convoy, which held 300 children, including a baby who had been born in Drancy, left the camp on July 31, 1944. *See also* AUSCHWITZ-BIRKENAU; DEATH CAMPS (WORLD WAR II); DEPORTATIONS; FINAL SOLUTION; FRANCE (WORLD WAR II); HOLOCAUST; WORLD WAR II.

Further Reading: Jeremy Josephs, *Swastika Over Paris* (1989); Serge Klarsfeld, *French Children of the Holocaust* (1996); Leni Yahil, *The Holocaust* (1990).

Dresden. *See* BOMBINGS (WORLD WAR II)

Drugs. *See* SOLDIERS, CHILD

Drummer Boys

For centuries, young boys have served as musicians, including drummer boys, with the military. Serving as drummers or buglers was one way for boys too young to serve legally as soldiers to join the military. During the 1700s, drummer boys were part of most wars, including the American and French Revolutions.

Prior to the late 1800s, military regiments in various countries used drums for numerous purposes in training, maneuvers, and on the battlefield. Drummers awakened troops in the morning and called them to meals. Drumbeats helped soldiers keep time during marches and drills. During battle, drummers beat out messages that told troops where to move on the battlefield. Soldiers relied on these sounds because smoke often prevented them from seeing hand signals from their superiors. The boys carried out other tasks, such as cutting soldiers' hair and caring for the wounded.

Jordan Noble, a 13-year-old African American, was among the drummer boys who served during the War of 1812. He responded to the call of Andrew Jackson when the general came to Noble's native Louisiana to fight the British. Noble was the drummer boy for Jackson's unit during the Battle of New Orleans. He continued to serve after the war ended in 1815 and may have gone with Jackson to fight the Seminole Indians in Florida. He rose to the position of principal musician, First Regiment, Louisiana Volunteers, during the Mexican War of 1846-1848. In 1860, he received a military medal.

Hundreds of drummer boys were killed during the American Civil War, and thousands more were wounded. Some showed unusual bravery. Author Jim Murphy (1990) recounted a story about a drummer boy who remained at his station despite heavy fire.

A cannon ball came bouncing across a corn field kicking up dirt and dust each time it struck the earth. Many of the men in our company took shelter behind a stone wall, but I stood where I was and never stopped drumming. An officer came by on horseback and chastised the men, saying "this boy puts you all to shame. Get up and move forward." We all began moving across the cornfield. . . . Even when the fighting was at its fiercest and I was frightened, I stood straight and did as I was ordered. . . . I felt I had to be a good example for the others.

As the Civil War continued, military officials decided that drummer boys should not be used during battle. Because the roar of cannons and rifles overpowered the drumbeats, bugles replaced drums as a way to send signals in battle. *See also* AMERICAN CIVIL WAR; CLEM, JOHN LINCOLN.

Further Reading: Robert Ewell Greene, *Black Defenders of America, 1775-1973* (1974); Jim Murphy, *The Boys' War* (1990); Catherine Reef, *Black Fighting Men* (1994); Richard Wheeler, *Voices of the Civil War* (1976).

Dugout. *See* AIR RAIDS

E

Education

War and post-war conditions impede the education of young people in numerous ways. Schooling is interrupted or cut short during air raids, when buildings are destroyed, or when students, parents, and teachers leave for the military. Students who are evacuated from their homes may move to places where they do not have access to schooling or do not speak the language. They may face other barriers to attending school or completing lessons. Occupation forces or wartime leaders have also shut down schools or banned certain people from attending. They have used schools for political purposes, as a place to indoctrinate or militarize youth.

The education of millions of youth was disrupted during World War II. Schools in England, Germany, Holland, Japan, and other countries were destroyed by bombings. Young people had to attend makeshift schools or study at home or outdoors. Schools were shut down in London several times during 1940 and 1941 when German bombings disrupted normal routines. As a result, many young people fell behind in their studies and had to make up their schoolwork later. Some dropped out permanently. Allied bombings in Germany and Japan likewise destroyed schools and disrupted school routines.

Government leaders often worried about what would happen if children did not attend school, especially in families where both parents were absent. Fathers were serving in the military and many mothers had taken jobs to support the family or to aid the war effort. Other women were doing volunteer work. Late in 1940, the head of the British Board of Education estimated that at least 400,000 children were going without an education. He said that some youths had become delinquents who stayed on the streets late at night with no adult supervision and had been caught stealing and vandalizing.

The extra responsibilities that are assigned to many youths during wartime can also hinder schoolwork. A British girl who was in her early teens during World War II described her life in a rural town where her mother was single-handedly rearing nine children. She and her sister, who were the oldest, helped their mother care for the younger ones.

> I was very poor and hopeless at school because I hardly ever went, because I had to see to the children. I had no friends because I had no time to make any. I loved my family but most of the time I wished I was an only child, because in school I was the lowest in my class and everybody said I was thick and lazy. I had no time to review for exams and hardly ever did homework. My life was babies, babies, and more babies. (Westall, 1985)

Some wartime leaders change the education system to further their particular goals. For example, after Adolf Hitler won power

Because of the destruction of their school during the Korean War, these Korean children take classes outdoors. *UPI/Corbis-Bettmann.*

in Germany in 1933, his regime tried to influence public opinion in every possible way by Nazifying all aspects of life. The government used schools to indoctrinate youth and build support for its political and military agenda. The Nazis ended parent-teacher groups, then dismissed Jewish teachers and eventually got rid of anyone who was not a Nazi Party member. They considered young minds to be especially vulnerable and used schools to rouse hatred toward Jews and promote conformity and loyalty.

New textbooks and teaching materials promoted Nazi ideals and gave students constant messages that Jews were to blame for Germany's problems and should be scorned. Reading assignments glorified Nazi characters and ideas and promoted racism toward Jews and others the Nazis disliked. Math problems also served these purposes. In one problem, students were told that Jews were "aliens in Germany," then asked to calculate the percentage of "aliens," using numbers of Jews in their calculations. School routines and rituals reinforced Nazism. Children were required to recite Nazi pledges, sing Nazi songs, and give the Nazi salute. Swastika flags hung in each classroom along with pictures of Adolf Hitler. Students who expressed admiration for the government were rewarded with praise and good grades; uncooperative students were punished.

By 1935, Jewish children in Germany were frequently harassed in the classroom and physically assaulted on their way to or from school. Some were ridiculed, banned from field trips and other activities, and given unfairly low marks for their assignments. Walter Weglyn, who was seven years old in 1933, later recalled that he was beaten up by gangs of Hitler Youth. One day his teacher came to school wearing a Nazi uniform and ordered him (the only Jewish child in class) to sing a popular Nazi song.

As a result of these kinds of abuses, many Jewish families removed children from school. Then, in 1935, laws were passed that banned them from attending. Underground or secret schools were set up in Jewish homes. Children in these covert schools arrived with books hidden under their clothing. During the lessons, people would listen for Nazi police. One popular place to hold these secret classes was the home of a shoemaker or tailor. If a raid did occur, children could hide their lesson books and begin playing. The teacher could pretend to be a customer conducting business.

After Germany invaded Poland in 1939, the Nazis decided that the Poles, whom they regarded as subhuman and inferior to themselves, should have little schooling. A high-ranking Nazi declared that "there must be no higher school than fourth grade. . . . The sole goal of this schooling is to teach them simple arithmetic, nothing above the number five hundred, writing one's name, and the doctrine that it is divine law to obey the Germans. I do not think that reading is desirable" (Stewart, 1992). It was also against the law to teach children about their Polish heritage or subjects that might inspire pride in their culture and history.

Many young people lost their teachers because the Nazis executed thousands of professors, teachers, and other intellectual and professional people in Poland and imprisoned thousands more. The Poles developed underground "flying schools" that met in various places whenever they could. About 5,300 teachers were working with 48,000 secondary school students during the year 1942-1943 in the area called the General Government, which was a portion of central Poland under Nazi occupation and included the cities of Warsaw and Cracow. In the lands that Germany had annexed in Poland, about 19,000 elementary school students and 1,400 teachers worked together in secret; 200 teachers taught nearly 1,700 students.

A Jewish student in Poland, Janina Bauman, described the situation as follows:

> The universities were closed, academic staff deported to concentration camps, secondary schools banned. In the primary schools which were open, Polish history and geography classes were prohibited. All this had triggered off an instant response in the nation. Teachers, parents, pupils themselves started up a whole system of underground education. The illegal courses began to function soon after the defeat. Germans sometimes took over boarding schools and forbade the best students from attending any classes. Catholic nuns and other Poles who ran these schools were ordered to teach according to German guidelines. (Bauman, 1945)

As the Germans occupied more countries during World War II, they instituted similar changes in the curriculum. In Holland, for example, Jewish and anti-German professors and teachers lost their jobs. In protest, some university students held demonstrations or went on strike. The Nazis removed texts and library books they did not like and banned classes teaching English. Nazis visited schools and promoted their political agenda. According to 14-year-old Jan Jonkheer of Amsterdam,

> The Nazis are trying all their tricks to win over the schoolchildren. They have given us sweets which most of us have put in the drain, and they have allowed the top class

to matriculate [move to the next level] without passing the exams (Cowan, 1969)

The Nazis also banned Jews in occupied countries from the public schools. Secret (and illegal) schools were formed in these countries and in Jewish ghettos. Groups were small and classes were held in people's apartments cellars, attics, or basements. Students had few materials and often shared the same book or writing materials. Despite the hazards, people continued to find ways to educate the young. School provided a way for young people to continue some normal routines under abnormal conditions. Besides promoting learning, which was valued by both students and parents, schools kept youth busy, gave them something positive to do, and sustained hope in the future.

When the Germans discovered schools in the Warsaw Ghetto, as they did at least twice in 1940, they shot the teachers and deported students to concentration camps.

Despite formidable obstacles, some students completed their education and were even able to graduate. Jews with strong connections found ways to bring Polish education inspectors into the Warsaw Ghetto to watch students take their final examinations and officially sign their diplomas. Kitty Hart, a Polish Jew who survived Auschwitz and death marches, was 13 when the war began and 18 at its end. She wrote in 1981, "Looking back, I think what makes me most bitter against the Nazis, even after all this time, is the education of which they robbed me. I've tried to make up the lost ground, but those lost years were never fully compensated for" (Hart, 1981).

The loss of educational opportunities plagued other young people during the last half of the twentieth century. Palestinians voiced deep concern about the problems of education for their youth growing up in the war-torn Middle East. Education has long been highly valued by Palestinians, who were once regarded as the best educated people in the Arab world. After thousands of Palestinians became refugees in the late 1940s, education was disrupted in numerous ways.

Makeshift schools were set up in refugee camps.

Schools were closed down during the late 1980s when strikes and demonstrations occurred regularly in the Middle East. Schools were under the control of the United Nations and the Israeli government, and Palestinian educators were not free to design curricula that met their specific needs. Students in the Gaza region were using educational materials used in Egyptian schools, while students living in the West Bank followed the curriculum used in Jordan. In 1993, more than 100 educators from the Israeli-occupied Gaza Strip and West Bank met to discuss ways to reform the education system and better meet the needs of their students. They created new books and materials that contained Palestinian history, geography, and culture. The educators said they aimed to develop materials that did not inflame old hatreds among the different groups in the region. Instead, these materials would present historical events from different points of view to encourage students to ask questions and explore the issues.

In its Convention on the Rights of the Child, the United Nations listed education as a basic right of children throughout the world. Relief organizations working to help youth in Bosnia, Sudan, Rwanda, and other war-torn places have addressed their educational needs along with providing food, shelter, clothing, and health care. *See also* AMERICAN FRIENDS SERVICE COMMITTEE (AFSC); BOMBINGS (WORLD WAR II); BOSNIA; CONVENTION ON THE RIGHTS OF THE CHILD; CUBAN REVOLUTION; EVACUATIONS (WORLD WAR II); GERMANY (WORLD WAR II); GHETTOS (WORLD WAR II); HITLER YOUTH; HOLLAND (WORLD WAR II); ITALY (WORLD WAR II); JAPAN (WORLD WAR II); LIBERIAN CIVIL WAR; POLAND (WORLD WAR II); REFUGEES; RUSSIAN REVOLUTION; RWANDA; SAVE THE CHILDREN; SUDAN; UNITED NATIONS CHILDREN'S FUND (UNICEF); WARSAW GHETTO; WORLD WAR I; WORLD WAR II.

Further Reading: Janina Bauman, *Winter in the Morning* (1945); Lore Cowan, ed. *Children of the Resistance* (1969); Kitty Hart, *Return to Auschwitz* (1971); Cathryn Long, *The Middle East in Search of Peace* (1994); Richard C. Lukas, *Did the Children Cry?*

(1996); Seymour Rossel, *The Holocaust* (1981); Arnold Rubin, *The Evil Men Do* (1977); Gail B. Stewart, *Life in the Warsaw Ghetto* (1992); Robert Westall, *Children of the Blitz* (1985).

Education for Peace

The United Nations Children's Fund (UNICEF) supports Education for Peace programs for youth in Lebanon, the former Yugoslavia, Sri Lanka, and other countries throughout the world. According to UNICEF, these programs aim "to develop skills and attitudes among young people; to help them peacefully resolve conflicts; to promote greater understanding among different groups; and to strengthen the values of tolerance, compassion, and respect for others."

UNICEF sponsors workshops and camps that bring together young people who live in communities on opposing sides of conflicts in their region. In addition, UNICEF provides booklets and other teaching materials for use in classrooms in the United States and other countries to raise students' awareness of global issues and the need for peaceful resolution of conflicts. The educational activities are geared for different age groups. Activities for younger children aim to foster self-respect and respect for the abilities of others, as well as differences among people. Older students are encouraged to consider how they would address specific social problems in a troubled region. They learn and practice ways to resolve specific conflicts in a cooperative manner. *See also* UNITED NATIONS CHILDREN'S FUND (UNICEF).

Further Reading: UNICEF, *Kids Helping Kids* (1996).

Einsatzgruppen

During World War II, Adolf Hitler and top Nazi officials organized mobile killing squads to murder Jews and other victims in Europe on a massive scale. In September 1939, before Germany invaded Poland, Nazi leaders planned to form special "action squads," called *Einsatzgruppen,* to carry out these killings in occupied territories. These squads killed more than one million Jewish men, women, and children and thousands of other non-Jewish civilians, many of them communists, whom the Nazis considered their political enemies. Youths under the age of 21 were among the members of these squads as were many of their victims.

Einsatzgruppen began operating during 1940 and 1941 in Eastern Europe; they followed German troops through Poland and the Soviet Union. Eyewitnesses described how the squads gathered large groups of Jews of all ages from towns and villages and forced them to board trucks that carried them to rural areas. They were ordered at gunpoint to dig a large hole in the ground and disrobe. The Nazis shot men, women, and children alongside the mass graves they had dug. Eyewitnesses also reported that the squads sometimes did not shoot children but instead buried them alive.

One such massacre occurred in Ejszyszki, a village in present-day Lithuania, on September 21, 1941. *Einsatzgruppen* drove 4,000 Jewish civilians to the local cemetery where they were shot to death. This village was one of hundreds of places where Jews were totally wiped out with no surviving children in the community. *See also* FINAL SOLUTION; GRAEBE, HERMANN; HOLOCAUST; MASSACRES; WORLD WAR II.

Further Reading: Daniel Goldhagen, *Hitler's Willing Executioners* (1996); Vera Laska, ed., *Women of the Resistance and in the Holocaust* (1984); John Mendelsohn, ed. *The Holocaust: Selected Documents in 18 Volumes* (1982); Carol Rittner and Sondra Meyers, eds., *The Courage to Care* (1986).

El Salvador

Civil war raged in this Central American country between 1980 and 1992. Death squads terrorized people, and mass killings occurred, including a massacre in El Limon on January 12, 1981 and in El Mozote on December 11, 1981. Children were orphaned as adults were killed in these and other civilian villages. In some cases, children were taken from their parents' arms by soldiers who said these children would be reared to serve the nation. Tens of thousands of people fled the country. As a result, thousands of children became refugees and the number of unaccompanied children rose as young people were separated from their families. As of 1995, nearly 190,000 Salvadoreans had sought asylum in the United States. More than 75,000 people had died.

Forced from their home by the fighting, this child and her grandmother take refuge in a shelter in San Salvador, El Salvador, in November 1989. *AP/Wide World Photos.*

Caring for children in the dangerous conditions brought on by this civil war was terribly difficult. The Women's Association of El Salvador worked with women's organizations around the world to raise money to evacuate children and build child care centers and bomb shelters, as well as to provide food and medicine. Child care centers found that young people who had witnessed killings and torture needed counseling along with a safe place to stay and material aid.

In 1991, the UCA (*Universidad Centroamericans*) Children of War conducted a survey project to better understand the needs of youth in El Salvador. Researchers found that of 246 children ages 10 to 16, 93 percent had been close to combat zones; 74 percent had been forced to flee their homes; 50 percent had lost close relatives or friends;

and 47 percent were forced to separate from their parents. Another survey was conducted two years later with 538 young people. It showed that nearly 30 percent suffered from depression, 72 percent felt anxiety, and 16.7 percent had exhibited aggressive behavior. World Vision and other non-governmental organizations worked in schools to help children who had been traumatized by the war.

In January 1995, a peace accord was reached between the Salvadorean Armed Forces and Farabundo Marti National Liberation Front (FMLN). Even after the fighting ended, land mines remained an ongoing threat to Salvadoreans. Children were hurt or killed after picking up land mines in the fields without realizing what they were. According to UNICEF, only about 20 percent of the children who were injured by these mines received any remedial therapy, most of the rest have had to fend for themselves— often resorting to begging or stealing to survive.

In 1992, UNICEF developed a Mine Awareness and Accident Prevention Project to educate people and remove the mines. Posters showing pictures of mines were posted so that young people would be able to identify them and leave them alone. They were urged to tell the authorities if they noticed any land mines. UNICEF also ran public education programs and distributed leaflets to Salvadorean families. Young people took part in the education program and helped to explain land mine safety to younger children. Both sides of the conflict described the location of hundreds of mines, and 425 were removed. Still, many more mines had been dropped by air and their whereabouts were unknown.

Years after the war ended, parents were also still searching for missing children. An independent organization called Pro-Busqueda (Association in Search of Disappeared Children), founded in 1994 by a Spanish-born Salvadorean Jesuit priest named Jon de Cortina and a Dutch man named Ralph Sprenkels, had been helping parents look for their children. As of 1999, the organization had reunited 98 disappeared children with their biological families and was still working on behalf of 434 families or children. Some of the children were adopted by people in foreign countries, including the United States.

One mother who did find missing children was Felipa Diaz, whose three children ages 11, 8, and 7 had disappeared from El Limon during the 1981 attack when that village was burned to the ground. In 1996, she was reunited with her son Ricardo, who was 8 years old when he vanished. During an interview in 1999, he told a journalist that soldiers had taken children from the village to their military base, where "They gave us out like chickens. They said, 'Anyone who wants one can have one'" (Rosenberg, 1999). Felipa's other son was found in Honduras, but her daughter was still missing as of 1999.

Other children had been adopted by families who believed that the children were orphans or had been abandoned by their families. Many children have not been reunited with their natural parents or have been traumatized to discover the circumstances of their adoptions. In some cases, adoptive families and biological families came from opposing political camps, causing more conflicts for the children. *See also* ADOPTION; LAND MINES.

Further Reading: Jose-Luis Henriquez, "Community-Based Mental Health Projects for Persons Affected by the War and Former Child Soldiers of the FMLN," in *Child Soldiers*, a report from a seminar by Radda Barnen and the Swedish Red Cross, February 12–13, 1994, Stockholm, Sweden; Maria de Lourdes, "Women in the Struggle for a New El Salvador," *Peace & Freedom,* September/October 1985, pp. 12ff; Larry Rohter, "Where Countless Died in '81, Horror Lives On in Salvador," *The New York Times,* February 12, 1996, p. 1ff; Tina Rosenberg, "What Did You Do in the War, Mama?" *The New York Times Sunday Magazine,* February 7, 1999, pp. 52–60; UNICEF, "Combating Land-Mines in El Salvador," in *The State of the World's Children, 1996,* (1996).

Elizabeth II (1926–)

Born the first of two daughters of the Duke and Duchess of York, Elizabeth became heir to the British throne when her father became King George VI in 1936 on the abdication of his brother, King Edward VIII. Elizabeth's mother, Elizabeth Bowes Lyon of Scotland, became Queen Consort. After Great Britain entered World War II in September 1939, life changed greatly for the royal family. Princess Elizabeth, then age 13, and her younger sister Margaret remained in London with their parents, although the family could have sent them away to Canada or to the countryside. The royal couple hoped that by remaining in the capital with their family, they could demonstrate solidarity with their people.

Elizabeth spent most of the war years at Windsor Castle, guarded by anti-aircraft guns and troops. The castle had bomb-proofed cellars and air-raid shelters in the courtyard. She witnessed the flames from the bombings and the destruction around the city. Sometimes the two young princesses accompanied their parents on tours of bomb-stricken areas to comfort the victims. Traditional celebrations, dances, and parties were curtailed during the war years, so Elizabeth spent many hours reading, studying, sketching, riding horses, or walking her dogs.

As a member of the royal family, Elizabeth took on special duties. She sometimes broadcast to other young people over the radio. In October 1940, she made a short speech to the people of the British Empire in which she assured them that "we children at home are full of cheerfulness and courage."

Like other Britons, Elizabeth had registered for war-service work at age 16 but her father refused to allow her to do anything dangerous. When she turned 19, she convinced him to let her do "real" war work. The princess became a Junior Officer in the Auxiliary Territorial Service (ATS). Elizabeth learned vehicle maintenance and driving and was photographed servicing trucks that were used to carry supplies for the military. She also learned how to drive a truck herself. At war's end in 1945, Elizabeth was permitted to join the throngs of people crowding in the streets below the balcony of the palace where the King and Queen stood waving. She wore her ATS uniform and cap and hoped she would not be recognized. In an interview years later, Elizabeth II recalled,

Fourteen-year-old Princess Elizabeth (right) and her sister Princess Margaret speak to the children of Great Britain in 1940. *Corbis/Hulton-Deutsch Collection.*

We cheered the King and Queen on the balcony and then walked miles through the streets. I remember the lines of unknown people linking arms and walking down Whitehall, all of us just swept along on a tide of happiness and relief. I remember the amazement of my cousin, just back from four and a half years in a Prisoner of War camp, walking freely with his family in the friendly throng. . . . I think it was one of the most memorable nights of my life. (Westall, quoting interview, 1985)

In 1952, after the death of her father, Elizabeth was crowned Queen Elizabeth II. She was a popular monarch, all the more so because her family had remained in London with her people during the tumultuous war years. *See also* BLITZ, LONDON; BOMBINGS (WORLD WAR II); GREAT BRITAIN (WORLD WAR II).

Further Reading: Judith Campbell, *Queen Elizabeth II, A Biography* (1980); Robert Westall, quoting from

a BBC radio broadcast, "The Way We Were," May 8, 1985.

Espionage

Young people have actively engaged in espionage (spying) during various wars. They have operated both officially and unofficially. Some took part in a single act or a few acts of espionage as the opportunity arose. Others took part in ongoing activities as part of a group or large network of spies. Many of these youths' names remained unknown, but others have been recognized for their exploits. Some of the following examples from different countries show ways in which teenagers have become espionage agents on behalf of a cause.

A teenage girl known simply as Marie became a spy during World War I. At age 14, she began working with the British secret service in Belgium to transport messages smuggled across the Belgium-Holland border to other places in Holland. For two years, Marie carried out her work, delivering reports twice a week from one agent to another. By the end of the war in 1918, she had learned how to write reports on the activities of the Germans around her area of Selzaete. She continued to work with the British intelligence network until she was captured by the Germans and sentenced to imprisonment for the duration of the war. Marie remained in prison for three months until the Germans surrendered. After her release, she was welcomed as a heroine by her fellow villagers. Captain Henry Landau, her contact and the leader of her espionage unit in Belgium, later wrote about Marie in his book *All's Fair: The Story of the British Secret Service Behind German Lines.*

During World War II, Tomas Santiago of Manila, a Filipino boy known as "Manila Boy," fought against the Japanese as a partisan. As the war was ending, he joined a communist organization that planned to overthrow the government. These revolutionaries, called Huks, operated as spies and attacked arsenals and government troops. Santiago was sent to assassinate a government official. However, after talking with his intended victim, he became convinced that this man could change the Philippine government for the better and unite the country, democratize institutions, and introduce reforms to help the poor. Santiago realigned himself with the government and told them what he knew about secret revolutionary plans. He also helped to convince some former communist underground fighters to join him. By gathering intelligence information, he was able to help the government arrest revolutionaries who planned to attack various people in the government with arms they had received from the Soviet Union.

As an ex-spy, Santiago organized welfare work to help children who had been orphaned during the fighting between the Huks and government troops. Some of them were left behind in Huk camps after their parents fled. He worked with the government to shape land reform policies, introduce rent controls, and

pass new laws that would punish soldiers who burned a house, raped, or stole from people. The government agreed to pardon ex-Huks, offering them land grants and helping them find jobs.

Another teenager, Helene Deschamps, worked with the French Resistance and as an agent with the American OSS during World War II. She lived undercover, using an assumed name in Vichy, where she gathered information about the Nazis to warn French partisans about upcoming raids. Later, Deschamps moved south to the town of Aix where she succeeded in locating a German PT-boat base. While fleeing from the Nazi police, she encountered two American pilots whose plane had been shot down and she guided them to safety. During her four years of espionage, Deschamps experienced many hardships as well as narrow escapes. She was arrested and interrogated but managed to outwit her captors. She was also betrayed, and shot at by Nazi collaborators. Some of her friends died while working with the resistance. Deschamps described her experiences in her autobiography entitled *Spyglass. See also* AMERICAN CIVIL WAR; AMERICAN REVOLUTION; BELGIUM (WORLD WAR II); BOYD, ISABELLE "BELLE"; DARRAGH, JOHN; RESISTANCE MOVEMENTS (WORLD WAR II).

Further Reading: Helene Deschamps, with Karyn Monget, *Spyglass* (1995); Barbara Nolen, ed., *Spies! Spies! Spies!* (1965); Kurt Singer, *Spy Stories from Asia* (1960).

Ethiopia

Civil war ravaged this East African country during the 1980s and early 1990s when government troops fought against the Eritrean and Tigre liberation forces. Civilian casualties in Ethiopia were high as starvation killed thousands of children and young adults. During the early 1980s, government troops burned hundreds of thousands of acres of food-producing land in Tigre in a scorched-earth policy designed to subdue resistance. Relief organizations sent food to relieve the serious shortages, but the government used most of these donations to feed government military forces rather than hungry civilians.

Some grain sent by the United Nations did reach people in the north. During 1991, as violence diminished, Ethiopia became a refuge for people fleeing from the war in neighboring Sudan. Sickly, hungry people who had lost everything arrived at refugee camps but had to flee again when the Ethiopian government changed once more in 1991.

Land mines remained a serious problem in Ethiopia and Eritrea during the 1990s. Between 1977 and 1999, about half of the estimated 12 million mines that were originally placed in Eritrea were removed. Thousands of civilians were killed by mines during these years, and most of the young casualties were hurt or killed while doing farmwork or going to fetch water.

In Ethiopia, land mines were causing between 5 and 10 casualties each week during the 1990s. A large-scale effort to demine the country began in 1995. *See also* AFRICA; REFUGEES; SUDAN.

Further Reading: UNICEF, *The State of the World's Children, 1996* (1996).

Euthanasia

Euthanasia is the act of killing or permitting the death of people who are hopelessly ill or injured for reasons of mercy. During the Holocaust of World War II, the Nazis discarded considerations of mercy as they murdered thousands of children who had physical or mental handicaps or incurable illnesses (for example, epilepsy). Leaders in Nazi Germany planned and carried out a program to eliminate people who had these conditions, or others they considered unfit to live, including children and youth who were too deformed or too sickly to work. These programs reflected Hitler's racial theories and were part of an overall design to create a "master race" of so-called "superior" people.

Early in World War II, in October 1939, Operation T-4 was set in motion. It was named for a Berlin address, Tiergartenstrasse 4, where the operations's headquarters were located. This program legalized the killing of people of all ages who were mentally or physically disabled. German doctors and health officials cooperated to find people who were targeted for death. Many of the child victims lived in institutions while some, like children with hearing disabilities, lived at home.

Victims were transported to one of six killing centers in Germany and Austria in buses with painted windows that blocked anyone from seeing in or out. They were then methodically killed in gas chambers or were given lethal injections. Some infants and very young children were starved to death. Their bodies were burned in crematoria to destroy evidence.

The German government notified the families that their loved ones had died of surgery, illness, or from natural causes. By 1941, people were increasingly suspicious about these deaths, and German Catholic clergy protested the killing of people with disabilities. Under pressure, the government ended the T-4 program, which had killed between 60,000 and 93,000 people. *See also* DEATH CAMPS (WORLD WAR II); GENOCIDE; FINAL SOLUTION; HITLER, ADOLF; HOLOCAUST; "MASTER RACE."

Further Reading: Henry Friedlander, *The Origins of Nazi Genocide* (1995); Ina Friedman, *The Other Victims* (1990); Hugh Gregory Gallager, *By Trust Betrayed* (1990).

Evacuations (World War II)

Children and young people have often been evacuated from war zones to protect them from injury and death. During World War II, families and numerous individual children were evacuated from areas that were likely to be bombing targets. They were transported to safer regions of their countries or moved abroad to the United States, Canada, and other countries where bombings were not occurring. Other children had to be evacuated because their homes had already been destroyed by bombings. A massive evacuation of youth was organized by the British government. Prime Minister Neville Chamberlain called these evacuations "the greatest social experiment which England has ever undertaken." The program was controversial. Some people feared it would hurt family life by separating children and parents.

After Great Britain declared war on Nazi Germany in 1939, Britain's leaders feared that London would be a major target of Nazi bombers. In September, some schoolchildren were evacuated from London. The government urged parents to send their children to the country or abroad. Some went by ship to the United States. In July, the S.S. *Britannic*, which held hundreds of young evacuees from Britain, reached New York harbor. They had endured a tense journey across the North Atlantic, dodging Nazi submarines.

Most Londoners reluctantly decided to send their children away, although thousands of other children remained in the city. In England, young people nicknamed these travelers "Vackies." Those who were evacuated could take one small suitcase and as much as they could wear or carry. Many children had tucked pictures of their parents and other family members into their pockets. Railroad stations were the scene of tearful partings. Many older children went to the station alone. While some young people were going to the homes of rural relatives, others would be living with strangers who had agreed to house them during this national emergency. Some children were frightened, but others viewed the trip as an adventure or vacation.

Boy Scouts and Girl Scouts were often assigned to meet the children at the station and serve refreshments, carry messages, and help small children. Children had their names written on pieces of paper that were pinned to their chests. They were fed milk and tinned corned beef before they arrived at their destinations. Host families varied in their treatment of the evacuees, whom they had been ordered by the government to house. Some evacuees were poor children from the slums who arrived at their foster homes malnourished, dirty, and infested with lice or other bugs. Some were not used to brushing their teeth or bathing regularly. Many children were also unruly and would not obey their hosts' directions. They faced adjustment problems as well as homesickness. However, many children enjoyed living in the country with room to play, fresh air, and farm foods. Some evacuees became much like another member of the host family.

When the winter of 1939-1940 brought no bombings, about 20,000 children were sent back to the cities. However, the Germans began an air battle over Britain in September 1940, at which time more English children were evacuated. Hundreds of thousands of youths were later removed from industrial areas and urban centers that were being bombed by the Germans. Some went to the English countryside; others were sent to Wales. People who had friends, relatives, or other connections in the United States or Canada sent their children to live with them for the rest of the war. Sea travel was hazardous, however. On September 17, 1940, 10 days after the Blitz began, the Germans torpedoed an evacuation ship in the North Atlantic. On board were 406 people, of whom 256 drowned, including 77 children.

Outside London, children living in towns that contained or were located near military installations were also evacuated. For instance, Lowestoft, the town nearest to Germany, was the headquarters of the Minesweeping Service and the site of a major naval base that housed more than 60,000 sailors during the war. Children and many mothers were evacuated from Lowestoft during the war, reducing the population of the town by about two-thirds in 1940.

Young people who were sent abroad suffered special problems. Some had trouble keeping in touch with their families, especially when ships carrying mail were torpedoed and did not reach their destinations. These young people worried about their parents' welfare during the bombings.

Evacuations took place in other countries besides England. After Holland and Belgium fell to German troops in spring 1940, many Dutch and Belgian children were also evacuated. Most were taken aboard boats to England. German children were also evacuated for safety reasons. In April 1941, about 1,000 children from Berlin were sent out of the country to Czechoslovakia. The government said these evacuations would protect young people now that the war was nearly two years old and intensifying. Parents were told that the children were being sent to East Prussia, but the trains took them to German-occupied Czechoslovakia. Teachers went with the children so they could continue their lessons. Some of these transports were led by older Hitler Youth members. At the camp in Czechoslovakia, the children did not have regular schooling and were basically inactive for several months. At the end of September 1941, the camps were disbanded and the children were returned to Berlin.

After Allied bombing raids over Japan increased in 1944, young schoolchildren were evacuated from Tokyo. Some went to stay with relatives in the country, but most went to camps where they lived with strangers. Groups of children, sometimes an entire class or school, travelled to the country with teachers, nurses, and school officials. They took backpacks and water bottles with them and sang songs along the way. Although many children felt sad, they knew they were expected to look brave and refrain from crying. Once they arrived at their destinations, they usually attended school part of the day and worked during the other half, usually in farming or industries. Housing for the children was set up in school buildings or empty religious temples. Many children became infested with lice, fleas, or ticks because they were crowded and could seldom bathe. Some homesick evacuees tried to run away. They followed lines of railroad tracks they thought would lead them back to the city. Those who became lost and were found by grownups along the way were sent back to the camps. Some of the runaway children reached Tokyo but were also sent back because their parents wanted them to stay away from the bombings.

During the war in Bosnia in the 1990s, children and others were evacuated from wartorn cities. One 1994 evacuation removed 1,000 people from Sarajevo. *See also* BLITZ, LONDON; BOMBINGS (WORLD WAR II); BOSNIA; CHILDREN'S TRANSPORTS (*KINDERTRANSPORTS*); EL SALVADOR; FINLAND (WORLD WAR II); FRANCE (WORLD WAR II); GERMANY (WORLD WAR II); GREAT BRITAIN (WORLD WAR II); JAPAN (WORLD WAR II); WORLD WAR II.

Further Reading: Jost Hermand, *A Hitler Youth in Poland* (1998); Ilse Koehn, *Mischling, Second Degree* (1977); Michael Kronenwetter, *Cities at War: London*

(1992); Dorothy Macardle, *Children of Europe* (1951); David E. Newton, *Cities at War: Tokyo* (1992); Robert Westall, *Children of the Blitz* (1985).

Executive Order 9066. *See* INTERNMENT CAMPS, U.S.

Experiments, Nazi

During World War II, Nazis used captive civilians as subjects for cruel physical experiments. The tests lacked a clear scientific purpose and did not follow standard medical practice or rules of medical ethics. Some procedures were conducted to let inexperienced physicians practice surgery and other techniques or to see the impact of new, untried treatments. Victims of these Nazi experiments included thousands of children and young people, among them a number of young twins. Those who did not die were often left with painful disabilities, emotional distress, and severe health problems.

Between 1941 and 1945, experiments were carried out on prisoners, most of whom were Jewish, at the concentration camp of Dachau in Germany, the first concentration camp to be set up by the Nazis (1933). Eyewitnesses later testified that medical students with little training performed hundreds of surgeries on the stomachs, gall bladders, spleens, throats, and other organs of healthy people. Numerous patients died in surgery.

At Dachau, people were infected with malaria by mosquito bite or injection. Others were forced into vans and subjected to high air pressure tests that killed many victims. In another set of experiments, people were placed in ice-cold water up to their necks to see how low the body temperature could descend before people died. Most of the 300 victims died.

Many experiments took place at the Auschwitz-Birkenau camp in Poland where the infamous Block Ten was located. Most of the victims of these experiments were Jewish. Among the victims were young Polish girls who received torturous treatments with no painkillers. Their captors infected them with gangrene, tetanus, or staphylococcus bacteria in their legs and arms, then tested them to see what kinds of treatments might work on German soldiers with these conditions.

In other experiments, doctors removed people's bones or parts of bones to see if they could transplant bones in German soldiers who had lost bones in combat. Victims died as a result of bleeding, infection, and blood poisoning. Nazi doctors also removed muscle tissues. Some healthy limbs were taken from prisoners, and Nazi doctors tried to attach them to German soldiers who had lost limbs during the war.

Other "experiments" were designed to find effective ways to sterilize people whom the Nazis had judged unfit to reproduce. In Block Ten, young women, many of them teenagers, were subjected to numerous surgeries. Teenage women were among the victims used for gynecological surgeries and tests that left them sick and disfigured and eventually killed them. Nazi doctors also injected dyes into people's eyes to see if the color could be changed, causing terrible pain and organ damage. Children who were twins were among the victims of these experiments.

On November 27, 1944, a group of 20 children were taken out of Auschwitz and moved to the concentration camp Neuengamme outside Hamburg, Germany. These children, some of whom were only five years old, became subjects of cruel experiments under the direction of Dr. Kurt Heissmeyer. Among the victims was a 12-year-old Jewish boy from Paris, Georges-Andre Kohn. He and the other children were injected with numerous disease organisms, such as tuberculosis bacilli. They were also subjected to incisions that left them weak and disfigured. In April 1945, as an Allied victory seemed imminent, the surviving victims of these experiments were taken from the camp to a building in Hamburg, where they were hanged in an effort to conceal what had been done to them. Four days later the camp at Neuengamme was liberated. After the war ended, the facts about these atrocities slowly came out. Some of the perpetrators were charged with war crimes and were prosecuted by an international war crimes tribunal.

Herta Oberhauser, another doctor at Auschwitz, also killed children during her experiments. She removed the limbs and vital organs of some children and was observed to rub ground glass and sawdust in their wounds. After the war, Oberhauser was convicted as a war criminal and sentenced to 20 years in prison, but she was released in 1952 and began practicing medicine in Stocksee, Germany, until her license was revoked in 1960. *See also* AUSCHWITZ-BIRKENAU; CHILDREN OF AUSCHWITZ NAZI DEADLY EXPERIMENTS SURVIVORS (CANDLES); DEATH CAMPS (WORLD WAR II); DEATH MARCHES; DEKEL, ALEX SCHLOMO; MENGELE, JOSEF; ROMANI (GYPSIES); WORLD WAR II.

Further Reading: Lucille Matalon Lagnado and Sheila Cohn Dekel, *Children of the Flames* (1991); Jeremy Josephs, *Swastika Over Paris* (1989); Robert Jay Lifton, *The Nazi Doctors* (1986); Miklos Nyiszli, *Auschwitz* (1986); Gisella Perl, *I Was a Doctor at Auschwitz* (1979).

F

Family Separations. *See* SEPARATIONS, FAMILY

Fatalities. *See* CASUALTIES, CIVILIAN; CASUALTIES, MILITARY

Feed the Children

Feed the Children is a non-profit Christian organization that provides food, clothing, educational supplies, medical equipment, and other materials to the victims of famine, drought, flood, war, and other disasters. The Reverend Larry Jones organized the group in 1970 and became its president. Donations to fund the programs come mostly from people in the United States. Based in Oklahoma City, Oklahoma, Feed the Children aids needy children overseas as well as in the United States. It has offices in more than 19 other countries, including countries in Africa, the Caribbean, Central and South America, the Middle East, Southeast Asia, Eastern Europe, and the former Soviet republics.

Larry Jones was moved to organize Feed the Children after he saw young people suffering in war-torn Haiti. As head of the organization, he visited war zones to supervise and to observe what was needed and how food deliveries could best be carried out. As of 1997, Feed the Children had distributed over 225 million pounds of relief commodities around the globe. These included ship-ments to needy children in Bosnia, Croatia, Haiti, and Somalia. Larry Jones has been commended for his humanitarian work by the governments of El Salvador, Guatemala, Iran, and Lebanon. In 1998 and 1999, Feed the Children aided children in war-torn Kosovo. *See also* FOOD; RELIEF ORGANIZATIONS.

Further Reading: Fact Sheet, Feed the Children, December 1997; Feed the Children (Larry Jones International Ministry) P.O. Box 36, Oklahoma City, OK 73101-0036.

Filipovic, Zlata (1980–)

One of the most detailed accounts of war from a child's viewpoint comes from the diary of Zlata Filipovic, who was 11 years old and living in Sarajevo in 1991 when fighting began in Bosnia. Filipovic had been keeping a diary when the war started and she managed to smuggle her written accounts out of the country with the help of the United Nations Children's Fund (UNICEF). The diary shows how her pre-war life of school, friends, sports, music, going out for pizza, and other adolescent activities turned into a fight to survive each day with her family. Gunfire destroyed much of the city, and there was no running water, electricity, or phone service. People cowered in cellars to avoid being killed by shells, and many went hungry or suffered from malnutrition. Zlata endured long periods of time with no eggs or fruit. School was often closed. She saw shops, churches, apartments, and other buildings turn to rubble.

In July 1994, 12-year-old Zlata Filipovic holds a copy of her published diary, which records her experiences during the war in Bosnia in the early 1990s. *AP/Wide World Photos.*

On May 23, 1992, Zlata described the chaotic scenes around her as follows: "SLAUGHTER! MASSACRE! HORROR! CRIME! BLOOD! SCREAMS! TEARS! DESPAIR!" In July 1993, she wrote, "SHOOTING, NO ELECTRICITY, NO WATER, NO GAS, NO FOOD. Almost no life." That year, a journalist who interviewed Zlata asked how many of her friends had died. She replied, "Too many to count." At Christmas that year, the family was finally able to leave Sarajevo and move temporarily to Paris. Filipovic's diary was published by the United Nations in 1994, then released around the world. She visited numerous cities to speak at public meetings about her wartime experiences and the impact of this war on children. The book and her presentations helped people to understand the suffering of children in war-torn Bosnia. *See also* BOSNIA; DIARIES.

Further Reading: Zlata Filipovic, *Zlata's Diary* (1994).

Films. *See* WAR FILMS

Final Solution

The term Final Solution refers to a plan devised by the Nazis under Adolf Hitler to kill all the Jews of Europe. Between 1931 and 1945, 1.5 million Jewish children died at the hands of the Nazis. In numerous writings and speeches, Hitler expressed zealous anti-Jewish feelings. He declared that "the final aim [of government] must be the deliberate removal of the Jews"(Payne, 1973). On January 20, 1942, top Nazi officials and leaders of the German government met at a villa in Berlin near the Wannsee Lake for what became known as the Wannsee Conference. SS Chief Reinhard Heydrich told the assembled men that the meeting had been called to discuss a "final solution to the Jewish question"—a code name for a plan of genocide, targeting all Jews (then numbering about 11 million) in Europe, along with others whom the Nazis considered unfit to live, mainly Romani (Gypsies). It was the first time in modern history that a nation had set out to methodically murder an entire group of people—men, women, and children.

Notes taken at the Wannsee Conference stated that "Europe is to be combed through from West to East in the course of the practical implementation of the final solution.... The evacuated Jews will be taken, group by group, to the so-called transit ghettos, in order to be transported further east from there." Plans for the Final Solution had been discussed before 1942, and the purpose of the conference was to enlist help from other government officials so that mass genocide could be carried out. By 1942, thousands of Jews had already been killed as a result of emigration, ghettos, overwork, starvation, and killing squads, but Nazi officials decided these methods were not fast or efficient enough. As the Nazi plan unfolded, Jews of all ages in Nazi-occupied lands were targeted for death.

After the conference, the Nazis arranged mass deportations of ghetto residents, sending them by train to death camps in Poland. Aided by local collaborators, they began rounding up any remaining Jews who had been in hiding or were using false identity papers to elude detection. *See also* DEATH CAMPS (WORLD WAR II); DEPORTATIONS; GENOCIDE; GHETTOS (WORLD WAR II); HITLER, ADOLF; HOLOCAUST; ROMANI (GYPSIES); ROUND-UPS; WORLD WAR II.

Further Reading: Lucy S. Davidowicz, *The War Against the Jews* (1975); Martin Gilbert, *The Macmillan Atlas of the Holocaust* (1982); John Mendelsohn, ed., *The Holocaust: Selected Documents in 18 Volumes* (1982); Robert Payne, *The Life and Death of Adolf Hitler* (1973).

Finland (World War II)

Finland and Russia were at war in 1939-1940, just as Nazi Germany began to invade other European nations. With men away fighting, women and boys began working in munitions plants. Very young children were evacuated from the country. Wearing nametags, they were sent by train and boat to safety in nearby Sweden, which remained neutral throughout World War II. A number of these evacuated children were orphaned by the war. They did not return to their former homes but stayed with their foster families in Sweden permanently.

During the war, Soviet aircraft bombed civilian targets. They also bombed trains on the Viipuri-Helsinki line that carried women and children westward. People hurried to shelters when sirens went off. A number of countries protested the bombing of civilian populations in Finland, and U.S. President Franklin Roosevelt issued a plea to the Soviet government to cease this kind of attack. Former President Herbert Hoover worked to organize relief efforts that shipped food and other supplies to Finland. In California, he made an impassioned speech protesting the Russian actions and their attacks that left Finland with "dead women and children in their streets" (Engle and Paananen, 1973). When the Russo-Finnish war ended, 25,000 people had died and 35,000 soldiers were wounded.

The conflict with the Soviet Union was over when Germany invaded Finland in 1942. Finnish leaders and journalists expressed their opposition, especially when the Nazis began persecuting Jews. The Germans insisted that the government turn over Jewish refugees living in Finland. Hitler intended to deport the 2,000 Finnish Jews who remained and he sent Heinrich Himmler, the head of all Nazi police, to expedite deportations. With Himmler was his personal physician, Felix Kersten, a native of Estonia who had once served with the Finnish Independence Army. While working as a mediator between the two sides, Kersten warned Finnish leaders about the Nazis' plans. He also advised Himmler that the Finns resented attacks on Jews and suggested that the Germans move slowly.

Finnish leaders became more determined to resist after their intelligence agents confirmed that the Nazis intended to kill the Jews they deported. Secretly, they made plans to transport Jewish refugees to neutral Sweden, if necessary. By late 1943, a few Jews had been arrested in Finland, but no groups had been deported. The war had intensified on several fronts, and German leaders gave up their fight to deport Jews from uncooperative Finland. *See also* DEPORTATIONS; SOVIET UNION (WORLD WAR II).

Further Reading: Eloise Engle and Lauri Paananen, *The Winter War* (1973); Philip Friedman, *Their Brother's Keepers* (1978).

Folded Crane Club

In 1958, the Folded Crane Club was founded by a Japanese man, Ichiro Kawamoto, who worked as a janitor at the Jogakuin Girls' School in Hiroshima. Kawamoto had done rescue work in Hiroshima after the atomic bomb struck the city on August 6, 1945. He witnessed the horrors of the bombing and was deeply upset when a girl named Sadako Sasaki and other children died from radiation sickness in the years that followed.

Kawamoto encouraged Sasaki's classmates to honor her, and the Folded Crane Club was formed. Members of the club asked the government to build the Children's Monument in the Hiroshima Peace Park. With his wife Tokie, Kawamoto organized the children to fold paper cranes in the traditional Japanese origami style. These cranes were placed at the foot of the monument. Young people in the Folded Crane Club, mostly girls in their early teens, also visited people in the hospital who were suffering from the long-term effects of the bombing. They wrote letters to world leaders protesting the nuclear arms race and urging them to work for peace and disarmament. Kawamoto told author Betty Lifton (1985), "I want them to grow up without prejudice toward anyone. It is another way of working for peace in our world." *See also* HIROSHIMA; JAPAN (WORLD WAR II); PEACE MONUMENT; RADIATION SICKNESS; SASAKI, SADAKO.

Further Reading: Betty Jean Lifton, *A Place Called Hiroshima* (1985).

Food

During wartime, young people often face food shortages that lead to hunger and starvation. Food may be rationed—doled out to people in limited quantities—to feed large numbers of people with a limited supply. Blockades or a lack of transportation may also prevent food from reaching people. Denying food to the population or preventing them from raising new food supplies are practices that have often been used as weapons of war to weaken, demoralize, and destroy the enemy.

The need for food can become a daily struggle, especially for young people in combat zones where food supplies, growing crops, or fields used for growing crops have been damaged or destroyed. To avoid starvation, young people may have to eat things they never ate before the war or find unpleasant. During World War II, for example, an English boy described eating whale meat that had been soaked for hours in vinegar to tenderize it. Other meals featured American dried eggs and sausage made without meat.

Jam, sugar, and tea were great luxuries during the Second World War years. Butter and other items were also rationed. As a result, young people could not enjoy certain traditional dishes, which meant changes in the meals they ate on holidays and special occasions. Families saved up ration coupons for sugar and butter so they could make cakes for birthdays or other occasions.

In many countries, young people have helped to raise food to supplement wartime supplies. For example, during World War II, Canadian and British children grew and harvested vegetables. Many school grounds were turned into fields for crops, and the children cultivated potatoes, carrots, cabbages, and other plants. Likewise, young people in Germany and Japan raised and harvested food. In the United States, children helped tend victory gardens to increase domestic food supplies, since large quantities of food were being sent to the military.

Some young people resorted to trading in the illegal black market during World War II. Black marketeers charge higher-than-normal prices for foods (and other goods) that are rationed or in short supply. To improve their food supply, young people risked the legal penalties of buying or selling food in the black market in occupied Europe. Some of them were caught and fined or imprisoned or both.

Young people forced to labor for the enemy have often been sent to do farmwork. During World War II, many young people from occupied Holland, Czechoslovakia, Poland, and the Soviet Union, among other countries, were obliged to plant and harvest food for the enemy either in their homelands, in Germany, or in another occupied country.

After wars end, food may be delivered quickly to relieve shortages. The military has often been the first vehicle for delivering food to newly liberated countries. Soon after the Allies arrived in Holland after World War II, Allied planes dropped food parcels down for the people. For the first time in years, young people in that country could enjoy real butter, margarine, bacon, sausages, cheese, and chocolate. Other tins contained dried egg powder. Such joyful scenes occurred in other European countries after both World War I and World War II.

Food shortages may plague countries long after wars end. A number of relief organizations have worked to provide food to young people in war-torn countries after the conflicts ceased. *See also* ADDAMS, JANE; AFRICA;

BOER WAR; BOSNIA; CARE; CONCENTRATION CAMPS (WORLD WAR II); DEATH CAMPS (WORLD WAR II); DRANCY; ETHIOPIA; FEED THE CHILDREN; FORCED LABOR (WORLD WAR II); FRANCE (WORLD WAR II); GENEVA CONVENTIONS; GERMANY (WORLD WAR II); GHETTOS (WORLD WAR II); HOLLAND (WORLD WAR II); HUNGER/MALNUTRITION; JAPAN (WORLD WAR II); MOZAMBIQUE; RATIONING; RELIEF ORGANIZATIONS; SAVE THE CHILDREN; SOVIET UNION (WORLD WAR II); UNITED NATIONS CHILDREN'S FUND (UNICEF); VICTORY GARDENS; WORLD WAR I; WORLD WAR II.

Further Reading: Eleanor Ayer, *Cities at War: Berlin* (1992); Michael Foreman, *War Boy* (1989); Tom Harrison, *Living Through the Blitz* (1976); Walter B. Maass, *The Netherlands at War* (1970). Alfred Price, *The Hardest Day* (1980); Dirk Van Der Heide (pseud.), *My Sister and I* (1941); Robert Westall, *Children of the Blitz* (1985).

Forced Labor (World War II)

Since ancient times, invading troops have sometimes forced captive peoples to perform labor. Forced labor (also called slave labor) occurred on a massive scale during World War II when the Nazis enslaved people from the nations they conquered. In Poland, Holland, and the Soviet Union, for instance, people were seized off the streets and taken to fill labor shortages in German factories and to work at jobs in agriculture. Between 1939 and 1945, around 10 to 15 percent of all Polish youths were sent to Germany for forced labor. Often, they were taken while they were away from home, and their families did not know what had happened to them.

Schools were a common site for Nazi raids. On one occasion, Nazis snatched students aged 12 to 16 as they left their trade school in Gorlice, Poland. They were loaded into trucks, driven to a train station, then taken to Germany. In all, about 390,000 young Poles were sent for forced labor in formerly Polish lands annexed by Germany. They made up about 25 percent of the labor force in Wartheland.

Youthful Polish laborers were made to clean up the mess that was left after the invasion and fighting ended in 1939. Outdoor jobs included building roads, bridges, canals, and railways. The Nazis also sent them to work in mines or in factories where they made war materiel such as ammunition. Others went to farms to raise and harvest food. For any job the Germans wanted done, they found free labor. A few jobs paid small wages, usually up to 40 cents a day. However, the prisoners themselves did not receive these wages; they were paid to the camps that had sent them to work.

The Nazis also forced young men in other occupied countries to work for them. In 1942, for example, an edict in Holland required all men between ages 18 and 40 to serve as a soldier or to work in a military industry. Nazi police searched for potential workers by raiding Dutch homes, schools, churches, and streets. A number of young men went into hiding or lived underground while working for the resistance to avoid this fate.

In her book *The Other Victims* (1990), author Ina Friedman described a Dutch family in which all three sons were abducted by Nazi police. Sixteen-year-old Dirk had seen his two brothers pulled off their bicycles and taken away. In July 1942, Nazis entered the bicycle repair shop where Dirk worked and seized him and nine others. Dirk was taken to the Ebenswald labor camp in Germany where he made metal pipes. There was little to eat except watery, contaminated soup, so he and his fellow workers ate mice and birds to survive. By the war's end, more than 300,000 Dutch men, many under age 21, had been forced into labor for the Nazis.

In Germany, some young prisoners were brought to places where Germans waited to "bid" on them. They worked on farms, in stone quarries, in munitions plants, in labor camps, and built roads and railroad tracks and demolished buildings. They labored for 12 hours a day and more after 1943. These workers were ill-fed and inadequately clothed. Often, their supervisors beat them or mistreated them in various ways. Some died from beatings, overwork, diseases, malnutrition, or when they were shot for breaking rules. Housing in the camps or barracks was usually unsanitary, and diseases were rampant.

Youths were forced to work in plants run by I.G. Farben, Siemens-Halske, and in the Krupp munitions plants, among others. They were paid far less than adults and their wages went to Nazi officials or factory owners, not the workers themselves. At first, children around age 14 and up were required to work for the Germans. As the war continued and the pool of older workers dwindled, increasingly younger children, ranging from 8 to 12 years old, were also forced to work.

Nazi decrees singled out Jews in particular for slave labor and sent them to do the most dangerous and deadliest types of work. In Poland, shortly after the German victory in 1939, a new decree stated: "All Jews from fourteen to sixty years of age are subject to forced labor." Young people were taken like others—either by some sort of notification that ordered them to report for work or by simply snatching them off the streets. After being captured, they were packed into boxcars and sent to Germany or other places.

At concentration camps and some death camps, people also had to labor, in most cases, until they died. They worked in stone quarries, camp kitchens, infirmaries, gas chambers, storage rooms, outdoor construction projects, factories at the camps, and other places. Slave laborers had to work long hours and received little food. They lacked adequate clothing and health care. Many died from hunger, disease, or the hazardous conditions in their work settings. They also died or suffered permanent physical problems resulting from beatings and other abuse by their captors. Some were put to death because they became sick or incapacitated.

Reuben Rosenberg, a Jewish boy from Lublin, Poland, was barely 12 when he was taken to a forced labor camp. While laboring at an aviation plant, he saw other boys die from overwork and starvation. Two were killed for stealing potatoes. Rosenberg recalled, "They were dragged to the cellar of the gendarmerie, where dogs bit them to death" (Ferencz, 1979). Rosenberg was next sent to work in an iron foundry at the Czestochowa camp. Workers there slept on crowded straw sacks infested with vermin. He later said, "There were some terrible ac-cidents in the workshops. Men fell asleep from hunger or fatigue at their machines, and their hands or feet would be torn away . . . " (Ferencz, 1979).

In a factory at the Flossenburg concentration camp, Rosenberg was ordered to make bazookas 13 hours a day. Five hundred people died within one two-week period. Rosenberg remembered, "To load bazookas we had to use picric acid and trotil. We worked without gas masks, and after a few weeks the lungs and feet would cave in. The young were chosen for this task. SS men would kill them while they worked " (Ferencz, 1979).

Hans Baermann, a young Jewish man from Cologne, Germany, endured forced labor at the Salaspils camp near the Riga ghetto in Latvia. In freezing weather, the workers built barracks and watchtowers. Their food consisted mostly of potato peelings and black bread. Inmates at the Mauthausen labor camp in Austria, mostly Jews, often died. Weak from overwork and lack of food, they were forced to haul immense rocks up 186 steps from the bottom to the top of the quarry. Those who did not work hard or fast enough risked being beaten, tortured, confined in a special cell, or shot. *See also* AUSCHWITZ-BIRKENAU; AUS-TRIA (WORLD WAR II); BAUM, FROIM; BAUM GROUP; CONCENTRATION CAMPS (WORLD WAR II); DEATH CAMPS (WORLD WAR II); GRAEBE, HERMANN; HART, KITTY FELIX; HOLLAND (WORLD WAR II); PACIFIC (WORLD WAR II); POLAND (WORLD WAR II); SCHINDLER, OSKAR.

Further Reading: Benjamin B. Ferencz, *Less Than Slaves* (1979); Ina Friedman, *The Other Victims* (1990); Milton Meltzer, *Never to Forget* (1976).

Fort Mims, Battle of. *See* AMERICAN INDIAN WARS

Foundlings (World War II)

During wartime, desperate parents have sometimes abandoned their children in the hope that it would save their lives. People who believed their children were doomed if they kept them have left them in places where they might be found by compassionate strangers who would take them in. During World War

II, some Jewish infants and young children became foundlings when their parents were on the verge of being deported or killed. Solomon Fleischman, a 16-year-old in Nazi-occupied Hungary in 1944, was one of 11 children. As the Nazis began deporting Jews, his parents sadly concluded that the family was too large to hide together and must be split up. He later told author Elaine Landau (1991) how his father gave each child some money to help him or her survive and tucked money into the clothing of his infant sister "in the hope that a kind Gentile might rescue her." (Landau, 1991)

In Poland and other occupied countries, convents were a common place for foundlings. People also found abandoned babies in empty homes, on doorsteps and porches, in parks, or at the edge of the woods. Author Richard C. Lukas (1994) wrote that 57 Jewish boys and girls were left at the home of Father Boduen in Warsaw during a three-month period in 1942. An order of Polish nuns called the Grey Sisters set up a special nursery near a hospital in Kielce in 1942 when the number of foundlings increased there.

People who feared they were about to be denounced (turned in to Nazi police for doing resistance work or because they were hiding Jews) also took children they were hiding to convents and other places. Some children whose parents had been killed made their way to these places on their own. Some nuns went looking for Jewish children who needed a place to hide.

Gilles Perrault, a teenager during the war, recalled the following story of how a baby was rescued in occupied Paris in 1942:

[A] man my age told me that his mother, a fervent Christian, had been warned about the roundup [of Jews], rushed to the Velodrome d'Hiver, and managed to get near the railings. A Jewish woman, jostled by the crowds, was able to pass her baby out. No words had been exchanged . . . . That child, brought up by its adopted family, now plays in the Orchestre de Paris. (Perrault, 1979)

After the war, surviving parents looked for their children. Some found them still living at convents and other institutions. Convents in Poland that were heavily involved in caring for such children included the Franciscan Sisters, the Ursulines, and the Little Servant Sisters of the Immaculate Conception.

Parents or family members who found young relatives after the war faced special problems and adjustments. Some children had become attached to the people they had been living with, sometimes for several years. Likewise, these families often grew to love the children and were distressed to part with them. In some cases, the children left with their biological families, never to return. Other times, they maintained warm relationships with their wartime families after they left the household. *See also* ADOPTION; DEPORTATIONS; FRANCE (WORLD WAR II); HIDDEN CHILDREN; HOLOCAUST; ORPHANS; RESCUERS (HOLOCAUST); RIGHTEOUS GENTILES; UNACCOMPANIED CHILDREN; WORLD WAR II.

Further Reading: Jean-Louis Besson, *October 1945: Childhood Memories of the War* (1995); Peter Hellman, *Avenue of the Righteous* (1980); Elaine Landau, *We Survived the Holocaust* (1991); Richard C. Lukas, *Did the Children Cry?* (1994); Gilles Perrault, *Paris under the Occupation* (1979); Kiryl Sosnowski, *The Tragedy of Children Under Nazi Rule* (1983).

France (World War II)

France entered World War II in 1939 after Germany bombed and invaded its ally, Poland. In June 1940, France fell to the Nazis after a swift, forceful German invasion. Germany annexed Alsace-Lorraine and divided France into two parts—the north, occupied by the Nazis, and the south, labeled a "Free Zone" under the aging military leader, Marshal Philippe Petain, and his government at Vichy. (By late 1942, the Nazis also occupied southern France.)

During the next four years, children and young people in France endured many deprivations and hardships. Young French Jews and young Jewish refugees living in France suffered deportation and death. Jean-Louis Besson, who was only seven years old in 1939, later recalled the start of the war:

September 3. It's war! England and France have declared war on Germany. . . . Ev-

In 1940, French refugees flee the German advance into their country. *Roger Viollet, Gamma Presse.*

eryone in the house is upset. War—I've been hearing about it for a long time now. Everyone's been very afraid of it, but they hoped that after the big war in 1914, which left millions dead, there would never be another. This is not to be. My father and Uncle Eugene agree that we can't let Hitler, Germany's leader, keep invading neighboring countries—our allies—and do nothing about it. . . . In the meantime . . . Papa will have to be a soldier (Besson, 1995).

Millions of refugees, mostly Jews, had fled to France from other European countries. When the Nazis marched into Paris in June 1940, about 5 million people lived there, more than double the pre-war population. The government in Paris advised people to evacuate the city, and a panic ensued. The southbound roads outside the city were jammed as 4 million people tried to leave, using cars, bicycles, ox-carts, on horseback, or on foot. Mothers could be seen pushing baby carriages. As masses of people clogged the roads, German warplanes dropped bombs. Many women and children were injured or killed as the moving mass of people trampled those who went too slowly or came to a stop. About 40,000 people died while trying to leave Paris. The rest went hungry for days until they reached their destinations because there was no food or water along the way.

Many of the refugees were children, who were taken to the countryside where adults thought they would be safe from bombings. The ministry of education helped to plan the evacuations of school-aged children, and many went to southern France, accompanied by their teachers. Other French people, especially the wealthy, tried to emigrate to other countries. During this mass emigration, some children were separated from their parents. Parents sought to find their children by posting notices in newspapers, which also published lists of children who had been located. Public notices on billboards throughout Paris showed where lost children could be picked up.

Life changed for the young people of France as curfews were imposed and food and other goods were rationed. New clothes were no longer available in stores. People could not buy soap, medicines, or leather shoes. When their feet grew or their old shoes wore out, some young people made themselves cardboard shoes with wooden soles.

Only a few people, such as doctors and Nazi officials and troops, were allowed to operate cars. Gasoline was scarce, and young people walked or biked when they wanted to go somewhere. Athletic teenagers could be seen bicycling at high speeds down French streets. Some enterprising youths earned money operating horse-drawn taxis or bicycle taxis.

In schools, the curricula were changed to suit the Nazis and textbooks were censored. The Germans removed certain pages and made other changes in history books. Interruptions occurred when students had to flee from their classrooms and remain in shelters during air raids. A number of young people missed classmates who had fled from the Nazis or been evacuated to the country.

By the winter of 1940–41, people were living with severe fuel shortages and could not heat their homes. Coal supplies were so low that people used balls made of compressed low-grade coal and warmed their beds with bricks heated in the oven, then wrapped up in a towel or rag. Children studied their lessons while wearing mittens and several layers of clothing, often padded with newspapers when they went outside. Families moved into one or two rooms of their homes to conserve fuel. Some spent hours inside the underground areas of the subway system or stood over sidewalk grilles to warm themselves. Electricity was so scarce that people felt lucky to have one light working at home.

Food was rationed, starting with bread, sugar, and noodles in August 1940, and followed by eggs, meat, butter, cheese, coffee, and cold cuts in October. After that came potatoes, chocolate, fresh fish, dried vegetables, milk, and wine. At the beginning of the occupation, the official daily allowance per adult was 1,200 calories, but most people could not obtain nearly enough food to equal that amount. The allowance included 12 ounces of bread per day, 12 ounces of meat per week, and 5 ounces of cheese per month. In addition, children were allowed small amounts of milk and an occasional egg. To supplement their meager meals, French schoolchildren were given pink vitamin pills and high-protein biscuits. They ate in government-run community restaurants to stay alive. As the war went on, these amounts were drastically reduced. After 1941, food was scarce, and people were subsisting on a few hundred calories a day. In the south of France, many people had only olives and fish that they caught themselves. In cities, markets that had once held ample supplies of food now offered few items—usually potatoes, rutabagas, carrots, turnips, cabbages, dried beans, noodles, and onions. Bread was dark in color because the bakers had limited amounts of flour. Some mixed straw with the flour to extend it.

To buy these small amounts of food, people had to line up for hours at a time. Young people were often sent to the market to wait in the lines, and stores had usually sold all their goods by mid-afternoon. Some only opened one or two days a week. As in other occupied lands, people relied on friends who lived in the country to help them obtain enough food, or they resorted to trading in the black market. Families raised rabbits in their homes and planted gardens wherever they could find a patch of ground. Gardens sprang up in parks, on rooftops, and on balconies. City pigeons, stray cats, and even pet cats and dogs were eaten when people became desperately hungry.

Young people played an active role in obtaining food, as well as helping to plant gardens at home. City children were sent on trips to the country to find food. In rural areas, children picked berries, mushrooms, herbs, and other wild foods. Children also helped collect money for the poor and elderly, a project called the National Relief. As they went door-to-door, they carried metal boxes for donations.

Curfews, blackouts, and a lack of food limited outings and entertaining. At home, many young people listened with their families to radios, which the Nazis had banned. For recreation, they went to more movies than usual. Young people often spent their leisure time at home reading or playing cards. Gilles Perrault, who was a high school student in Paris at that time, wrote, "Muffled in layers of woolens, with our gloves on, we read from nightfall, windows shuttered against a hostile world. Any book printed sold right out, and there were an enormous number published" (Perrault, 1979).

Young French women sometimes became romantically involved with German soldiers. They went out to dinner, to nightclubs, and to parties with these men, who could show them a good time, protect them from other Nazis, and provide such gifts as foods, textiles, and silk stockings, which were not available to other French citizens. Some of these girls were ostracized and labelled as traitors by other French citizens.

Everyday life held new dangers. Anyone who failed to move off the sidewalk when a German approached could be kicked, beaten, or arrested. Some young people criticized their elders for not fighting or resisting the Nazi invaders more vehemently. They became angry at the Nazi occupiers and sometimes took action themselves.

Jews in France faced far worse hardships, including imprisonment, deportation, and death. Between 1942 and 1944, 11,402 Jewish children were deported from France and sent to Nazi death camps. Only about 300 of them survived the war. Before they were deported, they were captured and held in detention centers, including the Velodrome d'Hiver and Drancy. Families were often separated before various members were sent to concentration camps in Poland and other places.

Some Jewish children were able to leave the country with assistance because France had many ports and bordered neutral Spain and Switzerland, as well as Italy, a country where about 80 percent of Jews survived the war. Some children managed to travel from France to Spain, then on to the United States, Africa, or Palestine. A Jewish assistance program called HICEM helped refugees. The Toulouse escape line was organized by a Jewish resistance group to help Jews in France after German troops occupied the entire country. The group managed to sneak about 7,500 Jews out of France to Spain. At least 600 of them were children and teenagers. The Spanish government insisted that they leave that country quickly and most went to either Portugal or the United States.

Thousands of Jewish children in France went into hiding during the occupation. More Jews sought hiding places beginning in 1942, when the Nazis began deporting Jews. The Nazis planned a massive round-up in Paris for July 16, but some French police and officials heard about it and warned Jews and members of the Resistance, which included a number of young people. Even so, the Nazis arrested about 11,000 people, including 4,000 children.

During the summer of 1942, high-ranking Nazis in France demanded that at least 50,000 Jews from southern France (the so-called Free Zone) be deported to concentration camps. To meet this quota, they suggested that the police round up children under age 16 along with adults. They hunted down 4,000 children who had been left behind when their parents were deported. Catholic and Protestant clergy saved about 12,000 Jewish children by hiding them in various places and smuggling some into Switzerland and Spain. *Amities Chretiennes* (Christian Friendship), a group of Catholics and Protestants who helped Jews in hiding, rescued many people. The group was directed by Catholic priest Father Pierre Chaillet and Protestant Pastor Marc Boegner. Chaillet published an important underground newspaper, *Notebooks of Christian Testimony,* beginning in 1941. In the region of his parish in Lyons, he hid hundreds of Jewish children who had been orphaned or left behind when their parents were arrested or deported. Many of them lived in monasteries or in the countryside with peasant families. In September 1942, officials of the Vichy government arrested Chaillet. He was imprisoned in a psychiatric ward for refusing to stop his resistance work, but other Jesuits continued the effort.

In August 1942, the Archbishop of Toulouse, Monsignor Jules Gerard Saliege (later Cardinal Saliege), protested the deportation of Jews and mourned the "dreadful spectacle of men, women, and children being treated like vile beasts; of families being torn apart and deported to unknown destinations." The archbishop asked Catholic families and religious institutions to aid Jews. Concerned clergy placed children in convents, homes, and other safe places, at the same time giving them false papers. Nuns who ran orphanages and boarding schools frequently hid Jewish children from the Nazis. Adults were also hidden in these places, sometimes disguised as clergy, servants, cooks, or gardeners.

The Allies liberated France late in 1944. Patriotic French punished young women who had been friendly to the Germans occupying their country, labelling them as collaborators. Angry neighbors shaved off the girls' hair and sometimes also painted swastikas on their bald heads. During the following winter, young Frenchwomen refrained from wearing hats or scarves so it would be clear that they, with full heads of hair, had not been among the traitors. *See also* CIMADE; DEPORTATIONS; DRANCY; ESPIONAGE; EXPERIMENTS, NAZI; HIDDEN CHILDREN; HOLOCAUST; HUNGER/MALNUTRITION; HARTZ, RUTH KAPP; LE CHAMBON-SUR-LIGNON; RIGHTEOUS GENTILES; RIVESALTES; ROUND-UPS; WORLD WAR II; ZAZOU.

Further Reading: Nathan Aaseng, *Cities at War: Paris* (1992); Jean-Louis Besson, *October 1945* (1995); M.R.D. Foot, *Resistance* (1977); Howard Greenfeld, *The Hidden Children* (1993); Serge Klarsfeld, *French Children of the Holocaust* (1996); Gilles Perrault, *Paris Under the Occupation* (1979); John F. Sweets, *The Politics of Resistance in France, 1940-1944* (1976); Jacqueline Wolf, *Take Care of Josette* (1981).

Frank, Anne (1930–1945)

The author of a famous diary, Anne Frank, a Jewish girl who lived in Amsterdam during World War II, is perhaps the best-known young victim of the Holocaust. Her first-person account of life in hiding in wartime Amsterdam has been printed in many languages and is read and dramatized throughout the world. At age three, Anne Frank arrived in Holland as a refugee from her native Germany. Her father Otto had relocated his food products business and moved the family to Amsterdam after the Nazis seized power in Germany in 1933. As a young child, Anne Frank enjoyed a loving family and comfortable life. She learned to speak Dutch quickly and made friends in her adopted land. As an adolescent, she especially liked the cinema and collected magazine pictures of her favorite film stars. People who knew her described Anne as bright, lovely, well-mannered, and sociable.

The Franks hoped they would be safe in neutral Holland, but the German invasion of Holland in May 1940 marked the onset of five long years of occupation. The Nazis enacted a series of laws that deprived Dutch Jews of their civil rights and proceeded to isolate and impoverish them. In the summer of 1941, Jewish children were banned from public schools and could not use swimming pools or certain other public facilities, including libraries. Anne and her sister began attending a Jewish school.

The Franks went into hiding in July 1942 after 16-year-old Margot received a card from the government ordering her to report for a work assignment in Germany. With the help of friends, the family lived in secret rooms above the warehouse attached to Otto Frank's business. Their lives were severely restricted because they could not go outdoors and had to be quiet all day. In time, the group increased to eight people as other Jews joined the Franks in hiding.

On Friday August 4, 1944, Nazis raided the building and located the secret door to the hiding place. The eight Jews and a man who was helping them were arrested and sent to concentration camps. At Bergen-Belsen in Germany, Anne and Margot contracted typhus, which killed many inmates at that crowded, unsanitary camp. The two young girls died just months before the war ended. Their mother died of illness at Auschwitz. Otto Frank survived and returned to Amsterdam where he lived for a while with his employee and friend, Miep Gies, and her husband Jan. Gies was able to give Frank his

Dit is een foto, zoals ik me zou wensen, altijd zo te zijn. Dan had ik nog wel een kans om naar Holywood te komen.
Anne Frank.
10 Oct. 1942

(translation)
"This is a photo as I would wish myself to look all the time. Then I would maybe have a chance to come to Hollywood."
Anne Frank, 10 Oct. 1942

This photo of teenage diarist Anne Frank also reproduces her signature and a page from her diary. *Corbis-Bettmann.*

daughter's diary and papers, which had been scattered on the floor after the Nazis arrested the group in the annex. Gies had saved the writings, hoping she could one day return them to Anne.

In 1947, friends convinced Otto Frank that the diary was an important literary and historical work that should be published. For the first small printing, the book was called *Het Achterhuis* ("The Hiding Place"); the diary was later published under the title *Anne Frank, The Diary of a Young Girl*. Within a decade, it had sold more than 50 million copies in dozens of different languages. A theatrical play, feature films, and television movies have also been based on the diary.

Anne Frank's diary has been described as a valuable historical record as well as a deeply personal document. It holds the hopes, fears, loves, and day-to-day thoughts of a teenager caught in a world turned upside down. At one point, Frank wrote, "I still believe, in spite of everything, that people are really good at heart." Arnold Rubin (1977) described the

diary's lasting appeal and message this way: "This is the magic of Anne Frank's diary: the light amid the darkness, the dreams amid despair, the idealism amid cynicism." *See also* BERGEN-BELSEN; DIARIES; GIES, MIEP AND GIES, JAN; HOLLAND (WORLD WAR II); HOLOCAUST.

Further Reading: Anne Frank, *The Diary of a Young Girl* (1967); Miep Gies, *Anne Frank Remembered* (1987); Willy Lindwer, *The Last Seven Months of Anne Frank* (1991); Arnold Rubin, *The Evil Men Do* (1977).

Free German Youth

Formed in the 1930s, the anti-fascist Free German Youth group was made up of young Germans in their late teens and early twenties who had fled to England. Many of these young people had actively opposed the Nazis and escaped before they were captured and punished. Others were political or Jewish refugees who had been transported to England for their safety when Nazi persecution and violence against Jews increased in the fall of 1938. Members of the Free German Youth held meetings in a camp near London, where they took part in hiking, singing, farming, and spirited political debates. Their Free German Youth Choir gave musical performances. Members also served as volunteers in a youth center and took classes to learn first aid and agricultural skills. The group helped other Jewish refugees to adjust as they moved to England during the war years.

Further Reading: Karen Gershon, ed., *We Came as Children: A Collective Autobiography* (1966).

French Revolution (1789–1799)

The French Revolution was the result of years of political unrest and widespread hunger and poverty among the masses of French people. The revolutionary movement caught fire in 1788 when noblemen demanded reforms that would give them more power and diminish the absolute power of the monarchy. Bad weather in 1788 led to low crop yields and a lack of flour and other foods. Wages were also lower. By 1789, members of the upper middle class and working people were clamoring for changes to reduce tax burdens and give people more representation in the government. Also by 1789, thousands of people in Paris were going hungry. The cost of bread, the mainstay of people's diets, kept increasing so that an average worker had to labor several days just to supply his family with bread for one week. People were forced to eat bread made with coarse grain mixed with bits of straw.

Intellectuals spearheaded the revolutionary effort, which by 1793 had brought down the monarchy and established a republic. Many university students also took part in the struggle to replace royal authority with a democracy. Children and teenagers joined their parents in demonstrating on the streets of Paris and other cities, demanding bread and political reforms. During these years, hungry children also begged in the streets and stood in long lines at bakeries to buy whatever food was available. Revolutionary young people could often be identified by their red caps and simpler styles of clothing, displaying the colors red, white, and blue. Girls and women were expected to wear a tri-colored cluster of feathers called a *cockade* attached to their hats when they were in public.

Some young people took an active role in revolutionary activities. Children whose fathers belonged to a political party called Jacobins, or Friends of the Constitution, attended that organization's social and political events. Young people took part in charitable work done by the Jacobins and attended processions where they sometimes were dressed as revolutionary heroes.

Education changed as well. Children of revolutionaries often went to so-called Sunday schools where they learned about the Declaration of the Rights of Man and the Citizen, which was the basic document of the Revolution. Parents also taught their children political ideas from the *Elements of Republican Instruction*. The question-answer format included passages like this: "Who are you?" "I am a child of the *Patrie*." "What are your riches?" "Liberty and egality." Literature was written for children to promote revolutionary ideals. Revolutionary leaders discussed how to set up public schools that would offer opportunities to all children.

Newborns were also given different kinds of names during these years. Many parents discarded the longstanding tradition of naming children for Catholic saints—for example, Antoine, Denis, Jeanne, Marie. Instead, they chose names from ancient Greek history, such as Brutus, or named their offspring after revolutionary heroes like Jean-Paul Marat. One patriotic Frenchman named his son Marat-Couthon-Pique and his daughter Civilization-Jemmapes-Republique.

Children of the nobility experienced different problems. In June 1791, the royal family, King Louis XVI, Queen Marie Antoinette, and their children, fled to Varennes. The children included a daughter, Marie-Therese Charlotte, born in 1778, and a son, the Duc de Normandie, born in 1785. (A son born in 1781 had died.) The family was captured and imprisoned by people who believed that the king was collaborating with counter-revolutionary forces outside the country. The children shared a cold cell with their parents in a prison called the Bastille for four months. They continued their lessons, played games, and were allowed to walk outdoors once a day.

Early in 1793, King Louis was sentenced to die as a traitor. Witnesses later said that his children could be heard lamenting loudly. The king's daughter recorded that he gave them his blessing and told his son to forgive his accusers and not to seek revenge. The king was beheaded in a public execution on January 21, 1793. In July, the queen was ordered to give up her son (the heir to the throne) so that he could be imprisoned in a different part of the building under the supervision of others. She was distressed to hear him crying from his room. The queen was guillotined on October 16, 1793, leaving the royal children orphans. The king's young son later died in prison of tuberculosis of the bones at age 10.

Universal conscription—the drafting of all eligible males—was ordered in August 1793. The Committee of Public Safety decreed that "The young men shall fight; the married men shall forge weapons and transport supplies; the women will make tents and serve in the hospitals; the children will make up old linen into lint . . . ." Among the teenaged soldiers was Xavier Vernere, who grew up in a rural area. He tried to enlist in the navy at age 14 but was rejected. In 1790, the army accepted him and he became a soldier in the French army the next year. As the war went on, soldiers complained that they did not have adequate supplies or food. They complained about the lack of bread and wine and about the high prices they were charged to buy these goods.

Executions by guillotine occurred by the hundreds, then thousands, each month during 1793 and 1794. Young people were also sometimes killed as traitors. People were killed for all kinds of reasons, such as printing counter-revolutionary writings, speaking against the Revolution, or merely because they were under suspicion or had been turned in by angry acquaintances. Fallen politicians were condemned. Whole families were executed during the Reign of Terror, as this period became known. Thousands of people also died of malnutrition or disease while they were confined in the crowded, filthy prisons. People of all ages lived in horrible fear of being arrested, and children were orphaned when their parents were killed.

Some young people took part in attacks on others. In late 1794, gangs of youths from different socio-economic classes attacked each other on the streets of Paris. Youths also joined crowds who stood in the streets to watch the thousands of beheadings that took place during the Revolution.

Further Reading: Vincent Cronin, *Louis and Antoinette* (1974); Norman Hampson, *A Social History of the French Revolution* (1964); Christopher Hibbert, *The Days of the French Revolution* (1980); John Hall Stewart, *A Documentary Survey of the French Revolution* (1951).

Fund Raising

Children and young people have participated in efforts to raise money for wartime purposes, particularly during World War II. Such efforts, whether compelled by the government or voluntary, were organized group activities or the actions of individuals. In Germany, Hitler Youth groups engaged in large-scale fund-raising during the Second World War. Different nations also involved schools in fund raising. A group might set out to raise a specific amount of money for a goal, such as to pay for a piece of military equipment. Money was also raised to send needed items to the war front or to people in need.

War stamps and war bonds were sold in schools throughout the United States. Young Americans saved millions of dollars in coins to buy bonds. They collected the stamps in booklets until they had purchased enough to exchange the books for bonds.

Sometimes children devised ways to raise money on their own and donate it for war use. For example, children who lived near orchards might ask permission to pick apples or other fruit. They would sell the fruit and send the money to funds being raised to buy military equipment or other things used by soldiers.

Each Halloween, children around the world also take part in a general fund-raising effort that benefits children who suffer from war and other problems. The United Nations Children's Fund (UNICEF) sponsors the "Trick-or-Treat for UNICEF" program and encourages children to help other children in need.

Individual children and groups of youth have organized their own fund-raising efforts to help children of war. They have been inspired by stories about the suffering of others told in the media or during programs or presentations they have attended at their schools, churches, or other places. *See also* AMERICAN CIVIL WAR; COLLECTION CENTER DRIVES (WORLD WAR II); HITLER YOUTH; SOMALIA; UNITED NATIONS CHILDREN'S FUND (UNICEF); WAR BONDS (U.S.); WORLD WAR I; WORLD WAR II.

Further Reading: Ilse Koehn, *Mischling Second Degree* (1977); Michael Kronenwetter, *Cities at War: London* (1992); Reader's Digest, *America in the '40s* (1998); Max Von Der Grun, *Howl Like the Wolves* (1980); Robert Westall, *Children of the Blitz* (1985).

G

Gage, Nicholas (1939–)

Nicholas Gage (Nikola Gatzoyiannis) was born the year World War II began in Europe and spent his early years in the village of Lia, Greece. There he survived both the Second World War and the devastating civil war that raged afterwards. During the latter conflict, communist guerillas fought against the government and its nationalist troops for control of Greece. By 1948, guerillas occupied Lia and the surrounding mountain region. That summer, in villages throughout Greece, the guerillas abducted Greek children, taking them away from their families to live in the Soviet Union and other Soviet bloc countries where they resided in special camps and were indoctrinated with communist ideals. Teenagers, both male and female, were conscripted to fight with the guerillas or sent to do other forced labor, such as growing and threshing wheat.

Cut off by the war from her husband, who had emigrated to the United States several years before, Gage's mother, 41-year-old Eleni Gatzoyiannis, defied these orders and arranged for her children to escape. Eleni and her older sister, who had also defied the guerillas' orders, and three other villagers were brutally tortured and put on trial. Local people were threatened and intimidated so they would testify against their neighbors. The trial was a mock proceeding because communist leaders in charge of the local gueril-

las had already ordered that Eleni and the other prisoners be found guilty. The five civilians from Lia were executed in late August 1948. During these months, guerilla leaders conducted similar trials and executions throughout Greece to terrorize people into submission.

Eleni Gatzoyiannis was one of 600,000 Greeks who lost their lives between 1940 and 1948 during the two wars that ravaged the country. Her courageous actions enabled her son and three of her daughters to escape being deported to Albania and Romania, where other Greek children were sent. The guerillas had captured her 15-year-old daughter and forced her to do hard labor and then to serve with communist troops fighting in Greece. She was finally able to escape and join her siblings in the United States in 1949.

After arriving in the U.S., Nicholas Gage lived in Worcester, Massachusetts, and went on to college, eventually became an investigative journalist. Tormented by his mother's fate, he began investigating her death and searching for her murderers in the 1970s. Gage interviewed numerous people in Greece and tracked down former guerillas who lived in Soviet-bloc countries to find out what happened during the war. His award-winning book, *Eleni*, was published in 1983 and made into a motion picture.

In telling his family's story, Gage showed the horrific impact of war on children and other civilians. He described the agony of those who saw their children seized and deported. One mother recalled how the guerillas took her son Vangeli in September 1948.

> There were about a dozen of us from Lia. Other groups of mothers and children came up the mountain from other villages. One boy had been bitten on the way by a rabid dog. "Don't worry, he'll be fine . . ." the guerillas told us. "Our doctors will take care of him." When they got to Albania, he went crazy. They shut him up in a room and tied him because he was biting his own hands. He died in terrible pain. . . . [Vangeli] was nine when he left, and when he came back, he was sixteen years old, but he looked twelve, no more, thin as an ax handle, his bones pushing through his skin. (Gage, 1983)

See also GREECE (WORLD WAR II).

Further Reading: Nicholas Gage, *Eleni* (1983).

Galicia. *See* UKRAINE (WORLD WAR II)

Gas Masks

Air raids and air-raid drills, in which children used gas masks, became common during World War II. After the war began, government officials in Great Britain, believing the German military would use poison gas against its enemies, issued gas masks to civilians. Even babies had gas masks, designed so that an adult would need to pump air into them. Horses and certain other animals also had masks. People even tried to obtain masks for their pets.

Children were expected to wear or carry their masks with them everywhere and some found it tiresome. At times, they played games with their masks and used them to hide special possessions. One 10-year-old English boy remembered the gas mask in "its clumsy cylindrical metal case. You had to carry it with you all the time, and the case bumped against your side most uncomfortably when you walked." Children often found it hard to breathe through the filters. The strong smell of rubber and the feeling of the mask covering their faces also upset some children. They

had trouble seeing through the eye holes and their skin became hot and sweaty.

A British propaganda poster that circulated during the war read: "Hitler will send no warning—so always carry your gas mask." Radio broadcasters urged mothers to "make

This little Israeli girl helps her father transport her gas mask during the Persian Gulf War of 1991. *Michel Eular, AP/Wide World Photos.*

a game of it" and call the mask a funny face "or something of the kind." To make them more agreeable to children, colorful red and blue rubber masks were made for them. Some masks were also designed to resemble Mickey Mouse to diminish young children's fears. During some drills to test the gas masks, children were led through air-raid shelters containing tear-gas. The masks were supposed to keep all this gas out. *See also* AIR RAIDS; ARAB-ISRAELI WARS; BLITZ, LONDON; BOMBINGS (WORLD WAR II); CHEMICAL WEAPONS; PERSIAN GULF WAR; WORLD WAR I; WORLD WAR II.

Further Reading: George Carter-Goldsmith, *The Battle of Britain—The Home Front* (1974); Marion Yass, *The Home Front, England* (1971).

Geiger, Emily (1763–c. 1780s)

Teenager Emily Geiger became a heroine for the colonial army during the American Revolution when she carried an important message to a key military leader. A native of South Carolina, Geiger rode off on her horse with a written message from General Nathaniel Greene, the leader of the colonial army's southern forces, to his fellow officer, General Thomas Sumter. British troops were attacking Greene's men, and he needed reinforcements from Sumter or his troops would be outnumbered.

On her way to Sumter's camp, Geiger was apprehended by British scouts. Peter Simons, who worked under the direction of Lord Rawdon, ordered her off her horse. Simons then summoned a Tory (British loyalist) woman to come and search Geiger in private for any messages or other military items. While Geiger was waiting for the woman to arrive, she quickly memorized the contents of the message. Then she broke it into tiny pieces and swallowed them to avoid discovery.

Since the British found no incriminating items on her, Geiger was set free. She proceeded to take a different, more obscure, route to Sumter and encountered no more Redcoats. In three days, she reached the colonial encampment and delivered the message she had memorized to General Sumter. He sent troops to Orangeburg to assist Greene in winning the Battle of Eutaw Springs.

Colonial supporters praised Geiger for her role in winning the battle, and her story was handed down to succeeding generations as an example of female heroism. After the war ended, she married Captain John Threwitz. Emily Geiger Threwitz died during the 1780s shortly after giving birth to her daughter Elizabeth. *See also* AMERICAN REVOLUTION; ESPIONAGE.

Further Reading: Donald Barr Chidsey, *The War in the South* (1969); Elizabeth Ellet, *Women of the Revolution* (1848); M. Foster Farley, "Emily Geiger's Ride," *South Carolina Magazine,* May/June 1976, pp. 10-11; Mollie Somerville, *Women of the American Revolution* (1974).

Geneva Conventions

After World War II ended in 1945, a series of four conventions were held in Geneva, Switzerland, to develop specific protocols that would protect civilians during war. Several provisions dealt primarily with the need to give special protection to children, both as combatants and as civilians. Those sections of the international agreement read, in part, as follows:

> Civilians . . . shall not be the object of indiscriminate attack, acts, or threats of violence.
>
> [Combatants should] allow the free passage of medical supplies, food and clothing for children, expectant mothers, maternity cases and nursing mothers.
>
> It is prohibited to attack, destroy, remove or render useless foodstuffs, crops, livestock, drinking water installations and supplies, irrigation works, etc.
>
> Sexual exploitation: Children shall be the object of special respect and shall be protected against any form of indecent assault.
>
> Unaccompanied children: The parties to the conflict shall endeavor to ensure that children who have been separated from their families are not left to their own resources.

Despite the conventions, numerous countries have violated these provisions in various wars that have taken place since 1945, especially in civil wars. Recent violations have occurred in Liberia, Mozambique, Rwanda, Bosnia, and Kosovo. Young civilians have been specifically targeted as well as killed and injured indiscriminately. The United Nations is working with other organizations to see that all nations follow the provisions in the Geneva Conventions and end the practice of using child soldiers. *See also* AFRICA; BOSNIA; CHECHNYA; CONVENTION ON THE RIGHTS OF THE CHILD; CLOTHING SHORTAGES (WORLD WAR II); FOOD; HUNGER/MALNUTRITION; SEXUAL ABUSE; UNACCOMPANIED CHILDREN; UNITED NATIONS CHILDREN'S FUND (UNICEF).

Further Reading: Maggie Black, *Children First* (1996); International Committee of the Red Cross (IRC) <Icrc.org>.

Genocide

The word "genocide" comes from the Greek word *genos*, meaning "race, nation, or tribe," and from the Latin word *caedere*, which means "to kill." It refers to an attempt to kill an entire group of people who belong to a particular race, nation, religion, ethnic group, or tribe. Children and young adults have been victims of genocide, along with adult members of targeted groups.

Dr. Raphael Lemkin (1900–1959), a Polish-born professor of international law, first coined the word "genocide. In 1921, while he was a university student, Lemkin was horrified to learn about a Turkish massacre of Armenians that had begun in 1915. When Lemkin asked why nobody had been arrested or put on trial for these murders, a professor told him that no existing laws covered such crimes. Later, Lemkin did extensive research into ancient and modern laws around the world. He wrote articles and books on these subjects and helped to write a new penal code for Poland, which was enacted in 1932.

During that decade, mass murders occurred in several places. More than 600 Syrian Christians were killed by Muslims in Iraq, and thousands of Ukrainians were killed by government troops in the Soviet Union in 1932–1933. When the League of Nations was organizing in the early 1920s, Lemkin proposed that a new crime be added to the list of international offenses, which then included piracy, slavery, and drug trafficking; he called the crime "barbarity," saying that it involved the "destruction of national, religious, and racial groups."

League of Nation delegates did not implement his idea, but Lemkin continued promoting the recognition of this crime with leaders from around the world. Pursued by the Nazis, Lemkin fled to Sweden where the minister of justice had offered him refuge. During the war, Lemkin taught at a university while studying the tactics used by Nazis in Germany and occupied countries. Along with some other observers, Lemkin concluded that the Nazis intended to kill all Jews and Romani (Gypsies). In one speech, British Prime Minister Winston Churchill alluded to the Nazis'

plans and said, "We are in the presence of a crime without a name."

Lemkin came up with a name—"genocide." He used it to describe the Nazi war against the Jews in his book *Axis Rule in Occupied Europe*, an analysis of Nazi law. The book was published in 1941 while Lemkin was living and teaching in the United States.

As the war continued, millions of children—Poles, Jews, non-Jews—were victimized between 1939 and 1945. As his troops were leaving for Poland, Hitler told his commanders, "I have sent to the East only my 'Death's Head Units' with the order to kill without pity or mercy all men, women, and children of Polish race or language. Only in such a way will we win the vital space we need" (Polish Ministry of Information, 1942).

Among the first victims of this genocidal policy were some Boy Scouts in Bydgoszcz, most of whom were between the ages of 12 and 16. German soldiers lined them up and shot them to death, along with a Catholic priest who came forward to give them the last rites. Young people in other towns and cities were also shot as a punishment for acting against the Germans or for no particular reason. When some Poles killed two German soldiers in Wawer, near Warsaw, soldiers shot every tenth person in the town. Thirty-four of these victims were under the age of 18. Young people were also shot for making anti-German remarks or showing what the Nazis regarded as negative attitudes toward Germans.

After the war, Lemkin attempted to have genocide added to charges made against Nazis on trial before the Nuremberg international war crimes tribunal, and he asked the United Nations to recognize genocide as a crime. In 1946, the United Nations declared in Resolution 96 that genocide was a crime under international law and was "contrary to the spirit and aims of the United Nations and condemned by the civilized world."

The Genocide Convention was held in 1949. Article III of this resolution makes it a crime to commit acts of genocide, to conspire to commit genocide, to directly and publicly incite anyone to commit genocide, to attempt to commit genocide, or to be complicit in acts of genocide. Public and private individuals alike may be arrested for these crimes and punished if convicted. On October 14, 1950, the United Nations Convention on the Prevention and Punishment of Genocide went into effect.

People around the world expressed horror as the extent of Nazi genocide came to light. Nazi Germany had targeted millions of civilians for death and carried out mass murders. They aimed to completely wipe out Jews and Romani and to dramatically reduce the numbers of Poles and Slavs in Eastern Europe. The latter groups were to be killed to create more living space for the German people. Children were targeted and murdered along with adults.

The following formal definition of genocide was developed in 1988 at the United Nations' Convention on the Prevention and Punishment of the Crime of Genocide:

> . . . genocide means any of the following acts committed with intent to destroy, in whole or in part, a nation, ethnical, racial or religious group, as such; a) killing members of the group; b) causing serious bodily or mental harm to members of the group; c) deliberately inflicting on the group conditions of life calculated to bring about its physical destruction in whole or in part; d) imposing measures intended to prevent births within the group; e) forcibly transferring children of the group to another group.

Such collective acts of violence against masses of people typically require some myth or theory to "justify" harming the targeted group, for example, by portraying them as evil, a threat to national security, subhuman, or unworthy of life. Genocide includes and even focuses on young people because they represent a new generation of their group. The Holocaust of World War II has become perhaps the best-known example of genocide in modern times. However, it was not the first genocide nor the last. Since World War II, genocide has been perpetrated in Tibet, Cambodia, Bosnia, and Africa, resulting in vast suffering and the deaths of untold numbers of young people. *See also* ARMENIAN-TURKISH CONFLICT; BOSNIA; CAMBODIA; DEATH CAMPS (WORLD WAR II); *EINSATZGRUPPEN*; FINAL SOLUTION; GUATEMALA; HOLOCAUST; LIBERIAN CIVIL WAR; "MASTER RACE"; ROMANI (GYPSIES); RWANDA; UKRAINE; WORLD WAR II; ZYKLON B.

Further Reading: Anti-Defamation League of B'Nai B'rith, *Witness to the Holocaust* (filmstrip); Richard A. Falk, Gabriel Kolko, and Robert Jay Lifton, *Crimes of War* (1971); Airey Neave, *On Trial at Nuremberg* (1978); Polish Ministry of Information, *Black Book of Poland* (1942); Statement by Hitler to Commanders, August 29, 1939, in U.S., Office of United States Chief of Counsel for Prosecution of Axis Criminality, *Nazi Conspiracy and Aggression* (1946); United Nations Convention on Genocide <http://www.traveller.com/~hrweb/legal/genocide.html>.

Germany (World War II)

During World War II, Germany was allied with Japan and Italy against the British, Americans, Russians, and other Allied Nations. German youth suffered in numerous ways during Adolf Hitler's Nazi regime and during the vast war that ensued after Germany invaded numerous European countries. Youth were affected both as combatants and on the home front. Jews were singled out for escalating persecution, and most German Jewish youth who did not escape the country before 1939 died in Nazi concentration and death camps.

After the war began in September 1939, the first big adjustment for many non-Jewish German children was seeing their fathers leave home for the army. They also heard adults debating the pros and cons of going to war, which most Germans had opposed because they had endured so many hardships and losses during World War I. However, early victories boosted patriotism. Young people supported the troops by sending them letters, cards, packages, and holiday greetings. They watched military parades and took part in rallies organized for young people.

Patriotic activities were often mandatory. People of all ages who might disagree with government policies had to be careful about expressing such sentiments because a large and active Nazi police system punished dis-

This poster warns German children of World War II not to touch unexploded incendiary bombs. *Hoover Institution Archives, GE 1202, Stanford University.*

senters. Children observed what happened to people who did not follow the rules, and were taught to denounce anyone who opposed the government, even their parents.

Patriotism was taught to children from an early age, and they were expected to greet all adults with the Nazi salute and the words, "Heil Hitler!" Schoolchildren saluted the Nazi flag each day and sang an anthem called "Germany Over All Others." Nazi propaganda pervaded the education system, and children were taught to have strong nationalistic attitudes and to put the interests of the state above their personal interests.

Imbued with these attitudes, some youths engaged in violence against anti-Nazis, Jews, and other people Hitler singled out for persecution. Gangs of Nazi youth were permitted and sometimes encouraged to brutalize Jews and those whom the Nazis called their enemies. During the mid-1930s, Hitler Youth sometimes attacked Jews as they walked to and from school or on city streets. Hostilities were also seen within the schools.

Teenage German boys were among the Nazis who violently attacked Jews and their homes, synagogues, businesses, and other property on November 9–10, 1938, an episode known as *Kristallnacht*—"the Night of Broken Glass." Other young Germans were victims or bystanders that night; still others helped friends and neighbors clean up or find a safe place to stay.

A minority of young people in Germany engaged in anti-Nazi resistance activities. They included a group called the *Edelweisspiraten* (Edelweiss Pirates) and *Swing-Jugend* ("swing youth"), so-named because they favored American swing music and resented censorship and the lack of freedom during the Nazi era. The *Edelweisspiraten* were mostly city youths between the ages of 14 and 18 who held non-skilled jobs. They sang anti-Nazi songs, wrote anti-Nazi graffiti, and sometimes attacked Hitler youth. "Pirates" in Cologne took part in more dangerous activities by helping German army deserters and raiding military supply depots. *Swing-Jugend,* who were mostly middle-class teenagers, expressed an interest in all things English; they spoke English, sang English songs, and wore English clothing. Nazi police arrested some members of both groups and publicly hung 12 of the *Edelweisspiraten* who took part in sabotage operations in Cologne. A few members from both groups were sent to concentration camps.

Resistance activities were difficult and hazardous because of the vast Nazi police system and numerous informers. Children found various ways to disobey the government. Some listened with their families to banned foreign radio stations, such as the British Broadcasting Corporation (BBC). A minority of young Germans refused to join Hitler Youth groups, for which they paid heavy penalties, including ostracism and exclusion from jobs, athletic teams, school activities, and university life. Their parents and other relatives were also harassed.

Bernt Engelmann, a teenager during the 1930s, grew up in a family that hated the Nazis; he later worked for the resistance and helped Jews escape from Germany. Engelmann (1996) described how his family disguised favorite books by Erich Maria Remarque, Jack London, and others: "Gradually they had wandered from my father's big bookcase to my shelves, after we had transformed them outwardly into old schoolbooks." Books were wrapped in blue waxed paper and given new titles that would be acceptable to the Nazis, e.g., Algebra, German Geography, and Racial Theory.

During the war, food, clothing, fuel, and other goods and materials were rationed. Even so, most people did not suffer from severe hunger until the last years of the war. Allied naval blockades prevented foods and other imports from reaching the country. Coal supplies were short throughout the war, forcing some schools to close. Children outside farm areas did not have much milk or fresh fruit. Meat was also scarce, and most vegetables for city children came from cans.

To increase food supplies, young people helped cultivate home and school gardens. Children living in the country picked wild nuts, berries, mushrooms, leaves, and herbs. Late in the war, people faced the possibility of starvation. Youthful members of the family were sent to farms to buy small quantities of milk and they walked long distances to obtain flour for bread. Food became more and more monotonous. For example, potato soup or cabbage was served several times a week, and portions were small.

Young people also worked in civil defense and took part in many war-related activities besides combat. They joined charitable drives, such as collecting money for the annual Winter Relief Fund. Young people collected donations, either by going door-to-door or standing at street corners. Most of the Winter Relief helped German soldiers at the front.

Just before World War II, German children had been told to save pfennigs (pennies) to contribute to the RLB (which stands for Air Protection League in German) and to form air protection groups in case of air raids. School was sometimes interrupted for air-raid drills. Young people practiced putting on gas masks that were issued to German citizens, then ran from classrooms to the shelters and back again. As a six-year-old, Elsbeth

Emmerich took part in air-raid drills at school.

> When the siren went we had to line up in twos and march in silence to the air raid shelter. It had bare brick walls and no windows. We were made to sit back-to-back on wooden benches. There were first-aid boxes, and gas masks hanging on hooks on the wall. They frightened me. We had to practice putting the gas masks on, and then sit there in silence till the siren sounded for the end of the drill. (Emmerich, 1991)

Bombings became a reality in 1941. Emmerich's home in Dusseldorf was heavily damaged by Allied bombs, after which the family moved to the village of Altenkirchen, which was also bombed. About two-thirds of the people in this village were killed during one bombing raid. She and her widowed mother and two sisters lived in several different apartments before the war ended. They lost most of their possessions as a result of bombings and thefts, which also became more common in the last year of the war.

Young German Jews experienced worse hardships. By 1941, Jews had been persecuted, stripped of their possessions, and imprisoned in ghettos. They were hunted down and sent to camps where they were systematically murdered. The Cologne ghetto in Germany was emptied along with others in October 1941. Thousands of Jewish men, women, and children were crammed into sealed freight cars and taken to Nazi concentration camps, primarily Auschwitz in Poland and Bergen-Belsen in Germany. Some children found hiding places with non-Jews, but few could find a way to leave Germany by this time. Most German Jewish youth died before 1945.

As the war continued, many children lost their fathers in combat, especially after Germany invaded the Soviet Union in 1941. Registered letters from the government brought news of the deaths of family members to homes throughout Germany. Many children lost more than one male relative—uncles, brothers, grandfathers, and cousins, as well as fathers.

Young men served in the military throughout the war, and more and even younger men were drafted as the war dragged on. Boys were taught military skills at a young age in the Hitler Youth program. Near the end of the war, teenagers served as messengers, ambulance drivers, and in other capacities. Ten-year-olds learned how to use rifles and, as they grew older, were taught to use such other weapons as machine guns, carbines, Luger handguns, grenades, and bazookas.

In the middle of 1943, a new tank division was formed with recruits ranging in age from 16 to 18. Some even younger boys were allowed to enlist and were trained in a camp in Belgium. The boys in this division fought in infantry units; in tank units and artillery regiments; and in engineering, reconnaissance, anti-tank, anti-aircraft, and communications units.

During 1943 and 1944, boys were being drafted at ages 14 and 15. A Hitler Youth unit fought against the Allied troops who launched the invasion of German-occupied France on D-Day in 1944. Led by 16-year-old Alfons Heck, nearly 200 teenage boys in this unit dug trenches on the Luxembourg border in an effort to keep the Allies out of Germany. Tens of thousands of teenage German soldiers also died on the Eastern Front fighting the Russians.

Young men were sent into hopeless battles in their tanks. In the Battle of Berlin in 1945, about 60,000 members of the People's Storm, many of them children and youth, fought without arms or equipment. Of the 5,000 Hitler Youth members who fought in this battle, only 500 survived. Another group of young men, called Werwolf, engaged in sabotage and tried to blow up Allied supply convoys or throw explosives behind enemy lines. As the war neared its end in 1945, Nazi leaders demanded that everyone work to defend the country. Boys 11 years old or even younger operated anti-tank weapons, while girls operated anti-aircraft batteries. When the war ended, some Allied soldiers were surprised to find 15- and 16-year-old German youths surrendering.

By the end of the war, numerous bombings had killed and injured civilians and destroyed homes all over the country. More than 5,500 children died in Hamburg when that city was bombed in July 1943. On February 13, 1945, Allied bombers from the Royal Air Force (RAF) attacked Dresden. The bombings were controversial because the city housed thousands of refugees and did not contain military bases. Other hard-hit cities included Dusseldorf, Nuremburg, and Cologne. Children who lived in these places became homeless and had to move to rural areas. Some remained homeless for months after the war.

Food shortages were critical. As Elsbeth Emmerich recalled,

> We had to find ways of managing. . . . My grandmother had to brave the train and return to the countryside. There were very few trains, and people were crammed into them like cattle, but in the country she could exchange some of our bits of jewellery or fur for a sack of potatoes. She said you had to sit on your potatoes on the way home or they'd be stolen. (Emmerich, 1991)

Post-war relief efforts focused on providing the basic needs of a defeated nation. Much of the aid that was sent by the United States and other nations was directed to German children and youth. *See also* ADOLF HITLER SCHOOLS; BAUM GROUP; BUCHENWALD; CONCENTRATION CAMPS (WORLD WAR II); D-DAY; DEPORTATIONS; EDUCATION; *EINSATZGRUPPEN*; EUTHANASIA; FINAL SOLUTION; FORCED LABOR (WORLD WAR II); HITLER, ADOLF; HITLER YOUTH; HOLOCAUST; JEHOVAH'S WITNESSES; *KRISTALLNACHT*; MARSHALL PLAN; RESISTANCE MOVEMENTS (WORLD WAR II); RIGHTEOUS GENTILES; SPORTS; THE WHITE ROSE; WORLD WAR I; WORLD WAR II.

Further Reading: David Altshuler, *Hitler's War Against the Jews* (1978); Elsbeth Emmerich, *My Childhood in Nazi Germany* (1991); Bernt Engelmann, *In Hitler's Germany* (1986); Robert Goldston, *The Life and Death of Nazi Germany* (1967); Ilse Koehn, *Mischling, Second Degree* (1977); Carol Rittner and John K. Roth, eds., *Different Voices* (1993); Max Von Der Grun, *Howl Like the Wolves: Growing Up in Nazi Germany* (1980).

Ghettos (World War II)

Thousands of Jewish youth died during the Nazi Holocaust of World War II after they were forced to live in closed ghettos in Poland, Lithuania, Holland, Latvia, Hungary, and German-occupied sections of the Soviet Union. Ghettos (certain portions of the city that were enclosed by high walls with locked, guarded entry ways) were overcrowded and unsanitary places where disease, starvation, exposure, and Nazi weapons daily claimed young victims and the lives of their family and friends. Armed guards patrolled the streets as well as the gates leading into the ghetto.

Ghettos in Poland were the largest. The Lodz Ghetto was about 1.5 miles square and confined 150,000 Jews, with seven to eight people crowding into each room. The Warsaw Ghetto was 1.6 square miles and contained from 400,000 to 600,000 people, with eight or more people crowded into each room and thousands homeless on the streets. About 100,000 Jewish children under age 15 were forced into the Warsaw Ghetto. In Hungary, the largest ghetto was in the capital, Budapest, but other ghettos were set up in Beregszasz and Szolos. In the Vilna Ghetto (Lithuania), 25,000 people were crowded into 72 buildings on five streets. The ghetto had two areas—one for people who were put to work, and the other a holding place for those to be sent to death camps. After the Vilna Ghetto opened in September 1941, residents held cultural events and organized two schools for young people, which were taught by a well-known professor from Vilna University. Physicians in the ghetto also gave free medical care.

Hunger and starvation were a continual misery for ghetto children. Jews received less than 500 calories a day, which was later reduced even more, to an average daily allotment of only 184 calories, which is less than 10 percent of what an average adult needs each day. One ghetto-dweller later described what hunger did to people.

> Starvation was the lament of the beggars sitting in the street with their homeless families. Starvation was the cry of the mothers whose newborn babies wasted away and died. Men fought tooth and nail over a raw potato. Children risked their lives smuggling in a handful of turnips, for which whole families were waiting.

A teenage girl who survived the ghetto later wrote that

> Walking on the streets was like a nightmare. On every block there were corpses, sometimes covered with paper, other times half naked—someone had already stolen pieces of their clothing. At first I could not look at them. I would get off the sidewalk in order to pass them as far away as I could. As days passed everyone grew used to the sight, but I couldn't. It seemed that those frozen bodies always had their eyes open and nobody would close them enough to shut them. . . . There was no such place as a morgue. Most of these corpses were taken by the garbage men—the streets had to be kept clean. (Berg, 1945)

Children suffering from extreme hunger and malnutrition became so thin their bones stuck out and their skin became dry and yellow in color. During the bitterly cold Polish winters, the Nazis did not allow ghetto dwellers coal or other fuel, and they confiscated any warm coats. Freezing children wore rags and torn clothing. People outside the wall heard the cries of hungry, cold infants and children.

Young people showed great courage and resilience. They smuggled in food to keep their families and others alive. One Jewish survivor of the ghetto later described the bravery of child smugglers:

> Once when I was walking along the wall, I came across a "smuggling operation" being carried out by children. The actual operation seemed to be over. There was only one thing left to do. The little Jewish boy on the other side of the wall had to slip back inside the ghetto through his hole, bringing with him the last piece of booty. Half the little boy was already visible when he began to cry out. At the same time, abuse in German could be heard from the Aryan side. I hurried to help the child, meaning to pull him quickly through the hole. Un-

happily, the boy's hips stuck fast in the gap in the wall. Using both hands, I tried with all my might to pull him through. He continued to scream dreadfully. I could hear the police on the other side beating him savagely. . . . When I finally succeeded in pulling the boy through the hole, he was already dying.

Resistance efforts also flourished in ghettos despite German military might and the difficulty of obtaining weapons. It is not clear exactly how many young people took part in ghetto fighting organizations, but historians have guessed that at least 2,000 youths actively fought, most of them teenagers. Of the 160,000 people who were trapped in the Lodz ghetto, about 1,000 survived the war, but few were young people. Most of the youths who survived were teenagers when they were taken from the ghetto to concentration camps. One of them was Ben Edelbaum, who was 15 years old in 1945. At Lodz, he was assigned to direct a work group of 12 boys in their early teens. Their job was to cut up fur coats, most of which had been stolen from Jews in occupied Europe, and make them into new coats for German soldiers fighting on the Russian front. As Edelbaum recalled, "We worked ten hours a day. We had nothing to eat except a bowl of hot broth and coffee. But we boys were very proud of the fact that we were doing grown-up work. It ensured our right to live" (Edelbaum, 1981).

At one point, the boys heard the Nazis planned to raid the ghetto and remove every remaining child. Edelbaum's group hoped to persuade the Germans they were too valuable to lose. They started making a beautiful Persian lamb coat for a German officer's wife, sewing the delicate skins after they finished their long regular workday. The coat was done in time for the woman's birthday, and the boys wrapped it up, attaching tags bearing their names, addresses, and ages. Ben Edelbaum obtained a special pass to deliver the coat to the Gestapo. A week later, the boys received a letter from the officer's wife, thanking each by name. She suggested that their group be sent on a week-long holiday

where they had fresh food, meat, and bread; slept on clean beds; and did not have to work. The comfort was short lived. Edelbaum was eventually sent to Auschwitz where he suffered terribly. At war's end, he weighed only 60 pounds. Of his whole family, only he and one sister survived.

Between 1942 and 1944, most ghettos were emptied and the surviving Jews were sent to camps. About 2 million people were removed during this time. By the summer of 1944, Jewish ghettos in Hungary were among the few remaining. Those would soon also be emptied as the Nazis made a massive effort to deport Hungarian Jews to death camps. *See also* ANIELEWICZ, MORDECHAI; BAUM, FROIM; BURZMINSKI, STEFANIA PODGORSKA; DEPORTATIONS; EDUCATION; FORCED LABOR (WORLD WAR II); HART, KITTY FELIX; HEHALUTZ; HOLOCAUST; HUNGARY (WORLD WAR II); JEWISH FIGHTERS ORGANIZATION (JFO); KORCZAK, JANUSZ; POLAND (WORLD WAR II); ROUND-UPS; WALLENBERG, RAOUL; WARSAW GHETTO; WORLD WAR II.

Further Reading: Stanislaw Adler, *In the Warsaw Ghetto* (1982); Reuben Ainzstein, *Jewish Resistance in Nazi Occupied Eastern Europe* (1974); Margaret Baldwin, *The Boys Who Saved the Children* (1991); Mary Berg, *Warsaw Ghetto Diary* (1945); Ben Edelbaum, *Growing Up in the Holocaust* (1980); Barbara Rogasky, *Smoke and Ashes* (1988); Gertrude Schneider, *Journey Into Terror* (1979); Gail B. Stewart, *Life in the Warsaw Ghetto* (1992); Liliana Zuker-Bujanowski, *Liliana's Journal* (1980).

Gies, Miep (1909–) and Gies, Jan (1906–1993)

Miep Gies and her husband Jan (given the pseudonym "Henk" in Anne Frank's diary) are two of the best-known rescuers of Jews during the Holocaust. Miep Gies, a native of Austria, first met the Frank family—Otto and Edith and their daughters Margot and Anne—in 1933 after she was hired at Travies and Company, the food products business Otto Frank operated in Amsterdam. They became friends and the Franks gave a wedding luncheon for Miep and Jan when they were married in 1941.

The Nazis invaded Holland in May 1940 and began to persecute Jews. Miep Gies told

Otto Frank that she would help his family if they had to go into hiding to escape the Nazis. The family went "underground" in 1942 after Margot was ordered to report for deportation to a German labor camp. They moved into secret rooms in the annex of the building where Frank's business was located, and where they had stored non-perishable food and other supplies.

Gies and her co-workers ran the business while they cared for those in hiding. Jan Gies used his position in the Amsterdam welfare department to help the Dutch resistance. He obtained extra food ration coupons for the Franks and other Jews and resistance workers. Among the other people who relied on the Gieses for help were two Jewish children whose parents had been arrested and a young man whom the Nazis wanted to arrest. The Gieses kept the children in their apartment, then found a safe house for them.

After the Franks went into hiding, four others, including a teenage boy, joined them. Miep Gies worked hard to keep them safe, healthy, and fed, a big challenge under the Germans' strict rationing system. To avoid suspicion, she went to different shops and bought a limited amount of food each trip. To encourage the people in the annex, Gies visited every day and brought books and magazines. She supplied Anne with paper for the diary she had started at age 13. Jan Gies also visited each afternoon.

As 1944 began, Nazi raids and arrests increased. Gies later said, "Daily, people in hiding were being captured. There were raids and betrayals. The price for turning in a Jew or any person in hiding was going up all the time" (Gies, 1987). On August 4, 1944, an armed policeman arrived at the office and ordered Gies and three other employees to stay put. The man who was managing the company in Otto Frank's absence was pulled into an office and interrogated. When Jan Gies came to meet his wife for lunch, Miep stopped him at the door and gave him a bag containing the illegal ration cards and papers she kept in her desk, saying quietly, "It's wrong here." Jan Gies hurried away but watched anxiously from a street corner to see what was happening.

Soon, Miep and her co-workers faced the interrogator, who seized the keys that fit the door of the hiding place. Shocked and grief-stricken, she heard her friends being led downstairs and onto the street. After they left, she and two co-workers entered the ransacked annex and rescued Anne's diary and other writings from the floor. Gies hid them, hoping to return them to Anne. The next day, Gies boldly entered Nazi headquarters and offered money for the Franks' release, but the officials refused.

When the war ended, only Otto Frank returned. He moved in with Jan and Miep Gies and remained there several years. In time, a letter notified Otto Frank that Anne and Margot had died of typhus at the Nazi camp, Bergen-Belsen. Gies gave Frank the diary she had saved, saying, "Here is your daughter Anne's legacy to you" (Gies, 1987). Anne Frank's diary became famous, but the Gieses shunned publicity. Finally, Miep Gies was persuaded to write her memoirs, which were published in 1987.

In 1993, Jan Gies died at age 87. The story of Jan and Miep Gies inspired a made-for-television movie, as well as a documentary that won an Academy Award in 1996. *See also* FRANK, ANNE; HOLLAND (WORLD WAR II); RIGHTEOUS GENTILES.

Further Reading: Miep Gies, *Anne Frank Remembered* (1987); "Jan Gies Dies at 87: Helped Anne Frank Hide in Amsterdam," *The New York Times,* January 28, 1993.

Goldszmidt, Henryk. *See* KORCZAK, JANUSZ

Graebe, Hermann

Hermann Graebe, a German construction engineer, rescued Jewish adults and children from the Nazis during World War II. In October 1942, Graebe was in Poland where he had been assigned to oversee the building of a German railroad facility. Graebe later testified under oath about the massacre he had witnessed at that time in Dubno. Armed German troops forced between 800 to 1,000 unarmed civilians ranging from infants to the elderly to undress, then step into a pit where they were shot to death. Graebe called it "the cruelest thing I have ever seen in my life . . . I think I shall carry that scene directly to my grave. . . . I kept saying to myself, 'Something has to be done.'" He was particularly haunted by images of a baby in the arms of its grandmother and a teenage girl as they were led, helplessly, to their deaths. Graebe decided to use his position to save lives. He hired Jewish workers for construction projects, and, as the word spread, Jews in hiding came to him for help. He eventually rescued more than 300 people in Poland, Germany, and the Ukraine.

After the war, Graebe's eyewitness testimony helped convict Nazi war criminals. He was the only German to testify on behalf of the prosecution at the Nuremberg war crimes trials held before an international panel of judges after the war. His written testimony was read at the 1961 trial of Adolf Eichmann, a major Nazi policy-maker during the Holocaust. Eichmann, who arranged for the deportations of hundreds of thousands of children and adults to deaths camps, was convicted in Israel for crimes against humanity. *See also* EINSATZGRUPPEN; FORCED LABOR (WORLD WAR II); GENOCIDE; HOLOCAUST; MASSACRES; RIGHTEOUS GENTILES.

Further Reading: Eve Fogelman, *Conscience and Courage* (1994); Milton Meltzer, *Rescuers: How Gentiles Saved Jews During the Holocaust* (1988); Carol Rittner and Sondra Meyers, *The Courage to Care* (1986).

Great Britain (World War II)

During World War II, Great Britain was one of the leaders of the Allied Nations fighting against the Axis powers—Germany, Japan, and Italy. Britain declared war on Germany in September 1939 after German troops invaded Poland, Britain's ally.

The war changed everyday life in many ways. Sea travel was restricted because German submarines had torpedoed ships bearing civilians. German blockades prevented cargo ships from bringing goods to Britain, so children went without certain foods, clothing, and other items. Some children wore wooden shoes when no leather shoes were available. Toys, new books, and furniture also were scarce.

After the United States entered the war in December 1941, packages from the U.S. occasionally brought children sweets and other welcome items. American soldiers and nurses stationed in England gave children chewing gum, candy, or food. They sponsored parties and holiday celebrations for young people near their bases. For some English children, this was the first time they had met Americans.

Along with clothing, gasoline, steel, rubber, coal, and certain other materials, food was rationed. The government issued ration coupons that people used to buy specified amounts of various foods, such as meat, butter, sugar, and produce. Some foods, such as bananas, were unavailable during the war. To ease food shortages, children helped their parents plant and harvest gardens. English victory gardens contained potatoes, carrots, tomatoes, radishes, and other vegetables. Schools also organized gardens, which were tended chiefly by schoolchildren, and the food was used for school lunches. Tens of thousands of city children joined harvest camps and worked on farms in the summer to raise more crops.

At age 16, all young people in Britain were required to register for essential war work. People of all ages and from every social and economic class took part. They worked in hospitals, factories, schools, civil defense, and other places. Boy Scouts and Girl Guides performed many tasks, including helping to evacuate children out of London and other endangered cities during the bombings. Older boys joined the Air Training Corps, the Army Cadets, and the Sea Cadets, groups that provided training the boys could use when they joined the military.

The largest evacuations of children during World War II took place in Great Britain. In 1939, about 827,000 unaccompanied children and 524,000 mothers with preschool children left English cities as part of the mass evacuations organized by the government. Other children were sent to rural England or abroad privately, by their families. About 80 percent of the children in the government program returned home early in 1940. Another evacuation took place during the Blitz that began in September 1940. In mid-1944, parents sent their children to Canada or the United States to escape German V-1 and V-2 rockets. Although more than 30,000 names were on a list of children whose parents wanted to send them to a safer place, sea travel was so perilous that only about 2,000 went to American foster homes as part of a program organized by the American Committee for the Evacuation of Children. In 1940, 37 children died while crossing the Atlantic when a German torpedo struck the *Arandara* en route to Canada.

See also AIR RAIDS; BLACKOUTS; BLITZ, LONDON; BOMBINGS (WORLD WAR II); CHILDREN'S TRANSPORTS (*KINDERTRANSPORTS*); CIVIL DEFENSE; CLOTHING SHORTAGES; COLLECTION CENTER DRIVES; DEFENSE PLANTS; EDUCATION; ELIZABETH II; EVACUATIONS; FOOD; GAS MASKS; HOLIDAYS; VICTORY GARDENS; VOLUNTEERS; WORLD WAR II.

Further Reading: Tom Harrison, *Living Through the Blitz* (1976); Norman Longmate, *How We Lived Then* (1971); Robert Westall, *Children of the Blitz* (1985).

Greece (World War II)

During World War II, German troops invaded Greece in April 1941 and occupied the country for four years. A bloody civil war followed the occupation, leading to more destruction and disorder throughout the late 1940s. Thousands of children lost one or more parents. In some cases, whole families were killed.

Greece was stripped of valuable resources, including food, resin, cotton, and leather. More than 40,000 Greeks, many of them children, starved to death during the first year of German occupation. They received inadequate rations of grain and other foodstuffs. Children lined up at soup kitchens to receive food, usually watery soup without much protein or fat. The supplies were so small that only about 25 percent of those who needed food could receive it from these places. People lived day by day on meager amounts of rice, sugar, and meat. Famine caused deaths and

malnutrition among children during and after the wars.

People living on farms were better able to find food than residents of Athens and other cities, especially the poor, who could not afford to buy food on the black market, where the rich could obtain food and other goods at inflated prices. Many women gave their food rations to their children. Children begged on the streets and searched trash cans for anything edible, including olive pits. They also gathered weeds and wild grass to eat.

Colds, flu, tuberculosis, and dysentery spread. People developed skin diseases due to vitamin deficiency, as well as anemia and stomach and intestinal disorders. Children's teeth softened and decayed from a lack of minerals and dental care. They also suffered emotional trauma from living in fear and deprivation.

Greek Jews and entire Jewish families were devastated during the Holocaust, and thousands died at the hands of the Nazis. Deportations of Greek Jews began late in 1942. Jews from the Salonika region were ordered into freight cars and told they were being sent to Poland to help found a new Jewish state. However, people became suspicious when they saw the brutal treatment of these deportees. They observed that elderly, sick, disabled, and mentally ill people were being sent away, too. The Red Cross was not able to locate any of these people after they were sent to Poland, where they died in Nazi concentration camps.

Giorgios Ioannou, a Greek novelist, later wrote about what his family witnessed in Salonika.

> Late one night, we heard sobbing in the kitchen. My father had returned. . . . He had been asked to drive a train with Jews right into Serbia and had seen terrible things with his own eyes. The Jews had already begun to die. The Germans stopped the train at a quiet spot—they had their plan. From inside, the Jews shouted and beat the wooden sides. Packed in as they were, they could not breathe and they had no water. The Germans, guns in hand, began opening the wagons, not however for the benefit of the Jews, but to steal their hidden jewelry, watches and coins. There

was much crying. From one wagon they threw out a young boy dead, and laid him—without of course burying him—in the ditch alongside the tracks. It seems he looked like my brother. (Mazower, 1993)

Nearly 49,000 Jews from northern Greece were taken to the death camp at Auschwitz-Birkenau during 1943. More than 37,000, including thousands of children, were killed at once. By 1947, fewer than 2,000 Jews could be found in Salonika. Eighty-nine percent of the Jews of Greece perished during the war. Among the children who survived the Holocaust in Greece was Paulette Pomeranz, who was seven years old in 1941. Pomeranz found refuge with a Greek family, who, aided by local villagers, saw that she had enough food and planned an escape route she could use in case of Nazi raids. Food was so scarce that people sometimes had only raisins to eat. The Nazis offered people rewards for turning in Jews, and Pomeranz feared somebody would become desperate enough to betray her, but this did not happen. Other Jews also received help from concerned non-Jewish Greeks, including public officials, religious leaders, artists, and others. As of 1997, 200 Greeks had been honored as Righteous Gentiles by Yad Vashem in Israel.

As the war continued, many mothers left home to take jobs to support their families. Fathers and older brothers had gone to the military or been forced to labor for the Germans. Forced labor was compulsory for Greek boys as of age 16. Families faced many problems. Mark Mazower (1993) described a young girl named Nausikaa who lived in a village near Kalamat. The Nazis burned her home. Her father was killed by the Germans in 1944, and her mother and older sister were imprisoned. She and another sister fled to Athens where they were homeless.

Many young people joined the army or were drafted into the service. Youths also took part in the anti-Nazi resistance. A resistance organization called EAM was involved with a group called the "Children's Front." When Athens was liberated on October 12, 1944, children from this group joined jubilant fellow Greeks for a victory parade.

When the Allies arrived in Greece after the war, they found a stricken people. Schools had been burned, and children and teachers were meeting outdoors, using rocks for desks. Thousands of homes had been destroyed; others were in ruins. Barefoot children in rags roamed the streets. Relief workers found gangs of orphans living on the streets. These homeless youth looked for odd jobs to buy food, one day at a time. Children played war games, and other aggressive activities were common among those who had grown up witnessing violence and death. These social and economic problems helped to foster political unrest that led to a civil war between Greek nationalists and communist revolutionaries in the late 1940s. *See also* GAGE, NICHOLAS; HOLOCAUST; KOMENO MASSACRE.

Further Reading: M.R.D. Foot, *Resistance* (1977); Mark Mazower, *Inside Hitler's Greece* (1993); Maxine B. Rosenberg, *Hiding to Survive* (1994).

Greece, Civil War. *See* GAGE, NICHOLAS

Grynszpan, Herschel (1921–)

In 1938, on the eve of World War II, Herschel Grynszpan was a 17-year-old German-Jewish refugee living with his uncle in Paris. In October, his family in Germany and thousands of other Polish-born Jews or those with Polish nationality were forced to leave behind their homes and possessions. They were taken from Germany to the Polish border and ordered at gunpoint to cross to the Polish side.

The exiles stayed in filthy stables, pigsties, and other makeshift shelters while the Polish government decided their fate. Eight thousand men, women, and children were trapped in the village of Zbaszyn; about 9,000 more waited in other towns without food.

Herschel Grynszpan was distraught after receiving a postcard from his sister, Berta, describing their ordeal. On November 7, 1938, he entered the German Embassy in Paris, where he encountered a minor official named Ernst Vom Rath. Grynszpan shot Vom Rath, saying it was "in the name of twelve thousand persecuted Jews" (Thalman and Feinermann, 1974). Grynszpan told police the Nazis had persecuted him and his family without cause. "Being a Jew is not a crime," he said. "I am not a dog. I have a right to live and the Jewish people have a right to exist on this earth" (Thalmann and Feinermann, 1974).

Vom Rath died two days later. German newspapers headlined the shooting and called it part of a worldwide Jewish conspiracy to murder Germans. Nazi officials used the shooting to rally public support for a violent attack on Jews that they had been planning for months. This attack took place on November 9-10, 1938, and became known as *Kristallnacht*—"the night of broken glass."

Sympathizers sent letters, telegrams, and money for Grynszpan's defense. A prominent non-Jewish, anti-Fascist attorney, Vincent de Moro-Giaferri, defended the teenager during his trial in France. Grynszpan was sentenced to prison rather than the death penalty. *See also* HOLOCAUST; *KRISTALLNACHT*.

Further Reading: Rosalind Herzfeld, "Recollections of Rosalind Herzfeld," *Jewish Chronicle*, September 28, 1979, p. 80; Arnold Rubin, *The Evil Men Do: The Story of the Nazis* (1977); Rita Thalmann and Emmanuel Feinermann, *Crystal Night* (1974).

Guatemala

Beginning in the late 1950s, a civil war raged in the Central American nation of Guatemala. That war would last for 36 years, reaching the highest level of violence during the 1980s, and some fighting continued into the 1990s. People of all ages, most of them indigenous people of Mayan descent, suffered and died, and Mayans were the victims of genocide. More than 200,000 were killed and between 40,000 and 80,000 people disappeared, presumed dead. About one million Guatemalans were widowed, orphaned, or displaced. More than 400 villages in the Ixil area were destroyed, forcing families to move, often far from their farmland. Many children and young adults were left homeless, and many lived on city streets where they resorted to begging or crime to survive.

To help street children in Guatemala City, a British organization called Toybox began operating outreach programs there in 1993. Toybox set up a training center and hostel that provides meals, showers, clean clothing,

and educational programs, and it established boys' and girls' homes on the outskirts of the city. Outreach teams go out at night to meet children and let them know they can find help at these facilities.

Hunger became widespread when entire villages were wiped out as a result of the "scorched earth" policy of government troops fighting leftist revolutionary groups. Soldiers burned buildings and crops, as well as crop-producing land. They arrested and executed people without due process of law. People who supported the labor movement or the plight of the poor were labeled as subversives. Eyewitnesses gave descriptions of brutal genocidal assaults on Mayan villages; for instance, in Huehuetenango, 352 men, women, and children were slaughtered by soldiers on July 17, 1982. Hundreds of other civilians were murdered that same day in San Francisco de Nenton. Investigations have uncovered the remains of massacred children in burial sites. One investigator said, "How can a man cut a child's throat? Must these things go on forever?" (Browne, 1999).

Male and female soldiers on both sides often joined the military when they were under age 21. Some joined the army in their teens and fought for years. Francisco Aguilar, for example, was a 17-year-old farmer when he joined the guerilla forces. He remained in the military for 18 years. Youths under 18 served in the army, civilian defense patrols, and guerilla units run by the National Revolutionary United Front (URNG). Often, such conscription was forced. Boys as young as 13 and 14 were taken to military encampments or guerilla hideouts.

Both the guerillas and national army soldiers forced young Mayan men to join them. The government forces used a tactic called "the grab." They encircled and closed off the roads to a village while sending troops inside. Soldiers invaded homes and took out young men between 15 and 21. To escape this fate, some young men joined guerilla bands.

The national army also organized youths age 13 and older into village civil guard units. Armed with sticks and machetes, they were expected to prevent armed invaders from taking food or other supplies. Luis Garcia, who was 15 in 1978, later recalled how guerillas terrorized his village, killing his father and demanding food and money from the poor citizens: "After that the guerillas came back to our house again, and this time they pointed a gun at me and stuck a knife in my throat and said they would kill me if I didn't join them." Garcia managed to escape to Mexico, and then fled to Florida to live with relatives who had escaped from Guatemala. At least 150,000 people fled from Guatemala to seek sanctuary elsewhere, including the United States. Thousands fled to Mexico where they lived in refugee camps, and some children died there from hunger and disease.

Children who remained in Guatemala lost access to education because priests and nuns were arrested and killed for running schools or informing people about their legal rights. Sometimes, whole villages were punished for supporting anti-government activities, and whole groups of people were executed. Children and adults were herded into local churches, which were then burned. Bodies of slain teachers and students were found in ditches.

Rural children suffered the most: Only about 50 percent of rural children ages 6 to 12 were attending school in 1996 and almost no teenagers. In cities, about 80 percent of children ages 6 to 12 attended school, and 25 percent of the children ages 13 to 17 were in school. Teenagers had also witnessed first-hand the worst years of the war, including killings, and had suffered displacement, persecution, and deprivation.

According to *Children and War*, a publication of Save the Children, "Today's Ixil teenagers remember what it was like to run from burning villages, watch soldiers shoot their families, hide out in inaccessible mountain areas for years, with little food and no shelter or school."

During and after the war, teenagers often bore heavy burdens and worked at low-paying jobs to help support their families. Boys did heavy farmwork. As of 1981, many youth were also forced to serve in the Civilian Defense Patrol units the government set up against the guerillas. Those who refused to serve in these patrols were subject to imprisonment and even death.

In the early 1990s, a committee of concerned Mayans proposed that youths be permitted to do national service to aid the country's economic, social, and cultural development rather than be forced to serve in the Civilian Defense Patrols. They hoped that these long-suffering young people would have the opportunity to rebuild their communities. The war officially ended in 1996. *See also* EL SALVADOR; SAVE THE CHILDREN

Further Reading: John M. Broder, "Clinton Offers His Apologies to Guatemala," *The New York Times* March 11, 1999, pp. A1, A10; Malcolm W. Browne, "Buried on a Hillside, Clues to Terror," *The New York Times* February 23, 1999, pp. F1, F4; Brook Larner, "Peasants Chafe at Forced Service," *The Christian Science Monitor*, January 15–21, 1989; Geoffrey Mohan, "After Guatemala's War, Difficulty of Disarming," *Newsday*, April 13, 1997, p. A08; *Child Soldiers*, report from a seminar by Radda Barnen and the Swedish Red Cross (1994); Save the Children, *Children and War* (1996); Lawana Hooper Trout, *The Maya* (1991).

Guernica

In 1937, during the Spanish Civil War (1936-1939), the town of Guernica (Guernica y Luno) in Vizcaya Province was held by Loyalist forces fighting against the fascist troops led by General Francisco Franco and supported by Nazi Germany. For three hours on April 26, 1937, German planes bombed this Basque city, causing death and destruction and killing children and young adult civilians.

Famed Spanish artist Pablo Picasso was saddened by photographs of the devastation in Guernica that appeared in the French press. He decided to pay tribute to the victims by painting a 26-foot-long mural. Picasso's *Guernica* took several weeks to complete and was exhibited in the Spanish Pavilion at the Paris World's Fair, which opened in June 1937. This abstract work of art shows the agonized faces of men, women, and children during the bombing of their town. Exhibited around the world, Picasso's *Guernica* has become a poignant symbol of the impact of war on civilians. Picasso also completed several more paintings and sketches of this tragedy.

Picasso, who lived in France during most of World War II, bitterly resented the Nazis and refused special favors they offered him because of his fame. When German officers visited Picasso's studio, the artist often handed them souvenir photographs of *Guernica*. On at least one occasion, an officer asked, "Did you do this?" and Picasso replied, "No, you did" (Rubin, 1980). *See also* SPANISH CIVIL WAR.

Further Reading: William Rubin, ed., *Pablo Picasso, A Retrospective* (1980).

Gulf War. *See* PERSIAN GULF WAR

Gulf War Syndrome

Gulf War Syndrome refers to the physical and mental health problems that have arisen since 1991 among Persian Gulf War veterans and their children. Veterans have complained of rashes, fatigue, vision problems, reduced immunity, headaches, muscle pains, abdominal pain, tumors, diarrhea, irregular body temperatures, and cancer. As a group, veterans suffered from higher-than-normal rates of the nerve-destroying condition known as Lou Gehrig's Disease (amyotrophic lateral sclerosis). By 1997, more than 70,000 Gulf War veterans and their dependents had claimed they had health problems related to service in the Gulf. Doctors, nurses, immunologists, and toxicologists have confirmed their claims.

Gulf veterans allege that children conceived after their service in the Gulf suffered from higher rates of birth defects and physical and mental disabilities and were more likely to be miscarried or stillborn than was true of the general population. In cases where veterans had children before and after serving in the Gulf, they asserted that those born before the war did not suffer from these problems.

The cause of Gulf War Syndrome has been the subject of much debate. Some analysts suspected chemical exposure. Support for this theory came from Czech chemical specialists located about 25 miles from the Iraqi border. They said their chemical detectors had gone off on January 19, 1991, after Allied warplanes bombed Iraq for the third day. These detectors showed the presence of sarin, an invisible nerve gas. Sarin can cause death within minutes.

Besides chemical weapons exposure, researchers have considered other causes: microorganisms caused by insect bites; toxic combinations of vaccines and other injections troops received before leaving for the Gulf; toxins from the oil-well fires set by Iraqi troops; and infectious agents, such as mycoplasmas. Early in 1997, Dr. Edward Hyman suggested that the veterans might be suffering from a serious bacterial infection rather than the effects of chemical exposure. Hyman had treated several veterans and their wives with antibiotics. Congress allocated $3 million for research into this possibility. Other researchers suggested there might be more than one cause, perhaps a combination of vaccinations and toxic exposure leading to immune system dysfunction.

In 1995, a presidential commission was appointed to study Gulf War illnesses and the impact on veterans, their children, and other family members. Meanwhile, veterans created the Gulf War Research Foundation to study these problems. Veterans have filed claims with the government for compensation and health care benefits for themselves and their affected children. In 1996, Congress looked at ways the government could help victims. However, veterans continue to assert that their claims are not receiving fair consideration and that the government has failed to fully investigate and explain their health problems. As of 1999, the causes of Gulf War Syndrome were still unclear. *See also* CHEMICAL WARFARE; PERSIAN GULF WAR.

Further Reading: Philip Hilts, "Researchers Say Chemicals May Have Led to War Illness," *The New York Times*, April 17, 1996, p. A17; Kenneth Millers, "The Tiny Victims of Desert Storm," *Life*, November 1995, pp. 46-52; Sarah Richardson, "Chemicals at War," *Discover*, January 1996, p. 19; Paul M. Rodriguez, "Sickness and Society," *Insight*, August 25, 1997, pp. 7–13; Kenneth Timmerman, "The Iraq Papers," *The New Republic*, January 29, 1996, p. 12+.

Gypsies. *See* ROMANI (GYPSIES)

H

Haiti. *See* REFUGEES

Hamas. *See* INTIFADA

Handicapped. *See* COMMITTEE OF RESPONSIBILITY (COR); EUTHANASIA; LAND MINES; VIETNAM WAR

Hanoi Peace Center. *See* AGENT ORANGE

Hart, Kitty Felix (1927–)

Kitty Felix Hart, a teenage survivor of the Holocaust, later described her ordeal in her memoir *Return to Auschwitz* (1971). A native of Bielsko, Poland, which lies near the Czech border, she was the daughter of a lawyer/businessman father and an English teacher mother. Although she was Jewish, Felix attended the Notre Dame Convent School along with Catholic and Protestant students. She excelled in academics and in swimming and other sports.

In 1939, when Felix was 12 and her brother Robert 17, Nazi Germany invaded Poland. Her father decided the family would be safer in central Poland so they moved to Lublin where they soon endured Nazi persecution and brutality. She was beaten one day for failing to move from the sidewalk to the gutter to make way for a German soldier.

Another time, a male friend of hers was shot for the same offense.

New laws banned Jews from attending school or working in certain trades and professions. Jews were forced to turn over money, furniture, clothes—eventually everything they owned—and move into the Lublin Ghetto. She joined other youths who smuggled food into the ghetto for the trapped, hungry people. She was caught several times and beaten. The family escaped from the ghetto and lived for a year on the estate of a Polish count. They had to move more than once to avoid Nazi round-ups. A priest helped the family obtain false documents so they could join a group of non-Jewish Poles who were shipped to Germany to do forced labor.

In 1942, when she was 15, Felix was captured by the Nazis and deported with her mother to Auschwitz, the notorious death camp in Poland. Despite many privations and narrow escapes, both women managed to survive. After the war, they went to a displaced persons' camp in Germany, then emigrated to Birmingham, England, where Felix's mother had relatives. She studied nursing, then radiography. She married and became the mother of two sons.

In *Return to Auschwitz*, Hart recounted her family's long struggle during the war and her memories of Auschwitz, including "the crack of whips, the screams, the dogs, [and] smelling the burning flesh." A documentary based on Hart's book was first shown on British television in 1978. *See also* AUSCHWITZ-BIRKENAU; DEATH CAMPS (WORLD WAR II); DEPORTATIONS; DISPLACED PERSONS (DPS) (WORLD WAR II); FORCED LABOR (WORLD WAR II); GHETTOS (WORLD WAR II); HOLOCAUST; POLAND (WORLD WAR II).

Further Reading: Kitty Felix Hart, *Return to Auschwitz* (1971).

Hartz, Ruth Kapp (1936-)

As a child, Ruth Kapp lived in France during World War II. Her family was Jewish and had fled from Germany after the Nazis rose to power in 1933 and began persecuting Jews. The Kapps found themselves on the run again in 1940 after the Nazis invaded and occupied France. During the war, the family lived in hiding, and Ruth was told to use a false, typically French name, "Renee," to hide her Jewish identity. All three Kapps owned fake identification cards. They fled from Paris to the south of France when the Nazis took control in the north. In Toulouse, they were sheltered by Catholic and Protestant villagers and surrounded by other French people who hid Jews and aided the resistance.

For several months during 1943, Kapp lived in a convent orphanage at Soreze. Knowing that some Catholic convents hid Jewish children, Nazis sometimes raided these institutions. One day, Ruth was in the infirmary receiving first aid when the nun in charge glanced out the window and cried, "Nazis!" She sent Ruth and another girl back to their classrooms. Kapp later recalled what happened next.

> As we reached the last steps, we heard male voices—German—issuing from the room on the right, which I was now certain was the Mother Superior's office. Perhaps the Nazis have come for Emmy, Jean-Claude, and me, I thought. Now everyone will know that I am Jewish. Should I try to run away? (Cretzmeyer, 1994)

Both girls stood listening silently as the German argued with Mother Superior, who persuaded him that the orphanage held only French children whose parents had died in the war. The officer finally left.

At times, when Nazis searched the convent, Kapp and the other Jewish children hid in a secret room. After five months, Kapp returned to her parents' hiding place above a tobacco shop in Arthes where they lived under the protection of a Catholic couple named Fedou. In this way, the Kapps survived the war.

Ruth Kapp Hartz later collaborated with author Stacy Cretzmeyer (1994) to produce a detailed account of her life in hiding and a description of the courageous people who risked their lives to save her family and other children in occupied France. *See also* FRANCE (WORLD WAR II); HIDDEN CHILDREN; HOLOCAUST; RIGHTEOUS GENTILES.

Further Reading: Stacy Cretzmeyer, *Your Name Is Renee* (1994).

Health Holidays. *See* HUNGER/MALNUTRITION

Heck, Alfons. *See* D-DAY; GERMANY (WORLD WAR II); HITLER YOUTH

Hehalutz

The Jewish resistance group Hehalutz developed in Bialystok, Poland, where Jews were being persecuted and killed by the Nazis during World War II. The first members of Hehalutz were part of a Zionist youth group headed by Mordecai Tenenbaum, who was 20 years old in 1939. Members of Hehalutz faced crucial decisions in 1941, when German killing squads called *Einsatzgruppen* were perpetrating mass murders of unarmed Jewish men, women, and children in their region. They debated whether they should try to escape to the forests, kill some of their tormentors, or organize more resistance activities. In the end, they decided their duty was to stay with the people in the Bialystok Ghetto and fight any way they could.

The ghetto was targeted for destruction in July 1943, when the Germans arrived with tanks, machine guns, and armored cars. A revolt began on August 15, when the Germans ordered that the remaining 40,000 people in the ghetto be deported to death camps. The ghetto fighters had few weapons and were crushed by German troops heavily armed with artillery and tanks. The Nazis killed virtually every Jew living in Bialystok, including the courageous youths of Hehalutz. Only a few managed to flee into the woods where they joined partisan units. *See also* HOLOCAUST; RESISTANCE MOVEMENTS (WORLD WAR II).

Further Reading: *Not Like Sheep to the Slaughter*, Ergo Home Video, 1991; Yuri Suhl, ed., *They Fought Back* (1975); Leni Yahil, *The Holocaust 1932-1945* (1990).

Hepburn, Audrey (1929–1993)

As a teenager in Holland during World War II, Audrey Hepburn worked with the anti-Nazi resistance. Later, she became an acclaimed actress and served as a special ambassador for the United Nations Children's Fund (UNICEF). The daughter of a British father and a Dutch mother, Hepburn was 10 when World War II broke out. She and her mother moved to a family estate in Arnhem after Great Britain entered the war. Holland seemed like a safe haven because it was neutral, but Germany invaded

Audrey Hepburn holds a child during her 1988 tour of Ethiopia as a UNICEF goodwill ambassador. *John Is, AP/Wide World Photos.*

the country in May 1940. At that time, Hepburn was a serious ballet student at the Arnhem Conservatory of Music.

Like many other young people, she experienced the problems and grief that accompanied occupation. Her education was often disrupted, and the lack of adequate nourishment left her thin and anemic, with lasting damage to her metabolism. The family's home was taken over by Nazis, so she and her mother moved to a small apartment. One of her half-brothers had fought with Dutch troops against the German invasion and had to go into hiding. In 1942, one of her uncles was executed for working with the Dutch resistance, and the next year, her other half-brother was taken to Germany for forced labor.

Hepburn and her classmates at the Conservatory performed in secret fund-raisers to aid the resistance, at which times the windows of the theater were covered with thick black curtains. She later said, "We danced to scratchy old recordings of highlights from *Swan Lake, The Nutcracker*, and *Giselle*, which has always been my favorite among the classical ballets" (Vermilye, 1995). At age 15, she sometimes carried messages and forged documents and ration cards for the resistance. Schoolbags provided a convenient place for young people to hide these papers. Sometimes, Hepburn secreted them in the lining of her ballet shoes.

After September 1944, when the Dutch resistance played a large role in the Allied offensive called Operation Market Garden, the Germans behaved even more harshly toward Dutch citizens. They destroyed much of Arnhem, including the Conservatory, and gave the people 24 hours to leave the city. Hepburn and her mother walked five miles to reach her grandfather's home in Velp. Along the way, they saw suffering refugees, some carrying dead relatives. Hepburn later recalled that babies were born on the side of the road and hundreds of people collapsed from hunger and exhaustion.

Commenting on those years, Hepburn told an interviewer that the war had taught her many lessons and made her "a realist."

She said, "I came out of the war thankful to be alive, aware that human relationships are the most important thing of all, far more than wealth, food, luxury, careers, or anything you can mention" (Woodward, 1984). Her sixteenth birthday on May 4, 1945, coincided with the liberation of western Holland by Canadian troops. After the war, the family was destitute. Hepburn and her mother moved to England where she resumed her dance training with the help of relatives. Hepburn's talent soon brought her roles onstage in England and the United States. She began her movie career in 1948 and went on to star in more than 30 films. In 1954, she won an Academy Award for her performance in *Roman Holiday.*

During the 1960s, Hepburn made fewer films and devoted herself to motherhood. However, in 1970, she readily agreed to film a documentary about UNICEF called "A World of Love," which aired in December. Hepburn said that she felt a debt of gratitude to UNICEF and other relief organizations, such as CARE, that had saved her and other children from hunger at the end of World War II.

In 1988, she assumed a prominent role for UNICEF as their goodwill ambassador. For the next four years, she visited war-torn countries, including El Salvador, Somalia, Vietnam, Ethiopia, and the Sudan, and acted as a spokesperson for children in Third World countries. Through speeches, public appearances, and fund-raisers, Hepburn helped increase public awareness of their needs. Although she had avoided interviews during her film career, Hepburn willingly granted them on behalf of UNICEF and said she was "glad I've got a name because I'm using it for all it's worth" (Vermilye, 1995).

During a 1992 trip to Somalia, Hepburn appeared ill. Although she was suffering from severe abdominal pains, she made a long trip to a refugee camp where hundreds of Somalian children had died. Hepburn was diagnosed with cancer shortly after she returned home. While recuperating from surgery, she received the Presidential Medal of Freedom, the highest civilian honor in the United States,

for her humanitarian work with UNICEF. In January 1993, Audrey Hepburn died at her home in rural Switzerland. UNICEF director James Grant said, "Children everywhere will feel her death as a painful and irreplaceable loss." The Audrey Hepburn Hollywood for Children Fund, chaired by her son Sean Ferrer, was established to raise money for children's charities around the world. *See also* CARE; HOLLAND (WORLD WAR II); SOMALIA; UNITED NATIONS CHILDREN'S FUND (UNICEF).

Further Reading: Jerry Vermilye, *Audrey Hepburn, Her Life and Her Career* (1995); Ian Woodward, *Audrey Hepburn* (1984).

Hidden Child Foundation/Anti-Defamation League (ADL)

The Hidden Child Foundation grew out of a meeting held in New York City in 1991 called the First International Gathering of Children Hidden During World War II. The meeting was attended by 1,600 Jewish men and women who had been hidden as children during the Holocaust to escape Nazi persecution and death. They came from countries around the world.

The Anti-Defamation League (ADL) sponsors the foundation. The ADL is a Jewish organization committed to educating people about religious and racial intolerance and exposing groups that promote bigotry. The ADL's executive director, Abraham Foxman, was himself hidden in Poland as a child by a Catholic nursemaid. Foxman described the conference as follows:

> We exchanged stories about our hiding places; how we lived for months in sewers, closets, barns, and fields; how we joined the partisans and fought the enemy; how we stayed alive. We examined the guilt that continues to haunt us; the pain we felt at losing our loved ones; our anger; our inability to speak of these experiences with our family; our identity crises; our confused, frightening, lost childhoods. . . . Everything we are committed to at the Anti-Defamation League has its roots, I believe, in the determination that children must never have to be hidden, ever again.

See also FRANCE (WORLD WAR II); FRANK, ANNE; GREECE (WORLD WAR II); HARTZ, RUTH KAPP; HIDDEN CHILDREN; HOLLAND (WORLD WAR II); HOLOCAUST; PRITCHARD, MARION VON BINSBERGEN; RESCUERS (HOLOCAUST); RIGHTEOUS GENTILES; TOLL, NELLY LANDAU; VOS, AART AND VOS, JOHTJE.

Further Reading: Howard Greenfeld, *The Hidden Children* (1993); Leora Kahn and Rachel Hager, eds., *When They Came to Take My Father* (1996); Jane Marks, *The Hidden Children* (1993).

Hidden Child Gathering. *See* HIDDEN CHILD FOUNDATION/ANTI-DEFAMATION LEAGUE (ADL)

Hidden Children

During World War II, thousands of Jewish youth went into hiding to escape the Nazi Holocaust. Of these children, between 10,000 and 100,000 escaped capture and survived. Most of these children went into hiding beginning in 1942. In January, the Nazis made specific plans to kill all remaining Jews in the lands occupied by Germany, which then included most of Europe. Hitler declared that Jews would be completely annihilated.

Parents dreaded parting with their children but decided this was the only way the family, or at least the child, could survive. Sometimes children were easier to hide than adults because they were not always required to carry identity papers to show their official status. Also, thousands of youth had been orphaned during the war. Families and institutions, such as convents, could represent Jewish children in their keeping as non-Jewish war orphans. Yet, hiding children in secret rooms or attics also posed added dangers. Babies might fret or cry out from hunger. Small children might talk, cough, giggle, or make some other noises during the day when visitors or repairmen were in the house or, even worse, during a Nazi raid.

Hiding people was complicated and dangerous. First, a suitable place had to be found or built, then disguised, whether in a home, store, cave, farmhouse, farm building, pigsty, or haystacks. Some young people hid in the mountains or woods or in underground bunkers. A few even hid in cemeteries. When a rescuer's household included children, special dangers existed there, too. Young children might unwittingly say the wrong thing in public and expose what was happening at home. In Nazi Germany, young people in Hitler Youth organizations were told to report anyone who spoke or acted against the government. Nonetheless, about one-fourth of the rescuers in a study conducted by researchers Samuel and Pearl Oliner had at least one child aged 10 or younger in their household during the war.

Finding a place for a child to hide was usually done through personal contacts. Some people turned to clergy, who helped to hide children in convents, monasteries, and orphanages run by religious groups. Thousands of children were sheltered in people's homes. When they could not find a safe house on their own, some parents turned to strangers in the resistance to hide their children.

To avoid detection, young people often moved from place to place during the war, depending on the circumstances. Teenager Jacques Van Dam survived the war by moving about in occupied Holland. First, he lived outside Amsterdam with one family, then left for the countryside, where a forester hid him. After several days, Van Dam moved to northern Holland to live with another family who had built a bunker in the floor of their home. He moved between this house and their bakery. For a few months, he stayed on a small barge until the Nazis began patrolling the lakes. Then Van Dam slept in haylofts.

Other children endured similar displacement, living in homes, convents, orphanages, city apartments, farms, and other places. Their experiences varied, depending on the nature of their rescuers and the locale. Some were able to continue studying or even attending school if their identity could be kept secret. Others were forced to stay indoors all day to avoid detection. They often lacked fresh air, physical exercise, and friends, and could not take part in the activities that make up a child's or teenager's normal daily life.

While some hidden children had ample food, others experienced hunger and malnutrition. Illness was another worry. When a hidden child became sick, it was sometimes not possible to find medicines or locate a doctor who could be trusted. Children hiding in attics or cellars had to be careful not to cough or sneeze, lest someone hear them and become suspicious. Some families who hid children received help from members of the resistance in their area or they bribed people to obtain medical care or other things they needed for the children they were sheltering.

After the war, former hidden children faced many adjustments. Some children were reunited with their families and had to become reacquainted. Many others found themselves orphans at the war's end, the only members of their families to survive. *See also* Displaced Persons (DPs) (World War II); Final Solution; France (World War II); Frank, Anne; Gies, Miep and Gies, Jan; Greece (World War II); Hartz, Ruth Kapp; Hidden Child Foundation/Anti-Defamation League (ADL); Holland (World War II); Holocaust; Hungary (World War II); Italy (World War II); Le Chambon-sur-Lignon; Poland (World War II); Pritchard, Marion von Binsbergen; Quakers (Society of Friends); Rescuers (Holocaust); Righteous Gentiles; Toll, Nelly Landau; Trocme, Andre and Trocme, Magda; Trocme, Daniel; Vos, Aart and Vos, Johtje; World War II.

Further Reading: Stacy Cretzmeyer, *Your Name Is Renee* (1994); Deborah Dwork, *Children with a Star* (1991); Eva Fogelman, *Conscience and Courage* (1994); Howard Greenfeld, *The Hidden Children* (1993); Donald Lowrie, *The Hunted Children* (1963); Robert Marshall, *In The Sewers of Lvov* (1991); Jane Marks, *The Hidden Children* (1993); Samuel P. Oliner and Pearl Oliner, *The Altruistic Personality: Rescuers of Jews in Nazi Europe* (1988); Maxine B. Rosenberg, *Hiding to Survive: Stories of Jewish Children Rescued from the Holocaust* (1994); Renee Roth-Hano, *Touch Wood* (1989).

Hill, Baylor

A detailed diary written by a teenager who served as a scout during the American Revolution shows the day-to-day life of a cavalry scout in the colonial army. The author of the diary, 16-year-old Baylor Hill of Virginia, joined the revolutionary forces in 1778 and observed that most of the other volunteers were young men like himself. After joining the combined troops serving under General George Washington, Hill saw fighting in Pennsylvania, Georgia, and South Carolina. His work was often tedious and difficult. To complicate matters, his commander was a Polish count, Casimir Pulaski, who did not speak much English, and his fellow scouts were often required to move about in unfamiliar territory searching for crossroads in the wilderness.

Hill's diary entries for the years 1779-1781 show that scouts rode or marched long distances, often in inclement weather, and received little help from local residents. Periodically, they were stricken with fevers and diseases or became prisoners of war. While scouting enemy lines on horseback in 1781, Hill was captured by the British, but survived the war and was freed in exchange for a British prisoner. After witnessing the British surrender at Yorktown, Hill returned to civilian life. *See also* American Revolution; Diaries.

Further Reading: P.M. Zall, *Becoming American* (1993).

Hindu-Muslim Riots (India)

In 1945, as India neared the end of its long struggle for independence from Great Britain, conflicts escalated between India's Muslims and Hindus. Muslims were a minority in India, and members of the newly formed Muslim League feared they would be poorly treated in a country governed by Hindus. In this heated atmosphere, children died and were injured as riots erupted in Calcutta on August 17, as each group attacked the other. Burnings, shootings, beatings, stabbings, and rapes took place in the city and surrounding area. People desecrated religious shrines. The death toll was 5,000 in just one day, and more than 15,000 people were injured. Orphaned children roamed the streets in terror. Many had witnessed the deaths of their parents.

In 1947, when India was declared independent, more fighting broke out between Hindus and Muslims. The Muslims, who were about one-fourth of the population, declared they would form a separate nation.

On August 15, after weeks of negotiations, the decision was made to partition India to form Hindu India and Muslim Pakistan. Pakistan was split into East and West, with East Pakistan breaking away with India's help in 1971 to form the country of Bangladesh.

Millions of Hindu and Muslim men, women, and children were now compelled to move from one section of the former India to the other. Thousands of peasants rolled carts along the roads, and women and small children walked or rode on donkeys. Babies were born on the roadsides. Thousands of people died during this mass migration, which soon turned violent. Hindus who resented the idea of Pakistani independence attacked Muslims and their homes and mosques. Both sides attacked groups of refugees from the opposite side.

News of the violence incited still more violence as people sought revenge. Thousands of soldiers tried without success to stop the violence. Fires spread throughout Delhi and thousands of people swarmed into unsanitary refugee camps. When the violence finally stopped, between 600,000 and one million people, about half of them youths, had died. Even after the fighting ended, children continued to suffer from homelessness, hunger, and diseases.

Further Reading: Penderel Moon, *Gandhi and Modern India* (1969); Mark Tully and Masani Zareer, *India: Forty Years of Independence* (1988).

Hiroshima

At about 8 a.m. on August 6, 1945, a U.S. B-29 bomber, the *Enola Gay*, dropped an atomic bomb on the city of Hiroshima, Japan, which had a population of about 380,000. This uranium bomb, the first atomic weapon ever used during wartime, had the force of 20 kilotons of TNT. It killed about 80,000 people, nearly all civilians, and injured thousands of others. About 250,000 people were left homeless.

In the days and years that followed, another 100,000 people would die from burns and radiation poisoning. Many others would suffer chronic health problems from the effects of the bombing and the radiation that blanketed the city for days after the bombing.

The morning of the bombing, children and young people were going about their usual activities. Many were eating breakfast or sitting in school classrooms. Others were outdoors, at home doing chores, or going to work. As the bomb fell, a blinding flash of light and loud boom were followed by a rush of extreme heat. Shock waves caused whole buildings to fall apart. Many people died instantly or soon after they were hit by flying pieces of wood, metal, glass, and other objects. Clouds of dust and smoke spread, along with flames, and Hiroshima suddenly grew dark. Later in the day, droplets of rain the color of soot fell from purplish clouds. This black rain stained clothing, wood, and other objects.

Casualties included thousands of youths. About 6,000 children and their teachers had been sent to the center of the city to help tear down houses in places where fire lanes were going to be built. Students from the All-Girls Hiroshima Commercial High School were working to clear out debris from houses that had been demolished. In another part of town, 150 first graders were playing outdoors. A group of eighth-grade girls were sitting near a Buddhist temple. Most of these people were killed when the bomb struck. Others suffered horrendous burns and died that same day.

Survivors who were not trapped under debris, or too injured to move, tried to escape the fires. They moved about in a daze and had bloody wounds and frizzled hair. Shredded flesh hung from their bodies. Some people were so badly burned that their facial features and limbs appeared to be melted; their faces often unrecognizable.

Children in the class of 18-year-old teacher Katsuko Horibe begged for a drink. Horibe led the terrified youngsters to the Motoyasu River but found the water covered with flames, debris, and dead bodies. Other young people suffered as family members, classmates, and coworkers died, and as they themselves endured terrible pain. As one severely burned teenager fled from the building where she worked, she heard survivors begging people to kill them because their pain was unbearable.

Some children died in their homes that day or shortly thereafter. A child recalled, "My little brother was burned on his face and hands and his face was all swollen. He was just three. He was a cute little brother but he died after a week" (Osada, 1963).

A number of children were orphaned. One 10-year-old girl searched for her family on the day after the bombing. Her mother lay in a hospital bed with severe burns covering her body. She was having trouble breathing. That night, she died.

Among those who came to help were female students who lived in the countryside around the city. Nurses in the Hiroshima hospitals directed these girls in cleaning up the wards, preparing and serving food, organizing supplies, and comforting patients. Medical supplies ran short, and people lacked adequate medicines and ointments to apply to burns. Some people used ashes on their wounds. Food and clean water were in short supply and workers could offer only a little rice and some biscuits to people whose injuries did not prevent them from eating.

A girl who was eight years old when the bomb fell said,

> When I think that all these things happened because of war, I hate it so that I can't stand it. With every year that passes I yearn more for my father and my brother so that I can hardly bear it. . . . From this day on I think from the bottom of my heart that we ought to throw away such barbaric things as atomic bombs and choose the path of peace. (Osada, 1963)

See also FOLDED CRANE CLUB; HIROSHIMA MAIDENS; JAPAN (WORLD WAR II); MUSHROOM CLUB; NAGASAKI; PEACE MONUMENT; RADIATION SICKNESS; SASAKI, SADAKO; WORLD WAR II.

Further Reading: Michihiko Hachiya, *Hiroshima Diary* (1969); Robert Jungk, *Children of the Ashes* (1961); Betty Jean Lifton, *A Place Called Hiroshima* (1985); Arata Osada, *Children of the A-Bomb* (1963); Robert Trumbull, *Nine Who Survived Hiroshima and Nagasaki* (1957).

Hiroshima Maidens

The atomic bombing of Hiroshima left many people with severely disfigured faces and bodies. Many lost fingers and limbs, and some young victims were scarred at especially vul-

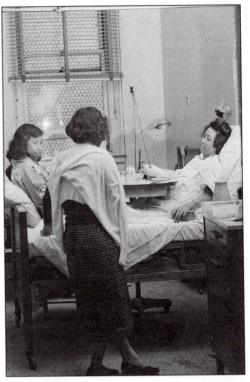

One of the Hiroshima maidens is shown in her hospital room. *Corbis-Bettmann.*

nerable ages. As the burns from the bombing healed, victims developed keloid scars—thick, rubbery, irregular-shaped patches of red tissue. Among these scarred victims were schoolgirls who had been outside clearing firelanes near the site where the bomb fell. One of them later recalled that people called her "A-Bomb Scar-Face" and other unkind names. After the war, some young women became so distressed by the rude stares and unpleasant remarks they received in public that they rarely went outside. They became recluses, giving up thoughts of marriage or careers.

Reverend Kyoshi Tanimoto organized a support group for these victims called the Society of Keloid Girls. The group offered a chance to meet with others who shared their plight and do sewing projects and other work. Tanimoto tried unsuccessfully to persuade the Japanese government to finance plastic surgery for the girls, who became known as A-Bomb Maidens—*Genbaku Otome*—or Hiroshima Maidens.

In 1955, 25 of these young women agreed to go to New York City to receive free plastic surgery and treatments in American hospitals. Surgeons had volunteered to try and restore the damage done to their skin, eyes, and other facial features. The women stayed in the New York City area with host families, including members of the Society of Friends (Quakers). Norman Cousins, the editor-in-chief of the *Saturday Review*, spearheaded the project after visiting Hiroshima and Reverend Tanimoto helped to implement this project. Cousins also developed fund-raising projects for orphans in Japan. He founded the Hiroshima Peace Center Foundation in New York City and stayed in contact with the young women from Hiroshima to help them after they had their surgery.

In addition to surgery and hospital treatments, the young women received cosmetic products. Make-up experts showed them how to minimize the appearance of their scars. They also received training in dressmaking and other job skills. The goal of these efforts was to help the women gain self-confidence and more strength to go on with their lives.

The press continued to take an active interest in the lives of the young women after their medical treatments ended. They noted that the surgery had been helpful, but, in many cases, the scars could still be seen. Some people back in Japan expressed resentment toward the young women and claimed their time abroad had made them more self-centered or "Americanized." Eventually, 12 of the women married and they had 19 healthy children among them. Some pursued higher education and new careers. For example, Masako Wado became a respected social worker; Tazuko Shibata became an executive in a company that manufactured electrical switches. Hideko Hirata, who had been doing volunteer social work, died in 1958 of stomach cancer that was probably caused by radiation. The maidens gradually withdrew from the public eye to their private lives as mothers, wives, and workers.

Three of the young women stayed, at least for a while, in the United States. Aided by Cousins, Shigeko Niimoto worked as a nurses' aide and then a home-care therapist and massage therapist while raising a son. She also became an anti-nuclear activist. Toyoko Morita graduated with honors from the Fashion Design Department of the Parsons School in New York City and then returned to Japan, where she opened her own fashion design house in Tokyo. Hiroko Tasaka married an American and lived in the United States until 1983 when her husband retired from his job and the couple moved to Japan. *See also* HIROSHIMA; RADIATION SICKNESS.

Further Reading: Rodney Barker, *The Hiroshima Maidens* (1985); Anne Chisholm, *Faces of Hiroshima* (1985); Betty Jean Lifton, *A Place Called Hiroshima.* (1985); Robert Jay Lifton, *Death in Life* (1982).

Hitler, Adolf (1889–1945)

As dictator of Nazi Germany from 1933 to 1945, Adolf Hitler created a powerful regime that almost conquered a continent and was responsible for the deaths of millions of people. Millions of young civilians were among the victims of Hitler's genocidal plan to destroy the Jews and Romani (Gypsies) and to eliminate many Poles and Slavs. Millions of young people suffered or died as a result of bombings, shellfire, Nazi occupation, persecution, imprisonment, or military executions, or while serving with military units that fought in World War II.

Hitler was born in Austria to a humble working-class family. A poor student, he failed to earn a certificate for completing secondary school, then failed to gain admission to the Academy of Fine Arts in Vienna, which dashed his dreams of becoming an artist. After moving to Vienna at age 20, Hitler eked out a living by painting houses and working at odd jobs. He developed intense anti-Semitic (anti-Jewish) attitudes that would become an obsession. During World War I, he fought as a combat soldier in the German army and was deeply upset when Germany lost the war. In 1919, he joined a political group made up of disgruntled veterans who shared his radical political attitudes. The group, which soon changed its name to the National Socialist German Workers' (Nazi) Party, was small in number and had no political power at that time.

The party slowly attracted more members throughout the 1920s. In 1923, Hitler led his supporters within the party in an unsuccessful attempt to take over the government. While in prison, Hitler wrote *Mein Kampf* (*My Struggle*), a book that set forth his plans for totalitarian government in Germany. The book contained unscientific "racial" theories that Hitler used to support his idea that certain Germans he called Aryans were meant to become a master race of superior people who would subjugate Poles, Slavs, and people of color. He blamed Jews for Germany's political and economic problems.

As the severe economic depression of the late 1920s and early 1930s crippled Germany, Hitler and his Nazi Party gained support. Hitler offered convenient excuses for the problems Germany faced and insisted that his party could solve these problems. He called for renewed German power and pride, which had been damaged by the nation's defeat in World War I and by the Versailles Treaty that had punished Germany for starting that war. In 1933, Hitler was named chancellor by President Paul von Hindenburg, who had recently defeated Hitler in the presidential election. Under Hitler's leadership, the Nazis, who were only one party in a coalition government, gradually squeezed out their rivals and took over every area of German life, stifling all dissent.

One key to Hitler's plans for a vast, powerful regime was a subservient population and an education system that pushed children to follow Nazi ideals. In his speeches and writings, Hitler said that German youth must be loyal and obedient to the state and violent toward Germany's enemies: "A youth will grow up before which the world will shrink back. A violently active, dominating, intrepid, brutal youth . . . indifferent to pain. No weakness or tenderness in it. I want to see once more in its eyes the gleam . . . of a beast of prey" (Green, 1980). In *Mein Kampf*, Hitler

stated that youth should be reared to become obedient soldiers.

The German education system under Hitler stressed Nazi racial theories and physical training, and strived to convince youth that Germans were a "superior race" above all others. Hitler wrote, "[A young person's] whole education and training must be so ordered as to give him the conviction that he is absolutely superior to others. Through his physical strength and dexterity, he must recover his faith in the invincibility of his whole people." Toward these ends, Hitler authorized a vast propaganda program with strict control of the schools and the media. He also established comprehensive Hitler Youth programs in which Nazi youth were taught that every activity should ultimately benefit the state.

Between 1939 and his death by suicide on April 30, 1945, Hitler presided over his country's invasion and occupation of numerous European countries and the Nazi war against the Jews, which became known as the Holocaust. As the leader of Nazi Germany, Hitler had a profound and devastating impact on millions of young people and on succeeding generations of German, Jewish, and other youths whose lives were affected by Nazism. That influence continues today as members of certain hate groups and perpetrators of hate crimes describe themselves as neo-Nazis and followers of Hitler's racist ideology. *See also* ADOLF HITLER SCHOOLS; CONCENTRATION CAMPS (WORLD WAR II); DEATH CAMPS (WORLD WAR II); DEATH MARCHES; EDUCATION; *EINSATZGRUPPEN*; FINAL SOLUTION; GERMANY (WORLD WAR II); HITLER YOUTH; HOLOCAUST; "MASTER RACE"; WORLD WAR II.

Further Reading: Alan Bullock, *Hitler, A Study in Tyranny* (1971); Robert Goldston, *The Life and Death of Nazi Germany* (1967); Adolf Hitler, *Mein Kampf* (1943); Max Von Der Grun, *Howl Like the Wolves* (1980); Burton H. Wolfe, *Hitler and the Nazis* (1970).

Hitler Youth

Shaping the attitudes, values, and behavior of young people was a priority for Adolf Hitler and the Nazi regime, and the Hitler Youth (*Hitlerjugend*) groups the Nazis established in 1926 were a key component of Nazism.

Adolf Hitler inspects members of the Hitler Youth in Berlin. *Corbis/Austrian Archives.*

The Hitler Youth promoted Nazi ideology and racial theories and involved youth in patriotic and political activities. Groups for young men stressed paramilitary activities designed to make them future soldiers.

The first Hitler Youth groups were designed for young men. Street fighting and other violence by Nazi youths prompted the German government to ban Hitler Youth and certain other Nazi groups on April 13, 1932, but they continued to meet. The ban was lifted later that year. When the Nazis came to power in 1933, they strengthened youth groups and sought recruits. Membership soared from about 120,00 to nearly 2.3 million. Large numbers of uniformed youth took part in Nazi Party rallies, celebrations, and ceremonies. By 1935, the Nazis had banned Catholic and all other youth groups. Only Hitler Youth groups were permitted.

With Baldur von Schirach as Reich Youth Leader, the groups were carefully reorganized. Von Schirach reported directly to Hitler. He wrote the theme song of the Hitler Youth, "Forward!", which glorified Hitler and Nazi ideals. Young singers pledged to "march for Hitler through night and through danger" (Stephens, 1973).

Hitler believed that childhood should end at age six, at which time children could enter Nazi Youth groups. Hitler described children as "the term we apply to those non-uniformed creatures of junior age group who have yet to attend an evening parade" (Heyes, 1993). In his view, children could be persuaded more easily to Nazi viewpoints because they could not remember life before Hitler nor any form of government besides Nazism.

The Hitler Youth organization contained several subgroups. Boys from 6 to 10, called Pimpfs, took part in some Nazi Youth activities. Records were kept of their achievements in athletics, outdoor activities such as pitching tents, and any service they gave the Nazi Party. At age 10, boys could join the *Jungvolk*. These boys wore uniforms of black shorts, brown shirts, heavy black shoes, a swastika armband, and daggers. Young men in the

Hitler Youth wore brown shirts but without the Nazi armbands of the Storm Troopers. Their uniforms had red swastika armbands. Winter uniforms were sometimes dark blue.

The youth organizations for girls were called *Jungmadel* (Young Maidens), for girls under 14, and *Bund Deutscher Madel* (League of German Maidens), for girls 14 to 18. Their uniforms included heavy marching shoes, blue skirts, white blouses, and neckerchiefs with a ring bearing the emblem of their group. Girls were also expected to build their physical strength but did not engage in the military activities boys did.

The official Hitler Youth handbook said that the foundation of the Nazi movement was "the perception of the unlikeness of men." Youth were taught that German blood was precious while people with "other" kinds of blood were less valuable than themselves and even unworthy of life. Rules were specific and strictly enforced. At his first Hitler Youth meeting, Hans Peter Richter was told that he had to give "absolute loyalty to the Fuhrer" and "unwavering dedication to the ideals of National Socialism" (Richter, 1972). The youth leader told the boys that the "enemies of the Fuhrer are your enemies, too, be they Jews, Bolsheviks, parsons, or whatever," and that "Sundays belong to the Hitler Youth, not to going to church" (Richter, 1972). Traditional religion was scorned and members were told not to attend services. Members were ordered to attend the Hitler Youth marches that were held on Sundays at the same time church services were being conducted. The movement also published its own *Hitler Youth Catechism* but the book was not popular.

More than 6 million boys and girls joined Hitler Youth groups even before joining became mandatory. Young people were encouraged to feel they were an important part of the Reich. With their left hands gripping the flag as three fingers of the right hand extended upward in the Nazi salute, Hitler Youth members swore the following oath: "I promise in the Hitler Youth to do my duty, at all times in love and faithfulness, to help the Fuhrer—so help me God." Starting in December 1936, the Hitler Youth Law required all youth between ages 10 and 18, both male and female, to join. The law simply stated that "The entire German youth within the borders of the Reich is organized into the Hitler Youth." Parents who failed to register 10-year-olds for Hitler Youth organizations could be fined or even imprisoned.

This vast organization was designed along paramilitary lines, with a system of ranks and promotions. The different branches of Hitler youth groups were divided into squads of 10 to 15 people and platoons of about 30 to 45 people. Youth attended training camps and leadership schools. For males, war games were the main part of their scheduled activities. By the time young men joined the Hitler Youth at age 14, most of their training was in military skills and exercises, such as rifle drills, training in the use of explosives and military equipment, and surviving at campsites.

By teaching youth competition and leader-follower relationships, the Nazis developed a vast pool of young men for future military troops. This training prepared them for tasks many would later assume in the German army or other Nazi organizations—police work, racial policy enforcement, concentration camp operations, death squads, or in deporting and resettling people the Nazis wanted removed from certain areas.

Other Hitler Youth activities included farmwork, fund raising, record-keeping, and charity work. Members took part in sports, camping trips, musical performances, hiking, country outings, and picnics and cookouts. Activities were made into competitions with quotas for each person and unit. For instance, when young people made toys and gifts to be given out at Christmas, their products were exhibited and they received rewards for the quality and quantity of their work. Awards were also given for outstanding work on farms or for collecting the most for German war relief.

Hitler Youth members were drawn into the excitement the Nazis fostered during the 1936 Summer Olympic Games in Berlin. Thousands of Hitler Youth joined the dramatic opening ceremonies. Some of them later recalled that the excitement and pageantry of this event made them feel strongly patriotic even when they and their families were not fond of Hitler or the Nazi regime.

Each year, September 10, was celebrated as the Day of Hitler Youth. Upwards of 80,000 young people attended a special ceremony at the Nuremberg Stadium. According to former Hitler youth leader Alfons Heck, Hitler told the 1938 gathering, "You my youth, are our nation's most precious guarantee for a great future, and you are destined to be the leaders of a glorious new order under the supremacy of National Socialism. Never forget that one day you will rule the world!" (Heck, 1985).

As time went on, new youth divisions were added: Motor Hitler Youth units, Marine units, and Flying Hitler Youth. One year in the Labor Service was compulsory at age 18. Girls did agricultural and homemaking work or took a job in a munitions factory, while boys did manual, agricultural, and construction work. Males were then drafted into the army. Girls were expected to become obedient wives and the mothers of strong, healthy German children.

One former Hitler Youth member summed up his experience as follows: "Exercises, lectures in history, political lectures, the purity of the Aryan race—a lot of what in later life you think is garbage. There were a lot of good things in it. And a lot of nonsense that the political people were trying to brainwash you with" (Richter, 1972). *See also* ADOLF HITLER SCHOOLS; D-DAY; EDUCATION; GERMANY (WORLD WAR II); HITLER, ADOLF; WORLD WAR II.

Further Reading: Alfons Heck, *A Child of Hitler* (1985); Eileen Heyes, *Children of the Swastika* (1993); Ilse Koehn, *Mischling, Second Degree* (1977); Melita Maschmann, *Account Rendered* (1965); Gerhard Rempel, *Hitler's Children* (1989); Hans Peter Richter, *I Was There* (1972); Frederick J. Stephens, *Hitler Youth* (1973).

Hitler's Children

The name Hitler's Children was given to children who were raised in state nursery schools in Germany during World War II. The mothers, many of whom were still in their teens, were mostly unwed young German women who had been encouraged to bear children for the Third Reich. They were urged to become pregnant by men in the SS (top-ranking Nazi officers) who were selected as especially good physical specimens. Nazi leaders encouraged all German women to have many children to ensure that the population would increase dramatically to build up future armies and replace men killed in battle. *See also* HITLER, ADOLF; LEBENSBORN; "MASTER RACE."

Further Reading: Catrine Clay and Michael Leapman, *Master Race* (1995).

Holidays

During wartime, children may not be able to celebrate birthdays, holidays, and other special occasions, or they may celebrate these occasions in different or unusual ways because money, food, or other commodities are scarce or expensive. When war involves religious oppression, such as during the Holocaust of World War II, people may also be forced to conduct religious observances secretly or lose the chance to mark such occasions. In some cases, survival is such a profound concern that holiday celebrations become less significant.

As war disrupts daily life, people live without luxuries or pleasures they may have taken for granted. During World War II, most people in England lacked enough butter, sugar, or other ingredients to make a traditional birthday cake. Others could not afford to pay the high costs of these ingredients. Some families decorated a hatbox to look like a birthday cake or put candles on a wooden "cake" that was used each time a family member had a birthday. Because gifts could rarely be purchased, children in various war-torn countries would make gifts for parents, siblings, friends, and relatives. During these years, simple gifts, or any gifts at all, were much appreciated. An English woman who was 10 in 1941 later recalled one Christmas in the middle of World War II:

> I had a pair of slacks (Mummy made them out of a blanket), a paint-book, a pencil-box, and a very nice handkerchief, a book

of poetry from Mummy, a bar of chocolate, a whole orange. I have a very nice present for Mummy. I made it myself, a kettle-holder. And a present for Daddy. I made it, it is a case with needles and cottons and buttons in, so when he goes away he can sew his buttons on. I also made him a shoe-polisher. (Westall, 1985)

In Japan, where most food was imported before World War II, young people missed the traditional herring's roe and chestnut sweets they had eaten on New Year's Eve before the war. Rice supplies grew scarce near the end of the war, so rice cakes, a tradition for parties, were seldom available.

Jewish children in hiding during World War II seldom had time or resources available for holiday celebrations. Still, people managed to mark special occasions whenever they could. While Anne Frank was hiding in secret rooms in a warehouse in Amsterdam, Holland, the non-Jews who were helping the family managed to find small gifts for the Franks' birthdays. One of Anne's gifts was a pair of second-hand red shoes with high heels, especially chosen for her sixteenth birthday. She had outgrown her clothing and enjoyed having something nice, like other young women. The Frank family carefully saved some butter and sugar to bake a cake for their rescuer friends.

In Budapest, Hungary, Gabor Kalman was in hiding from the Nazis when his tenth birthday arrived at the end of 1944.

> It is my tenth birthday. There are no birthday cake, guests, or gifts, but there are real fireworks outside and we hear heavy gunfire in the distance. It is snowing. Air raids are more frequent, but we are afraid to go down to the shelter. (Handler and Meschel, 1993)

Other Jews in hiding were gratified when the families who gave them shelter also helped them conduct their traditional religious celebrations. Even in the most grim circumstances, in concentration and death camps, such as Auschwitz, prisoners often fasted to mark certain Jewish holidays and found ways to pray together. A woman who survived Auschwitz with her mother later recalled that her mother saved two pieces of bread for her on her birthday—a gift of tremendous generosity in that place of starvation and death. *See also* AUSCHWITZ-BIRKENAU; FRANK, ANNE; RUSSIAN REVOLUTION; WORLD WAR I; WORLD WAR II.

Further Reading: Anne Frank, *The Diary of a Young Girl* (1967); Miep Gies, *Anne Frank Remembered* (1987); Andrew Handler and Susan V. Meschel, comps. *Young People Speak* (1993). Norman Longmate, *How We Lived Then* (1971); Robert Westall, *Children of the Blitz* (1985).

Holland (World War II)

World War II reached neutral Holland on May 10, 1940, when German ground troops and bombers launched a surprise attack. Young people awoke to hear strange rumbling noises and the worried voices of adults discussing the attack. They gathered around their radios as the government advised people to cover their windows with blackout paper and tape. A curfew was set for 8 p.m., and movies, schools, theaters, offices, and businesses closed abruptly. People hurried to shops to buy extra food before they closed for the day. Children who ventured outdoors to do errands scanned the sky nervously and ran for cover when they saw or heard a plane.

A woman from Eindhoven who was 15 years old at the time of the invasion later recalled feeling "pain and hopelessness."

> I remember the dreadful rules made by the German dictators. The noise of the dreaded jackboots as they marched through the towns. . . . I remember listening to the BBC [British Broadcasting Company] risking our lives, as this was punishable by death. At night the hidden radio was brought out and all members of the household would congregate for the news. (Westall, 1985)

The city of Rotterdam, which had no military base, was devastated as German bombs destroyed numerous homes and 750 city blocks, leaving 78,000 people homeless. Nine hundred people were killed, and thousands of others were injured. Drinking water and electricity were unavailable in hard-hit areas.

As German troops marched into every region, they removed Dutch flags and replaced them with Nazi swastika flags. They circulated printed materials urging people to support the Germans and told young Dutch men to join the German army. Some young people, such as 14-year-old Jan Jonkheer, resented Germans visiting their schools.

> The Nazis are trying all their tricks to win over the schoolchildren. They have given us sweets which most of us have put in the drain, and they have allowed the top class to matriculate without passing the exams. Our teacher says, "Be brave. Hold your heads up." (Cowan, 1969)

Jonkheer resented the laws the Nazis enacted as they crushed the Dutch democracy. They took over radio stations and movie theaters, playing only German music and showing only German films. Many books were banned, and young people were not allowed to take French or English language courses in school. Jonkheer joined other Dutch youths who organized resistance to the Nazis.

As the war went on, food became more scarce. By the fall of 1940, certain foods and other goods were rationed and people could only buy these things legally by using their ration coupons. Food, cows, coal, and other items from Holland were being shipped to Germany. Many schools closed for lack of fuel.

Young men in Holland faced the threat of being forced into labor for the Germans, often in hazardous jobs. During the early months of 1945, the Germans also began picking up young girls and Dutch women for forced labor. Soldiers with machine-guns arrested these girls and women on the streets and took them to work in German camps, kitchens, and military hospitals.

Among the most frightened young people in German-occupied Holland were Jewish refugees and Dutch Jews. During the early 1930s, about 25,000 German Jews had fled to Holland. Later, they were joined by thousands more refugees—Austrians, Czechs, Poles, and others. Dutch laws had permitted people of various faiths to worship freely since the 1600s, and Jews had not been attacked there as they sometimes were in Eastern Eu-

rope. The Dutch Nazi Party attracted some youths as well as older members, but most citizens opposed Nazism.

Leesha Rose, a Jew, was a 17-year-old student in Amsterdam when the Germans invaded Holland. Some of her friends and acquaintances tried to flee by sea. Only a few people managed to escape because German planes patrolled the harbors and shot at boats. However, one Dutch rescuer managed to get five carloads of Jewish orphans from Amsterdam onto a ship, and then to safety in England.

About 80 percent of the 140,000 Jews who lived in Holland in 1940 died during the Holocaust, despite a strong anti-Nazi resistance. The Nazis set up a harsh occupation government under the zealous Austrian Nazi, Arthur Seyss-Inquart. They lied to Dutch officials and Jewish leaders, saying that they would treat Jews fairly if people cooperated with them.

Holland, a flat, open country with no mountains and few forested areas, offered few good hiding places. The borders and surrounding countries, including Germany, were under Nazi control. To reach neutral Spain or Switzerland, refugees had to cross occupied France. German troops controlled Dutch canals, railroads, harbors, and bridges. Despite these risks, thousands of Dutch people, including young people, rescued Jews, either on their own or as part of a rescue network. The families of many rescuers included children and teenagers who kept their rescue activities secret and helped the people in hiding. Young people made sacrifices, such as not inviting friends to their homes while the family was hiding Jews during the war.

The last months of the war were marked by desperate hunger and fear as the Germans arrested more people. By April 1945, there was no electrical power or fuel in Holland, even for public kitchens. People wore dirty, ragged clothing and had no soap or hot running water for washing. For light, they used candle stumps or lit pieces of string they dipped in oil and floated in water.

On April 29, 1945, food packages dropped into the country from Allied planes, a sign that the war was finally ending. People cheered British, Canadian, and American planes from their roofs and balconies or hung out Dutch flags. Leesha Rose described the joy people felt as they opened these packages and found "cheese, meat, potatoes, flour, vegetables, tea, chocolate, and sugar" (Rose, 1978).

Dutch youth actively helped to rebuild the country after the war. They worked in hospitals and rest homes to help civilians and returning soldiers. They did construction work to put up housing, bridges, and farm buildings. Some drained land or worked on farms or in the dairy industry to increase food supplies.

The Dutch government arrested people who had helped the Germans or informed on people for aiding Jews. After the war, 50,000 Dutch people were convicted of treason. When both parents were in jail, communities set up homes for their children to live until their parents returned.

Surviving Dutch Jews faced painful adjustments as they returned to Holland and tried to resume their lives. Ida Vos, who was 13 in 1945, recalled that she was only in fifth grade because the war had interrupted her schooling. Even worse, many of her family members were gone: "I want to visit my grandparents, but I can't. I can't visit my cousins Marga and Meintje, either, for they are all dead. They were killed because they were Jews" (Vos, 1991).

In 1950, Dutch youth were honored for their contributions during the war. Princess Margriet and her mother, Queen Juliana, dedicated a statue in Amsterdam to "the courage of Dutch Youth through the ages." *See also* BOMBINGS (WORLD WAR II); FORCED LABOR (WORLD WAR II); FRANK, ANNE; GIES, MIEP AND GIES, JAN; HEPBURN, AUDREY; HOLOCAUST; HUNGER/MALNUTRITION; HUNGER WINTER; VOS, AART AND VOS, JOHTJE; WESTERWEEL, JOOP; WORLD WAR II.

Further Reading: Adriaan J. Barnouw, *The Pageant of Netherlands History* (1952); Lore Cowan, ed., *Children of the Resistance* (1969); Ina Friedman, *The Other Victims* (1990); Walter A. Maass, *The Netherlands at War* (1970); Leesha Rose, *The Tulips Are Red* (1978); Ida Vos, *Hide and Seek* (1991); Werner Warmbrunn, *The Dutch Under German Occupation* (1963).

Holocaust

The Holocaust refers to the methodical murder of approximately 6 million Jewish men, women, and children carried out by the Nazis during World War II. In 1933, the year the Nazis rose to power, Europe contained about 8 million Jews and about 300 million non-Jews. According to the United States Holocaust Memorial and Museum, between 1 and 1.5 million Holocaust victims were children under age 16. At least 1 million of these child victims were Jewish, with most of the rest being Romani (Gypsies) and children with disabilities killed in the Nazi "euthanasia" program.

The Nazi regime that rose in Germany under Adolf Hitler militarily occupied large parts of Europe and the western Soviet Union. Wherever the Nazis ruled, Jewish children were hunted, tortured, beaten, starved, deported, enslaved, and killed. In the early years of the regime, Jewish young people were cut off from schools, sports, friendships, and material support. Later, they endured family separations and deportations from their homelands. Millions of children suffered extreme deprivations and witnessed and experienced horrifying violence and brutality.

The Nazis caused further pain to Jewish children by forcing them to commit vile or humiliating acts against their parents and their religion. For example, Jewish boys were ordered to cut off their fathers' beards, which Jewish men grew in accordance with their Orthodox religious traditions. Some youths were sexually abused or humiliated, for example, by being forced to undress and dance or sing embarrassing songs.

To escape the Holocaust, thousands of Jewish youth in occupied countries were hidden or given new identities. They were compelled to deny or hide their religion and had to live in constant fear of being captured and killed. Those who were captured were sent to concentration or death camps run by the Nazis. At the camps, most children under 14 were killed at once and few young people of any age survived until the end of the war.

One of these survivors was Eugen Zuckermann (1926–1997), the son of a Czech mother and a Hungarian father. When he was three, his family moved to Berlin, Germany, but were expelled by the Nazis in 1939 and sent to Hungary. In 1944, when the family was living in the Miskolc Ghetto, he and his father and brother were sent by the Germans to forced labor camps. As a slave laborer in various camps, Zuckermann endured beatings, constant hunger, overwork, and exposure to cold. He was forced to take part in the death marches during the winter before the war ended. At Mauthausen, a camp in Austria, he labored long hours in a stone quarry where Nazi guards beat or shot people who displeased them. At this camp, about 1,000 people died each day from starvation. Many others died from diseases such as typhus.

When Zuckerman was finally liberated from Mauthausen in 1945 at age 19, he found out that his mother Malvina and his younger brother Artur and sister Klara had all been gassed at Auschwitz. In 1949, he moved to the United States where he lived in New York City and worked as a tailor. Zuckermann devoted his life to studying and learning about the Holocaust and urged other survivors to tell their stories and bear witness to what had happened. He was an active member of the Group Project for Holocaust Survivors and Their Children, which was founded in 1975.

In addition to Jews, the Nazis also targeted certain other groups for persecution and death during the Holocaust. These groups included the Romani (commonly but incorrectly called Gypsies), people with mental or physical handicaps, and homosexuals, who were sent to concentration camps and forced to wear labels in the form of pink triangles. Political opponents and communists, as well as Poles, Slavs, and people of color were also viewed as inferior under the Nazi concepts of a "Master Race," and were therefore also in danger of persecution and death. *See also* AUERBACHER, INGE; AUSCHWITZ-BIRKENAU; AUSTRIA (WORLD WAR II); BARBIE, KLAUS; BAUM, FROIM; BELGIUM (WORLD WAR II); BIELSKI BROTHERS; CHILDREN'S TRANSPORTS (*KINDERTRANSPORTS*); CONCENTRATION CAMPS (WORLD WAR II); DEATH CAMPS (WORLD WAR II); DEATH MARCHES; DEPORTATIONS; DISPLACED PERSONS (DPs) (WORLD WAR II); *EINSATZGRUPPEN*; EUTHANASIA; EXPERIMENTS, NAZI; FINAL SOLUTION; FORCED LABOR (WORLD WAR II); FRANK, ANNE; GENOCIDE; GHETTOS (WORLD WAR II); GREECE (WORLD WAR II); HART, KITTY FELIX; HIDDEN CHILDREN; HITLER, ADOLF; HITLER YOUTH; HOLLAND (WORLD WAR II); ITALY (WORLD WAR II); JEHOVAH'S WITNESSES; "MASTER RACE"; RESCUERS (HOLOCAUST); RESISTANCE MOVEMENTS (WORLD WAR II); RIGHTEOUS GENTILES; ROMANI (GYPSIES); ROUND-UPS; UNITED STATES HOLOCAUST MEMORIAL AND MUSEUM; WALLENBERG, RAOUL; WARSAW GHETTO; WORLD WAR II; ZYKLON B.

Further Reading: Barry Bearak, "Remembering One Who Remembered," *The New York Times*, December 11, 1997, pp. B1, B8; Howard Greenfeld, *The Hidden Children* (1993); Jack Kuper, *Child of the Holocaust* (1968); Maxine B. Rosenberg, *Hiding to Survive* (1994); Leni Yahil, *The Holocaust* (1990).

Home Guard. *See* CIVIL DEFENSE

Homelessness. *See* BLITZ, LONDON; BOMBINGS (WORLD WAR II); DISPLACED PERSONS (DPs) (WORLD WAR II); HIROSHIMA; NAGASAKI; NINOSHIMA; POLAND (WORLD WAR II); REFUGEES; UNACCOMPANIED CHILDREN; WORLD WAR II

Homosexuals. *See* HOLOCAUST

Hungary (World War II)

Hungary was allied with Nazi Germany and the Axis nations at the start of World War II. The Holocaust came late for Hungarian youth and their families. Hungarian Jews had been persecuted and deprived of legal rights and opportunities for education during the late 1930s but were not persecuted as severely or deported to concentration camps like Jews in other Nazi-dominated countries. Under Admiral Miklos Horthy, who became regent of Hungary in 1920, the country passed anti-Jewish laws between 1938 and 1942 but did not accede to Hitler's demands to deport Hungarian Jews to death camps. Horthy appointed an anti-Nazi prime minister, Miklos Kallay, in March 1942. Horthy and Kallay said that the Hungarian government must retain its independence and develop its own "Jewish policy."

Young people took part in political debates and sided with the fascist or anti-fascist sides. Some non-Jewish young men, teenagers as young as 14 and 15, joined the Arrow Cross, a right-wing militia group that terrorized Jews during the last months of World War II. The Arrow Cross was a fascist, anti-Semitic, and pro-Hitler militia organization in Hungary that recruited numerous young people. One division of fascist youths within the Arrow Cross, the Levente, consisted of teenagers who carried rifles and hand grenades.

During the war, Hungarians suffered from food shortages. Young Hungarians were forced to labor for the Germans after Germany took control of the country in 1944. They had to clear rubble from the streets, dig tank traps to stop Soviet tanks, and work in German-run factories. Fuel shortages meant that homes and schools often lacked heat, and some schools closed during the last year of the war. Other schools were closed down after the army requisitioned them for military use.

Jewish youth in Hungary suffered additional hardships. Gangs of Arrow Cross members attacked them on their way to and from school or in the streets. They were banned from schools, public recreation facilities, and sports teams, and then forced into ghettos.

On March 19, 1944, Hitler sent German troops into Hungary to take over the government. Pro-Nazi General Dome Sztojay was named prime minister. In May, Adolf Eichmann, the chief Nazi organizer of Jewish deportation to death camps, arrived to aggressively deport Jews. Hungarian police and Arrow Cross members helped him round up people from the countryside and send thousands to death camps, mainly Auschwitz.

Other Jews in the countryside were brutally attacked and killed. Within a few months, almost no Jewish men, women, or children remained in rural Hungary.

Meanwhile, Jews in Budapest and other cities were forced into specially marked buildings in sections of the city marked off as ghettos. People were put on starvation rations of fewer than 700 calories a day. In November 1944, after the Nazis sent her mother to a death camp, nine-year-old Martha Hentz was forced into a ghetto where she, her father, and grandmother lived with 14 people in one room. Hentz later recalled that

> There was no place to cook, but there was nothing to cook anyway. Fortunately the communal kitchen sent some food on most days. Beans one day, split peas the next. . . . During the day, if it was not extremely cold, the children walked around the fenced area of the ghetto. Corpses and dead horses lay scattered on the sidewalk. (Handler and Meschel, 1993)

Gangs of Arrow Cross members attacked people in the ghetto with impunity and committed savage acts. Sometimes they shot people at random; other times, they marched large groups to the river and shot them so their bodies fell into the water. When Nazi Germany occupied Hungary in 1944, their troops received help from members of the Arrow Cross and other collaborators as they rounded up, deported, and killed Jewish civilians during the last year of the war.

Ten-year-old Gabor Kalman had a narrow escape. He had arrived at a private school run by priests who were sheltering Jewish boys. His uncle picked him up the next day, saying he had found out that most of the boys there were Jewish so the school might not be safe. It was raided a few days later and all the boys were deported.

Solomon Fleischman, one of 11 children, was 16 in 1944 when the Nazis began rounding up Hungarian Jews. His father gave each of the children some money and urged them to scatter and try somehow to survive. Solomon hid with his uncle in a cellar beneath the apartment building where his family lived. After they ran out of food,

Fleischman asked the 14-year-old carpenter's apprentice who worked in the shops above the cellar to help. For the next few weeks, he brought back food he had obtained with Fleischman's ration coupons. Then the two men in hiding were discovered by Valeriu Moldovan, the Rumanian-born owner of the carpentry shop and father of two small children. He assured them that he would help. Refusing to accept any payment, Moldovan brought Fleischman and his uncle food and kept them informed about what was happening. He convinced other people not to turn the men in for the reward money. Late in 1944, after Russian troops liberated the town, Fleischman emerged from hiding. He was the only member of his immediate family to survive.

The last year of the war (1944–1945), brought hundreds of air raids that killed civilians and destroyed homes. People also went hungry as they huddled together in air-raid shelters and had no access to food. Some children faced these air raids alone because all the adults had been taken away for forced labor or deported to Nazi camps. During the many air raids that occurred in 1944, young people spent hours in shelters where they ate meals, played cards, and tried to occupy themselves. There was no electricity. One man later recalled that his uncle found a can of floor wax to use for light and he offered his shoelace as a candle wick. People starved to death because no food transports reached the cities.

Fighting between German and Russian troops marked the end of the war in Hungary. Gunfire in the streets killed some youth in the final days of the war when they ventured outside the shelters to get food and water. When the war finally ended, many young people were hungry, cold, and homeless. Children were also sick with dysentery, tuberculosis, pneumonia, scarlet fever, or other diseases. They died from the lack of heating fuel, nourishing food, and medicine. People from cities trekked long distances across icy rivers to find farms where they could trade jewelry and other valuables for some potatoes or flour.

Susan V. Meschel later recalled that her mother and some other women found a dead horse in the street and cut off the meat to make stew. She said, "My feet were frozen and I could not take my shoes off. My greatest desire was to go somewhere where I could take off my shoes and maybe even take a bath" (Handler and Meschel, 1993). Along with many young people who survived the war, Meschel would begin the difficult process of rebuilding her life in a war-torn country. *See also* GHETTOS (WORLD WAR II); HOLOCAUST; HUNGER/MALNUTRITION; RESISTANCE MOVEMENTS (WORLD WAR II); RIGHTEOUS GENTILES; SPORTS; WALLENBERG, RAOUL; WORLD WAR II.

Further Reading: Gay Block and Malka Drucker, *Rescuers* (1992); Andrew Handler and Susan V. Meschel, comps., *Young People Speak* (1993); Elaine Landau, *We Survived the Holocaust* (1991); Kati Marton, *A Race for Life* (1982).

Hunger/Malnutrition

Hunger and malnutrition are often serious problems for youth during wartime and can lead to illness, starvation, and death. After war's end, young people continue to suffer from a lack of adequate and nourishing food. Often, nutritious foods are not available and poverty and displacement make it harder for families to provide for their children. Because they are still growing and developing, young people typically encounter special problems when they lack adequate amounts of protein, vitamins, and other nutrients. They may suffer from stunted growth, skin diseases, symptoms of protein and vitamin deficiency, unhealthy bones and teeth, learning disabilities, and other problems.

After World War I, reports spread around the world that German children were starving. American physician Alice Hamilton visited war-torn Germany in 1919 and described the children's "sticklike legs, the swollen bellies, the ribs one could count, the shoulder blades sticking out like wings" (Hamilton, 1943). Children in Germany and Austria lacked basics like milk. Watery soup was sometimes the only food available. Without flour, people had to bake bread with sawdust and dried bark. Former enemies rallied to help these young victims of war.

A number of families participated in post-war hunger programs that arranged for children from working class families in Germany and Austria to go to Great Britain and The Netherlands where they received nourishing food in an effort to build up their health. The children stayed with foster families who could provide a healthy diet during these so-called "Health Holidays." In most cases, children returned to Germany after a doctor said they had recovered sufficiently. However, some children were so sickly and malnourished that their German families agreed to let them stay in Holland indefinitely.

World War II brought more widespread hunger as people in occupied countries struggled to avoid starvation and malnutrition. Because Adolf Hitler and his fellow German soldiers had sometimes gone hungry during World War I, he vowed that his soldiers during World War II would get the best foods available and that German civilians would have second priority over the occupied peoples. During the first years of the war, German soldiers had meat, poultry, dairy products, breads, and fruits and vegetables. They did not suffer serious shortages until near the end of the war.

After Germany invaded their country in 1939, Poles immediately faced food shortages. The occupation government rationed food strictly. Poles received far less food than their German counterparts, and food was shipped out of Poland to Germany. The Nazis had publicly stated that malnutrition would help them get rid of their enemies and was an especially effective way to kill children. Rations for Polish young people ages 14 to 20 were 33 percent less than for Germans of the same age; for children ages 10 to 14, they were 65 percent less; and for children under 10, they were 60 percent less. For Jewish youths, especially in the ghettos, amounts were far less. Malnutrition led to high rates of tuberculosis. Rickets—a disease of the bones caused by a lack of calcium and other minerals—increased by 70 to 90 percent among Polish children during the war years.

This poster was part of the American famine relief effort during World War I. *Hoover Institution Archives, Stanford University.*

Similarly, people in Holland suffered from lack of food during the five years of occupation that began in May 1940. A 15-year-old girl from Holland observed that

> Mothers would stand for hours in a queue with a bowl for some kohlrabi. Neither potatoes or kohlrabi were peeled before boiling . . . . The smell of this hash was unbelievable, but it was warm and stopped the hunger pains. Hunger is a pain that gnaws at your stomach and just will not go away. No matter how many cups of water one drank to fill that aching stomach, that dreadful feeling would not go away. (Westall, 1985)

Hunger reached drastic proportions in Hungary during the last months of World War II. As Susan V. Meschel later recalled, "I remember chewing a small, leathery piece of rancid bacon for more than a month. My mother found a sack of moldy, dry bread and by lengthy soaking and grinding made some round objects she called meatballs" (Handler and Meschel, 1993).

In Budapest, Hungary, Gabor Kalman recalled the struggle for food that he and his family faced while hiding from the Nazis: "We melt snow for drinking water, and I try to trap some city pigeons for dinner. When I finally succeed, I release the poor bird, for it is skinnier than we are. Our neighbors find a dead horse and happily return with frozen meat" (Handler and Meschel, 1993).

After the war ended, young people had high rates of diseases caused by the lack of specific nutrients. These diseases included rickets, anemia, scurvy, tuberculosis of the bones, and pellagra, a disease that affects the skin and nervous system. Children also suffered from such skin problems as boils, fistulas, infections, and rashes. Tooth decay and other dental problems were pervasive. Doctors noted that many children had large heads and small, bony bodies. Some were so weak they could not walk or talk. Infant mortality rates also increased. A survey by the Red Cross taken after World War II showed that the average child ate about half as many calories as he or she needed for normal growth and development. Between 1936 and 1944, the average height of boys declined by about three inches, while girls' heights declined by about four inches.

During the last half of the twentieth century, civil wars have brought hunger and starvation to many children. The scorched earth tactics used by military troops left people without food or any means to grow crops.

People who were uprooted from their homes lost their stored food and ability to produce food. The lack of tools and other supplies and lack of access to sources of water exacerbated these problems. Food supplies have also been purposely kept from civilian populations as a way to terrorize people and wear down their resistance.

Researchers measure the extent of malnutrition by comparing a child's height for age, weight for age, and weight for height with those of normally growing children. In August and September 1991, an international team of public health researchers studied malnutrition in Iraq after the Persian Gulf War of 1990–1991. They found that 29 percent of the children they studied were malnourished, which would translate to a total of 900,000 children in the country as a whole.

Hunger and malnutrition remained serious problems in Africa during various civil wars that continued into the late 1990s. The Sudan is one example. In 1996, MEDAIR, worked with UNICEF to assess the nutritional needs of children and implemented a program to supplement the diets of all children who fell below the 80 percent mark of weight for height. The program served 300 children supplementary biscuits, oil, sugar, and a nutritional product called Unimix. Children in the program gained weight and child mortality rates declined in the area served by the program.

In Liberia, where civil war had raged during the early 1990s, hunger and malnutrition afflicted tens of thousands of children. Fighting had cut off access to food supplies sent by humanitarian organizations, and people could not leave their homes to find food for fear of being struck by gunfire. Rebel groups often looted stores and places where food supplies were kept. In Tubmanburg, north of the capital of Monrovia, more than 20,000 people were suffering from severe malnutrition in 1996. Eighty-two percent of the children age 5 and under were malnourished, and many children had died from malnutrition. An organization called Action Against Hunger delivered food for 4,000 children in Tubmanburg and the United Nations World Food Program sent other large food shipments to the region.

The Children and Armed Conflict Unit (a project of the Children's Legal Centre and Human Rights Center, both based in Great Britain) studied the problem of hunger in Kosovo while it was monitoring the impact of that conflict on children. After war broke out in Kosovo in 1998, the organization found that children were going hungry. Food aid was inadequate for several reasons: Relief organizations had underestimated the number of children who would be displaced; the Serbian government had caused delays in shipping food and delivering it to children in need; Serbian troops had burned crops and let farm animals loose; and humanitarian agencies were unable to get free access to all the places children in need were living. Food rations consisted of flour, oil, sugar, rice and some salt, and children did not have access to fruit, vegetables, and foods rich in protein during the early months of the conflict. Baby food was also scarce, along with milk for children who were beyond breast-feeding age. As the war in Kosovo continued in 1999, providing for the nutritional needs of the hundreds of thousands of displaced children remained a challenge for relief organizations. *See also* AFRICA; AMERICAN FRIENDS SERVICE COMMITTEE (AFSC); BOER WAR; CHINESE CIVIL WAR; CUBAN REVOLUTION; DISEASE; FEED THE CHILDREN; FOOD; FRENCH REVOLUTION; GERMANY (WORLD WAR II); GHETTOS (WORLD WAR II); GREECE (WORLD WAR II); GUATEMALA; HOLLAND (WORLD WAR II); HUNGARY (WORLD WAR II); HUNGER WINTER; JAPAN (WORLD WAR II); KOSOVO; MARSHALL PLAN; PACIFIC (WORLD WAR II); POLAND (WORLD WAR II); RELIEF ORGANIZATIONS; RUSSIAN REVOLUTION; RWANDA; SOMALIA; UNITED NATIONS CHILDREN'S FUND (UNICEF); WARSAW GHETTO; WORLD WAR I; WORLD WAR II.

Further Reading: Mary Berg, *Warsaw Ghetto Diary* (1945); Douglas Botting, *The Aftermath: Europe* (1983); Andrew Handler and Susan V. Meschel, comps., *Young People Speak* (1993); Werner Warmbrunn, *The Dutch Under German Occupation* (1963); Robert Westall, *Children of the Blitz* (1985); Alexander Worth, *France: 1940-1955* (1956).

Hunger Winter (1944–1945)

In Holland, the last winter of World War II (1944–1945) was known as the "Hunger Winter" because food shortages, which had grown increasingly severe since 1940, reached a crisis. After the Germans first occupied Holland in May 1940, they began shipping food out of Holland to Germany and strictly rationed food in Holland. The Dutch had less and less food as the war continued. During the winter of 1944-1945, the Germans cut off food shipments by rail into Dutch cities and towns and frozen rivers prevented food from reaching people by barge. An estimated 400 people in Holland died each day of starvation during these grim months.

During the Hunger Winter, people from cities went on long hunger walks— *hongertochts*—in the countryside to trade furniture, musical instruments, silver, and other possessions for whatever food was available. Young people often accompanied their parents on these walks or went on their own. Some carried food in baby carriages or on their bicycles, while trying to avoid German patrols on the roads. Young people in the countryside tried to help these travelers by pointing out roads where they would not encounter patrols.

Most meals during this winter consisted of watery soups made with bits of unpeeled potatoes, turnips, wilted carrots, or dried beans. Many children lined up at public soup kitchens to eat broth made from sugar beets, potatoes, or carrots. During the Hunger Winter, public kitchens overflowed. About 300,000 people were served in Amsterdam. Many Dutch survived by eating tulip bulbs. *See also* HEPBURN, AUDREY; HOLLAND (WORLD WAR II); HUNGER/MALNUTRITION.

Further Reading: Miep Gies, *Anne Frank Remembered* (1987); Walter A. Maass, *The Netherlands at War: 1940-1945* (1970); Werner Warmbrunn, *The Dutch Under German Occupation* (1963).

I

Identity Papers

In Nazi-occupied countries during World War II, adults and young people over a specified age were required to carry identity papers that showed their name, age, and nationality. The authorities might ask for these papers at any time. Nazi officials marked the papers of Jews with a special stamp, such as a black letter "J." They also issued special work passes to people who were assigned to work projects or who were allowed to come and go through closed ghettos to get to factories outside ghetto walls.

Members of the resistance movements in Nazi-occupied countries secretly printed and distributed false identity papers and work passes. Young people often took part in this work, helping to forge documents and to deliver them. People who needed such documents asked people they trusted for help; others were contacted by members of the resistance, who gave them the papers they needed. For many young people, the possession of these documents meant the difference between life and death.

Because Jews were being hunted down and murdered, many tried to obtain false identity papers as well as a fake work card (called an *Ausweis*). Many young people survived because they succeeded in obtaining such fake identity papers. One young man from Poland later told author Joseph Ziemian (1975) that

I had a false Kennkarta (identity card issued by the Germans), a false Ausweis (certificate of employment), and a fabricated life history. Such a history, well thought out and memorised, was an indispensable condition of survival. Even when awakened from the deepest sleep, I could immediately trot out my "employment" and my "father's" name without a single mistake. (Ziemian, 1975)

To pass with a fake identity, it was essential to appear calm and to find ways to avoid Nazi police on the street, such as by blowing one's nose, shifting one's gaze to a shop window, or bending down to tie a shoe. *See also* Hartz, Ruth Kapp; Hidden Children; Italy (World War II); Jewish Fighters Organization (JFO); Resistance Movements (World War II); Wallenberg, Raoul.

Further Reading: Rose Zar, *In the Mouth of the Wolf* (1984); Joseph Ziemian, *The Cigarette Sellers of Three Crosses Square* (1975).

Imprisonment. *See* Prisoners

India. *See* Hindu-Muslim Riots (India); Massacres

Indian Wars. *See* American Indian Wars

International Committee of the Red Cross. *See* RED CROSS

International Rescue Committee (IRC)

The International Rescue Committee (IRC), a nonsectarian organization, was founded in 1933 by the world-famous physicist and Nobel Prize winning German-born scientist Albert Einstein. The purpose of this American-based nonprofit relief organization was to aid refugees in war-ravaged countries throughout the world. During the 1970s and 1980s, the IRC was active in Vietnam and ran recuperation centers for casualties of war, many of whom were children. These young people were the victims of bombings and explosions caused by minefields, and often suffered from malnutrition, which led to other health problems. The IRC has provided assistance to refugees in Cambodia, Afghanistan, Rwanda, and Bosnia and channels $80 million each year into its work for refugees. It has funded homes, schools, and hospitals and focuses on the needs of women and children. *See also* REFUGEES; VIETNAM WAR.

Further Reading: "Annual Report," "Fact Sheet," "Overseas Programs," IRC, 122 E. 42nd Street, New York, NY 10168-1289.

International Volunteer Services (IVS)

During the Vietnam War, the International Volunteer Services (IVS) organization operated as a privately run version of the Peace Corps. The IVS provided material aid and operated a number of hostels for street children in Saigon and other places. The group's goal was to provide shelter, food, clean clothing, and access to health and dental care. Volunteers learned the language and went to Vietnam to live and work with refugees.

While working at the Dong Tac refugee camp, author and IVS volunteer Thomas C. Fox met people who had faced the destruction and devastation of the war. One day, a 40-year-old peasant man walked up to him carrying the dead body of his four-year-old daughter, the victim of a bombing by U.S. planes. He said, "Tell President [Lyndon] Johnson how my daughter died" (Lifton, 1972).

The IVS operated refugee centers and homes for homeless children, such as the shoeshine center in Saigon, which gave each boy sheltered there a shoeshine kit and safe place to keep his earnings. The boys attended school and took part in recreational and artistic activities. Americans working with IVS helped the Vietnamese people learn the skills needed to take over and run the hostels for themselves to give them more independence and self-determination. IVS volunteers who opposed the Vietnam War tried to exert pressure on the government to end it. During the late 1960s, they petitioned President Johnson to stop the war. *See also* VIETNAM WAR.

Further Reading: Betty Jean Lifton and Thomas C. Fox, *Children of Vietnam* (1972).

Internment Camps, U.S.

In 1942, during World War II, internment camps for Japanese Americans were set up in the United States under the authorization of the "Civilian Exclusion Order." An estimated 110,000 to 120,000 people were forced into detention camps by the government. Camps were located in Rohwer, Arkansas; Poston, Arizona; Manzanar, California; Heart Mountain, Wyoming; Jerome, Arkansas; Topaz, Utah; Tule Lake, California; and Granada, Colorado, among other places.

When the United States entered the war on December 8, 1941, after the Japanese bombed Pearl Harbor, about 127,000 persons of Japanese ancestry lived in the United States. Most of these people lived in California, Washington, and Oregon. About two-thirds of them were U.S. citizens, while others had been barred from becoming citizens by laws that were passed by people who disliked Asians. Forced to remain aliens, these residents could not vote or own land or businesses in their own name. Their children, called Nisei, were U.S. citizens because they were born on U.S. soil.

After the attack on Pearl Harbor, people of Japanese ancestry were subject to racist attacks and the loss of various civil rights. Some Americans were suspicious of anyone with ties to Japan. There were rumors that the Japanese planned to attack the West Coast and that people of Japanese descent might help them through espionage or sabotage. People painted cruel messages on the homes, cars, and businesses of these people and vandalized their property. An article in *Life* magazine explained how to identify differences between the physical features of people of Japanese ancestry versus those of Chinese ancestry.

Government agents and men from the Federal Bureau of Investigation (FBI) visited towns and cities along the West Coast where people of Japanese ancestry lived and worked. They searched their homes and closed down businesses. Cameras, radios, and certain ceremonial weapons and other belongings, such as kitchen knives and flashlights, were confiscated or destroyed.

In Congress, lawmakers debated whether Japanese Americans posed a threat and even considered sending them out of the country. Eventually, some 120,000 were forced to leave their homes and interned in so-called relocation centers. Executive Order 9066, signed by President Franklin Roosevelt on February 19, 1942, legalized this action. It declared that people who had "a Japanese ancestry to any degree" were subject to internment.

Internment dramatically changed the lives of young people because their parents left behind jobs and sold businesses, often losing their savings in the process. They usually had to sell their homes, cars, tools, and other belongings, too, because these items might not be safe if left unattended for a long and un-

A Japanese American family is taken under guard to an internment camp in 1942. *Corbis.*

known period of time. Unscrupulous people exploited the chance to buy things at unfairly low prices. Sumiko Seo Seki later recalled, "We were only allowed to take with us just what we could carry. We left the crops that were about to be harvested"(Brimner, 1994).

Children were uprooted from their homes, neighborhoods, and schools. Before they were transported to the camps, internees were assigned a number and told they could bring only as much as they could carry by hand. Some people carried U.S. flags as they lined up in order of age, with the oldest member at the head of the line. Amy Iwasaki Mass was six years old at the time. She recalled, "I was scared. I was the youngest and I wanted to be closer to my parents" (Brimner, 1994).

They did not know where they were going. When they arrived, they had to sleep in smelly stables on straw-filled sacks. Armed soldiers and guard towers stood at the entrance to the camps, which were rimmed with barbed wire. The camps were not completed when the people first arrived, so they lived in crowded tar-paper barracks and used outhouses. A room measuring about 20 feet by 24 feet housed each family.

Food was also poor, mostly liver, sauerkraut, sardines, canned beans, sausage, and rice—far different from their usual meals, and hardly any fresh food. Months passed before schools were set up and recreation and religious programs began. Health care was another problem. Supplies of all kinds were inadequate. The U.S. military had first priority, then civilians, and last of all, the internees.

Children from warm climates like Hawaii and southern California lacked warm clothing for the cold winters. The Red Cross provided hats, sweaters, and mittens, and some children wore these items day and night to keep warm. In a 1987 interview, Norman Mineta, a Congressman from California, recalled the conditions at the camp in Heart Mountain, Wyoming, where his family was sent.

> I remember the sand whipping up into the barracks through the cracks in the floorboards. It was cold, bitterly cold, and since we were all from California, most people had to make do with light jackets and blankets. Of course we couldn't go shopping. There were 12,000 people in the camp living in crowded barracks. . . . We were treated as prisoners of war, really—not Americans. You have to imagine how we felt looking up at the guarded towers, knowing that their guns were pointed not outward but in, at us. (Mineta, 1987)

Older students had to interrupt their studies, and were not permitted to attend colleges or universities that had Reserve Officer Training Corps (ROTC) programs on campus. After several months passed, the American Friends Service Committee (AFSC) and some other religious groups were able to help obtain the release of thousands of interned students so they could return to school.

At the camps, young people tried to live as normally as possible. They joined scout troops and organized sports activities, such as baseball teams. Musical teens formed bands, and dances were held. The newly developing schools sponsored singing clubs, baton twirling groups, and other special interest groups. Some children planted gardens or took up arts and crafts. As camp conditions improved, young men found construction jobs building schools, churches, streets, and judo pavilions. People of all ages could attend classes in literature, needlework, judo, kendo, and Japanese crafts. The War Relocation Authority sponsored recreation programs in the camps. Groups of students were able to leave the camps to go on overnight camping trips and hikes with their leaders.

In 1943, the Japanese American Citizens League passed a resolution pledging that American-born (Nisei) men interned in camps would actively serve in the U.S. military. The government began setting up combat regiments made up of Nisei soldiers and distributed a controversial Loyalty Oath. People aged 17 or older had to sign the oath to join the military or look for jobs outside internment camps. Many children and their families were able to leave in 1943.

On December 18, 1944, the United States Supreme Court ruled on three landmark cases relating to internment. The Court declared that loyal citizens may not be held against their will in detention camps. As a result, all 10 internment camps were eventually closed down.

It was not until years later that Congress and others involved acknowledged the grievous wrong that had been done to Japanese Americans during the war. Two former internees brought lawsuits in federal court claiming that they had been improperly interned, in violation of their civil rights and due process of law. The court agreed. In 1980, Congress set up the Commission on Wartime Relocation and Internment of Civilians, charging its members with reviewing Executive Order 9066, which had authorized the internment. A report by the committee, *Personal Justice Denied*, was published in 1982. Five years later, a congressional bill sponsored by 74 senators declared that amends should be made to the victims of the internment. In 1988, the government formally apologized to those who had been interned. Token reparations in the amount of $20,000 per surviving internee were granted by the Senate and House. President Ronald Reagan signed the bill in August 1988. *See also* AMERICAN FRIENDS SERVICE COMMITTEE (AFSC); MANZANAR WAR RELOCATION CENTER; PEARL HARBOR; WORLD WAR II.

Further Reading: Larry Dane Brimner, *Voices from the Camps* (1994); Roger Daniels, *Concentration Camps U.S.A.* (1972); Roger Daniels, *The Decision to Relocate the Japanese Americans* (1975); Norman Mineta, "The Wounds of War," *"People,* 1987; Jayne Pettit, *A Time to Fight Back* (1996); Monica Itoi Stone, *Nisei Daughter* (1953); John Tateishi, *And Justice For All* (1984); Michi Weglyn, *Years of Infamy* (1976).

Interrogations

During wartime, young people have been subjected to interrogations that involved threats, emotional abuse, and physical violence. Interrogating children and young adults was a harsh reality during World War II. Nazi police and their collaborators, such as the Hungarian Arrow Cross, questioned children and pressured them to give incriminating information about parents, other family members, or neighbors. The officials sought information about where Jews and political opponents were hiding, as well as information about resistance activities. Sometimes they threatened to harm or kill other family members unless the victim gave them the information they sought.

Children whose parents were involved in resistance activities or were hiding Jews, which was illegal in Nazi-occupied countries, were at great risk. To prepare children for this possibility, young people were told how to mislead officials and to lie if necessary. Older youths who were themselves members of the resistance were also prepared for the possibility of interrogation. To prevent numerous arrests, members of resistance groups were told as little as possible about the other members and had minimal contact with them. People used false names even with members of their group.

When the Nazis discovered hiding places of Jews or other people they sought, they interrogated captives to get more information. In 1943, two houses for refugees in Le Chambon in southern France were raided by the Gestapo. Magda Trocme, the wife of the pastor Andre Trocme, one of the leaders of this effort, was in the house at the time and she pretended to be a maid. She later reported that the Gestapo had taken students into a room, one by one, and an agent interrogated them. Some children returned with bruises on their faces. In some cases, children were permanently injured as a result of physical abuse they endured during interrogations. *See also* ESPIONAGE; LE CHAMBON-SUR-LIGNON; RESCUERS (HOLOCAUST); RESISTANCE MOVEMENTS (WORLD WAR II); TROCME, ANDRE AND TROCME, MAGDA.

Further Reading: Ina Friedman, *The Other Victims* (1990); Philip Hallie, *Lest Innocent Blood Be Shed* (1979); Arnold Rubin, *The Evil Men Do* (1977).

Intifada

Tensions increased in the Middle East after Israel claimed new territory when it won a war against Egypt and Syria in 1967. Thousands of Palestinians became refugees in the years that followed. Late in 1987, children and teenagers were the major part of a Palestinian protest movement called the Intifada. They confronted Israeli soldiers on the West Bank of the Jordan River and the Gaza Strip and demanded that their homes and land be returned to them. As the troops pushed them back, the Palestinians threw stones, bottles, and other things at them. Israeli troops fired on the groups of protesters and children and teenagers were injured and killed, sparking reactions and criticism from people around the world.

The uprising spread throughout the Israeli-occupied territories and more violence took place, with more young casualties. Children and teenagers died and were injured daily as the Intifada continued. At first, the Israeli government stood firm and sent more troops into the area. At one point, Israeli Prime Minister Shamir banned television cameras and foreign news correspondents from both Gaza and the West Bank. By mid-1992, nearly 1,000 Palestinians and more than 40 Israelis had been killed, and the ongoing confrontations in the occupied regions

were hurting the Arab economy. *See also* ARAB-ISRAELI WARS; EDUCATION; REFUGEES.

Further Reading: David J. Abodaher, *Youth in the Middle East* (1991).

Iran-Iraq War (1980–1988)

Armed conflicts raged between the neighboring Middle Eastern countries of Iran and Iraq in the 1970s and 1980s. One major source of conflict concerned which nation should control an important waterway, the Shatt al-Arab, which borders both countries and leads into the Persian Gulf. The conflicts were also rooted in an earlier war, during the 1960s, when Kurds in Iraq (who made up about 20 percent of the population and were the largest non-Arab group living in Iraq) rebelled against the government and demanded their independence.

Kurdish guerilla bands received assistance and weapons from the government of Iran. In 1975, Iraqi leader Saddam Hussein reluctantly signed a treaty with Iran. However,

In December 1993, during another of the clashes that characterize the Palestinian Intifada, an Israeli border policeman detains a young Palestinian boy in East Jerusalem. *Jacqueline Arzt, AP/Wide World Photos.*

conflicts over land, mineral rights, and power in the region continued to fester. A new war between Iran and Iraq began in 1980. During that war, Iraqis attacked Kurds who lived in Iraq. Child soldiers were among the troops who fought with the Kurdish liberation movement, and some were as young as 12, while a substantial number were in their mid-teens.

Tens of thousands of child soldiers also fought with the Iraqi troops. The official age for conscription in Iraq was 18 at the time, but Saddam Hussein lowered it to 17. Some photos of uniformed soldiers holding rifles were of youths younger than 15, and journalists found some Iranian soldiers as young as 12. A large popular Iranian army and militia included youths between ages 16 and 18. Those units were disbanded in 1991.

Youth experienced many problems during the war, including homelessness, injuries, and death as missiles hit Bagdhad, the capital of Iraq, and other cities. Poverty rates increased as ports leading out of Iraq were involved in the fighting, disturbing international trade. By 1984, about one million refugees were struggling to survive, many living in tents. Oil facilities were destroyed or blockaded in both countries, and chemical, steel, and iron plants were bombed, all of which hurt the economy and led to poverty for many families.

The war cost tens of billions of dollars, and some analysts called it the most expensive border war in history and the bloodiest war ever fought in the Middle East. The Iraqi government levied special taxes on the people in 1983. In Iran, young people and adults collected money, jewelry, and other valuables to help finance the war effort.

In the oil-rich Iranian province of Khuzestan, bombs destroyed whole cities and thousands of civilians were killed and injured during these air raids. Iranian bombs also killed civilians in Iraq, and the Iranians used thousands of troops in what were called "human wave attacks," in which many soldiers lost their lives. *See also* CHEMICAL WARFARE; KURDS.

Further Reading: *Children Bearing Military Arms* (1984); Tahir-Kheli and Shaheen Ayubi, eds., *The Iran-Iraq War* (1983); Dorothea Woods, *Child Soldiers in Kurdistan* (1991).

Iraq. *See* IRAN-IRAQ WAR; PERSIAN GULF WAR

Ireland. *See* NORTHERN IRELAND; WORLD WAR II

Irish Republican Army (IRA). *See* NORTHERN IRELAND

Israel. *See* ARAB-ISRAELI WARS; CHEMICAL WARFARE; LEBANESE CIVIL WAR; REFUGEES

Italy (World War II)

In 1940, fascist Italy, led by dictator Benito Mussolini, sided with its ally Nazi Germany and declared war on Great Britain, France, and the rest of the Allied powers. In concert with German troops, Italian forces invaded North Africa and occupied certain surrounding countries, including Greece.

Early in the war, young Italian Jews and Jewish refugees in Italy were not persecuted as harshly as Jews in Germany or Nazi-occupied Europe. Mussolini, who rose to power in 1922, had criticized Hitler's anti-Semitic policies and compared them unfavorably with the policies of his own regime. Because of these policies, many Italian Jews supported Mussolini. However, as Germany and Italy became closely allied, Hitler pressured the Italian leader to pass laws that deprived Italian Jews of their civil rights, jobs, access to education, and property. In 1936 and 1938, new repressive anti-Jewish laws took effect. Jews could not own property over a certain value, which meant many children lost their standard of living and many families lost their livelihood.

In the wake of the 1936 laws, almost 5,700 Italian Jews converted to Catholicism. Children faced many adjustments as their familes fled to South America, Cuba, Switzerland, France, Spain, or the United States. Among those who emigrated were the two young children of Enrico Fermi, the famous physicist. Fermi's wife Laura was Jewish. In 1938, the family embarked for the United

States. Working with other scientists, many of them also refugees, Fermi later played a key role in building the atomic bomb.

Franca Ovazza, an Italian Jewish teenager, lived in Turin, Italy, in 1937. For several months, she attended a Swiss school with young women from different countries. "The world opened up for me. I was very proud of being from Italy, this great country that had become even greater with the African war. And in Switzerland, I suddenly realized this was not how the world saw it. Other people had freedom, they weren't grouped in uniforms. They saw Mussolini not as a great man but as an oppressor" (Stille, 1991). After she returned to Italy, Ovazza criticized the regime and was arrested and beaten by members of OVRA, the Italian secret police.

Because of the new laws, about 10,000 foreign Jews living in Italy in 1938 were arrested and interned in dismal camps over the next few years. The first prisoners were men between ages 18 and 60. Children had to leave their homes and live in huts their families were forced to build themselves. Food and water were inadequate. Illnesses such as malaria spread rapidly in the crowded, unsanitary conditions. People interned at Ferramonti worked hard to organize facilities, creating a nursery, library, school, theater, medical offices, pharmacy, and synagogue for the camp. Young people in the camp participated in sports.

Laws passed in July 1938 banned Jews from various jobs and professions. Franca Ovazza later recalled hearing about the new laws on the radio.

> When they announced that Jewish children would not be allowed to go to school again, we started crying and crying. That was the end of our world. . . . All our friends would be going on to university and we would be left outside. . . .My father was not able to work. My sister and I were not able to go to school. Those things were shattering to us. Everywhere you went you felt like a fly. (Stille, 1991)

Young Italian Jews attended schools run by the Jewish community. University professors who had been removed from their jobs brought their expertise to these schools. Fabio Della Seta told author Susan Zuccotti (1987) that the schools instilled more Jewish pride and taught students about famous Jews, such as scientist Albert Einstein, philosopher Baruch Spinoza, and author Franz Kafka. Some Jewish students were accepted as law students at the Pontificium Institutum Utriusque Iuris inside Vatican City. The Vatican also employed Jews who had lost their jobs because of the racial laws and helped some families to emigrate.

Meanwhile, thousands of young Italian soldiers under age 21 fought with the Axis troops. They had not been well-prepared for war, and tens of thousands of soldiers were captured by British and other Allied forces during 1941 and 1942. Thousands of young men perished on the Russian front while fighting with their German allies.

Young people living in Italy experienced severe food and clothing shortages and rationing as of 1942. As Allied bombs hit Italian targets, many people became homeless. Thousands of city-dwellers fled to the countryside, and urban factories and services did not operate. Workers went on strike to protest wartime conditions. By 1942, young men in many parts of Italy were being required to do forced labor, such as working on road crews or hauling coal or wood. Sometimes young women were also forced to do labor and might be assigned to sort fruit or work in a military barracks or hospital.

Starting in 1942, Hitler and his government demanded that Italian officials deport Jews to concentration camps, something the Italians had resisted. Mussolini continued to stall until he was overthrown in July 1943. Mussolini's fall brought relief to the vast majority of Italians, who hoped that the war would soon end. People celebrated when Allied troops landed in Sicily, and a new prime minister, Marshal Pietro Badoglio, signed an armistice with the Allies. However, in September 1943, German troops invaded Italy. The Italian army was not strong or large enough to drive them out, nor had enough Allied troops arrived. Badoglio had to surrender after three days.

German occupation brought extreme danger to Jews. Children and teenagers were among the first victims of Nazi atrocities. On September 16, 1943, Nazis arrested Jews staying at the Italian mountain resort town of Merano. A six-year-old child and 24 others were interrogated, beaten, and sent to German concentration camps, where only one adult survived the war. Two days later, 349 French Jewish refugees, men, women, and children, were arrested and deported to camps where all but nine died. SS troops hunted down Jews in other Italian villages near the Swiss border. Forty-nine people were shot; at least one teenage girl was raped before she was killed. Herbert Kappler, the German SS commander in Rome, was ordered to deport all Jews from Rome to Germany where, "regardless of nationality, age, sex, and personal conditions," they were to be "liquidated." A Nazi round-up known as the Black Sabbath raid occurred early on the morning of October 16, 1943. Nazi officials had guessed they would seize at least 8,000 people. Nine hours later, they had 1,259 captives, including 896 women and children.

Some children had been saved when adults quickly turned them over to non-Jews. The family of Marco Miele, 18 months old, let an unknown Catholic woman take him off the Germans' truck, claiming he was her baby. In another case, Arminio Wachsberger passed his two-year-old son to a janitor's wife when the Nazi guard was not looking. He was later reunited with his son after surviving the Nazi death camp at Auschwitz, where his wife and five-year-old daughter died. Thousands of Jews eluded the Nazis by hiding in Catholic monasteries, convents, the Vatican complex, or in private homes. Priests, monks, and nuns also helped Jews to escape. Catholic clergy issued thousands of false documents claiming that children had been baptized in the church before 1938.

During the Black Sabbath raid, Enrico and Grazia Di Veroli and their four children fled to the home of Catholic friends in a part of Rome called Trastavere. The friends shared their small food rations with the Di Verolis and the woman gave the children her bed. One of the children later recalled that a "lot of the people in the neighborhood knew we were Jews, and one person would bring us something to eat, another would bring something else, so that we didn't have to go out and risk being seen" (Stille, 1991). However, the family fled again after someone told the Germans they were there. By the end of the war, the Di Verolis had lived in seven different places, including convents.

Two brothers, Michele and Gianni, joined the anti-fascist resistance. At age 15, Michele Di Veroli and his father were killed during the massacre at Ardeatine Caves. On March 24, 1944, German SS men gathered 335 men and boys, of whom 77 were Jewish, and tied them together. They were forced inside a group of manmade caves near Rome and shot, one after the other, in retaliation for a partisan attack in which 33 German soldiers died. Another young victim of the massacre was 17-year-old Franco Di Consiglio. In several cases, brothers, fathers, and sons died together on that infamous day. The caves were sealed shut afterwards.

Most Italian police did not cooperate with the Nazis and even thwarted them. Police chief Mario di Nardis protected Jews in Aquila; Chief Giovanni Palatucci of Fiume was arrested and killed in Dachau after he helped Jews in his town. Mario de Marco, head of Rome's police department, refused to give the Nazis lists of Jewish residents. He secretly provided Roman Jews with false identity papers, saving many people from death. Nazi police arrested de Marco and tortured him, but he remained silent.

Many soldiers in Croatia and other Italian-occupied regions also refused to round up Jews for deportation. Croatian Jews were among those who found a safe haven in Italy until the German occupation.

When German troops arrived, a number of young soldiers deserted the Italian army and went home. Many joined partisan units fighting against the Germans. Thousands who were taken prisoner by the Germans died in prisoner of war camps.

Monsignor Hugh Joseph O'Flaherty, an Irish-born priest, helped to rescue Jews and others hunted by the Nazis. Posted at the Vatican, O'Flaherty hid thousands of people, some inside Vatican City and others throughout Rome. The priest often stood on the steps of St. Peter's Basilica where people in need could find him. One day in 1943, shortly after the Germans invaded Italy and reached Rome, a Jewish man approached O'Flaherty and showed him a heavy gold chain he had wrapped around his waist. The man said, "My wife and I expect to be arrested at any moment. We have no way of escaping. When we are taken to Germany we shall die. But we have a small son, he is only seven and too young to die in a Nazi gas chamber." The man asked O'Flaherty to hide his son and use the gold chain for his support. The Monsignor found a safe place for the boy and gave the parents false identity papers. The family survived, and, after the war, O'Flaherty returned the man's gold chain, saying, "I did not need it" (Gallagher, 1967).

Nazi police were suspicious of O'Flaherty, who was safe from arrest as long as he stayed behind a white line marking the border of Vatican City. However, the priest sometimes moved around Rome to make contact with other people in the resistance, usually disguised as a peasant. He managed to elude Nazi police.

One of the most heartening rescues of children took place in the Italian countryside. In 1942, the Jewish relief organization Delasem found 42 Jewish children between the ages of 9 and 21 hiding around Ljubljana, in the Italian zone of Yugoslavia. They were orphans who had survived Nazi massacres in Yugoslavia, Germany, Poland, Rumania, and Austria. Lelio Valobra, national director of Delasem, worked with the woman who headed the Slovenian Red Cross to pick up the children and bring them together in a safe part of Ljubljana. After the Italian government gave Valobra permission to bring the children to Italy, he took them to the Villa Emma, located in Nonantola, a village near Modena. Fifty more children, mostly Croatian, arrived in 1943. Villagers from Modena cooperated to provide food, medical care, and schooling for the children. Tradespeople taught them new skills. One family took two of the youngest children into their home to live. Other townspeople cooperated to provide false documents for the children. After the German occupation began, Nazis and a local Italian fascist raided the villa and found it empty. The 92 children had been hidden in the Catholic seminary and in private homes, where they remained until Italy was liberated in 1944.

Relief organizations helped some young Jews escape from Italy. Italian Jews set up Comasebit, which was based in the seaport city of Milan, to help refugees. The name was later changed to Delasem—*Delagazione Assist enza Emigrant Ebitei*. Much of its funding came from foreign bodies, mainly the Joint Distribution Committee in the United States.

After 1938, Delasem found homes abroad for some 5,000 Italian Jews, mostly young people. They moved to South America, North America, or Shanghai, China, with or without their families. Many Jews had been leaving by way of Genoa, but legal immigration from Genoa was banned as of 1940. Facing many dangers, young people left in boats that were smuggled from Genoa to southern France. From there, they tried to reach Spain or North Africa.

In 1943, German troops invaded Italy and banned Delasem, which was then working with members of the Italian clergy, including Pietro Cardinal Boetto, Father Francesco Repetto, and Father Benedetto, a French-born priest who relocated his resistance work to Italy in 1943. Benedetto's group, which included young Italian resistance workers, supplied thousands of fake identity papers and food ration cards to young Jews in hiding and to their families. *See also* HIDDEN CHILDREN; HOLOCAUST; RESCUERS (HOLOCAUST); RIGHTEOUS GENTILES; ROUND-UPS; WORLD WAR II.

Further Reading: J.P. Gallagher, *Scarlet Pimpernel of the Vatican* (1967); Raul Hilberg, *The Destruction of the European Jews* (1985); H. Stuart Hughes, *Prisoners of Hope* (1996); Alexander Ramati, *The Assisi Underground* (1978); Cecil Roth, *The History of the Jews in Venice* (1930); Alexander Stille, *Benevolence and Betrayal: Five Italian Jewish Families Under Fascism* (1991); Susan Zuccotti, *The Italians and the Holocaust* (1987).

J

Japan (World War II)

Japan invaded China and other Asian countries in the 1930s before World War II officially began in Europe in 1939. Japanese youth were exposed to stories, movies, and books that glorified the idea of war and Japanese military traditions. Patriotism was promoted in schools, and children attended parades to cheer soldiers. Boys enjoyed dressing up in the military uniforms of officers, and some showed their patriotism by wearing shirts made from Japanese flags.

A great celebration was held after the bombing of the U.S. naval base at Pearl Harbor on December 7, 1941. People lined the streets and threw flowers as the men who had carried out the bombing mission marched down the streets of Tokyo. Hiroko Nakamoto, age 11 at the time of Pearl Harbor, later recalled that there was no school on December 7 or 8.

> We were told to stay at home and listen to the news on the radio. . . . The radio was a government monopoly and nothing was broadcast now but news of the war, with martial music in between. . . . The radio addressed us children, saying we must work hard for our country and prepare for the future. We did not know exactly what was meant. (Nakamoto and Pace, 1970)

As the Japanese forces won victories in the Philippines, Hong Kong, Burma (now called the Myanmar Union), and French Indochina, young people were convinced, like their elders, that Japan could defeat any opponent.

As more fuel and ships were requisitioned by the navy for military purposes, deep-sea fish became unavailable. School lunches and other meals often featured squid, which could be caught near the shore, instead of other fish. Other common foods were rice balls, beans, pumpkins, and sometimes sweet potatoes. The rationing of rice began in 1940. By 1941, rice, fish, and vegetables were scarce. Meals consisted of a bowl of soup with a few noodles or some rice. People ate fruit and vegetable peels. They stood in line to buy food and other items. Serious fuel shortages made cooking difficult. Although children helped tend gardens and plant and harvest crops to increase the supply of food, they still often went hungry.

Fearing air attacks, some Japanese families devised home shelters where they could remain during air raids. Children helped collect paper and other materials used in the war effort. School uniforms were altered because of cloth shortages. Girls' skirts were cut shorter and collars were eliminated from their blouses. Other changes took place in schools as the war went on. English classes were abolished after the bombing of Pearl Harbor. Children spent less time on academic subjects and more time on drills and other activities that would help them in wartime, such as team games in which they moved buckets of water down a line of classmates toward a mock fire. Boys were taught how to shoot, using wooden rifles, and girls attended first-aid, cooking, and needlework classes. All Japanese children had to pass an athletic test as well as academic examinations to be admitted to high school.

By 1944, only a small percentage of children were still attending school. Many spent their days in war plants, where Japanese of all ages worked seven days a week producing ammunition and other military materials. For lunch, they often carried a patriotic dish called a "Japanese flag"—a red pickled plum set in the middle of some grain, often barley or wheat when rice was unavailable.

Young people performed many tasks in cities and in rural areas. They worked on farms to plant and harvest crops and gathered thousands of grasshoppers, which were used to protect crops and to make a protein-rich food for soldiers. Girls sewed buttons on uniforms, constructed parachutes, and replaced male workers who had left silk factories to enter the army. Girls also worked in bullet factories and made other military materials.

During the last months of the war, when food shortages were critical, each school-age child was required to collect at least five bushels of acorns each week. The nuts were processed into meal and flour. Even bamboo shoots and radishes were scarce. Food costs soared, and people ate small portions of boiled soybeans, grain, or potato soup. Lunch might be a sweet potato or some peanuts. Men hunted for small birds and animals their families could eat.

Fuel shortages meant that many homes were cold in the winter. In 1945, as shortages became critical, young people were assigned to dig up acres of pine tree roots, which were made into a kind of oil used to fuel airplanes. They also gathered charcoal, which was used to fuel military plants. While at work, most young people wore their school uniforms. Clothing of all kinds was scarce. Schools shut down as school buildings were often used to store army supplies.

Allied air attacks with napalm and incendiary bombs killed several hundred thousand civilians in 1945 and destroyed much of To-kyo. Among the dead was an entire class of sixth-grade students at a Tokyo school. They were killed by bombings on March 15, the day of their graduation ceremony. Homes, which were nearly all made of wood, were quickly destroyed in the fires set off by the bombings. Since homes were built close together, flames jumped quickly from house to house. Young people were put to work demolishing houses in the cities to create firebreaks. However, these firebreaks did not stop fires from spreading. Homelessness increased dramatically because of bombings and demolition. Seeing the bombers arrive day after day, many children believed they were doomed.

In April and May 1945, schoolchildren fought on Okinawa with swords. Early in the summer of 1945, as the threat of an Allied invasion of Japan grew, millions of children were ordered to join Japanese of all ages in a People's Volunteer Army, which was being readied to fight Allied invaders with knives and bamboo spears. By this time, food was so scarce that people were making dumplings from wild weeds and grasses mixed with acorn flour. They took carts to the country and traded possessions for potatoes, onions, rice, and peas. When nothing else was available, they made flour out of ground-up, edible weeds that children collected in fields or ate leaves, grasshoppers, or corn seeds. Some children became ill and died because they lacked proper nourishment and medicines.

In August 1945, after U.S. bombers dropped atomic bombs on the cities of Hiroshima and Nagasaki, Japan surrendered. By that time, half the country's cities were destroyed, and 800,000 civilians had died, including tens of thousands of children. Millions were homeless and hungry, and many children had no shoes and were dressed in rags. Crime and disorder were rampant. Phones and electricity did not work. Japanese youth also faced shortages of housing, food, clothing, and health care after the war. Children wore second-hand clothing or hand-me-downs from older siblings. Several families often lived together because housing was so scarce.

Conditions throughout Japan continued to worsen immediately after the war ended. Hunger, health problems, disorder and crime made daily life difficult. Millions of people had no place to live. Children and their families searched for food in rural areas. Desperately hungry people ate soup made from vegetable peels and stems and dumplings made from wild grasses and ground-up acorns. A black market thrived along with an increase in crime rates. One woman, who was seven years old in 1945, later wrote, "Many beggars appeared in front of the [train] station, and thieves and armed bandits have turned up one after the other, and it has become a world where you aren't safe for a minute" (Osada, 1963).

Schooling was also a major problem, especially in bomb-ravaged cities like Hiroshima and Nagasaki. When one school finally resumed in Nagasaki, a boy arrived to find that only four children in his class of about 60 were there that day. The building was also in bad shape. Some schools held classes outdoors and used tree trunks for seats. After Allied military troops arrived to enforce postwar laws, schools received supplies for children's lunches, including dried eggs, dried meats, canned foods, and tomato juice. Families were given flour and tinned corned beef.

Children feared the arrival of Allied troops, who were stationed in Japan after the war to enforce the terms of the Japanese surrender. They had heard that these men planned to enslave and hurt them. However, Allied soldiers had been told to treat people with the utmost respect. Many Japanese children were relieved to find that these men were kind and gave them candy and other foods. Funds sent by Allied countries helped to rebuild housing, schools, hospitals, utility plants, and other facilities and provided an income for Japanese people who were hired to do this reconstruction work. Children also helped to clear streets and repair their communities. They attended school outdoors until buildings were ready for use. People in Japan continued to rebuild their economy and political institutions for years after World War II was over. *See also* CHEMICAL WARFARE; EVACUA-

TIONS; HIROSHIMA; HIROSHIMA MAIDENS; HOLIDAYS; JAPAN-CHINA WAR; NAGASAKI; NINOSHIMA; PACIFIC (WORLD WAR II); PEARL HARBOR.

Further Reading: Anne Chisholm, *Faces of Hiroshima* (1985); Joseph C. Grew, *Ten Years in Japan* (1972); Tessa Morris-Suzuki, *Showa* (1985); Hiroko Nakamoto and M.M. Pace, *My Japan: 1930-51* (1970); Richard Storry, *A History of Modern Japan* (1960).

Japan-China War (1931–1945)

Youth in China and Japan experienced vast changes and hardships during the Japan-China war that began in 1931 when Japanese troops invaded northern Manchuria. Throughout the 1930s, Japan proceeded to attack various parts of China, including Shanghai and other cities. In Shanghai in 1937, Japanese troops massacred 300 communist leaders, young intellectuals and university students among them. Children in China saw fathers and other male relatives go off to war where many died or were injured. Many other children were forced to flee their homes with their families when Japanese tanks reached their towns.

Japanese forces approached Nanking, the Chinese capital, in January 1938. University students in Nanking helped their professors hide books and equipment before the Japanese arrived. Factories were also emptied of valuable machinery, which was taken to the west. Enraged by the strong Chinese defense of their capital, some Japanese troops reacted violently, and about 100,000 Chinese civilians died in the vicious attacks that became known as the Rape of Nanking. By the end of 1938, the Japanese controlled all the major cities in China.

Children in Japan were taught to be proud of their relatives who fought in these battles and learned to treat returning soldiers as heroes. In their games, they sometimes played out battle scenes they heard about at home or in school. At school, Japanese students marched, learned new patriotic and military songs, and waved flags at parades. Japanese boys also learned military drills. Kazuko Kiredel later recalled how schools celebrated Japanese military victories in China: "Students were all given a cookie that had a Japanese flag stuck into it. They marched around the school yard to celebrate the army's successes" (Newton, 1992).

Certain foods, such as rice, soy sauce, salt, and sugar, were being rationed. Children went without rice cakes and certain other treats they had enjoyed for school picnics. Gas and oil were also rationed, so charcoal was used for fuel. Children were taught that war was necessary for the Japanese people to survive because their land was small and lacked natural resources. They joined groups that were assigned to do civic work, distribute rations, and perform other war-related chores. During the winter, young people were told not to wear warm coats to remind them of the privations suffered by Japanese soldiers fighting in China.

By the late 1930s, Japan was allied with Nazi Germany and Italy. The Japanese attack on Pearl Harbor in December 1941 brought the United States into the war against Japan and merged the Japan-China War into World War II. Despite the growing war with the United States in the Pacific, Japanese troops continued to gain new territory in China. By 1944, the advancing Japanese were forcing hundreds of thousands of Chinese civilians to flee their homes. Children joined their parents to ride on mules and horses or to board boats, trains, or any transportation they could find. Millions of refugees could be seen camping out in rail yards. They slept outdoors as they waited for trains to arrive. Children gathered sticks or hot ashes from beneath the train engines that their families could use for cooking. Some were sent to beg for food. People had to pay high fares to purchase a place on a train. Some families committed suicide when they ran out of money and had no way to leave an endangered area.

Thousands of Chinese children died as they tried to escape. Some died on the train rides. Babies, who were strapped to their parents backs, were sometimes crushed or suffocated in the crowded cars. Refugees riding on the roofs of trains sometimes fell off and died. Hundreds of people of all ages were crushed to death in Kweilin when a locomo-

tive started while people were struggling to get into the train. More than a million made their way to safe places in the Chinese countryside. There, they struggled to find enough food and shelter to survive until the war ended in 1945. *See also* CHINESE CIVIL WAR; JAPAN (WORLD WAR II).

Further Reading: O. Edmund Clubb, *20th Century China* (1964); Hiroko Nakamoto and M.M. Pace, *My Japan: 1930-51* (1970); David E. Newton, *Cities at War: Tokyo* (1992).

Jehovah's Witnesses

Before and during World War II, Nazi Germany persecuted members of a small Christian sect known as the Jehovah's Witnesses. The Nazis hated the Jehovah's Witnesses because they refused to obey any human laws that contradicted their interpretation of the Bible, and because the Witnesses were pacifists who opposed war and refused to bear arms for Germany. These beliefs brought young Witnesses into direct conflict with Nazi laws that said citizens owed complete loyalty to the German government and its leader, Adolf Hitler. Many Nazi events, such as patriotic rallies and Hitler Youth meetings, were held on Sundays, so that people would have to attend government functions rather than religious services.

Witnesses refused to salute the Nazi flag, which was required of schoolchildren, or to take Nazi oaths, which demanded complete allegiance to Hitler and his government. In 1933, the government outlawed the Jehovah's Witnesses, whose leaders refused to join the Nazi Party. In 1935, the Nazis arrested about 6,000 young male Witnesses and sent them to concentration camps for refusing to serve in the military. At least 20,000 Witnesses from Germany and occupied countries died at the hands of the Nazis.

Children and youth suffered when parents lost their jobs and social welfare benefits or were imprisoned or executed because they refused to serve in the army or to denounce their religion. More than 800 children in Jehovah's Witnesses families were also forcibly taken away when their parents refused to sign loyalty oaths or join the army. Families were torn apart when children were sent to state-run institutions for "re-education" in Nazi doctrines.

Some young Jehovah's Witnesses resisted by reading and distributing banned papers, including their official church publication, *Der Wachturm* (*The Watchtower*). Witnesses also continued to hold banned Bible discussion groups. Hundreds of children saw their parents arrested. The father of Max Von Der Grun, who grew up in rural Germany during the 1930s, was among the Witnesses who brought the papers to Germany from Czechoslovakia, hidden inside the handlebars of a bicycle. In 1938, Von Der Grun's father was arrested by the Gestapo (Nazi special police) and sent to prison. For months, his family did not even know where he was because the police claimed they did not know his whereabouts.

Another Jehovah's Witness, Willibald Wohlfahrt, was 14 in 1941 when his brother was sent to a camp and another brother was killed for refusing to serve in the German military. He and his remaining siblings were sent away to Nazi-run institutions so they could be "re-educated" to support the Nazis. As the war neared its end in 1945, he and many other youths were sent to the front to dig trenches as part of home defense projects. Wohlfahrt was killed doing this work when he was only 17.

Children in the Kusserow family of Paderborn, Germany, also suffered during the war. The father, Franz Kusserow, was imprisoned for several years when he refused to sign Nazi oaths or serve in the army. In 1939, a Nazi policeman took 13-year-old Elisabeth and her two younger brothers to state boarding schools. Her mother was not even told of their whereabouts. Elisabeth Kusserow was finally able to return home when the war ended. Her mother and three of her sisters had been sent to concentration camps but survived. Two brothers had been killed for refusing to serve in the army; another had spent five years at the Dachau concentration camp near Munich, Germany, for refusing to give the Nazi salute. He returned gravely ill and died later in 1945. The survivors resumed their family life and remained loyal to their faith. *See also* GERMANY (WORLD WAR II; HOLOCAUST.

Further Reading: Eleanor Ayer, *Holocaust* (1997); Michael Berenbaum, ed., *A Mosaic of Victims* (1990); Ina Friedman, *The Other Victims* (1990); Max Von Der Grun, *Howl Like the Wolves* (1980).

Jewish Fighters Organization (JFO)

The Jewish Fighters Organization (JFO), which played a large role in the Warsaw Ghetto uprising of World War II, was led by Mordechai Anielewicz, who was in his early twenties during the war. In 1942, after Anielewicz became convinced that the Nazis intended to kill the Jews in Poland, he helped other Jews trapped inside the ghetto develop a secret fighting unit, even though they had no military training. The young people believed that they were doomed and should die fighting. Girls, boys, women, and men in the JFO drilled and trained. They managed to obtain a few weapons and made their own grenades. They also united with another group of ghetto fighters called the Jewish Military Union (JMO), led by Pinya Kartin, a young Jew who had fought with the Polish army.

Ghetto fighters built bunkers and organized themselves, making maps that showed details of the entire ghetto with places to attack and hide. By the fall of 1942, the JFO had about 400 members, about one-third of them women. Blonde, blue-eyed girls were sometimes given jobs as couriers because they could "pass" more easily as non-Jewish Poles, using false identity papers. They moved around outside the ghetto, carrying messages and seeking donations and supplies.

On Monday April 19, 1942, German troops attacked the ghetto. They encountered small group of fighters with their small collection of guns and homemade bombs. The 6,000 Germans were well supplied with machine guns, armed vehicles, tanks, motorcycles, and food and medical equipment. Nonetheless, the JFO hit some of the tanks with their homemade bombs and continued to fight for three weeks until they were defeated that May.

It is unclear whether Anielewicz was killed by poison gas thrown into a bunker or whether he committed suicide. In his last letter, he wrote, "The last wish of my life has been fulfilled. Jewish self-defense has become a fact. Jewish resistance and revenge have really happened. I am happy to have been one of the first Jewish fighters in the Ghetto" (Gutman, 1980). *See also* ANIELEWICZ, MORDECHAI; GHETTOS (WORLD WAR II); HOLOCAUST; RESISTANCE MOVEMENTS (WORLD WAR II); WARSAW GHETTO.

Further Reading: Reuben Ainzstein, The Warsaw Ghetto Revolt (1979); Israel Gutman, The Jews of Warsaw, 1939–1943 (1982); Bea Stadtler, *The Holocaust* (1973).

Joint Distribution Committee. *See* ITALY (WORLD WAR II); WALLENBERG, RAOUL

Jones, Larry. *See* FEED THE CHILDREN

Jungvolk. *See* HITLER YOUTH

K

Kalina, Antonin (1902– ?)

Antonin (Tony) Kalina helped hundreds of children survive the Holocaust of World War II. In 1939, a year after his Czech homeland was invaded and occupied by Nazi Germany, the 37-year-old Kalina was arrested for being a communist. After being held prisoner at various camps, he was sent to the Buchenwald concentration camp in Germany in 1944.

Kalina was named leader of Block 66, where he used his position to help inmates. Working with other sympathetic prisoners, he gathered Jewish children and other young people into his block. The boys came from different countries and ranged in age from 3 to 16. Kalina found ways to keep the Nazis from taking his young charges to their deaths, for example, by hanging quarantine signs on the door so guards would stay away. Besides protecting the boys, Kalina and the other men held classes in history and other subjects. They also devised ways to bring in extra food.

Near the end of the war, Kalina substituted the files of living children for others who had died. When the Nazis asked for specific children, he convinced them those children had already been taken away and could not be found. When Buchenwald was liberated in 1945, 1,300 boys and young men had survived thanks in large part to Kalina, who was later honored as a Righteous Gentile by the Israeli organization Yad Vashem. *See also*
CONCENTRATION CAMPS (WORLD WAR II); HOLOCAUST; RIGHTEOUS GENTILES; YAD VASHEM.

Further Reading: Gay Block and Malka Drucker, *Rescuers* (1992).

Kawamoto, Ichiro. *See* FOLDED CRANE CLUB

Kent State University. *See* ANTI-WAR MOVEMENT (VIETNAM WAR)

Kindertransport. See CHILDREN'S TRANSPORTS *(KINDERTRANSPORT)*

Kolbe, Maximilian (1944–)

Maximilian Kolbe, a Polish priest who headed the Franciscan monastery in Niepokalanow, Poland, during World War II, saved about 1,500 Jewish refugees, many of them children, from the Nazis. The priest also sheltered Christian Poles of all ages whom the Germans had expelled, along with Jews, from their homes in the Poznan region of Poland. When the Nazis discovered Kolbe was helping Jews, they sent him to the death camp at Auschwitz-Birkenau. While there, the priest ministered to other prisoners, who called him "The Saint of Auschwitz." Survivors later recalled his kindness. As a 13-year-old at Auschwitz, Sigmund Gorson was alone and in despair after the rest of his family was killed by the Nazis. Gorson said that Kolbe restored his faith in God.

> He was like an angel to me. Like a mother hen, he took me in his arms. He used to wipe away my tears. He knew I was a Jewish boy. That made no difference. His heart was bigger than persons—that is, whether they were Jewish, Catholic, or whatever. He loved everyone. He dispensed love and nothing but love. I will love him until the last moments of my life. (Treece, 1982)

See also AUSCHWITZ-BIRKENAU; HOLOCAUST; POLAND (WORLD WAR II).

Further Reading: Richard C. Lukas, *Did the Children Cry?* (1994); Patricia Treece, *A Man for Others* (1982).

Komeno Massacre

During World War II, German troops attacked the village of Komeno in western Greece, killing about 317 villagers, more than half of the civilian population. Among the dead were 74 children under the age of 10. Before the war, these villagers lived quietly as fishers, or by raising goats and sheep, and oranges and other crops. Italian forces occupied the region at the beginning of the war, but persecution did not begin until the Germans took over in 1943.

On August 12, 1943, Wehrmacht (German army) teams arrived and told their commander they had seen guerilla fighters near Komeno. About 100 Wehrmacht fighters were sent to invade Komeno on August 16. During a six-hour attack, they shot and killed the villagers. As they saw what was happening, people tried to flee. Some children and young people escaped by swimming across a river or hiding in thick canes that grew along its banks. Because these unarmed villagers did not fight back, no Germans were shot or killed during the massacre. Later, some of the troops said they opposed the attack and were upset about their role. One 19-year-old German soldier said, "Bodies lay everywhere. Some were still not dead. They moved and groaned. Two or three junior officers went slowly through the village and gave the dying 'mercy shots'" (Mazower, 1993).

The German commander ordered the men to collect cows, sheep, and any other food or items of value they could find. They were also ordered to set fire to every home that remained standing. See also GREECE (WORLD WAR II).

Further Reading: Mark Mazower, *Inside Hitler's Greece* (1993).

Korczak, Janusz (1879–1942)

Born Henryk Goldszmidt, this Polish neurologist and pediatrician became better known as Janusz Korczak, the pen name he used as a popular children's author during the 1920s and 1930s. During the Nazi Holocaust of the Second World War, Korczak became known as the "Father of Orphans." Korczak grew up in a middle-class home and graduated from the University of Warsaw. He studied medicine, specializing in pediatrics, then practiced among the children of poor families. Korczak devoted himself to children's emotional and social needs, as well as to their physical health. He worked for children's rights in the Polish legal system and wrote *How to Love a Child* and *The Child's Right to Respect*, which discussed ways to raise psychologically healthy children.

In 1911, Korczak set up his House of Orphans, one of the first institutions in the world to give loving care to orphaned children in a home-like setting. He and his assistants promoted self-confidence by letting the children help make some decisions. During these years, Korczak also became a children's author, whose tales about King Matt, the boy hero, were popular with children all over Poland. He read his stories over the radio, which earned him the nickname "Old Doctor of the Radio."

After World War II began, Korczak aided Jewish children persecuted by the Nazis. He and his colleague, Dr. Stefania Wilczynska ran a home for Jewish orphans in the Warsaw Ghetto at 33 Chlodna Street. Between 40 and 80 children ranging in age from about 2 to 12 lived there at any given time. Korczak tried to meet the emotional and physical needs of the children. He was upset to see them playing war games, such as digging graves or pretending to be ghetto guards who beat and insulted others. The staff encouraged spirituality and organized religious services on Jewish holy days.

At the end of July 1942, the Warsaw Ghetto was forcibly emptied as German soldiers deported thousands of residents. During these months, Korczak refused offers from Polish Christians to hide him from the Nazis. When Korczak's children were scheduled for deportation, the doctor was told he need not leave with them, but he insisted he would accompany the 192 children then under his care. Hillel Seidman, who watched the line of children stream out, described them as "small, tiny, rather precocious, emaciated, weak, shriveled and shrunk. They carry shabby packages; some have schoolbooks, notebooks under their arms. No one is crying. . . . The doctor is going with them, so what do they have to be afraid of? They are not alone; they are not abandoned."

Warsaw Ghetto diarist Mary Berg described the scene this way:

> Rows of children, holding each other by their little hands, began to walk out of the doorway. There were tiny tots of two or three years among them, while the oldest ones were perhaps thirteen. Each child carried a little bundle in his hand. All of them wore white aprons. They walked in ranks of two, calm, and even smiling. . . . At the end of the procession marched Dr. Korczak. (Berg, 1945)

Berg said that the doctor tenderly stroked their arms and patted their heads. When they reached the freight cars, the Nazis loaded all the children; Korczak and his nurses went along, telling them stories and comforting them. The entire group was killed in the gas chambers of the Treblinka death camp.

Further Reading: Mary Berg, *Warsaw Ghetto Diary* (1945); Wladyslaw Bartoszewski, *The Warsaw Ghetto: A Christian's Testimony* (1987); Betty Jean Lifton, *The King of Children* (1988).

Korean War (1950–1953)

Japan occupied Korea after the end of Japan's war against China in 1894 and set up a new government that treated Korea as an inferior

A young Korean boy prepares to leave home to join the army. *Corbis/Hulton-Deutsch Collection.*

colony, shutting down schools and censoring newspapers and books. Children suffered economically as their families' land and possessions were seized and Koreans lost their jobs to Japanese. Thousands of Koreans fled from this oppression.

Young students joined in protests against the Japanese regime. One of them, Syngman Rhee, wrote a revolutionary newspaper and led a group of patriots. After he was imprisoned by the Japanese from 1898 to 1904, Rhee went to the United States where he earned a Ph.D. from Princeton University, then formed a Korean government-in-exile in Hawaii. Another young opponent of the Japanese, Kim Il-sung, left Korea for the Soviet Union where he became a committed communist.

After World War II ended, these men became the leaders of a divided and unstable Korea. Syngman Rhee was elected president of South Korea and Kim Il-sung was installed by the Soviets as president of North Korea. Conflicts between North and South Korea heated up when troops from both sides moved beyond the 38th parallel, which had been declared the dividing line. In June 1950, North Korean troops invaded the South, initiating the Korean War, which eventually involved United Nations forces led by the United States as allies of the South, and Communist

China as ally of the North. In the three years of war that followed, 500,000 Koreans were killed. In South Korea alone, children and young adults were among 2.5 million people who became refugees after bombs demolished their homes.

After the war, many children went hungry because military tanks had ruined crops and irrigation ditches. Many areas lacked electrical power, clean water, and sanitary facilities, which increased rates of childhood diseases. United Nations forces had bombed hydroelectric power stations in North Korea and irrigation dams that supplied rice fields. Five million people relied on government assistance after the war, because they could no longer farm or because their workplaces had been destroyed, which left millions of Korean children in poverty. The process of rebuilding both Koreas would continued for decades.

Further Reading: Francis H. Heller, ed., *The Korean War* (1977); Robert Jackson, *Air War Over Korea* (1973).

Kosovo

Beginning in 1997, children suffered in numerous ways as fighting raged in the Kosovo region of the former Yugoslavia, now Serbia, which borders Albania and Macedonia. The population of Kosovo was more than 90 percent Albanian, and the ethnic Albanians had been resisting Serbian rule. The Serbs claimed that Kosovo was a holy place that belonged to them and that Albanians were attacking Serbs in the province. During 1997 and 1998, Serbian police forced tens of thousands of people from their homes and villages. Most of the refugees fled to Tirana, the nearby capitol of Albania. By mid-1998, almost 2,000 civilians had died. Humanitarian groups estimated that 700,000 persons had been displaced. Numerous villages had been totally destroyed. One refugee said, "Everyone is being attacked from three sides. Only the border area is safe. You flee or you die" (Hedges, 1998).

A cease-fire began in October 1998 but was not successful. Throughout early 1999, refugees continued to flee from Kosovo, on some days at the rate of more than 1,000 per hour. Most of them were women, children, and the elderly. Eyewitnesses described the small children who arrived in vans or on foot, tired, hungry, and frightened. They told journalists and members of humanitarian organizations that they had experienced brutal treatment from Serbian police and paramilitaries. Tens of thousands of men and boys had been rounded up and it was feared that untold numbers had been murdered. People described mass killings and brutal sexual assaults on young Kosovo women and girls. Thousands of children died and were injured by weapons; others died from malnutrition and disease. Refugees said that teenage boys were among those killed in massacres where men were rounded up and shot, presumably to prevent them from taking part in the Kosovo Liberation Army. Members of Human Rights Watch, Amnesty International, and other groups who interviewed refugees said they had found evidence of crimes against humanity which could be used to indict Serb leader Slobodan Milosevic and other Serbs who perpetrated these acts as war criminals.

By May 1999, an estimated 750,000 Kosovar refugees had fled to Albania, Macedonia, Montenegro, and Bosnia. More than 300,000 of those refugees were children under age 15, according to UNICEF. About 120,000 children had been separated from their families as of May 1999. The families had left behind their homes and other possessions. One woman told reporter John Kifner that Serb paramilitaries had pounded on her apartment door on the morning of March 29, and told her family that they had half an hour to leave. The troops had looted and smashed stores and religious buildings and were giving out Kosovar homes to Serb families. She and her husband were separated from his mother and their 18-month child during their flight across the Albanian border. She said, "Now we have nothing" (Kifner, 1999).

Refugee children showed signs of severe trauma and described seeing their homes burned, their relatives killed and beaten, and their female relatives and friends raped. An Italian pediatrician, Dr. Franco de Luca, said that as many as 40 percent of the children between ages 2 and 5 showed signs of serious psychological trauma (Smolowe, Fields-Meyer, Hewitt, 1999).

In April 1999, NATO forces launched a series of air-strikes against Yugoslavia to force the Milosevic government to change its policies. Bombings destroyed electrical facilities and buildings in Yugoslavia, disrupting children's lives in many ways. A doctor in a hospital unit for premature babies said that these infants would die if the generator they were using for power should fail. Children in Belgrade and other cities hid with their families in air-raid shelters when NATO bombs exploded nearby. One 5-year-old girl huddled in a corner during one such air-raid and told her mother, "I don't want to die" (Erlanger, 1999).

As of May 1999, more than 60 relief organizations from 35 countries were working to aid Kosovar refugees in Albania, a poor country with few resources to help the many refugees who had arrived there. UNICEF and the International Red Cross were working to reunite families that had been separated during their flight from Kosovo. Six reunification centers were opened in Skopje to help unaccompanied children find their relatives. UNICEF set up tent schools in Macedonia and brought in teachers and counselors for the children. UNICEF director Carol Bellamy said, "Bringing education and creative play back into children's lives provides them with much-needed routine at a time when their lives have been so shattered. Our hope is to engage them, to help them cope with their distress by getting them to draw, play soccer, read books and to do, as much as possible, what normal children do" (UNICEF Alert!, "Kosovo," 1999). UNICEF health teams worked to provide clean water, blankets, essential drugs, baby supplies, and medical supplies to treat respiratory illnesses and vaccinate children against measles, polio, and other diseases. Mobile health teams moved throughout the area to assist Kosovar refugees when they returned to their shattered homes in June 1999 after the Serbs withdrew and the NATO bombing ceased. *See also* AMERICARES; BOSNIA; CROATIA; REFUGEES.

Further Reading: Anthony DePalma, "Survivor Tells of Massacre at Kosovo Village," *The New York Times*, May 3, 1999, pp. A1, A13; Steven Erlanger, "Birthday in a Shelter with Fireworks," *The New York Times*, March 26, 1999, pp. A1, A10; Chris Hedges, "Refugees from Kosovo Cite a Bitter Choice: Flee or Die," *New York Times*, June 5, 1998, pp. A1, A4; John Kifner, "A Kosovo Family's Cry: 'Now We Have Nothing,'" *The New York Times*, May 29, 1999, pp. A1, A8; Mike O'Connor, "Attack by Serbs Shatters a Cease-Fire in Kosovo," *The New York Times*, December 25, 1998, pp. A1, A3; David Rohde, "In Macedonia, Lost Children Wait Helplessly for Reunions," *The New York Times*, April 27, 1999, pp. A1, A13; Laura Silberg and Allan Little, *Yugoslavia* (1997); Jill Smolowe, Thomas Fields-Meyer, and Bill Hewitt, "Who Will Save the Children," *People*, April 26, 1999, pp. 54-61; UNICEF Alert! "Kosovo," *UNICEF USA*, May 4, 1999.

Kristallnacht

On November 9, 1938, Nazi leaders organized a massive attack on Jews and their property throughout Germany and Austria, which Germany had annexed the previous March. The night these attacks began became known as *Kristallnacht* ("Crystal Night") or the "Night of the Broken Glass" because of all the Jewish shop windows that were smashed by the Nazis. The attacks were intended to look spontaneous, but documents from Nazi police files show that police throughout Germany received teletyped messages ahead of time, saying that violent outbreaks would occur and they should not interfere. Officials gave orders to attack and demolish Jewish synagogues, homes, businesses, and personal property. Hitler Youth were urged to take part. The head of the Gestapo (secret police), Heinrich Muller, ordered that preparations were "to be made for the arrest of about 20,000-30,000 Jews in the Reich. Wealthy Jews in particular are to be selected. More detailed instructions will be issued in the course of this night. Should in the forthcoming [action] Jews be found in possession of weapons, the most severe measures are to be taken" (Thalmann and Feinermann, 1974).

The attack was launched after teenager Herschel Grynzspan, a German Jewish refugee in Paris, shot a German official at the embassy. Grynzspan was enraged because Nazi officials had deported his family and thousands of other Jews of Polish ancestry. Newspapers wrote inflammatory articles calling the shooting part of a Jewish international plot. On November 8, one newspaper declared, "The Jewish attempt against the German Embassy in Paris will have, as everyone now knows, the most serious repercussions on the Jews." Another paper said,

> We shall no longer tolerate the hundreds of thousands of Jews within our territory who control entire streets of shops, who avail themselves of our public entertainments, and as foreign landlords pocket the wealth of German leaseholders while their brothers in religion incite war on Germany and assassinate German officials. (Thalmann and Feinermann, 1974)

Eyewitnesses, including foreign journalists and diplomats, later described what happened that night. Groups of stormtroopers, including young men under the age of 21, arrived in trucks in Jewish neighborhoods and began swinging clubs and smashing windows. They broke into people's homes, then terrorized families and destroyed furniture, mattresses, and paintings, and threw chairs, pianos, books, toys, and other things onto the streets. In Nuremberg, some 30,000 Nazis had joined an early evening rally where they were given hatchets and told to do whatever they wanted to the Jews.

Gangs violated Jewish cemeteries, ripping out tombstones and marking them with swastikas, and 7,500 Jewish stores were looted. Among those killed that night was an 18-year-old Jewish boy in Berlin who was thrown from a third-story window. All over the country, Jewish children saw their synagogues, homes, and family businesses smashed and set on fire, and Jewish religious objects destroyed. Hundreds of synagogues were vandalized and burned. Thugs tossed sacred religious books and objects onto bonfires, and non-Jewish children could be seen tossing them around and stepping on them.

Jewish youths joined those who tried to block the doors of synagogues and protect family members from beatings. They were chased down the streets and tormented. Nazis forced Jewish men to march to their synagogue and read portions of Hitler's book, *Mein Kampf.* Children saw their fathers dragged off to prison along with older boys. Lewis Schloss, who grew up in northeastern Germany and was 17 in 1938, recalled that "After they'd destroyed our store windows, they came upstairs to the apartment where we lived. The Nazis broke down our front door, destroyed our furniture, and threw our china out the windows. . . . A few hours later a group of Hitler's storm troopers and Nazi police returned. They arrested both my father and me" (Adler, 1989).

Schloss and his father were jailed for three weeks although they were not charged with a crime. They were en route to a concentration camp, but the officer who was taking them to their train was late, and they were sent home. Like many others, the Schlosses were ordered to clean up the debris in the street and pay someone to remove the broken glass. Their insurance company had to pay the German government, not the property owners. Schloss was required to buy new windows himself, then sell his business to a Nazi Party member for an unfairly low price.

Julius Rosensweig, a teenager in Frankfurt, Germany, remembered the aftermath of *Kristallnacht:* "A day or two later I saw Jewish-owned department stores all with broken windows. None of the stores reopened. They had no customers, no merchandise, no security. They were sold to gentiles [non-Jews] for almost nothing" (Adler, 1989).

After *Kristallnacht,* 30,000 Jewish men were taken by force to concentration camps where they were forced into hard labor. Many prisoners were tortured, and at least 1,000 were killed. Those who were released or ransomed were often sick and had head injuries, broken bones, and other health problems. Manfred Fulda later described his father's condition after he returned home: "He had lost eighty pounds. The Nazis had shaved off his entire beard. He had been severely beaten, and he was covered all over with bloody wounds" (Adler, 1989).

Thousands of children were left without a means of support, and people lived in fear. Some received help from abroad. People in Holland raised money to aid Jews who had been hurt during *Kristallnacht*. The Dutch and Belgian governments announced they would take in Jewish children even if they lacked immigration papers. British officials organized the World Movement for the Care of Children from Germany, a program to send endangered children to safe havens in Europe. Families grieved to send their children away but many felt this was their only way to survive. After 1938, it became increasingly difficult for people to obtain visas to leave Germany. Most of the Jews who were forced to remain in Germany died in the Nazi Holocaust. *See also* AUERBACHER, INGE; CHILDREN'S TRANSPORTS (*KINDERTRANSPORT*); CONCENTRATION CAMPS (WORLD WAR II); GRYNZSPAN, HERSCHEL; HITLER, ADOLF; HOLOCAUST.

Further Reading: David A. Adler, *We Remember the Holocaust* (1989); Martin Gilbert, *The Holocaust* (1985); Leora Kahn and Rachel Hager, eds., *When They Came to Take My Father* (1996); Elaine Landau, *We Survived the Holocaust* (1991); Seymour Rossel, *The Holocaust* (1981); Arnold Rubin, *The Evil Men Do* (1977); Rita Thalmann and Emmanuel Feinermann, *Crystal Night* (1974).

Kurds

The Kurdish peoples belong to different tribes that speak the same language, derived from Persian, and share the same customs. They live in Iran, Iraq, Syria, and Turkey. In 1961, Kurds in Iraq, where they made up about 20 percent of the population and were the largest non-Arab group, rebelled against the government, seeking their independence. Kurds formed guerilla bands that lived in isolated mountains and attacked Iraqis. These rebels received assistance and weapons from the government of Iran and its ally at the time, the United States. The conflict ended briefly in 1975 when Iraqi leader Saddam Hussein reluctantly signed a treaty with Iran to end the conflict.

However, the Kurds continued to feel oppressed by the Hussein regime. More than one million Kurdish refugees fled to Turkey and Iran during the early 1990s. Young people in the refugee camps suffered from hunger, diseases, and other deprivations. Their problems continued when Kurds in Turkey began their own war for independence against the Turkish government in 1979. During the early 1990s, recruits training in camps in Iraqi territory near the Turkish border included numerous adolescents of both genders. A Swiss journalist noted that about 20 percent of the trainees in one camp were young women and girls.

In April 1991, the Turkish army closed the border after thousands of Kurdish refugees had fled to Turkey from northern Iraq. Children were among the thousands of Kurds who were left stranded in the mountains without food or shelter. *See also* CHEMICAL WARFARE; IRAN-IRAQ WAR.

Further Reading: "A Stolen Future: Protecting the Rights of Refugee Children," Amnesty International, 1997.

L

Labor Camps. *See* CONCENTRATION CAMPS (WORLD WAR II); FORCED LABOR (WORLD WAR II)

Land Mines

Land mines (also called anti-personnel mines or APLs) are mechanical explosive weapons placed in the ground during wars to defend territory or impede the progress of enemy forces. As of summer 1997, land mines were killing or maiming about 25,000 people each year and 64 nations were affected by mines buried in their soil during past conflicts. In the late 1990s, someone in the world was being injured, maimed, or killed by a land mine every 22 seconds. Each month, at least 800 people were killed and 1,200 others injured. Many of these casualties were civilians.

Land mines have been called the most insidious, pernicious weapons being used by humankind. Because land mines do not discriminate, children have often been victims. Besides causing indiscriminate injuries and deaths, land mines interfere with movement and normal activities in former combat zones and impose other economic hardships by hindering farming, draining health care resources, and disabling people so they cannot work.

About half of the people hurt or killed by land mines each year are children. Children who are injured by land mines face special problems. Growing children need new prostheses (artificial limbs) about every six months. These limbs are expensive (about $125 each), especially for people living in countries where the average monthly wage is about $10-$15. Some children use crutches because they cannot afford a prosthesis. They may have to beg in the streets when their families cannot afford to support them. Being disabled in the developing world also means

Jody Williams, winner of the 1997 Nobel Peace Prize, presents "The Land Mine Monitor Report" at the United Nations in May 1999. *Shawn Baldwin, AP/Wide World Photos.*

fewer job opportunities and, for girls, limited marriage possibilities.

Land mines were first devised during World War I after military tanks came into use. To destroy tanks, armor-destroying mines were built and placed in the ground. These devices were followed by anti-personnel mines, positioned to hinder soldiers who were sent out to remove anti-tank mines. Land mines are built to explode when somebody steps on them or otherwise triggers the explosive. The primary purpose is to kill or injure enemy ground troops. Large land mines have enough force to destroy several small buildings.

When they bombed England during World War II, German planes sometimes used large parachutes to send down land mines packed with explosives. Some did not explode after hitting the ground. They remained inside empty buildings or on the ground. Injuries occurred when children or others accidentally triggered hidden mines. When unexploded land mines were identified, army personnel were usually sent to clear them out and remove the source of danger. Many remained, however, to cause unpredictable future damage.

By the 1990s, hundreds of thousands of people all over the world lived in places where land mines were a threat. About 110 million mines lay scattered in Central and South America, Southeast Asia, and elsewhere. As of 1997, Angola, the Balkans, Afghanistan, and Indochina had the highest number of undiscovered land mines.

During June 1997, the U.S. Congress discussed the Leahy-Hegel bill to destroy any remaining land mines still in place around the world. An outspoken supporter and co-sponsor of the bill was Democratic Senator Patrick Leahy of Vermont. Congress also considered a moratorium on the use of land mines. Speaking on behalf of the bill, Virginia Senator Charles Robb, a Vietnam War veteran, said that he looked forward to the time when an international agreement could be reached limiting the use of these devices. Senator Dick Durban pointed out that in poor and developing countries, the loss of a foot

can have far more devastating consequences than in the United States or other countries with excellent medical care and rehabilitation programs.

An international committee was formed at a conference on land mines that convened in Ottawa, Canada, in October 1996. The group began working to draft a treaty that would ban land mines. In 1997, citizens groups and nongovernmental institutions took active roles in gathering support for the International Compaign to Ban Land Mines. An alliance of 1,000 citizens' groups in more than 60 countries worked hard for the treaty. The cause gained publicity in the spring of 1997 when the Diana, Princess of Wales, visited with children and others who had been injured by land mine explosions. Before her death in the following August, Princess Diana helped make a documentary about land mines for British television. The public attention surrounding her death brought the cause further support.

Jody Williams of Putney, Vermont, a leader in the effort to ban land mines, began working with Vietnam veterans and other concerned citizens in 1992. In 1997, the 47-year-old Williams won the Nobel Peace Prize for her efforts to organize an international ban on land mines. Williams gave a keynote address on December 3, 1997, when leaders from around the world gathered to begin signing the treaty in Ottawa. More than 120 nations had agreed to ban the production, use, and stockpiling or transport of anti-personnel mines. (Anti-tank mines are not affected.) The treaty was to take effect within six months after 40 nations had signed it. At the meeting, Cirbekui Sommaruga, the president of the International Committee of the Red Cross, called the treaty a "victory for humanity" but said the real victory will come only after all the mines are cleared from fields and the thousands of people who are victimized each year receive care. Countries that sign the treaty have 10 years in which to destroy mines they have placed in the ground.

Among the nations that did not sign the treaty were Russia, China, and the United States. The U.S. objected to certain parts of the treaty but agreed to stop using land mines everywhere but in Korea as of 2003. The Pentagon began exploring alternatives to land mines in Korea, where the United States deemed their use necessary to protect U.S. troops. If an alternative is found, the U.S. plans to sign the treaty in 2006. The United States also agreed to increase the amount of money that it spent to remove land mines around the world from $80 million a year to more than $100 million in 1998. Other countries also agreed to devote more funds to clearing land mines. Canada said it would spend $75 million over the next five years and Norway agreed to commit $100 million.

On September 16, 1998, the 40th country ratified the treaty, which meant that it was binding under international law. The ban went into effect March 1999. *See also* ANGOLA; CAMBODIA; EL SALVADOR; MOZAMBIQUE; VIETNAM WAR.

Further Reading: Anthony DePalma, "As U.S. Looks On, 120 Nations Sign Treaty Banning Land Mines," *New York Times*, December 4, 1997, pp. A1, A14; International Committee of the Red Cross, "ICRC Assistance to Mine Victims," May 26, 1999; "Landmines—Not in Anyone's Back Yard," *FCNL Washington Newsletter*, June 1997, p. 3.

Le Chambon-sur-Lignon

During World War II, about 5,000 French villagers in the small mountain village of Le Chambon and the surrounding area in south-central France aided thousands of Jews, mostly children, who were fleeing from the Nazis. The villagers, Protestants of Huguenot descent and some Catholics, cooperated to hide Jews in private homes and in group homes, some of which were funded by international relief organizations. Children and young adults were among both the rescuers and the rescued.

Leaders of this effort included the village pastor, Andre Trocme, his wife, Magda, and the associate pastor, Edouard Theis. Trocme had praised the faith and commitment of the villagers when he arrived in the region with his wife and children in 1937. The rescue work began one winter day in 1941 when a German Jewish refugee arrived at the minister's house, where Magda Trocme was working in her kitchen. The cold, hungry woman explained that she had fled from northern France and heard that people in Le Chambon might help her. Magda Trocme offered her food, warm clothing, and shelter.

Realizing that many others needed help, Andre Trocme met with Burns Chalmers and other representatives of the American Quaker organization. They decided together that Le Chambon would hide refugees, especially children. Chalmers agreed to provide funds and some supplies. The village was well-suited for hiding refugees because it was set on a high plateau and surrounded by mountains. Trocme was a strong leader with a committed congregation. After the church council approved the plan, Jewish refugees were placed in private homes, more than 12 boarding houses, and several group homes sponsored by the World Council of Churches, Catholic groups, and the governments of Sweden and Switzerland. Adults were assigned to live in the homes with the children. The leaders of the effort believed that besides saving lives, they must try to restore the children's faith in humankind. Many of the young people were able to continue their schooling and take part in sports, music, and other normal activities during these years.

As more villagers joined the rescue effort, Trocme inspired them with sermons about overcoming evil with goodness. They were often in danger and survived several Nazi raids. One summer day in 1942, a local Nazi official came to Le Chambon and accused Trocme of hiding "a certain number of Jews, whose names I know" (Hallie, 1979). He ordered the clergyman to disclose their whereabouts or face arrest and deportation himself. Trocme refused. After the police left, Trocme asked local Boy Scouts to visit homes and farms to suggest that Jews hide in the woods for a day or two in case of a raid. Trocme was arrested more than once and he and Theis had to hide during the last year of the war, yet both survived.

Nazis did raid the village. During one raid, they arrested Daniel Trocme, Andre's cousin, and the boys living in that group home. All died in a Nazi camp. However, the Germans were dissuaded from taking more action because the Chambonais were so united and also because a high-ranking German officer in the region found ways to keep his comrades from pursuing them. This German, a former schoolteacher, was later publicly recognized by the French for his efforts to limit persecution and deportations in this region.

When the region was liberated in 1944, thousands of children had escaped death at the hands of the Nazis. Among them was Viennese refugee Elizabeth Koenig. She was 16 when she was sent to Le Chambon to live with the pastor's family and help with the four children. After the first children's home, called La Gespi, was set up, Koenig went to work there because she spoke German and French and could translate for the children. She left at the end of 1941 when her family was able to get visas to enter the United States.

Hanne Liebmann, a German Jewish child who was sheltered at Le Chambon, later said that

> Le Chambon was a very poor farming village, nothing much grows; so whatever they had, they shared with us. And if you are a family with small children and you take in one or two more mouths to feed, it is a sacrifice. And they didn't mind sacrificing, or even putting their lives at risk for us. And I think the great lesson we learned there has remained with us all our lives. (Shulman, 1998)

As an infant, Pierre Sauvage also lived in hiding in Le Chambon. Born in March 1944, he later said that he was "lucky to see the light of day in a place on earth singularly committed to my survival at a time when much of my family was disappearing into the abyss" (Rittner and Myers, 1986). Sauvage, who became a filmmaker, formed a group called The Friends of Le Chambon and served as its first president. During the 1980s, Sauvage made a documentary film, *Weapons of the Spirit*, about the rescue effort at Le Chambon. *See also* FRANCE (WORLD WAR II); HIDDEN CHILDREN; QUAKERS (SOCIETY OF FRIENDS); RED CROSS; RIGHTEOUS GENTILES; TROCME, ANDRE AND TROCME, MAGDA; TROCME, DANIEL.

Further Reading: Philip Hallie, *Lest Innocent Blood Be Shed* (1979); Carol Rittner and Sondra Myers, eds. *The Courage to Care* (1986); William Shulman, *Holocaust: Voices and Visions* (1998).

League of German Girls

Formed in 1927 but formally organized as the League of German Girls (*Bund Deutscher Madel* or BDM) in 1930, this Nazi youth group for young women was used to promote Adolf Hitler's political and military agenda during World War II. The league was part of the large and highly organized Hitler Youth organization in Germany. Young people were indoctrinated with the principles of Nazism and required to take part in activities to further the war effort after German armies began invading various countries in 1938. Girls in the BDM were expected to attend meetings and training sessions and to devote their time to civic activities. They volunteered to collect money, make and sell crafts and other products for the military, prepare and serve food at military and government events, and work in hospital and child care facilities.

They also helped to care for wounded soldiers in hospitals, assisted households with large families, and served refreshments at railroad stations to army troops leaving for the front. After German troops invaded Poland in 1939, girls from the Land Service division of the league were sent to northern Poland to help the troops move ethnic German families into the homes vacated by Poles who were forced to move into the southeastern portion of the country. As these ethnic Germans arrived from Russia and central Europe, the young women helped the children to learn German if they did not speak the language and they introduced them to German customs and the Hitler Youth movement. *See also* GERMANY (WORLD WAR II); HITLER YOUTH; HOLOCAUST.

Further Reading: Eileen Heyes, *Children of the Swastika* (1993); Ilse Koehn, *Mischling, Second Degree* (1977); Hans Peter Richter, *I Was There* (1972).

Lebanese Civil War (1975–1997)

Beginning in 1975, young people in Lebanon endured years of war, both internal and with neighboring countries in the Middle East. Tensions between Christians and Muslims erupted into violence in April 1975, when Muslim guerillas fought with members of the (Christian) Phalangist Party, which ruled Lebanon at that time. Muslims had once been a minority in Lebanon, but as they became a larger part of the population, they demanded a change in laws that required the ruler of the country to be a Maronite Catholic.

Children and young adults were among the estimated 300 to 350 casualties during the first week of conflict. As the fighting continued, more died and thousands of young people became homeless after shelling destroyed buildings. They suffered in terms of health, education, and economics. In 1980, an estimated 60,000 people had been killed during the Lebanese Civil War.

Young people were recruited as soldiers and were encouraged to attend military schools. Boys and girls between the ages of 8 and 14 were trained in military skills and guerilla warfare at programs run by the Palestinian Liberation Organization (PLO) in

A rescue worker carries an injured girl from the scene of a Beirut car bombing in 1986. *Reuters/Corbis-Bettmann.*

refugee camps in southern Lebanon. Their goal was to wrest Palestinian land from Israel. While visiting the region in 1980, author Thomas J. Abercrombie saw young boys called "Palestinian lion cubs"—commando trainees—training with rifles. The uniformed boys carried guns during school flag-raising ceremonies and other occasions. Girls of the same ages also carried rifles.

Many young people were the victims of sniper attacks or bombings. Terrorists had placed bombs in apartment buildings, grocery stores, parking lots, and other places, some of which were located near children's playgrounds. Families who fled from areas with heavy fighting sometimes returned to find their homes had been looted or taken over by soldiers or refugees from southern Lebanon. They were then forced to flee again. War also hindered the shipment of food and the availablity of safe drinking water. By 1990, for example, 66 percent of the urban water sources in Lebanon were contaminated.

Many young people served as combatants in the Lebanon wars. During the 1980s, training centers were operated for members of the youth branch of the PLO. Guerilla training was conducted for youths from the ages of 8 to 16, at which time some young men became full commanders. Young people, including Palestinian refugees, were given intense physical training and taught various military skills, including how to assemble and dismantle rifles.

In 1981 and 1982, air strikes by Israeli planes aiming at Palestinian targets killed hundreds of people and injured more. When the oil pipeline at Tyre was destroyed, many young people lost their jobs in this industry. Late in 1982, the Christian army in Lebanon attacked Palestinian camps in Beirut, killing hundreds of children and adults. More children became casualties during the heavy fighting and terrorist attacks that took place during the next six months. Refugees fled from their homes. David J. Abodaher described the lives of youth during this difficult time.

The young, especially the Christian youth, were in a constant state of torment. The

Syrian soldiers, many of them teenagers, themselves, teased and harassed Christians of both sexes. Boys were taunted with religious slurs. Girls were subjected to lewd remarks and suggestive invitations. So many incidents took place that girls of any age feared even walking to a nearby store alone. (Abodaher, 1991)

Abodaher described an incident in which a young Syrian soldier shot a young man who came to the rescue of his 16-year-old sister when she resisted the soldier's physical advances.

In 1985, Beirut was under siege during the civil war between the Palestinians and a group of Shiite Muslims called Amal. A large hospital was hit by bombs on May 31. Children were among the patients who were evacuated to the safest parts of the building. As the bombing continued and shooting occurred in the streets, wounded civilians were brought into hospitals for treatment. On one day, about 1,500 bombs were dropped during only three hours. As the violence continued, more young people became casualties. In 1989, for example, a 15-year-old Lebanese girl saw her parents killed after a Syrian soldier misfired his weapon and hit a gas tank, which exploded. The girl ran screaming from the blaze, her clothing on fire until bystanders managed to extinguish them. That same year, after President Assad of Syria ordered his military to stop Lebanese refugees from leaving the country, two young girls drowned in the port of Junni after Syrians fired with machine guns at a boatload of refugees.

A Lebanese Christian, Jean Chamoun, and a Palestinian, Mai Meeri, collaborated on a documentary film called *The War Generation* to show the impact of militarism and war on Lebanese youth. Some of the young people featured in the film began their military training at age 13. One boy commented that "War forces us to take up arms." Some young people fought on more than one side, joining the Muslims, Christians, Druze, or Palestinian groups. Many were not motivated by ideology but took part for other reasons, such as to protect themselves and their families or to escape poverty or because they lacked access to opportunities for jobs or education.

Although the United Nations Children's Fund (UNICEF) concluded that fewer than 1 percent of Lebanese children had taken part in combat, the organization worried that many young people had become resigned to living in a violent environment and that for those who stayed in the military, violence became a way of life. In 1989, UNICEF reached an agreement with the warring parties that permitted them to take children from different cultural and religious backgrounds to summer camps sponsored by UNICEF. Youth attending the camps took part in sports, drama, crafts, and other activities as they learned new conflict-resolution skills and heard about their fellow campers' different experiences and viewpoints. The Lebanese government later decided to make peace-education programs part of its national curriculum.

Lebanese and Israelis both suffered from terrorist attacks stemming from the Lebanese civil war. In April 1996, Israel and the Lebanese Shiite militia, Hezbollah, reached a cease-fire agreement. An international monitoring committee was assigned to oversee the truce. However, violence continued into 1997, when 41 civilians were killed and more than 130 were wounded in attacks by both sides. In August, 10 civilians died when Sidon and the surrounding area were bombed by the Israeli-backed South Lebanon Army militia. On November 23, 1997, mortar attacks by Lebanese guerillas killed nine Lebanese civilians, including a 7-year-old girl and her 16-year-old brother in the village of Beit Lif. Another 12 people were wounded.

Although the civil war officially ended in 1990, conflicts raged on between Israel and Lebanese guerillas known as the Hezbollah. Since 1985, Israeli soldiers had been stationed in southern Lebanon, along with South Lebanon Army militia, in an area Israel called the "security zone." Hezbollah was fighting to oust both troops from the area. Families living in the Beirut area or other vulnerable parts of southern Lebanon usually had underground shelters in their homes where they could go during an attack.

Children were victims in this conflict, even when they were living in camps set up by humanitarian agencies. For instance, in 1996, children were among the 100 civilians killed in Qana, a United Nations compound in south Lebanon, when it was shelled by Israeli long-range artillery. In December 1998, a woman and her six children, ages 2 to 13, were killed and her husband and seventh child, an 11-year-old boy, were both injured after Israeli warplanes attacked suspected guerilla bases in eastern Lebanon. The family had been working on a nearby farm. No peace agreement had been reached by mid-1999. *See also* ARAB-ISRAELI WARS; REFUGEES.

Further Reading: Thomas J. Abercrombie, "Islam's Heartland Up in Arms," *National Geographic*, September 1980, pp. 335-45; David Abodaher, *Youth in the Middle East* (1991); Judith Ennew and B. Milne, *The Next Generation: Lives of Third-World Children*, (1989); Mona Macksoud, *Lebanese Children and War*, UNICEF Conference on Peace-Building and Development of Lebanon, April, 1990; Ray Nordheim, "Playing the Death Game," *Newsweek*, January 6, 1986; Roger Rosenblatt, *Children of War* (1984).

Lebensborn

During World War II, Germany operated a program called Lebensborn ("source, or fountain, of life") to increase its population of infants whom the ruling Nazis considered "racially pure." Unmarried women, as well as wives, were urged to reproduce as long as both parents had pure German ancestry. Nazi official Heinrich Himmler declared that every SS man should father at least four children, so these men were encouraged to impregnate women. Under Himmler's direction, a chain of luxurious maternity homes was created in former hospitals, villas, resorts, and health spas throughout Germany. Pregnant unmarried women at these homes enjoyed comfortable rooms and excellent food. They were not forced to do heavy work; their main duty was to stay well and produce a healthy child. Guards patrolled the grounds of the homes to maintain privacy. Young nursing students worked in these maternity centers, caring for mothers and infants. The women could choose to raise their children or to have them sent to adoptive or foster homes.

After Germany invaded Poland in 1939, the Lebensborn program was expanded to include the adoption of Polish children between ages 6 and 10 with certain physical features. Some of these adoptees were war orphans, while others were children of Polish soldiers killed in the war or of Polish mothers and German soldiers. Still others were taken from their natural parents without consent.

The children were selected on the basis of age, health, and appearance. The ideal was a blond, blue-eyed child with fair skin, a long thin head, and other so-called "Aryan" features. An estimated 200,000 children were deported to Germany for this purpose. They were raised as Germans, taught to speak German, and socialized to think and act German in all respects. Adoptive parents were often told that these children—who were usually infants—were German war orphans.

After the war, international organizations and the families of missing children sought to locate them. One of these organizations, the United Nations Relief and Rehabilitation Administration (UNRRA), worked to repatriate Polish children who had been taken to Germany. They conducted searches and sought to reunite the young people with their families or to help older children who had lost their biological families to emigrate.

Their task was complicated because the Nazis usually destroyed records showing the children's origins. Officials at the orphanages where children had been kept were also uncooperative. Some German families quickly completed a legal adoption process before the child could be removed. Although prohibited by the Allied occupiers of post-war Germany, these adoptions took place nonetheless.

By the end of 1946, only 443 children had been found and identified. UNRRA continued the search and slowly located more children. In some places where local German officials claimed that no Polish children lived in the town, UNRRA found hundreds. For example, in Baden-Wurtemburg, officials identified 276 children from Poland; the Allies found 3,000. However, 80 percent of the missing children, most likely those who had been placed in private German homes, were never found.

Because many of the children had been taken from their birth families at a young age, they did not recall their pasts. Some were so attached to their German families that they refused to leave. Polish birth families faced agonizing situations when investigators told them their children would suffer great distress if they were returned to their original homes. *See also* ADOPTION; DISPLACED PERSONS (DPs) (WORLD WAR II); HITLER'S CHILDREN; "MASTER RACE"; POLAND (WORLD WAR II); POST-TRAUMATIC STRESS DISORDER (PTSD).

Further Reading: Robert Edwin Herzstein, *The Nazis* (1980); Richard C. Lukas, *Did the Children Cry?* (1994).

Lemkin, Raphael. *See* GENOCIDE

Leningrad, Siege of. *See* SOVIET UNION (WORLD WAR II)

Liberian Civil War (1989–1996)

The Liberian Civil War, which lasted from 1989 to 1996, saw the deaths of tens of thousands of children and young people and members of their families in this West African country. An estimated 250,000 people—10 percent of the total population—were killed during these years, while about 770,000 people became refugees. About 240,000 refugees returned to Liberia in 1998, but other refugees remained in neighboring countries.

War began in December 1989 at a time when the government was unstable and the country was under the control of a repressive regime. A warlord named Charles G. Taylor led his National Patriotic Liberation Front (NPLF) to invade Liberia from a bordering nation, Ivory Coast. Rival warlords led a group known as the United Liberia Movement for Democracy (ULIMO) against Taylor's troops. Troups from both sides killed many civilians—including children—in Monrovia, the Liberian capital. In 1990, the NPLF slew more than 600 people of all ages in a Lutheran church in Monrovia. This geno-cidal attack targeted people from the Gio and Mano tribal groups of northeastern Liberia, the region from which came many NPFL fighters.

In August 1990, militiamen came to Marshall, Liberia, and assembled Ghanian immigrants and their Liberian friends and sympathizers. They shot about 1,000 people to death. Children were brutally killed by soldiers who smashed their heads against palm trees. Other youths drowned while trying to swim across a river to a nearby island. Survivors either ran to safety or played dead on the ground until the soldiers left.

As different ethnic factions became involved in this conflict, the armies recruited boys as soldiers, and about 20,000 combatants—one-quarter of the total in 1990—were children. By the war's end, analysts estimated that about 20 percent of the soldiers had been between ages 15 and 17. The NPLF had a "small boys unit" whose members ranged in age from 6 to 20. Children as young as 7 could be seen wielding guns in combat. The director of the Liberian Red Cross said that some young boys joined the army to get a gun because this would help them to survive in the climate of violence. Others joined seeking revenge after family members were killed.

Lawrence Moore later told an interviewer for the *New York Times* about his life in the army. He had enlisted when he was 15 and said he did not give it much thought at the time. Most of his acquaintances were also joining militias because they were uneducated and had few options for the future. When Moore arrived at the front, he was happy to see his friends but suffered wounds to his hand and foot in his first battle. Moore recalled that after he returned to the front, "We were losing a lot of men, but we killed a lot of them too, plenty. One night, one of my friends died right in front of me. I felt very bad but I never stopped fighting. I said to myself, this is war" (French, 1998).

The war in Liberia was a forerunner of future African wars that would entail heavy civilian casualties, genocide, and the use of child soldiers. Heavy shelling of cities did not distinguish between military and civilian targets. Like Liberia, ethnic conflicts in Rwanda and Burundi, among other places, included hideous massacres of people and entire villages, as well as the use of children as combatants.

After the fighting stopped, concerned people called for war crimes trials. Janet Fleischman, director for Africa for Human Rights Watch, said, "All of the factions killed civilians, looted civilians, and raped civilians. And because they all took part in these acts, none of them have any interest in seeing any accounting for what happened" (French, 1998).

After the war ended in 1996, relief organizations worked to help young people adjust. A key goal was to help former child soldiers re-enter civilian life successfully. Demobilization programs sought to return young people to school or to vocational training programs and gave them access to halfway houses and drop-in support centers. Between November 1996 and August 1997, about 4,000 former child combatants had turned in weapons and enrolled in programs at educational centers run by British Save the Children. Yarkpawolow Hallay, an 18-year-old who had fought as a soldier for seven years, said, "I wanted to be a soldier but I have changed. I am taking a course. I want to be a social worker" (Coen, 1997). Una McCauley of Save the Children said, "They are normal children who want to go to school, who want to be loved by their families, and who want to be respected. If you can give them another channel of respect [other] than guns, then I think you open up a whole new way of looking at life" (Coen, 1997). *See also* AFRICA; MASSACRES; SIERRA LEONE; REFUGEES; SOLDIERS, CHILD.

Further Reading: Bob Coen (contributor), "Overcoming a Life of Warfare," CNN World News, August 29, 1997, at <http://cnn.co.uk/WORLD/9708/29/liberia>; Howard W. French, "Liberian Slayings Began Brutal Trend in Africa," *New York Times* February 4, 1998, p. A3; International Committee of the Red Cross, *Children and War* (1994).

Libya

In the 1980s, child soldiers fought for Libya, a nation in North Africa that had instituted universal military training for youth, starting at age 14. According to John Laffin, all children are taught to handle light-arms and every young person is a specialist in at least one field of warfare by the time he or she finishes secondary school or college. Libya also sponsored training camps for young Palestinian soldiers. As of 1982, local militia units were recruiting boys between the ages of 14 and 18. During fighting between Libya and Chad in the 1980s, troops from Chad claimed to have captured Libyan soldiers as young as 11. Libya occupied the Aozu strip during the 1980s and deployed numerous land mines that covered about one-tenth of the total land area in Chad. These land mines remained a threat to children's safety and interfered with people's ability to farm, travel, build homes, or develop industry in areas where mines might be located.

An American air raid on Libya took place in 1986. Conflicts between the United States and Libya escalated in August 1981 after two U.S. planes shot down two Libyan warplanes that attacked them over the Gulf of Sidra. There were rumors that U.S. intelligence agents had uncovered a plan by Libyan leader Colonel Muammar Qaddafi to have President Ronald Reagan assassinated. In response, American bombers attacked Libya on April 14, 1986. The bombings killed civilians, including children, in suburban areas outside Tripoli, the capital. One blast hit a park and children's playground in the suburb of Bin Ashur. The Libyan government also claimed that when bombs hit Qaddafi's palace, they killed his 15-month-old adopted daughter, Hanna.

Further Reading: "Libya's Hit Teams," *Time,* December 21, 1981; "Why Reagan Moved Against Libya's Qadhafi," *U.S. News and World Report,* December 21, 1981.

Lidice

In June 1942, the Nazis massacred many men and young boys in the village of Lidice, Czechoslovakia. The massacre took place after a top Nazi official, Reinhard Heydrich, was killed by members of the Czech resistance. Czechoslovakia had been suffering under a brutal Nazi occupation government since the country was forced to surrender to Germany early in 1939.

In revenge for Heydrich's assassination, the Nazis slaughtered villagers in Lidice beginning on the evening on June 9, 1942. Men and boys over age 15 (about 200 in all) were killed, and nearly 200 women and 91 children were sent to concentration camps, or, in the case of some of the children, to homes in Germany. The village was then burned to the ground and the ashes were bulldozed to wipe out any sign that it had ever existed.

News of the massacre of Lidice and other Nazi atrocities enraged the Allies, who began holding discussions about convening war crimes trials after the war to punish those who were responsible for the deaths in Lidice and for the deaths of millions of other civilians.

After the war ended, the Czechoslovak War Crimes Investigation Commission searched for any surviving children who had been taken from Lidice. German families had adopted some of the children. Of the 91 children who had been removed from the village at the time of the attack, only 16 could be found after the war, and only some of these could be reunited with their Czech parents. These children faced numerous adjustments. Some did not recognize their relatives and they had been taught to speak German, not Czech. The remaining children had either died or were living with German families who kept the children's identity secret. *See also* ADOPTION; LEBENSBORN

Further Reading: Eleanor Ayer, *A Firestorm Unleashed* (1998); Vera Laska, ed., *Women of the Resistance and in the Holocaust* (1984).

Lodz Ghetto. *See* GHETTOS (WORLD WAR II)

London. *See* BLITZ, LONDON

Long March

Beginning in October 1934, during the communist revolution in China, children were separated from their families when about 100,000 communists set out on what became

known as the Long March, a retreat from the opposing nationalist Chinese troops of Chiang Kai-shek. The communists spent a grueling year covering 6,000 miles as they moved from south toward the west and then north, trying to remain out of sight. The 100,000 people included members of the military and civilians of all ages. Communist leader Mao Tse-tung retreated with his supporters into mountainous areas where they hid from the Nationalists. In 1937, the two groups—nationalists and communists— joined forces against their common enemy, the Japanese.

Children who were too young to continue the march with their families were placed in the homes of peasant families. It was nearly 15 years later when the communist forces, now called the People's Liberation Army, gained control of the region where the Long March had begun. *See also* CHINESE CIVIL WAR; JAPAN-CHINA WAR.

Further Reading: John Robottom, *China in Revolution* (1969).

Long Walk

In 1863, young Navajos suffered from hunger, disease, and displacement after the U.S. cavalry forced thousands of Indians to leave their former homelands in the Southwest and move to Fort Sumner in eastern New Mexico—a tragic journey the Navajos called the "Long Walk." The Navajos had resisted efforts to remove them and were subjected to increasing violence during the early 1860s. The U.S. government wanted Navajo land opened for settlement and the mining of gold and other minerals. Also, Navajo and Apache warriors had been fighting against the white invaders since the early 1800s. U.S. army troops were authorized to attack Navajo villages, burn corn and vegetable crops, chop down orchards, and destroy buildings. Navajo children were among those who were shot and bayoneted on September 22, 1861, when violence erupted at Fort Wingate during a special horse race that was held each year between Indians and whites.

By 1863, thousands of young people and their families were homeless and thousands lacked food stores for the coming winter. They embarked on the Long Walk, a journey that took three weeks. Infants and children died of exposure and hunger along the way. Soldiers forced 8,000 Navajos to march on foot across mostly desert land to Fort Sumner on the Bosque Redondo Reservation in present-day New Mexico. At the fort, infant death rates were much higher than normal, and crops were so poor that children and others died from hunger and malnutrition. Diseases took the lives of hundreds of other children, who were weakened by malnutrition. About 2,000 people died at the fort from hunger and illness between 1863 and 1867. In 1868, the survivors were finally allowed to return to the driest and most remote of their lands, which were less appealing to white settlers. *See also* AMERICAN INDIAN WARS.

Further Reading: Lynn R. Bailey, *The Long Walk* (1964); Dee Brown, *Bury My Heart at Wounded Knee* (1971).

Ludington, Sybil (1761–1839)

During the American Revolution, 16-year-old Sybil Ludington made a famous ride to warn people that British troops were coming. Ludington rode 40 miles on her horse, Star, on the night of April 26, 1777, banging on the doors of people throughout the area around Danbury, Connecticut. Ludington lived in nearby Fredericksburg, New York, and her father, Colonel Henry Ludington, served as an American commander during the war. Aroused by Ludington, the local Patriots rode to the arsenal at Danbury where weapons and other supplies were being stored. They reached Danbury in time to prevent British troops from seizing the supplies. Colonial troops then gathered at Colonel Ludington's home. When around 2,000 British and Tory soldiers reached his residence, Colonel Ludington ordered them to return to their ships and they agreed. A statue of Sybil Ludington on horseback was erected in Danbury to commemorate the courage of this young Revolutionary War heroine. *See also* AMERICAN REVOLUTION.

Further Reading: Patricia Edwards Clyne, *Patriots in Petticoats* (1976); Selma Williams, *Demeter's Daughters* (1976).

Lusitania

On May 7, 1915, about nine months after the start of World War I in Europe, a German U-boat 20 torpedoed the luxury liner, *Lusitania*, off the southwest coast of Ireland. Some 1,200 men, women, and children, primarily from Great Britain and the United States, died when the ship sank. The elegantly appointed *Lusitania* had been in service since September 7, 1907, and was the largest and fastest ship of its day. The ship was hit on its way from New York to England. In an effort to save the babies, who had been sleeping in wicker baskets after lunch, the ship's crew tied lifejackets to the baskets. However, as the ship settled below the surface, turbulence in the water caused the baskets to overturn and the babies drowned. The ship sank in only 18 minutes.

After the blast, fewer than half of the 48 lifeboats were still operational, and only 6 were successfully launched. Some people were crushed as lifeboats fell on other boats full of passengers. Others were killed when the boats were put down too fast. Survivor Desmond Cox later recalled, "I was thrown in and then she [his mother] got in. This was the last lifeboat that was launched" (Simpson, 1983). Some mothers lashed themselves to their children before they leaped from the ship. Ten-year-old Frank Hook became separated from his sister and father. He was tossed around in the churning water and some men pulled him into a boat. He suffered a broken leg but was relieved to find his father alive in the hospital where he was taken.

Passengers struggled in cold water for hours because rescuers were far away. An SOS was received in Queenstown and fishermen and others took boats out to collect survivors. As each minute passed, more people died. Some child survivors were lifted up into fishing trawlers, where they were given mugs of hot tea. Among the dead people who were retrieved from the water was a mother with her two children tied to her.

The sinking of this passenger ship enraged Americans and roused indignation against the Germans. It helped to increase support for American entry into the war, something most

Americans had previously opposed. When the United States finally declared war on Germany in 1917, the sinking of the *Lusitania*, and the resulting deaths of American civilians, was a rallying point.

In later years, people found out that the *Lusitania* was not merely a passenger ship but had been carrying loads of ammunition from the United States for the British war effort.

Further Reading: Colin Simpson, *The Lusitania* (1983).

M

Manzanar War Relocation Center

In 1942, shortly after the United States entered World War II, more than 10,000 Japanese Americans were brought to Manzanar War Relocation Center in a desert valley in Inyo County, California. Manzanar was one of the largest internment camps set up by the federal government, allegedly to protect the internees. About 25 percent of the evacuees, who came from California, Oregon, Washington State, and Hawaii, were school-aged children; a number of others were younger, some of them infants.

Armed guards patrolled Manzanar. The internees lived with their families in barracks furnished with army cots and straw mattresses and they ate in group mess halls. They endured harsh conditions, including temperatures that could range from freezing to more than 110 degrees. Among the young people interned at Manzanar was Jeanne Wakatsuki, whose family had lived in California for years. Her father was a fisherman who had left Japan when he was 17, but laws that discriminated against Asians had prevented him from becoming a U.S. citizen. He and his wife had worked hard at different jobs to support their family. By 1940, when they celebrated their twenty-fifth wedding anniversary, they had a lovely home and looked forward to the future.

Jeanne was seven years old when Pearl Harbor was bombed in December 1941. In April 1942, she and her family were sent to Manzanar, where they were assigned to live in barracks made of pine planking and tar paper. Conditions worsened; the electricity went off regularly and the water supply failed. The latrines were inadequate for the large population. Refrigeration was poor, which meant the food often spoiled. Jeanne and her brothers and sister suffered from chronic stomach cramps and fevers. Like many internees, the family endured health problems and faced many difficulties both in the camp and when they tried to resume their lives afterward.

Internees were required to grow food in this dry, dusty location and succeeded in producing large crops of fruits and vegetables, which increased American food supplies during the war. Children helped with this farmwork and also raised animals. They attended school in the camp and joined scout troops and sports teams.

In September 1945, after the war with Japan was over, Manzanar was disbanded and the people who remained there began to leave. Some internees had left the camps earlier—to join the military, to attend college through special programs organized by Quakers, or to work in jobs that would aid the U.S. war effort. Many former internees spent months in shelters, hotels, army barracks, or public housing before they were able to move into a place of their own again. The internees faced many difficult adjustments. They had been forced to leave behind their homes, possessions, and businesses, often selling these things for ridiculously low prices. Many had put their possessions in storage but found these things were gone—either stolen or sold. They had also been treated as criminals and lost their rights during their time at the camp. One evacuee later said, "So much we left behind, but the most valuable thing I lost was my freedom" (Brimner, 1994). *See also* IN- TERNMENT CAMPS, U.S; PEARL HARBOR; UNITED STATES (WORLD WAR II); WORLD WAR II.

Further Reading: John Armor and Peter Wright, *Manzanar* (1988); Larry Dane Brimner, *Voices from the Camps* (1994); Roger Daniels, *Concentration Camps U.S.A.* (1972); Roger Daniels, *The Decision to Relocate the Japanese Americans* (1975); Monica Itoi Stone, *Nisei Daughter* (1953); Michi Weglyn, *Years of Infamy* (1976).

Marshall Plan

The Marshall Plan, a massive relief program, helped millions of children in Europe who were devastated by World War II. The war brought widespread hunger, homelessness, and unemployment, along with shortages of clothing and fuel. Many places lacked electrical power, drinking water, sanitation facilities, health care, and transportation. Hundreds of thousands of homes, as well as hospitals, schools, and other buildings, had been destroyed. Debris lay in bombed-out cities, and dead bodies still remained in the rubble of Warsaw and other cities.

In June 1947, former General George Marshall proposed that the United States design a large-scale plan to alleviate the suffering. U.S. leaders also believed that such a plan was important politically, as a way to prevent the spread of communism. The goal of the Marshall Plan was to promote self-sufficiency, with the United States providing materials and support to help Europeans help themselves.

The first shipment abroad in 1947 included 19,000 tons of meat, which was sent from Texas to France. Other shipments soon followed, bringing food, tools, fishing nets, fertilizer, machines, and other items. Through this program, the United States spent $15 billion over five years (about $88 billion to-

day). Farmers donated crops and supplies to their European counterparts. Companies like Volkswagen and Mercedes-Benz received funding for their businesses and were then able to employ people who needed jobs.

The program improved the lives of millions of children and young adults in war-torn Europe. On the fiftieth anniversary of the Marshall Plan, a German who was a teenager in the postwar years recalled how grateful he and his schoolmates felt when a truck arrived at his school bringing them soup and various supplies. This boy, Helmut Kohl, later became chancellor of Germany, which developed into a democratic and economically strong nation after the war.

Nations in Eastern Europe did not benefit from the Marshall Plan. The Soviet Union, then led by Joseph Stalin, barred the nations in the eastern (or communist) bloc from taking part. *See also* WORLD WAR II.

Further Reading: Robert J. Donovan, *The Second Victory: The Marshall Plan and the Postwar Revival of Europe* (1987); John Gimbel, *The Origins of the Marshall Plan* (1976); Susan M. Hartmann, *The Marshall Plan* (1968); Theodore A. Wilson, *The Marshall Plan, 1947-1951* (1977).

Martin, Joseph Plumb (1760–1833?)

As a teenager, Joseph Plumb Martin fought in the American Revolution. He later published his account of more than seven years service in the Continental Army. His memoir was based on the detailed journal he had kept during that time. Born in Massachusetts, Martin was raised on a farm in Connecticut. He was 15 when he enlisted in a regiment that was organized in his hometown in June 1776. His family had objected to his enlistment, but he received their consent after he decided to enlist for only six months.

After Martin arrived in New York, one of his first assignments was to join a group of men who rescued 2,500 barrels of flour from a storehouse that the British had planned to raid. During 1776, as part of George Washington's army, Martin participated in the battles of Long Island, Kip's Bay, Harlem Heights, and White Plains. He remained in the army beyond the six-month period even though he had experienced hunger, cold, and fatigue, and had been saddened by the sight of wounded men. During the 1777 campaign, he injured his foot and required surgery. His journal entries for that year describe long difficult marches, freezing weather, and severe hunger.

> In the cold month of November, without provisions, without Clothing, not a scrap of either shoes or stockings to my feet or legs, and in this condition to endure a siege in such a place as that, was appalling in the highest degree. (Martin, 1995)

Martin described weeks of subsisting on corned beef and hard bread, without tents, boots, shirts, and blankets. The men arrived at Valley Forge in Pennsylvania desperately hungry and thirsty. At one point, Martin obtained half a small pumpkin, which he cooked by making a small fire on the ground. His company continued to suffer hardships during the 1778 campaign. Martin took part in several battles that year but managed to stay alive. In 1779, he spent another terrible winter based in Morristown, New Jersey. Between battles, Martin was often assigned to sentry duty and spent many nights watching out for the British. He was present when the war ended in 1781 with the British surrender at Yorktown, Virginia, and remained with his military unit throughout 1781 and 1782 in case they were needed to maintain an uncertain peace.

In June 1783, he was honorably discharged and proceeded to teach school during the winter of 1783-1784. Then Martin settled in Maine where he married and had several children. In his community, he was known for his colorful, detailed stories about his war years. Friends encouraged him to put the entire story into book form, and it was published in 1830 under the title, *A Narrative of Some of the Adventures, Dangers, and Suffering of a Revolutionary Soldier, Interspersed with Anecdotes of Incidents, that Occurred within His Own Observation*. Years later, these reminiscences were fashioned into a book for young people. Joseph Martin's experiences resemble those of other young soldiers who fought in the Revolution on the American side. His account has been praised for its vivid details and good humor. It is regarded as more complete than the recordings of other revolutionary war soldiers although he was only 15 at the time he entered the army. *See also* AMERICAN REVOLUTION; DIARIES.

Further Reading: Joseph Plumb Martin, *Yankee Doodle Boy* (1995).

Massacres

Massacres—mass killings of people—have taken the lives of children and young adult civilians throughout history. Massacres may date back to ancient times. Archeological sites contain numerous human bones and skulls in mass graves, but historians are not sure if these were burial sites or the scenes of mass killings. Some massacres have been well documented. The sack of Antwerp by unpaid Spanish troops in 1576 was called the "Spanish Fury." When the fighting was over, about 17,000 men, women, and children were dead. According to an English eyewitness named George Gascoigne, the Spanish "slew great numbers of young children" (Carey, 1988).

Cawnpore, India, was the scene of a massacre in 1857. On July 15, native ruler Nana Sahib led a mutiny against the British. An entire garrison of British officials and residents, including more than 200 women and children, were killed with swords in a house known as the Bibigarh. The British retaliated by arresting and killing the leaders of the uprising, which spread to other towns across India during the summer and autumn.

During the Bulgarian revolt of 1876, Turkish soldiers brutally massacred civilians to suppress the Bulgarian independence movement. J.A. MacGahan, a reporter for the *London Daily News*, reached Batak, the scene of many killings, in August. He reported that the hillside surrounding the village was covered with skeletons and dead bodies of the victims. Some were clearly children and young people.

> On the other side of the way were the skeletons of two children lying side by side,

partly covered with stones, and with frightful sabre cuts in their little skulls. The number of children killed in these massacres is something enormous. . . . Before many of the doorways women were walking up and down wailing their funeral chant. One of them caught me by the arm and led me inside of the walls, and there in one corner, half covered with stones and mortar were the remains of another young girl, her long hair flowing wildly about among the stones and dust. And the mother fairly shrieked with agony, and beat her head madly against the wall. . . . A few steps further on sat a woman on a doorstep, rocking herself to and fro, and uttering moans heartrending beyond anything I could have imagined. Her head was buried in her hands, while her fingers were unconsciously twisting and tearing her hair as she gazed in her lap, where lay three little skulls. (Carey, 1988)

Nazi massacres of Jewish civilians killed tens of thousands of children and young people during the Holocaust of World War II. The so-called Bloody Thursday massacre occurred in Radom, Poland, on March 2, 1942; the Nazis entered the ghetto and shot 40 Jews in the streets at random. In the ghetto in Minsk, Russia, some 5,000 Jews were forced to the edge of the town. Adults were machine-gunned to death and fell into a mass grave; children were tossed alive into the pit where they suffocated to death. One of the most infamous World War II massacres took place in the Ukraine in a place called Babi Yar. About 30,000 Jewish men, women, and children were killed by Nazi killing squads (*Einsatzgruppen*) within a matter of hours. The killing squads massacred Jewish civilians throughout Poland and the Soviet Union.

During World War II, entire households and villages of people were sometimes killed by the Nazis for helping Jews or Allied troops. In Poland in July 1943, the Nazis burned more than 200 people alive for helping a Jewish partisan unit. The victims included 70 children, one only nine days old. The victims were forced into barns and houses that were then set on fire. In March 1943, the Nazis shot and killed 36 villagers in Przewrotne, Poland, for helping Jews. The villagers included four young people ranging in age from 2 months to 19 years.

During the last half of the twentieth century, massacres were perpetrated during civil wars in Europe, Asia, and Africa. *See also* AFRICA; ARMENIAN-TURKISH CONFLICT; BOSNIA; CAMBODIA; *EINSATZGRUPPEN*; EL SALVADOR; GENOCIDE; HOLOCAUST; LIBERIAN CIVIL WAR; LIDICE; MY LAI MASSACRE; ORADOUR-SUR-GLANE; PACIFIC (WORLD WAR II); RWANDA; WORLD WAR II.

Further Reading: John Carey, *Eyewitness to History* (1988); Richard C. Lukas, *Did the Children Cry?* (1994); Theodore Ropp, *War in the Modern World* (1962); Leni Yahil, *The Holocaust* (1990).

"Master Race"

The idea of a "master race" was central to the political agenda promoted in Germany and Europe by Adolf Hitler's Nazi (National Socialist Workers) Party during the 1930s and World War II. The Nazis indoctrinated and militarized youth to support and promote their vision of a glorious new Germany, composed of mentally and physically "superior" people who would rule over all others. This concept played a key role in Nazi activities during the Holocaust and World War II, when the Nazis perpetrated mass murder and euthanasia against people of all ages and deported millions of others. In addition to killing babies with certain mental and physical disabilities, the German government also worked to prevent the births of babies who did not have the desired traits and to increase the births of babies who were considered desirable.

Between 1933 and 1945, the Nazis spread their ideas through massive propaganda efforts, in newspapers, films, radio programs, and school textbooks. In the Nazi view, inferior humans included people who did not have Aryan or Nordic blood, including Slavic peoples, Asians, and Africans. The Nazis said that Poles, Latvians, Lithuanians, Estonians, Ukrainians, and Russians, among others, were subhumans—in German, *untermenschen*. As they conquered various countries during World War II, the Nazis attempted to subdue these groups by denying them civil rights and education and by using them as slaves. Jews and Romani (Gypsies) were viewed as having "inferior" blood and were targeted for total elimination.

The Nazis deemed certain people unworthy of life because they had incurable illnesses or disabilities that left them unable to work. Such people were to be eliminated through a program called Operation T-4. Moreover, people with certain kinds of handicaps and genetically transmitted conditions, such as mental retardation, were deemed unfit to reproduce. A program of sterilization was instigated to achieve that goal. Specific laws required people to prove they were "fit" to reproduce before they were allowed to marry. People with traits the Nazis did not want to be passed on to new generations were forced to undergo medical sterilization. A number of young people were subjected to this surgery, including some with conditions that were not genetic, such as deafness caused by disease.

To make their opinions look scientific, the Nazis developed various institutions to affirm their ideas about racism. They set up the Institute of Hereditary Biology and Race Research to study different ethnic groups and nationalities. In one series of studies, they measured people's facial features and skull bones, and categorized different shades of hair and eye colors. Scientists at the institute were told that all their work should support the Nazi political agenda. Their conclusions were presented as facts to children in German public schools.

Nazi books, articles, museum exhibits, and newsreels purported to show why certain races were inferior to Germanic peoples. Teachers were given new textbooks along with detailed instructions about how to teach racism and anti-Semitism (hatred of Jews) in their classrooms, beginning in the earliest grades. For example, *The Nazi Primer* described master humans, called Aryans or Nordic people, as being tall, pale-skinned, and blond, with eyes ranging from blue to grey. The text read, "The Nordic race is uncommonly gifted mentally. It is outstanding in truthfulness and energy. . . ."

To increase the Aryan population in Germany, thousands of blond, blue-eyed children in occupied Europe were kidnapped from their parents and sent to be Germanized—in Poland alone, some 200,000 children. Many Polish children who did not fit the physical ideal were killed or forced to perform slave labor or sterilized. Most kidnapped children were lost to their families forever because they died or were given new identities and could not be traced after the war. *See also* EDUCATION; EUTHANASIA; GENOCIDE; HITLER, ADOLF; HITLER YOUTH; HOLOCAUST; LEBENSBORN; OPERATION T-4; POLAND (WORLD WAR II); ROMANI (GYPSIES); WORLD WAR II.

Further Reading: George L. Mosse, ed., *Nazi Culture* (1981); Barbara Rogasky, *Smoke and Ashes* (1987); Bea Stadtler, *The Holocaust* (1973); Margot Stern Strom and William S. Parsons, *Facing History and Ourselves* (1978).

McBride, Maggie (1767–?)

Maggie McBride, a 14-year-old farm girl in 1781, became a heroine during the American Revolution. A native of Guilford County, North Carolina, McBride was familiar with the region around her home and was able to guide a group of Patriot soldiers to a camp in a dense pine forest where a group of Tories (British loyalists) had made camp. The Patriot troops then launched a surprise attack. As the shooting began, McBride leaped from her horse and ran several miles back home. *See also* AMERICAN REVOLUTION.

Further Reading: Selma Williams, *Demeter's Daughters* (1976).

McConnell, E.G. (1926–)

E.G. McConnell was one of the youngest soldiers to serve in the 761st Tank Battalion during World War II and one of more than 1 million African Americans who actively served during that war. In 1942, at age 16, he volunteered to serve in the army, lying about his age to qualify. McConnell traveled from his native New York City to begin basic training in Kentucky. His unit was then sent to Camp Claiborne in Louisiana where, as African Americans, they experienced racial prejudice.

McConnell and the other soldiers were deeply upset to find that German prisoners of war at the camp had more freedom to come and go on the post and in the nearby town than they did.

At Camp Hood in Texas, McConnell's group was reorganized as a medium tank battalion. His unit, Headquarters Company, was responsible for maintaining personnel files, supporting vehicle maintenance, and running an assault gun platoon, mortar platoon, and reconnaissance platoon. The treatment of African Americans at this base further discouraged McConnell: "I was a good soldier, but the South and segregation made me want to get out of the Army" (Pfeifer, 1994).

In August 1944, the battalion sailed to England on a British ship. By this time, O'Connell was one of only two men who had received special training on a part of a tank called a gyrostabilizer. He was assigned to the vehicle maintenance platoon and had specialized training in tank maintenance. The batallion arrived in England on September 8, 1944, and was posted in a small town in southern England where they awaited word to proceed across the English Channel to Omaha Beach on the French coast. He later recalled, "As we approached the Coast, there were sunken ships and debris everywhere. I never saw so much devastation in my life. How could anyone lose this much and still wage a major war?" (Pfeifer, 1994). McConnell and his fellow soldiers were heartened by the warm response of the French people who brought them food, drinks, and flowers.

On November 2, 1944, General George Patton told the men of the battalion, "You're the first Negro tankers to ever fight in the American army. I would never have asked for you if you weren't good. I have nothing but the best in my army. I don't care what color you are . . . everyone has their eyes on you and is expecting great things from you." Patton also spoke personally to McConnell, who was in the cannoneer's position in his tank: "I want you to use these . . . guns and shoot up everything you see. . . ." McConnell responded, "Yes, General" (Pfeifer, 1994).

Fighting bravely, the tank division headed northeast for the German border. They were later praised for their calmness and courage under fire, and a number of the men received medals. Several members of the division died or were wounded. They reached Germany on December 14, and were then ordered into Belgium, arriving on the front lines on December 31, 1944. They successfully forced the Germans to retreat from the city of Tillet and other parts of Belgium, then moved into Holland, where they received more training in preparation for fighting across the German border once again. In mid-March, they joined the 103rd Infantry Division of the Seventh United States Army, with whom they fought in southern France.

McConnell and his division were ordered to penetrate Germany's Siegfried Line, a 400-mile-long concrete and steel wall along the western border. With his battalion, McConnell traveled almost 2,000 miles and fought for 183 days without a break. He survived the war and returned home, a seasoned combat veteran barely 20 years old.

In 1949, his battalion began holding annual reunions. It took decades, however, before McConnell and his fellow veterans finally received a Presidential Unit Citation, which is the highest award given to combat units. A research team was assigned to look into their case, and, in 1978, Secretary of the Army Clifford Alexander announced that President Jimmy Carter would be giving their unit the citation. On April 20, 1978, McConnell was among the 200 veterans and their families who gathered at Fort Meyer, Virginia, for the ceremony. Each veteran received a letter from the president praising their "extraordinary gallantry, courage, professionalism, and high esprit de corps . . . in the accomplishment of unusually difficult and hazardous operations" and a blue pin they would wear as a lasting symbol of their award.

Further Reading: Mary Penick Motley, ed., *The Invisible Soldier* (1983); Kathryn Browne Pfeifer, *The 761st Tank Battalion* (1994).

Mein Kampf. *See* HITLER, ADOLF

Memorials. *See* ANIELEWICZ, MORDECHAI; LUDINGTON, SYBIL; PEACE MONUMENT; SASAKI, SADAKO; UNITED STATES HOLOCAUST MEMORIAL AND MUSEUM; YAD VASHEM

Mengele, Josef (1911–1979)

During World War II, a Nazi physician named Josef Mengele conducted cruel and deadly pseudo-medical experiments on death camp victims, many of whom were children. Nearly all of his victims were Jews, the main group targeted by the Nazis, and most of the subjects died. The notorious Mengele was called the "Angel of Death." As chief medical officer at Auschwitz, Mengele also played a key role in determining who would live or die by making "selections" when people arrived. Chilling first-person accounts describe how the elegantly dressed, white-gloved doctor with the glossy boots would determine their fate. He also sometimes chose people to be sent to the gas chambers at random during the day while making rounds of the camps. Young adults who survived the initial selection process at the camp later described the terror they felt when Mengele appeared.

Mengele was the son of a wealthy factory owner in Gunzburg, Germany. Before the war, he earned degrees in both medicine and genetics, then worked at the Institute of Hereditary Biology and Race Research, which Hitler's government set up to reaffirm Nazi beliefs about the inherent superiority or inferiority of different ethnic groups and nationalities. Institute scientists there wrote papers and conducted classes that supported the Nazis' political agenda. Mengele became a zealous advocate of these racial theories.

During the 1930s, Mengele joined the elite Nazi SS corps, then became a concentration camp physician after the war began. In 1943, he volunteered to work at the notorious Auschwitz-Birkenau death camp in Poland. Mengele stood near the gate where trainloads of captives arrived. With a motion of his thumb or his riding crop, he determined who would die. Mengele usually sent children straight to the death chambers, but he allowed twins and certain others, including dwarfs, to live so that he could experiment on them.

Nazi doctors in the camps were permitted to do whatever they wished to victims without presenting any credible medical rationale or adhering to laws or common medical standards or ethics. Subjects experienced grave pain and disability before they died. One twin, a child when he was imprisoned at Auschwitz, recalled how his brother was subjected to surgery that left him castrated, weak, and unable to walk. Like many children, the boy died. In one gruesome test, Mengele tried sewing twins together to see if he could turn them into Siamese twins. Of the approximately 3,000 twins victimized by Mengele, only about 200 survived.

In January 1945, when Allied troops were close to winning the war and liberating the death camps, Mengele vanished in the night. Convinced that his test results, tissue and organ specimens, documents, and reports were valuable, he took some of them with him and sent others to people in Germany before he fled. Aided by his family, Mengele hid in Germany until 1946, while members of the U.S. Army Counterintelligence Corps searched for him. Young people who had witnessed Mengele's activities spoke to the press, but most child survivors were trying to find any surviving family members and return home or trying to cope with the aftermath of their hideous experiences.

In 1945–1946, other war criminals received more attention than Mengele, in part because Allied authorities may not have known the extent of his crimes. Mengele made his way to Argentina, where he became part of a German community that included other Nazis. During the 1950s, he used his real name and even traveled to Europe where he joined his son Rolf for a ski trip in Switzerland. Rolf was told that Mengele was his uncle.

During the early 1960s, more efforts were made to locate Nazi war criminals in hiding. Israeli officials seized Adolf Eichmann, who had sent millions of Jews to their deaths. Eichmann was found guilty and received the death penalty. His trial, which was televised, brought worldwide attention to the Holocaust. Former child victims of Mengele's experiments found themselves reliving their ordeal and suffering from nightmares, depression, and other symptoms of stress.

Fearing capture, Mengele fled to Brazil where he lived under a false name. Friends continued to bring him letters and money from his family in Germany. However, family members grew less friendly through the years, and the German universities where Mengele received his training stripped him of his degrees. In 1979, Mengele apparently suffered a stroke and drowned while swimming with friends on a Brazilian beach.

In 1984, Holocaust survivors again publicized the atrocities Mengele had committed during the war. Several organizations and U.S. newspapers offered $4 million for his capture. The United States Department of Justice worked with the governments of West Germany and Israel to study the files each had gathered on Mengele and his whereabouts. People reported seeing Mengele in cities all over the world, but these leads turned out to be false.

German authorities searched the home of a German citizen who had helped Mengele through the years. They discovered Mengele's address in Brazil and addresses of his friends. Once in Brazil, investigators were told Mengele was dead and were led to a gravesite. In 1985, the body was exhumed and analyzed. Although an international team of scientists affirmed that the remains were Mengele's, controversy continued for years afterward. *See also* AUSCHWITZ-BIRKENAU; CHILDREN OF AUSCHWITZ NAZI DEADLY EXPERIMENTS SURVIVORS (CANDLES); CONCENTRATION CAMPS (WORLD WAR II); DEATH CAMPS (WORLD WAR II); DEKEL, ALEX SCHLOMO; EXPERIMENTS, NAZI; HOLOCAUST; "MASTER RACE"; ROMANI (GYPSIES); SELECTION PROCESS AT CONCENTRATION CAMPS (WORLD WAR II).

Further Reading: Israel Gutman and Michael Berenbaum, *Anatomy of the Auschwitz Death Camp* (1994); Michael Kater, *Doctors Under Hitler* (1989); Lucette Matalon Lagnado and Sheila Cohn Dekel, *Children of the Flames* (1991).

Messengers. *See* AMERICAL CIVIL WAR; AMERICAN REVOLUTION; BOYD, ISABELLE "BELLE"; DARRAGH, JOHN; ESPIONAGE; GEIGER, EMILY; JEWISH FIGHTERS ORGANIZATION (JFO); LUDINGTON, SYBIL; MOORE, BETH; RESISTANCE MOVEMENTS (WORLD WAR II)

Military Service. *See* AFRICA; AMERICAN CIVIL WAR; AMERICAN REVOLUTION; ARAB-ISRAELI WARS; BOSNIA; CASUALTIES, MILITARY; CHECHNYA; CHINESE CIVIL WAR; CONSCIENTIOUS OBJECTORS; CONSCRIPTION; CUBAN REVOLUTION; FRENCH REVOLUTION; GUATEMALA; IRAN-IRAQ WAR; KURDS; LIBERIAN CIVIL WAR; MOZAMBIQUE; PACIFIC (WORLD WAR II); PERSIAN GULF WAR; RWANDA; SELECTIVE SERVICE ACTS; SOLDIERS, CHILD; WORLD WAR I; WORLD WAR II; ZAIRE

Montagnards

The Montagnards, from the French word for "mountaineers," lived in mountainous regions and are considered to be the original, native inhabitants of Vietnam. They lived quietly as farmers, weaving cloth, which they sold to merchants. There were about 800,000 Montagnards living in the highlands of Vietnam when the Vietnam War reached its peak in the late 1960s.

The South Vietnamese government decided to remove the Montagnards from their villages so that the communist Viet Cong and the North Vietnamese troops could not take their food or use them as guides through the region. About 75 percent of these people were taken to resettlement camps where they suffered from mass epidemics of tuberculosis, cholera, and other diseases, and high death rates. Montagnards went hungry when they were unable to farm enough land and lacked work animals to grow enough food for their needs. They also lacked sources of clean water and the tools they needed to dig good wells.

Montagnard children became ill and died, and some were orphaned when disease struck their families. Young people also lost siblings. Older boys were forced to join military groups. Authors Betty Lifton and Thomas C. Fox interviewed a teenage girl named Nher who had lost both parents and her brothers. She and her nine-year-old sister were the only surviving family members. Nher said, "Before, we were very rich. We lived in a big house. We had cows, water buffaloes, and chickens. Now we have nothing. We are very hungry. Life is sad here" (Lifton and Fox, 1972). *See also* REFUGEES; VIETNAM WAR.

Further Reading: Betty Jean Lifton and Thomas C. Fox, *Children of Vietnam* (1972).

Moore, Beth

During the American Revolution, teenager Beth Moore carried an important message to Captain Wallace of the Patriot army. Moore and her family, who lived in Charleston, South Carolina, learned that British troops were planning a surprise attack on Wallace's camp, which was located up the river from their city. Moore devised a clever ruse involving herself, her brother, and his girlfriend. The three of them took a canoe out onto the river that evening, pretending to be enjoying a recreational boat ride. They managed to paddle to Wallace's camp and warn him so that he could relocate his men before the British arrived. *See also* AMERICAN REVOLUTION.

Mother Teresa (1910–1997)

Mother Teresa was renowned for her charitable work among the poor and her organized efforts to help people in war-torn and impoverished regions. This Catholic missionary nun was born Agnes Gonxha Bojaxhiu in Skopje in the former Yugoslav republic of Macedonia. She became a nun at age 18 and was sent first to Ireland, then to India where she taught at a school in Calcutta and lived in the convent of Loreto. While traveling to a religious retreat in 1946, Sister Teresa believed that God had commanded her to leave the convent and live among the "poorest of the poor," devoting her life to working with

these people outside the convent walls. In 1948, when she was allowed to leave the convent, she exchanged her black nun's habit for sandals and a white cotton sari with three blue stripes on it, and she pinned a small cross on her left shoulder.

For several months, Sister Teresa received training in providing health care and treating illness from nuns at the hospital in Patna. Then she began her missionary work and founded an order that grew to include more nuns. In Calcutta at this time, there were thousands of refugees from the India-Pakistan wars. As leader of their order, the Missionaries of Charity, she was called Mother Teresa. Mother Teresa had always been concerned about the poor, sick, dying, and most of all, children. During the long war in Lebanon, nuns from her order worked to rescue dozens of children who were endangered by the fighting. Her Missionaries of Charity order grew to include more than 4,000 sisters in countries around the world, and many of them helped children who suffered as a result of war. Among their other projects was an AIDS home in New York City. In 1979, Mother Teresa was awarded the Nobel Peace Prize. During the 1980s, Mother Teresa went to Northern Ireland, Israel, and Lebanon, among other places, to help those in need and promote the cause of peace.

Further Reading: Patricia Reilly Giff, *Mother Teresa* (1986).

Motherhood. *See* ADOPTION; HITLER'S CHILDREN; LEBENSBORN; PERSIAN GULF WAR; SEPARATIONS, FAMILY

Mozambique

Young people fought as soldiers and suffered from hunger, family separations, homelessness, a lack of health care, and other hardships when civil war ravaged the African nation of Mozambique. From 1976 to 1992, the Renamo (Mozambican National Resistance) fought the ruling government, called the Frelimo (Front for the Liberation of Mozambique). Between 1980 and 1988, about 490,000 children died in Mozambique from war-related causes. Drought and famine aggravated the suffering. Child victims could not receive health care when wartime conditions destroyed hospitals and damaged the infrastructure of the country. Between 1982 and 1986, more than 40 percent of the health care centers were destroyed. Transporting supplies across war zones was also difficult or impossible.

Families were torn apart. One night, young Absalao Paula Cumbane was sleeping when Renamo soldiers broke into the house and beat him and his mother and sisters. The soldiers seized the family and then split them up, forcing Absalao to join them as a soldier.

A number of other youths became soldiers. Observers from international relief organizations saw boys as young as 9 and 10 fighting with AK-47s. The Renamo forces contained at least 10,000 boy soldiers, some only 6 years old. Some of these children were brought out of orphanages, then given military training. Investigators found that their training often included physical abuse and terror to condition them to accept violence and act violently toward others.

Among these young soldiers was Rui Fernando, who was taken from an orphanage near Maputo at age 14. Fernando later told South African journalist John Fleming, "They made us do some terrible things. We were always attacking villages. Hardly ever military targets, only villages. We would go in at night and just start shooting; we would shoot at everything. It was always dark so I don't know if I ever killed anybody or not" (Fleming, 1996).

Peter Nkhonjera, a Save the Children coordinator in Mozambique, explained that commanders preferred child soldiers because they "are easy to organize, and they don't ask questions. In wartime, a commander wants total submission. You get that only from a child." Boy soldiers were killed not only by the enemy but sometimes by their own troops. Reporters found that when a boy disobeyed orders or his commanders decided he did not measure up, another soldier was ordered to kill him. These killings sometimes took place in front of the whole group as a lesson to the others.

The return of peace in 1992, did not restore normal conditions in Mozambique. Wartime spending had drastically cut funds that could be used for children's health care and the education system. Relief agencies helped stricken children. For example, Save the Children developed a program that was able to reunite about 8,000 children with their families after the war. They also helped people find out the fate of missing relatives. An estimated 200,000 children were orphaned or unaccompanied by a parent or adult after the war. Many of them were taken into the homes of extended family members or people who lived in their former communities before the war. According to UNICEF, the damage to the education system left two-thirds of the 2 million school-age children in Mozambique without access to schooling. One goal of the UNICEF programs in this country was to restore schools so that children could again become accustomed to structures and routines and engage in constructive peaceful activities.

Relief organizations found that some youth had serious emotional problems as a result of their experiences. Some were aggressive and antisocial, and often fearful. A number of former child soldiers found it hard to adjust to civilian life, which seemed boring compared to their wartime exploits. Others missed the comraderie of being in a fighting unit or the power they had had over their lives and the lives of others. Some were overwhelmed with guilt and shame for their actions as soldiers. *See also* AFRICA; SAVE THE CHILDREN; SOLDIERS, CHILD; UNACCOMPANIED CHILDREN; UNITED NATIONS CHILDREN'S FUND (UNICEF).

Further Reading: Maggie Black, *Children First: The Story of UNICEF Past and Present* (1996); Cole P. Dodge and M. Raundelen, eds., *Reaching Children in War: Sudan, Uganda, and Mozambique* (1991); John Fleming, "Children in Bondage," *World Press Review*, January 1996, p. 8; "War: The Heartbreak of Children Caught in Conflict," Save the Children at <http://www.savethechildren.org/war.html>.

Multiracial Children

Sexual relations between personnel attached to foreign armies and local residents have sometimes resulted in multiracial children (children with more than one racial heritage). Many of these children have faced special problems. During World War II, some German soldiers fathered children in France with women who had originally come from French colonies in Africa. The Nazi government under Adolf Hitler did not recognize these children as Germans and denied them rights and citizenship under German law because of their African heritage.

Children fathered by French soldiers during the French occupation of Indochina (later Vietnam, Cambodia, and Laos) were called *metis*. The French government took some responsibility for the children, who were allowed to obtain French citizenship and were eligible for funds to pursue an education either in France or Vietnam, depending on their choice.

More than 10,000 Amerasian children were fathered by American soldiers and civilians who were stationed in Vietnam during the 1960s and early 1970s. They were called *con lai*—"half breed children." Some of the mothers of the children were desperately poor women who became pregnant while working as prostitutes. Others had formed close relationships with soldiers and lived with them while they were stationed in Vietnam. After U.S. troops left, these children were usually abandoned by the fathers and remained in Vietnam. Other men left without realizing they had fathered a child or that their child would be born after their departure. More than half of the children later sought to find their fathers and many hoped to live in the United States, but few had the opportunity.

The problems of these children received increasing publicity during the 1970s. When U.S. troops left Vietnam, many jobs also disappeared. Poor single mothers were left to raise their children with even less money than they had before. Most were living in poverty and encountered discrimination and rejection from other Vietnamese. Mothers sometimes abandoned their children because they could not bear the public humiliation and stigma. Other mothers continued to raise their children, who were teased and excluded from childhood activities by their peers.

Authors Betty Lifton and Thomas C. Fox (1972) found that about 50 percent of the mixed-blood children left behind in Vietnam were part African American. These children were treated even more harshly than white Vietnamese children because Vietnam had a history of prejudice against people with darker skin. For years, the United States government did not assume financial responsibility for these children or offer them citizenship. The Department of Defense maintained that the plight of these children, while "unfortunate," was not within the proper scope of government intervention. During the 1970s, Congress passed several bills to promote the adoption of multiracial children and to send more aid to all Vietnamese children, without singling out those of mixed heritage.

An acclaimed Broadway musical, *Miss Saigon*, dramatized the plight of a young Vietnamese mother and her son after she was separated from the U.S. serviceman who fathered the boy before the fall of Saigon. *See also* ORPHANS; SEXUAL ABUSE; VIETNAM WAR.

Further Reading: Betty Jean Lifton and Thomas C. Fox, *Children of Vietnam* (1972).

Mushroom Club

The Mushroom Club was organized in Japan by parents whose children were exposed in utero (before birth) to the radiation emitted by the atomic bombings of Hiroshima and Nagasaki that ended World War II in 1945. Children born to women who were in the vicinity of the bombs during their pregnancy had higher rates of many disorders and diseases. For instance, women who were exposed early in pregnancy and located close to where the bomb exploded gave birth to children prone to disorders of the central nervous system. A number of these mothers suffered miscarriages. Some babies were born with smaller than normal brains and suffered from mental retardation. They often had kidney problems, eye problems, seizure disorders, high blood pressure, liver diseases, or dislocations of the hips. Many of the infants died before they reached their first birthday.

The 24 families who founded the Mushroom Club sought government aid to help them with the high costs of raising and caring for their disabled children. They did receive some financial aid, but it was a small amount and many parents still worried that their children would not have enough means to pay for their care after they, the parents, died. The group members offered each other emotional support as they sought practical ways to cope with numerous long-term problems. *See also* HIROSHIMA; JAPAN (WORLD WAR II); NAGASAKI.

Further Reading: John Hersey, *Hiroshima* (1988); Betty Jean Lifton, *A Place Called Hiroshima* (1985).

My Lai Massacre

Youths were among the casualties of the My Lai Massacre, which took place on March 16, 1968, during the Vietnam War. U.S. army troops from Charlie Company were brought by helicopter to a village called My Lai 4 in the district of Son My. Earlier that morning, helicopters had attacked the area. The U.S. troops were told the village was controlled by expert Viet Cong troops from North Vietnam. When the Americans arrived, they found unarmed villagers—men, women, children, and babies. People were fishing, walking to the market, working in their homes or gardens, or going about other ordinary activities.

During the hours that followed their arrival, the men in Charlie Company killed more than 500 people and destroyed their homes, livestock, and other possessions. Eyewitnesses reported that the servicemen shouted out the words "Viet Cong" as they committed these acts. They beat people and stabbed them with bayonets, setting fire to some victims. A number of women, including teenage girls, were raped. In all, 170 children were killed with machine guns, hand grenades, and other weapons. A survivor later wrote, "Our coastal village so green with coconut palms, bamboos and willows is now but heaps of ashes" (Lifton and Fox, 1972). Some of the villagers at My Lai tried to escape but found their way blocked by armed soldiers. A few who were not in the village that morning re-

turned to see My Lai in flames and dead bodies everywhere. Body parts lay scattered on the ground, and shocked survivors were weeping and burying the dead.

About 18 months later, concerned Americans called for an investigation as the details of the attack came to light. Photographs showed the shattered bodies of civilians who had died at My Lai, and eyewitnesses described the brutality they had seen. People asked how such an attack on civilians could have happened and who was ultimately responsible. One American soldier, Lt. William L. Calley, Jr., was court-martialed for his actions at My Lai. Warrant Officer Hugh Thompson, who would later testify about what he had seen, tried to rescue some victims. He and his crew chief Glenn Andreotta coaxed 10 frightened villagers out of a bunker and helped them into a helicopter so they could be safely removed from the area. Thompson later said that he and Andreotta then noticed something moving in a ditch: "He waded in among the dead and bloodied people and pulled out a little boy, about the same age as my son, who was 4 at the time. The boy was covered in blood, but he didn't have a scratch on him. We got back in and laid the kid over our laps. As we flew to a nearby orphanage, tears were screaming down our cheeks. I flew back to base and confronted my superiors" (Thompson, 1999).

Children were among the survivors of what became known as the My Lai Massacre. Author Thomas C. Fox later set out to find and interview survivors and get their view of what had happened. A 13-year-old girl named Do Thi Huu gave Fox the following account:

I was there that morning. It was early, about eight o'clock. The Americans had been firing into our village for about an hour. We all hid in our shelters under our huts. We were scared. But we knew only a few people ever died in the past when the bombs dropped on the houses.... But that morning was different. They were shouting for us to come out of our tents.... My father walked out first. As he stepped outside, one American soldier shot him. Shot him at the door. I cried. My mother screamed. . . . I cried. But the soldiers grabbed me and took me. . . . They took me and my mother. (Lifton and Fox, 1972)

Huu and her mother were made to join other villagers in a circle. The soldiers repeatedly took men from the circle and shot each one. Then several soldiers opened fire on the whole group and people fell dead on each other, screaming and crying. Huu survived because she was buried beneath several bodies. She waited until the soldiers were gone, then found that her mother was dead, as were her uncle, aunt, and other relatives and friends. Other children from My Lai lost grandparents, parents, and siblings. Many surviving children were plagued with nightmares afterwards. Tran Huyen told Fox, "I could not understand what had happened. Why American soldiers wanted to kill everyone in the village. All the children. . . . I still cry when I think of that day" (Lifton and Fox, 1972).

This gruesome massacre focused more attention on the question of how soldiers come to commit atrocities during wartime, and it focused attention on similar episodes in Vietnam and other places. In his book *My Lai 4*, author Seymour Hirsch quoted an American soldier as saying, "When they died, they didn't know why they were dying. And the people who were doing the killing, they didn't know why they were killing." *See also* VIETNAM WAR.

Further Reading: Richard A. Falk, Gabriel Kolko, and Robert Jay Lifton, *Crimes of War* (1971); Seymour Hirsch, *My Lai 4* (1970); Betty Jean Lifton and Thomas C. Fox, *Children of Vietnam* (1972); Hugh Thompson, "The Massacre at My Lai," *Newsweek* March 8, 1999, at <http://newsweek.org/nw-srv/printed/us/vn>.

Myanmar. *See* BURMA

N

Nagasaki

Thousands of young Japanese died when the second atomic weapon in history, a plutonium bomb, was dropped on Nagasaki, Japan, on August 9, 1945. Of a population of about 200,000, more than 70,000 people died, and more than one-third of the city was destroyed by the explosion and the resulting fires. After enduring two atomic bombings, Japanese leaders announced an unconditional surrender on August 14.

Kayano Nagai, who was four years old when the bomb fell on Nagasaki, described that day as follows:

> All of a sudden there was a great big flash, like lightning. . . . Then there was a big noise, then a big strong wind came and pushed me. I was scared. I got on the floor and stayed there with my hands over my ears. . . . From the other side of the big green mountain there was a great big red thing like a tree sticking up into the sky. It was a big big tree made out of fire. The top of it kept opening and opening and it looked as if it was alive. It kept swelling and swelling and it went up and up, higher and higher, like smoke from a chimney, right past the sky. . . . oh, so bright! It made my eyes hurt. (Nagai, 1951)

Ten-year-old Satoru Fukabori said, "I heard a plane go ZAA-aaooo, like they always did when they let go their bombs, then there was a flash, a bright-red-and-blue flash! Then there was a noise like WHEE-eesh!" (Nagai, 1951). A hot wind blew Satoru into the house, which caved in. Boards struck him and nails stuck in his skin. By the time his uncle rescued him from the debris, the whole town was on fire. People were moaning and hurrying to the city shelter for help. Satoru's mother and a baby had burned to death and his younger brother and sister died from wounds soon after the bombing. Another brother disappeared and nobody was sure how he died. Afterwards black smoke and greasy drops of black rain fell from the sky. Ten-year-old Makota Nagai lived in a town near Nagasaki. He recalled that the "leaves were torn off all the trees and came racing along. . . . It was getting dark and cold very fast. I thought an airplane must have crashed into the sun" (Nagai, 1951).

Shortly after the bombing, the Japanese military officials in control of the country agreed to surrender to the Allies. Kayano Nagai remembered the day Japan surrendered.

> Then we heard that Japan had lost the war. Daddy and everybody cried out loud just like children when they heard it. Daddy said I didn't have to hide in the air-raid shelter any more when I saw a plane, because the war was over and the planes weren't going to kill us any more. I was glad because I didn't want to die like Ritsuko and get all cold and be wrapped up in a straw mat and be carried to the graveyard. (Nagai, 1951)

In the wake of the bombing, young people were homeless and lacked food, clean drinking water, medical care, and other necessities. Five elementary schools and two junior high schools were among those that were destroyed. Schools had to close until new facilities could be arranged. One student recalled the time when school resumed.

> One day in October an order from the school was posted: "All pupils of Yamazato Grade School will assemble immediately in the school yard!" I went right to school. There were three teachers and about thirty pupils in the yard. Twenty-five teachers and about twelve hundred pupils had died. Another teacher and about three hundred pupils didn't turn up; they were out sick on account of wounds or atomic sickness. (Nagai, 1951)

In the aftermath of the bombing, victims suffered from a variety of health problems and genetic disturbances. Radiation sickness claimed many lives, and other young people were disfigured and maimed by the bombing. Some later died of cancer caused by exposure to radiation, or their children suffered from genetic problems caused by their parents' exposure to radiation. *See also* FOLDED CRANE CLUB; HIROSHIMA; HIROSHIMA MAIDENS; JAPAN (WORLD WAR II); MUSHROOM CLUB; PEACE MONUMENT; RADIATION SICKNESS; THE RIBBON.

Further Reading: Frank W. Chinnook, *Nagasaki* (1969); Takashi Nagai, *We of Nagasaki* (1951); Arata Osada, *Children of the A-Bomb* (1963).

Napalm. *See* PHUC, KIM; VIETNAM WAR

National Interreligious Service Board for Conscientious Objectors (NISBCO)

Founded in 1940, the National Interreligious Service Board for Conscientious Objectors (NISBCO) is a public education and advocacy organization, which, according to its purpose and policy statement, is "an association of religious bodies whose purpose is to defend and extend the rights of conscientious objectors to war and organized violence." Many of NISBCO's educational programs and much of its advocacy work involve teenagers and young people in their early twenties.

The association disseminates educational materials about conscientious objection and about the status and treatment of conscientious objectors in countries around the world. It helps conscientious objectors, most of them young men between 18 and 21, find alternative service in lieu of military service. NISBCO also encourages youth "to address issues of violence and militarism in their own communities." In its newsletter, *The Reporter for Conscience's Sake*, NISBCO features articles that investigate and strongly oppose the use of child soldiers as combatants in different countries. *See also* CONSCIENTIOUS OBJECTORS; CONSCRIPTION; SOLDIERS, CHILD.

Further Reading: "Purpose and Policy Statement" *The NISBCO Network*, 1996; *The Reporter for Conscience' Sake*, Autumn 1996; <http://www.nonviolence.org/nisbco>.

Native Americans. *See* AMERICAN INDIAN WARS; DEERFIELD RAID; LONG WALK; NAVAJO CODE TALKERS; NEZ PERCE WAR; SAND CREEK MASSACRE; SEMINOLE WARS; WOUNDED KNEE MASSACRE

Navajo Code Talkers

During World War II, young Navajos were among the 400 specially trained men known as the Navajo Code Talkers. These men worked with U.S. marine units in the Pacific theater to handle communications between top commanders so that these messages could not be decoded by the Japanese. The military code they used was based on the Navajo language, which was unfamiliar to other people because the Navajo lived in isolated areas and their language is considered difficult to learn.

Marine recruiters began seeking men for the code-talkers program in April 1942. They looked for healthy males between ages 18 and 35 who could speak English and had a solid education. Numerous recruits were in their teens and early twenties. Among the youngest was 15-year-old Dean Wilson, who pretended to be 18 so that he could enlist. Two

Two members of the Navajo Code Talkers in action in the South Pacific during World War II. *Corbis.*

18-year-old cousins—Preston Toledo and Frank Toledo—were also part of the program.

Besides their standard military training, the recruits were assigned the task of developing the code they would use. They studied hundreds of military terms and worked hard to figure out a corresponding Navajo term for each one. The code talkers had to memorize these words, since nothing could be written down and carried with them. Code talkers also learned how to assemble and disassemble radios that they would use in combat zones.

While serving in the South Pacific, the code talkers played key roles in Iwo Jima, Guadalcanal, Okinawa, and other major combat zones. In 1971, they received special citations from President Richard M. Nixon that recognized their courage, resourcefulness, and contributions to winning the war in the Pacific. The U.S. Senate later declared August 14, 1982, National Code Talkers Day. *See also* AMERICAN INDIAN WARS.

Further Reading: Nathan Aaseng, *Navajo Code Talkers* (1992); Alison R. Bernstein, *American Indians and World War II* (1991); Doris Paul, *Navajo Code Talkers* (1973).

Nazi Experiments. *See* EXPERIMENTS, NAZI

Netherlands. *See* HOLLAND (WORLD WAR II)

New Market, Battle of

During the American Civil War, about 280 cadets, aged 15 to 19, fought with the Confederate army in the Battle of New Market. The young men were students at the Virginia Military Institute (VMI). Some of these cadets had already served in the war. Among them was John Cabell Early, who had carried food and supplies to fighting soldiers when he was only 13 years old. In 1861, he was at the First Battle of Manassas, and at age 15, he served as a courier at the Battle of Gettysburg. Cadet John Horsely had enlisted at age 16 and fought at the Battle of Fredericksburg in December 1862.

When the Civil War began, VMI was closed as students went off to fight. But Confederate generals decided that the school should reopen to train officers and teach the students military strategy and tactics. On the morning of May 10, 1864, the cadets were informed that they were to join General John C. Breckenridge's troops in an attempt to halt a large group of Union soldiers who were coming through the Shenandoah Valley. About 27 cadets stayed behind to guard the academy.

After a long march, the cadets reached their destination. Breckenridge's army now included 3,500 infantry and 248 artillery troops. Another 1,500 soldiers were expected to join them. At the successful battle, which took place on May 15, the cadets were praised for their courage and skill. General Breckenridge told them "Young gentleman, I have you to thank for the result of today's operations" (Beller, 1991).

Four of the cadets died in the battle, and another died shortly thereafter. Five cadets also died later as a result of their wounds. Forty-five others had been wounded but survived. One of the young men who died was 18-year-old William Henry Cabell, who had been the best student in his class at VMI and was the cousin of General Breckenridge. His younger brother, Robert, who also fought in the battle, found his dead brother's body on the field. The casualty rate for the group of cadets was the highest of any unit that fought in the battle. One of the cadets, Moses Ezekiel, later became a world famous sculptor. He designed a monument to honor the brave young men who fought together at New Market. *See also* AMERICAN CIVIL WAR.

Further Reading: Susan Provost Beller, *Cadets at War* (1991).

Nez Perce War

The Nez Perce War was a series of battles between U.S. army troops and the Nez Perce Indians, whose ancestral lands lay in present-day Oregon and Idaho. In 1855, U.S. officials promised the Nez Perce that they could retain some of their homeland, including the Wallowa Valley, if they would sign a treaty ceding the rest of their lands to the government. General Isaac Stevens, governor of the Northwest Territory, assured them the government would honor this treaty—"So long as the sun travels across the sky shall this reservation belong to the Indians and no white man shall be allowed on it"(Beal, 1963). Nonetheless, white settlers moved on their land soon after the treaty was signed, and their numbers increased after gold was found on Nez Perce land in 1860. Whites built homes and other buildings and took Indian livestock and horses, but government officials refused to help when the Indians reported these offenses.

In 1863, white officials demanded still more land. Some chiefs of the Upper Nez Perce bands signed away large tracts in exchange for promises of homes, food, and other goods and moved to a reservation in Idaho. Most of the Nez Perce chiefs refused to sign, calling this agreement the "Thief Treaty." Among them was the respected leader of the Wallowa band, Tu-eka-kas. His son Hin-mah-too-yah-lat-kekt (known as Joseph) became chief after his death in 1871.

A new treaty was forced upon the Nez Perce in 1873 but it allowed the Wallowa band to keep most of their land. Under this agreement, white settlers were ordered to leave, but just one year later, the government refused to honor the treaty and let whites move in. White officials ordered the Wallowa Nez Perce to move to the reservation. Chief Joseph reminded them that his people had never agreed to give up these lands and recounted the promises white officials had made. Nonetheless, in May 1877, General Oliver Howard was assigned to take the Nez Perce to the Lapwai reservation. Howard told officials in Washington, D.C., that it was "a great mistake to take from Joseph and his band of Nez Perce Indians that valley," but he was ordered to proceed (Armstrong, 1971).

The Nez Perce were given only 30 days to reach Lapwai Reservation. Young people helped their elders rush to gather some of their thousands of horses and cattle and other belongings. Chief Joseph did not want war because the whites greatly outnumbered his men and had more arms. He tried to calm young warriors who wanted to fight. The band set off, crossing the swollen Snake River and the Salmon River, then made camp at Tolo Lake.

Fighting broke out on June 13, 1877, when young Nez Perce warriors killed some white settlers in revenge after whites killed a Nez Perce and beat one of their friends. Still hoping to avoid war, Chief Joseph had his group displayed a white flag of truce when some U.S. soldiers came into the camp a few days after the killings. The soldiers fired their rifles at the Indians carrying the flag. Indians nearby fired back, killing 12 soldiers. More people died in the shooting that followed.

Joseph decided to lead his band, which included his 12-year-old daughter and five of his other children, into Canada before General Howard's troops could overtake them. They embarked on a rough journey through Idaho, Wyoming, and Montana, through the steep Lolo Trail and across the rough Bitterroot Mountains. About 147 children were part of the group of 500 Nez Perce that undertook this 1,700-mile journey.

The Nez Perce were overtaken only 30 miles from the U.S.-Canadian border, at the Bear Paw Mountains of Montana. To save his people from hunger and freezing cold, Joseph surrendered. He emerged from the camp the morning of October 5 and handed his rifle to General Nelson A. Miles, saying,

> It is cold and we have no blankets. The little children are freezing to death. My people, some of them, have run away to the hills and have no blankets, no food. No one knows where they are—perhaps freezing to death. I want to have time to look for my children and see how many of them I can find. . . . My heart is sick and sad. From where the sun now stands, I will fight no more forever. (Armstrong, 1971)

Although Miles wanted to allow Joseph's band to move to the Lapwai Reservation, they were sent instead to North Dakota, then to Kansas and Oklahoma. These were hot, dry lands, quite different from their homelands. Children died of diseases and from drinking foul water. The dead included five of Chief Joseph's children, all of whom had managed to survive the Nez Perce War. Joseph's 12-year-old daughter was safe in Canada where she was sheltered with other Nez Perce who had reached Sitting Bull's camp. *See also* AMERICAN INDIAN WARS.

Further Reading: Virginia I. Armstrong, *I Have Spoken* (1971); Merrill L. Beal, *I Will Fight No More Forever* (1963); Alvin M. Josephy, Jr. et al., *The Patriot Chiefs* (1967); John D. McDermott, *Forlorn Hope* (1978).

Ninoshima

Called "Boy's Island," Ninoshima was the site of an orphanage that was opened for thousands of children whose parents died on August 6, 1945, after the bombing of Hiroshima, Japan. The United States dropped two atomic bombs on Japan, one on Hiroshima, to force Japan's surrender and end World War II.

In the fall of 1946, a schoolteacher named Yoshimaru Mori organized the institution at Ninoshima after he found 43 male orphans roaming the streets around the Hiroshima railroad station. He then brought in other youths, whom he discovered stealing and taking part in other criminal activities, including prostitution. The orphanage continued to operate into the 1980s, evolving into a home

and educational facility for homeless youths. *See also* HIROSHIMA; JAPAN (WORLD WAR II); NAGASAKI.

Further Reading: Betty Jean Lifton, *A Place Called Hiroshima* (1985); Arata Osada, *Children of the A-Bomb* (1963).

Nobel Peace Prize. *See* ADDAMS, JANE; AMERICAN FRIENDS SERVICE COMMITTEE (AFSC); MOTHER TERESA; UNITED NATIONS CHILDREN'S FUND (UNICEF); WIESEL, ELIE

Noble, Jordan. *See* DRUMMER BOYS

Northern Ireland

Conflicts in Northern Ireland led to years of suffering for both Catholic and Protestant youth and meant that many children grew up in a continual state of fear. The conflicts date back hundreds of years to the reign of Henry II of England. With the help of the only English Catholic pope in history, Pope Adrian IV, and Anglo-Norman troops, Henry gained control of Ireland. Three times, the Irish revolted but failed to regain their independence. After the Protestant Reformation took hold in England during the sixteenth and seventeenth centuries, Ireland remained mostly Catholic. Increasing numbers of English Protestants settled in Ireland and the English government displaced large numbers of Catholic Irish and gave their lands to English and Scottish settlers. They eventually dominated politics and society, making Irish Catholics a minority in parts of Northern Ireland. People were reduced to a state of poverty and experienced cultural and religious oppression. Fighting broke out during these years, and it affected civilians as well as soldiers. For example, in Drogheda in 1649, troops under the English ruler Oliver Cromwell massacred more than 3,000 Irish Catholic men, women, and children.

During the 1800s, nationalistic groups criticized British rule and continued to rebel. Although most of Ireland gained its independence in 1922, Northern Ireland remained part of the United Kingdom. The conflicts that occurred in the years that followed reflected disagreements over land and civil rights as well as religious differences.

Through the years, terrorism killed more civilians than soldiers. For example, in 1921 and 1922, groups of Protestant boys called the Murder Gang attacked Catholics at night in their homes, killing more than 400 people. The Irish Republican Army (IRA), which aimed to drive out the British army and achieve the unification of Ireland, planned and carried out terrorist attacks, both in Ireland and throughout Great Britain. Terrorist targets included movie theaters, stores, restaurants, bars, hotels, clubs, buses, trains, and other public buildings where people of all ages could be found. To fight the IRA, Protestants formed the Ulster Defense Associaton (UDA).

Large sections of Belfast, Londonderry, and Ulster were destroyed between 1960 and 1997. Thousands of people were killed, and tens of thousands were injured. Besides being victims themselves, young people suffered when friends and family members were hurt and killed. They lived amid the ruins caused by the conflicts—broken windows, barbed wire barricades, closed shops, bombed buildings. Children could not attend school or take part in their normal activities when buildings and other facilities were destroyed.

Youth in Northern Ireland grew up in an atmosphere of fear, sparked by random killings and bombings. The country was markedly divided, as young people lived among people of their own faith, attended schools with others of their own religion, and often had no friends or affiliations with members of the other group. Many young people were forbidden to associate with members of the other group or were afraid to walk outside their own Catholic or Protestant neighborhoods. Some youths formed gangs that attacked outsiders. Teenagers also joined their fellow Protestants or Catholics in organized groups run by the Orange Order (for Protestants) and the Knights of Columbus or Order of Hibernians (for Catholics).

Unrest grew during the late 1960s. On August 24, 1968, young people joined 4,000 marchers in Dublin for a planned, peaceful protest against discrimination. Police attacked a group of protesters on October 5, in Londonderry.

In 1969, British troops were stationed in Ulster to deal with mounting violence. Young people continued to become politically involved. A 21-year-old Catholic activist, Bernadette Devlin, won a seat in the British Parliament where she spoke fervently on behalf of the Catholic minority in Northern Ireland. Devlin and some friends had been beaten and jailed by police in 1968 while taking part in a student march from Belfast to Londonderry. She then joined student groups and committees that were dedicated to changing and improving conditions for Catholics in Northern Ireland.

Numerous deaths occurred in the ranks of both the IRA and UDA during the 1970s. A group of the IRA called Provisionals (Provos for short) lost 13 young boys in one year. To increase their ranks, these groups began recruiting teenagers, and they trained these young people and even younger ones to use weapons.

Two major outbreaks of violence occurred in 1972. On Bloody Sunday, Catholics marching in Londonderry were killed by British paratroopers. Car bombings by IRA guerrillas killed 11 people in Belfast. Young people witnessed a great deal of violence, including beatings, bomb blasts, shootings, and terrorist attacks in the streets.

Conor Cruise O'Brien wrote, "Young people in both parts of Ireland have been brought up to think of democracy as part of everyday humdrum existence, but of recourse to violence as something existing on a superior plane, not merely glorious but even sacred." Concerned adults believed that growing up in this tense atmosphere, in which the two sides expressed contempt for each other, would lead children to develop the same prejudices and hatreds.

A cease-fire held from September 1994 to February 1996, but was marred by bombs that killed two people and injured another 100 in London in February. During the ceasefire, mental health professionals working with traumatized young people observed that they suffered from long-term depression and anxiety and other signs of post-traumatic stress, the result of living with ongoing terrorism and unrest.

A 12-year-old girl from Belfast, Bridie Murphy, wrote in her diary in 1994: "I am frightened living on this street across from the Protestants. I am frightened they will come and kill us because this is the eleventh time they have shot people on our street. I don't know why they want to kill us" (Holliday, 1997).

Author Laurel Holliday interviewed people who grew up in Northern Ireland. They said that the emotions they experienced most frequently were fear, anger, and grief. Some people had nightmares about terrorists years after they reached adulthood.

Observers also expressed concern that children were becoming violent at such an early age. One observer said,

> A new generation seems to be entering the arena of intolerance. Children of eight to ten are throwing stones at the security forces and are taking sides. In the schools the teachers try to calm the troubled minds, and churchmen try to unite believers. But the London Sunday papers all expressed their consternation at what looks like a new Children's Crusade. The enthusiasm with which youth set fire to public buses brought a new dimension to the tensions. (Woods, 1997)

In 1998, serious peace negotiations took place with the help of foreign diplomats. On May 23, voters in Northern Ireland and the Irish Republic supported a peace agreement called the Ulster Accord. One Irish woman, interviewed by the press about her "yes" vote said, "It's very important for the grandchildren" (Hoge, 1998).

Yet, only two months later, three young Catholic brothers were killed when a firebomb was thrown into the window of their house early on a Sunday morning. The victims of this terrorism were Richard Quinn, age 11, and his brothers Mark, age 10, and Jason, age 9. The Quinn family lived in a predominantly Protestant building in the town of Ballymoney. This tragedy moved people around the world and emphasized the need for peace in Northern Ireland. A poem written by two teenagers who had known the three dead boys was read at their funeral. One line of the poem read: "Why would someone do this?" *See also* POST-TRAUMATIC STRESS DISORDER (PTSD).

Further Reading: Richard L. Berke, "In the End, Voters Found, a Real Chance at Peace Was Irresistible," *The New York Times* May 24, 1998, p. A6; Louis M. Cullen, *Life in Ireland* (1969); Warren Hoge, "Irish Voters, North and South, Give Resounding 'Yes' to Peace," *The New York Times* May 24, 1998, p. A1; Laurel Holliday, *Children of "The Troubles"* (1997); Dorothea Woods, *Children Bearing Military Arms* (1997).

Norway (World War II)

Invaded in May 1940, Norway was occupied by Nazi Germany until 1945. During those years, young Norwegians were subjected to curfews and suffered from numerous deprivations. Schoolteachers were ordered to tell students that the Germans were "friends" and that their takeover of Norway was an effort to "protect" Norwegian citizens from the British, not an invasion. The Germans seized raw materials, manufactured goods, and foodstuffs, and took charge of farms and the dairy industry. Norwegian cattle were removed to Germany, leaving children without milk, cheese, and other dairy items. Eggs were scarce and families were seldom able to obtain enough meat for more than one meal a month. Movies, radio, newspapers, and books were censored. Jews in Norway, who numbered 1,700, were persecuted and hunted down.

Young Norwegians also took an active part in the anti-Nazi resistance, which was organized at the start of the occupation. Underground newspapers flourished, and Norwegian students helped to publish and distribute them. Younger children also helped pass resistance papers from place to place.

When the Nazis set out to deport Jews in Norway, rescue groups worked to save them. About 800 were able to reach neutral Sweden, Norway's neighbor. One daring rescue occurred in Oslo, the capital, in November

1942. At a children's home where 22 Jewish refugee children from Austria and Czechoslovakia were living, a female doctor who worked at the home drove her car back and forth, picking up groups of children, then taking them to homes where people had agreed to hide them. Other children were

MED WAFFEN-SS OG DEN NORSKE LEGION MOT DEN FELLES FIENDE....

MOT BOLSJEVISMEN

This poster promotes the Waffen-SS units of the German Nordic Legion, a Nazi effort to encourage solidarity between the German and Norwegian peoples. *Hoover Institution Archives, GE 1986, Stanford University.*

transported on skis, along with family groups, across the border to neutral Sweden. Young skiers assisted in these rescues by leading people over the mountains and across the border.

Another child who escaped safely was Sara Hirschfeldt, who hid inside a coffin with her mother. A courageous neighbor, Helen Astrup, collected the coffin from a hospital and accompanied it by car to Oslo, supposedly for a funeral. German officials stopped the car and ordered everyone out so they could borrow the vehicle. The coffin with Sara and her mother inside was placed on the snowy ground, amidst Nazi guards. Astrup

told the Germans she felt ill and weak and sat on the coffin and began chatting with them as if nothing was wrong. Sara and her mother spent a long, terrifying hour before the car was returned, and the Germans allowed Astrup and the driver to put the coffin back inside and continue their journey to Oslo. From there, the Hirschfeldts were taken to Sweden.

Three children and their mother, Henriette Samuel, also fled with the help of Norwegian rescuers. Samuel received a telephone call one evening in November 1942 from Inge Sletten Fostyedt, a member of the resistance, who warned Samuel to wrap her children up well to protect them from the cold. Samuel quickly awakened the children and dressed them before Fostyedt arrived to escort them to homes where they stayed hidden for a month until they could board a boat for Sweden. The Samuels joined other children and their parents who rode to the boats on trucks that were supposedly carrying potatos. Inge Fostyedt later rescued others, including 14 Jewish Viennese refugees who were living at the children's home in Oslo. *See also* FINLAND (WORLD WAR II).

Further Reading: Helen Astrup and B.L. Jacot, *Oslo Intrigue* (1954); Dorothy Baden-Powell, *Operation Jupiter* (1982); Halvdan Koht, *Norway* (1941); Karen Larsen, *A History of Norway* (1948); Olav Riste and Berit Nokleby, *Norway 1940-45* (1970); Margaret Rossiter, *Women in the Resistance* (1986).

Nuclear Testing

Since the beginning of the nuclear age at the end of World War II, controversy has surrounded the potential hazards of nuclear weapons testing, especially as to how such testing might affect children. Atomic weapons were developed during World War II in the United States, and two atomic bombs were used against Japan in 1945. By 1949, the Soviet Union had also built nuclear weapons. An arms race ensued during the 1950s and persisted for decades. Nuclear testing was conducted by the United States, the Soviet Union, and several other countries as they developed and experimented with new weapons.

Almost from the beginning, scientists and concerned citizens discussed the health risks of radioactive fallout from the weapons tests. Opponents of nuclear testing described how fallout harms the atmosphere, soil, and water, as well as living creatures. Scientists have estimated that nuclear radiation affects a child's body 10 to 100 times more strongly than it does the body of an adult.

Between 1951 and 1958, the U.S. government conducted 119 tests of atomic bombs above ground in Nevada. After one test in Nevada in 1955, scientists at Los Alamos National Laboratory received reports that blue-colored snow fell for two days and children in New Mexico and Nevada suffered from reddened faces and swollen tongues. Cattle had inflamed udders and became sick; some died.

As a result of these and other tests conducted in the early 1960s, millions of Americans, especially children, were exposed to large amounts of radioactive iodine-131 in foods, such as milk, eggs, and leafy vegetables, and from breathing contaminated air. Scientists have linked exposure to this isotope to an increased risk for cancer of the thyroid gland. Children were at higher risk than adults because they have smaller thyroid glands and they drink more milk. The radioactive isotope accumulated in cow's milk after winds and rain scattered the fallout contaminating grasslands where cows grazed. Rain and hail carried the fallout to states as far away as North Dakota. Farm children and others who drank milk from backyard cows were exposed to more radiation than those who drank commercially processed milk because radioactivity decreased as the milk aged.

Scientists at the National Cancer Institute (NCI) later estimated that children between ages 3 months and 5 years were exposed to doses of Iodine-131 about 10 times greater than adults. NCI reports released in 1997 indicated that this exposure might eventually account for up to 25-50,000 cases of thyroid cancer in the United States among adults who were exposed as children.

Nuclear testing affected people around the world, including aboriginal people in Australia, Western Shoshone in Nevada, Yakima and other Native American groups in the Pacific Northwest, residents of northeastern Kazakstan, and Marshallese and Polynesian people in the South Pacific.

In March 1954, people in the Marshall Islands in the Pacific were exposed to radiation from the testing of thermonuclear weapons. The United States had tested nuclear weapons at a coral reef in Bikini Atoll, and contamination spread over an area covering some 20,000 square kilometers. Residents were evacuated two days after the test. Most of the people of Rongelap Atoll suffered from burns, nausea, and vomiting. Nearly all the children developed thyroid gland disorders and required surgery to have nodules removed from their thyroids. Although residents were allowed to return in 1957, radiation levels in the soil remained high and food had to be imported. Residents were evacuated again in 1978 because radioactive isotopes were entering the food chain. Opponents of nuclear testing cite the problems that these people experienced to show the potential hazards. *See also* COLD WAR; HIROSHIMA; NAGASAKI; RADIATION SICKNESS.

Further Reading: Glen Cheney, *They Never Knew: The Victims of Nuclear Testing* (1996); Sid Perkins, "Full Report of Nuclear Test Fallout Released," *Science News,* October 11, 1997, p 231; Keith Rogers, "Research Organization Seeks Radioactive Fallout Data," *Las Vegas Review-Journal,* September 20, 1997.

O

Occupation. *See* BELGIUM (WORLD WAR II); DENMARK (WORLD WAR II); FRANCE (WORLD WAR II); HOLLAND (WORLD WAR II); NORWAY (WORLD WAR II); PACIFIC (WORLD WAR II); POLAND (WORLD WAR II); WORLD WAR II

Oeuvre de Secours aux Enfants (OSE)

The *Oeuvre de Secours aux Enfants* (OSE) was a Jewish child-care and medical care agency in France that worked to help Jewish children get out of internment camps run by the Nazis in Vichy, France, during World War II. The group received help from other social welfare organizations in France, as well as from such American groups as the Quakers, the Unitarians, and the Young Women's Christian Association (YWCA). Some OSE workers were themselves young adults.

The OSE sought permission to remove children from the camps and take them to group homes where they were safer. In some cases, parents also sent their children to these homes because they believed this would keep them from being deported to Poland. Young people were often reluctant to leave their families behind in the camps, but parents persuaded them to go.

By 1943, when the Nazis began massive efforts to find and deport all Jews, the OSE and other groups began closing their group homes and hiding children in more obscure locations. The OSE went underground and relied more on resistance groups and *Le Comite de Nimes,* an ecumenical rescue group organized by Pastor Marc Boegner, head of the Protestant Church in France.

OSE workers who were Jewish used false identity papers as they carried out their tasks, including accompanying groups of children to their new hiding places. Members of the OSE also visited the children once they had been placed in homes to make sure that they had what they needed and to deliver food, ration coupons, and other needed supplies. *See also* FRANCE (WORLD WAR II); IDENTITY PAPERS; QUAKERS (SOCIETY OF FRIENDS); RESISTANCE MOVEMENTS (WORLD WAR II).

Further Reading: Leni Yahil, *The Holocaust* (1990).

Olympic Games. *See* SPORTS

Operation Babylift

In 1974, at the end of the Vietnam War, as tens of thousands of refugees fled Indochina, a group of agencies arranged to fly about 2,000 infants and toddlers to the United States. What became known as Operation Babylift had been organized after U.S. President Gerald Ford ordered an airlift of orphans, many of whom were fathered by Americans and who were being cared for in an American-run hospital in Saigon. In April

1975, orphanage workers and thousands of paid and unpaid volunteers, including Red Cross workers, prepared the children and cared for them during the airlift. The children were taken by vans and buses to the airport where they boarded C-5A cargo jets for the trip to the United States.

One plane carrying 250 orphans was forced to make a crash landing onto a field just outside Saigon shortly after it took off. A flight nurse on board the plane, Lt. Regina Aune, managed to open the emergency exit and walked back and forth through the waist-deep mud of the rice paddy where the plane lay to rescue children from the shattered plane. Aune, who had broken her leg and foot and a bone in her back in the crash, was later cited for heroism, as were the other 18 surviving crew members. *See also* VIETNAM WAR.

Further Reading: John L. Frisbee, "The Lady Was a Tiger," *Air Force Magazine,* June 1996; LeAnn Thieman, "Operation Babylift," *Newsweek,* March 8, 1999 at <http://newsweek.org/nw-srv/printed/us/vn/vn>; "Operation Babylift Helps Orphans Fleeing Southeast Asia" (1975) at <http://www.redcross.org>.

Operation Blessing International (OBI)

Operation Blessing International Relief and Development Corporation (OBI) helps youth in war-torn regions through its medical and hunger relief and development assistance programs. The goal of this non-profit humanitarian organization is to "relieve human suffering, to provide the basic necessities of life, to educate, and to develop healthy, self-sustaining communities, families and individuals."

Based in Virginia Beach, Virginia, OBI was founded in 1978 by religious broadcaster Pat Robertson and is registered with the Association of Evangelical Relief and Development Organizations (AERDO) and the United States Agency for International Development. OBI has worked in the United States and more than 70 other countries in times of disaster as well as time of war.

The international medical division of OBI operates the Flying Hospital with a staff of volunteers. Doctors and other personnel give

needed health care services and run training and education programs for health care workers and people in the community. OBI has distributed millions of pounds of food and other supplies through its Hunger Strike Force. Children in Rwanda were among those who benefited from OBI programs, delivered during the Rwandan Refugee Crisis of 1994. OBI was one of the first relief groups to arrive in Rwanda. Its Back-to-School and Bless-A-Child programs aided more than 7 million children between 1984 and 1998, by providing funds for orphanages, schools, and basic needs. *See also* RELIEF ORGANIZATIONS; RWANDA.

Further Reading: Operation Blessing International, Fact Sheet, 1998 (Contact OBI, 977 Centerville Turnpike, Virginia Beach, VA 23463).

Operation T-4

On September 1, 1939, as his troops were invading Poland, Nazi leader Adolf Hitler authorized Operation T-4, a program of euthanasia ("mercy killing"). Under Operation T-4, doctors were expected to kill people who were incurably sick (whom Hitler called "useless eaters") and other people the Nazis labelled "unworthy of life." Among the people the Nazis targeted for death were the senile; mentally retarded people of all ages; Jews in mental hospitals; people who had been treated in any hospital, asylum, or nursing home for at least five years; deformed newborns; people with epilepsy; invalids who could not work; and victims of any incurable disease that left them unable to work. Children were included in several of these categories and were put to death under the program.

As they implemented T-4, the Nazis used gas chambers for the first time as a method of killing. Gas was piped into sealed rooms using exhaust fumes from truck engines or tanks filled with carbon monoxide. Small groups of people were gassed in centers set up expressly for this purpose. Beginning in 1942, these methods were used on a massive scale to murder millions of Jews in gas chambers at the death camps.

The German public and German religious leaders gradually learned the truth about

Operation T-4 and pressured the government to end it in August 1941. By that time, more than 90,000 people had been killed, of whom more than 3,000 were children. *See also* DEATH CAMPS (WORLD WAR II); EUTHANASIA; "MASTER RACE."

Further Reading: Michael Kater, *Doctors Under Hitler* (1989); Leni Yahil, *The Holocaust* (1990).

Oradour-sur-Glane

On June 10, 1944, just days after the Allied landings in Normandy, Nazi troops in France launched several attacks on civilians. At Oradour-sur-Glane, a village in southern France, the Nazis decided to punish people for protecting Jewish refugees. The Nazis shot all the men in the village, then locked up about 500 women and children, along with the local Catholic priest, in the church. They burned these people alive and then burned the village to the ground.

After the massacre, workers searching for the charred bodies of the victims found the remains of two small boys lying hand in hand. A 46-year-old woman, Marguerite Roufflance, had survived by leaping from a church window to the ground. Her husband, brother, two sons, and a grandson were all killed in the massacre. She later gave an eye-witness account of the event. The French government decided to leave Oradour-sur-Glane the way it looked on the day of the massacre as a chilling reminder of the cruelty and barbarism of war. *See also* FRANCE (WORLD WAR II); MASSACRES.

Further Reading: Vera Laska, ed., *Women of the Resistance and in the Holocaust* (1984).

Orphans

Children are orphaned during wars as a result of bombings, the loss of parents in battle, or when parents are killed in concentration camps, forced labor camps, or political executions. Parents may also die from disease, malnutrition, or other conditions caused by wartime deprivations. Deliberate mass murders have also left children orphans. During World War II, for example, millions of Jewish men and women and hundreds of thou-

sands of Romani (Gypsies) were targeted for death by the Nazis. Thousands of children who managed to survive the Holocaust found themselves orphans when the war ended. Jewish orphans were housed in relocation centers, orphanages, and convents and monasteries throughout Europe. Some were adopted by families who hid them during the war. Others were taken to cities or countries where they had relatives, including Palestine (later Israel). The Israeli government also welcomed Jewish orphans into group-centered communities.

After the atomic bombings of Hiroshima and Nagasaki in Japan in 1945, many children found themselves orphaned. Some of them had been sent to stay with friends or relatives in parts of Japan that were not being bombed. In Koba, near Nagasaki, Makoto and Kayano Nagai lost their mother. Sadako and Sayoko Moriyama lost both parents and their brother and a sister. The woman who had to tell them this news was distraught. She said, "Telling her was like trying to spit out chestnut burrs. Sadako and Sayoko fell into each other's arms, weeping. All of a sudden, they found themselves orphans" (Nagai, 1951).

Children orphaned by war face many problems, especially when they have no relatives or friends to take them in. They may be placed in institutions or be forced to live on their own, roaming homeless in the streets. The International Committee of the Red Cross (IRC) and other relief organizations take an active role in helping to locate missing relatives or in placing homeless children with new families or in institutions.

Untold numbers of children around the world were orphaned during the last half of the twentieth century. According to some experts, by 1999, every 30 seconds, a child was made an orphan of war or disaster. In Afghanistan, thousands of children became orphans as a result of the civil wars that began there in 1979. The Tahia Maskan orphanage in the poor district of Kabal sheltered 500 children whose parents had died. In 1996, the orphanage ran out of funds and was not receiving support from the government.

There was no food, heating, or clothing available for the residents until the International Red Cross joined with the French-based organization *Médecins sans Frontierès* (Doctors without Borders), the World Food Programme, and Solidarités to provide food, firewood, shoes, and clothing. A French television reporter donated a cash prize to the orphanage that she had won for her coverage of the Afghan war.

In Liberia, thousands of children were born from unions of Liberian women and the United Nations and West African peacekeepers who were stationed in Liberia after the civil war ended. By March 1999, social workers had identified more than 5,000 children left behind by peacekeepers who had been pulled out of Liberia or who had died during the war. They believed that there were at least 15,000 multinational orphans in Liberia.

Humanitarian organizations developed programs to care for orphaned children in various countries. One of these organizations, Hope & Homes for Children, is part of Rotary International. It was founded by a British couple, Mark and Caroline Cook, and began its work in 1992 in the Balkans where Hope & Homes organized the rebuilding of orphanages in Lipik, Croatia, and Sarajevo, Bosnia. The organization went on to complete a home for 40 children in Sierra Leone and, in 1999, it planned to build orphanages in Albania, Mozambique, and Eritrea. Future orphanage sites included Rwanda, Somalia, Angola, Chechnya, and Sudan.

The civil war in Rwanda had left about 400,000 orphans. These youth often lacked the most basic necessities as well as a chance to gain an education. With aid from the International Red Cross, the Association for the Support of Survivors of the Genocide operated special educational programs for children who had lost both parents to genocide. One such school, for children 12 to 18, was located in Kanzenze in central Rwanda. The Red Cross was also paying for tuition and school kits for more than 1,400 orphans throughout Rwanda. *See also* ADOPTION; ARMENIAN-TURKISH CONFLICT; BOSNIA; DISPLACED PERSONS (DPs) (WORLD WAR II); FINLAND (WORLD WAR II); GERMANY, (WORLD WAR II); GHETTOS (WORLD WAR II); GREECE (WORLD WAR II); HIROSHIMA; KORCZAK, JANUSZ; LEBENSBORN; MASSACRES; MONTAGNARDS; MOZAMBIQUE; MULTIRACIAL CHILDREN; MY LAI MASSACRE; NAGASAKI; NINOSHIMA; POLAND (WORLD WAR II); ROMANI (GYPSIES); SEPARATIONS, FAMILY; UNACCOMPANIED CHILDREN; VIETNAM WAR.

Further Reading: Susan Johnson Hadler, et al., eds., *Lost in the Victory* (1998); Takashi Nagai, *We of Nagasaki* (1951); "Rwanda: Secondary School Education for Orphans," *ICRC News,* Dcember 11, 1997.

P

Pacific (World War II)

Japanese expansion in Asia and the Pacific merged into the war in Europe in 1941 when the Japanese attack on Pearl Harbor in Hawaii brought the United States into World War II against Japan and Germany. To gain support from their people, Japanese leaders propagated racist ideas and told them that Japanese were superior to other Asians, such as Chinese and Indians, and that white people would also eventually become slaves of the Japanese. These ideas were built into the school curriculum in Japan so that young people would develop such attitudes during their formative years.

As Japanese troops invaded other countries, massacres of civilians were perpetrated in the Pacific. During the 1930s, Japanese troops massacred civilians, including children and young adults, in China. Japanese soldiers had been told to kill the Chinese, whom their government labeled as "bandits" for opposing them. Sporadic killings took place in Chinese villages during the early 1930s. The Chinese city of Nanking fell on December 12, 1937. The mass executions, rapes, and random murders that were perpetrated here during the next six weeks by Japanese troops became known as the Rape of Nanking. Tens of thousands of children became homeless as homes and other buildings were destroyed by bombings. Historians estimate that at least 20,000 women were raped and 200,000 people were killed, including thousands of children.

On the same day that American military personnel and civilians were killed at Pearl Harbor, December 7, 1941, the Japanese attacked Guam and Hong Kong. On December 8, Wake Island fell. The Japanese military killed thousands of civilians in Singapore, Hong Kong, Borneo, Burma, Indonesia, the Philippines, and other places in Asia and the Pacific. In Hong Kong and Singapore, for example, eyewitnesses reported that Japanese soldiers murdered doctors, nurses, and hospital patients. Civilians, including infants and children, were bayoneted to death when Japanese troops attacked various cities and villages. Other methods of killing included machine guns, decapitation, drowning, and burning.

During the Japanese campaign to seize oil-rich Burma early in 1942, hundreds of thousands of people became refugees. With their families, young people from India, who had been living in Burma, fled the country. These people were also robbed, beaten, and raped by Burmese villagers who sided with the Japanese and who attacked Indian refugees as they moved across southern Burma. Most of the refugees had to walk and some tried to pull ox-carts bearing their household possessions along with children who were too small to walk. Nearly 90 percent of these refugees died of hunger, disease, exhaustion, or enemy attacks. Some 100,000 refugees reached safety, often by joining British troops who were leaving Burma. In May, some refugees who had attached themselves to troops under General Joseph Stilwell realized they would have to walk all the way to India. They were almost out of food and medicine and the monsoon was due to begin, which would cause the rivers to swell. As they moved toward India or China, refugees found that wells had been poisoned and Japanese supporters had burned ferry boats. A number of children died with their families while wandering in the mountains near Tibet. Others perished from smallpox, malaria, and cholera when these diseases spread among the groups of hungry, tired people.

During the Japanese conquest of the Philippines in 1941-1942, young people suffered terribly. Hunger and malnutrition were widespread and the occupying forces installed a strict new government. Youths were among the thousands of guerillas and millions of civilians who resisted the Japanese until the war ended. They carried messages, aided sabotage efforts, and raided Japanese camps and storage facilities. Some young spies disguised themselves as peddlers or beggars. Young people who were familiar with the Philippine coastline helped move food and equipment for the guerilla forces, which included young men and women. Young women also served as nurses for resisters and collected food and clothing for guerilla bands. Some served actively as spies, saboteurs, and fighters. They helped to make weapons, such as bows and arrows, because guns were scarce. Youthful Filipinos used their jobs in factories or offices to help the resistance.

The Japanese military forced thousands of young women from China, Korea, and other occupied countries into prostitution. They were imprisoned in brothels, where they were abused during the war. The military referred to these victims, who also included poor Japanese women, as "comfort girls." The women bore physical and emotional scars from their experiences long after the war ended in 1945.

As they took control of various countries, the Japanese announced that they had formed the Greater East Asia Co-Prosperity Sphere. However, they harshly dominated politics, industry, and laborers, which meant that people in the occupied countries experienced hardships and oppression, not economic benefits. According to John W. Dower (1986), "Untold millions of civilians died [between 1942 and 1945]—from fighting, atrocities, disastrous labor and economic policies, and the starvation and disease that followed the war destruction." The secret police, called the *Kempeitai,* enforced Japanese policies and terrorized local civilians.

People in occupied lands, including Indonesia, China, Korea, Java, Burma, and Southeast Asia, were ordered to labor for the Japanese in mines and heavy industry. These slave laborers built bridges, roads, and other structures. As able-bodied men were removed from their communities, children and young adults suffered from a lack of support that caused many deprivations. They were forced to take on difficult new roles to survive.

Hundreds of thousands of the forced laborers, many of them young people, died as a result of overwork, starvation, or abuse by their captors. Some also died on the boats that were taking them to work locations. Young men were among the 300,000 forced laborers taken to build the Burma-Siam railroad during 1942 and 1943. About 60,000 workers died in the jungle from malaria and other diseases or from abuse.

People in the Philippines endured a horrifying wave of violence near the end of World War II. Japanese aircraft bombed Manila, although it had been declared an open city. Later, when the war was nearly over, Japanese troops massacred about 100,000 people in the Philippines. Soldiers bayoneted children and shot people of all ages. They set fire to homes and shot people who were trying to flee. Rapes and looting were massive. Filipino hostages who were imprisoned in Christian churches in the old part of Manila, the capital, were tortured and killed. Thousands of children were among the wounded brought to the hospital.

A prominent Filipino journalist, Carlos Romulo, described the condition of his homeland when he returned with the Allied troops in 1945. The city of Manila was "black and gutted and reeking" with numerous corpses whose hands had been tied behind their backs before they were stabbed with bayonets. Romulo wrote, "I saw the bodies of priests, women, children, and babies that had been bayoneted for sport, survivors told us, by a soldiery gone mad with blood lust in defeat"(Carey, 1988).

On February 5, 1945, the people of Manila realized that they had been freed. Children joined men and women in the streets to celebrate. In the city of Santo Tomas, the people cheered and sang as the American flag was hung from the balcony of the university. Red Cross workers arrived, bringing former prisoners letters from their families and friends. The U.S. army delivered healthful food, including meat, milk, and other items the children had not had for several years. However, tens of thousands of people had become refugees—they were homeless, hungry, poor, and sick.

The Japanese military ordered Japanese civilians living in such Pacific battle zones as Guadalcanal and Okinawa to kill themselves before Allied troops arrived. Suicide was considered more honorable than surrender. Allied soldiers found the dead bodies of thousands of civilians in these island outposts, killed either by their own hand or by soldiers of their own military. About 95,000 civilians were dead when the Battle of Okinawa ended, through enemy fire, suicide, or at the hands of loved ones or the Japanese military. Japanese artists Iri and Maruki Toshi later painted a large mural that portrayed this tragic event.

After the war ended, war crimes trials were held in Tokyo, Japan. Eleven nations accused 28 Japanese military leaders of crimes against international law. *See also* ESPIONAGE; JAPAN-CHINA WAR; JAPAN (WORLD WAR II); PRISONERS; SEXUAL ABUSE.

Further Reading: Noel Barber, *Sinister Twilight* (1968); John Carey, *Eyewitness to History* (1988); John Costello, *The Pacific War, 1941–45* (1981); John W. Dower, *War without Mercy* (1986); James Fahey, *Pacific War Diary 1942–1945* (1963); Alfred W. McCoy, ed., *Southeast Asia Under Japanese Rule* (1980); Richard H. Minear, *Victors' Justice: The Tokyo

War Crimes Trial* (1971); Emily Van Sickle, *The Iron Gates of Santo Tomas* (1992).

Palestinians. *See* ARAB-ISRAELI-WARS; INTIFADA

Papanek, Ernst. *See* RESCUERS

Partisans. *See* BIELSKI BROTHERS; RESISTANCE MOVEMENTS (WORLD WAR II); WARSAW GHETTO

Peace Camps

Various organizations that promote world peace operate peace camps for youth to help them learn about the impact of war and how to find nonviolent solutions to problems. Some peace camps bring together young people from opposing sides of conflicts in their region. For example, camps have brought together youth from Catholic and Protestant families in Northern Ireland and from Israeli and Palestinian families. The Women's International League for Peace and Freedom (WILPF) has run many peace camps in different places. One program, "Little Friends for Peace," was developed in 1981 by Mary Joan and Larry Park, a teacher and family counselor team and the parents of six children. The Parks cover these kinds of topics: What is peace? Who are peacemakers? What can I do at home and in my neighborhood to promote peace? Children sing songs and hear from visitors who demonstrate peacemaking skills through puppet shows and other presentations. At the 1998 camp, held in Washington, D.C., participants heard letters from children in war-torn Bosnia and listened to survivors of the 1945 atomic bombing of Hiroshima.

The WILPF has worked with various religious groups, including the Society of Friends (Quakers), to fund and operate peace camps. In 1994, the WILPF and the Society of Friends started an annual children's peace camp in Norristown, Pennsylvania. At the 1998 camp, children ages 6 to 11 came from diverse backgrounds to study the following themes: peace with self, peace with others, peace in the community, peace in the environment, and peace in the global community. *See also* QUAKERS (SOCIETY OF FRIENDS); WOMEN'S INTERNATIONAL LEAGUE FOR PEACE AND FREEDOM (WILPF).

Further Reading: WILPF, "Peace Camping at the Congress," and "Norristown-area WILPF's Peace Camp," *Peace and Freedom*, Fall 1998.

Peace Monument

The Peace Monument was erected in Hiroshima, Japan, in 1958 in memory of Sadako Sasaki, a 12-year-old girl who died in 1955 as a result of radiation sickness caused by the atom bomb dropped on Hiroshima on August 6, 1945. The monument stands as a symbol of all the Japanese children who died as a result of the two atomic bombs the United States dropped on Japan to force an end to World War II in the Pacific.

Young people in Hiroshima promoted the idea of the memorial to commemorate the suffering Hiroshima's children experienced because of the bombings. They wrote to children all over Japan asking them to donate whatever money they could spare to this cause. The children also collected 7 million yen (about $20,000) to build the monument and found a prominent sculptor, Kazuo Kikuchi, to design it. The memorial, which was unveiled on Children's Day (May 5) 1958, features an oval granite pedestal—a symbol of Mt. Horai—upon which stands a young girl holding a golden folded crane. Below her on a mountain, a young girl and boy reach out toward the sky. The inscription on the base reads: "This is our cry, this is our prayer. Peace in the world." People from all over Japan have made 1,000 origami folded paper cranes that are hung within the pedestal. The monument is a significant part of the Peace Park in Hiroshima, site of an annual Peace Day ceremony. *See also* FOLDED CRANE CLUB; HIROSHIMA; NAGASAKI; RADIATION SICKNESS; SASAKI, SADAKO.

Further Reading: Penney Kome and Patrick Crean, eds., *Peace: A Dream Unfolding* (1986); Betty Jean Lifton, *A Place Called Hiroshima* (1985); Hitoshi Takayama, ed., *Hiroshima in Memoriam and Today* (1973).

Peace Park. *See* PEACE MONUMENT

Pearl Harbor

On December 7, 1941, the Japanese bombed the U.S. naval base at Pearl Harbor, Hawaii. The bombing affected the lives of young soldiers who were serving in the military at the base. Other young people who worked at the base or lived nearby were hurt or killed. In both the United States and Japan, children heard about the attack and wondered what would happen next. President Franklin Roosevelt asked Congress to declare war on Japan and its allies, including Nazi Germany, and the United States entered World War II. As a 6-year-old living in Pearl City, Dorinda Makanaonalani Nicholson saw the attack first-hand.

> Suddenly we heard the sound of low flying planes, then . . . .Almost immediately, loud explosions, followed by more planes passing directly over our house. . . [in the front yard]. We shielded our eyes from the early morning sun and looked up into the orange-red emblem of the Rising Sun. The planes were so low, just barely above the roof tops, that we could see the pilots' faces. (Nicholson, 1998)

Dorinda's father told her, her mother and her brother to get in the car so they could leave the harbor. Military vehicles were rushing people to their posts, and the roads were blocked. When they reached the road, Dorinda saw the devastated, burning ships in the harbor. She recalled, "The initial shock of that awful scene was soon replaced with waves of anxiety and panic sweeping over us" (Nicholson, 1998).

The family took refuge in a sugar cane field where they found several of their neighbors. Dorinda worried that her dog, which was back home, was frightened and had no one to feed her. After several hours, military police took all the families to a recreation hall at a nearby sugar mill, where they slept on the floor and worried that a Japanese invasion was imminent. They returned home five days later.

Sixteen-year-old John Garcia was employed by the Pearl Harbor Navy Yard as a pipe fitter's apprentice at that time. His grandmother awoke him that morning at about 8:00 a.m. and told him about the bombing. Garcia and other people who worked at Pearl Harbor were asked to report for work at once. When he arrived, ships were in flames. Garcia and the other employees spent much of the day diving into the water of the harbor retrieving bodies, some alive and some dead. In the weeks after the bombing, he and his coworkers repaired ships that could be salvaged. Garcia also suffered a personal tragedy that December day. His girlfriend of three years died after her house was hit during the bombing.

Sixteen-year-old Mary Ann Ramsey, the daughter of an American naval officer, lived near Pearl Harbor at the time of the Japanese air attack. She tried to help that day by sitting with dying men, holding and comforting each one in turn, and covering them with blankets. In the wake of the bombing, the wives and children of military personnel who lived in Pearl Harbor were evacuated to the mainland United States. During their trips to California, they rode on ships that were often crowded and whose crews were on the lookout for enemy fire.

Dot Chastney was in the fifth grade in New Jersey when she heard that Pearl Harbor had been bombed. She recalled that she asked her parents where Pearl Harbor was and they told her it was in Hawaii. Like most other Americans, her family listened to the radio that entire day. At school the next day, students also listened to the radio as President Roosevelt addressed the nation and announced that he had asked Congress to declare war. Chastney later told author Penny Colman that she kept wondering, "How are things going to change?" (Colman, 1995).

Dorinda Nicholson and her friends did not return to school after the attack until February 1942. Their school was used as a military hospital. Families prepared for possible future attacks by saving drinking water and food. People lined up at grocery stores to buy food and other supplies in case no ships could come to Pearl Harbor from the mainland.

Children walked down to the harbor to examine the sunken ships and to collect bullet casings. Although many children were sent to the mainland to live with relatives, Dorinda's family remained together in Hawaii throughout the war. The government decreed that everyone in Hawaii over age 6 had to be fingerprinted and carry an I.D. card at all times (to identify them in case of death). Bomb shelters and trenches were built, particularly near schools, and children took part in air-raid drills. Gas masks were also issued, and people were supposed to carry them at all times. Dorinda's 2-year-old brother had a mask that was almost as long as he was, and infants wore masks with bunny ears for decoration and a see-through window.

For Japanese-American children, the bombing ushered in a time of fear, uncertainty, and hardships. The FBI began investigating people of Japanese descent and arrested and questioned some of them about their activities. Curfews were imposed and people of Japanese descent had to stay at home between the hours of 7 p.m. and 7 a.m. They needed special permission to travel more than 25 miles from their homes. On February 19, 1942, President Franklin Roosevelt signed Executive Order 9066, which allowed the U.S. government to move people of Japanese ancestry from their homes on the West Coast to other places based on "military necessity." As a result, thousands of children were forced to move with their parents to internment camps. *See also* JAPAN (WORLD WAR II); INTERNMENT CAMPS, U.S.; UNITED STATES (WORLD WAR II).

Further Reading: Thomas B. Allen, "Pearl Harbor: A Return to the Day of Infamy," *National Geographic*, December 1991, pp. 62-63; Penny Colman, *Rosie the Riveter* (1995); Reader's Digest, *America in the '40s* (1998); Dorinda M. Nicholson, *Pearl Harbor Child* (1998); John Tateishi, *And Justice for All* (1984).

Persian Gulf War (1991)

Young soldiers fought on both sides of the Persian Gulf War, known in the United States as "Operation Desert Storm," which took place in January and February 1991. The United States, Great Britain, France, and Israel, along with other nations, fought as allies under the United Nations to drive Iraqi invaders from the small, oil-rich nation of Kuwait.

In August 1990, Iraqi leader Saddam Hussein speaks on television with a boy, one of the Western hostages taken by Hussein to forestall retaliation for Iraq's recent invasion of Kuwait. *AP/Wide World Photos.*

Iraq invaded neighboring Kuwait in July 1990 after years of border disputes and disagreements over oil production and other matters. Kuwaiti citizens claimed that Iraqi troops took valuables from the capital and attacked citizens. Iraqi President Saddam Hussein declared Kuwait a province of Iraq. Many young Kuwaitis and their families fled across the desert in cars, by camel, or on foot. The Iraqis permitted Egyptian citizens to leave Iraq peacefully during the war. Thousands of Egyptian men, women, and children arrived in refugee camps that were quickly set up in neighboring Jordan.

More than 100,000 people from Bangladesh were working in Iraq and Kuwait when the war began. These people were all discharged, and had to live in tents set up in refugee camps near the Iraqi-Turkey border. Children whose parents had been sent away from their jobs waited with other refugees in these desert camps until they could be resettled. The economic problems resulting from this war affected tens of thousands of these young people.

Some foreigners who lived in Iraq—from Ireland, Great Britain, France, Japan, Italy, and the United States—were taken hostage. Saddam Hussein sent hostages to strategic military installations in Iraq, as well as to dams and factories. He warned his opponents that if they bombed these places, they would kill the people imprisoned there. In September 1990, women and children were freed and allowed to leave Iraq.

One of the hostages was a young boy from Great Britain named Stuart Lockwood. Saddam Hussein appeared on television with Stuart, smiling at the boy and telling viewers that hostages were being treated well. In December, the Iraqi leader announced that Western hostages would be released.

On January 17, 1991, allied forces bombed the Iraqi capital, Baghdad. Iraqi planes bombed Israel near Tel Aviv, injuring a few people. The air campaign against Iraq caused billions of dollars of damage and destroyed factories and other civilian targets. The exact number of casualties has never been accurately determined but may have reached 100,000, including young people and children.

The fighting continued until Saddam Hussein pulled his troops out of Kuwait on February 27, 1991. By then, the Iraqis had spilled millions of gallons of oil from Kuwaiti oil fields into the sea and had also set fire to hundreds of oil wells. These acts polluted the water and air around Kuwait, damaging the environment.

Teenage soldiers fought in the Persian Gulf War. More than 200 of the troops sent from the United Kingdom were under 18 years old. They worked as weapons mechanics, radio operators, and in other jobs. After two 17-year-olds lost their lives during the war, some members of Parliament, as well as some British citizens, asked for changes in the policies that permitted persons under 18 to engage in combat. Journalists noted that boys as young as 12 were part of the Iraqi military. They took photographs of these boys training with AK-47 assault rifles.

This war marked the first time that American men and women served together as part of integrated military units in a war zone. Some of the servicewomen deployed to the Middle East during this conflict were mothers, which sparked a heated national debate over whether or not mothers of minor children should serve in combat-related positions. Supporters of a single military policy toward both men and women pointed out that more servicemen than servicewomen had children. They said that any parent who went to war was making a sacrifice for his or her country and that mothers and fathers should be treated the same. Opponents argued that motherhood was a special reason to bar women from action during wartime. Conservative spokeswoman and attorney Phyllis Schlafly, who favored traditional roles for women, said, "Pregnancy and motherhood are simply not compatible with military service. . . . The present policies are contrary to combat readiness, common sense and respect for family integrity" (Schlafly, 1991).

One of the most hotly debated issues during this war was whether or not women with children should be sent into combat. A number of magazines featured articles on this topic and *People* magazine ran an article called "Mom Goes to War," showing pictures of women saying good-bye to young children. A poll conducted by the Associated Press (AP) in February 1991 showed that Americans opposed sending mothers to the Gulf War by a margin of 2 to 1.

As a result of allied bombings, children in Iraq faced many hardships. Water delivery systems, electrical power stations, and sewage treatment plants throughout Iraq had been destroyed or seriously damaged. Ninety-five hospitals and medical centers were destroyed, as well as 80 percent of the country's farms and 90 percent of its fisheries.

At the end of that war, the United Nations imposed economic sanctions on Iraq. Most imports and all exports were frozen, and Iraq was not permitted to sell oil, which had brought more than 90 percent of the country's income. The embargo caused shortages, which led, in turn, to malnutrition among children, a lack of medical supplies, and the spread of disease. The World Health Organization (WHO) estimated that as of 1996, 100 children in Iraq were dying each day because of the sanctions. A Chicago-based organization called Voices in the Wilderness

to End the UN/U.S. Sanctions Against Iraq found that 567,000 children under the age of 5 were among the one million Iraqis who died in 1995 as a result of sanctions.

In 1997, UNICEF (the United Nations Children's Fund) reported that 25 percent of the children in Iraq faced death because of severe and chronic malnutrition, and 70 percent of the pregnant women in Iraq suffered from anemia. Visitors from humanitarian organizations saw children in hospitals and internal refugee centers suffering from diseases brought on by severe malnutrition

Late in 1997, the United Nations passed Resolution 986 called the "oil for food" plan. It permitted Iraq to sell $2 billion (later increased to $2.2 billion) worth of oil every six months in exchange for food and medicine. (An amount of $1.2 billion was first subtracted for United Nations operations and war reparations.) A committee of 15 nations had the right to approve or veto such exchanges. Although U.N. monitors said that the food and medicine were being efficiently distributed to the people of Iraq, they still only had about 10 percent of the food and medicine they needed. The plight of these children troubled people around the world who believed that these civilian children were innocent victims of political and military conflicts and prompted more relief efforts by AmeriCares and other organizations.

In April 1998, a group organized by the Church World Service, part of the National Council of Churches in the United States, brought food and medical supplies to Iraq to help the people who were suffering fom sanctions. Kara Newell, executive director of the American Friends Service Committee (AFSC), was part of the delegation to Iraq. She described the many problems she witnessed at a pediatric hospital, which lacked medicines, machine parts, disinfectants, sterilizers, and other supplies. She said that the breakdown in the sanitation system caused an increase in water-borne illnesses and prevented people from cleaning their homes and clothing: "We were in a children's ward and watched a baby die in an incubator, a full term child, who had a minor infection that simple antibiotics would have cured. . . . In the next ward there was a child who'd been in critical condition for 14 days and had hours to live. There are many more premature children . . . ." There were not enough doctors and nurses to care for the young patients. Newell said, "Pretty soon you're in a situation where you lose a whole generation of children because every child has some kind of brain damage or disease" (Weir, 1998).

Before sanctions were imposed, the Iraqi health care system was regarded as a model in the region and provided free care for all citizens. In 1998, delegates from relief organizations visited hospitals where doctors said there was a 500 percent increase in the cases of childhood leukemia. Some scientists attribute the dramatic increase in cancer to exposure to radioactive contamination caused by the uranium-tipped shells the allies used during the Gulf War. Often, the children suffering from leukemia could have been cured by medicines that were not available to them because of the sanctions.

In 1998, George Galloway, a member of the British Parliament, visited a Baghdad hospital and talked with Iraqi physicians about the unusually high rates of childhood cancer and infant mutations and abnormalities. These conditions were most common in areas that saw heavy fighting at the end of the war. Galloway said that allied nations should help to identify the source of the problems and provide drugs for these afflicted children: "Why not send a message to Iraqi children by sending an army of cancer experts laden with suitcases of cancer drugs to come and help the Iraqi health service—these heroes who are working in these conditions?" (BBC News Service, March 26, 1998)

The war also took its toll on Kuwaiti children. Of the estimated 1,082 Kuwaitis who were killed, 153 were children under age 13. Princess Hussa of Kuwait, whose son Ahmed was 4 years old during the war, worked with the anti-Iraqi resistance as a courier. She recalled, "You know that they [the Iraqi invaders] butchered boys and girls. I mean there were three boys, cut by a saw right through the stomach and left in the road, like pigeons

dumped in the street. The last five days just before the land attack were the worst. They started rounding up the boys and the men, and in three or four days they took about ten thousand civilians. I told my girlfriend, if anything happens to me, take my son and run away" (Lawrence, 1991).

Iraqi troops destroyed public utilities, electricity, water, and buildings in Kuwait, leaving some children homeless and without schools, clean water, and fuel. A number of young Kuwaiti women reported being sexually assaulted by the soldiers, and a number of them became pregnant, both of which socially stigmatized them in their conservative Muslim culture. Some of these young women killed themselves rather than bear a child under these circumstances. Some Kuwaiti children showed signs of post-traumatic stress syndrome when the war ended. Princess Hussa described her son's reactions: "He has not been allowed to be a child. . . . He is the same as the other children who lived through the war—they have all been living with fear" (Lawrence, 1991). *See also* AMERICAN FRIENDS SERVICE COMMITTEE (AFSC); AMERICARES FOUNDATION; GAS MASKS; GULF WAR SYNDROME; IRAN-IRAQ WAR; KURDS.

Further Reading: Gary Brown, "My Little Boy's Gone Off to War," *News of the World* (London), January 6, 1991; Elaine Donnelly, "Children Are Harmed When Mothers Serve in the Military," *Human Events,* March 16, 1991; Robert F. Dorr, *Desert Shield* (1991); Cynthia Enloe, *Does Khaki Become You? The Militarization of Women's Lives* (1988); "Gulf War Shells Could Be Causing Children's Cancers," BBC News Service, March 26, 1998 at <http://news1.thdo.bbc.co.uk/hi/english/world/middle_east>; G. Simon Harak, "Our Iraqi Children," *Conscious Living,* May/June 1998, pp. 3, 15; Tess Lawrence, "The Warrior Princess," *Mirabella,* August 1991, pp. 57-60; Molly Moore, "Women in the Battlefield—Gulf War Helps Bring Shift in Attitude," *Washington Post,* June 16, 1991; Charles Messenger, *Middle East* (1988); Tom Morgenthau, "The Military's New Image," *Newsweek,* March 11, 1991, pp. 50-51; Phyllis Schlafly, "The Combat Exclusion Law Is Necessary," in Carol Wekesser and Matthew Polesetsky, *Women in the Military* (1991); Carol Weir, "Friends in Iraq: An Interview with Kara Newell," *Friends Journal,* October 1998, pp. 17-22.

Peru

During a civil war that began in the 1970s in the South American nation of Peru, warring factions recruited soldiers under age 18. These young soldiers fought for the Peruvian army, the army's defense militias, the rebel group called the Maoist Shining Path, and the rebel forces of the Revolutionary Movement of Tupac Amaru (MRTA). Most of the young soldiers were poor youths from rural areas where millions of people were unemployed. Some young people were threatened with bodily harm if they did not join guerilla units or take part in certain battles in their region.

Shining Path operated training programs for young soldiers, who learned to make dynamite, use guns, and practiced mock attacks. As of 1993, more than 20 percent of the Shining Path troops were girls. They were taught to ardently support the goals of the group and to behave violently in combat situations. Young children were also used in terrorist activities. In October 1991, a nine-year-old boy working with the Shining Path group was assigned to place explosives beneath an electrical transmission tower. He died from injuries he sustained when a land mine that had been planted at the base of the tower exploded.

Other Peruvian youths joined the Tupac Amaru. Many of the young people who joined these troops lived in cities. Researchers Sandra and William Hazelton found that a number of children became soldiers because they admired the fine uniforms and equipment used by this group.

The civil war continued into the late 1990s. Journalists covering the war reported that child soldiers, both male and female, continued to fight. Two teenage girls fighting with the MRTA were killed in April 1997. At the war's end in 1999, an estimated 30,000 people had died and more than 600,000 had been displaced. Poverty was widespread, and about two-thirds of all children in war-torn regions were malnourished. Thousands of children had lost their fathers in the fighting and thousands more were orphaned as a result of killings by either the rebels or the Peruvian army.

However, immediate improvements began with the end of the fighting. Homes, schools, and playgrounds were beginning to be rebuilt, especially in Ayacucho Province, once the center of the Shining Path uprising. Children in rebel-controlled areas were once again able to call their parents "mama" and "papa," rather than "camarada," the term demanded by the rebels. Also, Indian and Christian religious ceremonies and holidays, which were banned by the Shining Path, were slowly being reinstated. *See also* RED CROSS; SOLDIERS, CHILD.

Further Reading: Duke University Institute of Policy Studies and Public Affairs, *Child Combatants* (1990); Clifford Krauss, "A Revolution Peru's Rebels Didn't Intend," *The New York Times,* August 29, 1999, pp. A-1, A-10; Sandra Way-Hazelton and William Hazelton, "The Shining Path and the Marxist Left," in David Palmer, ed., *Shining Path of Peru* (1992).

Peter, Prince of Yugoslavia

Seventeen-year-old Prince Peter became king of Yugoslavia during World War II, when his country was invaded by Nazi Germany. On March 25, 1941, Adolf Hitler planned to march across Yugoslavia on his way to invade Greece. The Yugoslavian prime minister signed the Tripartite Pact joining his country to the Axis nations of Germany, Japan, and Italy. Two days later, army generals rebelled against the prime minister and arrested government leaders. They crowned Prince Peter the new king of Yugoslavia. King Peter announced that his government would not join the Axis and would instead support the Allied cause. Throughout Yugoslavia, this stand gained popular support and people could be seen on the streets of Belgrade, the capital, telling the American press that they wished to join the Allies. Military leaders organized about 1.5 million troops to defend the Yugoslavian border from the German army.

In response, Hitler ordered his military staff to crush the rebellious Yugoslavians and ordered bombings, which began in early April. Young people were among the 17,000 people killed and the thousands who were badly injured during these air attacks. More than

10,000 buildings were destroyed leaving many families homeless. By April 22, the Germans had seized control of the country and announced that the Yugoslavian army would now be forced to join the Axis as stated in the Tripartite Pact. *See also* BOSNIA; KOSOVO; YUGOSLAVIA (WORLD WAR II).

Further Reading: Vera Laska, ed., *Women of the Resistance and in the Holocaust* (1984).

Philippines. *See* ESPIONAGE; PACIFIC (WORLD WAR II); PRISONERS

Phuc, Kim (1963–)

As a nine-year-old child in war-torn Vietnam, Kim Phuc appeared in a famous photograph that showed the brutal impact of war on children. Phuc was photographed by Nick Ut as she fled in pain, her clothes burned off, after a U.S. plane had dropped napalm on her village, Trang Bang. The aerial assault took place in June 1972. The photograph, which won a Pulitzer Prize, has often been reproduced and exhibited.

Nick Ut, a South Vietnamese-born photojournalist with the Associated Press, was himself only 22 when he took the award-winning photograph. His older brother, also a photographer, had been killed in 1965 while on assignment in North Vietnam. Recalling the day he encountered Kim Phuc, Ut said, "I saw the napalm explode, and I saw people carry children. They die. And after that, three or four children screaming. . . " (Gearan, 1997).

The picture devastated John Plummer, the 24-year-old helicopter pilot who had ordered the assault on Trang Bang. Plummer had been told there were no civilians in the area. For years after the war, he struggled with feelings of guilt. In 1990, after Plummer became a clergyman, he began to feel more at peace but still had nightmares and feelings of remorse. He wondered what had happened to the girl in the picture.

On November 11, 1997, Kim Phuc was a featured speaker at the Vietnam War Memorial in Washington, D.C., during the annual Veterans' Day service. Phuc was then 33 years old and a Canadian citizen. She still had scars

This famous Vietnam War photo, taken on June 8, 1972, shows Kim Phuc (center) running in terror down Route 1 after an American napalm attack on suspected Viet Cong positions. *Nick Ut/AP Wide World Photo.*

from the napalm on her arm, back, and neck and had undergone 17 operations through the years to heal the skin and relieve her pain. Plummer had heard Phuc would speak to the gathering, and he was in the audience that day. During her speech, Phuc said, "If I could talk face-to-face with the pilot who dropped the bombs, I would tell him we cannot change history, but we should try to do good things for the present and for the future to promote peace" (Gearan, 1997).

At the memorial service, Plummer wrote a note saying, "Kim, I am that man" and asked a police officer to deliver it to Phuc. He moved through the crowds and the two of them met. Plummer later recalled that he kept repeating the words, "I'm so sorry," and Kim Phuc said, "I forgive" (Gearan, 1997). *See also* VIETNAM WAR.

Further Reading: ABC's *Nightline* with Ted Koppel, June 6, 1997; Anne Gearan, "Embrace Silences Decades of Nightmares for Ex-Pilot; Vietnam: Girl in Famous War Photograph Meets Man Who Sent Bombers to Her Village," *Los Angeles Times*, April 20, 1997, p. A-2; Carlos Mendez, "Nick Ut: Capturing the Vietnam War in One Shudder of the Lens," *Asian Week*, May 5, 1995, pp. PG.

Pol Pot. *See* CAMBODIA

Poland (World War II)

On September 1, 1939, Nazi Germany invaded Poland with a heavy bombardment and thousands of tanks, triggering World War II in Europe. Many cities, including the capital, Warsaw, were devastated and tens of thousands of children were left hungry and homeless. Thousands of young people were killed and injured, both civilians and soldiers who fought in the Polish infantry and small air force.

A harsh Nazi occupation began. The Germans ousted Poles from regions they wanted for their own living space and for raw materials. Armed German troops were posted all over Poland. The Nazis viewed the Poles as inferior beings fit only for slave labor and for making Germany's war materials, and they sent young men and women into forced labor. Poles who could not work were to be

killed, along with many other people—influential clergy, labor leaders, intellectuals, and others who might provide leadership or challenge the Nazis. Children lost family members during these executions. Tens of thousands of young people were uprooted from their homes and forced to move to a different region.

In her diary, Mary Berg, a teenager during the invasion, described the dire food shortages in Warsaw. People stood in long lines for hours to obtain food and water. As they waited for food, they also risked being hit by bombs. Desperate people resorted to eating horses they found lying dead on the street.

The Nazis instituted new laws to limit the education of Polish children. A top Nazi official, Heinrich Himmler, said that Polish children should be taught "simple arithmetic up to 500, writing one's name, the lesson that it is a divine commandment to be obedient to the Germans; and to be honest, hardworking, and good. I do not think reading is required." The Nazis also decided to "Germanize" Polish children who had the appearance they regarded as desirable, or "Aryan"—blond, blue-eyed, fair-skinned. Himmler said they would carry out this plan, "If necessary by taking away their children and bringing them up with us" (Lukas, 1994).

Once in Poland, the Nazis began to isolate, impoverish, and terrorize Jews, as they did elsewhere. Although most Polish Jews were poor and had often been persecuted, they had built strong communities where children lived in close-knit families amid a culture rich in religious customs, literature, and the arts. Now they were driven from their homes. Lee Potasinski, who was seven years old in 1939, lived in the town of Jenju. His family had fled from Bendzin, where the Germans had burned all Jewish homes and synagogues. He recalled what happened four days after the Nazis invaded Poland:

> [T]he Germans decided to call all Jewish males into the market. And among them was my uncle. The Germans claimed, as they had all the males rounded up, that two German soldiers had been killed, which we found out was not true. And they took all

the males who were assembled at that time, and they were all shot. (Shulman, 1998)

In November, all Jews age 12 or older were ordered to wear a public label of their religion—a white armband with a blue Star of David. After the Warsaw Ghetto was built to confine and isolate Jews of all ages, more than 400,000 Jews from the city and surrounding area were ordered inside. Young people helped their parents carry the few belongings people were allowed to bring with them. Numerous people shared apartments inside the crowded ghetto. Thousands wandered the streets, homeless.

Between 1939 and 1941, Jews were also crammed into ghettos in Lublin and other Polish cities. Jewish young people from other occupied countries and Germany found themselves trapped. A few managed to escape and join anti-German partisan units that lived in Polish forests and rural areas.

Most Poles were bystanders to the persecution of Jews, while some helped the Nazis. Young men were among the members of gangs called *szmalcowniki* who tracked down Jews in hiding and demanded bribes in exchange for not exposing them and their protectors.

Thousands of Polish Jewish children went into hiding during the war. Some were taken into monasteries, convents, and other institutions, such as the Home of Father Boduen in Warsaw where about 200 young people hid under the supervision of Dr. Maria Prokopowicz-Wierzbowski. Polish nuns hid children in convents, often located in remote areas. According to Richard C. Lukas (1989), about two-thirds of the religious communities in Poland helped hide Jewish refugees during the Holocaust.

In Poland, the penalty for helping Jews was death, and some executions of entire families were carried out in public to scare local people into obeying the Nazis. Marilla Feld later recalled the risks: "We had heard of instances when not only an entire Polish family was shot, but the farm completely burned out—everything, the house, the animals, the farm equipment. The Germans so wanted to make sure that no Polish farmer would dare

harbor a Jew" (Laska, 1984). Because of these conditions, and because most of the Nazi death camps were located on Polish soil, 90 percent of the 3.3 million Jews who lived in Poland before the war died between 1939 and 1945. Nearly one million were children.

When World War II ended, more than 350,000 children in Poland were orphaned, abandoned, or neglected. Over one million had lost one or both parents and needed food, housing, and health care, among other things. Cities had been devastated and hospitals destroyed so health care facilities were grossly inadequate. Only 6,000 physicians were left in Poland to treat the sick and injured. For instance, a single 50-bed hospital for children remained in Warsaw to deal with the needs of the 90,000 children who lived in that city after the war. Some had been left blind, maimed, or wounded.

Children also had emotional wounds resulting from their wartime experiences. Some children who had witnessed horrors or atrocities became mute. Concentration camp survivors or Jewish children who had survived in hiding faced special problems. Many of them had no homes or families and were taken to new homes in other countries where the customs and language were unfamiliar. Young people in this devastated nation faced a long and difficult period of recovery. *See also* ADOPTION; ANIELEWICZ, MORDECHAI; BAUBLIS, PETRA; BAUM, FROIM; BERG, MARY; BURZMINSKI, STEFANIA PODGORSKA; DEATH CAMPS (WORLD WAR II); DEPORTATIONS; EDUCATION; FORCED LABOR (WORLD WAR II); GHETTOS (WORLD WAR II); HART, KITTY FELIX; HOLOCAUST; HUNGER/MALNUTRITION; JEWISH FIGHTERS ORGANIZATION (JFO); KOLBE, MAXIMILIAN; KORCZAK, JANUSZ; LEBENSBORN; "MASTER RACE"; ORPHANS; POST-TRAUMATIC STRESS DISORDER (PTSD); RESCUERS (HOLOCAUST); RESISTANCE MOVEMENTS (WORLD WAR II); RIGHTEOUS GENTILES; RINGELBLUM ARCHIVES; ROUND-UPS; SENDLER, IRENA; SEPARATIONS, FAMILY; TOLL, NELLY LANDAU; WARSAW GHETTO; ZEGOTA.

Further Reading: Mary Berg, *Warsaw Ghetto Diary* (1945); Vera Laska, ed., *Women of the Resistance and in the Holocaust* (1984); Richard C. Lukas, *Out of the Inferno: Poles Remember the Holocaust* (1989);

Richard C. Lukas, ed., *Did the Children Cry?* (1994); William Shulman, Holocaust: Voices and Visions (1998); Kiryl Sosnowski, *The Tragedy of Children Under Nazi Rule* (1983).

Post-Traumatic Stress Disorder (PTSD)

Post-traumatic stress disorders (PTSD) have afflicted untold numbers of young people who experienced the dangers and deprivations of war. The disorder can occur as a result of short-term trauma or when a person has endured long periods of fear, persecution, terrorism, loss, and hardship. PTSD may also afflict youths who have witnessed or engaged in brutal behavior. They may feel guilt over their wartime behavior, if, for example, they have engaged in lying, stealing, cheating, and other typically antisocial behavior.

Young people who sustain psychological scars from their war-related experiences may exhibit ongoing physical and behavioral symptoms of stress. The condition of young people after World War II shows how post-traumatic stress disorders can be manifested. Behavioral specialists who worked with children after the war found that many experienced ongoing fear, anxiety attacks, nightmares, facial ticks, fainting spells, enuresis, and intense sweating. In addition, many had flashbacks and suffered from depression. Nightmares or flashbacks were triggered by the smell of smoke or loud noises. Some children never felt safe. They were often insecure, distrustful, and suspicious of people's motives. Some young people were prone to amnesia and had trouble concentrating or sitting still. A number of children became overly shy, while others became aggressive and prone to angry outbursts. Still others coped by numbing themselves to emotions and showing intense apathy instead. Six years of war had taken away the childhoods of millions of young people throughout Europe and Asia.

Researchers noted that youthful Jewish survivors of the Holocaust of World War II, who were mostly over age 12, faced special problems and adjustments in addition to those of other young people. During the Nazi era, these youth had long been told they were inherently "bad" and unworthy of life. For years, they had been persecuted and had witnessed persecution of others. They had lost homes, family members, educational opportunities, community ties, and friends. One girl who was taken to a concentration camp in October 1940 summed up the feeling she had at that time: "Anything we ever knew that was civilized life had now disappeared in one quick stroke"(Bachrach, 1993).

During the last half of the twentieth century, signs of post-traumatic stress have often been observed in youths who endured wars in different parts of the world. Relief organizations have developed special programs to improve the emotional well-being of children who lived in war zones and who were child soldiers.

Relief workers observed high rates of post-traumatic stress disorders in children in Mozambique, where civil war raged for 16 years and thousands of child soldiers were involved in massacres. Former child soldiers reported experiencing flashbacks and exhibited aggressive behavior in their communities; suicide rates were also higher than normal among these youth.

Children in Guatemala showed signs of severe trauma. Eugenia Villareal, a Mexican sociologist and member of the Commission of Human Rights of the International Peace Research Association, studied the psychological effects of the long civil war on children who were forced to serve as soldiers or in the armed civil defense force. Her research team found that the children had been dehumanized, beaten, and degraded. The military forced indigenous youth to speak Spanish instead of their native languages. Young women in Guatemala who were raped and terrorized by the military also suffered from chronic fear, anxiety, and other symptoms of trauma.

Kuwaiti children showed signs of post-traumatic stress syndrome when the Persian Gulf War ended in 1991. In an interview late in 1991, Princess Hussa of Kuwait said of her 4-year-old son: "He has not been allowed to be a child. . . . He is the same as the other children who lived through the war—they have all been living with fear" (Lawrence, 1991).

Dr. Kueri Idrissov, who worked with children in war-torn Bosnia, said that child refugees and orphaned children were the most severely traumatized. "The ones who stayed in Grozny, and whose homes were destroyed and of course those who witnessed the death of family and friends—they're hyperactive, aggressive, and irritable. They can't concentrate properly, so it's hard for them to study. . . . They sleep badly with terrible nightmares, and a lot of them stammer or have nervous tics. Those are just some of the symptoms . . ." ("Children of Conflict," 1999).

For these children and hundreds of thousands of others around the world, the war did not end when the fighting stopped. Mental health workers estimate that during the 1990s, some 10 million children were psychologically traumatized by war ("Children of Conflict," 1999). *See also* ARMENIAN-TURKISH CONFLICT; BOSNIA; CHILDREN OF AUSCHWITZ NAZI DEADLY EXPERIMENTS SURVIVORS (CANDLES); EL SALVADOR; GREECE (WORLD WAR II); INTERNMENT CAMPS, U.S.; LIBERIAN CIVIL WAR; MOZAMBIQUE; NORTHERN IRELAND; POLAND (WORLD WAR II); RELIEF ORGANIZATIONS; RWANDA; SAVE THE CHILDREN; SOLDIERS, CHILD; UNITED NATIONS CHILDREN'S FUND (UNICEF).

Further Reading: Roberta J. Apfel and Bennett Simon, eds. *Minefields in Their Hearts: The Mental Health of Children in War and Communal Violence* (1996); Susan D. Bachrach, *Tell Them We Remember: The Story of the Holocaust* (1993); BBC World Service, "Children of Conflict, Wounded Children," at <http://www.bbc.co.uk/worldservice/childrenofconflict>; Helen Epstein, *Children of the Holocaust* (1979); Tom Harrison, *Living Through the Blitz* (1976); Flora Hogman, "Role Memories in Lives of World War II Orphans," *Journal of the American Academy of Child Psychiatry* 24, 1985, pp. 390-96; Zofia Kruk, *The Taste of Fear: A Polish Childhood in Germany* (1973); Tess Lawrence, "The Warrior Princess," *Mirabella,* August 1991, pp. 57-60; Dorothy Macardle, *Children of Europe* (1951); Graca Machel, *The Impact of Armed Conflict on Children* (1996); Judith Miller, *One by One: Facing the Holocaust* (1990); Aranka Siegal, *Upon the Head of a Goat: A Childhood in Hungary, 1939-1944* (1981).

Postwar Relief. *See* AMERICAN FRIENDS SERVICE COMMITTEE (AFSC); CARE; DISPLACED PERSONS (DPs) (WORLD WAR II); FEED THE CHILDREN; HIDDEN CHILD FOUNDATION/ANTI-DEFAMATION LEAGUE (ADL); HIDDEN CHILDREN; HOLOCAUST; HUNGER/MALNUTRITION; INTERNATIONAL RESCUE COMMITTEE (IRC); LIBERIAN CIVIL WAR; MARSHALL PLAN; MOZAMBIQUE; POLAND (WORLD WAR II); RED CROSS; REFUGEES; RELIEF ORGANIZATIONS; RWANDA; SAVE THE CHILDREN; SOMALIA; UNITED NATIONS CHILDREN'S FUND (UNICEF); VIETNAM WAR; WORLD WAR II

Prisoners

During wartime, young male combatants have been captured by enemy troops and confined in prisoner-of-war camps. Soldiers under the age of 21 have fought in numerous wars since the 1600s and were sometimes more vulnerable to being captured than soldiers with more experience. Conditions in prisoner-of-war camps have varied from war to war and from one country to another. The largest number of people were imprisoned during World War II when a total of 15 million men and women became prisoners of war (POWs). POWs had the highest chance of surviving if they were captured by American or British forces. In U.S. camps, German POWs ate plentiful, nutritious meals. They received 80 cents a day when they were put to work and could spend this money in the camps or save it. Allied soldiers captured by the Germans had higher rates of survival than those captured by the Japanese. However, Russian prisoners of war were treated more harshly by the Germans than were American or British prisoners. More than 50 percent of the 5.7 million soldiers captured by the Germans died in captivity. Of the 3.5 million German captives in Soviet camps, 1.5 million died. Allied POWs in German camps later said they did not receive enough food and that a typical meal was a piece of bread with watery soup. Prisoners often lost a great deal of weight. They passed the time reading or playing sports or card games.

During World War II, prisoners of the Japanese had the lowest rates of survival. They died as a result of starvation, overwork, disease, torture, death marches, and executions. Young soldiers were among the Americans and Filipinos who died after they became prisoners of the Japanese in April 1942 and were ordered to march across the jungle on the Bataan Peninsula in the Philippines. Seven thousand men died in the tropical sun from starvation, disease, or exhaustion on the Bataan Death March. Some were shot or beaten to death by their captors.

After the fall of Singapore in 1942, the Japanese put about 61,000 British, Dutch, and Australian POWs to work on a 260-mile railroad designed to carry supplies from Burma to Thailand. Young men made up a large portion of the 16,000 POWs who died while struggling to construct this road across the rough jungle and mountains and over streams and rivers.

Young civilians sometimes become prisoners during wartime. For example, during World War II, the Japanese captured thousands of American and European noncombatants as they invaded various outposts throughout Asia, such as the Philippines. Thousands of prisoners of all ages were interned at the San Tomas camp in the Philippines where they lived in overcrowded quarters and had little to eat. Whole families were crammed into small shantys made of pieces of wood, metal, and bamboo. Mothers and fathers helped their children survive by giving them part of their small food rations.

Dutch civilians were imprisoned in a jungle camp in Indonesia. Some children at the camp died of typhoid and other diseases. They had a poor diet and inadequate medical care. Sometimes the only food for the whole day consisted of watery soup or cornmeal mush. However, non-combatants living in prison compounds were allowed more freedom than imprisoned soldiers. For example, they were allowed to operate schools and churches.

Nazi Germany imprisoned millions of Jewish children and young adults during World War II. Along with civilians of all ages, they were rounded up and placed in transit camps, concentration camps, and death camps. The Nazis also pursued and arrested young members of the resistance in occupied countries, such as Holland, Belgium, Denmark, Poland, and France. These prisoners were interrogated and imprisoned for working against the Nazi regime. Likewise, in Germany, young people were imprisoned for acting or speaking against the regime, as well as for refusing to serve in the military or to give the Nazi salute. Imprisonment was used throughout the twentieth century in other countries during wars and revolutions as a way to intimidate people and subdue dissent.

Children have been captured and kept as prisoners during recent civil wars in Burma (Myanmar), Sierra Leone, Uganda, and other places. Former child soldiers reported that they were often abducted and kept in camps where their captors threatened to kill them if they did not fight with the troops. Sometimes, the children were captured by opposing troops during combat and forced to live in guarded camps and fight for the enemy. Children in Sierra Leone told relief workers that their captors made children kill or maim other children who tried to escape from these training camps. *See also* ADOPTION; AFGHANISTAN; ANGOLA; BOER WAR; CONCENTRATION CAMPS (WORLD WAR II); D-DAY; DEATH CAMPS (WORLD WAR II); DEPORTATIONS; DRANCY; FRENCH REVOLUTION; GHETTOS (WORLD WAR II); INTERNMENT CAMPS, U.S.; JEHOVAH'S WITNESSES; PACIFIC (WORLD WAR II); RED CROSS; RELIEF ORGANIZATIONS; RIVESALTES; ROMANOV CHILDREN; ROUND-UPS; RWANDA; SOLDIERS, CHILD; WARSAW GHETTO; WORLD WAR II.

Further Reading: Dieuwke Wendelaar Bonga, *Eight Prison Camps* (1996); Sheila Bruhn, *Diary of a Girl in Changi* (1994); Helen Colijn, *Song of Survival* (1997); Robert S. La Forte, ed., *Building the Death Railway* (1992); Eric Lomax, *The Railway Man* (1996); Celia Lucas, *Prisoners of Santo Tomas* (1997); U.S. Department of Health, Education, and Welfare, *Effects of Malnutrition and Other Hardships on the Mortality and Morbidity of Former United States Prisoners of War and Civilian Internees of World War II* (1956); Van Waterford, *Prisoners of the Japanese in World War II* (1994).

Pritchard, Marion von Binsbergen (1929–)

As a college student in Amsterdam, Holland, during World War II, Marion von Binsbergen Pritchard worked in the Dutch resistance against the Nazis who occupied her homeland. She and other students helped people in hiding and found hiding places for Jewish children and adults. Pritchard was roused to action after she witnessed a harrowing scene of violence against children on the streets of Amsterdam. As Germans were conducting a round-up, she saw them throwing babies and children from a Jewish children's home onto trucks. Pritchard recalled that "When they [the children] did not move fast enough the Nazis picked them up, by an arm, a leg, the hair. . . . To watch grown men treating children that way—I could not believe my eyes. I found myself literally crying with rage" (Rittner and Meyers, 1986).

She and a group of students began helping Jews escape from the Nazis. They provided hiding places, food, clothing, ration cards, false identity papers and work permits, and other things that these *onderduikers*—"divers"—needed. Members of their rescue group, most of them women, also escorted Jewish babies and children to their hiding places. Pritchard hid a man and his three children in the home she occupied outside Amsterdam. She registered three newborn babies as her own children so the government would list them as non-Jews and they would be spared from Nazi persecution and deportation. In all, Pritchard helped save 150 people, many of them children.

During the occupation years, Pritchard endured Nazi raids and was arrested, tortured, and imprisoned. After the war, she worked to help displaced persons (DPs) in European camps. She later married an American military officer and moved to Vermont, where she practiced psychoanalysis. Pritchard wrote and lectured on the subject of the Holocaust and human behavior. She was honored as a Righteous Gentile by Yad Vashem in Israel. *See also* DISPLACED PERSONS (DPs) (WORLD WAR II); HOLLAND (WORLD WAR II); RESISTANCE MOVEMENTS (WORLD WAR II); RIGHTEOUS GENTILES; YAD VASHEM.

Further Reading: Eva Fogelman, *Conscience and Courage* (1994); Carol Rittner and Sondra Meyers, eds., *The Courage to Care* (1986).

Protesters, War. *See* ANTI-WAR MOVEMENT (VIETNAM WAR); CONSCIENTIOUS OBJECTORS; CONSCRIPTION; JEHOVAH'S WITNESSES; QUAKERS (SOCIETY OF FRIENDS); RESISTANCE MOVEMENTS (WORLD WAR II); *TINKER V. DES MOINES*

Q

Quakers (Society of Friends)

The Society of Friends, known as the Quakers, is a religious group founded by Englishman George Fox during the seventeenth century. The group promotes pacifist beliefs based on the precept that no human or country should hate, or do violence against, another human or country; thus, young Friends have often become conscientious objectors or have performed relief work during and after wars rather than engage in combat.

Through the years, Friends have objected to participation in war and any kind of killing. In 1660, they drafted a declaration which said, in part, "Our principle is, and our practices have always been, to seek peace. . . ." A basic Quaker tenet is not to fight or make war "against any man with outward weapons, neither for the kingdom of Christ, nor for the kingdoms of this world" (Melter, 1985).

Members of the Society of Friends are urged to actively relieve human suffering and work for social justice. During wartime, Friends have aided people who suffered as a result of war and have worked to resist oppression and war in nonviolent ways. Toward that end, they set up hospitals, provided material assistance, and raised funds to help refugees on all sides of various wars.

During the Franco-Prussian War (1870-1871), British Quakers distributed food, clothing, and medicine to thousands of children in war-torn Europe. They brought farming equipment, seeds, livestock, and other supplies to farm families whose crops had been destroyed. They also helped rebuild homes in areas of Alsace-Lorraine that had been ruined by siege. Five years later, Quakers helped thousands of Bulgarian refugees from Turkish persecution by building homes and seven new schools in that country.

During World War I, the American Friends Service Committee (AFSC) was formed to aid victims and provide alternative service opportunities for young men who would not fight for reasons of conscience. The AFSC contributed money and humanpower to the post-war relief effort. Friends brought clothing, food, and health care supplies to Germany and ran programs to feed students at German universities.

In the 1930s, when the Nazis rose to power in Germany and began persecuting Jews, Quakers helped people who wished to leave the country and settle in new communities. Quakers were harassed by Nazi police, and Nazis monitored their religious services. Quaker families living in Berlin hid Jews from the Nazis, although they did not openly talk about their activities at that time, even with one another. Elisabeth Abegg, a teacher who had been fired by the Nazis in 1941 for her anti-Nazi beliefs, hid several Jews in her apartment and ran a secret day school for children who were banned from German public schools.

Quaker relief organizations operated before, during, and after fighting broke out in World War II. They aided Jews and other refugees from fascism to escape Nazi-occupied countries and worked with other organizations that were assisting children, for example, the *Oeuvre de Secours aux Enfants* (OSE) in France. Quakers also operated relief missions in Gurs and other Nazi concentration camps in France and other countries.

Quakers were sometimes able to help children escape from these camps. Some young refugees were taken to Le Chambon-sur-Lignon, a mountain village that sheltered thousands of Jews, mostly children, during the war. American Burns Chalmers, the head of the regional Quaker office in southern France, helped coordinate these projects with the religious leaders of Le Chambon. Quakers provided money to help run some of the homes. Chalmers told Pastor Andre Trocme, a leader of the rescue effort in Le Chambon, "If the parents are nonetheless deported, we take charge of the children, and we arrange that they be boarded outside of the camps" (Hallie, 1979). After the Nazis drove Quaker relief organizations out of southern France, couriers from Geneva, Switzerland, brought money to keep the safe homes operating. Some Quakers were arrested and shot while doing this dangerous work.

After World War II ended in 1945, Quakers took part in relief work that helped children and young people in Europe and Asia. American Friend, Dr. Floyd Schmoe, organized a project called Peace Houses to provide homes for people in bombed-out Hiroshima, Japan. Schmoe, his wife, and people from different countries built homes, which the Japanese government then rented to needy people for just one dollar a month. Homeless Japanese children greatly benefited from this project.

Since 1945, through the AFSC and other endeavors, Friends have actively worked to help youth during wartime and after wars ended in countries around the world, including Southeast Asia, Guatemala, Bosnia, and throughout Africa. *See also* AMERICAN FRIENDS SERVICE COMMITTEE (AFSC); CONSCIENTIOUS OBJECTORS; DARRAGH, JOHN; HIDDEN CHILDREN; HIROSHIMA MAIDENS; HOLOCAUST; INTERNMENT CAMPS, U.S.; LE CHAMBON-SUR-LIGNON; *OEUVRE DE SECOURS AUX ENFANTS* (OSE).

Further Reading: Philip Hallie, *Lest Innocent Blood Be Shed* (1979); Hans A. Schmitt, *Quakers and Nazis* (1997).

Queen Anne's War. *See* DEERFIELD RAID

R

Radiation Sickness

Thousands of Japanese youth were among the civilians who suffered from radiation sickness after the United States dropped two atomic bombs on Japan in August 1945 to end World War II. The radiation emitted from the weapons damaged their blood cells and various body organs. Bomb survivors—known as *hibakusha*—were prone to numerous, unpredictable health problems, some of which were fatal. People who were in the closest contact with the rubble and the ground contaminated by the bombs were most likely to become seriously ill. Corpses were also radioactive, so people who handled bodies and buried them after the bombings frequently became sick. Because it was typhoon season when the bombs fell, heavy rains eventually wiped away some radioactivity, but radiation remained in the environment for months after the bombings.

One common early symptom of radiation poisoning was hair loss. While using a comb, children found clumps of hair falling out. Victims suffered from terrible stomach pains, bloody diarrhea, vomiting, and fevers. They developed sores on their bodies. Hemorrhaging throughout their bodies caused blood to show up in their urine and mouths. Small red dots or purple blotches appeared on victims' skin where blood vessels close to the surface had burst. Bomb survivors also suffered from cataracts, anemia, and other problems the doctors labeled "atomic bomb weakness symptoms." Children who did not have severe wounds died for no apparent reason.

At the time of the bombing, the Japanese government did not inform people that the bomb was a nuclear weapon. Many doctors were puzzled by the strange symptoms they saw. Laboratory tests showed that affected people had fewer white cells (which fight disease) than normal. In the months and years that followed the bombing, survivors had higher rates of cancer, including leukemia and malignant tumors, than other people.

A Japanese boy named Nagatoshi was three years old when the bomb fell on his city, Nagasaki. After the bombing, he suffered from fever and diarrhea and his hair fell out, but he seemed to recover. Three years later, when Nagatoshi was in second grade, he complained of chest pains. During the next year, Nagatoshi became weak and tired and lost his appetite. He grew too weak to stand, then experienced fainting spells, a sore throat, fever, and cough. Doctors at the Atomic Bomb Casualty Commission diagnosed him with A-bomb disease. He died at age nine of pneumonia. Radiation in his body had destroyed his immune system, which no longer functioned effectively to fight diseases.

Radiation sickness also affected future generations. Children born to A-bomb survivors who had been exposed to radiation were more prone to blood disorders and cancers than were people in the general population.

The children of women who were pregnant at the time of the bombing were often born with physical abnormalities, such as smaller-than-normal heads. These babies also were more likely to have mental and physical delays in their development after they were born. Studies showed that bomb survivors had suffered damage to the chromosomes, the part of the cell that passes traits from parent to offspring.

People in other countries have also suffered from the effects of radiation as a result of nuclear testing or from working in laboratories and factories where nuclear weapons were developed and made. An estimated 220,000 American servicemen were exposed to nuclear radiation during the time they were stationed in Japan or while witnessing atmospheric nuclear tests in the United States. This exposure affected both them and their families.

Scientists have been studying the long-term impact of nuclear testing on people who lived in the American Southwest where nuclear tests were conducted in desert areas during the early 1950s and on people who worked in nuclear-weapons facilities. Between 1943 and 1990, more than 660,000 people in the United States worked in such places. In 1988, a bill was enacted by the U.S. Congress to provide some financial compensation for atomic veterans who develop cancer. *See also* FOLDED CRANE CLUB; HIROSHIMA; HIROSHIMA MAIDENS; MUSHROOM CLUB; NAGASAKI; NUCLEAR TESTING; PEACE MONUMENT; THE RIBBON; SASAKI, SADAKO.

Further Reading: Anne Chisholm, *Faces of Hiroshima* (1985); Kome, Penney, and Patrick Crean, eds., *Peace: A Dream Unfolding* (1986); Clifford T. Honicker, "The Hidden Files," *New York Times Sunday Magazine*, November 19, 1989, p. 39+; Robert Jay Lifton, *Death in Life: Survivors of Hiroshima* (1982); Arata Osada, *Children of the A-Bomb* (1963).

Rape. *See* SEXUAL ABUSE

Rationing

During wartime, young people have experienced the impact of rationing—the doling out of food, clothing, fuels, and other necessary materials in limited amounts. Rationing provides a way to distribute scarce materials throughout the population. Rationing tends to be stricter in countries where military activities are most intense and where foods and other supplies are used to feed, clothe, and support troops and to build and fuel military equipment. Rationing is also stricter when a country depends on imports that cannot be obtained in wartime because of combat, blockades, or the failure of transportation systems.

During World War I and World War II, youth in the United States, Great Britain, and other countries worked as volunteers in ration centers, giving out ration coupon and point books to people in the community. Ration cards or coupons allowed people to buy a certain item or amount of food—for example, a pair of shoes, a half pound of flour, or two ounces of cheese. They had to present both their money and their ration card to legally obtain the item in question. Within families, young people were often in charge of keeping track of the ration books and coupons. They were also frequently sent out to buy various items, a job that required standing in lines for long periods of time.

Occupied nations have often resorted to strict rationing when invaders seized food, clothing, and raw materials for their own use. During World War II, rationing left many young people in Europe in a state of chronic hunger and malnutrition. Some families became so hungry they forged ration cards to get enough food. Black markets also flourished in some countries as people paid more money to obtain items illegally or sold things illegally themselves. Children were sometimes sent to stores to buy food with forged cards, or even to trade with black marketeers, because they appeared more innocent. Children also helped people in the resistance deliver forged ration cards for people who were hiding from the enemy.

No combat occurred within the United States during either of the world wars, but rationing was introduced to provide enough food and supplies for the military. During 1942 and 1943, the government passed laws that limited the amounts of fuel, rubber, metal, nylon, and certain foods that were used by the military. Children ate more candies and desserts made with honey and molasses because white sugar was rationed. Families used their cars less often during World War II when gasoline was in short supply, and they put retread tires on their cars. *See also* GHETTOS (WORLD WAR II); GERMANY (WORLD WAR II); GREAT BRITAIN (WORLD WAR II); HIDDEN CHILDREN; HOLLAND (WORLD WAR II); HUNGER/MALNUTRITION; JAPAN (WORLD WAR II); RESISTANCE MOVEMENTS (WORLD WAR II); UNITED STATES (WORLD WAR II); VICTORY GARDENS.

Further Reading: Stan Cohen, *V for Victory: America's Home Front During World War II* (1991); Archie Satterfield, *Home Front* (1981).

Red Cross

Red Cross organizations have provided wartime relief and post-war assistance to youth around the world. The International Committee of the Red Cross (ICRC), often shortened to Red Cross, was founded by Henri Dunant, a Swiss businessman. In 1859, Dunant was horrified when he witnessed the lack of care available for thousands of wounded soldiers at the Battle of Solferino in Italy during the Franco-Austrian war. Dunant believed that neutral organizations could bring relief to all victims of war, and he set forth his ideas in a book called *Origins of the Red Cross,* which was published in 1862. After Dunant and his supporters appealed to an international conference held in Geneva, Switzerland, in 1863, the Geneva Convention of 1864 agreed to establish the Permanent International Committee for Relief to Wounded Combatants, which evolved into the International Committee of the Red Cross. The symbol comes from reversing the colors on the Swiss flag, which consists of a white cross on a red ground.

The American Red Cross, now the largest volunteer service organization in the United States, was founded by Clara Barton, a former schoolteacher from Massachusetts. Barton had overcome many barriers to gain permission from the United States government to care for soldiers on the battlefields of the Civil War. Wounded soldiers were dying because they had to wait too long for medical assistance. Barton and some nurses under her direction went into combat zones to care for the wounded and organize field hospitals. After the war, Barton helped families find out what had happened to loved ones who were missing in action.

During a visit to Europe undertaken for health reasons, Barton learned about Henri Dunant's work and the Red Cross. She returned home and waged a long campaign to found the American Red Cross (ARC). As the ARC's first president, Barton expanded the role of the American organization to give relief to victims of both natural and human disasters. The Red Cross provides health care and health and safety education to people in remote areas and conducts many other programs, including blood collection drives.

During World War I, Red Cross organizations were active in war-torn Europe. The ICRC and Red Cross organizations from the United States and European countries ran canteens, health clinics, hospitals, and soup kitchens. Children benefited from these goods and services, as did the rest of their families. Young soldiers visited canteens and relied on other Red Cross services. Many other young people served as Red Cross volunteers, helping to staff canteens, clinics, and other facilities. The Red Cross also helped refugees who were driven out of their countries. It arranged for prisoner exchanges and helped people trace missing relatives. It sent letters from prisoners of war to their families.

The Red Cross raised more than $730 million for its relief programs during World War II. The programs to collect and ship blood products reduced the death rate to 50 percent of the rate during World War I. Young people worked as volunteers during blood drives. They completed junior nurses' aide courses to ease the shortage of nurses in hospitals and other health care settings after many nurses left to serve in the military. In addition, young people rolled bandages, prepared and wrapped packages, handled mail, and performed many other necessary tasks.

Red Cross workers in Europe also aided children who were imprisoned in concentration camps. In Nazi-occupied France, Red Cross workers, many of them from Sweden, helped children in Drancy, Pithiviers, and other camps by bringing them extra food and packages from relief agencies and helping them receive and send letters. Workers were sometimes able to smuggle Jewish children out of these camps and into safe houses.

Hanne Liebmann, a German Jewish child imprisoned at the concentration camp at Gurs, France, later described the conditions she endured before receiving help from the Red Cross.

> We were put in . . . very flimsy wooden barracks. There was absolutely nothing in those barracks. . . . The barracks were covered with a single layer of tarpaper which in many places was torn, and water would come down on us. . . . we had to sleep on the floor. . . . There was no privacy. (Shulman, 1998)

Liebmann and her fellow prisoners had little to eat—small amounts of bread, watery coffee, brown sugar, and thin vegetable soup. During one period, their only food was pumpkin. The Children's Division of the Swiss Red Cross gave the young people an additional meal in the morning and tried to help those who were ill. On September 8, 1941, a social worker took Liebmann and six other children from the camp and brought them safely to the village of Le Chambon where people were sheltering thousands of Jewish children. There, Liebmann lived in a group home run by the Swiss Red Cross and survived the war.

Red Cross workers also helped children who were imprisoned in Asia during World War II. For example, children as well as adult civilians were kept in a Japanese-run prison in San Tomas in the Philippines, among other places. By 1944, prison officials had reduced their rations to some rice and one vegetable per day. Red Cross kits containing canned and dried foods, vitamins, cheese, and medicine helped people survive.

Along with providing material relief to children in need, the Red Cross carries out a wide range of educational and social work activities that help youth. In Peru during the early 1990s, the Red Cross prepared a school magazine for adolescents living in war zones. The magazine discussed humanitarian principles and key points of international law. It was intended to inform young people about these principles and laws and encourage them to discuss them with each other and in legal or military situations they might encounter.

The ICRC won the Nobel Peace Prize in 1917, 1944, and 1963. *See also* LE CHAMBON-SUR-LIGNON; PRISONERS; RELIEF ORGANIZATIONS; SPANISH-AMERICAN WAR; TEREZIN (THERESIENSTADT); UNITED STATES (WORLD WAR II); VOLUNTEERS; WALLENBERG, RAOUL; WORLD WAR I; WORLD WAR II.

Further Reading: Jeremy Josephs, *Swastika Over Paris* (1989); Louise Levathes, "The American Red Cross: A Century of Service," *National Geographic,* June 1981, pp. 777-91; William Shulman, *Holocaust: Voices and Visions* (1998).

Refugees

Refugees are persons who flee from their homes or countries to escape war or persecution. During the late twentieth century alone, millions of people became refugees as a result of wars in Asia, Africa, the Middle East, and Central America. In some cases, refugees were forced out of their homes or communities by enemy forces. In other cases, they left after bombings demolished their homes or because their crops or means of raising food or making a living had been destroyed.

Young refugees need food, clothing, bedding, shelter, soap and water, medicine, and health care. Children who become refugees face additional problems when separated from their families, sources of support, and such community structures as schools. They may be unable to pursue their education and often lose touch with their relatives and cultural heritage. They may also suffer from emotional trauma because of these losses and as a result of witnessing wartime horrors and being violently displaced.

During the twentieth century, bombings left many young people homeless refugees. World War I marked the first time aerial bombs were used in warfare. Air raids en-

A Vietnamese mother and her children swim across a river to escape fighting during the Vietnam War. *Kyoichi Sawada, Corbis-Bettmann.*

abled enemy troops to destroy larger areas than ever before, and homes and crops were destroyed. During World War II, bombings left millions of people homeless in numerous countries in both Allied and Axis countries and the nations they occupied or bombed.

Thousands of Jewish youth became refugees before, during, and after World War II. After Adolf Hitler rose to power in Germany in 1933 and began the persecution of Jews, many Jewish families fled to other European countries, such as Holland, Czechoslovakia, Hungary, or France, or even to North or South America. Among those who fled from Germany to Holland was the family of Otto Frank, whose teenage daughter Anne wrote a famous diary about her life in hiding during the war.

Some Jews became refugees in more than one country because they were caught in the ever-widening Nazi net. Clara Isaacman's family moved from Romania to Antwerp, Belgium, in 1932 after her father was beaten by anti-Jewish thugs on a public street. In Belgium, the family rebuilt their lives and Clara and her three siblings attended school and learned a new language. By early 1938, their relatives were urging them to leave Europe completely because of the Nazi threat. Clara's father told his brother, "World opinion will stop Hitler. And we can't run again. Once is enough" (Isaacman, 1984).

When World War II began, more Jewish youth tried to leave Nazi-occupied lands, but by 1940, German troops had invaded and occupied Czechoslovakia, Poland, Norway, Denmark, Holland, Luxembourg, Begium, and France. Clara Isaacman's family again faced anti-Jewish laws, restrictions, and propaganda. Like many others, they were trapped for the duration of the war.

Strict quotas limited the number of refugees who could leave Europe during the 1930s. Before World War II began, some agencies worked to help Jewish children escape persecution. The British Academic Exchange Service permitted some Jewish refugees to come to Great Britain as students. In the United States, Congress considered the Child Refugee Bill (Wagner-Rogers Bill), which would have admitted thousands of Jewish youth above the immigration quotas. The bill had strong support from First Lady Eleanor Roosevelt but failed to pass.

Also in 1938, an international conference was held in Evian, France, to discuss the plight of refugees in Nazi Germany. However, most of the 32 nations represented at the conference did not offer to accept more Jewish refugees. A notable exception was the Dominican Republic in the Caribbean, which offered refuge to 100,000 people. Holland and Denmark said they would accept additional Jewish refugees and would take Jewish children even without immigration papers.

The number of refugees increased dramatically after World War II ended in 1945. Millions of displaced persons (DPs), including orphaned children, needed food and housing. Relief organizations worked to reunite families and meet young refugees' needs while finding places for them to resettle. Some refugees spent years in war-ravaged countries before they could legally emigrate to North America or Palestine, which became the state of Israel in 1948.

After the United Nations decreed that a portion of the former Palestine would become the Jewish state of Israel, large numbers of Arab Palestinians became refugees. By 1967, hundreds of thousands of young people were among the one million Palestinian refugees who lived in shanty towns built by the United Nations Relief and Rehabilitation Administration (UNRRA) along the border of their former lands.

When the 1967 Six-Day War between Israel and the Arab states began, some of these Palestinian refugees anticipated an Arab victory and began moving with their cart-loads of belongings along the roads toward their former homes. Tanks and trucks staffed with Arab soldiers were also moving along these roads, which were bombed on Monday June 6, by Israeli fighter planes. The camp build-ings that housed the refugees were not hit, but some of the people walking on the roads died from the air strikes. Because debris blocked the roads so that food and other supplies could not reach the camps that week, children endured hunger and other deprivations. Young Palestinian refugees continued to suffer in the decades that followed.

Young refugees suffered greatly during the last half of the twentieth century, especially in civil wars. African youth were among the millions who became refugees during the last decades of the century. In 1994, for example, refugees from Rwanda fled to Zaire and tens of thousands camped in Goma, just across the border of Zaire. Cholera broke out in the camps at Goma because of unsanitary conditions, overcrowding, and lack of medicine and adequate food. At least 50,000 people, mostly children and women, died there.

A military coup unseated the elected government of Haiti in September 1991. In an effort to pressure the new leaders to restore democracy and civil rights, the United Nations imposed economic sanctions on the country. They voted to halt most shipments to Haiti, except for food and medicine. Thousands of Haitians fled the country. Known as Haitian Boat People, they tried to make their way by sea to the United States, Cuba, Panama, the Bahamas, or the Dominican Republic. Boats of refugees found in U.S. waters were intercepted by U.S. Coast Guard vessels and returned to Haiti, the result of a government policy that was implemented in 1992. Children were among those who died when their overcrowded or flimsy boats sank.

After President Bill Clinton took office in 1993, he implemented a new policy of screening Haitian refugees to determine whether they could be admitted to the United States as political refugees. To implement the policy, the U.S. Navy ship *Comfort* was positioned in Kingston Harbor to interview refugees. A journalist who visited the *Comfort* in June 1994 observed how children and adults were treated on the ship. People were given food and water and those who felt sick were placed in hospital beds: "Up a ramp on another level of the ship, they're photographed, sorted into family groups, and tagged with unremovable identity bracelets" ("Fatalities Among . . ." (1994). Then Creole-speaking interpreters talked with the Haitians and showed them how to fill out applications for political asylum and to help them through their interview. This policy enabled some Haitian youth to begin new lives in the United States. *See also* ARAB-ISRAELI WARS; ARMENIAN-TURKISH CONFLICT; BOMBINGS (WORLD WAR II); BOSNIA; CAMBODIA; CHECHNYA; CHILD-REFUGEE BILL (WAGNER-ROGERS BILL); CHILDREN'S TRANSPORTS (*KINDERTRANSPORT*); DISPLACED PERSONS (DPS) (WORLD WAR II); GREECE (WORLD WAR II); HARTZ, RUTH KAPP; HINDU-MUSLIM RIOTS (INDIA); LE CHAMBON-SUR-LIGNON; LIBERIAN CIVIL WAR; QUAKERS (SOCIETY OF FRIENDS); RELIEF ORGANIZATIONS; RUSSIAN REVOLUTION; RWANDA; SHANGHAI (WORLD WAR II); SOMALIA; UNACCOMPANIED CHILDREN; UNITED NATIONS RELIEF AND REHABILITATION ADMINISTRATION (UNRRA); VIETNAM WAR; WORLD WAR II; ZAIRE.

Further Reading: Associated Press, *Lightning Out of Israel* (1967); "Fatalities Among Haitian Boat People Increasing," National Public Radio (NPR), "Morning Edition," July 5, 1994; Clara Isaacman, as told to Joan Adess Grossman, *Clara's Story* (1984); Joanna Macrae and Anthony Zwi, eds., *War and Hunger* (1994); Office of the United Nations High Commissioner for Refugees, *Refugees at a Glance* (1995); "A Stolen Future," Amnesty International, 1977 at <http://www.amnesty.org/aiweek/aiweek97>; United Nations Children's Fund (UNICEF), *The State of the World's Children, 1996* (1996).

Relief Organizations

Numerous local, national, and international organizations have worked to help youth cope with the problems of war and its aftermath. Relief organizations provide food, clothing, shelter, educational supplies, medicine, health care, and a variety of social services, including psychological counseling and programs to reunite families. Some organizations, including the American Friends Service Committee (AFSC), were founded during World War I, when relief was needed on a massive scale. The Fellowship of Reconciliation (FOR), founded in England in 1914, also helped young people during wartime. During World War II, FOR helped rescue Jews and refugees from the Nazis. The group joined other organizations protesting the mandatory military draft and helped young conscientious objectors legally avoid taking part in combat.

Relief agencies operated on a large scale during World War II. A number of new programs were developed, and new relief organizations sprang up as needs arose in various European countries. Some organizations, such as the Polish Zegota, were organized by resistance groups to save the lives of people being hunted by the Nazis. Such organizations were founded in occupied France, Belgium, Holland, Italy, and other countries. They were able to hide Jewish children from the Nazis during the war.

After World War II ended, many organizations helped survivors recover and rebuild their lives. Among these hundreds of organizations were the United Nations Relief and Rehabilitation Agency (UNRRA), Young Men's Christian Association (YMCA), Quaker Relief Mission, British Save the Children Fund, American Relief for Poland, International Committee of the Red Cross (ICRC), American Red Cross (ARC), War Relief Services of the National Catholic Welfare Conference, and the American Joint Distribution Committee. In addition, new relief organizations—for example, CARE—were organized.

An organization called Concern, which became one of the largest international relief agencies in the world, worked with youth in war-torn countries. Volunteers helped families, supplied nurses for hospitals and homes, and provided food and other supplies as needed. Concern also tried to reunite unaccompanied children with their relatives. Workers went into villages with descriptions of unaccompanied children and asked local women to help them find the children's families.

Some organizations work primarily with refugees. The American Refugee Committee, a nonprofit organization based in Minneapolis, Minnesota, provides health care and self-help training for refugees around the world. The committee has helped youth in Zaire, Somalia, Rwanda, and Sudan, among other places. The United Nations also has a special division called the High Commissioner for Refugees to study the problems of refugees around the world and to recommend solutions. *See also* AMERICAN FRIENDS SERVICE COMMITTEE (AFSC); AMERICAN NEAR EAST REFUGEE AID (ANERA); AMERICARES FOUNDATION; ARMENIAN-TURKISH CONFLICT; CARE; CIMADE; COMMITTEE OF RESPONSIBILITY (COR); FEED THE CHILDREN; INTERNATIONAL RESCUE COMMITTEE (IRC); INTERNATIONAL VOLUNTEER SERVICES (IVS); *OEUVRE DE SECOURS AUX ENFANTS* (OSE); OPERATION BLESSING INTERNATIONAL (OBI); RED CROSS; REFUGEES; SAVE THE CHILDREN; SAVE THE CHILDREN ALLIANCE (INTERNATIONAL SAVE THE CHILDREN ALLIANCE); UNITED NATIONS CHILDREN'S FUND (UNICEF); UNITED NATIONS RELIEF AND REHABILITATION ADMINISTRATION (UNRRA); WAR CHILD; WORLD WAR II; ZEGOTA.

Further Reading: Millard J. Burr, *Requiem for the Sudan* (1995); Robert F. Gorman, *Historical Dictionary of Refugee and Disaster Relief Organizations* (1994); John E. Hutchinson, *Champions of Charity: War and the Rise of the Red Cross* (1997); Krishna Kumar, *Rebuilding Society After Civil War* (1996); Oliver Ramsbotham, with Tom Woodhouse, *Humanitarian Intervention in Contemporary Conflict* (1996); Arthur R. Simon, *Bread for the World* (1984).

Rescuers (Holocaust)

During World War II, young people helped rescue Jewish men, women, and children from Nazi persecution. Jews of all ages were persecuted in many ways—deprived of civil rights, ostracized, impoverished, and imprisoned—then systematically murdered. During this persecution, which became known as the Holocaust, some people living in Hitler's Germany or in Nazi-occupied territories became perpetrators or collaborators with the Nazis; the majority of non-Nazi Europeans were bystanders.

A minority of people helped the oppressed and actively rescued others, many of them children and young people. Rescuers included courageous young people, some only in their teens. Adults who helped and hid Jews also often had children in their families, and these children aided in the rescue work, kept the family's secret, and made sacrifices so their families could help others.

Researchers and authors Samuel and Pearl Oliner (1988) (Samuel Oliner was himself rescued as a child in Nazi-occupied Poland), studied more than 700 rescuers and their activities during the Holocaust. Rescuers provided Jews with food, clothing, medicine, money, shelter, transportation, and other basic needs. Some rescuers helped Jews escape Nazi-occupied lands or hid them in private homes, institutions, and other places. They created and distributed fake identity papers, work papers, food ration cards, and other documents Jews needed to live underground.

Rescuers who helped children find hiding places might also arrange for their transportation, accompany them to these places, and continue to visit them afterwards to make sure they were safe. Among these rescuers was Austrian Ernst Papanek, who worked to save children in southern France and Paris during the war. Rescuers came from all types of jobs and professions and every social and economic class. They had different religious and political beliefs. Thousands of rescuers were members of the clergy or religious orders. An estimated 5,000 Jewish children survived by hiding in monasteries and convents during the war.

In Poland, where the Nazis harshly persecuted the whole nation, the penalty for helping Jews was death, even when the rescuer was a child. The Nazi occupation put Poles on low food rations, so they had little to share. Yet, thousands of Poles saved lives. Some of them were remarkable young people. Holocaust survivor Liliana Zuker-Bujanowska later recalled how her family's 17-year-old maid helped her in the Warsaw Ghetto. Another Pole, Marisia Szul, was 15 when an 11-year-old Jewish girl, Frieda Saperstein, asked her to shelter herself, her mother, her baby brother, and a family friend. Szul lived in a tiny cottage but let the family stay in a barn in the yard where they hid all day, only moving about to bathe and do other necessary things at night. Szul did not turn in the family even when she was tortured during an interrogation by Nazi police. Explaining her actions during the war, Szul later said, "If I live, why couldn't somebody else? God gave life to everybody; . . . everybody has a right to live in this world" (Laska, 1984).

Halina Martin, another Polish rescuer, owned a large estate in Tarczyn. She began hiding Jews and donating money to help them early in the war when she became aware of Nazi brutality, especially toward children. One day when Nazis were conducting a major round-up of Jews in her region, Martin, aided by friends, some Polish police, and workers from her estate, tried to save as many people as possible, including a Jewish infant. After the round-up, laborers found a Jewish boy unconscious in a potato field. Martin later described his emaciated appearance.

> The bony arm that protruded from his tattered threadbare coat showed that he had been starved to the limit. His huge, grown man's shoes were well-worn. Flies settled around him. I gently rolled the boy on his back and lifted his hand from his face. The whites of his eyes were visible under the half-closed lids. The parted lips hardly took in any air. (Oliner, 1988)

After the boy had rested and eaten some food inside Martin's home, local police took him to a safe haven.

Martin had to face a Nazi interrogator who suspected she was aiding Jews. Eyewitnesses said she angrily told the officer,

> Listen, you. I'm a mother. For me, a child's a child whether it be German, Turkish, Jewish, Chinese, or Polish. If I find one lying in a ditch, I'll always feed it. You threaten death? Fine! I'd rather not live in a world where a woman, a mother, can't help a child. You can shoot me, hang me. Do you have children? Where? Are they in Berlin? Under the falling bombs? Who's going to help them when they're lying wounded in a ditch somewhere? (Oliner, 1988)

Many rescuers risked death. In Poland, Nazis sometimes forced whole towns to witness public hangings of Jews and the families, including children, who had helped them. Even so, about one-fourth of the more than 700 rescuers in a study conducted by Samuel and Pearl Oliner had at least one child aged 10 or younger. Father Jonas in Vidukle, Lithuania, died trying to defend some children. When he saw that the Jews in his city were being forced inside the synagogue and would soon be killed, he hid 30 Jewish children in his church. The Germans broke inside and demanded that he give them up. Father Jonas told the Germans they would have to kill him first. They shot him at once and proceeded to murder the defenseless children.

Hungarian Malka Csizmadia was 17 when the Nazis built a ghetto in her village, Satoraljaujhely. As time went on, they imprisoned Jewish residents. When Csizmadia saw the abandoned homes, with food still on the tables and children's toys lying on the floor, she decided to do something. Her mother joined her in rescuing several men from the ghetto before the Nazis could deport them. The two women arranged hiding places for the men in local farms, then personally took the men, disguised as peasant women, to these places.

Rescue activities often continued for years. More than 70 percent of the rescuers in the Oliners' study began aiding Jews by 1942 or before, and 65 percent continued until the war's end in 1945. About 56 percent were involved for two to five years or more. Nearly 65 percent helped more than 5 people, while 15 percent helped more than 100. More than half of these rescuers helped people they had not known before the war; nearly 90 percent helped at least one total stranger.

Even in Germany, with millions of Nazi Party members and supporters, strict laws, and prevalent police and informers, some people rejected anti-Jewish propaganda and helped Jews. About 25,000 German Jews survived the war. Some were aided by organized groups but most were saved by individual Germans.

Most rescuers remained unknown after the war. Many of them chose not to talk about their experiences. As the years went by, they were urged to speak about what they had seen and done, by journalists, historians, and authors, among others. Some received public recognition for their rescue work. Thousands of non-Jews who risked their lives during the Holocaust to save Jews out of humanitarianism, not for material gain, have been awarded the title Righteous Gentile by Yad Vashem (The Martyrs' and Heroes' Remembrance Authority) in Israel. *See also* Baublis, Petra; Belgium (World War II); Burzminski, Stefania Podgorska; CENTOS; CIMADE; Denmark (World War II); France (World War II); Gies, Miep and Gies, Jan; Graebe, Hermann; Hartz, Ruth Kapp; Hidden Children; Holland (World War II); Holocaust; Italy (World War II); Kalina, Antonin; Le Chambon-sur-Lignon; Norway (World War II); Pritchard, Marion von Binsbergen; Quakers (Society of Friends); Resistance Movements (World War II); Righteous Gentiles; Schindler, Oskar; Sendler, Irena; Simaite, Anna; Toll, Nelly Landau; Trocme, Andre and Trocme, Magda; Trocme, Daniel; Ukraine; Vos, Aart and Vos, Johtje; Wallenberg, Raoul; Westerweel, Joop; World War II; Yad Vashem; Zahajkewycz, Orest and Zahajkewycz, Helena.

Further Reading: Gay Block and Malka Drucker, *Rescuers* (1992); Vera Laska, ed., *Women of the Resistance and in the Holocaust* (1984); Richard C. Lukas, *Did the Children Cry?* (1994); Samuel P. Oliner and Pearl M. Oliner, *The Altruistic Personality: Rescuers of Jews in Nazi Europe* (1988); Carol Rittner and Sondra Meyers, eds., *The Courage to Care* (1986).

Resistance Movements (World War II)

Despite grave dangers, the World War II invasion and occupation of their homelands drove many young people in many countries to engage in resistance activities against the occupying forces. Some resistance was peaceful, but many other youths took up arms. Youthful resisters served as couriers, messengers, and spies and took part in sabotage, in printing and distributing resistance literature, in rescuing hunted people, in making and distributing false identity papers and ration cards, in hiding refugees, and in destroying enemy supplies and records.

The Germans sometimes offered children food and other bribes to gain information about the resistance. They encouraged them to report on parents or family members who were involved in resistance activities. They also brought children and teenagers into police headquarters to interrogate them about their family's activities when they suspected family members were involved in the resistance. Children endured physical and mental abuse during these interrogations.

In Nazi-occupied Europe, young people undertook various resistance activities. In Holland, youth were among the Dutch men who attacked German police in Amsterdam in 1941 and then organized the dock-workers' strike in February. Youths blew up railroad lines and trains carrying German supplies. They showed their hostility toward the Germans by wearing the Dutch national color (orange) and growing orange flowers, which were then legally banned in Holland because orange was the color of the Dutch royal family.

In Denmark, young people, particularly students, ran illegal presses to publish hundreds of anti-Nazi pamphlets and newspapers. They operated fishing vessels that carried Jews to neutral Sweden during a massive rescue that kept Jews from being deported by the Nazis. Other young people helped destroy records that showed where Jewish families lived in their towns. To show their defiance, young Danes wore the national colors, red and white, and took part in mass outdoor gatherings where people sang patriotic songs. They painted red "Vs" for victory on the windshields of German vehicles and slashed their tires. Some tried to knock down German soldiers with their bicycles.

French youth also showed their contempt for the Nazis. On November 11, 1940, several months after the occupation began, French students organized a demonstration. They chose this day, because it was the anniversary of France's victory over Germany in World War I. Thousands of high school and college students marched down the Champs Elysees, the most prominent boulevard in Paris, singing the national anthem and waving French flags. Boldly, they chanted, "Long Live France!" and "Down with Hitler!" German soldiers and police dispersed the crowds with clubs. Most of the 123 people who were arrested were high school students; some were sent to prison. Young French people also initiated and participated in spontaneous acts of protest. In June 1941, they joined with their elders in wearing a black ribbon to mark the day France had fallen to the Nazis one year earlier.

The French resistance was especially large and well-organized. Of the more than 200 acts of resistance it undertook in December 1941, many were carried out by young people. The Nazis arrested 27 youths, including 15-year-old Andre Kirschen, in 1941 and early 1942. These youths were put on trial in the spring of 1942 and found guilty. Because Kirschen was younger than 16, he could not be executed for his actions, but 23 other young men were shot by Nazi firing squads, and a young woman was guillotined. Nazi secret police killed Kirschen's brother and father while he was imprisoned.

In Greece, the national youth organization (EPON) did relief work and aided the anti-German resistance. Teenagers, both rural and urban, and younger children called Little Eagles—*Aetopoula*—worked against the invaders. A group called *Homeros* rescued Jews. Although females in rural Greece were traditionally expected to remain in domestic roles, girls and young women were also active in the resistance. They carried messages and brought food and other supplies to guerilla fighters hiding in the mountains. Some defied their parents' wishes to become involved.

Youths also took an active part in armed resistance. For example, about 5,000 young partisans fought against the Nazis in Poland after the Germans invaded that country in September 1939. Young Poles planted explosives in Nazi offices and blew up trains carrying supplies. Among those partisans was Byrna Bar Oni of Byten, Poland, who was in her late teens during the war.

Jewish youth were targeted for death and imprisoned in ghettos and camps. Nevertheless, some managed to help organize resistance as partisans and in ghettos, as well as in towns and cities throughout occupied Europe where they lived underground. For in-

stance, a Jewish teenager who was being transported to the Treblinka death camp threw a hand grenade at the camp guards. Others fought back physically when they were attacked. Jewish youth in Hungary carried out numerous acts of resistance and helped plant explosives in Gestapo buildings. Jewish youth also worked with resistance groups to fight the Nazis and help other Jews. In occupied France, young Jews with false identity papers worked with the *Oeuvres Secours des Enfants* (OSE). They cared for Jewish children living in group homes. After 1943, they helped move these children out of the homes and into convents, monasteries, or the homes of non-Jews who had agreed to hide them from the Nazis.

No accurate figures are available for the number of young people who joined fighting organizations in the Jewish ghettos in Poland or who joined partisan units in eastern Poland. Some historians have estimated that more than 2,000 teenagers actively fought in the ghettos, and about 5,000 young people fought with partisan units. Many teenage partisans who escaped from transports or ghettos made their way into the forests of Poland or the Ukraine. A few survived in the forest, eating what they could find or obtaining food and clothing from non-Jews until they could join partisan groups.

Some youths, such as 17-year-old Zofia Yamaika from Warsaw, died fighting with partisan groups. She managed to escape from a train that was taking her to a death camp. With the help of strangers in a rural area, she went underground and eventually joined a partisan group. Yamaika led some reconnaissance missions and helped derail German trains before being killed during a fight with German troops.

During World War II, young people in occupied countries engaged in sabotage as part of their resistance work against the invaders. In Europe, such resistance took place in France, Holland, Denmark, Poland, Hungary, and Belgium, among other places. Youth in the Philippines and other Asian countries occupied by the Japanese also engaged in sabotage.

In Belgium, a group of young Jews targeted trains carrying supplies to Germany. Raw materials from their country were typically shipped by rail, where the group could plant explosives along the tracks or plant flammable materials inside the cars. They also planted bombs on German ships.

Other European youth in occupied countries planted bombs in Nazi buildings or trucks and slashed the tires of their vehicles. They helped to blow up factories the Germans used to make ammunition, guns, and other military supplies, as well as service stations the Germans used for their vehicles. Besides planting these weapons, young people helped to construct the homemade bombs that were used by saboteurs.

In Amsterdam, teenager Jan Jonkheer and his schoolmates took part in sabotage operations. One night, Jan and his friend Piet volunteered to do some farmwork in the evening so they could help the resistance. They carried parcels of explosives with them on a truck that was delivering beets to a storehouse where they were supposed to unload the beets. As other members of the resistance took the parcels and tied them to some nearby railroad tracks, the boys kept watch along the railway line. While they were driving back to the farm, they heard the explosion. *See also* ANIELEWICZ, MORDECHAI; BAUM GROUP; BELGIUM (WORLD WAR II); BICYCLES; BIELSKI BROTHERS; DENMARK (WORLD WAR II); ESPIONAGE; GERMANY (WORLD WAR II); GHETTOS (WORLD WAR II); GIES, MIEP AND GIES, JAN; HEHALUTZ; HEPBURN, AUDREY; HOLLAND (WORLD WAR II); IDENTITY PAPERS; INTERROGATIONS; ITALY (WORLD WAR II); JEHOVAH'S WITNESSES; JEWISH FIGHTERS ORGANIZATION (JFO); *OEUVRES DE SECOURS AUX ENFANTS* (OSE); ROMANI (GYPSIES); SIMA; "THE SIXTH"; UKRAINE (WORLD WAR II); UNDERGROUND PRESSES; VIETNAM WAR; WARSAW GHETTO; THE WHITE ROSE; WORLD WAR II; ZAZOU; ZEGOTA.

Further Reading: Lore Cowan, ed., *Children of the Resistance* (1969); M.D.R. Foot, *Resistance* (1977); Schmuel Krakowski, *The War of the Doomed* (1984); Vera Laska, *Women of the Resistance and in the Holocaust* (1984); Don Lawson, *The French Resistance* (1984); Jane Marks, *The Hidden Children* (1993); Margaret Rossiter, *Women in the Resistance* (1986); Yuri Suhl, ed., *They Fought Back* (1975); Dirk Van der Heide (pseud.), *My Sister and I* (1941).

Revolutionary War. *See* AMERICAN REVOLUTION

The Ribbon

To mark the fortieth anniversary of the atomic bombings of Hiroshima and Nagasaki and make a vivid plea for peace, hundreds of thousands of people throughout the world made banners that were joined to make The Ribbon. On August 4, 1985, this peace ribbon, which measured more than 10 miles in length, was used to encircle the Pentagon, seat of the U.S. military establishment, in Arlington, Virginia.

The idea for this peace ribbon came from Justine Merritt, a former teacher and a grandmother of seven. After attending a religious retreat, Merritt found herself becoming increasingly concerned about the fate of new generations in a nuclear age. She came up with the idea of a huge embroidered ribbon that could be wrapped around the Pentagon "like tying a ribbon around your finger. It will serve as a gentle reminder that we love the earth and its people" (*The Ribbon*, 1985).

Because Merritt could not finance this project alone, she asked everyone on her Christmas card list to make a yard-long tapestry based on the theme "What I cannot bear to think of as lost in a nuclear war." These people were urged, in turn, to recruit everyone on their holiday mailing list and other friends. The number of participants grew to include many people, including artists and craftspeople, who contributed to this huge needlework project. The panels, most of which measured 36 by 18 inches, were diverse—silk-screened, painted, tie-dyed, appliqued, quilted—in myriad colors.

Many children and young people helped make panels. Children worked on panels in schools and Sunday school classes, as well as during church youth group meetings. Students in college art departments also designed and completed panels. Some panels were joint efforts involving children from different countries. A group of children in Largo, Maryland, collaborated with children from the Soviet Embassy School to make a Soviet-American segment for the Ribbon. Children in the Netherlands worked with adults to create a panel featuring colorful tulips.

Young people also marched with adults at the Pentagon when the panel was unfurled. Merritt said she hoped that,

> With its palm prints of infants, its footprints of toddlers, its applique of the Golden Gate Bridge or the New York skyline, its quilted pizza or embroidered flowers . . . [the Ribbon] will encourage [leaders from around the world] to move ahead with greater resolve, to move ahead cautiously, not always easily, but continuously, toward a planet without nuclear weapons. (*The Ribbon*, 1985)

Further Reading: *The Ribbon: A Celebration of Life* (1985).

Righteous Gentiles

Thousands of people who rescued Jews during the Holocaust of World War II have been formally honored by Yad Vashem (the Martyrs' and Heroes' Remembrance Authority) in Israel as Righteous Gentiles. These courageous people, many of whom saved children and young people, include rescuers who were young adults at that time. To be designated a Righteous Gentile, a person must have helped to save the life of one or more Jews during the period of Nazi persecution in Europe, without having done so for material gain. The Righteous Gentile's behavior must surpass ordinary help, such as having given someone food, although Yad Vashem notes that any helping activity is praiseworthy. Besides refusing to do evil, to be honored by Yad Vashem, a person must have taken positive action to help Jews despite the risks or hardships involved. Yad Vashem examines eyewitness testimony from Holocaust survivors to determine who qualifies for this honor.

As of 1997, 13,700 Righteous Gentiles had been recognized by Yad Vashem. Among them is Oskar Schindler, whose saving of more than 1,100 Jews was depicted in the 1993 film *Schindler's List*. A carob tree in honor of each individual is planted along the Avenue of the Righteous or on a terraced hillside located beyond the plaza near the Holocaust Museum. A plaque on the tree contains the name and nationality of the honored person. Righteous Gentiles also receive a certificate and an engraved medal from Yad Vashem. The front of the medal shows an arm reaching up through barbed wire toward a globe; the other side features a view of Yad Vashem. Inscribed on the medal are these words from the holy book called the *Talmud*: "Whoever saves a single soul, it is as if he had saved the whole world." *See also* BURZMINSKA, STEFANIA PODGORSKA; DENMARK (WORLD WAR II); GIES, MIEP AND GIES, JAN; HARTZ, RUTH KAPP; HIDDEN CHILDREN; HOLLAND (WORLD WAR II); HOLOCAUST; ITALY (WORLD WAR II); LE CHAMBON-SUR-LIGNON; NORWAY (WORLD WAR II); POLAND (WORLD WAR II); PRITCHARD, MARION VON BINSBERGEN; RESCUERS (HOLOCAUST); SCHINDLER, OSKAR; SENDLER, IRINA; SIMAITE, ANNA; TROCME, ANDRE AND TROCME, MAGDA; TROCME, DANIEL; UKRAINE; VOS, AART AND VOS, JOHTJE; WALLENBERG, RAOUL; WESTERWEEL, JOOP; WORLD WAR II; YAD VASHEM; ZAHAJKEWYCZ, OREST AND ZAHAJKEWYCZ, HELENA.

Further Reading: Eva Fogelman, *Conscience and Courage: Rescuers of Jews During the Holocaust* (1994); Information from Yad Vashem at <www.yadvashem.org.il>.

Ringelblum Archives

During World War II, university professor and Jewish historian Emmanuel Ringelblum mobilized young people in the Warsaw Ghetto to create a historical record of their lives under Nazi oppression. Ringelblum was forced into the Warsaw Ghetto in 1941 and kept a written diary of his experiences. He was determined to compile written records that would bear witness to what happened in the ghetto during the Nazi occupation. To carry out this task, Ringelblum organized a team of researchers that included young people. The group met secretly each week to present their reports and writings and discuss their work. In addition to their diaries and journals, they accumulated other important papers, some of them from the Germans. They kept leaflets, underground newspapers, poems, drawings, maps, photos, and copies of decrees. Those who worked with the group knew they risked death or severe punishment if they were caught.

When the Nazis began deporting residents from the ghetto in 1942, Ringelblum's group buried their materials. With help from the Polish underground, the group was also able to smuggle some documents and information about the ghetto to England. This material included the information that 164 young German Jews, mostly members of pioneering youth movements, had been sent to the death camp at Treblinka in April 1942. Some of the writings and documents compiled by Ringelblum's group were discovered after the war. They provide important information about how people lived and died in the ghetto and about the lives of young Jews during the Holocaust. On May 7, 1944, the Nazis executed Emmanuel Ringelblum and his wife and child on the ruins of the Warsaw Ghetto. *See also* DIARIES; HOLOCAUST; WARSAW GHETTO.

Further Reading: Chaim A. Kaplan, *Scroll of Agony* (1973); Emmanuel Ringelblum, *Notes from the Warsaw Ghetto* (1958).

Rivesaltes

During World War II, many young people suffered and perished at the Nazi concentration camp at Rivesaltes in southern France. Jews from Poland, Germany, and other countries were sent here, sometimes as a stopping place on the way to Drancy, another camp in France, from which they were usually sent to Auschwitz, a death camp in Poland. In 1940, children and the elderly made up most of the transports of people who came to Rivesaltes from Germany and the Alsace-Lorraine region of France. Many children died along the way or perished in the camp from disease or malnutrition.

A minority of youth managed to escape from Rivesaltes and survive the war. Born in Lodz, Poland, 13-year-old Henri Parens arrived at Rivesaltes with his mother. Together, they devised a plan for Henri's escape, choosing May Day, May 1, 1942, as a good day for the attempt because May Day was a European holiday when fewer guards might be posted. Following his mother's directions, Henri walked through a specific area of the camp, reached a highway, then boarded a train to Marseilles where he located a Jewish social services agency. The agency sent him to a home for refugee children in Boulouris, a town in southern France. About 30 young people hid in this villa during the war. More than 18,000 people, including thousands of children, eventually spent time at the Rivesaltes camp. They included Jews, Romani (Gypsies), and Spanish refugees.

German refugees David Katz, age 12, and his parents also were imprisoned in Rivesaltes in the summer of 1942. The camp was hot and unsanitary, and the hordes of mosquitoes spread typhus, malaria, and other diseases. Members of the *Oeuvre de Secours aux Enfants (OSE)*, a French children's aid group, managed to secure the release of some of the children in the camp, including David, whose parents insisted that he save himself. He was taken to an orphanage in Limoges where he lived for a time before Nazis raided the area. Katz survived the war in a series of hiding places in France. When the war ended, he found out that his parents had both died in the Auschwitz death camp. *See also* CONCENTRATION CAMPS (WORLD WAR II); DRANCY; FRANCE (WORLD WAR II); HOLOCAUST; *OEUVRE DE SECOURS AUX ENFANTS*.

Further Reading: Deborah Dwork, *Children with a Star: Jewish Youth in Nazi Europe* (1991); John F. Sweets, *The Politics of Resistance in France, 1940-1944* (1976).

Romani (Gypsies)

During the Holocaust of World War II, Nazi Germany planned the annihilation of all Romani (commonly but incorrectly called Gypsies) in Europe. An estimated 700,000 Romani lived in Europe before the war began. About one-third—some 200,000 to 250,000 people—died in death camps or were murdered by the Nazi mobile killing squads called *Einsatzgruppen*. Thousands of other Romani were sterilized, tortured, and injured.

During the 1300s, Romani from two different tribes—Roma and Sinti—came to Europe from India. The Romani were skillful weavers, jewelry-makers, basket-makers, musicians, and dancers. They were often persecuted because of their unfamiliar customs and dark skin and were denied access to craft guilds and other ways of making a living. Governments in countries where they settled often passed laws against them. In some cases, officials offered bounties to people who killed Romani.

When the Nazis came to power in Germany in 1933, they required Romani of all ages to register with the government. During this process, children were photographed and fingerprinted. The Nazis claimed the Romani had "evil blood" and denied any rights to a person who had at least two Romani great-grandparents. Nazi laws declared that Romani were "unfit for human reproduction" and "not worthy of living." This persecution intensified in the mid-1930s. In 1936, a group of Romani who lived in Germany were arrested and taken to Dachau, a concentration camp near Munich, Germany.

Beginning in 1939, young Romani were sent to concentration camps. The first mass arrests took place in Germany and Austria, followed by large-scale round-ups in 1941 and 1943, during which Romani were arrested in Poland, Yugoslavia, Hungary, Romania, Belgium, The Netherlands, and Czechoslovakia. Large numbers of children were among these deportees. Some young Romani eluded their captors, and some joined resistance groups fighting against the Nazis. Their fellow partisans said that Gypsy youth, often armed only with knives, displayed uncommon courage as they fought against heavily armed soldiers. A number of Romani tried to reach Spain to escape persecution.

At the Sachsenhausen concentration camp in Austria, Romani children and adults were subjected to cruel Nazi experiments. Young men and women were sterilized as part of the Nazi genocidal plan to wipe out their bloodlines. At the Ravensbruck camp, 55 doctors sterilized 120 young Romani girls. During the experiments, the victims were denied any pain-killing anesthesia.

By 1942, Nazi officials were actively killing groups of Romani both in camps and in the countryside. Death squads rounded up men, women, and children in the Crimea, Baltic states, and Ukraine and shot them around mass graves. In December 1941, 800 men, women and children were shot by Nazi killing squads. Yugoslav peasants reported hearing the cries of children who were being taken away by truck to be killed. About 19,000 were gassed to death in August 1943. Seventeen-year-old Maria Sava Moise barely escaped death when Romani in her region were deported in cattle cars to the Ukraine. Moise later said that the group was "marched to a farm and left in open fields to die slowly" (Ayer, 1998). Her sister died in that field, but Maria was saved because her father, a member of the Romanian army, was stationed nearby. He was able to smuggle his daughter out on a troop train heading back to Romania.

Large numbers of Romani were later sent to death camps. Thousands of Romani were kept in what was called the Gypsy Family Camp at Auschwitz, the notorious death camp in Poland. Their one "privilege" in the camp was being allowed to stay together as families. Parents encouraged the children to play games amd learn traditional songs. The Nazi director of Auschwitz, Dr. Josef Mengele, sometimes removed Romani children for his "medical experiments." In an area called the Revier, Romani between ages 8 and 18 were subjected to X-ray experimentation. Women were sterilized in a painful and dangerous way by having a solution of silver nitrate injected into their oviducts (egg-carrying ducts). The resulting inflammation caused terrible pain and other symptoms and closed the oviducts permanently, making the women infertile. The solution could also seep into other areas of the body. At least four girls were known to have died in agonizing pain from peritonitis (inflammation of the stomach) after this procedure. During one week in 1942, more than 100 children were sterilized in this way.

Conditions worsened during late 1943 and early 1944. By this time, Nazi leaders had decided to exterminate all Romani, just as they planned to kill all Jews. By 1944, many Romani children were dead or dying of illness and starvation. The Gypsy camp at Auschwitz was liquidated in August 1944. On the evening of August 2, the camp was shut down. A Jewish prisoner at Auschwitz, Menache Lorinczi, who was 10 at the time, later recalled that night.

> We heard a terrible cry. The Romani (Gypsies) knew they were going to be put to death, and they cried all night. They had been at Auschwitz a long time. They had seen the Jews arriving at the ramps, had watched the selections where old people and children went to the gas chambers. (Lagnado and Dekel, 1991)

Families were separated. A few adults were sent to Germany as slave laborers, but about 3,000 of the women, children, and elderly Romani at the camp were killed. Historians estimate that between 70,000 to 200,000 Romani children were killed by the Nazis during the war. A few Romani youths managed to escape round-ups, deportations, and death at the camps and joined resistance groups and partisan units who fought to defeat their oppressors. *See also* AUSCHWITZ-BIRKENAU; EXPERIMENTS, NAZI; GENOCIDE; HOLOCAUST; "MASTER RACE"; MENGELE, JOSEF.

Further Reading: Eleanor Ayer, *Holocaust* (1998); Ina Friedman, *The Other Victims* (1990); Lucette Matalon Lagnado and Sheila Cohn Dekel, *Children of the Flames* (1991); Vera Laska, ed., *Women of the Resistance and in the Holocaust* (1984); Jan Yoors, *Crossings* (1971).

Romanov Children

During the Russian Revolution of 1917-1918, the five children of the last Romanov ruler of Russia, Tsar Nicholas II, were killed, along with their parents, by Bolshevik revolutionaries. The murdered children included four Grand Duchesses: Olga, 23; Tatiana, 21; Marie, 19; and Anastasia, 17. The youngest child, and only son, was 14-year-old Alexis,

who had been born with the incurable hereditary disease hemophilia.

After the February Revolution in 1917, Tsar Nicholas II abdicated and different revolutionary factions vied for power. The family was forced to live under house arrest in various places while the new government decided their fate. During their months in captivity at Governor's House, the five young people tried to continue their lessons, to cook, to do needlework, and to walk outdoors when that was permitted. At night, they read, played card games with their parents, and made up plays. They performed these plays for the grown-ups, who included some family servants as well as the former tsar and his wife Alexandra.

Because the family was not allowed to go out to church, an altar and chapel were improvised inside Governor's House. Photographs taken by the children's English-born tutor, Charles Sydney Gibbes, show that the girls had put family photos and religious icons on the walls of the room where they slept.

In spring 1918, Nicholas, Alexandra, and the five children were taken to Ipatiev House in Ekaterinburg in Siberia where they were held hostage for several months. The family was under constant guard and the young people could not even use a bathroom without supervision. They had little to eat—black bread, tea, some soup or cooked potatoes—and shared a common bowl of food, which they were forced to eat without utensils. The family was unable to obtain the medicines they needed for Alexis. They were allowed only two 30-minute walks each day. Observers later said they prayed often and read the Bible together.

The Romanovs were killed in the basement of the house in Ekaterinburg on July 16, 1918. An eyewitness to the murders, Pavel Medvedev, later said, "Shortly after one o'clock a.m., the Tsar, the Tsaritsa, their four daughters, the maid, the doctor, the cook and the waiter left their rooms. The Tsar carried the heir in his arms" (Trewin, 1975).

The entire family was shot numerous times; the soldiers used pistols at close range and then followed with bayonets. The guards had been ordered to kill the family by Bol-

Tzar Nicholas II of Russia (second from left) stands next to his four daughters and his son Alexis (foreground). The entire family was executed by the Bolsheviks in 1918. *Corbis/Hulton-Deutsch Collection.*

shevik leaders in Moscow who feared that anti-revolutionary forces heading toward Ekaterinburg might free the tsar and reinstate the Russian monarchy.

For years, mystery shrouded the exact circumstances of the deaths and the location of the bodies. In the decades that followed, several women claimed to be the Grand Duchess Anastasia. The most persistent and convincing claimant was Anna Anderson, who maintained that she was Anastasia right up to her death in the United States in 1984.

In the 1990s, DNA experts conducted genetic testing on tissue that had been taken from Anna Anderson during surgery and subsequently stored in a hospital laboratory. The DNA did not match samples taken from members of the Romanov family but did match the DNA from members of a humble family in Poland. Most historians have since concluded that all seven members of the Romanov family died in July 1918. *See also* RUSSIAN REVOLUTION.

Further Reading: Robert K. Massie, *Nicholas and Alexandra* (1967); Robert K. Massie, *The Romanovs* (1995); J.C. Trewin, *The House of Special Purpose* (1975).

Rosie the Riveter

During World War II, as men went off to war, young women in the United States took jobs in the defense industry. They worked in steel mills, shipyards, factories, lumberyards, and other places making planes, ships, munitions, and other necessary war materials. They became electricians, welders, mechanics, boilermakers, streetcar operators, bus drivers, and crane operators, among other things. Of the six million women who took these jobs, a number were between the ages of 18 and 21. Young men below the draft age of 18 also filled defense plant jobs.

On May 29, 1943, the cover of the *Saturday Evening Post* featured a painting of "Rosie the Riveter" by artist Norman Rockwell. The model for the picture was 19-year-old Mary

This *Saturday Evening Post* cover from May 1943 offers Norman Rockwell's depiction of "Rosie the Riveter." *Library of Congress LC-USZ-62-75181.*

Doyle of Arlington, Vermont. A song about "Rosie the Riveter" was also popular during the war. Throughout the United States, various young plant workers named Rosie appeared in photos that showed them doing their factory jobs and on posters and in newsreels and films. *See also* DEFENSE PLANTS; UNITED STATES (WORLD WAR II).

Further Reading: Penny Colman, *Rosie the Riveter* (1995).

Rotterdam. *See* HOLLAND (WORLD WAR II)

Round-Ups

During World War II, Nazis and their collaborators in various occupied countries seized millions of youths during round-ups of Jews who were then deported to concentration and death camps. Round-ups took place in Germany, Austria, Poland, France, Holland, Romania, Bulgaria, Yugoslavia, Hungary, Italy, and other Nazi-occupied countries. In some places, notably Denmark,

organized, large-scale resistance prevented the Nazis from rounding up large numbers of people.

Round-ups occurred in rural areas and cities and in ghettos where large groups of Jews had already been imprisoned. These arrests were highly organized, and victims were often harshly treated. People who tried to resist were beaten or shot; non-Jews who tried to help could be beaten, arrested, or killed.

Sometimes thousands of people were seized during Nazi round-ups. On the night of July 16-17, 1942, nearly 13,000 foreign-born Jews living in France were arrested during the massive raids conducted by the Nazis and their collaborators. Nine thousand adults were deported to the Auschwitz death camp in Poland. The 4,000 children were deported a few weeks later, and none of them survived the war. These children, whose parents had already been deported, had to face death alone.

One witness to a round-up in Krakow, Poland, later told author David A. Adler how children in the Bochnia Ghetto were taken away by Nazis.

> First they took the older children and then the younger ones. I saw mothers holding onto their children's clothing and begging, begging the Nazis, "Please, please don't take my child." By the time the children were loaded into open trucks, the mothers were exhausted from crying. Then, while everyone watched, one of the Nazis took a machine gun and shot a few of the grieving mothers. (Adler, 1989)

In her diary, teenager Janina Bauman described a round-up that took place in August 1942 in the Warsaw Ghetto.

> From our fifth-floor flat, we heard the uproar of troops bursting into the courtyard, the ear-splitting whistle, the loud cry: "*Alle Juden raus, schnell, schnell, alle Juden herunter*" ("All Jews out, quick, quick, all Jews down here") repeated in Polish. Then the sounds of dozens of feet running down, down to disaster. Then shouts, screaming, whistles, lamenting in the courtyard. . . . Two single shots. . . . A turmoil of violence and misery. . . . Soon we heard a rumble

of heavy boots climbing up the stairs, of smashed locks and doors flung open by force; the hunters were searching through the flats. (Bauman, 1945)

Ben Edelbaum, who was born in 1928, recalled what happened in the Lodz Ghetto when he was a teenager imprisoned there.

The Nazis would come for us in the night or the early morning. It was always the same. We awoke to the sounds of screams and shots. People ran in panic from street to street, trying to escape. Of course, there was no escape. Little children were dragged from their mothers' arms. Husbands were taken from their wives. Grandparents were torn from their families. Sometimes we heard shots. (Baldwin, 1991)

One day, the Nazis took Edelbaum's 13-year-old friend Sala, who had long feared arrest; the Nazis grabbed the girl away from her parent and loaded her onto a truck, along with other children. Sala had once asked Edelbaum, "Why did this have to happen to us? Why were we born now?" (Baldwin, 1981). *See also* BAUM, FROIM; DENMARK (WORLD WAR II); DEPORTATIONS; DRANCY; FINLAND (WORLD WAR II); FRANCE (WORLD WAR II); GHETTOS (WORLD WAR II); HIDDEN CHILDREN; HOLLAND (WORLD WAR II); HUNGARY (WORLD WAR II); ITALY (WORLD WAR II); KORCZAK, JANUSZ; PRITCHARD, MARION VON BINSBERGEN; RESCUERS (HOLOCAUST); RESISTANCE MOVEMENTS (WORLD WAR II); RIVESALTES; SEPARATIONS, FAMILY; "THE SIXTH"; WORLD WAR II; YUGOSLAVIA (WORLD WAR II).

Further Reading: David A. Adler, *We Remember the Holocaust* (1989); Margaret Baldwin, *The Boys Who Saved the Children* (1991); Janina Bauman, *Winter in the Morning* (1945); Gilles Perrault, *Paris Under the Occupation* (1979).

Russia (World War II). *See* SOVIET UNION (WORLD WAR II)

Russian Revolution (1917)

Young people in Russia played a major role in sparking the revolution that led to the end of tsarist rule in 1917 and created a new political and economic system based on communist ideals drawn from the writings of Karl Marx and others. Children and young people also suffered many hardships because of the revolution and during the subsequent civil war of the early 1920s. In the decades leading up to the revolution, students from Russian schools and universities were involved in efforts to overthrow the tsarist system. They joined discussion groups and radical political movements that advocated major changes. Young people made up a large number of the revolutionaries who moved into the Russian countryside during the late 1800s to teach illiterate peasants how to read and to spread their Marxist political philosophy. Most of these revolutionaries were students in universities, technical schools, and high schools. Thousands of young people also traveled around the Russian countryside in the summer of 1874 to help the peasants deal with a severe famine and to gain support for political change.

That year, tsarist police arrested 1,600 young people, many of whom were between the ages of 16 and 20, on charges of joining illegal organizations that aimed to overthrow the government. Sixty-five of these youths were convicted and sentenced to hard labor in Siberia for as long as 10 years. Young people also became terrorists. Some used guns or bombs to attack members of the Russian imperial family or high-ranking officials. A 19-year-old man named Rysakov threw the bomb that killed Tsar Alexander II in 1881. He and other members of his group, The People's Will, which organized the assassination, were tried, convicted, and publicly hung.

By 1905, a number of Russians were committed to asking their leaders for change. On January 22, 1905, youths were among the victims of the incident that became known as Bloody Sunday. About 200,000 men, women, and children had gathered for a march organized by an Orthodox priest named Father Gapon, who had written the tsar a letter informing him that the march would take place. He assured the tsar that the march would be peaceful and that the people had a petition they would present to him at the Winter Palace. The petition asked the tsar to improve the wages and working conditions of the poor. However, the tsar did not appear to receive the petition and military guards were sent to stop the march. They shot at the crowds, killing more than 500 people and wounding thousands more.

The February Revolution that prompted the tsar to abdicate in 1917 was relatively peaceful. However, once the tsar was overthrown, various groups, including the Bolsheviks (later called Communists) vied with one another for power within the provisional government. After the Bolshevik Revolution in November 1917, during which the Bolsheviks seized power, a civil war erupted in Russia between the Bolshevik (Red) forces and the counter-revolutionary (White) forces. The children of families that supported the revolution joined adults in building trenches and barricades for the Red Guard in Petrograd (later Leningrad), so the Bolsheviks could keep out their enemies. Thousands of young people who were involved in this effort carried rifles, picks, spades, and cartridge belts.

During the fighting and violence that ensued after the tsar abdicated, many young people went hungry. Families had to trade valuables for food, and meals often consisted of only bread and water, dried beans, or oats that had once been used for horse feed. Margarita Zarudny, a child during this time, later recalled that, "One time my aunt and uncle brought home a little round sack of sunflower seeds. They'd swapped a dress for them" (Lourie, 1991). These seeds had to last for days, so the family doled them out slowly.

Some children moved with their families from one town to another, taking refuge in different parts of Russia to escape the fighting and to find food and shelter. Among these people was Kyra Karadja, who was nine in 1917. After her father was arrested by Bolsheviks because he had once been a government official, she and her siblings fled to the home of an aunt in Petrograd. Later, they stayed with other relatives in the Caucasus region. Eventually reunited, the whole family went to the United States as refugees.

In 1918, food shortages were acute and rationing was enforced. Karadja stood in lines to receive rations of bread and dried beans. Schoolchildren were given small meals that usually consisted of cornbread and tea with some brown sugar. Clothing was also in short supply, and young people wore the same shabby, mended clothing over and over. Children had rope-soled sandals for everyday wear; their regular shoes, reserved for special occasions, were often too tight.

Among the most famous young victims of the revolution were the four daughters and one son of the former Russian tsar, Nicholas II. Nicholas, his wife Alexandra, the five children, and several servants were all murdered in 1918. The Romanov children ranged in age from 14 to 23 when they died.

During the civil war, some families were impoversihed when the new Bolshevik government confiscated private property, such as livestock, buildings, mills, and tools. Government committees decided how food and other scarce necessities should be distributed. Children died and became ill as hunger, death, and destruction plagued rural areas. Food shortages were aggravated by drought and locusts, which further reduced crop yields. By 1921, about 7.5 million Russians had died of starvation, illness, or exposure.

After the revolution, young people faced numerous adjustments. Some of them became embroiled in political battles in their schools. Youths who remained loyal to the tsar or to religious traditions, which were banned by the communist government, were harassed by fellow students and school officials who supported the new regime. Those who spoke out against the government risked arrest. Young people were expected to join Leagues of Young Communists and other groups that were set up to support the new government. The league conducted classes and told youth that religious teachings were false and that they should renounce religion, along with many other features of tsarist Russia. Young people who supported communist ideals worked hard to build a new society and some became leaders of youth groups in their schools and communities. *See also* ROMANOV CHILDREN; UKRAINE; WILD CHILDREN.

Further Reading: Kyra Karadja, *Kyra's Story* (1975); Richard Lourie, *Russia Speaks* (1991); Richard Pipes, *The Russian Revolution* (1990).

Rwanda

In the twentieth century, millions of people died and millions more suffered during brutal tribal conflicts and civil wars that erupted in the east central African nation of Rwanda. During these conflicts, hundreds of thousands of children were the victims of genocide, mutilations, and sexual assaults, and many others succumbed to hunger, disease, and other war-related hardships.

For centuries, people populated this region because of its rich soil. The Hutu and Tutsi peoples had lived in the region since at least 800 B.C., but around A.D. 1500, Tutsi rulers took control of the area and forced the Hutu into a lower social class. Europeans colonized the region during the 1800s, and Belgium gained control of Rwanda after World War I ended in 1918. European colonial governments promoted disunity and conflicts among the tribes to better maintain their own control.

In the 1950s, Rwanda became independent, but violence recurred as Hutus and Tutsis vied for power. In 1965-1966, Tutsi troops killed some 5,000 Hutu civilians. Fighting also occurred between northern and southern Tutsi. From 1972 to 1974, between 80,000 and 200,000 Hutu civilians were murdered and another 150,000 fled as refugees. During the 1980s, the Hutus organized their own troops and attacked and killed thousands of Tutsi. Tutsi troops retaliated by slaughtering an estimated 20,000 Hutus.

Civil war broke out in 1990 when the Tutsi-led Rwandan Patriotic Front fought the Rwandan army, which was dominated by Hutus. Civilians, including youth, were killed on both sides. More deaths occurred in 1993 as leaders on both sides advocated killing people of all ages whom they labeled as enemies. Tutsis killed between 30,000 and 50,000 Hutus. About 600,000 people, mostly Hutus, fled the country.

The suffering in the region continued after Tutsi extremists seized power in the neighboring country of Burundi in 1994-1995; they extinguished Hutu neighborhoods in the Zairean capital, Kinshasa. A devastating massacre took place in Rukara in May 1994. Hundreds of Tutsis sought refuge inside a Roman Catholic Church because people had been able to rely on the tradition of receiving sanctuary inside a church, which most armies around the world have viewed as "off limits." The priest gathered vegetables for the refugees to eat. When about 600 men left the church to seek protection from the local officials, they were attacked and killed by Hutu militia

Afterwards, soldiers blasted through the church door with a grenade and fired on the women and children hiding inside, using bullets, grenades, and mortars. Father Oreste Incimatata, who hid in the rectory during the massacre, claimed that the women and children cried and prayed during their ordeal and moans could be heard for hours afterward. Reporters who visited this village and others in the region saw dozens of corpses, empty villages, and abandoned fields.

The two sides were close to reaching a settlement to end the fighting in 1994, and Rwandan refugees had hopes of returning to their country when Hutu extremists gained control of Rwanda and began mass killings of Tutsis.

Another 500,000 people, mostly Tutsis and moderate Hutus, were massacred in 1994. Army leaders urged peasants to take up arms against the Tutsis, and whole families were sometimes killed at once. They were shot, clubbed, and stabbed with machetes. Some were tortured and assaulted before they were killed.

Some 2 million Hutu refugees poured into Zaire, Tanzania, and Burundi, and the war spread into Zaire, where Hutu soldiers fought against Tutsis and other local ethnic groups. To help feed these displaced people, the World Food Programme of the United Nations staged a huge airlift, bringing in several hundred tons of grain each day in the spring and early summer. Relief workers from CARE and

Save the Children also helped those who were injured and sick.

However, the refugees were so numerous and lacked so many things that thousands died from disease and malnutrition. Overcrowding and the lack of sanitary facilities, medicines, and nutritious foods aggravated their plight. Malaria, a disease carried by mosquitoes, and cholera struck the camps. A cholera epidemic claimed the lives of many children during the summer of 1994. This disease, which is spread through contaminated water, causes severe diarrhea that can lead to fatal dehydration, especially in children. Young people made up the majority of the hundreds of people who died each day in late July.

Thousands of unaccompanied children were placed at the Ndosho refugee camp in Goma, just over the border in Zaire. Some of them had made their way to Zaire alone after seeing their families killed by rival tribes, often in their own homes. Thatched huts were hastily set up to accommodate refugees. Visitors to this camp heard sorrowful children crying out for their parents. Young people from Zaire were among the volunteers who worked at the camps distributing food and clothing. UNICEF workers brought clean water, sacks of wheat, powdered milk, medicines, and fluids to help treat children suffering from diarrhea.

By 1995, the population of Rwanda had fallen from 7.9 million to 5 million. An estimated 114,000 children were separated from their families. As of 1995, some 2 million refugees from this war-torn region remained in camps sponsored by the United Nations in Tanzania and Zaire. In 1996, the government of Tanzania ordered Rwandan refugees to leave because of the strain their presence had placed on the Tanzanian economy. Refugees had cut down large areas of trees for firewood. After the Rwandans left, however, about 100,000 refugees from Zaire and 150,000 from Burundi sought refuge in Tanzania.

Human rights groups estimated that a Rwandan refugee was dying every minute. The capital, Kigali, was devastated. The United Nations sent peacekeeping forces to prevent further outbreaks of violence. Although the war officially ended in 1995, fighting continued off and on and spread to the adjoining Congo in 1996, where many Hutu refugees were killed. The major battles then returned to Rwanda where Hutu rebels killed Tutsi civilians in 1997. The Rwandan Army, dominated by a Tutsi minority, was in conflict with Hutu guerilla bands that said they planned to kill all Tutsis and take control of the government.

On December 11, 1997, Hutu guerillas killed 272 people and wounded hundreds of others at a Tutsi refugee camp. Babies and children of all ages were among the victims, many of whom were slashed with machetes. As refugees continued to suffer and people continued to live with the threat of violence, the United Nations and the international court began investigating the war in Rwanda. Nearly 90,000 men were arrested and charged with war crimes. A United Nations tribunal in Tanzania began conducting the first war crimes trials seen in Rwanda and Burundi.

Human rights groups estimate that the conflicts between tribes led to more than one million deaths. The children who survived being killed outright suffered from malnutrition, starvation, diseases, and the loss of one or both parents. They were also among the more than one million people left homeless by the fighting and destruction.

Food supplies remained a problem because the war had damaged fields, grazing lands, crops, and livestock. Poor families no longer had the cattle, coffee crops, or tools they needed to subsist. The infrastructure of the country was gravely damaged. Relief organizations opened orphanages for homeless children whose parents had died. A director of an orphanage in Rwanda described some of the violence inflicted on children in the region: "Children received machete blows to their heads, children were shot, children were stoned, children were executed after listening to long speeches about why they must be killed."

Rwandan children needed many kinds of help after the fighting subsided. The United Nations Children's Fund (UNICEF) operated the Trauma Recovery Program to address their short- and long-term needs and to help them recover from the stress of being surrounded by violence. Their goal was to help young people reintegrate themselves into community life. An outpatient clinic in Kigali was organized to provide services for severely traumatized children. *See also* AFRICA; GENOCIDE; OPERATION BLESSING INTERNATIONAL (OBI); POST-TRAUMATIC STRESS DISORDER (PTSD); SOLDIERS, CHILD; UNACCOMPANIED CHILDREN; UNITED NATIONS CHILDREN'S FUND (UNICEF).

Further Reading: Joshua Hammer, "The Killing Fields," *Newsweek,* May 23, 1994, pp. 46-47; James C. McKinley, Jr., "Machete Returns to Rwanda, Rekindling a Genocidal War," *New York Times,* December 15, 1997, pp. A1, A12; James C. McKinley, "Searching in Vain for Rwanda's High Ground," *New York Times,* December 21, 1997, p. 3; Gerard Prunier, *The Rwanda Crisis* (1995).

S

Sabotage. *See* Resistance Movements (World War II)

Sack of Antwerp. *See* Massacres

Sack of Magdeburg. *See* Thirty Years' War

St. Louis

Young Jewish refugees found themselves stranded and imperiled when the steamship *St. Louis* was not allowed to complete its planned journey to a safe haven on the brink of World War II. On May 13, 1939, the *St. Louis* left Nazi Germany bound for Cuba. The 937 Jewish refugees on board, including entire families, all had visas—legal permits—to enter Cuba. Some of them had paid a great deal of money, sometimes everything they had, to get these visas and pay for their passage out of Germany.

When they arrived, the Cuban government refused to let them disembark. They then tried to enter the United States, but the U.S. Coast Guard was ordered to keep the ship away from U.S. ports. The passengers watched the American coastline as the ship wandered up and down the Atlantic during the end of May. The *St. Louis* was finally ordered back to Germany by the shipping line.

When the ship reached England on June 6, the British government agreed to accept one-fourth of the people on board. The rest went to Holland, France, and Belgium. As a result, most of the passengers were forced to endure Nazi occupation when those countries were invaded in 1940. More than half of them died during the Holocaust. Some of the children who survived lost their parents. Among them was Heinz Blumenstein who went to Holland with his mother Else after the ship returned to Europe. The Blumensteins were hidden separately by the Dutch resistance, but Else was discovered and deported to the death camp at Auschwitz, where she died.

Other ships filled with Jewish refugees also met a tragic fate. The *Struma* left Germany with Jewish refugees in 1942. Seventy Jewish children died when the ship sank in the Black Sea after no country would allow it to enter. *See also* Holocaust; Refugees; World War II.

Further Reading: David A. Adler, *We Remember the Holocaust* (1989); Henry L. Feingold, *The Politics of Rescue* (1970).

Sand Creek Massacre

On November 28, 1864, U.S. troops led by Colonel John Chivington attacked a Cheyenne-Arapaho encampment at Sand Creek, Colorado. Of the 600 Indians in the camp, two-thirds were women and children. Only about 60 men were present that morning, most of them elderly; the younger men had gone hunting. As the troops approached, people ran screaming from their tents. Mothers helped dozens of children hurry toward the tent of their leader, the peace-loving Chief Black Kettle, who had raised a U.S. flag, along with a white flag of truce. Black Kettle had recently negotiated with white leaders at the nearby fort and had been assured that no harm would come to his people.

Nonetheless, the soldiers opened fire on the unarmed civilians, killing young people of all ages. Eyewitnesses reported that the Indians were slaughtered indiscriminately with bullets and bayonets. Soldier Robert Bent later said,

> I saw a little girl about five years of age who had been hid in the sand; two soldiers discovered her, drew their pistols and shot her, and then pulled her out of the sand by the arm. I saw quite a number of infants in arms killed with their mothers. (Hoig, 1961)

After nightfall, survivors emerged from their hiding places and found that 105 women and children were dead, as well as 28 men. George Bent, owner of a fort in the region, later said,

> As we rode into that camp there was a terrible scene. Everyone was crying, even the warriors, and the women and children screaming and wailing. Nearly everyone present had lost some relatives or friends, and many of them in their grief were gashing themselves with their knives until the blood flowed in streams. (Hyde, 1968)

Stories about the atrocities committed at Sand Creek moved some whites to question military policies toward Native Americans. U.S. government officials ordered a military investigation of the massacre. Meanwhile, the Cheyenne abandoned hope of reaching a nonviolent settlement with whites after their peace-seeking chiefs were killed at Sand Creek. Warriors began planning attacks against whites, which sparked a widespread war between Native Americans and whites in the West. When U.S. officials sent an emissary, Medicine Calf Beckwourth, to visit Black Kettle and seek a new peace agreement, he found Chief Leg-in-the-Water had taken his place. Leg-in-the-Water said,

The white man has taken our country, killed all of our game; was not satisfied with that, but killed our wives and children. Now no peace. We want to go and meet our families in the spirit land. We loved the whites until we found out they lied to us, and robbed us of what we had. We have raised the battle ax until death.

True to their word, the Cheyenne joined Arapaho and Sioux warriors to attack whites. Young people were among those killed or injured in Indian attacks on settlements, wagon trains, stage stations, and military outposts. Indians destroyed telegraph wires and railroad cars and seized food supplies.

The U.S. Congress conducted an inquiry into the Sand Creek massacre and condemned Colonel Chivington, calling his actions an "outrage . . . gross and wanton" (Brown, 1970). Chivington resigned from his position.

Further Reading: Dee Brown, *Bury My Heart at Wounded Knee* (1971); Stan Hoig, *The Sand Creek Massacre* (1961); George E. Hyde, *The Life of George Bent* (1968).

Sasaki, Sadako (1943–1955)

When the atomic bomb hit Hiroshima, Japan, on August 6, 1945, Sadako Sasaki was barely two years old. She was at home with her mother and older brother, and the three of them fled to the Ota River where they remained on a boat that day. Radioactive black rain from the bombing fell on these three survivors and other people in Hiroshima. For years, Sadako Sasaki seemed to be healthy. In the fall of 1954, she was the fastest runner in her class at the Noborimachi Elementary School. However, she soon began to complain of fatigue and then she fainted in school. In February 1955, she was taken to the A-Bomb Hospital for medical tests. Blood analyses showed that Sasaki had acute leukemia, a cancer of the blood. Even though Sasaki was a mile away from the site where the bomb fell, she had received harmful doses of radiation.

The brave young girl fought to live. She set herself the task of making 1,000 paper cranes in the traditional Japanese origami style of folding paper. An old legend said that cranes live for 1,000 years; from this came the idea that by making a thousand paper cranes, a person could have a wish granted by the gods. After the bomb fell on Hiroshima, people all over Japan had made paper cranes and sent them to friends, relatives, and strangers in the hospitals.

Sadako Sasaki completed 964 cranes before she died on October 25, 1955. Friends and relatives made enough cranes to equal 1,000 and these were buried with her. Her class at school collected Sadako's letters and writings and they were published in a book called *Kokeshi*. A play about Sadako Sasaki, *A Thousand Cranes*, has been published and performed around the world.

Sasaki's classmates organized a Folded Crane Club in her honor and collected money for the construction of a monument in memory of Sasaki and other young victims of the atomic bombs. The monument, built in 1958, features a statue of Sadako built in the Hiroshima Peace Park. She stands atop the Mountain of Paradise—Mount Horai—holding a golden crane whose wings are spread in her outstretched hands.

On Peace Day each August, Japanese children lay garlands of paper cranes at the base of the statue. Engraved there are these words: "This is our cry, this is our prayer. Peace in the world." About a million people visit the Peace Monument in Hiroshima each year. *See also* FOLDED CRANE CLUB; HIROSHIMA; JAPAN (WORLD WAR II); PEACE MONUMENT; RADIATION SICKNESS; WORLD PEACE PROJECT FOR CHILDREN.

Further Reading: Betty Jean Lifton, *A Place Called Hiroshima* (1985); Masamoto Nasu, *Children of the Paper Crane* (1996).

Save the Children

Save the Children is a private, nonsectarian, tax-exempt organization committed to helping children through community development programs. Their programs focus on family and community activities that make people more self-sufficient and capable of solving their own problems. Many of these programs help children in war-torn countries.

The founder of Save the Children, Eglantyne Jebb, was born in Ireland and grew up in a prosperous family in England. She devoted much of her time to community outreach activities, particularly on behalf of children. She and her sister Dorothy Buxton established Save the Children in 1919 to relieve the suffering of children in Europe after World War I and during the Russian Revolution. Jebb spoke eloquently on behalf of suffering children, saying, "Humanity owes the child the best it has to give." In 1923, Jebb wrote the Children's Charter, which sets forth the guiding principles of the organization and later influenced the Convention on the Rights of the Child, which was adopted by the United Nations General Assembly in 1989.

Save the Children in America was organized in 1932 during the Great Depression to help children in the southern Appalachian region of the United States. Beginning in 1938, funds donated by sponsors were used to run schoolhouses in this mountainous region and to provide food, books, and school supplies for children. The organization expanded to help children around the world and has often aided young victims of war. In 1940, Save the Children launched a program in which individual sponsors gave $30 a month to help a needy child in war-torn Europe. A total of 12,000 European children were sponsored by the end of the war. Refugees and displaced children received special attention. During this time, more programs to sponsor needy children in the United States were also started. A program to aid children in Korea was organized when the Korean conflict raged in 1951.

After World War II, Save the Children began using its resources to improve the lives of families and communities so it could have a greater impact on the quality of a child's life over a longer period of time. When the organization helped children in war-torn Bangladesh, for instance, it developed programs called "high-impact." These programs aimed to promote long-term improvements in the economy and elevate levels of health, nutrition, sanitation, training, and education. Toward that end, money was used to hire teachers and health workers, administer vaccines, teach mothers how to care for babies, dig wells for safe sources of water, and provide loans for small businesses. The goal of these programs is to break the cycle of poverty that prevents children from growing up and reaching their potential.

Save the Children worked in war-torn Lebanon during the 1970s and 1980s. Thousands of children received aid during the civil war that afflicted youth and their families, particularly in Beirut. The organization operated health care centers and brought medical supplies into the region, provided loans for people who needed to build new businesses, and repaired schools and homes.

To help children in war-torn Bosnia in the 1990s, Save the Children set up community pre-schools to provide nourishing meals and safe playgrounds for young children. About 18,000 village children were involved in these programs as of 1997. Save the Children set up over 890 preschools serving more than 24,000 children. Teachers and staff members came from local communities and the schools became self-sustaining.

Save the Children helped thousands of children in Afghanistan and Angola to recognize and cope with the danger of land mines. The organization developed a comprehensive program to clear mines in Angola and help children detect them in the ground.

As of 1997, Save the Children was operating in six regions of the world: the United States, South Central Asia, Southeast Asia, the Middle East, western and southern Africa, and Latin America and the Caribbean. There were more than 90,000 sponsorships.

During 1998 and 1999, Save the Children developed transit centers to help former child soldiers in Liberia to return to normal civilian life. In war-torn Sudan, the organization helped to relieve widespread hunger among people who had been displaced by the fighting. In addition to bringing food and water, Save the Children provided families with cooking pots, seeds, tools, and fishing gear so they could help themselves. In Central America, Save the Children continued to work with children who were living on the streets of Guatemala and Nicaragua after they lost their parents during the civil wars of the

1980s. The organization was supporting the work of The Child Search Association in El Salvador to help reunite "disappeared" children with their natural families. *See also* AFGHANISTAN; ANGOLA; BOSNIA; LAND MINES; LEBANESE CIVIL WAR; LIBERIAN CIVIL WAR; MOZAMBIQUE; RELIEF ORGANIZATIONS; UNACCOMPANIED CHILDREN.

Further Reading: Fact Sheet, "Children and War," October 31, 1996; Laura Herbst, *Children in War* (1995); "The Work Continues in War-Torn Bosnia," *Save the Children Impact*, 1997.

Save the Children Alliance (International Save the Children Alliance)

The Save the Children Alliance is the world's largest and oldest group of nongovernmental organizations working for the welfare of children. The Alliance is made up of 24 independent organizations that work together in more than 100 nations to aid children in need as the result of war, poverty, or natural disasters. The Save the Children Alliance also advocates for children and has actively worked for 10 years to help draft and gain worldwide support for the United Nations Declaration on the Rights of the Child, which was adopted unanimously in November 1989. Save the Children U.S., founded in 1932, is a member of the Alliance. Another member, Save the Children Sweden (Radda Barnum) has compiled information about child soldiers and worked vigorously to end the practice of using children as military combatants. *See also* DENMARK (WORLD WAR II); FINLAND (WORLD WAR II); NORWAY (WORLD WAR II); RED CROSS; RELIEF ORGANIZATIONS; SAVE THE CHILDREN; SCANDINAVIA (WORLD WAR II); UNACCOMPANIED CHILDREN; WALLENBERG, RAOUL.

Further Reading: International Save the Children Alliance at <http://www.savechildren.or.jp/alliance/>.

Scandinavia (World War II). *See* DENMARK (WORLD WAR II; FINLAND (WORLD WAR II); NORWAY (WORLD WAR II); RED CROSS; WALLENBERG, RAOUL

Schindler, Oskar (1908–1974)

During World War II, Oskar Schindler saved more than 1,100 Jews, including youths, from being deported to Nazi death camps.

Oskar Schindler, an Austrian businessman, saved over 1,000 Jews during World War II. *Corbis-Bettmann.*

Schindler was born in 1908 in Zwittau, then part of Austria. In 1938, he joined the Nazi Party but later lost enthusiasm for its agenda. He became a successful businessman with luxurious tastes. During the war, Schindler's enamelware factory in Cracow, Poland, produced army equipment. In 1940, German officials insisted that he use Jewish prisoners as laborers and pay their wages directly to the Nazis. Schindler complied, but was known to treat his workers decently.

In June 1942, Schindler saw SS men shooting and beating unarmed Jews during a round-up and was especially distressed by their brutality toward children. He helped smuggle children out of the Cracow Ghetto to Polish convents and carried messages between parents and hidden children. Schindler also enlarged his plant and added workers, regardless of their skills. He let them produce substandard materials that would weaken the German war effort. He transported money from an organization in Hungary to Jewish resistance leaders in Poland. In 1943, Schindler convinced the Nazis to transfer workers from the nearby Plaszow labor camp, where they were brutalized, to his factory grounds. Schindler was arrested and interrogated several times by Nazi officials, but influential friends secured his release. He protected his workers by giving officials expensive liquor, diamonds, and other valuables.

In 1944, Germany faced military defeat, and the Nazis escalated attacks on Jews. To save his workers, Schindler asked officials to let him build a new factory and camp near his birthplace. He paid them large sums of money to let him take along hundreds of workers whose names appeared on his now famous "list." These workers were able to escape death.

As the German army withdrew, Soviet troops approached this new camp. Schindler and his wife Emilie fled to Switzerland, carrying a letter of gratitude written by people he had helped and a gold ring they made for him, inscribed: "He who saves a single life saves the world entire."

After the war, the Schindlers moved to Argentina with help from a Jewish relief group. Oskar Schindler returned to Germany in 1958 but never recovered financially and relied on assistance from Jews he had saved during the war. In 1963, Schindler was named a Righteous Gentile, the third person to be so honored by Yad Vashem in Israel. He died in 1974 and was buried in a Catholic cemetery in Jerusalem. A book about his life, *Schindler's List,* was the basis of an acclaimed 1993 feature film by the same name produced by Steven Spielberg. *See also* Holocaust; Righteous Gentiles; World War II.

Further Reading: Thomas Keneally, *Schindler's List* (1982).

Scholl, Hans and Scholl, Sophie. *See* THE WHITE ROSE

Scouts, Military. *See* AMERICAN REVOLUTION; HILL, BAYLOR; MOORE, BETH

Selection Process at Concentration Camps (World War II)

During the Holocaust of World War II, the Nazis under Adolf Hitler sent millions of men, women, and children to concentration and death camps, where a selection process took place as they arrived. New prisoners were directed to line up and were examined before being told to move either to the right or the left. Those sent to the right were selected to work, which meant they would not be killed outright. Those sent to the left were taken to gas chambers where they were killed and then cremated.

Young children were nearly always quickly sent to their deaths. A person had to look at least 14 to pass this first selection. Visibly pregnant women were also killed. Rudolf Hess, the Nazi SS commander at Auschwitz-Birkenau, the notorious death camp, later told a war crimes tribunal about the selection process.

> We had two SS doctors on duty at Auschwitz to examine incoming transports of prisoners. These would be marched by one of the doctors, who would make spot decisions as they walked by. Those who were fit to work would be sent into the camp. Others were sent immediately to the extermination plants. Children of tender years were invariably exterminated since because of their youth they were unable to work. (Canot, 1983)

Another person reported that

> When it came [the children's] turn to stand before this automaton [the man making the selections], they stretched out their pitiful arms and pleaded and beseeched, "Please, Herr General. Look how strong I am. I can work. I want to live. See how strong." But this calculating machine in human guise swung the finger to the left. They all went to the gas chambers. German economy had no use for the efforts of a twelve-year-old.

See also AUSCHWITZ-BIRKENAU; DEATH CAMPS (WORLD WAR II); DEPORTATIONS; FINAL SOLUTION; GENOCIDE; HOLOCAUST; "MASTER RACE"; MENGELE, JOSEF.

Further Reading: Azriel Eisenberg, ed., *The Lost Generation* (1982); Miklos Nyiszli, *Auschwitz* (1986); Barbara Rogasky, *Smoke and Ashes* (1988).

Selective Service Acts

At various times in American history, the United States Congress has passed selective service acts that required young people to register with military boards so that they could be called to serve. In May 1917, Congress passed a selective service act that required men between the ages of 21 and 31 to register for the military draft. In 1940, the year after World War II began in Europe, the United States passed the Selective Training and Service Act, the first peace-time draft law. All men between the ages of 21 and 35 were required to register for the draft with local boards. The law exempted some fathers from being drafted into the service, but these exemptions were limited after the U.S. entered World War II in December 1941. The ages were also expanded to include men between ages 18 and 65, although men in the oldest groups were not actually drafted.

Youths have sometimes protested laws that require them to register for military service. Eight Protestant students at the Union Theological Seminary were among the first to refuse to register for the draft or apply for any legal exemptions. They wrote a statement declaring their opposition to the Selective Service Act itself, which they claimed was a part of the "whole war system." The students were sentenced to serve prison terms.

The draft was ended in the United States in 1973 when Congress approved a law that created an all-volunteer army. As of 1997, young men in the United States were still required to register with the Selective Service at age 18 but were not subject to mandatory service. *See also* AMERICAN CIVIL WAR; CONSCRIPTION; CONSCIENTIOUS OBJECTORS.

Further Reading: Frederick C. Giffin, *Six Who Protested* (1977); Alice Lynd, ed., *We Won't Go* (1968); Milton Meltzer, *Ain't Gonna Study War No More* (1985).

Seminole Wars (1835–1842)

Occurring between 1835 and 1842, the Seminole Wars between U.S. troops and the Seminole Indians of present-day Florida were the bloodiest and longest American Indian

Wars. The Seminoles had migrated south to Florida during the 1700s and 1800s. By the 1830s, other states along the east coast, including Georgia, had forcibly removed the vast majority of Indians living within their borders. They ignored previous treaties made with such peoples as the Cherokee and Creek, and forced Indians of all ages to relocate in unsettled, and mostly dry, regions west of the Mississippi River in present-day Oklahoma.

Whites in Florida wanted the Seminole to move to the Indian Territory in Oklahoma, but the Seminole chief Osceola organized an effective resistance effort, and many young Seminole warriors helped their elders delay removal. After years of bitter fighting, the Seminole were defeated and were forced to move west. Young people were among the casualties as the Indians made the long journey west, hungry and exposed to the elements. Others died once they reached the reservations, where the climate was hot and dry, unlike the humid region they had inhabited in the Southeast.

Further Reading: John Bemrose, *Reminiscences of the Second Seminole War* (1966); Edwin C. McReynolds, *The Seminoles* (1957).

Sendler, Irena (1910–)

Irena Sendler, a Polish social worker, saved the lives of Jewish children during World War II. As part of the Social Welfare Department of the Municipal Administration of Warsaw, Sendler worked with the *Rada Glowna Opiekuncza* (the Central Welfare Council), an agency that served adults and children. The council ran more than 1,000 facilities, including nurseries, soup kitchens, and hospices where some 200,000 to 300,000 people received help between 1941 and 1943. Children received food, clothing, and health care.

During the year 1941, children under age 15 made up about 42 percent of those helped by the council. Beginning in 1942, Nazi officials limited the council's activities. They banned the distribution of food to Polish children in 1943, at which time the Nazi occupation regime subjected Poles to strict food rationing. Sendler began working with CENTOS, a Jewish relief organization; she wore a Jewish armband so she could enter the Warsaw Ghetto. When the ghetto was sealed, Sendler obtained documents that allowed her and an associate, Irena Schultz, to move in and out. The two women helped at least 3,000 people during the war with their relief activities.

When the Nazis began rounding up Jews, Sendler was appointed to head the Zegota Children's Bureau, whose goal was to save as many Jewish children from the Nazis as possible. She had already rescued many children from the ghetto and knew about people and agencies that would help the rescue effort, including convents, special child care centers, agencies, and private homes. Zegota had more than 2,600 children in hiding at any given time. About 500 were in convents, 200 were in the Home of Father Boduen, 500 were in places run by *Rada,* and 1,300 were in private homes or living with partisans in the countryside.

Sendler later said that as the ghettos were being liquidated, people begged her and other rescuers to hide their children. Sendler later recalled ruefully, "I couldn't even guarantee that I would get them past the sentry" (Lukas, 1994). She and other rescuers were in constant danger. In her home, Sendler had hidden the names and addresses of the children under the care of Zegota. The Gestapo arrested and questioned her more than once and searched her home but found nothing. In October 1943, Sendler was arrested and tortured in Pawiak prison. Friends bribed an official to obtain her release, and Sendler lived in hiding until the war ended. During that time, her mother died, and she could not attend the funeral. Sendler survived the war and was later honored as a Righteous Gentile by Yad Vashem in Israel. *See also* CENTOS; HOLOCAUST; POLAND (WORLD WAR II); RESCUERS (HOLOCAUST); RIGHTEOUS GENTILES; WARSAW GHETTO; YAD VASHEM; ZEGOTA.

Further Reading: Fact Sheet, "Irena Sendler," Jewish Foundation for the Righteous, New York City, 1997; Richard C. Lukas, *Did the Children Cry?* (1994); Yad Vashem Archives, File #153.

Separations, Family

War often separates family members, sometimes leaving children completely on their own. Parents are separated from their children when they leave home to serve in the military. Separations also occur when family members are sent to forced labor, deported, imprisoned, or killed. During civil wars, such as those occurring in the twentieth century in Russia, Greece, Rwanda, and Somalia, children have been taken away from their parents and forced to serve with the military or in labor projects that aid the military. They have also been sent to institutions or camps to be indoctrinated with the political beliefs of their captors.

In some cases, separations are planned, as when parents allow their children to be evacuated or hidden for safety reasons. Evacuations took place in England, Germany, and Japan, among other places, during World War II when bombing raids endangered certain areas. Children in these situations were often reluctant to leave.

European Jewish families experienced massive separations during the Holocaust of World War II when millions of Jews of all ages were deported by the Nazis and killed. Before the war, some Jewish parents in Europe allowed their children to emigrate alone, when they had an opportunity, to escape dangers in their homeland. Late in 1938, the family of teenager Helga Katz hoped to emigrate from Germany, where they were being persecuted because they were Jews. Helga's 16-year-old brother had already gone to live with relatives in the United States to avoid being drafted by the German army. Katz was able to leave in the summer of 1939, to live as a sponsored domestic worker in England.

Katz never saw her parents again. Her father committed suicide after hearing that he was going to be seized by Nazi police and, in 1942, her mother was sent to a death camp. Katz, who later became a U.S. citizen and teacher, said, "All my other relatives, my mother's entire family and my father's entire family—those who were Jewish—all emigrated legally or illegally . . . . They're so widely spread now" (Rubin, 1977).

As Jews were being forced onto trains that would take them to their deaths, some terrified mothers could be seen tossing their babies from the cars in the hope that a kind stranger might rescue the child. Jews were also separated after they reached concentration camps. To gain more cooperation, the Nazis falsely promised to keep families together, but once they reached the camps, families were torn apart. As new arrivals were "selected" for work or death at the camps, children who appeared younger than 14, pregnant women, the sick, and the elderly were almost always sent to the gas chambers. Adults who looked strong enough were put to work. When families were not deported together, they were separated when they were imprisoned at different camps.

In Asian countries, Japanese invaders separated family members by sending people to forced labor. Korean women were taken away to brothels where they were forced to serve the Japanese military as sex slaves.

Post-war conditions can also bring separations. After World War I, doctors urged some families in Germany and Austria to send their malnourished children to Holland where they would live with a foster family and receive nourishing food and care. Some children were so thin and sickly that they stayed for months, even years. A number of these youths became so attached to their foster families that they remained in Holland or maintained close ties with these families throughout their lives.

During the last decades of the twentieth century, tens of thousands of unaccompanied children were seen in many war-torn countries, including Bosnia, Liberia, Rwanda, Somalia, and Zaire. Relief organizations working to help youth in these countries tried to reunite them with family members whenever possible. *See also* ADOPTION; BOSNIA; CONCENTRATION CAMPS (WORLD WAR II); DEATH CAMPS (WORLD WAR II); DEPORTATIONS; DISPLACED PERSONS (DPs) (WORLD WAR II); EL SALVADOR; EVACUATIONS (WORLD WAR II); FORCED LABOR (WORLD WAR II); FOUNDLINGS (WORLD WAR II); GAGE, NICHOLAS; GIES, MIEP AND GIES, JAN; GREECE (WORLD WAR II); GUA-

TEMALA; HIDDEN CHILDREN; HOLOCAUST; JEHOVAH'S WITNESSES; LEBENSBORN; LIBERIAN CIVIL WAR; ORPHANS; POLAND (WORLD WAR II); PRISONERS; REFUGEES; RIVESALTES; ROUND-UPS; RWANDA; SAVE THE CHILDREN; SELECTION PROCESS AT CONCENTRATION CAMPS (WORLD WAR II); SIERRA LEONE; SOMALIA; SOVIET UNION (WORLD WAR II); UNACCOMPANIED CHILDREN; UNITED STATES (WORLD WAR II); WORLD WAR I; WORLD WAR II.

Further Reading: Deborah Dwork, *Children with a Star* (1991); Arnold Rubin, *The Evil Men Do* (1977); United Nations Children's Fund (UNICEF), *The State of the World's Children, 1996* (1996).

Sexual Abuse

During wars, especially ethnic conflicts, children and young adults have been victims of rape and other forms of sexual abuse. Wartime violence against women dates back thousands of years. Conquering armies sometimes considered captured women part of the "spoils of war," to be confiscated and used as they saw fit, just like the land and the material wealth of the conquered people. In the 1990s, sexual intimidation and degradation have been specifically employed as tools of war to terrorize and degrade the opposition.

Troops have raped girls and women as punishment in places where people strongly resisted their invasions. For example, in A.D. 60, when Roman legions claimed her kingdom in Britain, Queen Boadicea refused to turn over her late husband's jewels and the horses and other valuables she controlled. To punish her, the Romans raped the queen's two daughters.

Besides being violently attacked, young people have been forced to trade sexual favors to survive. Some have agreed to unwanted sexual advances when members of the military threatened their lives or those of their families or threatened to starve them if they did not comply.

During World War II, Japanese troops raped numerous women in Asia, including Chinese, Koreans, and Filipinas. Young women in occupied Asian countries, notably Korea, were forced to live in brothels and serve as prostitutes for Japanese soldiers.

Long after the war ended, these victims were still asking for an apology and some kind of reparations for their suffering.

Some women from Poland, the Soviet Union, and other occupied countries who were sent to Germany as forced laborers were sexually abused, although Germans were officially forbidden to have sexual relations with Jews, Poles, or Slavs. Until February 1943, women from Poland or Eastern Europe who became pregnant in Germany were allowed to return home to deliver their babies. However, labor shortages became so acute that year that many women were forced to have abortions or to send their babies to German orphanages so they could continue working unencumbered by children. Infants in these orphanages lived in rough wooden barracks and many died from illnesses or inadequate milk rations. The mortality rate was above 25 percent. According to Richard C. Lukas (1994), 350 to 400 of these infants died during the last 10 months of the war.

In the 1990s, during the civil war in the former Yugoslavia, thousands of teenage girls in Bosnia, Herzegovina, and Croatia were raped by Serbian soldiers and many ended up bearing children fathered by their enemy. These rapes and impregnations were the results of genocidal policies meant to destroy an enemy's bloodlines and cultural ties. Rape was used as a tactic to drive the Bosnians from their homes and terrorize the civilian population. A fact-finding team from the European Community estimated that more than 20,000 Muslim women were raped in Bosnia between 1992 and 1996. Bosnia's Interior Ministry believes the number is more accurately around 50,000. The subject of rape is an especially sensitive one in Bosnia, and victims have sometimes felt too ashamed to come forward. One victim said that for her rapist "There is not a punishment strong enough for what he has done to me. He has wounded me in a way I will never heal."

One of the most tragic results of these rapes is the fate of the so-called "children of hate"—the children who were conceived as a result of rape. A number of women who became pregnant after being raped chose to have abortions, but some could not. Some distraught mothers abandoned their unwanted babies, who reminded them of the horror they had experienced. Some of the abandoned babies found loving homes, while others were turned over to relief agencies. For example, Human Relief International, an Islamic organization, has taken care of some abandoned babies. Bosnian families, who were earning, on average, about $100 a month in 1996, were seldom able to afford more children.

Sexual violence also occurred during various African civil wars. The extent of such abuse cannot be fully reported because governments often conceal such incidents. In addition, few people have investigated the sexual abuse of young male soldiers. Thousands of adolescent girls in Rwanda were also raped by soldiers of the opposing forces during the war between Hutus and Tutsis. Tens of thousands of Tutsi girls were victims of sexual abuse, often accompanied by beatings and mutilation. The defeated Hutu army took some women to Zaire and imprisoned them as sexual slaves. Human rights groups and the Rwandan government estimate that between 2,000 and 5,000 children were born to Tutsi women as a result of rape. Abortion is illegal in Rwanda, so nearly all the impregnated women gave birth. Women who bore these children were often shunned by fellow villagers who regarded rape as a disgrace for the victim. As a result, some women abandoned their infants or killed themselves in despair. During the first four months of 1995, 80 babies were abandoned by their mothers in the maternity ward of Kigali Central Hospital. Many abandoned babies ended up in orphanages that lacked enough food, safe water, and staff members to take care of them. The Belgian Red Cross was among the organizations that set up clean orphanages with trained nurses to care for these children.

One Tutsi mother who kept her baby after being raped expressed mixed feelings about the child, as she recalled the agony of the day he was conceived. She was raped by a Hutu militiaman, part of a gang that killed her mother, husband, and brother. She told a journalist, "If there had been a means of aborting, I would have done it. But now I am obliged to take care of this child. I am obliged to love him" (Sullivan, 1996).

Some young female soldiers have also reported being raped or coerced into having unwanted sexual relations. They have told investigators that they were ordered to serve as the "wives" of male soldiers to help these males deal with stress and fear. In Mozambique, UNICEF investigators found that young male soldiers in the Renamo camps were encouraged to violate young girls. Similar stories came from Liberia, Sierra Leone, and Uganda.

International health organizations have found higher rates of sexually transmitted diseases, especially HIV/AIDS, in countries ravaged by civil war, such as Rwanda and Uganda. Rape and the trading of sexual favors for food and protection led to high rates of these diseases. The effects of these diseases are far-reaching. According to a UNICEF report called *The State of the World's Children, 1996*, as a result of sexual abuse, "the next generation is at an even greater disadvantage, as more children are born with AIDS or are orphaned."

Women's organizations and human rights organizations have advocated that rape be recognized as a crime against humanity and as a form of genocide. The International Criminal Court that convened in 1998 to prosecute war crimes in the Balkans and Rwanda supported this idea. *See also* Bosnia; Concentration Camps (World War II); Forced Labor (World War II); Geneva Conventions; Genocide; Holocaust; Japan-China War; Liberian Civil War; Massacres; Mozambique; My Lai Massacre; Pacific (World War II); Poland (World War II); Rwanda; Sierra Leone; Soldiers, Child; Uganda.

Further Reading: Laura A. Barnitz, *Child Soldiers* (1997); Stacy Sullivan, "Born Under a Bad Sign," *Newsweek*, September 23, 1996; Antonia Fraser, *Heroes and Heroines* (1980); Vera Laska, ed., *Women of the Resistance and in the Holocaust* (1984); Richard C. Lukas, *Did the Children Cry?* (1994); United Nation's Children's Fund (UNICEF), *The State of the World's Children, 1996* (1996).

Shanghai (World War II)

From 1933 to 1945, a number of young European refugees from Nazi persecution made their way to Shanghai, China. Though overcrowded and rife with poverty, Shanghai was a place refugees could live without a visa. Parts of this port city were occupied by the Japanese; the rest of the city was under International Settlement Control.

In 1939, 14-year-old Henry Compart arrived with his parents from Berlin, Germany. They, along with other Jewish refugees, received help from the local Jewish community and the American Jewish Joint Distribution Committee. Young Jews were able to attend a Jewish school that opened that autumn and could join the Shanghai Jewish Youth Association. Compart recalled, "We kept maps detailing the progress of the war. But we didn't know anything about the concentration camps. We didn't know what was going on in Germany. . . . We had relatives there but we never heard from them again" (Kahn and Hagar, 1996).

After the Japanese bombed Pearl Harbor in 1941, new problems arose for the people of Shanghai; the Japanese brought in more troops and moved tanks into the International Settlement area. Jews were forced to live in a certain restricted part of Shanghai. There were no basements, so during the bombings, Compart recalled sitting in a room with a washbasin over his head. His family survived the war and later emigrated to the United States. *See also* JAPAN-CHINA WAR; PEARL HARBOR.

Further Reading: Leora Kahn and Rachel Hager, eds., *When They Came to Take My Father* (1996).

Shoah. *See* HOLOCAUST

Sierra Leone

During a civil war that began in 1991, tens of thousands of children and teenagers died, were forced to serve in the military, and lost their homes and loved ones in Sierra Leone, a country in West Africa. The war was rooted in years of misrule and conflicts between poor rural people and the wealthier classes. Between 1991 and 1999, half of the people in Sierra Leone fled the country, making them the largest refugee group in Africa. Thousands of children were orphaned.

Both the rebels and the pro-government forces, called the Kamajors, recruited child soldiers, and both sides waged brutal attacks on civilians of all ages. Children were mutilated and killed by machetes, gunfire, and land mines. In Freetown, rebels carried out a brutal attack in which they amputated the limbs of about 1,500 people and killed an unknown number of others. Teenagers made up a large portion of the troops known as the Revolutionary United Front (RUF), which took part in this attack. Eyewitnesses said the teen soldiers seemed unconcerned about their own safety as they infiltrated the city of Freetown and terrorized the population. In other places, children were abducted after RUF or Kamajor troops attacked and destroyed their villages. The children were imprisoned in camps and many were forced to serve as soldiers. Some managed to escape and make their way to orphanages run by relief organizations.

Young refugees described being raped, beaten, and mutilated. Some had to watch as family members were brutally killed. In May 1998, UNICEF Director Carol Bellamy said, "The children of Sierra Leone have had three strikes against them. . . . First, they were made into child soldiers; then they became targets during recent atrocities; and now they are largely forgotten by the international community" (UNICEF, 1998). *See also* AFRICA.

Further Reading: Elizabeth Blunt, "Sierra Leone's Rebel Teenage Army," BBC News, January 12, 1999; Caroline Hawley, "A Country Torn by Conflict," BBC News, May 19, 1999 at <http://news2.thdo.bbc.co.uk/hi/english/special_report>; "Latest Developments Affecting Children: Action Needed Against Sierra Leone Atrocities," *UNICEF Newsline*, May 22, 1998.

Sima (1930?–)

The young woman who became known by the name "Sima" was part of the underground resistance during World War II. At age 12, she was smuggling people out of the Minsk Ghetto, taking them to the forests of Staroje-Sielo. Jacob Greenstein, a partisan who fought the Nazis in that region (Byelorussia), described this courageous Jewish teenager in his memoirs. Her parents had been killed. When she first began her underground work, she carried messages or ran errands.

> No assignment was too difficult for Sima. Before going out on a mission, she listened carefully to the given instruction; then she would repeat what she was told, trying hard not to miss a single word. Her small pistol was always in the special pocket sewn into her coat . . . . On cold winter nights, Sima would sneak out of the ghetto through an opening beneath the barbed wire fence. She returned to the ghetto through the cemetery. . . . After the liquidation of the Minsk ghetto, Sima participated in the combat operations of the partisan detachment. (Meltzer, 1976)

Sima survived the war. In the summer of 1944, she was part of a group of partisans who marched in triumph through the city of Minsk.

Further Reading: Milton Meltzer, *Never to Forget: The Jews of the Holocaust* (1976).

Simaite, Anna

Anna Simaite of Riga, Lithuania, a teacher and literary critic, was director of the cataloguing department at the Vilna University library when World War II began. During the Holocaust, she rescued Jewish children and adults from the Vilna Ghetto. In Vilna, more than 25,000 Jewish men, women, and children were crowded into a few buildings on five streets. They lacked food, warm clothing, medicines, running water, and decent sanitary facilities. People died on the streets from disease and hunger.

Simaite later told author Philip Friedman that she could not stand by and watch this suffering: "I could no longer go on with my work. I could not remain in my study. I could not eat. . . " (Friedman, 1978). The Nazis had banned non-Jews from the ghetto, but Simaite convinced officials she must go inside to retrieve valuable books for the library. At considerable risk, she carried messages, food, and sometimes weapons inside the ghetto. Simaite removed rare Jewish books,

documents, and ghetto diaries and hid them at the university.

When the police began deporting ghetto residents, Simaite smuggled out Jewish children and took them to the homes of non-Jews who hid them. By 1942, the Nazis suspected Simaite was working with the resistance, and she was forced underground where she continued her rescue work.

Simaite was arrested in 1944 and convicted of crimes against the Nazi regime. She was sentenced to die, but officials at Vilna University were able to have her sentence reduced to imprisonment. Simaite was sent to the concentration camp at Dachau, then to a camp in France. She was gravely ill when the Allies arrived at the camp. After a hospital stay, Simaite moved to Paris and worked as a dishwasher. Several of the Jews she had helped offered to support her, but she declined.

One of the children Simaite rescued in Vilna, Tania Wachsman, had moved to Israel where she married and had two children. In 1953, Wachsman insisted that her rescuer—whom she called, "My dear Mother"—come to live with her family. Anna Simaite finally agreed and arrived in Israel, where she was honored as a Righteous Gentile. *See also* GHETTOS (WORLD WAR II); HOLOCAUST; RESCUERS (HOLOCAUST); RIGHTEOUS GENTILES.

Further Reading: Philip Friedman, *Their Brothers' Keepers* (1978); Milton Meltzer, *Rescue: The Story of How Gentiles Saved Jews During the Holocaust* (1988).

Singapore (World War II)

In 1942, Singapore, an island nation off the Malay Peninsula in Southeast Asia, was occupied by Japanese troops. Young people suffered from hunger and other deprivations as the occupying forces took food and other resources out of Singapore for their own use. Japanese lawmakers and officials also imposed curfews, rationing, censorship, and other restrictions.

Japanese officials immediately made all Europeans in Singapore prisoners of war. Children of civilian POWS were interned with their parents in Changi Prison, Selarang Barracks, Sime Road Camp, and other camps. Able-bodied people were forced to clean up debris and bury the dead. They also worked to restore water lines and electrical power.

The Japanese occupation forces placed barbed wire across roads to form roadblocks and guards stood in these places. People were ordered to bow to Japanese soldiers or they would be beaten. Chinese living in Singapore were singled out for special punishments. Chinese men between the ages of 18 and 50, along with some women and children, were ordered to report for interrogation at various military centers. Thousands of these people were labeled as anti-Japanese, often on the basis of no evidence. Youth were among those who were executed after these hearings.

The Japanese occupation set up schools designed to influence youth to learn Japanese language and culture, and students were forced to sing the Japanese national anthem. Theaters showed only Japanese films, and radio stations and newspapers were also under Japanese control. Young people under age 21 were among the 7,000 resisters who took part in the Malayan People's Anti-Japanese Army (MPAJA).

Some people tried to flee to allied countries. On February 19, 1942, a ship containing refugees from Singapore, the *Tanjong Penang*, was hit by a Japanese submarine. On board were 250 women and children accompanied by nurses from Great Britain, the ship's destination. The blast sunk the ship. Some of the surviving adults managed to get hold of a raft, and they picked up a few other survivors. One of the British nurses later reported that she and another group floating on a raft moved around the wreckage searching for survivors. They found six children, including two babies under one year of age. Without food or water, and exposed to the tropical sun and storms, these children all died at sea. It was four days before the adults were picked up by a Japanese cruiser, which then took them to a prisoner-of-war camp.

After the war ended in 1945, conditions were still harsh for youth living in Singapore and other parts of Malaysia. They endured food shortages, rationing, a lack of clothing

and school supplies, malnutrition, and disease. The British military administration set up some relief programs. Many young people who lived through the war were among those who worked for a free, independent Singapore after the war. *See also* PACIFIC (WORLD WAR II).

Further Reading: Louis Allen, *Singapore 1941–42* (1992); Sheila Bruhn, *Diary of a Girl in Changi* (1994).

Six-Day War (1967). *See* ARAB-ISRAELI WARS

"The Sixth"

This French World War II resistance group was made up of young people between the ages of 11 and 18. They had been left without parents after the Nazis conducted a huge round-up and deportation of Jews in Paris on July 16, 1942. After escaping deportation to Poland themselves, the youths banded together. Some joined existing resistance groups, but 88 of them worked with an underground group that sprang from the Jewish Scout Movement. This group became known as "The Sixth." Most of their resistance work involved expert forgery of documents that Jews could show Nazi police to convince them they were non-Jews. Members of the group also helped other Jews, especially those who were refugees from other countries, to find safe hiding places. The hiding places were often arranged with the help of Catholic and French clergy.

Some members of The Sixth helped people escape from occupied France across the mountains into Spain. It is believed this youth resistance group rescued more than 3,000 adults and 1,000 children. Thirty members of The Sixth lost their lives during the war. They were either shot by Nazis or died in death camps after being captured. *See also* DEPORTATIONS; FRANCE (WORLD WAR II); HOLOCAUST; RESISTANCE MOVEMENTS (WORLD WAR II); ROUND-UPS; SEPARATIONS, FAMILY.

Further Reading: Nathan Aaseng, *Cities at War: Paris* (1992); Henri Nogueres, *Histoire de la Resistance en France* (1967).

Slave Labor. *See* CONCENTRATION CAMPS (WORLD WAR II); FORCED LABOR (WORLD WAR II); GHETTOS (WORLD WAR II); HOLLAND (WORLD WAR II); ITALY (WORLD WAR II); PACIFIC (WORLD WAR II); SOVIET UNION (WORLD WAR II)

Smith, Samantha (1972–1985)

Samantha Smith became famous at age 10 for her efforts to promote peace and understanding between the United States and the Soviet Union, countries that had been engaged in a Cold War since World War II ended in 1945. Smith, a native of Maine, became so concerned about the nuclear arms race and tense relations between the two countries that she wrote a letter to Soviet leader Yuri Andropov in November 1982. Smith's letter read as follows:

> Dear Mr. Andropov,
>
> My name is Samantha Smith. I am ten years old. Congratulations on your new job. I have been worrying about Russia and the United States getting into a nuclear war. Are you going to vote to have a war or not? If you aren't, please tell me how you are going to help to not have a war . . . the world is for us to live together in peace and not to fight.
>
> Sincerely,
> Samantha Smith

Andropov replied with a letter of his own the next spring, and the news media interviewed Smith and she appeared on television shows to discuss her letter and her concerns about world peace.

At the invitation of Soviet leaders, Smith and her parents visited the Soviet Union in July 1983. They traveled to Moscow, the Crimea, and Leningrad, stopping at tourist sites and meeting young people and various officials. When she returned to the United States, Smith wrote a book called *Journey to the Soviet Union.* She said that she had made new friends who showed her people are the same, no matter where they live.

Smith became an unofficial ambassador of peace as she continued to travel. In Janu-

ary 1984, her family went to Japan, where people called her the "Angel of Peace." She continued to appear on different television shows where she discussed her experiences. This led to a chance to try out for a part in a new television series called *Lime Street.* By September of 1985, she had filmed four episodes of the show. She and her father were traveling home from England when their plane crashed just 30 miles from home. Samantha and her father and the other six people on the plane were killed. *See also* COLD WAR.

Further Reading: Anne Galicich, *Samantha Smith: A Journey for Peace* (1987); Patricia Stone Martin, *Samantha Smith, Young Ambassador* (1987); Samantha Smith, *Journey to the Soviet Union* (1985).

Soldiers, Child

The term "child soldiers" typically refers to soldiers under the age of 18 who participate voluntarily or involuntarily in armed military organizations. Throughout history, children (usually defined as anyone under the age of 18) have taken part in armed conflicts as combatants. For example, in ancient Greece, young people in Sparta went to war, and some members of the Roman legions were teenagers. Scandinavian youth also fought as Vikings, and youth in medieval times were among the knights who engaged in combat.

During various wars, some countries deliberately recruited young teenagers as soldiers while others set the age for enlistment at 17 or 18. In the United States, teenagers below the legal minimum age for joining the military were sometimes able to join by pretending they were older. Youths under age 18 fought in the American Revolution and the Civil War. In some documented cases, Americans as young as 15 fought in World War I.

During World War II, the average age of enlisted men in the U.S. military was about 26, but combatants in all branches included thousands of men younger than 21. After World War II ended, the governments of many countries began to set 17 or 18 as the minimum age for military service. New national and international laws were made to reflect these limits. International laws set 15 as the minimum age for combatants, although groups like the United Nations Children's Fund (UNICEF) argued that it should be set higher.

The Vietnam War became known as "America's first teenage-war" because the average age of U.S. combatants in that war was only 19. Vietnamese youth also served as combatants for both the North and South. Many teenaged soldiers on both sides died, while thousands of others were wounded and disabled.

A movement to ban child soldiers grew during the 1990s. Organizations that oppose the use of child soldiers estimated that, as of 1997, 200,000 to 250,000 youths under age 18 were taking part in armed conflicts in some 34 countries on any given day. The exact number may be higher because of efforts to hide the existence and extent of child soldiers. Nevertheless, cases of soldiers as young as 5 have been documented.

Studies of child soldiers have shown that most are males, but females were also recruited. According to a report by Youth Advocate Program International (YAP-I), about one-third of the child soldiers in El Salvador, Ethiopia, and Uganda were female. Investigators from Amnesty International found that females, especially orphans, were recruited by guerilla movements in Sri Lanka, Peru, Turkey, and Eritrea.

Girl child soldiers may suffer from additional burdens, according to humanitarian observers. They may be forced to serve as sexual servants, suicide bombers, and martyrs. Those who become pregnant may be forced to undergo unsafe abortions. In some countries, virgins are kidnapped as sexual servants so that male soldiers do not contract AIDS, but the young women often become infected. When the conflicts end, girl soldiers may again suffer more than males. They may be forgotten and have more trouble gaining acceptance in their communities. Studies showed that many former girl soldiers resorted to prostitution or criminality to survive. During the 1980s, a civil war af-

fected young people in Sri Lanka in numerous ways. Child soldiers took part in the conflict, and investigators found that orphans in Tamil, including girls, were recruited by the LTTE (Tamil Tigers), the rebel forces. According to Amnesty International's Swedish branch, the girl soldiers received rigorous physical and mental military training. When they completed their training, each was given a cyanide capsule to carry on a string around her neck so she could kill herself by biting down on the capsule if captured.

Authors Rachel Brett and Margaret McCallin (1996) found that several factors made a child far more likely to become a soldier: 1) extreme poverty, 2) the loss of parents and family, 3) weakened ties with family members, 4) living in a combat zone, and 5) the destruction of the child's immediate society, including homes, schools, places of worship, and hospitals. Children in refugee camps and orphanages were especially vulnerable to pressure to join military organizations after a conflict erupted.

The United Nations found that in some countries, children were recruited off the streets in poor sections of cities. Forced conscription took place in schools, athletic fields, movie theaters, bus stops, and other places where youths were likely to be found. Some military organizations threatened children or their families with violence if a child did not join them.

A research project conducted by the United Nations, *Study on the Impact of Armed Conflict on Children* (1996), confirmed that most children who become soldiers are motivated by poverty. Poor children and orphans are more likely to be targeted for recruitment and training and are sometimes coerced into joining the military. Some children volunteer for military service to escape hunger and homelessness. The military may offer to pay wages directly to their families, who are often in great need. Military life also offers these youths a sense of belonging, comradeship, and security. It may give them a chance for revenge for the killing of family members or friends or for destroying their property or communities.

Military leaders in many countries have found children to be convenient subjects for training purposes, especially since the advent of new types of weapons, including lighter weight guns. Young soldiers may be willing to take more risks because they are less fearful. Author Raymond J. Toney pointed out that children "are easily recruited and indoctrinated, present a small target and lack the judgment that adults normally possess, rendering them fierce and fearless killers" (Toney, 1997).

Once recruited, child soldiers may be assigned to various duties, such as cooking, putting up tents, checking for land mines, or digging latrines at campsites. Some are used to guard prisoners, spy, or carry messages or supplies. Young soldiers may also be ordered to kill, rape, or torture people, or to carry out suicide missions. According to Toney, military groups also work to desensitize these young recruits to violence and encourage them to carry out aggressive and brutal acts: "They are often encouraged to engage in sexual activity with prostitutes and civilian victims of war. . . . Children are often exposed to brutal 'hazing' rituals involving extreme physical and psychological violence. There are reports of children being forced to ritualistically drink human and animal blood prior to combat" (Toney, 1997).

Child soldiers may die or be taken prisoner when they are too weak or sick to keep up with their group and are left behind. A report by Youth Advocate Program International (YAP-I) claimed that during the Iran-Iraq War (1980-1988), thousands of Iranian children were sent ahead of adult soldiers in case there were minefields. These children, who had been told they would be heroes if they died, wore necklaces around their necks bearing "the keys to heaven." Investigators believe about 90 percent of them died.

Children in the military receive different treatment, depending on where they live and the type of war in which they fight. While some child soldiers are not mistreated, others have been subjected to physical and emotional abuse and ordered to take deadly risks. Some of them are also given drugs or alcohol to alter their mood before they are sent into combat. According to YAP-I, child combatants have reported being given a variety of substances, including marijuana, cocaine, amphetamines, and cane juice mixed with gunpowder.

The impact of these experiences can last for years, even for life. Child soldiers may have trouble resuming civilian life when they leave the military. They may turn to criminal activity or be exploited by experienced criminals who use them to further their goals. They often receive little or no help in re-entering the community.

International organizations and human rights groups have faced enormous problems trying to enforce laws regarding child soldiers. Many modern conflicts have been internal ones, civil wars fought between different factions within the same country. These groups may ignore both national and international laws.

Child soldiers were the subject of intense discussion at the Convention on the Rights of the Child, sponsored by the United Nations (UN). Work on the drafting of the convention began in 1979—the International Year of the Child—by a working group established by the Commission on Human Rights. It was unanimously adopted by the United Nations General Assembly on November 20, 1989 and opened for signature January 26, 1990. That day, 61 countries signed it, a record first-day response. Seven months later, on September 2, 1990, the convention entered into force after the twentieth state had ratified it. Ratification will be unanimous after two more states ratify the convention.

The UN Committee on the Rights of the Child has urged that nations throughout the world set the minimum age for conscription into the military at 18. As of 1999, the committee was continuing to work for universal acceptance of this age limit on conscription. *See also* AFGHANISTAN; AMERICAN CIVIL WAR; BURMA; CAMBODIA; CONSCRIPTION; CONVENTION ON THE RIGHTS OF THE CHILD; GENEVA CONVENTIONS; LEBANON; LIBERIAN CIVIL WAR; MOZAMBIQUE; RWANDA; SIERRE LEONE; SOMALIA; SUDAN; UGANDA.

Further Reading: Laura A. Barnitz, *Child Soldiers* (1997); Rachel Brett and Margaret McCallin, *Children:*

The Invisible Soldiers (1996); Guy S. Goodwin-Gill and Ilene Cohn, *Child Soldiers* (1994); Raymond J. Toney, "The Children of War," *Christian Social Action*, March 1997, pp. 36-39; United Nations Children's Fund (UNICEF), *The State of the World's Children, 1996* (1996).

Somalia

Young people fled from Somalia, a country in northeastern Africa, which was devastated by a violent civil war during the 1980s and early 1990s. Thousands of refugees left the famine-stricken southern part of the country as Somali troops fought against nationalists, who took over in 1989. By March 1992, members of the Migration and Refugee Assistance (MRA) in Washington, DC, estimated that 160,000 Somalis had fled because of the civil war. Many arrived in Kenya near death from hunger and exposure.

A report issued by UNICEF claimed that, as of 1992, half of all Somali children under age five had died by year's end. The vast majority perished because of malnutrition and disease; bullets claimed around 2 percent of these children. One of the most profound effects of the war on children was the loss of educational opportunities. The illiteracy rate was almost 100 percent in 1993 because schools all over Somalia were shut down during the war. The country lacked the resources to revive the school system after the war ended.

Relief groups and concerned individuals tried to help. In 1992, a group of American schoolchildren began a project to aid Somali children in the farming community of Dhoqoshay. They launched a program they called "Children Helping Children—Horn of Africa Relief." Nine-year-old Daniel Perry of Washington, DC, came up with the idea of helping the children, and his classmates at the Mater Amoris Montessori School in Ashton, Maryland, joined the effort. They held fund-raisers for Somalia and packed supplies that could be sent to Dhoqoshay, where the money they raised was used to build a school.

Mohamud Jama who grew up in the village of Dhoqoshay, later attended school in the United States and became an official at

the United Nations. He returned to Dhoqoshay to deliver the supplies and tell the people about the relief effort organized by the Mater Amoris school. Jama continued to visit the school and carried letters and messages back and forth between the American and African children. Schools in several other states heard about the project and joined the Somalian relief effort. *See also* AFRICA; HEPBURN, AUDREY; RELIEF ORGANIZATIONS; SOLDIERS, CHILD; UNITED NATIONS CHILDREN'S FUND (UNICEF).

Further Reading: William Barnhill, "Children's Crusade for Somalia," *Good Housekeeping*, April 1993, p. 90ff; United Nations Children's Fund (UNICEF), *The State of the World's Children, 1996* (1996).

South Pacific (World War II). *See* PACIFIC (WORLD WAR II)

Soviet Union (World War II)

Youth in the Soviet Union were actively involved, both in the military and as civilians, during World War II. In June 1941, Nazi Germany attacked the Soviet Union, despite the fact that the two nations had signed a mutual non-aggression pact in 1939. The Soviet Union, under Premier Josef Stalin, then joined Great Britain, France, and the other Allied Nations in fighting against Adolf Hitler's Germany.

Tatjana Wassiljewa, a 13-year-old living outside Leningrad in 1941, later recalled that on the evening of the invasion, she and her friends "played soldier" and staged mock battles. Within two weeks, food was becoming harder to obtain and children helped to gather wild berries and mushrooms. They could see troop carriers and military vehicles belonging to their own Red Army moving along the countryside. German bombings began in July, and young people learned to run for cover or hurry into air-raid shelters. By August, bombings were occurring each night. Wassiljewa's family spent those hours in the cellar until their home was destroyed by bomb-fire, after which they moved in with neighbors.

During World War II, Soviet schoolboys in besieged Leningrad assemble machine guns for the Red Army. *Itar-Tass/Sovfoto.*

As German tanks swept across Russia, millions of people, both military and civilians, died. Stalin instigated a "scorched earth" policy, telling people to burn thousands of acres of crops before the Germans could use them to supply their troops. While the destruction of crops deprived German troops of food, it also meant that many Russians went hungry. In some places, even water was rationed. People planted vegetables in spaces where food might grow and tended these small gardens carefully, even when shooting was taking place nearby.

German troops occupied Tatjana Wassiljewa's town in September 1941. They seized Russian men as prisoners and beat others. German patrols searched homes, and forbade children from gathering wild berries and other foods in the woods. Families went hungry because their garden produce was used up; they killed goats and other animals for food. By December, Wassiljewa's family was starving and her mother was too weak to walk. They survived by killing the family's pet cat, then by making mush out of grated birch-bark. That winter, Wassiljewa set out

in freezing weather to find some food for her family. After weeks of wandering, she reached a home where kind people gave her a sack of corn to take home. The corn ran out by April. By then, her father had died.

An example of a community that endured numerous attacks was the town of Belgorod in southern Russia, which became part of the battlefront. Germans first arrived there in October 1941, and again in July 1943. By the time the German and Russian troops had finished fighting in the area, only 140 of the town's 34,000 citizens remained in Belgorod. The rest had either died, become soldiers, or fled.

Jews in the Soviet Union were targeted for death. Thousands were killed by mobile killing squads called *Einsatzgruppen,* which were sent from Germany to follow the military into Russia. Some young Russian Jews managed to escape being sent to ghettos and death camps. They made their way into the countryside and fought with partisan units.

Every Soviet citizen, whether male or female, could be conscripted into the army.

Teenage boys and girls were among those who served. As men left factory jobs to fight the invaders, children went to work making rifles, grenades, and other military equipment. Many young girls won awards for their high level of production. Youths also worked on farms where they helped raise food for military and civilian needs.

During the siege of Leningrad, which began in September 1941, German troops cut off the city from the rest of Russia and blocked food from reaching the starving population of about 3 million, as well as the 200,000 defense troops in the city. Rations dwindled to a small piece of bread for each person daily. Desperate people resorted to eating moldy food, then leather, lipstick, and carpenter's glue. Stacks of dead bodies lined the streets; people were too weak from hunger and sickness to bury them. The siege continued through 1942. During one three-week period in August and September, more than 11,000 people died. Homeless people wandered the streets or could be seen lying against piles of debris. Orphaned children begged for food. Many children and young adults died from bombardment, starvation, disease, or exposure, especially during the bitterly cold winter of 1941-1942.

Aleksandr A. Fadeyev, who arrived in Leningrad in the spring of 1942, later described the plight of youth there.

> In April, when I first saw the Leningrad children, they had already emerged from the most difficult period of their lives, but the hard experience of the winter was still imprinted on their faces and was still reflected in their games. It was reflected in the way many of the children played all by themselves; in the way that, even in their collective games, they played in silence, with grave faces. I saw the faces of children which expressed so grown-up a seriousness, children's eyes which reflected such thoughtfulness and sorrow, that those faces and eyes told one more than could be gathered from all the stories of the horrors of famine. (Carey, 1988)

The people of Leningrad worked valiantly to save children, and managed to evacuate many of them. Youths who remained in the city during the siege received special attention to help them deal with the problems it had caused. Kindergartens were set up for young children so they could study and play as normally as possible. Citizens contributed food and time to help these children. More than 1.5 million people died during the siege.

Young Soviets were also used as forced laborers. In May 1942, Tatjana Wassiljewa was taken to Germany on a train, where she had only some bread to eat during the trip west. When they arrived at a warehouse, they were hosed down, naked, by German men, then inspected by adults who had come to choose workers. Tatjana Wassiljewa worked in fields, weeding, then was sent to a factory that manufactured books. She was continually tired and hungry but stayed alive. Other young Soviets died from hunger and overwork or were seriously injured when they were forced to do dangerous, difficult jobs for the Germans.

The factory was bombed in November 1944, but Wassiljewa survived. She managed to escape from the region and went to Belgium, along with other refugees. She was not able to reach the Soviet Union again until 1946. Back home, she heard dreadful stories about the suffering that took place while she was gone. Finally, in 1947, Wassiljewa returned to school to begin studying to become a teacher. Years after the war, she would write in her diary that she was still often hungry and light-headed. Her account of her life during the war years, *Hostage to War,* was published in translation in 1997.

More than 13 million Russian civilians died during the war, along with 7 million soldiers. People throughout the nation endured hunger, and 25 million people became homeless as a result of World War II. *See also* SIMA; UKRAINE; UKRAINE (WORLD WAR II); WORLD WAR II.

Further Reading: John Carey, *Eyewitness to History* (1988); John Erickson, *The Road to Stalingrad* (1975); John Keegan, *The Second World War* (1989); Theodore Ropp, *War in the Modern World* (1962); Tatjana Wassiljewa, *Hostage to War* (1997).

Spanish-American War (1898)

The Spanish-American War of 1898 was fought to liberate Cuba from Spanish rule. Conflicts had raged for years, especially during the Ten Years' War (1868-1878) between rebels and the Cuban government, in which atrocities against civilians were committed on both sides. Sugar plantations were destroyed, causing widespread hunger and poverty among Cuban youth. The Spaniards who ruled the region, called *peninsulares*, killed whole villages of men, women, and children if people in the village were suspected of sheltering rebels.

After Governor-General Weyler came from Spain to take charge of Cuba in 1896, he ordered the burning of many sugar cane fields and moved people out of rural areas. Cubans were herded into concentration camps near cities and were kept under surveillance.

Clara Barton, an American Civil War nurse and the founder of the American Red Cross, brought some supplies from the United States to the stricken Cubans. She saw villages and towns that had been destroyed and was distressed about the plight of Cuban children. Barton visited a camp in Havana, which she later described in her book, *The Red Cross*.

> [O]ver four hundred women and children in the most pitiable condition possible for humans to be in and live . . . . The death record counted out a dozen or more every twenty-four hours and the grim, terrible pile of black coffins that confronted one at the very doorway told each famishing (sic) applicant on her entrance what her exit was likely to be. . . . Some were mere skeletons, others swollen out of all human shape. (Barton, 1895)

Stories like these (and some that were invented by people who wanted to arouse anti-Spanish sentiments) angered Americans. During the 1890s, they complained when Spaniards searched arriving American ships for arms or rebels. In 1897, Spanish officials stopped the steamer *Olivette* and seized a Cuban girl named Evangelina Cisneros, whom they accused of being a spy. She was searched by a female inspector, then released.

However, U.S. journalists who supported Cuban rebels exaggerated the story to arouse more sympathy for Cuba. The incident involving Cisneros became a rallying cry for Americans who wanted the United States to help rebels fight a war against Spain.

The United States declared war in August 1898. On February 15, the USS *Maine* exploded in the harbor of Havana, Cuba. The ship was destroyed and at least 263 people, including young crew-members, were killed. The cause of the blast was unclear. It may have occurred from a gas leak in the ship's bunkers. People who supported the Cuban rebels blamed it on Spanish fire and called for war.

During the war that followed, young civilians continued to suffer from food shortages, homelessness, and other deprivations. Young soldiers died on both sides. Cuba won its independence from Spain when the war ended in December 1900 in a Spanish defeat.

Further Reading: Clara Barton, *The Red Cross* (1895); Bernard A. Weisberger, *The American Newspaperman* (1962); Irving Werstein, *1898: The Spanish-American War* (1966).

Spanish Civil War (1936–1939)

Young men fought on both sides of the Spanish Civil War, which pitted the Nationalist (fascist) forces led by General Francisco Franco against the Republican government and its Loyalist troops. In addition to Spaniards, young men from other countries, including France, Italy, the United States, and Germany, took part in this war. The 500 young men who made up the American Abraham Lincoln Battalion of the Fifth International Brigade were mostly students who went to Spain to support the Republicans fighting against Franco's Nationalist rebels. More than half of the men in this battalion were killed or wounded at a battle in Jarama in 1937. Some international volunteers sided with Franco's troops, including young men from Ireland and the Soviet Union.

Young Spanish civilians experienced many changes during and after the war. Women between the ages of 17 and 35 were recruited

Young Spanish soldiers on drill during the Spanish Civil War of the late 1930s. *Corbis/Hulton-Deutsch Collection.*

for war work, whereas in the past they had been expected to remain in domestic roles. By 1936, social mores had changed. Young women could be seen walking alone on city streets without a male escort, which was once considered vital to preserve one's reputation. Homeless, hungry children could be seen begging. Private property was taken over by the new Franco government, so middle- and upper-income children saw big changes in their families' way of life.

Cities were under siege, and people went hungry. Children had to stay inside and endure blackouts at night. More thousands became hungry as farmers lacked the seeds and other things they needed to sustain food production. Thousands of children also became orphans and were homeless. To aid orphans, the widow of Onesimo Redondo, a fascist officer under General Franco, founded a relief organization called Winter Help. It was expanded and renamed Social Help to meet growing needs as the war continued.

As Franco's troops occupied various cities, schoolchildren were taught that they should make sacrifices for the country. Religious practices, which had been removed from public schools when Spain was a republic, were brought back. Children recited prayers, and Catholic religious objects were returned to schools.

Bombings were carried out against civilian areas. During heavy bombing, some families slept outside so they would not be buried under the rubble if their homes were hit. Some fled to the subways for safe havens. Refugees headed across the border to France. The bombing of the ancient Basque city of Guernica aroused protests from around the world. On April 26, 1937, German bombers launched the attack on market day, when people from the surrounding area crowded the town. They dropped nine incendiary and explosive bombs, which destroyed the main part of the city and killed 1,600 people, wounding at least 1,000 others. Two days later, Guernica and Durango were both taken over by Nationalist troops. The governments of England and France sent ships to carry several thousand Basque children to safe havens in their countries. The children lived either in special camps that had been set up for them or in private homes.

After their city was besieged by rebel troops in October 1936, people in Madrid tried to survive, but they ran out of food. German and Italian bombers hit the city, causing property damage. Children helped their elders build trenches and defenses. They could be seen carrying shovels and axes along the streets of Madrid. By spring 1939, 300 people were dying each day of starvation as they subsisted on a few ounces of bread per person per day. Children lacked shoes and warm clothing, as well as food.

After Franco's fascist troops took over Madrid in 1939, hundreds of food trucks arrived, and cats were let loose to kill the booming rat population. About 600,000 people had been killed, mostly in battle. Thousands of others had become refugees there and in Barcelona, which also fell as the Nationalists won the war. *See also* GUERNICA.

Further Reading: Segismundo Casado, *The Last Days of Madrid* (1939); Robert Goldston, *The Civil War in Spain* (1966).

Spiegel, Zvi (1915–)

As a young man imprisoned in a Nazi camp during World War II, Zvi Spiegel tried to help a group of children survive during and after the Holocaust. A native of Budapest, Hungary, Spiegel grew up in Munkacs, Czechoslovakia. At age 21, he was drafted into the Czech army where he rose to officer's rank. Because he was Jewish, Spiegel was sent to various labor camps after World War II began and the Nazis were in control of his country.

In 1944, when the Nazis deported Jews from the ghetto near his hometown, Spiegel and his family were sent to the notorious death camp at Auschwitz-Birkenau. He and his twin sister Magda escaped immediate death in the gas chambers, where his parents and Magda's seven-year-old son were killed upon arrival. Zvi and Magda were sent to the "Twins' Block," where Dr. Josef Mengele and other Nazi scientists kept human subjects for their cruel and unethical "medical" experiments. Mengele had a keen interest in twins and believed they could provide important information about heredity. He hoped that

this information would help the Nazis develop a "master race" and find ways to extinguish human traits they deemed undesirable.

Mengele placed Spiegel in charge of the twin boys, most of them children, at the camp. They called him "Twins' Father." Spiegel was sometimes able to influence Mengele to give him more food for the children in his care. In at least one case, he falsified documents and turned two brothers into twins so they could stay alive. Spiegel also organized classes in math, history, geography, and other subjects he recalled from his own schooling. He tried to help the children cope with the brutal conditions and daily tragedies at the camp. Many of the children had seen their whole families killed there, and the Twins' Block stood near the crematorium where dead bodies were burned day and night.

Spiegel later told author Lucette Lagnado that he distrusted Mengele: "I felt he could change his mind about the twins at any time and have us all killed. And so my strategy was to have the twins maintain as low a profile as possible—and keep out of Mengele's way" (Lagnado and Dekel, 1991). To keep up the boys' spirits, Spiegel promised them he would take them back to their homes when the war ended. Late in 1944, as Germany lost ground and Russian troops approached, the Nazis hastened to kill any prisoners still alive at Auschwitz, including the surviving twins. Spiegel interceded with Mengele to keep the twins alive. Some were taken on a Death March out of the camp in mid-winter and forced to walk, on foot, across Poland into Czechoslovakia, then Germany. Others remained in the barracks and were freed by the Allies in January. Spiegel had remained with the children. On January 28, he left the camp with about 36 children heading for their first stop, Cracow, Poland.

Spiegel tried to track down any surviving relatives and accompanied some children to their home towns. Along the way, he convinced Russian guards and soldiers to give them food and let them pass through borders. By this time, the rail system was destroyed and the former prisoners could not persuade anyone to give them a car. When transportation finally became available, Spiegel made sure the children were taken safely to their destinations and gave them all the information he had gathered about them so they could try to find their families. *See also* AUSCHWITZ-BIRKENAU; CHILDREN OF AUSCHWITZ NAZI DEADLY EXPERIMENTS SURVIVORS (CANDLES); DEATH CAMPS (WORLD WAR II); DEPORTATIONS; EXPERIMENTS, NAZI; HOLOCAUST; "MASTER RACE"; MENGELE, JOSEF; PRISONERS.

Further Reading: Lucette Matalon Lagnado and Sheila Cohn Dekel, *Children of the Flames* (1991); Robert Jay Lifton, *The Nazi Doctors* (1986).

Sports

Normal activities for young people, including sports and athletic competitions, are disrupted by war. The Olympic Games, which were created to develop international fellowship and goodwill, have sometimes been suspended during wartime, and young athletes have lost their chance to compete. Athletic coaches may also leave to join the military or flee the country as refugees. Sports facilities close down for lack of fuel, equipment, personnel, and funds. Teams broke up as children were evacuated to different places for reasons of safety.

During the 1930s and 1940s, young athletes were strongly affected by politics and war. After Adolf Hitler became the leader of Germany in 1933, his Nazi Party passed new laws that deprived Jews of civil liberties and banned them from numerous activities and from sports teams, sports organizations, and regional and national competitions.

In choosing its Olympic teams for the 1936 Berlin Games, Germany excluded top Jewish athletes. Among the many Jewish athetes who suffered was Margarethe (Gretel) Bergmann, an outstanding track and field athlete. She was also ousted from her soccer club and played informally with other Jewish soccer players who had also been banned from their regular teams. Although Bergmann had long planned to pursue physical education studies after high school, she and other Jews were banned from attending German universities.

After she and her family moved to England, Bergmann won the British high jump event in 1934. She hoped to compete for Great Britain in the Olympics but was ordered back to Germany to try out for the German team instead. In fall 1935, German officials set up a training facility in Baden for a few Jewish athletes. By this time, the United States and some other countries had criticized Germany for persecuting Jewish athletes. In response, German officials allowed Bergmann and fencer Helene Mayer (whose father was Jewish and whose mother was Christian) to train with the German Olympic team. Mayer had won a gold medal in women's fencing at the 1928 Olympics and a silver medal in 1932 at the Olympics in Los Angeles.

On June 30, 1936, Gretel Bergmann recorded a high jump of 5 feet, 3 inches, which was then the record for German women. Nevertheless, she was notified that she had not been selected for the German team that would go to the Olympics. The 1936 Summer Olympics, held in Berlin, were in many ways a political spectacle designed to glorify Nazism. Thousands of young Germans marched or played musical instruments in the elaborate parades and ceremonies. They included 28,000 members of the Hitler Youth, the Nazi organization for boys, and the *Bund Deutscher Madchen*, the national organization for girls. Young people were also among the thousands of spectators at the games. They saw Germany's best male track and field athletes defeated by American college student Jesse Owens, who won four gold medals— in the 100-meter dash, the long jump, the 200-meter race, and as part of the U.S. men's 400-meter relay team. Although Owens was African American (a race the Nazis regarded as "inferior"), German schoolchildren cheered for Owens and sought his autograph.

The Olympic Games scheduled for 1940 and 1944 were canceled because of World War II. Young people were most affected because they made up the majority of athletes on the teams. Some of these athletes fought as soldiers, served with women's corps or volunteer organizations, or worked in war-related industries. Many never again competed as top athletes.

Years later, in 1980, U.S. athletes were not permitted to compete in the Moscow Summer Olympics for political reasons. U.S. President Jimmy Carter made this decision to protest the invasion of Afghanistan by Soviet Russia. Young athletes expressed different opinions about the boycott. Some of them supported the president; others strongly believed the United States should compete. Athletes who had reached their peak performance that year lost the chance to demonstrate their best work at the Olympics.

Save the Children and other relief organizations have developed sports programs in Liberia, Sudan, and other war-torn regions as one way to help young people resume more normal lives. They regard organized sports activities as another way to help youth, especially former child soldiers, to take part in routine activities after the trauma of war. In some cases, former combatants have participated in football games and other team sports with their former enemies. *See also* HITLER YOUTH.

Further Reading: Tony Gentry, *Jesse Owens* (1990); Richard D. Mandel, *The Nazi Olympics* (1971); Robert Slater, *Great Jews in Sports* (1983).

Stalin, Josef. *See* SOVIET UNION (WORLD WAR II); UKRAINE

Student Nurse Corps. *See* CADET NURSE CORPS

Sudan

Children were caught in the crossfire of civil wars that began in southern Sudan during the 1950s as government forces opposed a liberation army of rebels. The war was complicated by conflicts between Muslims and Christians, which had erupted intermittently despite intermarriages and social mixing. Young men died while serving in the army. In Khartoum, the national capital, high school students were being inducted into the army as soon as they graduated. Military recruiters took to the streets and apprehended eli-

gible young men from buses and other public places. The draft and conscription tactics were widely criticized and groups of mothers were arrested for publicly protesting the draft.

Young men tried to avoid being inducted. Some fled from Khartoum when they reached draft age. Some families who could afford the costs sent their sons abroad to avoid service, while others deliberately kept their sons from receiving high school diplomas so they would remain ineligible for service. One protesting mother, Fawzia Fadil, said, "When we go to market, everyone is talking about how 'I'm not sending my son anymore to final exams.' This regime is killing our children" (McKinley, 1998).

Children suffered from numerous other problems as the war greatly increased Sudan's refugee population. Tens of thousands of people left southern Sudan, which was occupied by rebels, and moved to central and northern Sudan. About 650,000 lived in Khartoum by 1998. By that year, an estimated 4 million people had become refugees.

Inflation soared because goods and food could only be flown in at high prices and planes had to risk gunfire to land. Hunger was widespread during this long war. By 1998, an estimated 2 million people were in need of food and other supplies. Malnutrition was rampant, especially in southern Sudan. One resident, a chief of the Kuku tribes in Juba, the capital of southern Sudan, said, "One is hungry, and the hunger brings weakness and disease, and there is a lack of medicine. We lost many people, especially old people and young children" (McKinley, 1998). As more people fled from the areas of most intense armed conflict in the south, the North and South Kordofan States became overcrowded, and children suffered from the lack of safe water, food, and other goods and services.

During the war, UNICEF—the United Nations Children's Fund—was able to help some children by bringing in food and medical supplies. They developed the concept of "Children as Zones of Peace" in which certain areas were designated as safe for children and were declared off-limits to combatants. Patrick McCormick, who worked for UNICEF in New York City, said, "There are places where medical supplies can get through, where there is no fighting and children are protected." Save the Children also worked to ease the suffering in Sudan which continued after a cease-fire was declared in 1997. In July 1998, Save the Children instituted the Sudan Emergency Appeal, which raised nearly $400,000 to fund programs in Sudan. The Save the Children Alliance worked to meet the emergency needs of children and to support families in Sudan. *See also* AFRICA; REFUGEES; SAVE THE CHILDREN; SAVE THE CHILDREN ALLIANCE (INTERNATIONAL SAVE THE CHILDREN ALLIANCE); SOLDIERS, CHILD; UNITED NATIONS CHILDREN'S FUND (UNICEF).

Further Reading: James C. McKinley, Jr., "Many in Sudan Tired of a War without End," *New York Times,* March 3, 1998, p. A6; Save the Children, "Emergency in Sudan Continues," *Impact,* 10, 2, 1998, p. 7.

Sweden. *See* DENMARK (WORLD WAR II); LE CHAMBON-SUR-LIGNON; NORWAY (WORLD WAR II); RED CROSS; WALLENBERG, RAOUL

Szeptycki, Andreas. *See* UKRAINE (WORLD WAR II)

Szold, Henrietta. *See* YOUTH ALIYAH

T

Terezin (Theresienstadt)

During World War II, the Nazis under Adolf Hitler imprisoned thousands of children in the Terezin concentration camp in Czechoslovakia. The camp was first designated as a place where elderly Jews would be sent to live, as well as other privileged prisoners. Terezin was to be a "model" camp that could be shown to visitors from the International Red Cross and other humanitarian organizations as "proof" that Jews were being treated humanely in the camps. Because of this, Terezin appeared much more attractive than other concentration and death camps. Propaganda photographs from the camp showed children smiling and playing, eating hearty meals, and sleeping comfortably on their own beds. Camp buildings were labeled as cafes, banks, and bakeries. Prisoners worked in an art studio and at other jobs and took part in seemingly normal activities. However, the camp was quite different when visitors were not around, and the photographs were deceptive. Visitors were also served better food than the prisoners received. Sick, dying, and starving prisoners were hidden from their view.

During the war, the camp became overcrowded and was used as a way-station or transit camp, from which Jews were sent to other camps, usually to die. More than 90,000 people lived in a place that had been designed for about 7,000. By 1942, about 131 people were dying each day at Terezin.

Along with the elderly, young Jews were sent to Terezin. Thousands of children were brought to the camp from all over occupied Europe. Between 1942 and 1945, about 15,000 children under the age of 15 arrived. Most of these children were orphans, although a few families arrived together. Children lived together in barracks, about 20 to 30 in each room. Those over the age of 14 were forced to labor in the fields or to dig ditches, build roads, or clean the camp. Of the thousands of children who were sent to Terezin, only about 100 survived the war. None of the survivors was younger than age 14. Most of the children who spent time in Terezin were then sent away and murdered in other camps, such as Auschwitz-Birkenau. Terezin was liberated in 1945.

Younger children who were imprisoned at Terezin produced artwork, stories, and poems, some of which have been preserved and exhibited around the world. They show the brutal scenes of war the children witnessed and their fears of death and starvation, as well as the day-to-day deprivations they suffered. Many of these drawings and writings are part of a collection entitled *I Never Saw Another Butterfly. See also* AUERBACHER, INGE; CONCENTRATION CAMPS (WORLD WAR II); HOLOCAUST.

Further Reading: Gerald Green, *The Artists of Terezin,* (1969); Marie Rut Krizkova, *We Are Children Just the Same: Vedem, the Secret Magazine by the Boys of Terezin* (1995); Hana Volavkova, ed., *I Never Saw*

Another Butterfly: Children's Drawings and Poems from Terezin Concentration Camp, 1942-1944 (1993).

Terrorism. *See* ARAB-ISRAELI WARS; BIOLOGICAL WARFARE; CHEMICAL WARFARE; LEBANESE CIVIL WAR; NORTHERN IRELAND; KURDS; VIETNAM WAR

Tet Offensive. *See* VIETNAM WAR

Theresienstadt. *See* TEREZIN (THERESIENSTADT)

Thirty Years' War (1618–1648)

The Thirty Years' War (1616-1648) involved most countries in Western Europe and was fought primarily on German soil. The war was characterized by religious animosity between Catholics and Protestants and territorial conflicts among rulers in Germany, Austria, Sweden and France. It marked the first time that wartime civilian casualties outnumbered military casualties. Children and young adults suffered as mercenary troops moved across Germany during these years, bringing diseases and taking food, cattle, horses, and necessities from peasants. Many young people became refugees as their communities were destroyed. Large numbers of young soldiers also fought and died during this long war. An estimated 30,000 even fought on each side during this war and took part in more battles over a longer period of time than in previous wars.

The largest number of young civilians died during what was known as the Sack of Magdeburg (Germany) in 1631. Military discipline broke down after troops won a victory in the region. Fires broke out in different parts of Magdeburg, and the wooden homes burst into flames, leaving thousands homeless. When the war ended in 1648 with the Treaty of Westphalia, Germany's population had gone from 21 million to 13 million. The population of the Holy Roman Empire declined by 15 to 20 percent. In Bohemia, 29,000 villages had been totally destroyed.

Further Reading: Mark Kishlansky et al., *Civilization in the West* (1999); Stephen J. Lee, *The Thirty Years War/30 Years Later* (1991); Peter Limm, *The Thirty Years War* (1984).

A Thousand Cranes. *See* SASAKI, SADAKO

Tinker, John. *See* TINKER V. DES MOINES

Tinker, Mary Beth. *See* TINKER V. DES MOINES

Tinker v. Des Moines (1968)

Teenage anti-war protestors were the plaintiffs in the case *Tinker v. Des Moines*, which was decided by the United States Supreme Court in 1968. Mary Beth Tinker, her brother John Tinker, and their friend Christopher Eckhardt had been suspended from their high school in Des Moines, Iowa, for wearing black armbands as a symbolic protest against the Vietnam War. The students were told they could not wear these armbands in school; they, in turn, said such a prohibition violated their First Amendment right to free speech.

The matter was debated at local school board meetings and in newspapers and on television. The Tinkers had support from their parents, who also opposed the war. However, some people in the community became angry enough to send the family written death threats and make hostile phone calls to their home. The American Civil Liberties Union (ACLU) represented the young people in a lawsuit, in which they claimed a First Amendment right to peacefully express their political viewpoint so long as they did not disrupt school activities. The school administrators disagreed, saying the school was not an appropriate forum for these kinds of displays. The trial court agreed with the school as did the appeals court.

The students asked the United States Supreme Court to consider their case, and a ruling in their favor was handed down in 1968. Speaking for the Court, Justice Abe Fortas declared that the wearing of black armbands was a form of symbolic, or non-verbal, speech protected by the First Amendment to the United States Constitution. Fortas declared that school officials must find a compelling interest was at stake to deny students this right. He defined a compelling interest as more than a "vague fear of disturbance," as something that would materially disrupt classwork or disturb the rights of other people in the school. *See also* ANTI-WAR MOVEMENT (VIETNAM WAR); VIETNAM WAR.

Further Reading: Peter Irons, *The Courage of Their Convictions* (1988); Doreen Rappaport, *Tinker v. Des Moines: Student Rights on Trial* (1993).

Toll, Nelly Landau (1935-)

Artist and author Nelly Landau Toll wrote an absorbing first-person account of her life in hiding as a Jewish child in Poland during the Holocaust. From 1943 to 1945, Toll kept a diary to express her feelings and painted to help pass the long months she and her mother spent hidden day and night. Her vivid watercolor paintings show a child's longing to move about freely and enjoy nature, school, playmates, and other normal activities.

Toll first went into hiding one afternoon in 1943 soon after her family was sent to the Lwow Ghetto in Poland. For days, she had seen Nazis rounding up people who never returned. Under cover of a bitter storm, her mother slipped Nelly outside the ghetto and she hid for several months with a Catholic family. She had to return to the ghetto after a boarder at the house became suspicious. In a desperate effort to escape Poland, Nelly and her parents joined a group that paid a German major to take them to Hungary. However, the German abandoned them near the border and disappeared. Betrayed, the group barely escaped the Nazi killing squads that were operating nearby and returned to the Lwow Ghetto.

In 1943, Nelly and her mother found refuge with a middle-aged Polish couple named Wojtek. Inside their tiny two-room apartment was a small space built inside the bedroom wall where they could hide in case of Nazi raids. They had to stay quiet at all times, never moving or using the toilet unless someone else was at home.

A friend of Mrs. Wojtek's brought Nelly books, a diary, and watercolor paints and paper, and she began keeping a journal. In her book, Toll described the constant fear she faced.

> Outside, the Nazi storm kept sweeping through the streets. More Jews in hiding were being discovered daily; the police relied on the tip-offs of neighbors ready for a reward and used vicious dogs to search for Jews. More than once I watched, riveted, my eyes filled with tears, as these victims were pushed roughly past our window by the armed Gestapo. (Toll, 1993)

The days passed slowly and fearfully. When Nelly became ill with scarlet fever in December 1943, her mother had no medicine. Late in the war, a grenade crashed through the window and left imbedded metal in her mother's foot, causing a nasty wound. Nelly and her mother had several narrow escapes as the Nazis and their collaborators conducted random searches. Despite the risks, the Wojteks kept them in their home until the Soviet army arrived in July 1944. They were relieved to be free but saddened when they found out that Nelly's father had been killed by the Nazis.

After the war, Nelly Toll met other former hidden children. One six-year-old boy and his father had lived for nearly a year in a graveyard where an old Ukrainian gravedigger brought them food, blankets, and other things. Another boy was hidden by his Polish nanny. Still others had stayed in an underground bunker outside a Polish village for two years, aided by a peasant and forester.

Toll's book, *Behind the Secret Window* (1993), based on her childhood memories, details this harrowing time and shows life before and right after the war. Several of Toll's paintings are reproduced with the text. They have been exhibited around the world. *See also* GHETTOS (WORLD WAR II); HIDDEN CHILDREN; HOLOCAUST; POLAND (WORLD WAR II); RESCUERS (HOLOCAUST).

Further Reading: Nelly S. Toll, *Behind the Secret Window: A Memoir of a Hidden Childhood During World War II* (1993).

Treblinka

During the Holocaust, Treblinka, Poland, was the site of one of the six death camps operated by the Nazis for the purpose of genocide. Of 400,000 Jews taken to this death camp during the first months of its operation, between July and September 1942, 90,000 were children. About 750,000 Jews were gassed to death in this camp during the 14 months it was in operation. *See also* DEATH CAMPS (WORLD WAR II); FINAL SOLUTION; HOLOCAUST; KORCZAK, JANUSZ.

Trocme, Andre (1901–1971) and Trocme, Magda (1902–1996)

Pastor Andre Trocme and his wife Magda took leading roles in helping a community in southern France save thousands of Jews, mainly children, during World War II. Trocme was a pacifist Huguenot minister who had worked among laborers and the poor before arriving in Le Chambon-sur-Lignon, in the mountains of southern France. He and his co-pastor, Edouard Theis, founded the Cevenol School, which prepared youths for university study and was dedicated to principles of nonviolence, tolerance, and social justice.

The Trocmes began helping Jewish refugees in 1941 when a woman who had fled Nazi Germany arrived at their home. Magda Trocme immediately offered the woman shelter, food, and warm clothing. She and Andre believed that more refugees might arrive and they should be prepared to help. After conferring with church leaders and Quaker relief organization leaders in the region, Trocme decided Le Chambon would offer group homes and private homes to shelter refugees, mostly children, who eventually numbered around 5,000.

Magda Trocme was involved in many aspects of the rescue work. She taught at the Cevenol School, helped organize the group homes, and continued to manage her own household, which included four young children—Jacques, Daniel, Jean-Pierre, and Nelly. The children also felt a responsibility to do what they could to help. As an adult,

Nelly Trocme Hewitt, who later moved to the United States, recalled that

> In school it was an unspoken assumption that one was not to ask where or how these [refugee children] came into our midst. Despite the language barrier, we understood that they had suffered. . . . We tried to make them feel welcome. (Hallie, 1979)

Between 1941 and 1944, Le Chambon was raided several times and Pastor Trocme was interrogated by Nazi police. He refused to acknowledge the presence of Jews at Le Chambon or provide any information to the Nazis, even after he was jailed. In July 1943, a member of the French resistance told the pastor that the Nazis planned to assassinate him and were offering a reward or bounty to anyone who killed him. Trocme was reluctant to leave the village, believing that he should continue to guide people in their dangerous work. However, high church officials urged him to leave until the danger was over. Trocme finally fled to avoid endangering his family. While he was in hiding, he was arrested and had some narrow escapes. In the meantime, Magda Trocme continued her difficult work. Of those times, she would later say, "Each person, each day, did what seemed necessary" (Rittner and Myers, 1986).

In June 1944, shortly after the D-Day invasion brought the Allies into France, Andre Trocme returned home. The Trocmes were later recognized as Righteous Gentiles. Trocme's citation from the state of Israel says that the courageous pastor, "at peril of his life, saved Jews during the epoch of extermination."

After the war, the Trocmes continued to work for the causes they believed in. They helped found an international organization called the House of Reconciliation in Versailles, France. The organization is dedicated to the principles of peace and justice. *See also* FRANCE (WORLD WAR II); HIDDEN CHILDREN; LE CHAMBON-SUR-LIGNON; TROCME, DANIEL.

Further Reading: Philip Hallie, *Lest Innocent Blood Be Shed* (1979); Carol Rittner and Sondra Myers, eds., *The Courage to Care* (1986).

Trocme, Daniel (1916?–1944)

Daniel Trocme, a cousin of Pastor Andre Trocme, was the director of the first group home set up for refugee children in a French community that rescued about 5,000 Jews, mostly children, during World War II. The house was called the Crickets and was located about two miles from the center of the mountain village of Le Chambon-sur-Lignon. Later, Trocme took charge of a second house for boys called the House of the Rocks.

Trocme was the son of a prominent educator and one of eight children. He had been teaching in his father's school, Ecole des Roches, during the year 1940-1941. Although he had a heart ailment that made it difficult for him to live at high altitudes, Daniel Trocme answered his cousin's call to come to Le Chambon. As a "house father," he educated the boys in his care and also worked tirelessly to meet their other needs, staying up late to cook soup for their meal the next day and replacing their worn-out shoe soles with pieces of leather tires. He regarded children as the weakest and most helpless victims of the Nazi Holocaust.

Nazi special police—the Gestapo—raided Crickets and the House of the Rocks in the summer of 1943. It was the only time they succeeded in raiding a home in Le Chambon before the occupants could sneak out and hide elsewhere. The Germans arrested Trocme and the children. As one Jewish boy was being harassed, a Nazi officer hit him with holy objects the boy had received at his Bar Mitzvah, a Jewish ceremony that marks a young man's coming-of-age. As he left, Daniel told Magda Trocme, his cousin's wife,

"Write immediately to my parents. Tell them I'll send them news as soon as I can. Tell them I'm okay, and not to worry. And remind them how much I like traveling" (Hallie, 1979). He and the boys, most of whom were between ages 14 and 15, were forced onto buses.

News of Daniel Trocme's whereabouts reached Le Chambon about a year later. Most of the boys who had been deported never returned, but one of them managed to escape from a Nazi camp and make his way back to the village. He said that Daniel Trocme had been taken to the death camp Majdanek in eastern Poland. The Germans had accused him of being Jewish because he showed so much concern for the boys in his care. After Russian soldiers liberated Majdanek in 1945, an investigation into camp records showed that Daniel Trocme was gassed to death on April 4, 1944. He was later honored posthumously by Yad Vashem in Israel as a Righteous Gentile. *See also* LE CHAMBON-SUR-LIGNON; TROCME, ANDRE AND TROCME, MAGDA; RIGHTEOUS GENTILES; YAD VASHEM.

Further Reading: Philip Hallie, *Lest Innocent Blood Be Shed* (1979).

Tuczno Ghetto. *See* UKRAINE (WORLD WAR II)

Twins' Block. *See* CHILDREN OF AUSCHWITZ NAZI DEADLY EXPERIMENTS SURVIVORS (CANDLES); DEKEL, ALEX SCHLOMO; EXPERIMENTS, NAZI; MENGELE, JOSEF; SPIEGEL, ZVI

U

Uganda

During the second half of the twentieth century, civil wars in the central African nation of Uganda affected the lives of thousands of young people. Conflicts between northerners and southerners, which involve longstanding religious and territorial disputes, were exacerbated during British colonial days when people in the south were recruited for civil service positions while northerners were primarily recruited into the army. Southern Ugandans became more educated and prosperous while the Acholi tribal group, which inhabits the northernmost districts of Uganda, remained poor. Civilians suffered from hunger and lived in fear of being attacked. Youths were also conscripted for military service, sometimes against their will. In 1971, an army officer named Idi Amin Dada led a coup that overthrew President Milton Obote, who had support from the Acholi. Amin pledged to reform the country and improve living conditions, but instead he instituted a brutal military regime. Amin ordered the massacre of young Acholi and Langi soldiers who had fought against him. Within a year, other prominent Ugandans, including doctors, professors, government officials, and army officers from tribes Amin disliked were also executed. Children lost parents and other relatives, and many others feared their families would become targets.

Asian youth living in Uganda were forced to leave the country. In September 1972, Amin declared that all Asians must leave, even those who were legally citizens. More than 70,000 people left for India and Pakistan, taking almost nothing along with them. Some fled to Kenya and made their way to Great Britain or North America where they struggled to start new lives. When Amin nationalized businesses in Uganda, many foreigners left, and the economy suffered, bringing shortages of food, fuel, cooking oil, and many manufactured goods. Prices soared, and people could not obtain things they needed.

In 1976, government-ordered massacres of Kenyans in Uganda took place in Jinja and other towns and villages. Thousands more Ugandans fled when Amin banned 26 Christian groups and had some religious leaders killed. He also banned European tourists from the country.

Among those who protested Amin's actions were students at Makerere University. The government imprisoned these students and forced others to leave Uganda. Human rights organizations later estimated that 300,000 people were killed during Idi Amin's regime (1971-1979). Illiteracy increased as schools shut down, children became orphans, and educational opportunities declined.

Children's lives did not improve much when Milton Obote returned to power in 1979 after his supporters overthrew Idi Amin.

Violence continued as opposition movements fought for control of Uganda, and young civilians were among the dead and injured, along with young soldiers. About 200,000 people died during Obote's term in office. After Tito Okeloo Lutwa came into power and installed a military government in 1985, his opponents, resistance troops led by Yoweri Museveni, tried to gain control. Fighting with the resistance were many young soldiers; about 10 percent of them were under the age of 15. Many of these young men had become orphans during the previous wars. Museveni's troops, the National Resistance Army (later renamed the Uganda People's Defense force or UPDF), were regarded as well-disciplined and were praised for not exploiting people in Uganda. A victorious Museveni took charge of the country in January 1986 and pledged to rebuild the economy and reform the government. However, fighting continued, and members of the UPDF sometimes sought revenge against the Acholi rebels and were known to harass villagers and loot and steal cattle.

Military factions in Uganda have continued to use young people to fight for them. In northern Uganda in 1996, a rebel group called the Lord's Resistance Army (LRA) was attacking both civilians and soldiers in that region. Working out of southern Sudan, the LRA kidnapped children for military purposes. Hundreds of children, some as young as 8 or 9, were seized by guerillas and taken to LRA camps across the Sudanese border. Some of these children were later rescued and reported that they had experienced brutality in the camps, including beatings and torture. They told representatives from relief organizations that they often had only yams or wild plants to eat while they were in the camps.

In October 1996, the LRA abducted a group of 139 girls, most of them between the ages of 15 and 17, from St. Mary's, a Catholic boarding school in Aboke. They raided the school at night, looted the clinic, set fire to several buildings, and destroyed a school vehicle. By 1998, the LRA had abducted at least 8,000 children, according to UNICEF, and from 2,000-4,000 remained in captivity. Children who were abducted into the LRA

later testified that they were forced to carry heavy army supplies, steal food, take part in looting raids, and beat and kill fellow captives who tried to escape. Young girls were forced to become sexual servants for soldiers. The children suffered from constant hunger, fear, and beatings, and their feet became swollen and infected from the long walks. One child told representatives from Human Rights Watch/Africa, "with any load you must struggle to carry it, or otherwise the rebels say, 'You are becoming stubborn and rebellious!' And they kill you. If your feet swell, they also kill you" (Human Rights Watch, 1997).

By 1997, hundreds of thousands of northern Ugandans had been displaced from their homes, and agriculture had nearly halted. Schools, hospitals, and other community buildings had been destroyed. For example, in 1996, in the district of Gulu, the number of functioning schools fell from 199 to 64. Representatives from Human Rights Watch and UNICEF reported that children in Uganda suffered the most during the war. Thousands had died or been injured by land mines, gunshots, and other weapons. Others died from malnutrition or from malaria, measles, or other infectious diseases that spread quickly among the weakened population. According to Human Rights Watch, "The children of northern Uganda are the victims of atrocious human rights violations of a severity that is difficult to imagine, and the actions of the Lord's Resistance Army violate the most basic principles both of customary international law and of human morality" (Human Rights Watch/Africa, 1997).

Further Reading: Laura Barnitz, *Child Soldiers* (1997); Human Rights Watch/Africa, Human Rights Watch Children's Rights Project, *The Scars of Death: Children Abducted by the Lord's Resistance Army in Uganda* (1997); Thomas P. Ofcansky, *Uganda, Tarnished Pearl of Africa* (1996).

Ukraine

During the 1930s, hundreds of thousands of children starved to death in the Ukraine during conflicts between Ukrainian nationalists and the government of the Soviet Union (USSR). Under Premier Joseph Stalin, Soviet leaders decided that people in this Soviet republic would no longer be permitted to own private farms. The Ukraine was a major grain producer, and Stalin wanted to turn all the land into collective farms under the control of the government.

Under the new policy, no grain from a collective farm would be distributed to the farmers, known as kulaks, until the government quota was met, and Stalin increased the quota for the Ukraine by 44 percent, leaving no grain to feed the peasants. Meanwhile, there was plenty of grain and other foods being shipped throughout the Soviet Union and abroad. When Ukrainians resisted this effort, Stalin sent armed troops to fight them, and thousands of people were killed. The Ukraine declared that it wished to become independent of the Soviet Union. To prevent this from happening, Stalin ordered that almost all Ukrainian wheat be removed and he banned any grain from being shipped into the region.

Red Army troops sealed roads and rail lines to prevent anything from reaching the Ukraine. Seed stocks, grain, silage, farm animals, and fuel were seized. If a man, woman, or child was caught taking even one handful of grain for their own use or stealing a bit of coal from a train, they could be deported or even executed. People died of cold, hunger, and disease, especially during the bitter winter of 1932-1933. Children were forced to eat bark, roots, even leather boots and belts, to survive another day.

From the year 1929 to the year 1938, the number of 7-year-old children in the Ukraine decreased by about 600,000, as shown by school enrollment figures kept by the Soviet government. All the other Soviet republics showed an increase in the number of children who enrolled that year in school.

Eyewitnesses later described the horror of the famine. Soviet official Victor Kravchenko said, "The most terrifying sights were the little children with skeleton limbs dangling from balloon-like abdomens. Starvation had wiped every trace of youth from their faces, turning them into tortured gargoyles—only in their eyes still lingered the reminder of childhood" (Kravchenko, 1944). As a result, during the years 1932 and 1933, more than 3 million people in this region died of starvation. Some people regarded this as an act of genocide by Stalin's government. *See also* GENOCIDE; RUSSIAN REVOLUTION; SOVIET UNION (WORLD WAR II); UKRAINE (WORLD WAR II).

Further Reading: W.E.D. Allen, *The Ukraine* (1941); Martin Gilbert, *Russian History Atlas* (1972); Victor Kravchenko, *I Chose Freedom* (1989); Eric Margolis, "Remembering Ukraine's Unknown Holocaust," *The Toronto Sun*, December 13, 1998; reprinted at <http://mykola.com/famine.html>; George Vernadsky, *A History of Russia* (1954); Bernard D. Wolfe, *Krushchev and Stalin's Ghost* (1957).

Ukraine (World War II)

During World War II, Jewish youth were persecuted and killed by the thousands in the Ukraine, then part of the Soviet Union (USSR). Nearly 2 million Jews lived in the Soviet Ukraine and the Soviet Baltic states of Lithuania, Estonia, and Latvia. In 1939, Hitler made a non-aggression pact with the Soviet Union, giving the Soviets control over the Baltic states and pledging he would not invade the USSR. However, Hitler broke the pact in June 1941 when he invaded the Soviet Union. Massacres occurred in the Ukraine when Nazi mobile killing squads (*Einsatzgruppen)* followed the invading forces into the Soviet Union. The squads rounded up and shot Jewish men, women, and children. Whole villages were emptied and people were forced to march into remote areas where they had to dig mass graves, then stand naked near the pits, where they were shot.

In 1942, the Germans built a wall around the Jewish community of Tuczno, turning it into a ghetto. That autumn, armed Germans and Ukrainians tried to deport the 3,000 Jews trapped inside. Spurred by young people, ghetto residents decided to resist. They filled all available containers with kerosene and set fire to the ghetto. In the confusion that followed, the Jews of Tuczno were able to smash the ghetto fence. Youths then attacked the armed soldiers with hatchets and other weapons. Other people threw home-made grenades at the troops. Most of the Jews were able to escape into the forest where youths joined partisan groups.

Although some Ukrainians helped the Nazis round up and kill Jewish civilians, others tried to help the Jews. One staunch anti-Nazi was the head of the Ukrainian Greek Catholic Church in Galicia and archbishop of Lwow, Andreas Szeptycki (1865–1944). A well-traveled man in his seventies, Szeptycki was known as a scholar and master of several languages, including Hebrew. When Szeptycki realized that the Nazis and their Ukrainian collaborators were murdering thousands of Jews, Szeptycki wrote a critical pastoral letter titled "Thou Shalt Not Murder!" Every priest in his region had to read the letter at weekly church services and Szeptycki ordered that clergy reporting to him must take action to save Jews. Szeptycki warned people that God would punish those who took part in these murders. He confronted Nazi officials and secretly hid people inside his church. Szeptycki was later honored as a Righteous Gentile by Yad Vashem in Israel.

Non-Jewish children in the Ukraine also suffered greatly. During three years of German occupation that began in June 1941, Ukrainians endured devastating losses and millions of civilians lost their lives. The Nazis regarded the people as "sub-humans" and wanted the fertile Ukraine as more living space for Germans. Toward that end, Hitler ordered that the army use brutal means to fight Ukrainians, including women and children.

Ukrainians suffered more losses as a result of their own government's policies. After Hitler's armies invaded the Soviet Union, Russian dictator Joseph Stalin ordered the farmers to destroy all crops, machinery, and materials that might be used by the Germans. Soviet guerilla units were ordered to set fire to forests, stores, and transports. Six million cattle were removed from the Ukraine and sent east, along with 300,000 tractors and other goods.

In 1941, Nazi leaders discussed the possibility of slaughtering all Ukrainian men over age 15 but decided to use them as slave laborers instead. When few men volunteered to go to Germany as laborers, they were forced to do so. During the war, over 2.3 million Ukrainian men and women, many of them teenagers, were forced into labor, and tens of thousands of them died. Children lost their parents and other relatives when these adults were sent to Germany and forced to work for the Nazis. Because they considered Ukrainians to be inferior to themselves, many German officers beat and terrorized these slave laborers, who had to work in mines, factories, agricultural settings, and as domestic servants.

Ukrainian schools were also closed down in 1942, according to an order from Hitler. He stated that Ukrainian children should receive "the crudest kind of education necessary for communication between them and their German masters" (Dallin, 1956). Schools and colleges serving students over 15 years old were closed, and students and teachers were sent into forced labor. All schools above grade four were shut down in January 1942.

Massacres were also perpetrated in thousands of Ukrainian villages. On September 23, 1942, German troops burned down Kortelisy and killed the 2,892 men, women, and children who lived there. At least 160 Nazi concentration camps were also constructed on Ukrainian soil. The commandant of the Yanivska camp in Lvov, Gustav Wilhaus, was known to shoot children and other inmates for target practice.

By war's end, Ukraine had lost more people than any other country in Europe. Estimates range from 7.5 million to nearly 14 million, which included about 600,000 Ukrainian Jews. The country had also been devastated, leaving surviving youth without the barest necessities, including homes. More than 2 million homes and apartments had been burned by Hitler's troops. Enemy troops had poisoned wells and destroyed rail lines and industrial facilties, leaving people with no means of support. *See also* RESISTANCE MOVEMENTS (WORLD WAR II); RIGHTEOUS GENTILES; SOVIET UNION (WORLD WAR II); UKRAINE; ZAHAJKEWYCZ, OREST AND ZAHAJKEWYCZ, HELENA.

Further Reading: M. P. Bazhan, ed., *Soviet Ukraine* (1969); Yury Boshyk, ed. *Ukraine During World War*

II (1986); Robert Conquest, *The Harvest of Sorrow* (1986); Walter Duranty, *USSR: The Story of Soviet Russia* (1944); Philip Friedman, *Their Brother's Keeper* (1978); Andrew Gregorovich, "World War II Tragedies: Villages of Lidice, Czechoslovakia and Kortelisy, Ukraine," *Forum: A Ukrainian Review* (Scranton, PA) 67, Winter 1986, p. 31; Leo Heiman, "They Saved Jews: Ukrainian Patriots Defied Nazis," *Ukrainian Quarterly*, 17, 4, Winter 1961, pp. 320-32; J. Joesten, "Hitler's Fiasco in Ukraine," *Foreign Affairs*, 21, no. 2, January 1943, pp. 331-39; Ihor Kamenetsky, *Hitler's Occupation of Ukraine 1941-1944* (1956); Ihor Kamenetsky, *Secret Nazi Plans for Eastern Europe* (1961); George Vernadsky, *A History of Russia* (1954).

Unaccompanied Children

One of the most common and serious consequences of war is unaccompanied children—children who are left on their own, with no caring adult family members in their lives during or after the conflict. Sometimes tens of thousands of unaccompanied children can be found in war-torn regions. These youths may have no means of support and lack food, clothing, shelter, and other needs. They may also lack adults to protect them from danger or exploitation or to supervise their activities and provide guidance and role models. With no means of support, some drop out of school and look for jobs or become delinquent. They are also vulnerable to criminals who use children for their illegal activities.

Relief organizations work to provide for the physical needs of unaccompanied children and also aim to reunite family members through tracing and searches. Between 1988 and 1995, Save the Children operated a family reunification program for unaccompanied children in Mozambique, where civil war had left children orphans or separated them from their families. Save the Children trained 13,000 volunteers to track down family members and they succeeded in registering 18,000 unaccompanied children. Of these, 14,000 were reunited with their families as of 1996.

In the 1990s, the war in the African nation of Rwanda resulted in thousands of unaccompanied Hutu and Tutsi children. During the Rwandan civil war, Save the Children worked to organize a similar program with other relief organizations. The organi-

zations set up foster homes for children who could not be reunited with their families. Hundreds of children were living at the Unaccompanied Children's Centers in Butare as of 1996. Between 1994 and 1998, the Red Cross helped to reunite thousand of unaccompanied Rwandan children with at least one relative.

Working with the United Nations High Commissioner for Refugees (UNHCR), the United Nations Children's Fund (UNICEF), and other organizations, the Red Cross set up a vast tracing program to help unaccompanied children locate family members. Children were interviewed, then registered and listed in computer databases. Dozens of staff members processed the information at a central location in Nairobi. The information also became available on a worldwide network so that children who were evacuated to Uganda, Kenya, Tanzania, Zaire, or other countries could be traced. Parents searching for missing children could fill out tracing requests and radio was also used to reunite families. In cases where no relatives remained alive, these organizations worked to place unaccompanied children in homes or institutions. *See also* ADOPTION; AFRICA; ARMENIAN-TURKISH CONFLICT; CONVENTION ON THE RIGHTS OF THE CHILD; GENEVA CONVENTIONS; GREECE (WORLD WAR II); HIROSHIMA; NINOSHIMA; ORPHANS; RWANDA; SEPARATIONS, FAMILY; UNITED NATIONS CHILDREN'S FUND (UNICEF); WILD CHILDREN.

Further Reading: International Committee of the Red Cross (ICRC), "Help Us Find Our Families—Rwanda: Unaccompanied Children," at <http://www.icrc.org>.

Underground Presses

Young people have been involved in producing newspapers and other written materials for underground resistance movements in occupied countries. They have also played a key role in distributing such materials. Some underground papers have also been written for young people, to give them encouragement during wartime and to address their special needs and interests.

Resistance papers were especially common during World War II in Europe. Hundreds of underground presses flourished in Poland, France, Belgium, Norway, Denmark, Luxembourg, Czechoslovakia, Holland, and other countries occupied by Nazis. (Such papers were banned by the Germans in countries they occupied during both world wars.) Among other things, underground papers contained messages from resistance movements operating in these countries, inspirational articles and poetry, uncensored news from the war front and from other nations, and humorous items—for instance, cartoons or jokes that ridiculed Hitler and the Nazis. Sometimes, the papers announced upcoming events, such as labor strikes, and encouraged people to take part. The papers also urged displays of patriotism, such as the wearing of national colors on special days. Students were told about upcoming anti-Nazi demonstrations. Danes were reminded to observe the annual moment of silence, something they did as a group each year on the day the Germans first invaded their country.

A 17-year-old in Copenhagen, Denmark, had distributed an anti-Nazi leaflet on the same day as the German invasion. Arne Sejr and his fellow students passed out sheets that urged their fellow Danes "to spoil everything that might help the Germans and to defend every person persecuted by the Germans" (Werstein, 1967). His group proceeded to write and distribute an underground paper called *Students' Service* during the occupation. Most of the people involved in the writing and distribution were teenagers; the oldest person in the group was 25.

Poland had more underground papers than other occupied countries—between 1,200 and 1,400 titles. Young people helped to print and distribute them. Some publications were aimed at children and discussed scouting and other activities that were of special interest to young people.

Throughout Nazi-occupied Europe, university student organizations published illegal newspapers. When the Nazis found illegal presses, they often shot all the people involved, as well as whole families whose members were involved, and entire neighborhoods. The courageous youth frequently carried the forbidden papers inside parts of their bicycles or hidden in other ingenious places. Teenage boys or girls who were caught carrying these papers were imprisoned, and some were shot.

In occupied Belgium, a 12-year-old boy named Peter Brouet took an active role in smuggling copies of *La Libre Belgique*, an underground paper. His grandfather had been one of the main publishers of a paper by that same name during World War I, and Peter's father had been among the children who secretly distributed it. Now Peter and his father continued the tradition. Peter's mother helped distribute the papers and organized other women to help. They placed papers in market baskets, mailboxes, train compartments, and trolley cars, and even on teacher's desks at school. The paper appeared at a time when Belgians were distressed over Nazi deportations of Belgian Jews. Friends and neighbors of the Brouets were among those who were seized from their homes during this time. *See also* BICYCLES; DENMARK (WORLD WAR II); HOLLAND (WORLD WAR II); JEHOVAH'S WITNESSES; NORWAY (WORLD WAR II); RESISTANCE MOVEMENTS (WORLD WAR II); THE WHITE ROSE.

Further Reading: Lore Cowan, ed., *Children of the Resistance* (1969); Irving Werstein, *That Denmark Might Live* (1967).

UNICEF. *See* UNITED NATIONS CHILDREN'S FUND (UNICEF)

United Nations Children's Fund (UNICEF)

Founded in 1946, the United Nations Children's Fund (UNICEF) was originally called the United Nations International Children's Emergency Fund. UNICEF is a leading organization devoted to promoting the health and safety of children around the world. UNICEF was founded to provide emergency relief for children who needed help after World War II. For its continuing work, UNICEF won the Nobel Peace Prize in 1965.

The first programs, which targeted children in war-torn China and Europe, began on a small scale as UNICEF provided dried milk and other basic needs. In 1949,

UNICEF began its annual Christmas card sale to raise money for programs. The card was based on a water-color painting by a 7-year-old girl from Czechoslovakia. She had sent the painting after the war as a way of thanking UNICEF for the help it sent to people in her village.

Throughout its history, UNICEF has focused attention on, and designed many relief programs for, children afflicted by war. The 1996 UNICEF report, *The State of the World's Children*, describes the horrifying impact of war on children, showing how millions have died, been disabled, suffered from illnesses, and been left orphaned, homeless, or separated from their parents during the last decades of the twentieth century. The report also describes hunger and starvation, the lives of child soldiers, and the emotional traumas suffered by children of war.

In 1995, UNICEF set forth its *Anti-War Agenda* for children, which calls for

an end to the recruitment and conscription into the military of children under the age of 18, for a ban on the manufacture, use, stockpiling, and sale of all anti-personnel land-mines and for strengthening of procedures to monitor and prosecute war crimes. The Agenda also urges support for long-term development, reconciliation, rehabilitation and education for peace.

Statistics show that, between 1940 and 1995, the lives of about 2.5 million children were saved through UNICEF programs that provided health care (including immunization against infectious diseases) and improved nutrition and education. During the 1960s, UNICEF programs focused on reducing poverty among the world's children.

Young people have also contributed their time and money to UNICEF programs that help other children in need. American children have taken part in an annual tradition called "Trick or Treat for UNICEF," collecting donations for this organization on Halloween night instead of treats for themselves.

During 1998 and 1999, UNICEF continued to expand its organized relief efforts and to promote international laws and policies that benefit children. In October 1998, UNICEF issued a statement saying that forcing children to fight or otherwise serve in armed conflicts is a major violation of human rights and should be recognized as a war crime by the International Criminal Court. UNICEF also supported a ruling in September 1998 in which the International Criminal Tribunal in Rwanda recognized that genocide includes crimes of sexual violence committed in the course of armed conflict. The organization approved that court's convictions of certain Rwandan leaders for the crime of genocide. Through various books, pamphlets, *Newsline*, and other publications, UNICEF informs the public about the many problems of children afflicted by war. UNICEF has become the world's largest relief organization for children, devoting about $800 million annually to various programs that benefit young people in more than 160 countries. *See also* AFRICA; ANGOLA; BOSNIA; EL SALVADOR; HEPBURN, AUDREY; LEBANESE CIVIL WAR; LIBERIAN CIVIL WAR; MOZAMBIQUE; RELIEF ORGANIZATIONS; RWANDA; SOLDIERS, CHILD; SUDAN; UGANDA.

Further Reading: United Nations Children's Fund (UNICEF), *Anti-personnel Land-mines: A Scourge on Children* (1994); UNICEF, *First Call for Children: World Declaration and Plan of Action from the World Summit for Children, Convention on the Rights of the Child* (1995); UNICEF, *The State of the World's Children, 1996* (1996).

United Nations Emergency Children's Fund. *See* UNITED NATIONS CHILDREN'S FUND (UNICEF)

United Nations Relief and Rehabilitation Administration (UNRRA)

The United Nations Relief and Rehabilitation Administration (UNRRA) worked to provide help to war-torn countries after World War II. With funding from 52 counries, UNRRA provided food, medical supplies, and shelter for European countries such as Poland, which received the largest amount of aid, a total of $480 million worth of materials between 1945 and 1947. Most aid was in the form of food. Hospitals received much-needed equipment, such as X-ray machines, medicines, and surgical instruments.

The UNRRA returned 7 million displaced persons to their countries of origin and also worked to repatriate tens of thousands of Polish children who had been taken to Germany for Germanization. (About 200,000 children were deported to Germany between 1939 and 1945 as part of a program called Lebensborn.) UNRRA searched for these young people and sought to reunite them with their families or helped older children with no families to emigrate. Although people in Poland expressed their gratitude for this aid, Cold War tensions ended UNRRA programs in that country.

The UNRRA also helped children who were orphaned by the Holocaust to find relatives or new homes. In 1947, most UNRRA programs ended in Europe, although the organization continued to work in China until 1949. At that time, UNRRA was disbanded and its functions were assigned to other United Nations divisions that aid refugees and children. *See also* ADOPTION; ARAB-ISRAELI WARS; CHINESE CIVIL WAR; LEBENSBORN; REFUGEES; UNITED NATIONS CHILDREN'S FUND (UNICEF).

Further Reading: Richard Lukas, *Did the Children Cry?* (1994); Stanley Meisler, *United Nations: The First Fifty Years* (1997); United Nations, "Global Achievements" and "Milestones," at <http://www.orgun>.

United States (World War II)

Americans did not suffer the effects of occupation or fighting on U.S. soil during World War II. Young Americans suffered in various other ways as brothers, fathers, sisters, cousins, and other relatives and friends went to fight in the European or Pacific theaters. American youth also learned to do without a variety of things people had once taken for granted. Rubber, gasoline, nylon, and heating oil were in short supply. As a result, no new bicycles were made for consumers during the war years of 1941 to 1945. A number of other new items were not available during the war years, including flashlights, batteries, certain toys and games, vacuum cleaners, toasters, vending machines, and

washing machines. Factories were producing war materials instead. Also, the metals needed to make these items were needed to manufacture weapons, tanks, and other military materiel. Fiberboard school lunch boxes replaced metal ones. The kit used to make these boxes was called a "victory kit."

As rationing laws made many items unavailable, young women tried to make their nylon stockings last as long as possible. Shoes were rationed. Young people also learned to eat meals made with limited quantities of meat, butter, sugar, coffee, and various canned fruits and vegetables. Sweets were seen more rarely. Because they could not obtain much gasoline, people organized carpools and families did not take automobile drives as a leisure activity. They also used more public transportation.

Ships that had carried certain goods and materials from other countries were now devoted to carrying military troops and supplies. Bubble gum disappeared and was replaced by a grainy version that was made without chicle, an ingredient that was not available during the war. Sugar, butter, tea, cooking oil, canned foods, coffee, and a number of other foods were rationed. Each man, woman, and child received a ration book with pages of stamps that showed how many stamps were needed to purchase a given item. To buy an item, a person had to present the right number of stamps, along with enough money to buy it. Many young people were given the job of shopping and managing the ration books for the family. They also helped collect materials that were being used for the war effort, such as scrap metal, newspapers, tin cans, rubber, and aluminum items. Used nylon and silk stockings were required to make parachutes. Families saved cooking fats that contained glycerin, which was used in the making of the black powder found in bullets.

Groups of students and individual young people took part in national drives to collect these kinds of materials. They dug up old railroad tracks and went door-to-door for scrap metal and rubber items—tires, raincoats, bathing caps, and garden hoses. Towns had collection centers for newspapers and cooking fat, and encouraged families to grow additional food in backyard victory gardens. Children also wrote letters and cards to service-people and prepared gifts and boxes of items that could be sent to people in the military.

The only known civilian casualties on American soil were Elyse (Mrs. Archie) Mitchell and five children from her Sunday school class. They were killed on May 5, 1945, near Bly, Oregon, after they went into the woods for a picnic and encountered an unexploded aerial bomb that the Japanese had launched toward the Pacific coast of the United States. The bomb exploded when a child examined it. This explosive was one of more than 9,000 that had been launched in bomb-carrying balloons by the Japanese. The bombs held timers that were supposed to release them on American soil, where they were expected to explode when they landed. A few hundred were found but they did not explode as planned.

As the war ended in 1945, food restrictions were lifted. Newspaper articles in September announced that the U.S. Department of Agriculture had ended bans on whipping cream and increased the supply of butter, canned salmon, and ice cream available to civilians now that military orders for these items had declined. *See also* COLLECTION CENTER DRIVES; INTERNMENT CAMPS, U.S.; PEARL HARBOR; VICTORY GARDENS; WAR BONDS (U.S.).

Further Reading: Stan Cohen, *V for Victory: America's Home Front During World War II* (1991); Penny Colman, *Rosie the Riveter* (1995); Dorinda M. Nicholson, *Pearl Harbor Child* (1998); Reader's Digest, *America in the '40s*, (1998); Archie Satterfield, *Home Front* (1981); William M. Tuttle, *Daddy's Gone to War* (1995).

United States Holocaust Memorial and Museum

Located in Washington, D.C., the United States Holocaust Memorial and Museum was dedicated in 1993. Visitors to the museum are given identification cards to carry as they walk through the various areas. These replica cards bear the name and picture of a Holocaust victim and include some basic facts about that person and his or her experiences.

People walk from one exhibit to the next along bridges with glass sides. One set of glass panels contains thousands of names of villages and towns that the Nazis attacked or destroyed during the Holocaust. A tribute to the villagers in one such town, Eishishok in Lithuania, is shown in a display called the Tower of Faces. In September 1941, Nazis executed all but 29 of the 3,400 Jews who once lived there. Four-year-old Yaffa Sonenson was one of these 29 survivors. She later put together this collection of 6,000 photographs that shows how people lived in this town before the war. The collection includes family pictures and photographs of children at play, school, and religious celebrations.

Among the items on display at the memorial are works of art and writings by young people. Clothing, toys, and personal possessions are also exhibited and serve as a poignant reminder of the youngest victims of the Holocaust. The Wall of Remembrance at the memorial was built to commemorate these young victims. On the wall are 3,000 hand-painted ceramic tiles made by elementary and middle-school American students.

The tiles were created after students studied the Holocaust, and they express the young people's thoughts and feelings about this horrendous chapter in human history. Some tiles feature pictures, such as the face of a crying child. Others contain such words as, "Hope lives when people remember" and "The hurt still lives." Yet another tile contains one word: "Why?" *See also* HOLOCAUST.

Further Reading: Eleanor H. Ayer, *The United States Holocaust Memorial Museum* (1994); Jeshajahu Weinberg and Rina Elielhi, *The Holocaust Museum in Washington* (1995).

United States School Garden Army (U.S.S.G.A.). *See* WORLD WAR I

Untermenschen. See "MASTER RACE"

V

Velodrome d'Hiver. *See* FRANCE (WORLD WAR II); ROUND-UPS

Victory Gardens

To increase food supplies during World War II, people in Great Britain, the United States, and other countries planted gardens in their backyards and some public places and called them victory gardens. American gardens could be seen in sports fields, parks, parking lots, zoos, and other places where a patch of ground could be tended. About 33 percent of the vegetables eaten in the U.S. during 1943 came from some 20 million home gardens. At one point during the war, victory gardens supplied 40 percent of the vegetables eaten throughout the nation. Young people played a major role in planting, tending, and harvesting crops from victory gardens.

These youth helped to cultivate gardens at home and in the community. Some young people worked in victory gardens as part of a group, such as Boy Scouts, Girl Scouts, or 4-H clubs. A typical victory garden included tomatoes, potatoes, green beans, and carrots.

One Midwesterner who was 8 years old during the war recalled that a local company offered prizes, in the form of war bonds, to children who started a victory garden. He said, "My brother and I both had victory gardens, so we both got $25 war bonds . . . " (Woodburn, 1999). *See also* GREAT BRITAIN (WORLD WAR II); UNITED STATES (WORLD WAR II).

Further Reading: Amy Bentley, *Eating for Victory* (1998); Indiana Historical Society <http://www2.ihs1830.org/ihs1830/war2.htm>; Dorinda M. Nicholson, *Pearl Harbor Child* (1998); Reader's Digest, *America in the '40s* (1998); Kate Woodburn, "Civilians Did Their Part to Aid the War Effort," *Moline Dispatch* Publishing Company at <http://www.qconline.com/progress99/2ration2.shtml>.

New York City children work on a rooftop victory garden during World War II. *Corbis-Bettmann.*

Vietnam War (1965–1975)

Although the Vietnam War began in 1959 after communist guerillas from South Vietnam (Vietcong), supported by the North Vietnamese government, tried to overthrow their leaders, extensive American involvement did not begin until 1965. The conflict expanded into a civil war, in which both sides received support from other countries. Conflicts in the former French Indochina (Vietnam, Cambodia, and Laos) dated back to 1946 when native Asians asserted their independence from the French colonial administration. Communist revolutionary leader Ho Chin Minh's Viet Minh troops overthrew the Vietnamese emperor and set up the republic of North Vietnam with its capital in Hanoi. The French supported the former emperor, who set up a new government in South Vietnam, with its capital in Saigon, leaving the country divided. Fighting continued between the French and Viet Minh until the French surrendered in 1954.

With backing from the United States, the new South Vietnamese leader, Ngo Dinh Diem, said the South wished to remain independent and would not be reunited with the north under Ho Chi Minh's leadership. From 1957 through 1959, more Vietcong moved to South Vietnam and attacked Diem's military installations.

During the early 1960s, while North Vietnam received help from the Soviet Union, the United States supported the South Vietnamese government by sending supplies and military equipment and advisors. By 1964, the U.S. was sending thousands of troops as well as more war material. Young men fought as combatants during the war, which escalated during the late 1960s. Vietnam has been called the first "Teenage War" in American history because the average age of U.S. combatants was 19. By comparison, the average age of combatants in World War II was 26.

Vietnamese youth aided the military on both sides in different ways. For example, at age 12, Mguyen To Manh worked with the Viet Minh forces that fought against the French (who occupied the country until 1954), and he helped to dig a 200-mile tunnel in Saigon, the capital of South Vietnam, where revolutionaries could hide and store supplies. This underground network was finished by the Vietcong during the late 1950s and provided a subterranean place for living, sleeping, eating, hospitals, workshops, and printing presses. Some children were used

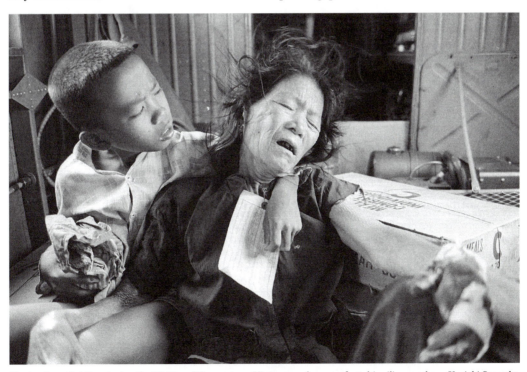

Fleeing from fighting during the Vietnam War, a young Vietnamese boy comforts his ailing mother. *Kyoichi Sawada, Corbis-Bettmann.*

as decoys, couriers, spies, and saboteurs. At age 18, Vietnamese boys were drafted into the army.

Young civilians were especially vulnerable to injury and death because the whole country became a battlefield. Guerilla units sometimes hid in villages where children lived, and these villages were bombed and attacked by opposing troops. Bombings left children blind, deaf, and missing hands, feet, and legs. Some were hurt by playing in fields that hid explosives and land mines. American authors Betty Jean Lifton and Thomas C. Fox (1972) described the following scene at a hospital in Vietnam during the early 1970s:

> Walking through the hot, overcrowded hospital wards in Vietnam, one can see children lying two to a bed or on stretchers on the floor. There are children burned like paper dolls by napalm, paralyzed children as still as the air. Children who have lost arms and legs. Children receiving free limbs from USAID the way our children receive lollipops. A gift from the generous Americans. A souvenir of war.

At least one million children, and probably more, were killed in Vietnam during this long war. Many children were also orphaned or left homeless in city streets; they carried the emotional scars that come from such losses and from family separations. Young children experienced terror as bombs dropped and they were confused about what was happening. They had recurring nightmares long after the war ended in 1975. Needy or homeless young people often migrated to Saigon, the South Vietnamese capital, and other large cities. The wartime economy brought severe inflation and insufficient housing for the swelling population. Poor children often dropped out of school by the sixth grade to work.

Street-children sometimes became pickpockets, hustlers, prostitutes, or smugglers. They became known as *Bui Doi*—the "dust of life"—because they were swept around the way wind blows dust through the air. Millions of Vietnamese were uprooted; their villages were destroyed or identified as areas where bombs might be dropped on a regular basis. Some people were resettled so they could not grow crops that would be used by enemy troops. Tens of thousands of refugees crowded into various camps where they lived in tents or shacks after leaving their homes and plots of land.

These displacements hindered normal family and community life and spiritual customs. The war-related deaths of fathers and older brothers deprived youth of sources of support and their family role models. Mothers were forced to take on menial jobs, leaving children alone more than usual. Some youth saw their sisters turn to prostitution as the only way they could earn enough money to survive. Crime increased throughout the land. More young people also used drugs, such as marijuana, amphetamines, and heroin. Some ended up in jail at ages as young as 13 for crimes involving drugs and theft.

Vietnamese youth typically helped parents care for younger siblings, but the war brought them many more duties and responsibilities. Some older children had to care for and support several brothers and sisters, raising food, cleaning house, and nursing ill family members. Youths also worked hard in fields at young ages to replace their elders.

In crowded conditions, with a lack of enough nourishing food, children often became ill. Epidemics of cholera, measles, polio, and plague spread. Some children suffered grievous injuries from land mines while trying to grow food. At the same time, medical services were in short supply because so many Vietnamese doctors had left for the military or emigrated to other countries. By the early 1970s, there were only about 300 doctors available in Saigon for a population of 3 million people. The 16 million people in South Vietnam had only about 1,000 doctors. International organizations such as Children's Medical Relief International came to help these victims.

By the early 1970s, at least 100,000 children had been separated from their families, either by death or because they were abandoned when parents could no longer take care of them. Abandoned children were often infants left at hospital doorsteps. Vietnamese culture was family centered, and relatives would have normally taken in children whose parents died. Wartime conditions made this unfeasible for many families and orphanages sprang up around Vietnam. Some were run by religious groups, such as Buddhist nuns. These institutions struggled to care for the large numbers of children. They did not receive enough money from the government, or have enough staff members or health care equipment. Orphanages received some supplies, clothing, and food from the U.S. Army, CARE, and Catholic Relief Services.

After Saigon fell to the North Vietnamese in April 1975, more than 2 million Vietnamese left the country and became refugees. More than one million moved to the United States, requiring more adjustments for children and young people.

On January 31, 1968, thousands of young people were killed and injured when forces from North Vietnam launched the Tet Offensive, a carefully planned attack on 30 South Vietnamese cities. Thousands of guerillas infiltrated Hue and other cities by quietly arriving in town and then hiding in the homes of local citizens who could not resist these armed soldiers. The guerillas took control of numerous official buildings in Saigon and other cities. In Hue, the old capital of the country, they also freed more than 1,000 political prisoners from the city jail.

For nearly a month, fighting continued, mostly in the streets. When it ended, the city of Hue had suffered more than $20 million in damage. About 5,000 civilians were dead and many others were injured. They included family members of South Vietnamese military officers whose wives and children were sometimes killed inside their homes. *See also* AMERICAN FRIENDS SERVICE COMMITTEE (AFSC); ANTI-WAR MOVEMENT; BICYCLES; CAMBODIA; COMMITTEE OF RESPONSIBILITY (COR); INTERNATIONAL RESCUE COMMITTEE (IRC); INTERNATIONAL VOLUNTEER SERVICES (IVS); MONTAGNARDS; MULTIRACIAL CHILDREN; MY LAI MASSACRE; ORPHANS; PHUC, KIM; REFUGEES; WILD CHILDREN.

Further Reading: John Carey, *Eyewitness to History* (1988); Betty Jean Lifton and Thomas C. Fox, *Children of Vietnam* (1972); Michael Maclear, *The Ten Thousand Day War: Vietnam 1945-1975* (1981);

Phuong Trieu, "The School on the Front Line," in *Between Two Fires: The Unheard Voices of Vietnam* (1970).

Volunteers

Youth have served as volunteers during wartime in various capacities. For example, young women have worked in hospitals to assist doctors and nurses caring for injured or sick soldiers. They carried meals and fresh water, helped soldiers write letters or read their mail, changed bedding, and did cleaning chores, all of which enabled trained personnel to spend more time giving critical care. Some youths have become involved when they belonged to organizations such as the Young Men's Christian Association (YMCA), scouts, or other groups that found people to staff particular programs and services in wartime.

Young people volunteered in many capacities during World War I and World War II. They served as nurse's aides for the Red Cross, as ambulance drivers and civil defense wardens, and in fire brigades. In Great Britain, women between ages 18 and 50 signed up for National Service and could also be drafted. During the Second World War, some teenagers took part in the Women's Land Army as farmworkers. Girl Scouts were among the volunteers who helped at the train stations when children were being evacuated from London and other cities that were expected to be bombed.

Teenage girls helped staff canteens in the United States and European countries during World War II. They joined thousands of other volunteers to meet the social needs of military personnel. Canteens were set up in communities throughout the U.S. in church basements and other public buildings located near military bases or other places where large numbers of servicemen could be found. Canteens were also set up overseas in places chosen by the military. Members of the American Red Cross (ARC), Young Men's Christian Association (YMCA), Salvation Army, and Knights of Columbus were among those who staffed these gathering places. Many Canadian citizens also became volunteers to help the Allied cause in Europe.

The canteens served refreshments and organized other social activities, such as dances, card games, and pancake breakfasts. They featured reading rooms and places where people could gather to talk. Volunteers managed to find furnishings and accessories for their canteens, often decorating the walls with war posters.

Young women who worked in the canteens cooked and served food, and helped soldiers write letters, shop for gifts, mend clothing, and do other tasks. Most received no salaries for this work, although their travel and other expenses were paid. Canteen work was popular, and there were often more volunteers for overseas spots than the number of volunteers that were needed.

After World War II ended, children volunteered to help with numerous post-war relief projects. They worked in hospitals and displaced person camps, distributed food and other supplies, cleaned up debris, did farmwork, and helped to repair and rebuild streets, buildings, and municipal facilities.

During the late twentieth century, young volunteers have been active in war-torn countries in Europe, Africa, Asia, and Central and South America. Some of these youth have worked in refugee camps set up to help people who were displaced by wars. *See also* AMERICAN CIVIL WAR; AMERICAN REVOLUTION; COLLECTION CENTER DRIVES (WORLD WAR II); ELIZABETH II; GREAT BRITAIN (WORLD WAR II); HITLER YOUTH; INTERNATIONAL VOLUNTEER SERVICES (IVS); QUAKERS (SOCIETY OF FRIENDS); RATIONING; RED CROSS; VICTORY GARDENS; WAR BONDS (U.S.); WORLD WAR I; WORLD WAR II; ZAIRE.

Further Reading: Alma Lutz, ed., *With Love, Jane: Letters from American Women on the War Fronts* (1945); Walter B. Maass, *The Netherlands at War* (1970); Reader's Digest, *America in the '40s* (1998).

Vos, Aart (1906–1990) and Vos, Johtje (1909–)

During World War II, Aart and Johtje Vos hid 36 Jews in their home in Laren, outside Amsterdam, Holland. Among the Jews were several children whose parents had been deported or killed by the Nazis. The Voses' rescue work began when they agreed to safeguard a suitcase for a Jewish friend who feared he might be deported after German troops invaded Holland in May 1940. Johtje Vos later described how their recue efforts escalated from that start: "And then a week later, somebody would ask you, 'Well, my child is in danger.' So we said, 'Of course, bring him here.' Then two people said, 'Well, we don't know where to go'" (Rittner and Myers, 1986).

Within months, the Voses were deeply involved with a rescue network and more people sought refuge at their home, which stood near a wooded area on a dead-end road outside Amsterdam. Inside their shed under a coal bin with a false bottom, the Voses built a tunnel that led into the woods. People could flee through the tunnel when Nazis raided the neighborhood, which happened regularly. The Voses were both interrogated by Nazi police more than once.

The Voses also had four young children of their own. The children knew the family was hiding Jews and helped to keep the household running and ensure that the Nazis did not discover their secret. At one point, Johtje Vos's mother expressed her fears that the couple was endangering their children by doing rescue work. Johtje Vos replied that she and Aart had thought carefully about the situation and decided it was vital for them to set this kind of moral example for their children. Despite some narrow escapes, everyone survived.

After the war, Aart and Johtje Vos moved to the United States where they continued to work for humanitarian causes and social justice. They were honored by Yad Vashem as Righteous Gentiles. *See also* HOLLAND (WORLD WAR II); HOLOCAUST; RESCUERS (HOLOCAUST); RIGHTEOUS GENTILES; YAD VASHEM.

Further Reading: Gay Block and Malka Drucker, *Rescuers* (1992); Carol Rittner and Sondra Meyers, *The Courage to Care* (1986).

W

Wagner-Rogers Bill. *See* CHILD REFU-GEE BILL

Wallenberg, Raoul (1912–?)

In 1944, Swedish diplomat Raoul Wallenberg saved thousands of Hungarian Jews, many of them children and young people, from being sent to Nazi death camps. Born in 1912 to a prominent, wealthy family, Wallenberg was expected to join the family banking business, but decided to study architecture. He excelled in this field and in foreign languages while earning a degree at the University of Michigan.

After Wallenberg graduated in 1935, he worked in South Africa, then in Palestine, where he met refugees from Europe. Wallenberg often declared that he also had some Jewish roots on his mother's side of the family. His grandmother's grandfather was among the first Jews to settle in Sweden. After leaving Palestine, Wallenberg became the international director of a food import-export firm in Sweden. His partner, Soloman Lauer, was a Hungarian Jew. As Wallenberg conducted business throughout Europe, he saw brutality toward Jews and heard about Nazi atrocities and the death camps.

By 1944, most Jewish communities in Europe had been destroyed. A high-ranking Nazi official, Adolf Eichmann, prepared to deport and kill Hungarian Jews, starting with those in rural areas. The United States had set up a War Refugee Board (WRB) to save Jews, and the board finally took strong action. WRB officials met with a committee in Stockholm, the capital of Sweden, to discuss ways to rescue Hungarian Jews. The committee asked Wallenberg to lead this rescue mission and he agreed. He was given a diplomatic title, staff, and funding.

When Wallenberg arrived in Hungary in June, about 230,000 of the 700,000 Jews who had lived in pre-war Hungary remained alive, most of them in Budapest. Wallenberg hired hundreds of Jews to work with his staff, who bought and rented buildings for their activities, giving them names like "Red Cross" or "Swedish Research Institute." These buildings were safe houses for Jews, who also received official-looking identity papers that Wallenberg had designed. These protective passes (*schutzpasses*) were shown to German and Hungarian police to prove the bearer had protection from the Swedish government. Wallenberg and his staff handed out thousands of passes.

Peter Tarian, who was eight years old in 1944, said, "Raoul Wallenberg had indeed saved my life by creating a haven for thousands of Jews including Panni's family [his relatives] in Swedish protected houses. He was also instrumental in establishing the international ghetto where my mother and I had been able to stay earlier. Finally he had saved the life of my aunt Agnes by preventing the demolition of the ghetto" (Handler and Meschel, 1993).

One of the protected houses was an orphanage that housed 79 children. Agnes Adachi, a young Jewish woman who worked with the Swedish ligation, later wrote,

> Hardly was there a day when he did not visit them. One day, after being away . . . saving other people, he arrived back in Budapest to find that all the children but one had been brutally killed by the Arrow Cross men. This was the first time we saw Raoul really desperate. He went down on his knees and cried. (Adachi, 1989)

The only survivor of this massacre was a small boy who hid under a chair. When the shooting stopped, he fled out the back door and searched for his mother on the street. They found each other and survived the war hiding in one of Wallenberg's safe houses.

During the late summer, deportations from Hungary slowed down, but in October 1944, the Germans seized control of the government and installed a new leader, the Hungarian Nazi Ferenc Szalasi. As the new government began killing and deporting Jews, Wallenberg issued more passes and created new safe houses, rousing the Swiss and Vatican governments to do likewise. Wallenberg literally pulled people out of lines heading for the railroad station and off the departing trains. He bribed and threatened officials to save lives.

Nearly 150,000 Jews were alive in Hungary when Russian soldiers liberated the country in February 1945. Wallenberg arranged to meet with Soviet commanders to discuss ways to help survivors after the war. It is not clear what happened at this meeting, but Wallenberg was taken into custody and disappeared, probably into the Soviet prison system. The Soviets may have thought he was a spy or feared that he would thwart their plans to make Hungary a socialist nation after the war. The Soviet government later said that Wallenberg died in prison during the 1950s, but his body was never returned to his family. Some ex-prisoners claimed they saw him alive as late as the 1970s.

U.S. Congressman Thomas Lantos, who lived in one of the Wallenberg safe houses as a teenager in war-time Hungary, was among those who renewed efforts to determine Wallenberg's fate, which was still unknown in the 1990s. Lantos also urged the Senate to grant Wallenberg honorary U.S. citizenship. When President Ronald Reagan signed this resolution into law on October 5, 1981, Wallenberg became the third person ever to receive this honor. Wallenberg has also been named a Righteous Gentile by Yad Vashem. The United States Postal Service issued a commemorative stamp in his honor in 1996. *See also* HUNGARY, (WORLD WAR II); RIGHTEOUS GENTILES; YAD VASHEM.

Further Reading: Agnes Adachi, *Child of the Winds* (1989); Andrew Handler and Susan V. Meschel, comps., *Young People Speak: Surviving the Holocaust in Hungary* (1993); Kati Marton, *Wallenberg* (1982).

Wannsee Conference. *See* FINAL SOLUTION

War Bonds (U.S.)

During World War II, Americans bought war bonds to help finance the war effort. Eight large, national bond drives were held in the United States between 1941 and 1945. Celebrities, radio announcers, and filmstrips urged citizens to show their patriotism by buying bonds on a regular basis. Posters and print ads exhorted them to "Buy War Bonds!" Newspapers recognized young people in the community who sold large numbers of bonds. For example, on May 6, 1943, an article written by William Gorton in the *Gettysburg (Pennsylvania) Times* announced that 20 of the carriers for the newspaper had set a record by selling almost 160,000 war stamps in one week. This meant that these boys and girls, who lived in the Adams County area, had raised nearly $16,000 for the war effort that week. The article went on to say that *Times* carriers had sold more than 2 million war stamps during the recent big war bonds drive. The six children who had sold the most won special awards and their pictures appeared in the newspaper.

Most American children bought war bonds, too, using their spending money or the money they earned by working. Bonds

This World War I poster promotes the selling of war bonds. *Hoover Institution Archives, US 1175, Stanford University.*

were sold at movie theaters, schools, grocery stores, and other places. Young people could purchase war-bond stamps with a dime or a quarter, then paste the stamps in war-bond booklets. When they had accrued $18.75 worth of stamps, the book was complete and could be exchanged for a bond that would be worth $25.00 in 10 years. Children who lived in New York City could watch an ongoing tally of war bond sales. A giant cash register was set up in Times Square to show the dollar amount of bonds sold in New York State. *See also* UNITED STATES (WORLD WAR II); VICTORY GARDENS; WORLD WAR II.

Further Reading: Penny Colman, *Rosie the Riveter* (1995); Dorinda Nicholson, *Pearl Harbor Child* (1998); Readers' Digest, *America in the '40s* (1998)

War Child

War Child, founded in 1993 by film makers Bill Leeson and David Wilson, is an international relief organization that provides aid to children in war zones and refugee camps and helps children adjust and return to their homes to rebuild their lives after wars end. The organization was formed after the founders were moved by the plight of children in Bosnia. With funds raised through entertainment events and public appeals, they provided clothing, food, medical equipment, and other items to children of all ages and ethnic backgrounds. Additional funding from other sources enabled War Child to set up large-scale meal programs, medical projects, educational and social programs, and reconstruction projects. These included an orphanage for 40 children under age 6 in Tuzla and the establishment of the Pavarotti Music Centre in 1997 (named for one of its patrons, opera star Luciano Pavarotti).

By 1999, War Child had funded a mobile clinic in Lebanon, provided support for Tibetan refugees in Nepal, and assisted homeless youth in Central America, South Africa, Rwanda, Ethiopia, and Sudan. The organization provided health care assistance in Zaire, sent food during the war in Chechnya, helped with a school rebuilding project in Azerbaijan, and established a mobile medical clinic and school meals program for Liberian refugees living in camps in Ghana. War Child was carrying out numerous other projects to aid child victims of war and planned more for the future.

War Child has brought musical instruments and equipment to children in the former Yugoslavia and other places, along with musical and dance training programs. Patrons of the organization include well-known musicians and other performers who have raised millions of dollars for relief programs.

Further Reading: "Helping the Innocent Victims of War" and "War Child Projects" at <http://www.warchild. org>.

War Films

Dozens of feature films and documentaries have portrayed the impact of war on children and teenagers. Some of these films, which have been made in North and South America, Europe, Asia, Africa and Australia, have focused specifically on children as soldiers, casualties, refugees, displaced people, orphans, and survivors. The vast majority of war films deal with World War II, although some show the impact of other wars on younger family members. Examples are *War and Peace* (1956) based on Russian Leo Tolstoy's novel about the Napoleonic Wars and *Dr. Zhivago* (1969), a dramatization of Boris Pasternak's novel about the Russian Revolution. The 1938 film *Marie Antoinette* includes some scenes portraying the experiences of young people and the royal children during the French Revolution. A view of war through the eyes of young soldiers fighting in World War I was vividly portrayed in the award-winning film, *All Quiet on the Western Front* (1930), based on the novel by Eric Remarque.

Numerous films during the 1940s dealt with World War II, and some showed young people on the home front. Wartime life in an English village was the subject of *Mrs. Miniver* (1942), in which one of the main characters, a young girl, is killed in an air raid. The year 1942 brought *Journey for Margaret,* which showed the plight of children left homeless by the bombings of Great Britain. A 1944 film, *Since You Went Away,* dramatized the lives of a mother and her teenaged daughters on the American homefront after the husband/father left for war. *Racing with the Moon* (1984), set in small-town California, told the story of the romantic relationships between teenage girls and young men who are about to leave for the military. The 1946 film *The Best Years of Our Lives* showed the problems and adjustments that veterans and their families faced after the war. The role of a young sailor who lost both hands in combat was portrayed by Harold Russell, who brought his real-life experience to the film.

Hitler's Children (1943) gave a view of youth under the Nazi regime in Germany. *Swing Kids,* released in 1992, portrayed young Germans who opposed Nazism and embraced democratic values and the American "swing" music of the 1940s. Families staying at a Yugoslav resort overtaken by Nazis during World War II are shown in the film *The Summer of the White Roses.*

A number of films deal with the Holocaust. Vittorio De Sica's *The Garden of the Finzi-Continis* (1972) shows life in Italy during World War II. Adapted from a novel by Giorgio Bassani that is based on his youth, it tells the story of a wealthy Jewish family who were deported by the Nazis after the Italian government surrendered to the Allies in 1944. More than one film has been made about Anne Frank. *The Diary of Anne Frank,* released in 1959, was based on Frank's diary and showed the family's life in hiding and arrest. *Au Revoir Les Enfants (Good-bye Children),* a feature film by the acclaimed French producer/director Louis Malle, was based on Malle's childhood experiences during World War II. Malle attended a private school in France where school officials agreed to hide Jewish boys so they could elude the Nazis, who were rounding up Jews in France and deporting them to concentration camps. A television series called *Holocaust* premiered in 1981 in the United States. Based on an historical novel by Gerald Green, the series personalized the suffering of millions of Jews by showing the experiences of the Weiss family, including their three children, Karl, Rudy, and Anna. The series was later shown around the world and sparked renewed discussions about the Nazi era in Germany, where the government has encouraged studies of Nazism and the Holocaust in public schools. *Miracle at Midnight,* a 1998 made-for-television movie, portrays the courage of Danish families who helped to rescue Jews from Nazi-occupied Denmark in 1943. The film was produced by John Davis, an American film-maker whose Danish father-in-law, George Hubner, was 15 years old when his family took part in the rescue effort by hiding a Jewish family.

Empire of the Sun, a 1987 film, portrays the struggles of a 12-year-old British boy who becomes separated from his upper-class colonial parents in occupied Shanghai during World War II. It was produced by Steven Spielberg, who later produced and directed *Schindler's List,* a film about the Holocaust. In one memorable scene, Oskar Schindler is deeply upset by the sight of a child victim, a little girl wearing a red coat, the only color in this black-and-white film.

A 1995 Chinese film titled *Red Cherry* tells the true story of two Chinese children who were hidden in a Russian boarding school in Moscow after their parents, who were communists, were killed by the Chinese nationalist army. The children endured terrible hardships after the German army invaded Russia in 1941. *Earth*, a 1999 film by Indian filmmaker Deepa Mehta, portrays the suffering and massive displacement that occurred in 1947 when British India was divided into the separate nations of India and Pakistan. A child plays a major role in the film.

The Vietnam War is the subject *of Born on the Fourth of July,* which shows the transformation of a young enlisted soldier, who is seriously injured in Vietnam, into a war protester. *The Killing Fields* showed the tragic fate of civilians of all ages in Cambodia. *Casualties of War,* the story of a young American soldier who witnesses the brutal rape and murder of a Vietnamese girl by members of his unit, was based on real events. *See also* AYLWARD, GLADYS; DISPLACED PERSONS (DP) (WORLD WAR II); FRANK, ANNE; GIES, MIEP AND GIES, JAN; LE CHAMBON-SUR-LIGNON; SCHINDLER, OSKAR

War Games. *See* WAR TOYS

War of 1812. *See* BATES, REBECCA AND BATES, ABIGAIL; DRUMMER BOYS

War Toys

War toys include items made for children to use while engaging in military play, pretending to be soldiers or engaging in mock battles. Examples include toy guns, swords, and other weapons, as well as toy soldiers, tanks, warplanes, missiles, or action figures used in combat. Children may also wear child-sized uniforms or other costumes designed for such activities. These items have been made for centuries and may be especially prevalent during wartime.

In May 1996, three teenage South Dakota boys take a break from a paintball game, a popular war game of the 1990s. *Sandra Korkow, Brookings Register, AP/ Wide World Photos.*

Modern toy soldiers were made and sold in Germany during the mid-1700s. After 1850, they also became popular in Great Britain and other countries. Children could collect models of soldiers of various ranks wearing different uniforms and insignia; they could also collect horses, nurses, tents, wagons, band instruments, and other military paraphernalia to help them set up battle scenes, maneuvers, and parades.

Children also played at being soldiers themselves. On April 28, 1917, a newspaper ran a story about a tragic and uncommon event: A nine-year-old African-American boy in New York, Maurice Holloway, died during a war game. He and his friends were playing near a large boulder, and Maurice was defending the embankment where the boulder was located against the others, who were pretending to be German soldiers. The article noted that, "Many of [the other neighborhood boys] would play they were soldiers on one side or the other, but not so Maurice. He must always be on the American side or he would have nothing to do with the game." When the boys' activity shook the boulder loose, it fell on Maurice and crushed him to death.

During wars, or in periods just prior to wars, numerous war toys and games may appear in stores or become increasingly popular. Sometimes governments encourage these toys and games to create an atmosphere that glorifies war and military activities. An American official visiting Japan in the early 1930s noted the large stocks of war-related toys. He wrote, "A glimpse at any toy shop, and they are numerous in Japan, will reveal the military inclinations of the people. There one can find toy soldiers, tanks, helmets, uniforms, rifles, armored motor cars, airplanes, anti-aircraft guns, howitzers, cannons, besides the usual pop guns, bugles, and drums" (Nakamoto and Pace, 1970). Wooden rifles were another popular item. War games were also popular with Japanese boys in the 1930s. They held mock battles like those they had heard about from soldiers who had returned from Manchuria. They used bamboo poles for rifles and made small buildings into forts. Saito Mutsuo later recalled how he and his friends pretended to be the "Three Bomb Heroes of Shanghai":

> Three of the boys would get a large log of wood and tie it to their backs with string, to be the "bomb," and the rest of us would be the enemy guards and so on. We were very impressed by the story of the Three Bomb Heroes. We were told that only Japanese soldiers could do something like that. (Nakamoto and Pace, 1970)

In the United States, many war toys have been associated with popular movies and television shows. For instance, in the 1980s, action figures and paraphernalia drawn from the "Rambo" movies, a series featuring a U.S. soldier who fought in the Vietnam War, were widely sold in the United States.

Many war toys have also been manufactured and purchased during peacetime. For example, in the United States, between 1982 and 1985, sales of war toys climbed by 350 percent and had gross sales of more than $842 million a year. During the 1980s, these kinds of toys made up the leading category of toy sales in the United States. Five or more of the 10 best-selling toys were war-related.

Critics have claimed that war toys foster aggressive attitudes and lead to an acceptance of the idea of war. The Jane Addams Peace Association, part of the Women's International League for Peace and Freedom (WILPF), has urged adults not to buy these kinds of toys and to promote other types of toys and play activities for children. The association publishes books and pamphlets on this subject and offers educational kits for teachers to use when discussing the negative effects of war toys.

In a 1986 article called "Killers in Your Toy Box," the famous pediatrician and author of books on child development, Dr. Benjamin Spock, said, "War toys prepare children for war and other kinds of violence. If that is not what you want, don't buy those toys."

The Peace Pledge Union also criticized these toys, saying,

> War toys help to "legitimize" and "make natural" a most unnatural and barbaric activity. . . . By buying war toys and by not discouraging children from playing with them, we are in a small but far from insignificant way supporting a view of the world where war—the arbitrary killing of strangers—is seen as "natural" and inevitable. . . and the pain of others is simply not real. (Kome and Cream, 1986)

During the 1990s, violent video games featuring attacks on people and various military activities became more popular and numerous. Critics charged that these games numb children to the suffering of others and create an atmosphere in which violence and war can more easily occur. In *The Cooperative Sports and Games Book* (1978), Terry Orlick wrote that war games and war toys and violent sports "teach children that it is perfectly acceptable to hit, push, shove, and otherwise mistreat human beings."

Concerned parents pressured some toy companies to stop selling particularly violent games. In December 1993, the Senate Judiciary and Government Affairs Committee began holding congressional hearings on the subject of violent video games and created the Video Game Rating System of 1994 to help parents evaluate the games. A group of parents, teachers, and other citizens formed the Recreational Software Advisory Council (RSAC), which developed its own set of guidelines. *See also* AMERICAN CIVIL WAR; JAPAN (WORLD WAR II).

Further Reading: Penney Kome and Patrick Crean, eds., *Peace: A Dream Unfolding* (1986); Tessa Morris-Suzuki, *Showa* (1985); Hiroko Nakamoto and M.M. Pace, *My Japan* (1970); Terry Orlick, *The Cooperative Sports and Games Book* (1978).

Warsaw Ghetto

During World War II, the Nazis set up an enclosed area in Warsaw, the capital of Poland, as a prison for Jews. The Nazis hoped that by isolating and impoverishing the Jews many would die. The Nazis steadily deported those who survived the ghetto to death camps. Children not only endured the awful conditions but some had to survive without their parents, who might be dead, missing, hiding, or in prison.

Thousands of Jews from Poland and other countries were forced into the Warsaw Ghetto, an area about 1.5 miles square surrounded by walls nine feet high. People moving into the ghetto could bring very little—some clothing, bedding, cooking pots, and small furnishings. They were not allowed to use cars or horses to help transport these goods, so people pushed carts and baby-carriages carrying their belongings into the ghetto.

Among the most pitiful victims were the children. One eyewitness described them as having "yellow skin that looks like parchment. . . . They crawl on all fours, groaning" (Berg, 1945).

Hunger was a constant problem because the Nazis allowed the imprisoned Jews only starvation rations. Chaim Kaplan, author of *Scroll of Agony: The Warsaw Diary* (1973), wrote the following:

Thus at one intersection you encounter a group of children of poverty ranging in age from four to ten, the emissaries of mothers and fathers who supervise them from

With their hands raised, Polish Jews, including many children, are marched out of the Warsaw Ghetto to Nazi death camps. *Corbis.*

the sidelines. They sing, and their voices are pleasant and their songs permeated with Jewish sorrow and grief. The music touches your heartstrings. Little groups of idlers and strollers stand near the childish quartet, their eyes filled with tears; they find it hard to leave.

Janina Bauman, a teenager at the time, later escaped from the ghetto. She kept a diary that detailed daily life behind the walls. In April 1941, she wrote that

> Two little boys are begging in the street next to our gate. I see them every time I go out. Or they might be girls. I don't know. Their heads are shaven, clothes in rags, their frightfully emaciated faces bring to mind birds rather than human beings. Their huge black eyes, though, are human; so full of sadness . . . They don't move, they don't speak. The little one sits on the pavement, the bigger one just stands there with his claw of a hand stretched out. (Bauman, 1945)

Young people in the Warsaw Ghetto tried to grow food on any patches of land they could find. These included places where houses had burned down, as well as on rooftops. Children often became smugglers because they could move in and out of small cracks in the ghetto walls or fences more easily than grownups. Poles on the other side might also be more willing to give food to a starving child than to an adult. Most smugglers were between ages 7 and 14; some were as young as 5. When trying to squeeze through barbed wire, they often wrapped themselves in burlap sacks. A popular song in the ghetto paid tribute to the young smugglers.

> Over the wall, through holes, and past the guard,
> Through the wires, ruins, and fences,
> Plucky, hungry, and determined,
> I sneak through, dart like a cat.

Young smugglers risked being shot or savagely beaten. One boy was trying to climb over the wall into the ghetto. As his helper got ready to throw up a sack of food, he was shot reaching out to catch it.

Besides going hungry, people lacked fuel and warm clothing. Some were also homeless. A young girl wrote, "Sometimes a mother cuddles a child frozen to death and tries to warm the inanimate little body. Sometimes a child huddles against his mother, thinking she is asleep and trying to waken her, while, in fact, she is dead."

Young people sparked the Warsaw Ghetto uprising against German troops that occurred during the summer of 1944. After the Nazis began deporting large numbers of people to death camps, people began meeting to discuss what they should do, and many youths wanted to stop cooperating. Diarist Mary Berg, who was 16 at the time, wrote, "Some people demand that a protest be organized. This is the voice of the youth; our elders consider this . . . a dangerous idea. We are cut off from the world. There are no radios, no telephones, no newspapers" (Berg, 1945).

During the war, some of these youths had participated in resistance activities conducted by the Polish Home Army (A.K.) and the People's Army (A.I.). Besides joining the armed fighting, young people helped build stone and brick barricades in the streets. They rescued the wounded and those who were hurt during bombing raids. As fires broke out, they used buckets, pans, and kettles to carry water from the few available sources left.

When the Warsaw Ghetto residents began their armed revolt, a 17-year-old girl played a leading role by throwing a grenade into a group of SS men who had come to arrest people for deportation to death camps. At least 12 of these Nazis died in the blast. The Jewish Fighters Organization (JFO) led the resistance fighters, who held off the Germans for several weeks with far less equipment, people, and supplies. In the end, they were defeated by tanks sent inside the ghetto to fire at the buildings and send poison fumes into the fighters' hiding places.

Survivor Reva Kibort, now living in the United States, later recalled

> I remember my grandmother and my little cousin slowly starving to death. I remember so many people living in our apartment—no one had any privacy or room to

move. I can remember dead bodies outside in the courtyard, on the streets. I remember the Germans and their dogs . . . But the thing that bothers me most—the worst thing the Germans did to me in Warsaw was to deprive me of a childhood. I had no school, no friends, no life other than watching those around me die.

The poetry and other writings of children living in the Warsaw Ghetto have been preserved and can be read in books, including Michael Berenbaum's *The World Must Know: The History of the United States Holocaust Memorial Museum. See also* ANIELEWICZ, MORDECHAI; BAUM, FROIM; BERG, MARY; EDUCATION; GHETTOS (WORLD WAR II); HOLOCAUST; JEWISH FIGHTERS ORGANIZATION (JFO); KORCZAK, JANUSZ; TOLL, NELLY LANDAU.

Further Reading: Janina Bauman, *Winter in the Morning: A Young Girl's Life in the Warsaw Ghetto and Beyond* (1945); Mary Berg, *Warsaw Ghetto Diary* (1945); Lucy S. Dawidowicz, *The War Against the Jews* (1975); Bernard Goldstein, *The Stars Bear Witness* (1949); Chaim Kaplan, *Scroll of Agony* (1973); Gail B. Stewart, *Life in the Warsaw Ghetto (The Way People Live)* (1995).

Westerweel, Joop (1898–1944)

Joop Westerweel, a Dutch-born teacher, led a group of people who helped about 200 Jewish young people and children escape Nazi Europe during the Holocaust of World War II. Westerweel was a pacifist living and working in the Dutch town of Bilthoven when the war broke out. After anti-Jewish laws were passed, he helped Jews by renting apartments in his own name so that these families could live in them with less fear of being discovered by the Nazis.

In 1942, Jewish students who belonged to a group called *Aliyat Ha-Noar* (Youth Aliyah) asked Westerweel to help children escape from Holland. He agreed at once, later explaining, "I felt I had reached a dead end. When one tries to teach in the face of this humiliation to humanity, it is impossible" (Stadtler, 1973). Through this escape network, Jews were smuggled from France and Holland through Belgium and France and into neutral Switzerland or Spain. Westerweel served as a guide on several of these escape

trips. His wife Wilhelmina (Will) was also an active member of the rescue group.

In March 1944, the 45-year-old Westerweel was captured by Nazis during one of his missions to France as he was helping two young Jewish girls escape from Holland. His captors tortured him, but Westerweel refused to name any other members of the resistance. He was executed on August 11, 1944. Will Westerweel and other members of the group continued Joop's work after his death.

Before he was killed, Westerweel urged others to resist evil and continue helping people in need. In one letter, he wrote, "If we do not meet again, I hope what we did together will remain a sacred memory for life." Sophie Nussbaum, one of the young people he saved, later said, "I'll never forget him. In those dark days, he was the only spark of humanity" (Stadtler, 1973).

Joop Westerweel has been honored as a Righteous Gentile by Yad Vashem in Jerusalem, Israel. In his honor, a forest was planted in northern Israel in 1953. *See also* HOLLAND (WORLD WAR II); HOLOCAUST; RIGHTEOUS GENTILES; YAD VASHEM; YOUTH ALIYAH.

Further Reading: Gay Block and Malka Drucker, *Rescuers* (1992); Bea Stadtler, *The Holocaust* (1973).

The White Rose

In 1942 and 1943, a group of German college students published anti-Nazi pamphlets called "Leaflets of the White Rose." Leaders of the White Rose movement were a brother and sister, Hans and Sophie Scholl, and their friends Christopher Probst and Alexander Schmorell. These four and the others in the White Rose group had once been members of the Hitler Youth but were now disgusted by the hatred and military aggression they observed in their country under Hitler. They were also appalled by the atrocities perpetrated by the German army, which young soldiers returning from battle described for them.

From the University of Munich, the students wrote and printed leaflets that they said were intended "to strive for the renewal of the mortally wounded German spirit." They referred to Hitler and his government as "fascist criminals" and an "evil regime." Flyers also declared that Germans were "guilty, guilty, guilty" of allowing this evil to flourish in their country. Leaflets were placed in public telephone booths, mailed to professors and students, and distributed to other universities by couriers.

Four different White Rose pamphlets suggested ways to resist the Nazi regime through acts of sabotage and a refusal to serve in the military. Besides dropping these leaflets onto the streets, the students also painted the walls of the university and other public sites with the words "Down with Hitler!" "Freedom!" and "Hitler the Mass Murderer!"

Nazi officials were determined to discover who was responsible for these acts. The student leaders were identified, arrested, and found guilty of "high treason." On February 22, 1943, Hans and Sophie Scholl and Christopher Probst, all in their early twenties, were put to death by beheading. As he was about to die, Hans Scholl cried, "Long live freedom!" Three other members of the White Rose were also beheaded in July 1944. *See also* GERMANY (WORLD WAR II); HITLER YOUTH; RESISTANCE MOVEMENTS (WORLD WAR II).

Further Reading: Inge Scholl, *The White Rose* (1983).

Wiesel, Elie (1930–)

A native of Sighet in Transylvania (Romania), Elie Wiesel was 14 when he was deported, along with the rest of his family, to the Nazi death camp at Auschwitz-Birkenau. During the selection process at the camp, Wiesel and his father were ordered to line up on the left. His mother and sisters were sent to the right; they were killed in the gas chambers. During the next year, Wiesel endured beatings, starvation, exhaustion, and exposure.

Wiesel and his father were still alive in Auschwitz in late 1944 as the Allies approached the camp. In December 1944, Nazi troops hurried to evacuate the survivors from the camp and took them on forced "death marches" to Germany. Wiesel was taken to

A Holocaust survivor and winner of the 1968 Nobel Peace Prize, Elie Wiesel helped organize the United States Holocaust Memorial and Museum. *Tim Sloan, Corbis/AFP.*

Buchenwald where he and some 21,900 other prisoners were liberated by Allied troops on April 10, 1945. His father died from dysentery, starvation, and exposure to freezing weather.

Wiesel later wrote that he and his fellow prisoners were "tormented with hunger," having eaten nothing but grass and potato peelings for the previous six days. They hurried to the supply area of the camp to get some food, and Wiesel became sick with food poisoning. While he was hospitalized, he was shocked by the sight of his reflection in the mirror and later said it was as if "a corpse gazed back at me" (Wiesel, *Night,* 1972).

After the war, Wiesel moved to France and was reunited with his two older sisters. He studied philosophy at the Sorbonne in Paris and taught the Hebrew language while pursuing a career as a journalist.

In 1958, Wiesel published *Night*, a moving account of his experiences during the Holocaust, and is regarded as the first person to use that term to describe the Nazi war against the Jews. He wrote other novels based on his life and encouraged other survivors to share their experiences as humankind struggled to understand what had happened and why. In 1968, Elie Wiesel, who became a U.S. citizen, was awarded the Nobel Peace Prize.

Besides bearing witness to the suffering of Holocaust victims, Wiesel also paid tribute to those who helped others instead of being bystanders, saying, "One person of integrity can make the difference between life and death" (Rittner and Myers, 1986). Wiesel played a key role in organizing conferences to recognize the people who rescued Jews during the Holocaust and also helped to serve as chairman of the United States Holocaust Memorial and Museum. The author of numerous books, articles and essays, Wiesel speaks out for victims of injustice throughout the world. *See also* AUSCHWITZ-BIRKENAU; DEATH MARCHES.

Further Reading: Carol Rittner and Sondra Meyers, eds., *The Courage to Care* (1986); Elie Wiesel, *Night* (1972); Elie Wiesel, *All Rivers Run to the Sea* (1995).

Wild Children

The term "wild children" referred to bands of unaccompanied children in the Soviet Union after the Russian Revolution of 1917. Thousands of children displaced by the Bolshevik Revolution roamed the countryside after 1917; many were accused of crimes, including stealing, looting, black marketeering, and terrorizing people. They survived by whatever means they could, legal or illegal, and were often exploited by adults.

Similar problems have occurred in other war-torn countries, such as in Japan after the atomic bombings in 1945, and in Vietnam during and after the Vietnam War of the 1960s and 1970s. Most gangs of unaccompanied children in Vietnam were made up of males.

During the late twentieth century, groups of unaccompanied children in other war-torn countries, such as Uganda, Rwanda, Sierra Leone, and Colombia sometimes banded together and engaged in delinquent behavior. Relief organizations such as War Child, Save the Children, and UNICEF tried to help these children find stable homes and enroll in school or job training programs that would help them survive in more constructive ways. *See also* AFRICA; NINOSHIMA; RUSSIAN REVOLUTION; VIETNAM WAR.

Further Reading: Betty Jean Lifton and Thomas C. Fox, *Children of Vietnam* (1972); Harrison E. Salisbury, *Russia in Revolution: 1900-1930* (1978).

Williams, Jody. *See* LAND MINES

Wolfe, James (1727–1759)

James Wolfe, who was born in Kent, England, to a military family, was only 15 when he enlisted in the army. He became well-known for his military achievements at a young age. Although Wolfe was not a large, strongly-built man, he worked hard and developed strong tactical skills. Throughout his short life, he continued to educate himself by studying languages, engineering, artillery, and mathematics, among other subjects.

For his first assignment, he was sent to Flanders (in present-day Belgium). Since the 1600s, the British and their allies had been involved in periodic fighting against the French for control of this region. In June 1743, Wolfe and his regiment were involved in heavy fighting. As a result of his performance, he was promoted to adjutant, and, less than one month later, to lieutenant. His commander recalled him to Great Britain to help quell a Jacobite uprising in Scotland when Scottish nationalists who supported the Stuart family as the rightful rulers of their country fought against the forces of the Duke of Cumberland in 1745. He fought at the Battle of Falkirk and the Battle of Culloden, where the Jacobites were defeated.

After he returned to Flanders, Wolfe was wounded. He continued his military career and became a brigade-major at 21, an amazing achievement. He reached the ranks of major, then lieutenant-colonel, during his twenties.

Stories circulated that Wolfe had refused orders to kill men wounded on the battlefield and had once told his commanding officer, "I can never consent to becoming an executioner" (Fraser, 1980).

During the French and Indian War, Wolfe lead a British expedition against Quebec, the capital of French Canada. Although the British won the battle and captured Quebec,

Wolfe was fatally wounded in the chest, dying on the field at the age of 32.

Further Reading: Antonia Fraser, *Heroes and Heroines* (1980).

Women's International League for Peace and Freedom (WILPF)

The Women's International League for Peace and Freedom (WILPF) was organized at the second International Congress of Women held in 1915 in The Hague, Holland. Women from neutral countries and from countries then involved in World War I came together to discuss ways to promote peace. It was the first time in history that women from warring nations had met to discuss ways to end the fighting.

By 1919, the group had expanded and decided to adopt a formal constitution stating the aims of an international women's movement for peace. Along with many other activities, the WILPF has focused attention on the impact of war on children. The group has also sponsored meetings to discuss the impact of war and nuclear radiation on children.

A branch of the WILPF, the Jane Addams Peace Association (JAPA), was formed in 1948. JAPA sponsored the Art for World Friendship program from 1946 to 1968. More than one million children from the five major continents exchanged original pictures containing themes of goodwill and peace. Each year, JAPA and the WILPF sponsor the Jane Addams Book Award given to a children's book that most effectively promotes the cause of peace, equality, social justice, and world community. The WILPF also produces educational materials designed to help young people understand the roots of war and violence and to learn peaceful ways of resolving conflicts. *See also* ADDAMS, JANE; PEACE CAMPS; WAR TOYS.

Further Reading: Gertrude Bussey and Margaret Tims, *Pioneers for Peace* (1980); Women's International League for Peace and Freedom (WILPF), *Peace & Freedom,* September/October 1995.

Work Camps. *See* CONCENTRATION CAMPS (WORLD WAR II); FORCED LABOR (WORLD WAR II)

World Health Organization (WHO)

Founded in 1948, the World Health Organization (WHO) is committed to helping all peoples attain the highest possible level of health. The WHO Constitution defines health as "a state of complete physical, mental and social well-being and not merely the absence of disease or infirmity." To carry out its mission, WHO engages in numerous research, relief, consulting, training, and public education projects.

Many WHO projects focus on the promotion of child health and direct health care for children. WHO, which is part of the United Nations, often collaborates with the United Nations Children's Fund (UNICEF) to help children whose health has been adversely affected by wartime or post-war conditions. Regional WHO offices in Africa, Asia, Europe, and other places around the world have assisted children in war zones and in refugee camps. *See also* UNITED NATIONS CHILDREN'S FUND (UNICEF).

Further Reading: "About WHO: Achievements and Challenges," "Mission Statement," and "Integrated Management of Childhood Illness," Fact Sheets, World Health Organization, 1998; WHO Web site <http://www.who.ch/aboutwho/achievements.htm>.

World Movement for the Care of Children from Germany. *See* CHILDREN'S TRANSPORTS (*KINDERTRANSPORT*)

World Peace Project for Children (WPPC)

The World Peace Project for Children (WPPC), which is based in Seattle, Washington, was founded in 1997 as a non-profit organization devoted to peace education for children. It offers educational programs and activities that involve music, art, and volunteerism. The WPPC sponsors a peace club with members from different countries and a peace choir that that has performed for community events in the Seattle area and at an international conference in Japan held to promote peace. The club has promoted its causes and activities via the internet at <www.sadako.org>. The Internet has enabled children and educators to become involved with other people around the world who are interested in this project.

In 1999, the WPPC launched a peace project for the beginning of the new millennium. Thousands of children took part in a project to build the world's largest origami peace crane, which the group planned to place at the monument for Sadako Sasaki in Seattle, Washington. The children wrote peace messages on 2,000 pieces of paper that were used to make the crane. *See also* FOLDED CRANE CLUB; SASAKI, SADAKO.

Further Reading: "History of the World Peace Project for Children at <www.sadako.org>."

World Summit for Children. *See* UNITED NATIONS CHILDREN'S FUND (UNICEF)

World War I (1914–1918)

Millions of young people in numerous countries felt the impact of World War I, the most destructive war that had occurred up to that time. The war caused an estimated 20 million casualties worldwide; foot soldiers, which included teenagers and men in their early twenties, experienced especially high rates of death and injury. Millions of civilians died of hunger and the diseases that flourished among people weakened by malnutrition and other conditions brought on by the war.

The events that led to the war began on a June morning in 1914. A 19-year-old Bosnian student from Belgrade, Gavrilo Princip, shot and killed Archduke Franz Ferdinand of Austria-Hungary and his wife as they were driving along the streets of Sarajevo in an open automobile. Princip was part of a group that despised Austrian rule over Bosnia and hoped to liberate their country. Because the group had traveled through adjacent Serbia, the

Austrian government blamed Serbia for the assassinations. Within a month, Austria-Hungary declared war on Serbia, an act that brought Russia into the war on Serbia's side and Germany into the war as an ally of Austria-Hungary. France came into the war against Germany, which was then the largest and best-armed military power in the world. When Germany invaded Belgium, Great Britain, the strongest naval power in the world, declared war on Germany on August 4. The First World War would eventually involve Italy, Turkey, Bulgaria, Japan, Brazil, San Marino, Siam, Honduras, the United States, and other countries.

Young men in these countries were moved to fight by strong patriotic feelings. Patriotism boosted American recruitment when the United States entered the war in 1917. One oft-used enlistment poster in the United States featured the image of a mother and child drowning after their ship was torpedoed by a German U-Boat. During their training, young soldiers learned how to use new kinds of machine guns, artillery, aircraft, and other equipment. The first tanks ever used in warfare also appeared on the battlefield. The British developed tanks and used them successfully beginning in 1916. Young soldiers faced the horrors of trench warfare on the western front of France and the eastern front of Russia. Soldiers were also exposed to poison gas during this war. The Germans used poison gas for the first time in the Second Battle of Ypres in the spring of 1915. World War I also marked the first time air bombardments were used against civilians, and air raids were directed against non-military targets. In Great Britain, about 4,000 civilians were killed or wounded by German air raids. Germans used zeppelins to bomb England. On June 13, 1917, an air raid of 18 German Gothas hit England during the day and a 100-pound bomb hit a school in Poplar, killing 46 children. Other children died or were injured by the 30 tons of bombs dropped on London during the war.

The use of mass armies and mass production also meant that more and more civilians were affected by war. Support from war factories and civilians, including young

These Russian children were taken prisoner by German troops in 1915. *Roger Viollet, Gamma Presse.*

people, helped those men fighting on the battlefields. Resources such as food, chemicals, metals, cloth, ships, fuels, rubber, and machinery had to be distributed to both the war fronts and the home fronts. Limitations on materials meant that baby carriages used more wood than metal, and fewer bicycles were made during the war.

Naval blockakes and the sinking of ships at sea resulted in shortages of many items in both the countries at war and in neutral nations, such as Holland and the Scandinavian countries. Coal, oil, fertilizer, and grains were among the commodities these countries imported before the war. Millions of tons of shipping were sunk by mines and torpedoes. Food prices rose dramatically because of these shortages, and children had less to eat because food was rationed or sometimes not available. Less milk and meat were produced in Germany, France, and the United Kingdom between 1914 and 1918.

German youth suffered from hunger because British blockades prevented various items, including many foods, from reaching their country. Young people helped collect scrap metal for the war effort. In German classrooms, students put small German flags onto the sites of German military victories on various European battlefields. Teenagers also worked as Red Cross volunteers to tend wounded soldiers in the hospitals.

German-occupied Belgium suffered from terrible shortages of food, clothing, and fuel. Many people were homeless after the war, and the Belgian economy was damaged. Towns throughout France lay in ruins, and millions of people were hungry. During the war, teenagers helped out in defense plants. British teenage girls were in demand to make fuses for artillery shells and to fill shell casings with explosives. Some girls working in European factories died from exposure to toxic chemicals or gases. Young people in France, Germany, and Great Britain had more chores to do at home because their mothers worked in factories, or delivered coal, mail, milk, or vegetables, or drove trucks or worked on farms. Young girls joined their mothers at gatherings to knit scarves and gloves for the military or to roll bandages.

American college students were among those who volunteered to go to Europe to help the Allies before the United States joined the war in 1917. Men worked in the American Field Ambulance service, a privately operated organization that rescued wounded soldiers on the battlefield. Some of these young drivers were killed by enemy fire while they were driving patients to city hospitals. They saw badly wounded soldiers and witnessed tragic scenes. One young American driver, Arthur Taber, wrote to his mother about a funeral he had attended for a fallen French soldier.

I had already been through the hospital and seen ghastly wounds and the shattered remains of men—all sorts of things . . . I noticed a group of a few women and children and a few soldiers waiting by one of the entrances to the hospital. . . . it was in their attitude that they betrayed the utter dejection of their grief . . . ." (Churchill, 1968)

American civilians were killed before the United States entered the war. Some died at sea when German submarines torpedoed their ships. The most infamous of these sinkings was the *Lusitania*, which occurred in May 1915. In 1916, 14 Americans died when an Italian ocean liner called the *Ancona* was sunk by an Austrian submarine.

When the United States declared war on Germany, former President Theodore Roosevelt's three sons wanted to enlist. The youngest, Quentin, age 20, had back problems but was admitted to an air training school near New York City. Young men left universities to enlist in the armed services. On Registration Day, June 5, 1917, nearly 10 million men between ages 21 and 31 registered their names with the government at local draft board offices.

Younger Americans became involved in the war effort in diverse ways. The Girl Scouts collected peach pits that were burned and used for the charcoal in soldiers' gas masks. The U.S. Committee on Public Information designated the Boy Scouts of America as the president's official messengers during the war. Scouts helped distribute pamphlets from the government that told citizens to buy war bonds, conserve food, and not waste coal or other fuel. Booklets written for the Scouts instructed them in patriotic ways to behave during the war. It told them how to look neat and clean in their uniforms and admonished them to be polite at all times to represent their country well.

War posters addressed the nation's youth: "Boys and Girls! You Can Help Your Uncle Sam Win the War. Save Your Quarters; Buy War Savings Stamps." At movie theaters, children saw public service messages urging them to buy war stamps and to sign "Food Pledge Cards." By signing the cards, people pledged to eat less meat, pork, wheat, and sugar, which were then sent to Europe. Young people also helped their parents tend gardens and can fruits and vegetables for winter use. They learned to eat bread made with oats, to forego meat on Tuesdays and wheat on Mondays, and to "clean their plates."

About 5 million young people worked after school and on weekends at public vegetable gardens located in parks, school-yards, and private estates. They were members of the United States School Garden Army, entitled to wear special U.S.S.G.A. armbands, and equipped with hoes and shovels. This produce was shipped to feed hungry troops and citizens in France and England. U.S.S.G.A. volunteers also earned money to buy thrift stamps to fill their Liberty bond cards. Some youths planted extra grass to feed cattle. Young men in the Northwest over age 16 were excused from school in the spring of 1918 to help plant wheat.

The war did not reach U.S. shores, but some German-American families experienced harassment and discrimination. Children were teased because of their national origins, and German language classes were banned in American schools. Anti-German feelings even caused people to change the way they talked. New names were given to foods and other items of German origin: frankfurters became "Liberty sausages"; dachshunds were now "Liberty dogs"; sauerkraut was renamed "Liberty cabbage."

Schools also became involved in wartime activities. Teachers discussed patriotism and students were taught about the misdeeds of German leaders. Students were also assigned to write essays on subjects related to the war, such as conserving food, or the need for the Allies to defeat Germany. On November 11, 1918, the war ended, and young people throughout the U.S. left school to take to the streets and celebrate with their elders.

The war had killed millions of soldiers and had wounded millions more, most of them young men. Some disabled soldiers were seen begging on the streets to survive. Marriage rates declined in countries where millions of young men had been killed in the prime of life. Millions of children suffered from poverty when the family wage-earner was killed during the war. British soldier Wilfred Owen, who was 21 when the war began in 1914, expressed the misery of the soldier in his poetry. In "Anthem for Doomed Youth," he wrote, "What passing-bells for those who died as cattle? Only the monstrous anger of the guns. Only the stuttering rifles' rapid rattle" (Falls, 1961). Owen was killed on the Western Front in 1918.

Civilians in war-torn countries were hungry and sickly. A number of young men returned home missing eyes or limbs or with severe scars. About 100,000 civilians had died at sea and in air raids, while millions more died from disease, famine, and starvation. During the war, about 4 million Armenians, Syrians, Greeks, and Jews had been victims of massacres. An influenza epidemic that spread across the world from the spring of 1918 to the spring of 1919 killed another 6 million people, many of them youths. Wartime deprivations and conditions were blamed for the massive deaths caused by the flu epidemic, which found people in a malnourished and weakened state.

A future U.S. president played a key role in relief efforts. Herbert Hoover, an engineer and self-made millionaire, had retired in 1914 at age 40 to do humanitarian work. As World War I began, he organized the Commission for the Relief of Belgium, which sent $1 billion in U.S. government loans and private funds to that ravaged country between 1914 and 1919. In 1917, Hoover was appointed the director of the Food Administration,

which shipped food to needy persons overseas while maintaining enough food at home. After the war ended in 1918, Hoover directed the American Relief Administration that sent tons of food, clothing, and medical supplies to European refugees. Millions of children needed food, and the problem was aggravated when famine struck the Soviet Union. Although Hoover and other U.S. leaders opposed communism, American relief was extended to Eastern Europe and the Soviet Union. When he was criticized for helping the Soviet people, Hoover said, "Twenty million people are starving. Whatever their politics, they shall be fed" (Freidel, 1975).

Although World War I was supposed to be the "war to end all wars," a second world war, one that was even more disastrous for young people, engulfed the world in the late 1930s. *See also* Addams, Jane; Armenian-Turkish Conflict; Chemical Warfare; Espionage; Gas Masks; Hunger/Malnutrition; *Lusitania*; Russian Revolution; Selective Service Acts; Underground Presses.

Further Reading: Allen Churchill, *Over Here* (1968); Cyril Falls, *The Great War* (1961); Pierce G. Fredericks, *The Great Adventure: America in the First World War* (1960); Frank Freidel, *The Presidents of the United States of America* (1975); Emmet J. Scott, *Scott's Official History of the American Negro in the World War* (1919); Louis L. Snyder, *Historic Documents of World War I* (1958); Mark Sullivan, *Our Times: The United States, 1900-1925* (1933).

World War II (1939–1945)

Untold numbers of children throughout the world, mainly in Europe, Asia, and the South Pacific, suffered the horrors of World War II (1939-1945). Millions were killed, injured, or rendered homeless by bombardment with conventional or nuclear weapons. Neutral nations were not spared from attacks. For example, Ireland was neutral during World War II but was still affected. German bombers hit some parts of the country. An area near Dublin was hit in 1941, destroying numerous homes and other buildings and killing many civilians. Neutral Holland and Belgium were also invaded and occupied by the Nazis, as were Norway and Denmark.

Children were affected by the war in numerous other ways. Many became fatherless or lost brothers and other relatives when men were killed in battle. They were orphaned when their parents died from warfare or from diseases, hard labor, starvation, or direct enemy actions, such as executions or massacres. Children were sometimes specifically targeted for imprisonment and death. Hunger and starvation also plagued young people in Europe, Asia, and other regions affected by the conflict both during and after the war. Occupying forces confiscated local food supplies, fuel, livestock, clothing, and other goods, which they used for their own armies or shipped to the military or civilians in their homeland.

Millions of young people were forced into slave labor in special camps far away from their homes. In Europe, these laborers included young men and, sometimes, young women, from Holland, Poland, France, and other Nazi-occupied nations. The Japanese also forced young men from occupied Asian countries into labor. Hundreds of thousands of slave laborers died.

Youths were also sent to concentration camps or death camps where millions perished. In Europe, the Nazis targeted Jews and Romani (Gypsies) of all ages for deportation and death. About 1.5 million Jewish youth and thousands of Romani youth perished.

Young soldiers from Allied and Axis nations died or were injured during the war. The first U.S. soldiers to die during the war were killed on October 31, 1940, when the USS destroyer *Reuben James* was blown up between Ireland and Iceland while guarding convoys of cargo ships filled with war materiel bound for Great Britain. Among the dead was 20-year-old Leonidas Dickerson of Virginia, a member of the destroyer's 100-person crew.

Family separations frequently occurred because people left to serve in the military or were involuntarily sent to do forced labor or were imprisoned. Many Jewish children were sent to other countries, if they could escape from the Nazis, or went into hiding, sometimes separately from other family members.

Some families had more than one member serving in the military during the war. In February 1941, the three Joffrion boys of Donaldsville, Louisiana, enlisted in the U.S. Army Air Corps. They included Leonard, age 20, Ray, age 18, and Olin, age 17.

Men under age 21 served with various national navies during the war. For example, in Great Britain, they served on crews aboard tankers in the Atlantic. One such ship was torpedoed by a German warship in January 1941 off the coast of Scotland. Aboard were a 20-year-old third mate and a 17-year-old radioman. They were among those who escaped onto lifeboats and were rescued by a Canadian ship.

Many military and civilian youths acted courageously. Civilian youths took part in resistance activities and rescue work. Some risked their lives for others. For example, youths helped rescue Allied troops stranded on a beach in Dunkirk, France, in 1940. About 500,000 troops were trapped along the English Channel after trying to stop German troops from invading Belgium and France. German troops and tanks gathered to push them toward the sea. Teenagers helped other civilians who went to rescue them with small motorboats and fishing vessels. More than 338,000 British and French soldiers were able to board these boats and escape to England during the amazing rescue known as the "miracle of Dunkirk." *See also* ADOPTION; BAUBLIS, PETRAS; BELGIUM (WORLD WAR II); BOMBINGS (WORLD WAR II); CADET NURSE CORPS; CARE; CASUALTIES, CIVILIAN; CASUALTIES, MILITARY; CHILDREN'S TRANSPORTS (*KINDERTRANSPORT*); CIMADE; CLOTHING SHORTAGES; COLLECTION CENTER DRIVES; CONCENTRATION CAMPS (WORLD WAR II); CONSCRIPTION; DEATH CAMPS (WORLD WAR II); DENMARK (WORLD WAR II); DEPORTATIONS; DISPLACED PERSONS (DPs) (WORLD WAR II); EDUCATION; *EINSATZGRUPPEN;* EXPERIMENTS, NAZI; FINLAND (WORLD WAR II); FOOD; FORCED LABOR (WORLD WAR II); FRANCE (WORLD WAR II); FRANK, ANNE; GERMANY (WORLD WAR II); GHETTOS (WORLD WAR II); GREECE (WORLD WAR II); HIDDEN CHILDREN; HIROSHIMA; HITLER, ADOLF; HOLIDAYS; HOL-

LAND (WORLD WAR II); HOLOCAUST; HUNGARY (WORLD WAR II); HUNGER/MALNUTRITION; INTERNMENT CAMPS, U.S.; INTERROGATIONS; ITALY (WORLD WAR II); JAPAN (WORLD WAR II); JEHOVAH'S WITNESSES; LE CHAMBON-SUR-LIGNON; LEBENSBORN; MARSHALL PLAN; MASSACRES; NAGASAKI; NORWAY (WORLD WAR II); *OEUVRE DE SECOURS DES ENFANTS* (OSE); ORPHANS; PACIFIC (WORLD WAR II); PEARL HARBOR; POLAND (WORLD WAR II); POST-TRAUMATIC STRESS DISORDER (PTSD); QUAKERS (SOCIETY OF FRIENDS); RATIONING; RED CROSS; REFUGEES; RELIEF ORGANIZATIONS; RESCUERS (HOLOCAUST); RESISTANCE MOVEMENTS (WORLD WAR II); ROMANI (GYPSIES); ROUND-UPS; SELECTIVE SERVICE ACTS; SEPARATIONS, FAMILY; SEXUAL ABUSE; SHANGHAI (WORLD WAR II); SINGAPORE (WORLD WAR II); SOVIET UNION (WORLD WAR II); *ST. LOUIS*; UKRAINE (WORLD WAR II); VICTORY GARDENS; VOLUNTEERS; WAR BONDS (U.S.); WAR TOYS; *ZAZOU*; ZEGOTA.

Further Reading: Jack Coggins, *The Fighting Man* (1966); Penny Colman, *Rosie the Riveter* (1995); John Keegan, *The Second World War* (1989); Thomas Leonard, *Day by Day: The Forties* (1977); Reader's Digest, *America in the '40s* (1998); Michi Weglyn, *Years of Infamy* (1976).

Wounded Knee Massacre

U.S. cavalry troops attacked Sioux Indians encamped at Wounded Knee Creek, South Dakota, in December 1890. The camp contained about 120 men and 230 women and children. These Sioux had left the reservation and were traveling toward the Pine Ridge Agency to surrender when they were surrounded and taken to Wounded Knee Creek, where the U.S. soldiers demanded that they surrender all guns and other weapons. The troops then separated the men from the women and children, taking them to another place. Eyewitnesses later said that one unruly member of the Indian group managed to keep a gun and fired it. The troops then started firing their guns, killing people indiscriminately.

About 300 of the Indians died at the hands of the cavalry during the attack. Most of the Indians were unarmed. After trying to defend themselves with clubs, knives, or hands, they tried to flee. The cavalry opened fire with four large guns positioned on a hill overlooking the camp and killed or wounded more than half of the Indians.

Besides the dead, there were 47 women and children among the wounded. They, along with four men who were still alive, were taken by wagons to the Pine Ridge Reservation and had to stay in the open air during the bitter cold weather until shelter was found for them in an abandoned Episcopal mission.

Louise Weasel Bear, who escaped death that day, later said, "We tried to run but they shot us like we were a buffalo. I know there are some good white people, but the soldiers must be mean to shoot children and women. Indian soldiers would not do that to white children" (McGregor, 1940). The massacre at Wounded Knee marked the end of the Indian Wars in the west. Two eyewitnesses, Turning Hawk and American Horse, later testified to the Commissioner of Indian Affairs about the details. American Horse said, "[T]he killing of the young boys and girls who are to go to make up the future strength of the Indian people, is the saddest part of the whole affair and we feel it very sorely" (McGregor, 1940). *See also* AMERICAN INDIAN WARS.

Further Reading: Dee Brown, *Bury My Heart at Wounded Knee* (1971); James H. McGregor, *The Wounded Knee Massacre from the Viewpoint of the Sioux* (1940).

Writers. *See* BERG, MARY; DIARIES; FRANK, ANNE; GIES, MIEP AND GIES, JAN; HART, KITTY FELIX; RINGELBLUM ARCHIVES; TOLL, NELLY LANDAU; WARSAW GHETTO; WIESEL, ELIE

Y

Yad Vashem

In August 1953, the Israeli Parliament passed the Martyrs' and Heroes' Remembrance Law, which set up Yad Vashem (from the Hebrew words "lasting memorial," or "monument and a name"). Located in Jerusalem, the Martyrs' and Heroes' Remembrance Authority is a center for research on the Holocaust, or Shoah in Hebrew. During this tragic era before and during World War II, about 6 million Jews were killed by the Nazis under Adolf Hitler.

Yad Vashem contains a museum, library, and numerous historical materials and artifacts. Among the thousands of taped testimonies from Holocaust survivors are many accounts from people who were children or teenagers during their ordeal. The memorial also includes poignant reminders of the millions of children who died and suffered during the Holocaust. A special memorial for Jewish children killed by the Nazis is located beneath the Children's Garden. Designed by architect Moshe Safdie, the memorial features a dark room that contains panels of mirrors and five memorial candles. The design of the mirrors multiplies the flames of those five candles into 1.5 million lights, one for each child who died. A somber recorded voice reads the names, ages, and countries of all the children, one by one. The last item visitors see at the memorial is a child's high-topped shoe placed in the exit hall. This shoe is a bitter reminder of the fact that children were targeted for death by the Nazis.

Yad Vashem is also authorized to identify and honor Righteous Gentiles, defined as "high-minded Gentiles who risked their lives to save Jews" during the Holocaust. Some of these Gentiles were teenagers during the war. Carob trees with plaques identifying these courageous rescuers line the Avenue of the Righteous and can be seen on a hillside near the Holocaust Museum. *See also* BELGIUM (WORLD WAR II); BURZMINSKI, STEFANIA PODGORSKA; DENMARK (WORLD WAR II); FRANCE (WORLD WAR II); GIES, MIEP AND GIES, JAN; GRAEBE, HERMANN; HIDDEN CHILDREN; HOLOCAUST; ITALY (WORLD WAR II); KALINA, ANTONIN; KOLBE, MAXIMILIAN; LE CHAMBON-SUR-LIGNON; PRITCHARD, MARION VON BINSBERGEN; RESCUERS (HOLOCAUST); RIGHTEOUS GENTILES; SCHINDLER, OSKAR; SENDLER, IRINA; TROCME, ANDRE AND TROCME, MAGDA; TROCME, DANIEL; VOS, AART AND VOS, JOHTJE; WALLENBERG, RAOUL; WESTERWEEL, JOOP; WORLD WAR II; ZAHAJKEWYCZ, OREST AND ZAHAJKEWYCZ, HELENA.

Further Reading: Yad Vashem Fact Sheets, "About Yad Vashem," "Remembrance," "Education," "Righteous Among the Nations," at <www.yadvashem.org>.

Young Vanguards. *See* CHINESE CIVIL WAR; JAPAN-CHINA WAR

Youth Advocate Program International (YAP-I)

The Youth Advocate Program International (YAP-I) was founded in 1994 as an outgrowth of the National Youth Advocate Program in the United States. YAP-I promotes the rights and well-being of youth throughout the world. The organization is particularly concerned with the plight of troubled and needy youth and those victimized by armed conflict and by state and personal violence.

YAP-I states its goals and services to be as follows:

> Provide advice and counsel to youth advocate programs in nations throughout the world

> Support and conduct training programs and conferences devoted to the rights and well-being of youth

> Carry out research, publish materials, and act as an information clearinghouse for international youth issues

> Work for the development of international legal norms and procedures for the protection of youth.

Among other activities, YAP-I worked with other organizations to promote ratification of the United Nations Convention on the Rights of the Child and an end to child labor. Consultants from YAP-I met with people in different countries to develop programs that would address particular problems created by war and other disasters.

Further Reading: Youth Advocate Program International Fact Sheets "Who Are We?" "Activities," "Publications," at <www.yapi.org>.

Youth Aliyah

Youth Aliyah, a group for young Jews in Europe, was set up by Recha Freyer on January 30, 1933, the day Adolf Hitler and his Nazi Party took control of Germany. The group was directed by Henrietta Szold. The daughter of a Jewish rabbi living in Baltimore, Maryland, Szold became a teacher and conducted classes in English and American culture for European immigrants who had moved to the United States.

She then worked as an editor for the Jewish Publication Society of America, which specializes in works by Jewish authors and materials about Jewish history, people, and culture. Beginning in the 1890s, Szold translated six volumes of Louis Ginzberg's famous work *The Legends of the Jews.* This task occupied some of her time for the next 27 years.

In 1909, Szold visited Palestine, a small country in the Middle East that many Jews regarded as their ancestral homeland. They hoped to build a Jewish state there. Szold found that children living in Palestine lacked proper health care, sanitation, and other necessities. She founded an organization in the United States called Hadassah, which worked to raise money for projects in Palestine. The Young Judaea was the Hadassah youth group. Szold also connected Hadassah with the Jewish youth group, *Hatzofim.*

In 1920, Szold moved to Palestine and became the director of the health services organization she had founded in 1912. During the early 1930s, she saw an urgent need to help youth in Nazi Germany. In numerous countries, young Jews were banned from joining scouting groups and Youth Aliyah offered them opportunities to do similar activities. To prepare them to survive and work in new places, the group stressed outdoor activities and taught members skills in farming, building, and related jobs.

Youth Aliyah helped thousands of young people leave Nazi-occupied countries during the Holocaust. Many young people in the group hoped to emigrate to Palestine, which was then under British control. At that time, British ships patrolled the borders and the British government set strict limits on Jewish immigration. Youth Aliyah arranged to transport a number of people on secret ships that sailed for Palestine. Between 1934 and 1948, Youth Aliyah helped to resettle 30,353 young adults and children from Romania, Cyprus, Turkey, Denmark, Hungary, and other countries. As young people arrived in Palestine from Nazi-occupied countries and war-torn areas, Szold helped them begin new lives in the Jewish homeland. *See also* HOLOCAUST; WESTERWEEL, JOOP.

Further Reading: Leni Yahil, *The Holocaust* (1990).

Yugoslavia (World War II)

In retaliation for an announcement by the Yugoslavian government that the nation would join the Allies, German warplanes bombed Yugoslavia for 72 hours starting on Sunday April 6, 1941. Belgrade, the capital, was devastated and homeless children roamed the streets begging for food. A number of children were left orphaned by the bombings.

After the Nazis occupied Yugoslavia, they divided the country into two sections, Serbia and Croatia, to be controlled by Germany and its allies, Hungary and fascist Italy. Young people were among the Yugoslav partisans who resisted and tried to sabotage the occupying forces.

A group called the Ustasha, under the control of Ante Pavelic, supported the Nazis and their ideology. The Ustasha attacked Serbs, who were a minority population in Croatia. They killed hundreds of thousands of Serbs and threatened others who did not change their religion from Muslim to Catholic. Serbs also followed the Nazis in killing Jews and Romani (Gypsies). Witnesses said that the Ustasha attacked and murdered children as well as adults.

Jewish citizens felt threatened as Nazis moved into the country. Samuel and Erna Nachmias and their three children fled from Croatia in July 1941 to a seaside town controlled by Italian troops, who were known to treat Jews less harshly. In September 1943, the Italians were overcome by German troops, and Jews in the region faced persecution and death. Notices were posted in public places announcing that anyone who hid Jews would face the death penalty.

Thousands of Jewish young people were killed in Croatia during the Holocaust. Some were gassed inside specially equiped vans; their bodies were later discovered in mass graves. Croats used axes to brutally kill both Serbs and Jews in concentration camps. Holocaust historian Leni Yahil (1990) wrote, "In 1942 there were 24,000 children in the infamous Jasenovac Camp. Half of them were murdered; the remaining children were released owing to Red Cross pressure. Many, however, later died of the aftereffects of their imprisonment." *See also* HOLOCAUST; PETER, PRINCE OF YUGOSLAVIA.

Further Reading: Leni Yahil, *The Holocaust* (1990).

Z

Zahajkewycz, Orest (1926–) and Zahajkewycz, Helena (1921–)

Orest and Helena Zahajkewycz were two young Ukrainians who rescued Jews from the Nazis during the Holocaust of World War II. Orest and Helena Zahajkewycz were 16 and 20 years old, respectively, in 1941. Their family, who were members of the Greek Orthodox faith, lived in Peremyshl, a city with about 50,000 people, and their parents were teachers. They had Jewish friends, including a family named Shefler who had once lived in the same apartment building.

The Nazis sent Orest and other young men to work in a German military supply factory where his co-workers included Jews from the ghetto. By 1941, older Jews were being sent away from the ghetto by train to places unknown. Soon, Orest and his co-workers noticed that shirts with bullet-like holes in them were arriving at the factory for the use of the Germans. They concluded that the shirts had belonged to Jews, who were being shot by the Nazis.

The Zahajkewyzc family hid a Jewish doctor, then a man and woman who told the family they were their "last hope." After a few weeks, Orest and Helena bought the couple train tickets to Poland and escorted them safely to their destinations. The family also hid Edzo Shefler and his wife for 10 months, first in their cellar, then in a hiding place they built in their pantry, during the last year of the war. In 1985, Orest and Helena were reunited with the Sheflers in Israel where they were honored as Righteous Gentiles by Yad Vashem. *See also* RIGHTEOUS GENTILES; UKRAINE (WORLD WAR II); YAD VASHEM.

Further Reading: Gay Block and Malka Drucker, *Rescuers* (1992).

Zaire (Democratic Republic of the Congo)

Zaire, the former Belgian Congo, is the second largest country on the African continent south of the Sahara. From the 1960s to the 1990s, civil war and war in neighboring Rwanda took a heavy toll on Zaire, its people, and its resources. Foreign aid sent to Zaire might have relieved some problems suffered by youth but was instead exploited by the government, which also used the country's mineral wealth to serve the elite rather than the poor.

Zaire has seen fighting between Hutu and Tutsi peoples, who have lived there for centuries. When these groups fought bloody wars against each other in neighboring Rwanda, the Hutu received some help from Zairean troops. Hutus and Tutsis in Zaire clashed, and local people clashed with local groups in Zaire's North Kivu province. In 1996, rebels staged an uprising against the corrupt government. Civilians complained that government troops stole food and other things from civilians.

The thousands of refugees in Zaire in the 1990s included many children who suffered from hunger, disease, and lack of adequate shelter and health care. During just one month in 1994, a cholera epidemic at the Goma camp in eastern Zaire killed 50,000 people. Relief organizations working with youth in Zaire also found numerous unaccompanied children. Some children were taken in by families in the area, who might take in as many as 9 or 10 children. Others were placed in group homes or orphanages run by relief groups. To help locate children's families, the organization Doctors without Borders worked with Radio Agatachya in Zaire. *See also* AFRICA; GENOCIDE; REFUGEES; RELIEF ORGANIZATIONS; RWANDA; SOLDIERS, CHILD; UNACCOMPANIED CHILDREN.

Further Reading: Joanna Macrae and Anthony Zwi, eds., *War and Hunger* (1994); United Nations Children's Fund (UNICEF), *The State of the World's Children, 1996* (1996).

Zazou

Between 1940 and 1944, during the Nazi occupation of France, some Parisian youth protested against the Nazis by joining a movement called *zazou*. Young people in this movement could be spotted by their odd, trademark clothing and hairdos: long, too-large jackets, dingy shoes, wool ties, and oiled hair for young men and short pleated skirts, loose jackets, heavy flat shoes, and long hair for young women. They often carried umbrellas and wore dark glasses, indoors as well as out.

The *zazou* danced to swing music, which the Nazis had banned in Germany and tried to restrain throughout occupied Europe. Some youth also joined those protestors who painted "V" signs (for victory) on French buildings. They annoyed the Germans by laughing at German-produced films, which were shown in French theaters, and by mocking German soldiers. Some adults criticized these young people for their unconventional appearance and behavior, but the *zazou* felt it was important to rebel against the Germans and what they stood for. They resented the precise, orderly ways in which the Nazis con-

trolled France and the way they repressed human rights during the years of occupation. *See also* FRANCE (WORLD WAR II).

Further Reading: David Pryce-Jones, *Paris in the Third Reich* (1981); John F. Sweets, *The Politics of Resistance in France, 1940-1944* (1976).

Zegota

A Polish rescue group, the Zegota or *Rada Pomocy Zydom*—Council for Aid to Jews—was made up of Jews and Catholic intellectuals and political activists. Sponsored by the London-based Polish government in exile, the group was created near the end of 1942 and cooperated with the Polish underground and with Jewish and Polish resistance groups. The group was most active in large cities like Warsaw, Cracow, and Lublin. The Zegota received funds from foreign Jewish organizations. It provided those in need with food, hiding places, medical care, and forged identity papers.

Wladyslawa Choms headed the Lwow branch of the Zegota and may have saved hundreds of people. She personally took care of 60 children whom she had smuggled from the ghetto. She and her associates used resourceful methods, moving children through sewers under the streets at night or using garbage wagons to transport them by day. They carried sacks of bread into the ghetto, then used these empty sacks to sneak Jewish children out. Her organization provided Jews with food, money, and medical care inside and outside the ghetto. They also provided people with false identity and work papers. It is estimated that the Zegota hid and saved more than 2,500 Jewish children in Warsaw alone during the war by placing them with families or in Catholic or secular institutions. *See also* HOLOCAUST; IDENTITY PAPERS; POLAND (WORLD WAR II); RESCUERS (HOLOCAUST); SENDLER, IRENA.

Further Reading: Richard C. Lukas, *Out of the Inferno: Poles Remember the Holocaust* (1989); Nechama Tec, *When Light Pierced the Darkness: Christian Rescue of Poles in Occupied Poland* (1986); Irene Tomaszewski and Tecia Werbowski, *Zegota: The Rescue of Jews in Wartime Poland* (1994).

Zones of Peace, Children as. *See*
BOSNIA; UNITED NATIONS CHILDREN'S
FUND (UNICEF)

Zyklon B

Zyklon B, a poison made of hydrogen cyanide, was used to kill rats and other vermin and to disinfect rooms and clothing. During World War II, the Nazis used it in the form of a gas to systematically murder Jews and other people in death camps set up for mass killings. The Nazis first tested methods of killing people by gas when they piped carbon monoxide into sealed vans that they moved from place to place, mostly in Poland and Nazi-occupied regions of the Soviet Union. Among the first victims were Romani (Gypsy) children.

In 1941, after Nazi leaders devised a plan of genocide they called The Final Solution, they sought a method that would kill groups of people quickly and with the least trouble and expense. Once they settled on poison gas as the preferred method, German firms competed to supply the poisonous substance to the death camps, with the Dessauer Works, which made and sold Zyklon, winning the contract.

Zyklon B came in the form of crystals inside blue-colored capsules that were then packed into canisters. The crystals turned into poison gas when they were exposed to the air. They were released through the ceilings of death chambers that the Nazis misrepresented to the victims as "showers." People inside died from asphyxiation as poison gas filled their lungs. This painful process could take from 3 to 15 minutes, sometimes longer.

A monoxide type gas was first tested at a death camp called Belzec in Poland late in 1942. Children were among the first victims at Belzec. Kurt Gerstein, a German SS of-

ficer who had been sent to Belzec to deliver the poison, was horrified by what he had seen. Gerstein informed a Swedish diplomat and other people he hoped might take action, but his story was not believed at that time. Gerstein reported that he had seen 45 cars with about 6,700 people, including children, arrive at Belzec in August. Ukrainian guards had ordered them all off the train, inside which about 1,450 already lay dead. The people were forced to remove all their clothing, then were whipped. Their hair was shorn.

> Then the procession started to move. With a lovely young girl at the front. They all walked along the path, all naked, men, women, and children. . . . Mothers with their babies at the breast came up, hesitated, and entered the death chambers.

The victims were told to inhale deeply, that the air inside would help kill any infections or illness. Some guessed their fate. Any who resisted were pushed into the chambers with whips. Many prayed. It took about 32 minutes before the last people in the chambers had died.

Gerstein also reported that "The corpses were thrown out . . . . Children's bodies flew through the air." After dentists removed any gold fillings they could find in the teeth of these corpses, their remains were buried in pits.

Killings by poison gas continued until 1945 when the Allies defeated Hitler's armies and liberated the death camps. By then, millions had been murdered. *See also* AUSCHWITZ-BIRKENAU; DEATH CAMPS (WORLD WAR II); EUTHANASIA; FINAL SOLUTION; GENOCIDE; HOLOCAUST; OPERATION T-4.

Further Reading: Konnilyn Feig, *Hitler's Death Camps* (1979); Isaac Gutman, ed., *Encyclopedia of the Holocaust,* 4 vols. (1995).

BIBLIOGRAPHY

Aaseng, Nathan. *Cities at War: Paris*. New York: Macmillan, 1992.

———. *Navajo Code Talkers*. New York: Walker, 1992.

Abodaher, David J. *Youth in the Middle East: Voices of Despair*. New York: Franklin Watts, 1991.

Adachi, Agnes. *Child of the Winds*. Chicago: Adams Press, 1989.

Addams, Jane. *Twenty Years at Hull-House*. New York: The Macmillan Company, 1910.

———. *The Second Twenty Years at Hull-House*. New York: The Macmillan Company, 1930.

Adler, David A. *We Remember the Holocaust*. New York: Henry Holt, 1989.

———. *Child of the Warsaw Ghetto*. New York: Holiday House, 1995.

Adler, Stanislaw. *In the Warsaw Ghetto, 1940-1943*. Jerusalem: Yad Vashem, 1982.

Africa Watch, Human Rights Watch Staff. *Mozambique: Conspicuous Destruction*. New York: Human Rights Watch, 1992.

Ainzstein, Reuben. *Jewish Resistance in Nazi Occupied Eastern Europe*. New York: Barnes and Noble, 1974.

———. *The Warsaw Ghetto Revolt*. New York: Holocaust Library, 1979.

Allen, Louis. *Singapore, 1941-42*. London: Frank Cass & Co., 1992.

Allen, W.E.D. *The Ukraine: A History*. Portland, OR: International Specialized Book Services, Cambridge University Press, 1941.

Almond, Mark. *Europe's Backyard War: The War in the Balkans*. Portsmouth, NH: Heinemann, 1994.

Altman, Susan. *Extraordinary Black Americans from Colonial to Contemporary Times*. Chicago: Children's Press, 1989.

Altshuler, David. *Hitler's War Against the Jews*. New York: Behrman House, 1978.

Amnesty International. "A Stolen Future: Protecting the Rights of Refugee Children." New York: Amnesty International, 1997.

Anderson, Trezzvant W. *Come Out Fighting: The Epic Tale of the 761st Tank Battalion, 1942–1945*. Salzburg: Salzburger Druckerei und Verlag, 1945.

Andrist, Ralph K. *The Long Death: The Last Days of the Plains Indians*. New York: Macmillan, 1964.

Anticaglia, Elizabeth. *Heroines of '76*. New York: Walker, 1975.

Apfel, Roberta J. and Bennett Simon, eds. *Minefields in Their Hearts: The Mental Health of Children in War and Communal Violence*. New Haven, CT: Yale University Press, 1996.

Arad, Yitzhak. *Ghetto in Flames: The Struggle and Destruction of the Jews in Vilna in the Holocaust*. New York: Holocaust Publications, 1982.

Armor, John, and Peter Wright. *Manzanar.* New York: Times Books, 1988.

Armstrong, John A. *Ukrainian Nationalism 1939-45.* New York: Columbia University Press, 1955.

Armstrong, Virginia I. *I Have Spoken: A Documentary History of Chief Joseph.* Athens, OH: Sage Books, 1971.

Arney, George. *Afghanistan.* London: Mandarin, 1989.

Aroneau, Eugene. *Inside the Concentration Camps: Eyewitness Accounts of Life in Hitler's Death Camps.* Translated by Thomas Whissen. Westport, CT: Praeger Publishers, 1996.

Ashman, Charles, and Robert J. Wagman, *The Nazi Hunters.* New York: Pharos, 1988.

Asprey, Robert B. *War in the Shadows: The Guerilla in History.* Garden City, NY: Doubleday & Co., Inc., 1975.

Associated Press. *Lightning Out of Israel: The Six-Day War in the Middle East.* New York: Associated Press, 1967.

Astrup, Helen and B.L. Jacot, *Oslo Intrigue: A Woman's Memoir of the Norwegian Resistance.* New York: McGraw Hill, 1954.

Auerbacher, Inge. *I Am a Star: Child of the Holocaust.* New York: Prentice-Hall, 1985.

Avriel, Ehud. *Open the Gates! The Dramatic Personal Story of "Illegal" Immigration to Israel.* New York: Atheneum, 1975.

Ayer, Eleanor. *Cities at War: Berlin.* New York: Macmillan, 1992.

———. *The United States Holocaust Memorial Museum: American Keeps the Memory Alive.* New York: Dillon Press, 1994.

———. *Holocaust: A Firestorm Unleashed.* Woodbridge, CT: Blackbirch Press, 1998.

Aynes, Edith. *From Nightingale to Eagle: The Army Nurses History.* Englewood Cliffs, NJ: Prentice Hall, 1973.

Bachrach, Susan D. *Tell Them We Remember: The Story of the Holocaust.* Boston: Little, Brown, 1993.

Baden-Powell, Dorothy. *Operation Jupiter: SOE's Secret War in Norway.* London: Hale, 1982.

Baer, Edith. *A Frost in the Night: Girlhood on the Eve of the Third Reich.* New York: Pantheon, 1980.

Bailey, Lynn R. *The Long Walk.* Los Angeles: Westernlore Press, 1964.

Bailey, Ronald H. *Partisans and Guerrillas.* New York: Time-Life Books, 1978.

Bainton, Roland H. *Christian Attitudes Toward War and Peace.* New York: Abingdon, 1960.

Bakeless, Katherine, and Bakeless, John. *Spies of the Revolution.* Philadelphia: Lippincott, 1962.

Baldwin, Margaret. *The Boys Who Saved the Children.* New York: Julian Press, 1991.

Barber, Noel. *Sinister Twilight: The Fall and Rise Again of Singapore.* Boston: Houghton-Mifflin, 1968.

Barfod, Jorgen. *The Holocaust Failed in Denmark.* Copenhagen: Frihedsmuseets Venners, 1985.

Barkai, Meyer, ed. and trans. *The Fighting Ghettos.* Philadelphia: J.B. Lippincott Co., 1962.

Barker, Rodney. *The Hiroshima Maidens.* New York: Viking, 1985.

Barnitz, Laura A. *Child Soldiers: Youth Who Participate in Armed Conflict.* Washington, DC: Youth Advocate International, 1997.

Barnouw, Adriaan J. *The Pageant of Netherlands History.* New York: Longman, Greens and Company, 1952.

Barson, Michael. *Better Red Than Dead.* New York: Hyperion, 1992.

Barton, Clara. *The Red Cross.* Washington, DC: The Red Cross, 1895.

Bartoszewski, Wladyslav. *The Warsaw Ghetto: A Christian's Testimony.* Boston: Beacon Press, 1987.

Bauer, Yehuda. *Fight and Rescue: The Organized Escape of the Survivors of Eastern Europe, 1945-1948.* New York: Random House, 1970.

———. *The Holocaust in Historical Perspective.* Seattle: University of Washington Press, 1978.

———. *American Jewry and the Holocaust: The American Joint Distribution Committee, 1939-1945.* Detroit: Wayne State University Press, 1981.

————. *A History of the Holocaust.* New York: Franklin Watts, 1982.

Bauman, Janina. *Winter in the Morning: A Young Girl's Life in the Warsaw Ghetto and Beyond.* London: Virago Press, 1945.

Baxter, Craig. *Bangladesh: From a Nation to a State.* New York: Westview Press, 1997.

Baynes, Norman H., ed. *The Speeches of Adolf Hitler.* New York: Howard Fertig, 1969.

Bazhan, M.P., ed. *Soviet Ukraine.* Kiev: Editorial Office of the Ukrainian Soviet Encyclopedia, Academy of Sciences of the Ukrainian SSR, 1969.

Beal, Merrill L. *I Will Fight No More Forever: Chief Joseph and the Nez Perce War.* Seattle: University of Washington Press, 1963.

Beasley, W.G. *The Modern History of Japan.* New York: Praeger, 1963.

Becker, Elizabeth. *The Armies of Cambodia.* Paris: Presses de la Cite, 1986.

Bedoukian, Kerop. *Some of Us Survived: The Story of an Armenian Boy.* New York: Farrar Straus Giroux, 1979.

Beller, Susan Provost. *Cadets at War: The True Story of the Battle of New Market.* White Hall, VA: Shoe Tree Press, 1991.

Bemrose, John. *Reminiscences of the Second Seminole War.* Edited by John K. Mahon. Gainesville: University of Florida Press, 1966.

Bentley, Amy. *Eating for Victory.* Evanston: University of Illinois Press, 1998.

Bentwich, Norman. *They Found Refuge.* London: Crescent Press, 1956.

Berenbaum, Michael, ed. *A Mosaic of Victims: Non-Jews Persecuted and Murdered by the Nazis.* New York: New York University Press, 1990.

Berg, Mary. *Warsaw Ghetto Diary.* New York: L.B. Fischer, 1945.

Bernstein, Alison R. *American Indians and World War II: Toward a New Era in Indian Affairs.* Norman: University of Oklahoma Press, 1991.

Besson, Jean-Louis. *October 45: Childhood Memories of the War.* San Diego: Harcourt Brace & Co., 1995.

Bierman, John. *Righteous Gentile: The Story of Raoul Wallenberg, Missing Hero of the Holocaust.* New York: Viking, 1981.

Bills, Scott L., ed. *Kent State/May 4: Echoes Through a Decade.* Kent, OH: Kent State University Press, 1988.

Bischoff, Ralph F. *Nazi Conquest Through German Culture.* Cambridge, MA: Harvard University Press, 1942.

Black, Maggie. *Children First: The Story of UNICEF Past and Present.* New York: Oxford University Press, 1996.

Black, Wallace B. and Jean F. Blashfield. *Battle of the Bulge.* New York: Crestwood House, 1993.

Blackman, Ellen. *Harvest in the Snow: My Crusade to Rescue the Lost Children of Bosnia.* Washington, DC: Brassey's Inc., 1997.

Bles, Mark. *Child at War: The True Story of a Belgian Resistance Fighter.* New York: Mercury House, 1991.

Block, Gay, and Malka Drucker. *Rescuers: Portraits of Moral Courage in the Holocaust.* New York: Holmes and Meier, 1992.

Blomqvist, Ulla, ed. *Protection of Children in Refugee Emergencies.* Stockholm, Sweden: Radda Barnen (Save the Children), 1995.

Boas, Jacob. *We Are Witnesses: The Diaries of Five Teenagers Who Died in the Holocaust.* New York: Henry Holt, 1995.

Bonavia, David. *Peking.* New York: Time-Life Books, 1978.

Bonga, Dieuwke Wendelaar. *Eight Prison Camps: A Dutch Family in Japanese Java.* Athens, OH: Ohio University Press, 1996.

Boshyk, Yury, ed. *Ukraine During World War II: History and its Aftermath.* Edmonton: Canadian Institute of Ukrainian Studies, University of Alberta, 1986.

Botting, Douglas. *The Aftermath: Europe.* Alexandria, VA: Time-Life Books, 1983.

Bower, Tom. *Klaus Barbie: The Butcher of Lyons.* London: Corgi Books, 1984.

Breitman, Richard and Alan M. Kraut. *American Refugee Policy and European Jewry, 1933–1945.* Bloomington: Indiana University Press, 1987.

Bibliography

Brett, Rachel and Margaret McCallin. *Children: The Invisible Soldiers*. Vaxjo, Sweden: Radda Barnen (Save the Children), 1996.

Breznitz, S. *Memory Fields: The Legacy of a Wartime Childhood in Czechoslovakia*. New York: Knopf, 1992.

Brimner, Larry Dane. *Voices from the Camps: Internment of Japanese Americans During World War II*. New York: Franklin Watts, 1994.

Brock, Peter. *Pacifism in the United States from Colonial Era to the First World War*. Princeton: Princeton University Press, 1968.

Brown, Deė. *Bury My Heart at Wounded Knee: An Indian History of the American West*. New York: Henry Holt, 1971.

Brown, Maggie, Helen Charney, and Celia Pettym, eds. *Children Separated by War: Family Tracing and Reunification*. London: Save the Children UK, 1995.

Brown, Wallace. *The Good Americans: The Loyalists in the American Revolution*. New York: William Morrow, 1969.

Bruhn, Sheila. *Diary of a Girl in Changi, 1941-1945*. Cincinnati, OH: Seven Hills Book Distributors, 1994.

Bullock, Alan. *Hitler: A Study in Tyranny*. New York: Harper and Row, 1971.

———. *Hitler and Stalin: Parallel Lives*. New York: Knopf, 1992.

Burden, Hamilton T. *The Nuremberg Party Rallies: 1923-1939*. New York: Frederick A. Praeger, 1967.

Burgess, Alan. *The Small Woman*. London: Evans Brothers, 1957.

Burr, J. Millard. *Requiem for the Sudan*. Boulder, CO: Westview Press, 1995.

Bussey, Gertrude, and Margaret Tims. *Pioneers for Peace: Women's International League for Peace and Freedom, 1915-1965*. Oxford, England: Alden Press, 1980.

Caidin, Martin, and Jay Barbree. *Bicycles in War*. New York: Hawthorn Books, 1974.

Cameron, James. *The African Revolution*. London: Thames and Hudson, 1961.

Campbell, Judith. *Queen Elizabeth II, A Biography*. New York: Crown, 1980.

Cannon, Terence. *Revolutionary Cuba*. New York: Thomas Y. Crowell, 1981.

Carey, John. *Eyewitness to History*. Cambridge, MA: Harvard University Press, 1988.

Carmer, Carl, ed. *A Cavalcade of Young Americans*. New York: Lothrop, Lee and Shepard, 1958.

Carse, Robert. *Keepers of the Light*. New York: Scribner's, 1969.

Carter-Goldsmith, George. *The Battle of Britain—The Home Front*. London: Mason and Lipscomb, 1974.

Casado, Segismundo. *The Last Days of Madrid*. London: P. Davies, 1939.

Cataldi, Anna. *Letters from Sarajevo: Voices of a Besieged City*. London: Element Books, Ltd., 1994.

Catton, Bruce. *This Hallowed Ground: The Story of the Union Side of the Civil War*. Garden City, NY: Doubleday, 1956.

Chaikin, Miriam. *A Nightmare in History: The Holocaust 1933-1945*. New York: Clarion, 1987.

Chary, Frederick B. *The Bulgarian Jews and the Final Solution, 1940-1933*. Pittsburgh: University of Pittsburgh Press, 1972.

Cheney, Glen. *They Never Knew: The Victims of Nuclear Testing*. Danbury, CT: Franklin Watts, 1996.

Chidsey, Donald Barr. *The War in the South*. New York: Crown, 1969.

Child Soldiers. Report from a Seminar by Radda Barnen and the Swedish Red Cross, Stockholm, Sweden, February 1994.

Children Bearing Military Arms. Geneva: Quaker United Nations Office, 1984.

Chinnook, Frank W. *Nagasaki: The Forgotten Bomb*. Cleveland: World Publishing Co., 1969.

Chisholm, Anne. *Faces of Hiroshima*. London: Jonathan Cape, 1985.

Chole, Eshetu, ed. *Children of War in the Horn of Africa: The Bitter Harvest of Armed Conflict in Ethiopia, Sudan, Somania, and Djibouti*. Addis-Ababa, Ethiopia: Inter-Africa Group, 1992.

Chuikov, Vasili I. *The Battle for Stalingrad.* Translated by Harold Silver. New York: Holt, Rinehart, and Winston, 1964.

Chung, Ly Qui. *Between Two Fires: Unheard Voices of Vietnam.* New York: Praeger, 1970.

Churchill, Allen. *Over Here.* New York: Dodd, Mead, and Company, 1968.

Churchill, Randolph S., and Churchill, Winston S. *The Six Day War.* Boston: Houghton Mifflin, 1967.

Claghorn, Charles E. *Women Patriots of the American Revolution: A Biographical Dictionary.* Metuchen, NJ: Scarecrow Press, 1991.

Clay, Catrine, and Michael Leapman. *Master Race.* London: Hodder and Stoughton, 1995.

Clubb, O. Edmund. *20th Century China.* New York: Columbia University Press, 1964.

Clyne, Patricia Edwards. *Patriots in Petticoats.* New York: Dodd, Mead, 1976.

Coggins, Jack. *The Fighting Man: An Illustrated History of the World's Greatest Fighting Forces Through the Ages.* Garden City, NY: Doubleday, 1966.

Cohen, Stan. *V for Victory: America's Home Front During World War II.* Missoula, MT: Pictorial Histories Publishers, 1991.

Cohn, Ilene, and Guy Goodman-Gill. *Child Soldiers: The Role of Children in Armed Conflicts.* Oxford: Clarendon Press, 1994.

Colijn, Helen. *Song of Survival: Women Interned.* Ashland, OR: White Cloud, 1997.

Colman, Penny. *Rosie the Riveter: Women Working on the Home Front in World War II.* New York: Crown, 1995.

Commager, Henry Steele, and Morris, Richard B., eds. *The Spirit of "Seventy-Six": The Story of the American Revolution as Told by Participants.* New York: Harper & Row, 1967.

Connor, R.D.W. *Makers of North Carolina History.* Raleigh, NC: Alfred Williams and Co., 1930.

Conquest, Robert. *The Harvest of Sorrow.* Edmonton: University of Alberta Press, 1986.

Costello, John. *The Pacific War, 1941-45.* New York: Quill, 1981.

Council for the Protection of Monuments to Struggle and Martyrdom. *The World Remembers Those Children.* Warsaw, Poland: Ruch Publishers, 1971.

Cowan, Lore, ed. *Children of the Resistance.* New York: Meredith Press, 1969.

Cretzmeyer, Stacy. *Your Name Is Renee: Ruth's Story as a Hidden Child.* Brunswick, ME: Biddle Publishing Co., 1994.

Cronin, Vincent. *Louis and Antoinette.* New York: William Morrow, 1974.

Cullen, Louis M. *Life in Ireland.* New York: G.P. Putnam's, 1969.

Czech, Danuta. *The Auschwitz Chronicle.* New York: Henry Holt, 1997.

Dallin, Alexander. *German Rule in Russia 1941-1945.* London: Macmillan, 1957.

Daniels, Roger. *Concentration Camps U.S.A.* New York: Holt, Rinehart, & Winston, 1972.

———. *The Decision to Relocate the Japanese Americans.* Boston: Lippincott, 1975.

———. *Concentration Camps North America.* Malabar, FL: R.E. Krieger, 1981.

Dank, Milton. *The Dangerous Game.* Philadelphia: J.B. Lippincott, 1977.

Dawidowicz, Lucy S. *The War Against the Jews, 1933-1945.* New York: Holt, Rinehart, and Winston, 1975.

———. *The Holocaust and History.* Cambridge, MA: Harvard University Press, 1981.

Davis, Burke. *The Civil War: Strange and Fascinating Facts.* New York: Holt, Rinehart, and Winston, 1982.

Davis, Curtis Carroll. *Belle Boyd in Camp and Prison.* South Brunswick, NJ: T. Joseloff, 1968.

Davis, Daniel S. *Behind Barbed Wire.* New York: Dutton, 1982.

De Jong, Louis. *The Lion Rampant: The Story of Holland's Resistance to the Nazis.* Translated by Joseph W.F. Stoppelman. New York: Querido, 1945.

Debo, Angie. *A History of the Indians of the United States.* Norman: University of Oklahoma Press, 1970.

DePauw, Linda Grant. *Founding Mothers.* Boston: Houghton Mifflin, 1975.

Des Pres, Terrence. *The Survivor: An Anatomy of Life in the Death Camps.* New York: Oxford University Press, 1976.

Deschamps, Helene, with Kathryn Monget. *Spyglass! An Autobiography.* New York: Henry Holt, 1995.

Dippel, John V.H. *Bound Upon a Wheel of Fire.* New York: Basic Books, 1996.

Dodge, Cole P. and M. Raundelen, eds. *Reaching Children in War: Sudan, Uganda and Mozambique.* Uppsala, Sweden: Sigma Forlag, 1991.

Donia, Robert, and John V.A. Fine. *Bosnia and Hercegovina Betrayed.* New York: Columbia University Press, 1994.

Donovan, Robert J. *The Second Victory: The Marshall Plan and the Postwar Revival of Europe.* New York: Madison Books, 1987.

Dorr, Robert F. *Desert Shield: The Build-up: The Complete Story.* Osceola, WI: Motorbooks, 1991.

Dower, John W. *War without Mercy: Race & Power in the Pacific War.* New York: Pantheon, 1986.

Downey, Fairfax. *Indian-Fighting Army.* New York: Scribner's, 1941.

Drucker, Olga Levy. *Kindertransport.* New York: Henry Holt, 1992.

Dudley, William, ed. *The Middle East: Opposing Viewpoints.* San Diego: Greenhaven Press, 1992.

Duke University Institute of Policy Studies and Public Affairs. *Child Combatants: Countries in Which Children Under 15 Years Have Participated in Armed Conflicts.* Durham, NC: Duke University, 1990.

Dupuy, R. Ernest, and Trevor N. Dupuy, *The Encyclopedia of Military History.* New York: Harper & Row, 1977.

Duranty, Walter. *USSR: The Story of Soviet Russia.* New York: 1944.

Dwork, Deborah. *Children with a Star: Jewish Youth in Nazi Europe.* New Haven, CT: Yale University Press, 1991.

Dyer, Gwynne. *War.* New York: Crown, 1985.

Dyson, Freeman. *Weapons and Hope.* New York: Harper & Row, 1984.

Edelbaum, Ben. *Growing up in the Holocaust.* Kansas City, MO: Self-published, 1980.

Edelheit, Hershel, and Abraham J. Edelheit. *A World in Turmoil: An Integrated Chronology of the Holocaust and World War II.* Westport, CT: Greenwood Press, 1991.

Edmonds, Beverly C. and William R. Ferneckes. *Children's Rights.* Denver: ABC-CLIO, 1996.

Eisenberg, Azriel, ed. *The Lost Generation: Children in the Holocaust.* New York: Pilgrim Press, 1982.

El Zein, Ali, et al. *Situation Analysis and Surveys on Child Health in Lebanon.* Beirut: UNICEF, 1993.

Ellet, Elizabeth. *Women of the American Revolution.* Washington, DC: New York: Baker & Scribner, 1848.

Elson, Robert T. *Prelude to War.* New York: Time-Life Books, 1976.

Emmerich, Elsbeth. *My Childhood in Nazi Germany.* New York: Bookwright Press, 1991.

Engelmann, Bernt. *In Hitler's Germany: Everyday Life in the Third Reich.* New York: Alfred Knopf, 1986.

Engle, Eloise, and Lauri Paananen. *The Winter War: The Russo-Finnish Conflict.* New York: Charles Scribner's Sons, 1973.

Enloe, Cynthia. *Does Khaki Become You? The Militarization of Women's Lives.* London: Pandora, 1988.

Ennew, Judith, and B. Milne, *The Next Generation: Lives of Third-World Children.* London: Zed Books, 1989.

Epstein, Helen. *Children of the Holocaust.* New York: G.P. Putnam's Sons, 1979.

Erickson, John. *The Road to Stalingrad.* London: Weidenfeld and Nicholson, 1975.

Fabre, Emil C., ed. *God's Underground.* Translated by William and Patricia Nottingham. St. Louis: Bethany, 1970.

Fahey, James. *Pacific War Diary.* Boston: Houghton Mifflin, 1963.

Falik, Odie B. *Crimson Desert: Indian Wars of the American Southwest.* New York: Oxford University Press, 1974.

Falk, Richard A., Gabriel Kolko, and Robert Jay Lifton. *Crimes of War.* New York: Random House, 1971.

Falls, Cyril. *The Great War 1914-1918.* New York: Putnam, 1961.

Farrell, John C. *Beloved Lady: A History of Jane Addams' Ideas on Reform and Peace.* Baltimore, MD: Johns Hopkins University Press, 1967.

Fatou, Paul. *Letters of a Civil War Surgeon.* Purdue, IN: Purdue University, 1961.

Feig, Konnilyn. *Hitler's Death Camps.* New York: Holmes and Meier, 1979.

Feingold, Henry L. *The Politics of Rescue: The Roosevelt Administration and the Holocaust, 1938-1945.* New Brunswick, NJ: Rutgers University Press, 1970.

Feller, Carolyn M., and Constance J. Moore, eds. *Highlights in the History of the Army Nurse Corps.* Washington, DC: U.S. Office of Military History, 1945.

Ferencz, Benjamin B. *Less Than Slaves: Jewish Forced Labor and the Quest for Compensation.* Cambridge, MA: Harvard University Press, 1979.

Filipovic, Zlata. *Zlata's Diary.* New York: Viking, 1994.

Fittko, Lisa. *Escape Through the Pyrenees.* Translated by David Koblick. Evanston, IL: Northwestern University Press, 1991.

Flannery, Edward H. *The Anguish of the Jews.* New York: Paulist Press, 1985.

Fleming, Gerald. *Hitler and the Final Solution.* Berkeley: University of California Press, 1982.

Flender, Harold. *Rescue in Denmark.* New York: Holocaust Library, 1963.

Fogelman, Eva. *Conscience and Courage.* New York: Doubleday, 1994.

Foot, M.D.R. *Resistance: European Resistance to Nazism.* London: Metheun, 1977.

Foreman, Michael. *War Boy.* New York: Arcade, 1989.

Foster, Annie. *From Emergency to Empowerment: The Role of Education for Refugee Communities.* Washington, DC: Academy for National Development, 1995.

Frank, Anne. *The Diary of a Young Girl.* Translated by B. M. Mooyart-Doubleday. Garden City, NY: Doubleday, 1967.

Fraser, Antonia. *Heroes and Heroines.* New York: A & W Publishers, 1980.

Fredericks, Pierce G. *The Great Adventure: America in the First World War.* New York: Dutton, 1960.

Freidel, Frank. *The Presidents of the United States of America.* Washington, DC: National Geographic Society, 1975.

Friedlander, Henry. *The Origins of Nazi Genocide: From Euthanasia to the Final Solution.* Chapel Hill: University of North Carolina Press, 1995.

Friedman, Ina. *Escape or Die: True Stories of People Who Survived the Holocaust.* Reading, MA: Addison-Wesley, 1982.

———. *The Other Victims: First-Person Stories of Non-Jews Persecuted by the Nazis.* Boston: Houghton-Mifflin, 1990.

Friedman, Philip. *Their Brothers' Keepers: The Christian Heroes and Heroines Who Helped the Oppressed Escape the Nazi Terror.* New York: Crown, 1978.

———. *Roads to Extinction: Essays on the Holocaust.* New York: Jewish Publication Society of America, 1980.

Gaffen, Fred. *Forgotten Soldiers.* Penticton, British Columbia: Theytus Books, 1985.

Gage, Nicholas. *Eleni.* New York: Ballantine Books, 1983.

Galicich, Anne. *Samantha Smith: A Journey for Peace.* Minneapolis: Dillon Press, 1987.

Gallagher, Hugh Gregory. *By Trust Betrayed: Patients, Physicians, and the License to Kill in the Third Reich.* New York: Henry Holt, 1990.

Gallagher, J.P. *Scarlet Pimpernel of the Vatican.* Toronto: Ryerson Publishing Co., 1967.

Games, Sonia. *Escape Into Darkness: The True Story of a Young Woman's Extraordinary Survival During World War II.* New York: Shapolsky, 1991.

Garlan, Yvon. *War in the Ancient World: A Social History.* New York: W.W. Norton, 1975.

Gaucher, Roland. *Opposition in the U.S.S.R. 1917-1967.* New York: Funk & Wagnalls, 1969.

Gentry, Tony. *Jesse Owens.* New York: Chelsea House, 1990.

Gershon, Karen, ed. *We Came as Children: A Collective Autobiography.* New York: Harcourt, 1966.

Gies, Miep, with Alison Leslie Gold. *Anne Frank Remembered.* New York: Simon and Schuster, 1987.

Giff, Patricia Reilly. *Mother Teresa.* New York: Viking, 1986.

Giffin, Frederick C. *Six Who Protested: Radical Opposition to the First World War.* Port Washington, NY: Kennikat Press, 1977.

Gilbert, Martin. *Russian History Atlas.* New York: Macmillan, 1972.

———. *Final Journey: The Fate of the Jews in Nazi Europe.* Boston: Allen and Unwin, 1979.

———. *The Macmillan Atlas of the Holocaust.* New York: Macmillan, 1982.

———. *The Holocaust.* New York: Holt, Rinehart, and Winston, 1985.

———. *The Boys: The Story of 732 Young Concentration Camp Survivors.* New York: Henry Holt, 1997.

Gimbel, John. *The Origins of the Marshall Plan.* Stanford, CA: Stanford University Press, 1976.

Glatstein, Jacob, ed. *Anthology of Holocaust Literature.* New York: Atheneum, 1972.

Glenny, Misha. *The Fall of Yugoslavia: The Third Balkan War.* London: Penguin, 1992.

Gluck, Sherna Berger. *Rosie the Riveter Revisited: Women, the War, and Social Change.* Boston: G.K. Hall, 1987.

Goldberger, Leo, ed. *The Rescue of the Danish Jews: Moral Courage Under Stress.* New York: New York University Press, 1987.

Goldhagen, Daniel. *Hitler's Willing Executioners: Ordinary Germans and the Holocaust.* New York: Knopf, 1996.

Goldstein, Bernard. *The Stars Bear Witness.* New York: Viking Press, 1949.

Goldston, Robert. *The Civil War in Spain.* Indianapolis: Bobbs Merrill, 1966.

———. *The Life and Death of Nazi Germany.* New York: Fawcett, 1967.

Goodwin-Gill, Guy S., and Ilene Cohn. *Child Soldiers: A Study on behalf of the Henry Dunant Institute, Geneva.* New York: Oxford University Press, 1994.

Gordon, Sarah. *Hitler, Germans, and the "Jewish Question."* Princeton, NJ: Princeton University Press, 1984.

Goris, Jan-Albert. *Belgium in Bondage.* New York: I.B. Fisher, 1943.

Gorman, Robert F. *Historical Dictionary of Refugee and Disaster Relief Organizations.* Lanham, MD: Scarecrow Press, 1994.

Green, Gerald. *The Artists of Terezin.* New York: Hawthorne, 1969.

Greenberg, Keith, and John Isaac. *Children in Crisis: Bosnia.* Woodbridge, CT.: Blackbirch Press, 1997.

———. *Children in Crisis: The Middle East.* Woodbridge, CT: Blackbirch Press, 1997.

Greene, Robert Ewell. *Black Defenders of America, 1775-1973.* Chicago: Johnson Publishing Company, 1974.

Greenfeld, Howard. *The Hidden Children.* New York: Houghton Mifflin, 1993.

Gregorovich, Andrew. *Jewish-Ukrainian Bibliography: A Brief Selected Bibliography of Resources in English.* Toronto: Forum, 1994.

Grew, Joseph C. *Ten Years in Japan.* New York: Arno, 1972.

Grinnell, George Bird. *The Fighting Cheyennes.* New York: Scribner's, 1961.

Gross, Jan Tomasz. *Polish Society Under German Occupation.* Princeton, NJ: Princeton University Press, 1979.

Gross, Leonard. *The Last Jews in Berlin.* New York: Simon and Schuster, 1982.

Grunberger, Richard. *The 12-Year Reich: A Social History of Nazi Germany, 1933-1945.* New York: Holt, Rinehart and Winston, 1971.

Gutman, Israel. *The Jews of Warsaw: 1939-1943: Ghetto, Underground, Revolt.* Bloomington: Indiana University Press, 1982.

————. *Resistance: The Warsaw Ghetto Uprising.* Boston: Houghton Mifflin, 1994.

————, ed. *Encyclopedia of the Holocaust.* 4 vols. New York: Macmillan, 1995.

Gutman, Israel, and Michael Berenbaum. *Anatomy of the Auschwitz Death Camp.* Bloomington: Indiana University Press, 1994.

Guttman, Allen. *The Olympics: A History of the Games.* Champaign-Urbana: University of Illinois Press, 1992.

Hachiya, Michihiko. *Hiroshima Diary: the Journal of a Japanese Physician.* Translated by W. Wells. Chapel Hill: University of North Carolina Press, 1969.

Hadler, Susan Johnson, et al., eds. *Lost in the Victory: Reflections of American War Orphans of World War II.* Denton: University of North Texas Press, 1998.

Halberstam, David. *The Fifties.* New York: Villard, 1993.

Halliday, F.E. *England: A Concise History.* London: Thames and Hudson, 1989.

Hallie, Philip. *Lest Innocent Blood Be Shed: The Story of the Village of Le Chambon and How Goodness Happened There.* New York: Harper and Row, 1979.

Hamilton, Alice. *Exploring the Dangerous Trades: The Autobiography of Alice Hamilton.* Boston: Little, Brown, 1943.

Hamilton, Edward P. *The French and Indian Wars.* Garden City, NY: Doubleday, 1962.

Hammarberg, Thomas. *Making Reality of the Rights of the Child: The United Nations Convention: What It Says and How It Can Change the Status of Children.* Stockholm: Radda Barnen (Swedish Save the Children), 1990.

Hampson, Norman. *A Social History of the French Revolution.* London: Routledge, 1964.

Hanaford, Phebe A. *Daughters of America.* Boston: True & Co., 1882.

Handler, Andrew, and Susan V. Meschel, comps. *Young People Speak: Surviving the Holocaust in Hungary.* New York: Watts, 1993.

Hanser, Richard. *A Noble Treason: The Revolt of the Munich Students Against Hitler.* New York: Putnam, 1979.

Harris, Mark Jonathan, Franklin D.M. Mitchell, and Steven J. Schecter. *Homefront.* New York: Putnam, 1984.

Harris, Robert, and Jeremy Paxton. *A Higher Form of Killing: The Secret Story of Gas and Germ Warfare.* London: Chatto and Windus, 1982.

Harrison, Tom. *Living Through the Blitz.* London: Collins, 1976.

Hart, Kitty. *Return to Auschwitz.* New York: Atheneum, 1971.

Hartmann, Susan M. *The Marshall Plan.* Columbus, OH: C.E. Merrill, 1968.

Heck, Alfons. *A Child of Hitler.* Frederick, CO: Renaissance House, 1985.

Heidler, David S. and Jeanne T. Heidler, eds. *Encyclopedia of the War of 1812.* Denver: ABC-CLIO, 1997.

Heike, Wolf-Dietrich. *The Ukrainian Division "Galicia" 1943-45: A Memoir.* Toronto: Shevchenko Scientific Society, 1988.

Heller, Celia S. *On the Edge of Destruction: Jews in Poland Between the Two World Wars.* New York: Schocken, 1977

Heller, Francis H. ed., *The Korean War: A 25-Year Perspective.* Lawrence: The Regents Press of Kansas, 1977.

Hellman, Peter. *Avenue of the Righteous: Portraits in Uncommon Courage of Christians and the Jews They Saved from Hitler.* New York: Atheneum, 1980.

Henry, Clarissa, and Marc Hillel. *Children of the SS.* Translated by Eric Mosbacher. London: Hutchinson, 1975.

Hensley, Thomas R., et al. *The Kent State Incident: Impact of the Judicial Process on Public Attitudes.* Westport, CT: Greenwood Press, 1981.

Herbst, Laura. *Children in War: Community Strategies for Healing.* Durham, NC: Save the Children Federation with Hart Leadership Program, Terry Sanford Institute of Public Policy, Duke University, 1995.

Hermand, Jost. *A Hitler Youth in Poland: The Nazis' Program for Evacuating Children During World War II*. Translated by Margot Battauer Dembo. Evanston, IL: Northwestern University Press, 1998.

Hersey, John. *Hiroshima*. New York: Knopf, 1988.

Herzer, Ivo. *The Italian Refuge: Rescue of Jews During the Holocaust*. Washington: Catholic University Press, 1989.

Herzstein, Robert Edwin. *The Nazis*. Alexandria, VA: Time-Life Books, 1980.

Heyes, Eileen. *Children of the Swastika: The Hitler Youth*. Brookfield, CT: The Millbrook Press, 1993.

Hibbert, Christopher. *The Days of the French Revolution*. New York: William Morrow, 1980.

Hilberg, Raul. *The Destruction of the European Jews*. New York: Holmes and Meier, 1985.

———. *Perpetrators, Victims, Bystanders: The Jewish Catastrophe 1933-1945*. New York: HarperCollins, 1992.

Hingley, Ronald. *A Concise History of Russia*. New York: Viking, 1972.

Hirsch, Seymour. *My Lai 4*. New York: Random House, 1970.

Hitler, Adolf. *Mein Kampf*. Translated by Ralph Manheim. Boston: Houghton Mifflin, 1943.

Hoare, Robert. *World War One*. London: Macdonald and Co., 1973.

Hoff, Rhoda. *China: Adventures in Eyewitness History*. New York: H.Z. Walch, 1965.

Hoffman, Peter. *The History of the German Resistance 1933-1945*. Cambridge, MA: The MIT Press, 1997.

Hoig, Stan. *The Sand Creek Massacre*. Norman: University of Oklahoma Press, 1961.

Holliday, Laurel, ed. *Children in the Holocaust and World War II: Their Secret Diaries*. New York: Washington Square Press, 1996.

Holliday, Laurel. *Children of "The Troubles": Our Lives in the Crossfire of Northern Ireland*. New York: Simon and Schuster, 1997.

Horwitz, Gordon J. *In the Shadow of Death: Living Outside the Gates of Mauthausen*. New York: Free Press, 1990.

Hsieh Ping-ying. *Girl Rebel*. New York: John Day Co., 1940.

Hughes, H. Stuart. *Prisoners of Hope: The Silver Age of the Italian Jews, 1924-1974*. Cambridge, MA: Harvard University Press, 1996.

Human Rights Watch/Africa. *The Scars of Death: Children Abducted by the Lord's Resistance Army in Uganda*. New York: Human Rights Watch, 1997.

Hutchinson, John E. *Champions of Charity: War and the Rise of the Red Cross*. Boulder, CO: Westview Press, 1997.

Hyde, George E. *The Life of George Bent, Written from His Letters*. Norman: University of Oklahoma Press, 1968.

International Committee of the Red Cross. *The Geneva Convention of August 12, 1949*. Geneva, IRCR, 1949.

———. *Children and War*. Geneva: ICRC, 1994.

Irons, Peter. *The Courage of Their Convictions: Sixteen Americans Who Fought Their Way to the Supreme Court*. New York: Free Press, 1988.

Isaacman, Clara, as told to Joan Adess Grossman. *Clara's Story*. Philadelphia: Jewish Publication Society, 1984.

Jackson, Donald Dale. *The Civil War: Twenty Million Yankees, The Northern Home Front*. New York: Time-Life Books, 1985.

Jackson, Robert. *Air War Over Korea*. New York: Scribner's, 1973.

Jagchid, Sechin. *Essays in Mongolian Studies*. Provo, UT: Brigham Young University, 1988.

Jahoda, Gloria. *The Trail of Tears: The Story of the American Indian Removals, 1813-1855*. New York: Holt, Rinehart, and Winston, 1975.

Johnson, Emily Cooper, ed. *Jane Addams: A Centennial Reader*. New York: Macmillan, 1960.

Jones, Gregg. *The Red Revolution: Inside the Philippine Guerilla Movement*. San Francisco: Westview Press, 1989.

Jones, Rufus M. *The Quaker in the American Colonies*. New York: Russell & Russell, 1962.

Josephs, Jeremy. *Swastika Over Paris: The Fate of the Jews in France*. New York: Arcade, 1989.

Josephy, Alvin M., Jr. et al. *The Patriot Chiefs*. New York: Viking, 1967.

———. *Red Power: The American Indians' Fight for Freedom*. New York: American Heritage Press, 1971.

Jungk, Robert. *Children of the Ashes*. New York: Harcourt, Brace, 1961.

Kahn, Leora, and Rachel Hager, eds., *When They Came to Take My Father: Voices of the Holocaust*. New York: Arcade, 1996.

Kamenetsky, Ihor. *Hitler's Occupation of Ukraine 1941-1944*. Milwaukee: Marquette University Press, 1956.

———. *Secret Nazi Plans for Eastern Europe: A Study of Lebensraum Policies*. New York: Bookman, 1961.

———. *The Tragedy of Vinnytsia: Materials on Stalin's Policy of Extermination in Ukraine During the Great Purge 1936-1938*. Toronto: Ukrainian Historical Association, 1989.

Kaplan, Chaim A. *Scroll of Agony: The Warsaw Diary of Chaim A. Kaplan*. Translated and edited by Abraham I. Katsh. New York: Collier, 1973.

Karadja, Kyra. *Kyra's Story: Reminiscences of a Girlhood in Revolutionary Russia*. New York: William Morrow, 1975.

Kater, Michael H. *Doctors Under Hitler*. Chapel Hill: University of North Carolina Press, 1989.

Katz, Alfred. *Poland's Ghettos at War*. New York: Twayne Publishers, 1970.

Keegan, John. *The Second World War*. London: Hutchinson, 1989.

———. *A History of Warfare*. New York: Knopf, 1993.

Kelly, Lawrence C. *The Navajo Indians and Federal Indian Policy, 1900-1935*. Tucson: University of Arizona Press, 1968.

Keneally, Thomas. *Schindler's List*. New York: Simon and Schuster, 1982.

Kennedy, David M. *Over Here: The First World War and American Society*. New York: Oxford University Press, 1980.

Kenrick, Donald and Grattan Puxon. *The Destiny of Europe's Gypsies*. New York: Basic Books, 1972.

Kermish, Joseph, ed. *To Live with Honor and Die with Honor*. Jerusalem: Yad Vashem, 1986.

Kidron, Michael, and Dan Smith. *The New State of War and Peace: An International Atlas*. New York: Simon and Schuster, 1997.

Kishlansky, Mark A. et al. *Civilization in the West*. 3rd ed. New York: Longman, 1998.

Klarsfeld, Serge. *French Children of the Holocaust*. New York: New York University Press, 1996.

———. *The Children of Izieu*. New York: Abrams, 1984.

Kluger, Ruth, and Peggy Mann. *The Secret Ship*. New York: Doubleday, 1978.

Koch, H.W. *The Hitler Youth: Origins and Development 1922-1945*. New York: Stein and Day, 1975.

Koehn, Ilse. *Mischling, Second Degree*. New York: Greenwillow, 1977.

Koht, Halvdan. *Norway: Neutral and Invaded*. London and Melbourne: Hutchinson and Co., 1941.

Kome, Penney and Patrick Crean, eds. *Peace: A Dream Unfolding*. San Francisco: Sierra Club, 1986.

Kops, Bernard. *The World Is a Wedding*. New York: Coward, McCann, 1963.

Korczak, Janusz. *The Warsaw Ghetto Memoirs of Janusz Korczak*. Translated by E.P. Kulawiec. Washington, DC: University Press of America, 1978.

Kort, Michael. *The Cold War*. Brookfield, CT.: The Millbrook Press, 1994.

Kovner, Abba, ed. *Childhood Under Fire: Stories, Poems, and Drawings by Children During the Six Days War*. Tel Aviv, Israel: Sifriat Poalim, 1971.

Krakowski, Schmuel. Translated by Orah Blaustein. *The War of the Doomed: Jewish Armed Resistance in Poland, 1942-1944*. New York: Holmes and Meier, 1984.

Kranzler, David. *Japanese, Nazis, and Jews: The Jewish Refugee Community of Shanghai, 1938-1945*. New York: Yeshiva University, 1976.

Kratoska, Paul H. *The Japanese Occupation of Malaya: A Social and Economic History*. Honolulu: University of Hawaii Press, 1998.

Kravchenko, Victor. *I Chose Freedom*. New York: Transaction, 1989.

Krizkova, Marie Rut. *We Are Children Just the Same: Vedem, the Secret Magazine by the Boys of Terezin*. Philadelphia: Jewish Publication Society, 1995.

Kronenwetter, Michael. *Cities at War: London*. New York: Macmillan, 1992.

———. *Protest!* New York: Twenty-First Century Books, 1996.

Kruk, Zofia. *The Taste of Fear: A Polish Childhood in Germany, 1939-46*. London: Hutchinson, 1973.

Kuchler-Silberman, Lena. *One Hundred Children*. New York: Doubleday, 1961.

Kumar, Krishna. *Rebuilding Society After Civil War*. Boulder CO: Lynne Rienner Publishers, 1996.

Kumar, Ravinder. *The Emergence of Modern India*. New Delhi, India: Manohar Publications, 1990.

Kuper, Jack. *Child of the Holocaust*. Garden City, NY: Doubleday and Co., 1968.

Kurzman, Dan. *The Bravest Battle*. New York: G.P. Putnam's Sons, 1976.

La Forte, Robert S., ed. *Building the Death Railway*. Wilmington, DE: Scholarly Resources Inc., 1992.

Laffin, John. *War Annual II: A Guide to Contemporary Wars and Conflicts*. London: Brassey's Defence Publishers, 1988.

Lagnado, Lucette Matalon, and Sheila Cohn Dekel, *Children of the Flames: Dr. Josef Mengele and the Untold Story of the Twins of Auschwitz*. New York: William Morrow, 1991.

Landau, Elaine. *Chemical and Biological Warfare*. New York: Dutton, 1991.

———. *We Survived the Holocaust*. New York: Franklin Watts, 1991.

Lappin, Ben. *The Redeemed Children: The Story of the Rescue of War Orphans by the Jewish Community of Toronto*. Toronto: University of Toronto Press, 1963.

Larsen, Karen. *A History of Norway*. Princeton, NJ: Princeton University Press, 1948.

Lash, Joseph P. *Eleanor and Franklin*. New York: W.W. Norton, 1971.

Laska, Vera, ed. *Women of the Resistance and in the Holocaust*. Westport, CT: Greenwood Press, 1984.

Lawson, Don. *The French Resistance*. New York: Wanderer Books, 1984.

Le Boucher, F. *The Incredible Mission of Father Benoit*. Translated by J.F. Bernard. New York: Doubleday, 1969.

Lee, Irvin H. *Negro Medal of Honor Men*. New York: Dodd, Mead, Co., 1967.

Lee, Stephen J. *The Thirty Years War/30 Years Later*. London, New York: Routledge, 1991.

Leonard, Thomas. *Day by Day: The Forties*. New York: Facts on File, 1977.

Lessing, Doris. *The Wind Blows Away Our Words*. London: Pan Books, 1987.

Lester, Elenore. *Wallenberg: The Man in the Iron Web*. Englewood Cliffs, NJ: Prentice-Hall, 1982.

Levi, Primo. *Survival in Auschwitz*. Translated by Stuart Woolf. New York: Collier Books, 1971.

———. *Moments of Reprieve*. New York: Viking Penguin, 1987.

Levin, Nora. *The Holocaust: The Destruction of European Jewry, 1933-1945*. New York: Crowell, 1968.

Lewin, Abraham. *A Cup of Tears: A Diary of the Warsaw Ghetto*. Oxford: Basil Blackwell, 1988.

Lifton, Betty Jean. *A Place Called Hiroshima*. Tokyo: Kodansha International, 1985.

———. *The King of Children: A Biography of Janusz Korczak*. New York: Farrar, Straus, Giroux, 1988.

Lifton, Betty Jean, and Thomas C. Fox. *Children of Vietnam*. New York: Atheneum, 1972.

Lifton, Robert Jay. *Death in Life: Survivors of Hiroshima.* New York: Basic Books, 1982.

———. *The Nazi Doctors: Medical Killing and the Psychology of Genocide.* New York: Basic Books, 1986.

Limm, Peter. *The Thirty Years War.* London, New York: Longman, 1984.

Lindwer, Willy. *The Last Seven Months of Anne Frank.* New York: Random House, 1991.

Lomax, Eric. *The Railway Man.* New York: Balantine, 1996.

Long, Cathryn. *The Middle East in Search of Peace.* Brookfield, CT: The Millbrook Press, 1996.

Longmate, Norman. *How We Lived Then.* London: Hutchinson, 1971.

Lourie, Richard. *Russia Speaks: An Oral History from the Revolution.* New York: HarperCollins, 1991.

Lowrie, Donald. *The Hunted Children.* New York: W.W. Norton, 1963.

Lucas, Celia. *Prisoners of Santo Tomas.* London: Pen and Sword Books, Ltd., 1997.

Lukas, Richard C. *The Forgotten Holocaust: The Poles Under German Occupation, 1939-1944.* Lexington: University Press of Kentucky, 1986.

———, ed. *Out of the Inferno: Poles Remember the Holocaust.* Lexington: University Press of Kentucky, 1989.

———. *Did the Children Cry? Hitler's War against Jewish and Polish Children, 1939-1945.* New York: Hippocrene Books, 1994.

Lutz, Alma, ed. *With Love, Jane: Letters from American Women on the War Fronts.* New York: John Day, 1945.

Lynd, Alice, ed. *We Won't Go: Personal Accounts of War Objectors.* Boston: Beacon Press, 1968.

Maass, Walter B. *The Netherlands at War: 1940–1945.* New York: Abelard-Schuman, 1970.

Macardle, Dorothy. *Children of Europe: A Study of Children of Liberated Countries; Their War-Time Experiences, Their Reactions, and Their Needs, with a Note on Germany.* Boston: Beacon Press, 1951.

MacGregor, James H. *The Wounded Knee Massacre from the Viewpoint of the Survivors.* Baltimore: Wirth Brothers, 1940.

Machel, Graca. *Impact of Armed Conflict on Children.* New York: United Nations, 1996.

Macksoud, Mona. *Lebanese Children and War.* UNICEF Conference on Peace-Building and Development of Lebanon (April 1990). New York: UNICEF, 1990.

Maclear, Michael. *The Ten Thousand Day War: Vietnam 1945-1975.* New York: Avon, 1981.

Macleish, Roderick. *The Sun Stood Still: Israel and the Arabs at War.* New York: Atheneum, 1967.

Macpherson, Martin, ed. *Child Soldiers: The Recruitment of Children into Armed Forces and Their Participation in Hostilities.* London: Quaker Peace and Service Report, United Kingdom, 1992.

Macrae, Joanna, and Anthony Zwi, eds. *War and Hunger.* London: Zed Books in association with Save the Children (UK), 1994.

Mandel, Richard D. *The Nazi Olympics.* New York: Macmillan, 1971.

Manning, Clarence A. *Ukraine Under the Soviets.* New York: Bookman, 1953.

Markle, Donald E. *Spies and Spymasters of the Civil War.* New York: Hippocrene, 1994.

Marks, Jane. *The Hidden Children: The Secret Survivors of the Holocaust.* New York: Fawcett Columbine, 1993.

Marley, David F. *War of the Americas: A Chronology of Armed Conflict in the New World, 1492 to the Present.* Denver: ABC-CLIO, 1998.

Marrus, Michael R. *The Holocaust in History.* Hanover, NH: University Press of New England, 1987.

Marrus, Michael R., and Robert O. Paxton. *Vichy France and the Jews.* New York: Basic Books, 1981.

Marshall, Robert. *In The Sewers of Lvov: The Last Sanctuary from the Holocaust.* New York: Scribner's, 1991.

Marten, James. *The Children's Civil War.* Chapel Hill: University of North Carolina Press, 1998.

Martin, Joseph Plumb. *Yankee Doodle Boy.* Edited by George Scheer. New York: Harmony Press, 1995.

Martin, Patricia Stone. *Samantha Smith, Young Ambassador.* Vero Beach, FL: Rourke Enterprises, 1987.

Marton, Kati. *Wallenberg.* New York: Random House, 1982.

Maschmann, Melita. *Account Rendered: A Dossier on My Former Self.* Translated by Geoffrey Strachan. New York: Abelard-Schuman, 1965.

Massie, Robert K. *Nicholas and Alexandra.* New York: Atheneum, 1967.

———. *The Romanovs: The Final Chapter.* New York: Random House, 1995.

Mazower, Mark. *Inside Hitler's Greece: The Experience of Occupation, 1941-44.* New Haven, CT: Yale University Press, 1993.

McCallin, Margaret, ed. *The Psychological Well-Being of Refugee Children: Research, Practice and Policy Issues.* Geneva: International Catholic Child Bureau, 1992.

McCoy, Alfred W., ed. *Southeast Asia Under Japanese Rule.* New Haven, CT: Yale University Southeast Studies, 1980.

McDermott, Jeanne. *The Killing Winds: The Menace of Biological Warfare.* New York: Arbor House, 1987.

McDermott, John D. *Forlorn Hope: The Battle of White Bird Canyon and the Beginning of the Nez Perce War.* Boise: Idaho Historical Society, 1978.

McGregor, James H. *The Wounded Knee Masacre from the Viewpoint of the Sioux.* Minneapolis: Land Press, 1940.

McKee, Alexander. *Dresden 1945: The Devil's Tinderbox.* London: Souvenir Press, 1982.

McReynolds, Edwin C. *The Seminoles.* Norman: University of Oklahoma Press, 1957.

Meisler, Stanley. *United Nations: The First Fifty Years.* New York: Atlantic Monthly Press, 1997.

Meltzer, Milton. *Never to Forget: The Jews of the Holocaust.* New York: Harper & Row, 1976.

———. *Ain't Gonna Study War No More.* New York: Harper & Row, 1985.

———. *Rescue: The Story of How Gentiles Saved Jews During the Holocaust.* New York: Harper and Row, 1988.

Mendelsohn, Everett. *A Compassionate Peace: A Future for Israel, Palestine, and the Middle East.* New York: Hill and Wang, 1989.

Mendelsohn, John, ed. *The Holocaust: Selected Documents in 18 Volumes.* New York: Garland, 1982.

Messenger, Charles. *Middle East.* New York: Franklin Watts, 1988.

Miller, Donald E., and Lorna Touryan Miller. *Survivors: An Oral History of the Armenian Genocide.* Berkeley: University of California Press, 1993.

Miller, Judith. *One by One by One: Facing the Holocaust.* New York: Simon and Schuster, 1990.

Milton, Mayer. *They Thought They Were Free: The Germans, 1933-1945.* Chicago: University of Chicago Press, 1966.

Minear, Larry and Thomas G. Weiss. *Humanitarian Action in Times of War.* Boulder, CO: Lynne Rienner Publishers, 1994.

Minear, Richard H. *Victors' Justice: The Tokyo War Crimes Trial.* Princeton, NJ: Princeton University Press, 1971.

Moon, Penderel. *Gandhi and Modern India.* New York: Norton, 1969.

Morris, Benny. *The Birth of the Palestinian Refugee Problem, 1947-1949.* New York: Cambridge University Press, 1987.

Morris-Suzuki, Tessa. *Showa: An Inside History of Hirohito's Japan.* New York: Schocken, 1985.

Moser, Don. *China-Burma-India.* New York: Time-Life Books, 1978.

Mosse, George L., ed. *Nazi Culture.* New York: Schocken Books, 1981.

Motley, Mary Penick, ed. and comp. *The Invisible Soldier: The Experiences of the Black Soldier.* Detroit: Wayne State University, 1983.

Moyer, Nancy. *Escape from the Killing Fields: One Girl Who Survived the Cambodian Holocaust.* Grand Rapids, MI: Zondervan Publishing House, 1991.

Mullen, Robert W. *Blacks in America's Wars: The Shift in Attitudes from the Revolutionary War to Vietnam.* New York: Monad Press, 1973.

Murphy, Jim. *The Boys' War: Confederate and Union Soldiers Talk About the Civil War.* New York: Clarion, 1990.

Nagai, Takashi. *We of Nagasaki: The Story of Survivors in an Atomic Wasteland.* New York: Meredith Press, 1951.

Nakamoto, Hiroko, and M.M. Pace, *My Japan: 1930-51.* New York: McGraw Hill, 1970.

Nasu, Masamoto. *Children of the Paper Crane: The Story of Sadako Sasaki and Her Struggle with the A-Bomb Disease.* Translated by Elizabeth W. Baldwin et al. Armonk, NY: M.E. Sharpe, 1996.

Neave, Airey. *Little Cyclone.* London: Hodder and Stoughton, 1954.

————. *On Trial at Nuremberg.* Boston: Little, Brown, 1978.

Newton, David E. *Cities at War: Tokyo.* New York: Macmillan, 1992.

NGO Committee on UNICEF Working Group on Children in Armed Conflict. *Summary of International Treaties to Protect Children in Armed Conflict.* New York: UNICEF, 1993.

Ngor, Haing. *A Cambodian Odyssey.* New York: Macmillan, 1987.

Nicholson, Dorinda M. *Pearl Harbor Child.* Honolulu: Arizona Memorial Museum Association, 1998.

Nir, Yehuda. *The Lost Childhood.* San Diego: Harcourt, Brace, Jovanovich, 1989.

Nogueres, Henri. *Histoire de la Resistance en France.* Paris: Robert Laffont, 1967.

Nolen, Barbara, ed. *Spies! Spies! Spies!* New York: Franklin Watts, 1965.

Norton, Mary Beth. *Liberty's Daughters: The Revolutionary Experience of American Women, 1750-1800.* Boston: Little Brown, 1975.

Nyiszli, Miklos. *Auschwitz: An Eyewitness Account of Mengele's Infamous Death Camp.* New York: Seaver, 1986.

O'Ballance, Edgar. *Civil War in Bosnia.* New York: St. Martin's Press, 1995.

Ofcansky, Thomas P. *Uganda, Tarnished Pearl of Africa.* Boulder, CO: Westview Press, 1996.

Office of the United Nations High Commissioner of Refugees. *Refugees at a Glance.* Geneva: UNHCR, 1995.

Oliner, Samuel P., and Pearl M. Oliner, *The Altruistic Personality: Rescuers of Jews in Nazi Europe.* New York: The Free Press, 1988.

Orlick, Terry. *The Cooperative Sports and Games Book.* New York: Pantheon, 1978.

Osada, Arata. *Children of the A-Bomb.* Translated by Jean Dan and Ruth Sieben-Morgan. New York: Putnam, 1963.

Ousseimi, Maria. *Caught in the Crossfire: Growing Up in a War Zone.* New York: Walker & Co., 1995.

Overseas Press Club. *How I Got That Story: Top Reporters Give the Behind-the-Scenes Story of Covering Great News Events.* New York: Dutton, 1967.

Palmer, David, ed. *Shining Path of Peru.* London: Hurst and Co., 1992.

Parrish, David. *The Cold War Encyclopedia.* New York: Twenty-First Century Books, 1996.

Paul, Doris. *Navajo Code Talkers.* Philadelphia: Dorrance, 1973.

Payne, Robert. *The Life and Death of Adolf Hitler.* New York: Praeger, 1973.

Peck, Jim. *We Who Would Not Kill.* New York: Lyle Stuart, 1958.

Perez, Louis A., Jr. *Cuba Between Reform and Revolution.* New York: Oxford University Press, Inc., 1988.

Perl, Gisella. *I Was a Doctor at Auschwitz.* New York: Arno Press, 1979.

Perrault, Gilles. *Paris Under the Occupation.* New York: Vendome, 1979.

Petrow, Richard. *The Bitter Years: The Invasion of Denmark and Norway.* New York: Morrow, 1974.

Pettit, Jayne. *A Time to Fight Back: True Stories of Wartime Resistance.* Boston: Houghton Mifflin, 1996.

Pfeifer, Kathryn Browne. *The 761st Tank Battalion.* New York: Twenty-First Century Books, 1994.

Philbin, Marianne, ed. *The Ribbon: A Celebration of Life.* Asheville, NC: Lark Books, 1985.

Pipes, Richard. *The Russian Revolution.* New York: Random House, 1990.

Plant, Richard. *The Pink Triangle: The Nazi War Against Homosexuals.* New York: Henry Holt, 1986.

Polish Ministry of Information. *Black Book of Poland.* New York: G.P. Putnam's, 1942.

Prakashan, Kranti. *Genocide of Hindus and Buddhists in East Pakistan (Bangladesh).* Delhi, India: Kranti Prakashan,, 1980.

Pran, Dith, compiler. *Children of Cambodia's Killing Fields: Memoirs by Survivors.* New Haven, CT: Yale University Press, 1997.

Prasad, Devi, and Tony Smythe. *Concription: A World Survey.* London: War Resisters International, 1968.

Pratt, John Clark. *Vietnam Voices: Perspectives on the War Years.* New York: Viking, 1984.

Presser, Jacob. *The Destruction of the Dutch Jews.* New York: Dutton, 1969.

Price, Alfred. *The Hardest Day.* New York: Scribner's, 1980.

Prunier, Gerard. *The Rwanda Crisis: History of a Genocide.* New York: Columbia University Press, 1995.

Pryce-Jones, David. *Paris in the Third Reich: A History of the German Occupation, 1940–1944.* New York: Holt, Reinhart, and Winston, 1981.

Pyszka, Wieslaw, ed. *The Warsaw Ghetto.* Poland: Interpress Publishers, 1988.

Rabinsky, Leatrice, and Gertrude Mann. *Journey of Conscience: Young People Respond to the Holocaust.* Cleveland: William Collins Publishers, Inc., 1979.

Ramati, Alexander, as told by Padre Rufino Niccacci. *The Assisi Underground.* New York: Stein & Day, 1978.

Ramsbotham, Oliver, with Tom Woodhouse. *Humanitarian Intervention in Contemporary Conflict.* Cambridge, MA: Polity Press, 1996.

Rappaport, Doreen. *Tinker vs. Des Moines: Student Rights on Trial.* New York: HarperCollins, 1993.

Rautkallio, Hannu. *Finland and the Holocaust: The Rescue of Finland's Jews.* New York: Holocaust Library, 1987.

Raviv, Amiram, Louis Oppenheimer, and Daniel Bar-Tal, eds. *How Children Understand War and Peace: A Call for International Peace Education.* San Francisco: Jossey-Bass, 1999.

Reader's Digest. *America in the '40s.* Pleasantville, NY: The Reader's Digest Association, Inc., 1998.

Reef, Catherine. *Civil War Soldiers.* New York: Twenty-First Century Books, 1992.

———. *Black Fighting Men: A Proud History.* New York: Twenty-First Century Books, 1994.

Remak, Joachim. *The Nazi Years: A Documentary History.* New York: Simon and Schuster, 1969.

Rempel, Gerhard. *Hitler's Children: The Hitler Youth and the SS.* Chapel Hill: University of North Carolina Press, 1989.

Resnick, Abraham. *The Holocaust.* San Diego: Lucent Books, 1991.

Ressler, Everett M. *Evacuation of Children from Conflict Areas: Considerations and Guidelines.* Geneva: UNHCR, 1992.

Ressler, Everett M., Joanne Marie Tortorici, and Alex Marcelino. *Children in War: A Guide to the Provision of Services.* New York: UNICEF, 1993.

The Ribbon: A Celebration of Life. Asheville, NC: Lark Books, 1985.

Richter, Hans Peter. *I Was There.* Translated by Edite Kroll. New York: Holt, Rinehart, and Winston, 1972.

Ringelblum, Emmanuel. *Notes from the Warsaw Ghetto: The Journal of Emmanuel Ringelblum.* Edited and translated by Jacob Sloan. New York: McGraw-Hill, 1958.

Riste, Olav, and Berit Nokleby. *Norway: 1940-45: The Resistance Movement.* Oslo: Tanum, 1970.

Rittner, Carol, and John K. Roth, eds. *Different Voices: Women and the Holocaust.* New York: Paragon House, 1993.

Rittner, Carol, and Sondra Meyers, eds. *The Courage to Care: Rescuers of Jews During the Holocaust.* New York: Oxford University Press, 1986.

Roberson, John R. *China from Manchu to Mao (1699-1976).* New York: Athenuem, 1980.

Roberts, Jack L. *The Importance of Oskar Schindler.* San Diego: Lucent Books, 1996.

Roberts, Mary M. *American Nursing: History and Interpretation.* New York: Macmillan, 1954.

Robertson, James I. *The Civil War: Tenting Tonight, the Soldier's Life.* Alexandria, VA: Time-Life Books, 1984.

Robottom, John. *China in Revolution.* New York: McGraw Hill, 1969.

Rogasky, Barbara. *Smoke and Ashes: The Story of the Holocaust.* New York: Holiday House, 1988.

Roi, Emilie. *A Different Story: About a Danish Girl in World War Two.* Dallas: Rossel Books, 1987.

Roland, Charles G. *Courage Under Siege: Starvation, Disease, and Death in the Warsaw Ghetto.* New York: Oxford University Press, 1992.

Ropp, Theodore. *War in the Modern World.* New York: Collier, 1962.

Rose, Leesha. *The Tulips Are Red.* New York: A.S. Barnes and Co., 1978.

Rosenberg, Maxine B. *Hiding to Survive: Stories of Jewish Children Rescued from the Holocaust.* New York: Clarion, 1994.

Rosenblatt, Roger. *Children of War.* New York: Anchor Books, 1984.

Rossel, Seymour. *The Holocaust.* New York: Franklin Watts, 1981.

Rossiter, Caleb S. *The Chimes of Freedom Flashing: A Personal History of the Vietnam Anti-War Movement and the 1960s.* Self-published by the author, 1998.

Rossiter, Margaret. *Women in the Resistance.* New York: Praeger, 1986.

Roth, Cecil. *The History of the Jews in Venice.* Philadelphia: Jewish Publication Society of America, 1930.

Roth-Hano, Renee. *Touch Wood: A Girlhood in Occupied France.* New York: Puffin, 1989.

Rubin, Arnold. *The Evil Men Do: The Story of the Nazis.* New York: Julian Messner, 1977.

Rubin, Barnett R. *The Search for Peace in Afghanistan.* New Haven, CT: Yale University Press, 1999.

Rubin, William, ed. *Pablo Picasso, A Retrospective.* New York: The Museum of Modern Art, 1980.

Salisbury, Harrison E. *Russia in Revolution: 1900-1930.* New York: Holt, Rinehart, and Winston, 1978.

Samuels, Klara. *God Does Play Dice.* Philadelphia: BainBridge Books, 1999.

Satterfield, Archie. *Home Front: An Oral History of the War Years in America, 1941-1945.* New York: Playboy Press, 1981.

Save the Children Federation. *Children and War: Facts.* Westport, CT: Save the Children, October 1996.

————. *Promoting Psychosocial Well-Being Among Children Affected by Armed Conflict and Displacement.* Geneva Switzerland: International Save the Children Federation, 1996.

Schlissel, Lillian, ed. *Conscience in America: A Documentary History of Conscientious Objection in America, 1757-1967.* New York: Dutton, 1968.

Schmitt, Hans A. *Quakers and Nazis: Inner Light in Outer Darkness.* Columbia: University of Missouri, 1997.

Schneider, Gertrude. *Journey Into Terror: The Story of the Riga Ghetto.* New York: Ark House, 1979.

Scholl, Inge. *The White Rose: Munich 1942–1943.* Translated by Arthur R. Schultz. Middletown, CT: Wesleyan University Press, 1983.

Scituate Town Report: Paper Read at a Meeting of the Chief Justice Cushing Chapter D.A.R. (September 5, 1908).

Scott, Emmet J. *Scott's Official History of the American Negro in the World War.* New York: Arno Press, 1919.

Senesh, Hannah. *Hannah Senesh: Her Life and Diary.* New York: Schocken, 1972.

Seth, Ronald. *Some of My Favorite Spies.* Philadelphia: Chilton Book Co., 1968.

Sherrow, Victoria. *Cities at War: Amsterdam.* New York: Macmillan, 1992.

Shirer, William. *The Rise and Fall of the Third Reich.* New York: Simon and Schuster, 1959.

———. *The Nightmare Years.* New York: Simon and Schuster, 1984.

Shulman, William. *Holocaust: Voices and Visions: A Collection of Primary Sources.* Woodbridge, CT: Blackbirch Press, 1998.

Siegal, Aranka. *Upon the Head of a Goat: A Childhood in Hungary 1939-1944.* New York: Farrar, Straus, Giroux, 1981.

Silberg, Laura, and Allan Little. *Yugoslavia: Death of a Nation.* New York: Penguin, 1997.

Simon, Arthur R. *Bread for the World.* New York: Paulist Press, 1984.

Simpson, Colin. *The Lusitania.* New York: Penguin, 1983.

Singer, Elisabeth. *Children of the Apocalypse.* London: Hodder and Stoughton, 1967.

Singer, Kurt. *Spy Stories from Asia.* New York: W. Funk, 1960.

Slater, Robert. *Great Jews in Sports.* Middle Village, NY: Jonathan David Publishers, Inc., 1983.

Smith, Dan, et al. *The State of War and Peace Atlas.* 3rd ed. New York: Penguin, 1997.

Smith, George Winston, and Charles Judah, *Life in the North During the Civil War.* Albuquerque: University of New Mexico Press, 1966.

Smith, Samantha. *Journey to the Soviet Union.* Boston: Little, Brown, 1985.

Snow, Edward Rowe. *The Lighthouses of New England, 1716-1973.* New York: Dodd, Mead, 1984.

Snyder, Louis L. *Historical Documents of World War I.* Westport, CT: Greenwood Press, 1958.

Somerville, Mollie. *Women of the American Revolution.* Washington, DC: National Society, Daughters of the American Revolution, 1974.

Sosnowski, Kiryl. *The Tragedy of Children Under Nazi Rule.* New York: Howard Fertig, 1983.

Stadtler, Bea. *The Holocaust: A History of Courage and Resistance.* New York: Behrman House, 1973.

Steinberg, Rafael. *Island Fighting World War II.* New York: Time-Life Books, 1978.

Stephens, Frederick J. *Hitler Youth: History, Organisation, Uniforms and Insignia.* London: Almark Publishing, 1973.

Stewart, Gail B. *Life in the Warsaw Ghetto.* San Diego: Lucent Books, 1992.

Stewart, John Hall. *A Documentary Survey of the French Revolution.* New York: Macmillan, 1951.

Stille, Alexander. *Benevolence and Betrayal: Five Italian Jewish Families Under Fascism.* New York: Simon and Schuster, 1991.

Stone, Monica Itoi. *Nisei Daughter.* Boston: Atlantic Monthly Press, 1953.

Storry, Richard. *A History of Modern Japan.* New York: Penguin, 1960.

Strom, Margot Stern, and William S. Parsons. *Facing History and Ourselves: Holocaust and Human Behavior.* Strom and Parsons, 1978.

Sugihara, Yukiko. *Visas For Life.* Translated by Hiroki Sugihara. San Francisco: Edu-Comm. Plus, 1995.

Suhl, Yuri, ed. and trans. *They Fought Back: The Story of Jewish Resistance in Nazi Europe.* New York: Schocken, 1975.

Sullivan, Mark. *Our Times: The United States, 1900-1925.* New York: Scribner's, 1933.

Sully, Francois. *Age of the Guerilla: The New Warfare.* New York: Parent's Magazine Press, 1968.

———, ed. *We the Vietnamese: Voices from Vietnam.* New York: Praeger, 1971.

Sweets, John F. *The Politics of Resistance in France, 1940-1944.* Dekalb: Northern Illinois University, 1976.

Tahir-Kheli and Shaheen Ayubi, eds., *The Iran-Iraq War*. San Francisco: Praeger, 1983.

Takayama, Hitoshi, ed. *Hiroshima in Memoriam and Today*. Hiroshima, Japan: Hiroshima Peace Center, 1973.

Tateishi, John. *And Justice for All: An Oral History of the Japanese American Detention Camps*. New York: Random House, 1984.

Tec, Nechama. *Dry Tears: The Story of a Lost Childhood*. New York: Oxford University Press, 1984.

———. *When Light Pierced the Darkness: Christian Rescue of Jews in Occupied Poland*. New York: Oxford Press, 1986.

———. *Defiance: The Bielski Partisans*. New York: Oxford University Press, 1993.

Tehir-Kheli, Shirin, and Shaheen Ayubi, eds. *The Iran-Iraq War: New Weapons, Old Conflicts*. New York: Praeger, 1983.

Ten Boom, Carrie. *The Hiding Place*. New York: Bantam, 1974.

Thalmann, Rita, and Emmanuel Feinermann. *Crystal Night: 9-10 November 1938*. Translated by Giles Cremonesi. New York: Coward McCann and Geoghegan, 1974.

Thomas, Hugh. *The Cuban Revolution*. New York: Harper & Row, 1977.

Thompson, Robert Smith. *The Missiles of October: The Declassified Story of John F. Kennedy and the Cuban Missile Crisis*. New York: Simon and Schuster, 1992.

Timm, R.W. *Forty Years in Bangladesh*. Dhaka, Bangladesh: Caritas Bangladesh, 1995.

Toll, Nelly S. *Behind the Secret Window: A Memoir of a Hidden Childhood During World War II*. New York: Dial, 1993.

Tomaszewski, Irene, and Tecia Werbowski. *Zegota: The Rescue of Jews in Wartime Poland*. Montreal: Price-Patterson, 1994.

Treece, Patricia. *A Man for Others: Maximilian Kolbe, Saint of Auschwitz in the Words of Those Who Knew Him*. San Francisco: Harper and Row, 1982.

Trewin, J.C. *The House of Special Purpose: An Intimate Portrait of the Last Days of the Russian Imperial Family*. New York: Stein and Day, 1975.

Trout, Lawana Hooper. *The Maya*. New York: Chelsea House, 1991.

Trumbull, Robert. *Nine Who Survived Hiroshima and Nagasaki*. New York: Dutton, 1957.

Tully, Mark, and Masani Zareer. *India: Forty Years of Independence*. New York: Braziller, 1988.

Tuttle, William M. *Daddy's Gone to War: The Second World War in the Lives of America's Children*. New York: Oxford University Press, 1995.

United Nations Children's Fund (UNICEF). *The State of the World's Children, 1989*. UNICEF: New York, 1988.

———. *Children on the Front Lines*. New York: UNICEF, 1989.

———. *Convention on the Rights of the Child*. New York: UNICEF, 1989.

———. *Anti-personnel Land-mines: A Scourge on Children*. New York: UNICEF, 1994.

———. *I Dream of Peace*. New York: HarperCollins, 1994.

———. *First Call for Children: World Declaration and Plan of Action from the World Summit for Children, Convention on the Rights of the Child*. New York: UNICEF, 1995.

———. *Kids Helping Kids*. New York: UNICEF, 1996.

———. *The Progress of Nations, 1996*. New York: UNICEF, 1996.

———. *The State of the World's Children, 1996*. Oxford: Oxford University Press, 1996.

United Nations High Commissioner for Refugees. *Refugee Children: Guidelines on Protection and Care*. Geneva: UNHCR, 1994.

———. *Sexual Violence Against Refugees: Guidelines on Prevention and Response*. Geneva, UNHCR, 1995.

U.S. Department of Health, Education, and Welfare. *Effects of Malnutrition and Other Hardships on the Mortality and Morbidity of Former United States Pris-*

oners of War and Civilian Internees of World War II. Washington, DC: U.S. Government Printing Office, 1956.

U.S. Department of the Army. *Highlights of the History of the Army Nurse Corps.* 1987.

U.S. Office of United States Chief of Counsel for Prosecution of Axis Criminality. *Nazi Conspiracy and Aggression.* 10 vols. Washington, DC: U.S. Government Printing Office, 1946, vol. vii, p. 753.

Van der Heide, Dirk (pseud.). *My Sister and I: The Story of a Dutch Boy Refugee.* New York: Harcourt, 1941.

Van Sickle, Emily. *The Iron Gates of Santo Tomas.* Chicago: Academy Chicago Publishers, 1992.

Vermilye, Jerry. *Audrey Hepburn, Her Life and Her Career.* New York: Citadel Press, 1995.

Vernadsky, George. *A History of Russia.* New Haven, CT: Yale University Press, 1954.

Vestal, Stanley. *Sitting Bull: Champion of the Sioux.* Norman: University of Oklahoma Press, 1957.

Vinke, Hermann. *The Short Life of Sophie Scholl.* Cambridge, MA: Harper & Row, 1984.

Viorst, Milton. *Fire in the Streets: America in the 1960s.* New York: Simon and Schuster, 1979.

Vittachi, Varinda Tarzie. *Between the Guns: Children as a Zone of Peace.* London: Hodder and Stoughton, 1993.

Volavkova, Hana, ed. *I Never Saw Another Butterfly: Children's Drawings and Poems from Terezin Concentration Camp, 1942–1944.* New York: Schocken, 1993.

Von Der Grun, Max. *Howl Like the Wolves: Growing Up in Nazi Germany.* Translated by Jan Van Heurk. New York: William Morrow, 1980.

Vos, Ida. *Hide and Seek.* Boston: Houghton Mifflin, 1991.

Wales, Nym. *Inside Red China.* New York: Doubleday, Doran and Company, 1939.

———. *Red Dust: Autobiographies of Chinese Communists.* Stanford, CA: Stanford University Press, 1952.

Ward, Geoffrey C., with Ric Burns and Ken Burns. *The Civil War.* New York: Alfred Knopf, 1990.

Warmbrunn, Werner. *The Dutch Under German Occupation: 1940-1945.* Stanford, CA: Stanford University Press, 1963.

Wassiljewa, Tatjana. *Hostage to War: A True Story.* Translated by Anna Trenter. New York: Scholastic, 1997.

Waterford, Van. *Prisoners of the Japanese in World War II.* Jefferson, NC: McFarland and Co., 1994.

Wechter, Nell Wise. *Betsy Dowdy's Ride.* Winston-Salem, NC: John F. Blair, 1960.

Weglyn, Michi. *Years of Infamy.* New York: Morrow Quill Paperbacks, 1976.

Weinberg, Jeshajahu, and Rina Eliehi. *The Holocaust Museum in Washington.* New York: Rizzoli International Publications, 1995.

Weinstein, F.S. *A Hidden Childhood: A Jewish Girl's Sanctuary in a French Convent, 1942-1945.* New York: Farrar, Straus, Giroux, 1985.

Weisberger, Bernard A. *The American Newspaperman.* University of Chicago Press, 1962.

Wekesser, Carol, and Matthew Polesetsky, eds. *Women in the Military.* San Diego: Greenhaven Press, 1991.

Werbell, Frederick E., and Thurston Clarke, *Lost Hero: The Mystery of Raoul Wallenberg.* New York: McGraw-Hill, 1982.

Werber, Jack, and William B. Helmreich. *Saving Children: Diary of a Buchenwald Survivor and Rescuer.* New York: Transaction Publishers, 1996.

Werner, Emmy E. *Reluctant Witnesses: Children's Voices From the Civil War.* New York: Perseus Books Group, 1999.

Werstein, Irving. *1898: The Spanish-American War.* New York: Cooper Square Publications, 1966.

———. *That Denmark Might Live: The Saga of the Danish Resistance in World War II.* Philadelphia: Macrae Smith, 1967.

———. *The Uprising of the Warsaw Ghetto.* New York: W. W. Norton, 1968.

Westall, Robert. *Children of the Blitz: Memories of Wartime Childhood.* New York: Viking, 1985.

Wheeler, Richard. *Voices of the Civil War.* New York: Thomas Y. Crowell, 1976.

Whitman, Sylvia. *V Is For Victory: The American Home Front During World War II.* Minneapolis: Lerner, 1993.

Wiesel, Elie. *Night.* New York: Avon Books, 1972.

―――. *All Rivers Run to the Sea.* New York: Schocken, 1995.

Wiesenthal, Simon. *The Murderers Among Us.* New York: McGraw Hill, 1967.

Wilkins, Thurman. *Cherokee Tragedy.* New York: Macmillan, 1970.

Williams, John. *The Redeemed Captive, Returning to Zion.* Edited by E. Clark. Amherst: University of Massachusetts Press, 1976.

Williams, Selma. *Demeter's Daughters: The Women Who Founded America 1587-1787.* New York: Atheneum, 1976.

Wilson, Dick. *The Long March: The Epic of Chinese Communism's Survival, 1935.* New York: Viking, 1971.

Wilson, Theodore A. *The Marshall Plan, 1947–1951.* New York: Foreign Policy Association, 1977.

Wise, Nancy Baker, and Christy Wise. *A Mouthful of Rivets: Women at Work in World War II.* San Francisco: Jossey-Bass, 1994.

Wolf, Jacqueline. *Take Care of Josette: A Memoir in Defense of Occupied France.* New York: Franklin Watts, 1981.

Wolfe, Bertram D. *Krushchev and Stalin's Ghost.* New York: Praeger, 1957.

Wolfe, Burton H. *Hitler and the Nazis.* New York: Putnam, 1970.

Woods, Dorothea. *Child Soldiers in Kurdistan.* Geneva: Quaker United Nations Office, 1991.

―――. *Children Bearing Arms in the War Between Iraq and the Coalition (Gulf War).* Geneva, Switzerland: Quaker United Nations Office, 1991.

―――, ed. *Child Soldiers.* Geneva, Switzerland: Quaker Peace and Service (International Division of the British Society of Friends [Quakers]), September 1993.

Woodward, Ian. *Audrey Hepburn.* New York: St. Martin's Press, 1984.

World Conference on Religion and Peace. *Children and Violent Conflict.* New York: World Conference on Religion and Peace, 1995.

Worth, Alexander. *France: 1940-1955.* New York: Holt, 1956.

Wyden, Peter. *Bay of Pigs: The Untold Story.* New York: Simon and Schuster, 1979.

Wyman, Mark. *DP: Europe's Displaced Persons, 1945-1951.* Philadelphia: Balch Institute Press, n.d.

Yahil, Leni. *The Rescue of Danish Jewry: Test of a Democracy.* Philadelphia: The Jewish Publication Society, 1969.

―――. *The Holocaust: The Fate of European Jewry, 1932-1945.* New York: Oxford University Press, 1990.

Yass, Marion. *The Home Front, England: 1939-1945.* London: Wayland Publishers, 1971.

Yoors, Jan. *Crossings: A Journal of Survival and Resistance in World War II.* New York: Simon and Schuster, 1971.

Zall, P.M. *Becoming American: Young People in the American Revolution.* Hamden, CT: Linnet Books, 1993.

Zar, Rose. *In the Mouth of the Wolf.* Philadelphia: The Jewish Publication Society of America, 1984.

Zeinert, Karen. *Those Remarkable Women of the American Revolution.* Brookfield, CT: The Millbrook Press, 1996.

―――. *Those Courageous Women of the Civil War.* Brookfield, CT: The Millbrook Press, 1998.

Ziemian, Joseph. *The Cigarette Sellers of Three Crosses Square.* Trans by Janina David. Minneapolis: Lerner, 1975.

Zinn, Howard. *A People's History of the United States.* New York: Harper & Row, 1980.

Zuccotti, Susan. *The Italians and the Holocaust.* New York: Basic Books, 1987.

Zuker-Bujanowski, Liliana. *Liliana's Journal: Warsaw, 1939-1945.* New York: Dial, 1980.

Zutt, Johannes. *Children of War: Wandering Alone in Southern Sudan.* New York: UNICEF, 1994.

Zyberg, Michael. *A Warsaw Diary: 1939-1945.* London: Vallentine, Mitchell, 1969.

Web Sites

American Friends Service Committee (AFSC): <afscinfo@afsc.org>

AmeriCares: <http://www.americares.org/>

Amnesty International: <http://amnesty.org>

CARE: <http://www.care.org/html>

Feed the Children: <http://www.feedthechildren.org>

Human Rights Watch: <http://www.hrw.org/>

International Committee of the Red Cross: <http://www.icrc.org>

National Interreligious Service Board for Conscientious Objectors (NIBSCO): <nibsco@igc.apc.org>

Operation Blessing International (OPI): <http:www.ob.org/>

Red Cross: <http://redcross.org>

Samaritan's Purse: <http://www.samaritan.org>

United Nations Children's Fund (UNICEF): <http://www.unicef.org>

United Nations Convention on Genocide: <http:www.traveller.com/~hrweb/legal/genocide.html>

War Child: <http://www.warchild.org>

Women's International League for Peace and Freedom (WILPF): <http://wilpf.got.net/>

World Health Organization (WHO): <http://www.who.ch/aboutwho/achievements.htm>

Yad Vashem: <www.yad-vashem.org.il>

Youth Advocate International Program (YAP-I): <yapi@igc.apc.org>

INDEX

by Virgil Diodato

Index

Index

Index

Index

Index

Index

Index

Index

Index

Victoria Sherrow is a freelance author who has published numerous adult and young adult books in the fields of history, social issues, biography, and science. Her recent books have included titles on the Holocaust, bioethics, and the Great Depression. She authored the encyclopedias *Women in Sports* and *Women and the Military* (1996 RUSA/ALA Outstanding Reference Source award winner). She is currently preparing another Oryx title, *For Appearances' Sake: The Historical Encyclopedia of Good Looks, Beauty, and Grooming.*